The Social Engagement
of Social Science

A series in three volumes

Volume I: *The Socio-Psychological Perspective*
Volume II: *The Socio-Technical Perspective*
Volume III: *The Socio-Ecological Perspective*

The University of Pennsylvania Press joins the Editors in expressing thanks to the *Ecology of Work Conferences* for their generosity in supporting the production of these volumes and to the Busch Center for underwriting the publication.

The Social Engagement of Social Science

A Tavistock Anthology

Edited by Eric Trist and Hugh Murray

Assistant Editor: Beulah Trist

Volume II:
The Socio-Technical Perspective

University of Pennsylvania Press
Philadelphia

Permission is acknowledged to reprint portions and excerpts from published materials:

L. Davis. "The Coming Crisis for Production Management." *International Journal of Production Research,* 9 (1971): 65–82.
L. Davis and S. Sullivan. "A Labor-Management Contract and the Quality of Working Life." *Journal of Occupational Behaviour,* 1 (1980): 29–41.
F. Emery. *Futures We Are In.* Leiden: Martinus Nijhoff, 1976.
F. Emery and E. Thorsrud. *Democracy at Work.* Leiden: Martinus Nijhoff, 1976.
P.G. Herbst. *Alternatives to Hierarchies.* Leiden: Martinus Nijhoff, 1976.
G. Morgan. "Organizational Choice and the New Technology." In *Learning Works: Searching for Organizational Futures.* Edited by S. Wright and D. Morley. Toronto: ABL Group, Faculty of Environmental Studies, York University, 1989.
P. Hill. *Towards a New Philosophy of Management.* London: Gower Press, 1971.
C.H. Pava. *Managing New Office Technology: An Organizational Strategy.* New York: Free Press, 1983.
E. Trist. "The Evolution of Socio-Technical Systems." In *Perspectives on Organizational Design and Behavior.* Edited by A.H. Van de Ven and W.F. Joyce. New York: John Wiley, 1981.
E. Trist and C. Dwyer. "The Limits of Laissez-Faire as a Socio-Technical Change Strategy." In *The Innovative Organization: Productivity Programs in Action.* Edited by R. Zager and M. Rosow. New York and Oxford: Pergamon Press, 1982.

Library of Congress Cataloging-in-Publication Data
The Social engagement of social science.
    Includes bibliographical references and indexes.
    Contents: v. 1. The socio-psychological perspective — v. 2. the socio-technical perspective.
    1. Social psychology. 2. Social psychiatry. I. Tavistock Institute of Human Relations.
II. Trist, E. L. III. Murray, Hugh, Dr.
HM251.S67124 1990   302   89-28856
ISBN 0-8122-8912-6 (v. 1)
ISBN 0-8122-8193-4 (v. 2)

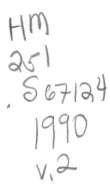

These volumes are dedicated to
DR. A.T. MACBETH WILSON
Founder Member and Chairman (1948–1958)
Tavistock Institute of Human Relations

Contents

Preface

The Tavistock Institute of Human Relations, a novel, interdisciplinary, action-oriented research organization, was founded in London in 1946 with the aid of a grant from the Rockefeller Foundation. It was set up for the specific purpose of actively relating the psychological and social sciences to the needs and concerns of society. In sustaining this endeavor for more than forty years, it has won international recognition.

The circumstances of World War II brought together an unusually talented group of psychiatrists, clinical and social psychologists and anthropologists in the setting of the British Army, where they developed a number of radical innovations in social psychiatry and applied social science. They became known as the "Tavistock Group" because the core members had been at the pre-war Tavistock Clinic. Though only some of them continued their involvement with the post-war Tavistock organization, those who did built on the war-time achievements to introduce a number of far-reaching developments in several fields. This style of research related theory and practice in a new mode. In these volumes this style is called "The Social Engagement of Social Science."

The word "engagement" (which echoes French Existentialist usage) has been chosen as the best single word to represent the process by which social scientists endeavor actively to relate themselves in relevant and meaningful ways to society. This overall orientation is reflected in what the editors have called "perspectives," of which there are three: the socio-psychological, the socio-technical and the socio-ecological. These perspectives are explained in the Series Introduction on the Foundation and Development of the Institute. They have evolved from each other in relation to societal change. They are interdependent, yet each has its own focus and is represented in a separate volume.

The Institute's theories and projects have resulted in a considerable number of books, many of which are regarded as classics. A large collection of articles of continuing interest are dispersed through various journals. There is a further collection of little-known manuscripts containing some outstanding contributions. These have been available only in document series maintained by the Institute and two or three closely related centers. This body of work by many hands has never been gathered together. The present volumes offer a comprehensive selection of these writings—a Tavistock anthology.

There are now very few people left who were at the Institute at the beginning of this saga. As a founder member and sometime Chairman I felt I should undertake the required compilation. Having been in the United States for more than twenty years, however, I needed a co-editor still on the scene in London. Accordingly, I invited one of my oldest colleagues, Dr. Hugh Murray, to join me.

All the contributions contain innovations in social psychiatry and the social sciences, either in concept or in the nature of the projects undertaken; these have led in many cases to widespread developments in their fields and in some cases to the foundation of entirely new fields. They look backward to show the origin, in the period following World War II, of much in current theory and practice whose historic depth is not widely known or appreciated. They look forward to show the continuing relevance of the material presented to tasks that lie ahead in many areas of the social sciences and, more widely, to the post-industrial social order that is beginning to emerge from the "turbulence" of the present.

In order to allow the inclusion of as many contributions as possible, the Volume and Theme introductions have been kept short. The papers—many of them recent—are primarily by members of the founding generation and their successors over the following two decades, whether they are still at the Institute or have moved elsewhere, as most of them have. Some of the papers are by authors from related centers that developed later. This wide dispersal of people has enabled the original tradition to be enriched by developments in different settings in institutes and university departments in Commonwealth and European countries and in the United States. In this way, new insights have been added to those of the founding body. From its beginnings as simply an organization in London, the Tavistock has become an international network.

More than half the contributions have been remodeled or specially written for these volumes. Many have one or more co-authors, as befits an enterprise characterized by a group orientation. Co-authors have not necessarily been members of the Institute.

The three volumes comprising *The Social Engagement of Social Science* are dedicated to Dr. A.T. Macbeth Wilson, affectionately known to us all as "Tommy." He was the one senior psychiatrist involved at the beginning who chose to stay with the separately incorporated Institute when the Clinic entered the National Health Service in 1948. He was endowed with what C. Wright Mills called "the sociological imagination." His seminal contributions date from the pre-war period and continued uninterrupted thereafter. Throughout his years as Chairman (1948–58) he carried the main burden when the Institute was struggling to find an independent identity.

Gainesville
Florida

Eric Trist

Eric Trist and Hugh Murray

Historical Overview
The Foundation and Development
of the Tavistock Institute

The Formative Years

The Founding Tradition

PRE-WAR ANTECEDENTS

After the fall of France in 1941, the Royal Air Force, by winning the Battle of Britain, prevented German invasion of the British Isles. The evacuation from the Dunkirk beaches prevented the capture of the core of the regular army, including many of the generals who were later to distinguish themselves. There was, therefore, a chance to fight again but there was no land army of any size to do so. It was thus imperative that Britain build a large land army in a hurry. Attempts to meet this need created immense problems in the utilization of human resources (problems far more severe for the army than for the other services), but no measures tried in the first few months seemed to be effective.

In 1941 a group of psychiatrists at the Tavistock Clinic saw that the right questions were asked in Parliament in order to secure the means to try new measures. As a result they were asked to join the Directorate of Army Psychiatry, and did so as a group.

To understand how such a small group was able to be so influential, we must go back to the period immediately after World War I when there was a growing recognition that neurotic disabilities were not merely transitory phenomena related to the stress of war, but were endemic and pervasive in a modern society. In order to respond to the "felt social need" thus arising, the Tavistock Institute of Medical Psychology (better known as the Tavistock Clinic), the parent body of the post-World War II Institute, was founded in 1920 as a voluntary outpatient clinic to explore the implications for treatment and research.

The founding group comprised many of the key doctors who had been concerned with neurosis in World War I. They included general physicians and neurologists, as well as psychiatrists, and one or two multiply trained individuals who combined psychology and anthropology with medicine. The group, therefore, showed from the beginning the preparedness to be linked to the social sciences and to general medicine, as well as to psychiatry, which has characterized it ever since.

Interest focussed on the then new "dynamic psychologies" as representing the direction which offered most hope. Because of the uncertain and confused state of knowledge in these fields, tolerance of different viewpoints was part of the undertaking and the Tavistock Clinic functioned as a mediating institution, a clearing-house where the views of several contending parties could be aired. On the one hand were the adherents of Freud, Jung and Adler, who were preoccupied with establishing their own professional societies and advancing their own theories. On the other were a neurologically oriented general psychiatry, a somatically oriented general medicine and a surrounding society puzzled, bewildered, intrigued and frightened by the new knowledge of the unconscious and its implications for important areas of life.

Because "authoritarian" government of the medical kind in a pathfinding organization such as the Tavistock Clinic proved dysfunctional, a transition to a collegiate professional democracy took place in the early 1930s, when problems arising from the Depression shook many cherished beliefs and raised new questions concerning the role of social factors in psychological illness. This organizational revolution brought to the front a younger generation of clinicians with a level of ability and a maverick quality that would otherwise have been lost.*

This younger group now began to take on a conceptual direction consonant with the emergent "object relations approach" in psychoanalysis. The object relations approach emphasized relationships rather than instinctual drives and psychic energy.

As Dicks's (1970) history (*Fifty Years of the Tavistock Clinic*) shows, there were great variations in the quality of the services offered by the pre-war Clinic. Among the 80 physicians who contributed six hours a week, many had little or no psychiatric training. Nevertheless, by the beginning of World War II the Tavistock had attained international standing. It had developed links with organizations in the main Commonwealth countries and the United States, and had undertaken systematic research and teaching. It had obtained pe-

---

*The staff now elected as their Director Jack Rawlings Rees, grouped around whom were Henry Dicks, Ronald Hargreaves, Tommy Wilson and Wilfred Bion, all of whom subsequently made world-wide reputations. They would have left the Tavistock had it not been for the opportunities opened up by the organizational revolution.

ripheral academic standing in London University with six recognized teachers. The outbreak of war, however, prevented this arrangement from being implemented.

WAR-TIME BREAKTHROUGHS

The group who entered the Directorate of Army Psychiatry took a novel approach to the human resource problems facing the army. Rather than remain in base hospitals they went out into the field to find out from commanding officers what they saw as their most pressing problems. They would listen to their troubled military clients as an analyst would to a patient, believing that the "real" problems would surface as trust became established, and that constructive ideas about dealing with them would emerge. The concept thence arose of "command" psychiatry, in which a psychiatrist with a roving commission was attached to each of the five Army Commanders in Home Forces.

A relationship of critical importance was formed between the Clinic's Ronald Hargreaves, as command psychiatrist, and Sir Ronald Adam, the Army Commander in Northern Command. When Adam became Adjutant General, the second highest post in the army, he was able to implement policies that Hargreaves and he had adumbrated. New military institutions had to be created to carry them out. The institution-building process entailed:

- Earning the right to be consulted on emergent problems for which there was no solution in traditional military procedures, e.g., the problem of officer selection.
- Making preliminary studies to identify a path of solution—the investigation of morale in Officer Cadet Training Units.
- Designing a pilot model in collaboration with military personnel which embodied the required remedial measures—the Experimental War Office Selection Board.
- Handing over the developed model to military control with the psychiatric and psychological staff falling back into advisory roles or where possible removing themselves entirely—the War Office Selection Boards (WOSBs) and Civil Resettlement Units (CRUs) for repatriated prisoners of war.
- Disseminating the developed model, securing broad acceptance for it and training large numbers of soldiers to occupy the required roles, e.g., CRUs.

To meet these large scale tasks the range of disciplines was extended from psychiatry and clinical psychology to social psychology, sociology and anthropology. The members of these various disciplines were held together by participation in common operational tasks in an action frame of reference. To varying extents they began to learn each others' skills. The group became, to use a term that arose after the war in a project concerned with alternative forms of organization in the mining industry, a "composite" work group (Trist et al., 1963/Vol. I).

Undertaking practical tasks that sought to resolve operational crises generated insights that led towards new theory. This process was familiar to those members of the group who were practicing psychiatrists, but it was new to those coming from other disciplines. This led to a generalized concept of professionalism.

The innovations introduced during the war years consisted of a series of "inventions":

- Command psychiatry as a reconnaissance activity leading to the identification of critical problems.
- Social psychiatry as a policy science permitting preventive intervention in large scale problems.
- The co-creation with the military of new institutions to implement these policies.
- The therapeutic community as a new mode of treatment.
- Cultural psychiatry for the analysis of the enemy mentality.

By the end of the war a considerable number of psychiatrists and social scientists had become involved in this comprehensive set of innovative applications of concepts of social psychiatry. They saw in these approaches a significance which did not seem to be limited by the condition of war, and were determined to explore their relevance for the civilian society. Obviously, individual programs could not be transferred without considerable modification; entirely new lines of development would have to be worked out. Nevertheless, a new action-oriented philosophy of relating psychiatry and the social sciences to society had become a reality in practice. This event signified the social engagement of social science.

Post-War Transformation

OPERATION PHOENIX

New questions now arose. Who would be the next pioneers? Who would accept the risks, which were great? Could a setting be found that could nurture the new endeavors? An answer to these questions came about in the following way.

Toward the end of the war the existence of a democratic tradition in the Tavistock Clinic made possible the election by the whole staff (through a postal ballot) of an Interim Planning Committee (IPC) to consider the future of the organization. The election gave power to those who had led the work in the Army.* The IPC began meeting in the autumn of 1945 to work out a re-definition of the Clinic's mission in light of the experiences gained during the war. The IPC was chaired by Wilfred Bion, who used his new findings about groups to clarify issues and reduce conflicts within the planning group itself. Council approved its report by the end of that year.

The IPC made a crucial decision in recognition of an impending political event—the then new Labour Government's intimation that it would in 1948 create a National Health Service. The IPC resolved:

- To build up the Clinic to enter the National Health Service fully equipped with the kind of staff who could be entrusted with the task of discovering the role of out-patient psychiatry, based on a dynamic approach and oriented towards the social sciences, in the as yet unknown setting of a national health service.
- Separately to incorporate the Institute of Human Relations for the study of wider social problems not accepted as in the area of mental health.

This readiness enabled the IPC in 1945 to attract the attention of Alan Gregg, Medical Director of the Rockefeller Foundation, who was touring the various institutions that had been involved in war medicine. He was interested in finding out if there was a group committed to undertaking, under conditions of peace, the kind of social psychiatry that had developed in the army under conditions of war. So began a process that led the Rockefeller Foundation in 1946 to make a grant of untied funds without which the IPC's post-war plan could not have been carried out.

The Rockefeller grant led to the birth of the Tavistock Institute of Human Relations, constituted at first as a division of the Tavistock Clinic. With these funds it became possible to obtain for the then joint organization a nucleus of full-time senior staff who would otherwise have been scattered in universities and hospitals throughout the country and abroad.

A Professional Committee (PC), with Rees in the chair, and a small Techni-cal Executive representing the new permanent staff, chaired by Bion, came into existence in February 1946. These arrangements lasted until the separate

*The six elected members were J.R. Rees, who was later to found the World Federation of Mental Health; Leonard Browne, who became a prominent Alderman in the London County Council; Henry Dicks, who founded the field of cultural psychiatry; Ronald Hargreaves, who became Deputy Director of the World Health Organization; Mary Luff, who retired after the war; and Tommy Wilson, who became Chairman of the Tavistock Institute. The IPC met twice a week for two or three hours in the evenings. There were rarely any absentees. The group co-opted two people not previously at the Clinic—Jock Sutherland, a psychiatrist, who was to become Director of the post-war Clinic, and Eric Trist, a social psychologist, who was later to succeed Wilson as the Institute's Chairman. Both had played prominent parts in the war-time developments.

incorporation of the Institute in September, 1947. The situation required the transformation of a large part-time staff, appropriate for the pre-war Clinic as a voluntary out-patient hospital, into a small nucleus of full-timers, supported by others giving substantial proportions of their time, and committed to the redefined mission of the post-war organization. Decisions were taken as to who should stay, who should leave and who should be added. Criteria included willingness to participate in the redefined social mission and to undergo psychoanalysis if they had not already done so. This critical episode became known as Operation Phoenix.*

As regards the requirement for psychoanalysis, it was felt that object relations theory had proved its relevance during the war in the social as well as the clinical field. It represented the most advanced body of psychological knowledge then available which could provide a common foundation for those who would in various ways be continuing, in the peace, the work begun under war conditions.

Training would be in the hands of the British Psycho-Analytical Society, and social applications in the hands of the Institute. This understanding equilibrated relations between the two bodies. The Society agreed to provide training analysts for acceptable candidates, whether they were going to become full-time analysts, mix psychoanalytic practice with broader endeavors in the health field or use psychoanalytic understanding outside the health area in organizational and social projects. The Society, therefore, recognized the relevance for psychoanalysis of work in the social field, while the Institute affirmed the importance of psychoanalysis for psycho-social studies. In this way some 15 individuals, some in the Clinic and some in the Institute, most of them in mid-life, undertook personal psychoanalysis as part of the enterprise of building the new Tavistock. It was a major "experiment," the outcome of which could not be known for a number of years.

The PC now faced painful tasks. When the decisions stemming from Operation Phoenix began to be implemented, a great deal of guilt developed over the termination of most of the pre-war staff who in one way or another did not meet the criteria for inclusion in the post-war body. An abdication crisis ensued. The PC agreed to stay in power only after a searching self-examination that enabled them to separate task-oriented factors from the tangle of personal feelings. Tension and confusion developed throughout the entire organization. Bion resigned as Chairman of the Technical Executive and restricted himself to

---

*In addition to Sutherland and Trist, a number of other outsiders who had played prominent roles in the war-time effort were brought in at this point. John Bowlby, a child psychiatrist and analyst, was made head of what he came to call the Department for Children and Parents. (The other senior psychiatrists appointed to the Clinic were all from the wider Tavistock group.) Elliott Jaques, a young Canadian psychiatrist and psychologist, was invited to join the Institute and played a prominent role during the five years he stayed.

the role of social therapist to an overall staff group that held weekly meetings to work through these matters. Without them the post-war organization could scarcely have survived its conflicts. Our first experiment with group methods was on ourselves.

THE JOINT ORGANIZATION

In preparing to enter the National Health Service (NHS) the Clinic had to develop therapeutic methods that would allow the maintenance of a patient load sufficiently large to satisfy the new authorities that out-patient psychotherapy could be cost effective. War-time experience suggested that the best prospect would lie in group treatment. Accordingly, the PC asked Bion, considering his special achievements in this field, to pioneer this endeavor. His response was to put up a notice which became celebrated—"You can have group treatment now or wait a year for individual treatment." The groups he started, however, were not only patient groups but groups with industrial managers and with people from the educational world. He was developing a general method reflected in a series of papers in *Human Relations* (Bion, 1948–51), which put forward entirely new theory. By the time the Clinic entered the NHS most of the psychiatrists were taking groups, though none used precisely Bion's methods.

Meanwhile, in the Department for Children and Parents, Bowlby (1949/ Vol. I) laid the foundations of family therapy. Also at this time he began his world famous studies of mother/child separation.

Another major and still continuing enterprise that began during this early period emerged from a crisis in the Family Welfare Association (FWA), which co-ordinated family case work in the London area. The coming of the welfare state rendered unnecessary its task of dispensing material aid to the poor. Its offices were now besieged by clients with social and emotional problems with which its staff were unable to deal. Through Wilson (1949) the Institute was consulted. An attempt to train FWA staff proved unsuccessful. The Institute therefore set up within its own boundary what was called the Family Discussion Bureau (FDB), which later became the Institute for Marital Studies (IMS). This created the first non-medical channel in Britain for professional work with families. In time it was supported by the government through the Home Office.

Michael Balint, one of the senior analysts at the Clinic, introduced a group method of training family welfare workers in which stress was laid on making them aware of their counter-transferences: their projections of their own problems onto their clients. Balint later developed these methods for training large numbers of health professionals, including general physicians (Balint, 1954). This allowed the Clinic to have a multiplier effect which, along with group treatment and the inauguration of family therapy, showed that what had been learnt in the Army about using scarce resources to meet the needs of large scale systems could be applied in the civilian society in entirely new ways.

Hostility to the Institute's work, however, developed in the academic world. The Medical Research Council dismissed the first draft of the WOSB write-up as being of only historical, not scientific, interest. No further funds were granted.

Several strategic moves were nevertheless made to establish the Tavistock's academic claims. There was very little chance at that time of getting much of its work accepted by existing journals. A new journal was needed that would manifest the connection between field theory and object-relations psycho-analysis. With Lewin's group in the U.S., the Research Center for Group Dynamics, now at the University of Michigan, the Institute created a new international journal, *Human Relations,* whose purpose was to further the integration of psychology and the social sciences and relate theory to practice.

In 1947 a publishing company—Tavistock Publications—was founded, which in the longer run succeeded in finding a home in a major publishing house (the Sweet and Maxwell Group) while retaining its own imprint. A joint library was also established with the Clinic that provided the best collection of books and journals then available in London in the psycho- and socio-dynamic fields. This was needed for teaching as well as research purposes. John Rickman, a senior analyst closely associated with the Tavistock, said that there should be no therapy without research and no research without therapy and that the Institute should offer training in all the main areas of its work.

By the time the Institute was separately incorporated there was a staff of eight with Wilson as chairman. Six of the eight had taken part in one or other of the war-time projects. The disciplines included psychology, anthropology, economics, education and mathematics.

Achieving a Working Identity

INDUSTRIAL ACTION RESEARCH

By 1948 the British economy was in serious trouble. The pound had been devalued, productivity was low and there was a scarcity of capital for invest-ment in new technology. The government formed an Industrial Productivity Committee which had a Human Factors Panel. This made grants for research aiming to secure improved productivity through better use of human resources. The grants were for three years and were administered by the Medical Research Council. The Institute proposed three projects, all of which were accepted. The first focussed on internal relations within a single firm (from the board to the

shop floor) with the aim of identifying means of improving cooperation between management and labor and also between levels of management; the
second focussed on organizational innovations that could raise productivity;
the third pioneered a new form of post-graduate education for field workers in
applied social research.

A site for the first project was obtained in the London factories of a light
engineering concern (the Glacier Metal Company) whose managing director
had a special interest in the social sciences. The project, headed by Elliott
Jaques, led to far-reaching changes in the organization and culture of the firm.
A novel role was elaborated that enabled process consultation to take place
across areas of conflict. Some radically new concepts were formulated such as
the use of social structure as a defense against anxiety (Jaques, 1953/Vol. I).
Jaques's (1951) book, *The Changing Culture of a Factory,* was the first major
publication of the Institute after it became independent. While it was an
immense success in the literature, being reprinted many times, no requests
were received to continue this kind of work. As Jaques said at the time, the
answer from the field was silence.

A component of the second project, under Eric Trist, led to the discovery of
self-regulating work groups in a coal mine—the first intimation that a new
paradigm of work might be emerging along the lines indicated by the Institute's
work with groups. It opened up the study of "socio-technical systems" which
has become world-wide.

The training program for the six industrial fellows was for two years and
experience based. All participated in a common project (the Glacier Project)
while each took part in another Institute project. To gain direct experience of
unconscious factors in group life each was placed in a therapy group. To gain
experience of managing their own group life they met regularly with a staff
member in attendance. Each had a personal tutor. After the first year they
returned to their industries to see what new perceptions they had gained and
reported on them to a meeting of Institute staff. They also attended regular staff
seminars at which all projects were discussed. This was the first opportunity
which the Institute had to apply its methods in training. It was, however, too
experience based to receive favor at that time.

Consultancy Developments

With the ending of the government's Human Factors Panel, no further research
funds were available from British sources. Though Rockefeller help continued, the Institute had to develop its work in the consultancy field and prove
that it could pay its way by directly meeting client needs while at the same time
furthering social science objectives.

Further work in the socio-technical field was arrested in the coal industry, but unexpected circumstances yielded an opportunity in India to work collaboratively with the Calico Mills, a subsidiary of Sarabhai Industries, in Ahmedabad. In view of his experience of the tropics, the MC selected A.K. Rice to go to India as the project officer. He proposed that a group of workers should take charge of a group of looms. The idea was taken up spontaneously by the workers in the automatic loom shed who secured management permission to try out a scheme of their own creation. This led to developments that continued for 25 years showing that the socio-technical concept was applicable in the culture of a very different kind of society.

Unilever had established a working relationship with the Institute immediately after the war. It was now expanding. It needed to recruit and train a large number of high caliber managers. The Chairman, Lord Heyworth, had been interested in the WOSBs and approached the Institute for assistance. The result was the joint development of the Unilever Companies' Management Development Scheme based on a modification of WOSB methods. This led to a still continuing collaborative relationship, with many ramifications, of which Harold Bridger has been the architect.

With the profusion of new products in the 1950s, advertising agencies and the marketing departments of firms were under pressure to develop new methods for increasing sales. Motivation research had made its appearance but was narrowly conceived. One or two trial projects gave rise to a new concept which brought together Lewinian and psychoanalytic thinking—the pleasure foods region. This consisted of products of little or no nutritional value that were consumed, often in excess, because of their power to afford oral satisfactions which reduced anxiety and relieved stress.

Early studies by Menzies and Trist (1989) concerned ice cream and confectionery. Later studies by Emery (Emery et al., 1968) and Ackoff and Emery (1972) concerned smoking and drinking. The smoking study identified the affect of distress, as formulated by Silvan Tomkins (1962), as a continuing negative state (as distinct from acute anxiety and depression) which required repeated relief such as smoking affords. The drinking study produced a new social theory of drinking behavior that distinguished between social, "reparative" and indulgent drinking, only the last leading to alcoholism.

As regards the consultancy style that developed, the method was adopted of having two Institute staff attend the early meetings. This was both to obtain binocular vision and to show that the relationship was with an organization and not simply with an individual. With only one person, the dangers of transference and counter-transference would have been greater. A project officer was appointed. After the opening stage the second staff member remained largely outside the project so that a more objective appreciation could be made. Other staff were added as required by project assignments.

The funding crisis had proved a blessing in disguise. The Institute had now proved to itself that it could earn a substantial part of its living from private industry. Though it still needed support from foundations and government funding agencies, it was no longer completely dependent on them. It needed these funds to add a research dimension to projects that clients could not be expected to pay for and to cover the costs of writing up the results.

Toward an Optimum Balance

In 1954 the Institute succeeded once more in obtaining research funds. A four-year grant enabled the socio-technical studies in the coal industry to be resumed through the government's Department of Scientific and Industrial Research (DSIR) which administered counterpart US/UK funds that were part of the Marshall Plan. The Nuffield Foundation supported the research component of the family studies program, while the Home Office supported the operational part.

The most difficult funds to obtain were untied funds such as had been provided by the Rockefeller Foundation. As no further grants of this kind were available, a development charge was added to all consultancy projects so that a special reserve could be built up to tide staff over between projects and to enable them to be taken out of the field to write up work that had already been done. It was felt that 15 percent of the Institute's income should be from untied funds. A much larger proportion—35 percent—should be sought from foundations or government for specific long range projects of a primarily research character, though the research would largely be action research. Experience in the consultancy field had now shown that long range projects with serious social science outcome could be obtained of a kind too unconventional to be supported by foundations or governments. These could account for another 30 percent of income. Experience had also shown the value of short-range projects which could lead into new areas. The remaining 20 percent of income could best be generated by projects of this kind.

Another dimension concerned the sectors of society in which the projects would take place. The aim was to have work going on in more than one sector, though the larger proportion would be in industry. By 1961 there were nine industrial projects and six in other sectors.

Separately categorized were projects related to the Clinic, which was regarded solely as a treatment institution by the NHS. As originally intended, however, it was developing large research and training programs. These were financed by foundation grants, especially from the U.S., and were administered by the Institute through what was called the Research and Training Committee (RTC). Some of the Institute's own activities came into this area.

The RTC succeeded in resolving conflicts as to which projects should be put forward for funding.

Among such Institute activities was a program to develop new projective tests and to train people in their use. This led during the 1970s to the creation of the British Society for Projective Psychology through which a large number of clinical psychologists have been trained. New Tavistock tests which were widely adopted included Phillipson's Object Relations Technique. His book with R.D. Laing (Laing et al., 1966), *Interpersonal Perception,* opened up fresh ground. A leading part in these developments was played by Theodora Alcock (1963), recognized world-wide as a Rorschach expert, who was kept on by the Institute when she reached the retiring age in the NHS. This path of development represents a pioneer effort that would not otherwise have taken place.

Of crucial importance was the duration of projects. Action research projects concerned with change tend to be long-range as they unfold in unpredictable ways. Projects lasting more than three years were regarded as being in the long-range category, those between 18 months and three years were considered medium-range, and those lasting six to 18 months short-range. A balance was needed between these types of duration. In addition, it was found advantageous to keep going a few very brief exploratory assignments as these sometimes opened up new areas and led to innovative developments which could not be foreseen.

In the industrial sector, socio-technical studies continued in the coal industry and then in industries with advanced technologies, both funded through DSIR. There was also a program of research on labor turnover, absence and sickness (Hill and Trist, 1955/Vol. I). Under conditions of full employment there was widespread concern about these phenomena. New theory and a new practical approach emerged.

Towards the end of the 1950s problems of quite a new kind began to be brought to the Institute. They arose from changes taking place in the wider contextual environment and led to what has been called the socio-ecological perspective. These problems and the theories and methods to deal with them are encompassed in Volume III. The opportunities to build up this perspective came initially from exploratory projects with Bristol Siddeley Engines, the National Farmers' Union and a Unilever subsidiary in the food industry, all of which were facing major changes in their contextual environments. (These changes were not understood.)

As regards other social sectors, the work in family studies produced a major book by Elizabeth Bott (1957) entitled *Family and Social Network* (also Bott, 1955/Vol. I). This put the concept of network, as distinct from that of group, firmly on the social science map and generated a whole new literature. The Prison Commissioners asked the Tavistock to test the value of a scheme for greatly increasing time spent in "association," which had been successfully tried out in the Norwich local prison. A systematic action research study was carried out of its adaptation in Bristol. The prison officers' union, the inmates, and the staff immediately reporting to the Governor were all involved. This study, which broke new theoretical ground, was carried out by Emery (1970/ Vol. I). Also during this time Dicks (1970/Vol. I) completed studies of the Russian national character at the Harvard Center for Russian Studies. They were a sequel to his work on the German national character during World War II to which he returned in *Licensed Mass Murder* (Dicks, 1972). These studies established a firm empirical base on which cultural psychology using psychoanalytic findings could develop.

Another development during this period was the creation, in collaboration with the University of Leicester, of a U.K. equivalent to the form of sensitivity training pioneered by the National Training Laboratories for Group Development in the United States. This is still continuing. An overall review of it is given by Miller in Vol. I. Two other models were developed (Bridger, Vol. I; Higgin and Hjelholt, Vol. I), the idea being to experiment with alternative forms. These are also still evolving.

A basic pattern could now be discerned in the projects of the Institute:
- They were all responses to macro- or meta-problems emerging in the society with which the Institute, in Sommerhoff's (1950) terms, became directively correlated.
- Access to organizations struggling with meta-problems was initially obtained through networks of individuals who had come to know about the Institute's work during World War II. As time went on the initiating individuals became people with whom the Institute had made contact in the post-war period.
- There was not yet a wide appreciation of these emergent meta-problems so that the connections through which the Institute could become directively correlated with them were scarce and fragile. To discover the role of networks in this situation was new learning.
- The projects were carried out by interdisciplinary teams with the project officer having a second staff member as his consultant. Later on these teams became joint with internal groups in the client organization. Project reviews took place not so much in Institute seminars as in joint meetings with these internal groups.
- Though seminal projects might begin from short-term relations, those with the most significance as regards the advance of basic social scientific knowledge depended on very long relationships being maintained with client organizations or other sponsoring agencies. Change processes take time. They unfold in interactions between the system and its environment in complex ways which are not predictable. One is able to understand the

course of a social process only so far as it has manifested itself and then only so far as one is able to stay with it.

- Clients actively collaborated with the Institute. The projects were joint enterprises of action research and social learning. No results were published without the agreement of all parties.
- Great stress was laid on "working through" difficulties and conflicts by analogy with the psychoanalytic method. Not that interpretations of a psychoanalytic kind were directly made. Jaques called the process "social analysis." No standardized procedures, however, were established. Suitable interpretative languages had to evolve in different projects and some of the methods introduced were manufactured more by the clients than by the Institute.
- The aim was to build social science capabilities into organizations that they could then develop by and for themselves.
- Some of the innovations were ahead of their time, often by a number of years. There was little recognition of their significance and no short-term diffusion of the practices involved.
- New theory was as apt to be generated by research paid for by client organizations as by work paid for by research-funding agencies. One of the functions of the latter was to fund work in which organizations would be willing to collaborate operationally, but for the scientific analysis of which they were not yet willing to pay. There were, of course, other projects which could only be initiated if research funds were available.
- The aim was eventually to secure publication at a fully scientific level, but this had sometimes to be delayed for several years and sometimes never emerged at all. Those concerned were often understandably unwilling for work to be made public that described internal processes of a sensitive kind or led to changes the outcome of which could not be assessed for a long time.

This pattern established the Institute's working identity. It expresses what is meant by the social engagement of social science. It treated all projects as opportunities for organizational and personal learning, both for the client and for itself. Though this basic pattern has since undergone much elaboration and improvement, its fundamental character has remained the same.

The Sequel

Division into Two Groups

Before describing how this division came about, it will be convenient to outline the Institute's structure and mode of functioning. It is an independent, not-for-profit organization based on an Association of five hundred members—well-wishers in key positions in the medical and academic worlds and also in industry and other social sectors. To obtain such a support base became possible only after prolonged effort. At this time, at its annual meeting, the Association elected a small working Council that met with the Management Committee (MC) every quarter. Members of the MC were nominated by the staff and approved by the Council so that it could operate with a double sanction. The MC proposed its own chairman but the Council had to confirm the appointment. The MC met weekly to guide all aspects of the Institute's affairs as a group.

The permanent staff were of four grades—consultants, principal project officers, project officers and assistant project officers. When the Institute was separately incorporated in 1947 there were eight staff members, in 1961 there were 22. A pension scheme had been negotiated by the Secretary after persisting difficulties. This gave a much needed addition to security which, during the formative years, had been exceedingly low. There were a number of people on temporary assignment and many overseas visitors, especially from the United States, who usually stayed a year. Administration was in the hands of a professional secretary, Sidney Gray, who had voting rights as a member of the MC.

The MC met with the consultants quarterly and once every year with the whole staff for a period of two days. There were fortnightly seminars to discuss project and theoretical matters. The Council insisted that members of MC be of professorial status. Salary scales had to be approved by the whole staff and were in line with those of the universities, the Scientific Civil Service and the National Health Service. This system had functioned well; relations in working groups had been good. A strong collegiate culture had persisted from the war and was strengthened by the Institute having to contend with a largely hostile environment.

In 1958 Wilson had left to take up the position of strategic adviser to Unilever world-wide. This was the first time a social scientist (other than an economist) had been asked to fill a strategic position at this level in industry. For ten years a balanced relationship had existed between Wilson and Trist, as chairman and deputy chairman. Wilson was a man of daring seminal insights. He had immense prestige in both the medical and non-medical worlds and an exceedingly wide range of contacts. He was adept at negotiations with government and foundations, and opened up diverse channels which led to new projects. Trist had complementary capacities in formulating concepts, project design and research methodology and in acting as mentor to the growing body of younger staff who required rapid development. This partnership, however, was no longer an organizational necessity; there was now a well-developed staff, several of whom were active in finding and maintaining projects and in coming forward with new ideas and methods.

The Institute had become over-busy with its growing project portfolio. The quarterly meetings with the consultants and the annual retreats were not kept up. The place that had so strongly affirmed the need to pay attention to the process side of organizational life had been neglecting its own. With the departure of Wilson, the MC should have asked for a radical reappraisal of the whole situation; but the requisite meetings with the consultants and with the staff as a whole were never called. It was assumed that the status quo would continue and that Trist would become chairman with indefinite tenure. It was as though a quasi-dynastic myth had inadvertently crept in to a supposedly democratic process.

The staff was now beyond the limits of the small face-to-face group it had been in 1948. There was a far greater range of interests, capabilities and projects and the problem of managing the Institute as a single unit grew correspondingly greater.

Conflicts, latent for some time, came to a head while Trist was in California on sabbatical. Rice, as Acting Chairman, proposed that the Institute should divide into three self-accounting project groups. This division was resisted by many of the senior staff who wished to preserve the unity of the whole. The differences were partly personal, partly professional, but there was also disagreement over the direction in which the Institute should best develop in the increasingly turbulent environment and how it should be shaped to meet the new challenges. On Trist's return an attempt was made to resolve the differences but in the end two groups were formed, the larger around Trist (the Human Resources Centre) and the smaller (the Centre for Applied Social Research) around Rice.

Though not ideal, the partition provided a "good enough" solution, to use Winnicott's (1965) term. Each group proceeded to work productively on its own lines.

The Matrix

The expansion of the Clinic and Institute during the 1950s led to the need for more space. The Ministry of Health offered to build new premises in the Swiss Cottage district of Hampstead on the other side of Regent's Park from the existing set of buildings and the question arose as to whether the Ministry would agree to the inclusion of activities of the Institute that were not health related. The Minister at first said, "No." Sir Hugh Beaver, the then Chairman of the Council, had become convinced of the need to keep the Clinic and Institute together and persuaded the Ministry to allow all activities to be included so that the overall unity could be preserved.

The 1960s were now beginning. Many changes and developments had taken place. How far was the original definition of mission, made 15 years ago, still applicable? How far was the requirement of psychoanalysis for all still relevant? How to find a formulation that would no longer make the Institute appear as a para-medical organization but would express the broader idea of the social engagement of social science. Emery came up with the notion that everything it did—clinical and non-clinical—was at a more general level concerned with improving what he called "the important practical affairs of man." He prepared a document along these lines which was accepted by the Council.

The Institute continued to administer the Clinic's research and training activities, which had grown into a large enterprise. Bowlby had molded them into what he called the School of Family Psychiatry and Community Mental Health. An attempt was made to get the School affiliated to one of the London medical schools but the Tavistock was still too marginal and too identified with psychoanalysis to be countenanced.

Another development which began at about this time led to the setting up of an Institute for Operational Research. A growing number of management and decision scientists had become concerned that the capture of operational research (OR) by academic departments focussed on mathematical model-making was leading OR away from its original mission of dealing with real-world problems. They were interested in establishing a connection with the social sciences. Russell Ackoff of the University of Pennsylvania, a leading authority on OR, who was in England on sabbatical during 1962–63, suggested setting up an institute for operational research in the Tavistock orbit in conjunction with the British Operational Research Society. This suggestion came to fruition. Ackoff also found a British colleague, Neil Jessop, a mathematical statistician with social science interests, who was willing to give up a senior post in industry to head up the new enterprise.

There had been a large-scale development of OR in Britain in industry but nothing had been done in the public sector, outside defense. If it were to enter the policy field where problems were often ill-defined, ambiguous and interest-group-driven, OR had to find new concepts and methods to which the social sciences could contribute. OR people had found that their recommendations were only too often left on the shelf. They needed to involve the various stakeholders far more than had been their custom, to admit the limits of rationality, to pay attention to unconscious factors in organizational life and to acquire process skills in dealing with them. The OR people had considerable experience in dealing with large-scale problems at the multi-organizational level which the Institute was just beginning to enter and for which it lacked concepts and methodologies. On both sides there was a need to establish common ground and to find an organizational setting in which this could be explored. The status of an independent unit within the Tavistock orbit provided the required conditions. The new unit became known as the Institute for Operational Research (IOR).

The Family Discussion Bureau had also developed into a large undertaking of national standing. It needed a suitable identity to pursue its mission of setting up a non-medical but professional channel for dealing with marital difficulties. The title of the Institute for Marital Studies was proposed and accepted. It became an autonomous unit within the Tavistock orbit (Woodhouse, Vol. I).

There were now five units: those deriving from the original Management Committee—the Human Resources Centre (HRC) and the Centre for Applied Social Research (CASR); the School of Family Psychiatry and Community Mental Health; the Institute for Marital Studies; and the Institute for Operational Research. The Institute had become what Stringer (1967) called a multi-organization, a federation of interacting units with the same overall mission of furthering the social engagement of social science. Emery suggested that it had acquired the character of a social matrix—a nourishing and facilitating environment for all components. This matrix form of organization had the merit of showing to the external world that the overall mission could be pursued in different but nevertheless related ways.

The mutation required a new organizational structure. While each unit worked out its own form of internal governance the overall organization was steered by a Joint Committee of the Council and Staff, chaired by Sir Hugh Beaver with Trist as staff convener.

The broader formulation of mission and the greater variety of activities and people made it no longer possible or desirable that all staff should undergo psychoanalysis. This had been falling into disuse since 1958 and became a matter of individual choice. Awareness of psychoanalytic concepts and their relevance in the social field had become more widely accepted. They were absorbed "by osmosis." Moreover, one or two people with strongly Jungian views regarding archetypes and the collective unconscious were now on the staff. It was also found that capacity to work with groups and the process side of organizational life was to a considerable extent a personal endowment. Some of the best practitioners were "naturals." Nevertheless, a number of people continued to enter analysis and several became analysts.

The matrix worked well for several years. Major new projects were undertaken and a number of influential books produced. The HRC, for example, embarked on what became known as the Norwegian Industrial Democracy Project (Thorsrud and Emery, 1964; Emery and Thorsrud, 1969; 1977) and the Shell Management Philosophy Project (Hill, 1971). The CASR was instrumental in setting up an activity in the United States based on the Tavistock/Leicester Group Relations Training Conferences and Rice (1965) published a general account of this field. Miller and Rice (1967) published their now classic book *Systems of Organization*. The IOR broke new ground with a project in which they worked collaboratively with the HRC on urban planning. It was jointly carried out with the city of Coventry with the support of the Nuffield Foundation (Friend and Jessop, 1969). The Institute for Marital Studies, having published a book, *Marriage: Studies in Emotional Conflict and Growth* (Pincus, 1960), which stated its theories and procedures, secured a multiplier effect by training case workers from a large number of organizations and extending its influence into continental Europe.

There were unanticipated developments. Several key people left the HRC. At the end of 1966, Trist was appointed to a professorship at the University of California (Los Angeles). Emery returned to Australia in 1969 as a Senior Fellow in the Research School of the Social Sciences at the Australian National University. In 1971 van Beinum went back to Holland to develop a new Department of Continuing Management Education at Erasmus University and in 1974 Higgin left to set up a similar department at the University of Loughborough. Pollock became a full-time analyst. Growing out of his work with Unilever, Bridger instituted a unit of his own—a network organization for career counselling. These individuals had all been at the Institute either from the beginning or for a great number of years. Though the moves all made sense and led to the appearance of new nodes in an emerging international network, they severely reduced the capacity of the HRC. The CASR was greatly impeded by the unexpected death of A.K. Rice at the height of his powers.

The IOR also suffered the death of its first leader, Neil Jessop, but the type of social-science-linked OR that he was developing created such a demand that the unit underwent extraordinary growth. It established offices in Coventry and Edinburgh in addition to the London base; at its peak it had 20 professional staff, more than all the other units taken together. Three books—*Communications in the Building Industry* (Higgin and Jessop, 1963), *Local Government and Strategic Choice* (Friend and Jessop, 1969) and *Public Planning: The Inter-Corporate Dimension* (Friend, Power and Yewlett, 1974)—established its academic reputation. The theory and practice of reticulist planning which it introduced are now taught in planning schools throughout the world.

In the mid-1970s, the International Monetary Fund intervened dramatically in the British economy. Public spending was cut by four-and-a-half billion pounds sterling. This meant that the funds for the large IOR programs with government departments were instantly cut and reductions in staff took place. The larger parts of HRC and IOR merged to form a unit subsequently known as the Centre for Organizational and Operational Research (COOR). In the early 1980s even more drastic measures became necessary; all the working groups became one unit in which the members were on individual contract. There were no reserves to tide people over between projects.

It seemed that the Institute might go under but this did not happen. None of those left wanted the organization to die. They had the tenacity to keep it going and have been rewarded by seeing it re-expand and enter new areas of activity in which a younger generation has the task of proving itself. The 1987 annual report showed a staff of 20.

During the financial crisis the IMS could no longer accept the risk of remaining within the Institute. A new host organization was available in the Tavistock Institute of Medical Psychology, kept in existence for just such a need. IMS's sponsors preferred this arrangement with its even closer connections with the Clinic.

Recently, the Clinic has acquired university status by becoming affiliated with Brunel University in north-west London. There is no teaching hospital at Brunel. There is, however, an inter-disciplinary Department of Social Science founded by Elliott Jaques, one of the Tavistock founder members. New opportunities, therefore, open up. The search for university status by the Clinic and the School of Family Psychiatry and Community Mental Health has ended in a novel way that by-passed the medical school connection. This development was without precedent in Britain.

The International Network

With the establishment of the matrix there began to emerge an international network of Tavistock-like centers. These came into existence through the efforts of pioneering individuals who had spent some time at the Tavistock or through the migration of Tavistock staff to these new settings. The growth of such a network was inherent in much that had been going on for several years, but events in the 1970s and early 1980s prompted its actualization. Some of the projects were (and are) joint undertakings between people at the Tavistock and people in the other centers. A number of new endeavors have been large in scale and have emerged in the socio-ecological perspective. They have needed more resources than the Institute alone could supply. They have often been international in scope and it has been necessary for them to be mediated by organizations in the countries primarily concerned.

Work in these different settings has had a far-reaching effect on the concepts and methods employed. It is rarely the case that a single setting can carry forward a major innovative task for more than a limited period of time. The variety created by multiple settings sooner or later becomes a necessary factor in maintaining social innovation.

The following tables summarize what has emerged. Table 1 briefly describes the centers or nodes and the principal initiating individuals. The entries are by country in the order in which they commenced operation. Table 2 shows how far the movement was from the Tavistock to the node or in the other direction. Visits were often for several months or a year. Some key individuals migrated permanently or for several years, playing major institution-building roles.

The network in its present state of evolution may be characterized as follows:

- All nodes express the philosophy of the social engagement of social science. The engagement is with meta-problems that are generic and field determined rather than with issue-specific single problems.
- The work is future oriented and concerned with the transition to the post industrial social order and the paradigm shift which this entails.
- Since they are concerned with bringing about basic change, the activities undertaken encounter opposition. This makes it hard for the various nodes to acquire the resources they need.
- This situation creates severe stress which in turn generates internal strain in both organizations and individuals.
- The nodes have been developed by pioneering individuals who gather groups around them and connect with similar individuals in one or more of the other nodes.
- Though most of the nodes have existed for a considerable number of years they are, nevertheless, temporary systems. Unless they can engage with the next round of critical problems they have no further useful function.
- The nodes wax and wane, go out of existence or trigger new developments elsewhere.
- A number of them are no longer linked with the London organization.
- Apart from the London center, the most densely connected are the Work Research Institute, Oslo; the Centre for Continuing Education, Canberra; the University of Pennsylvania group and the Faculty of Environmental Studies, York University, Toronto.
- Several centers have added new ideas beyond the scope of the original organization. This is particularly true of the four mentioned above in which very substantial advances have been, and are being, made both conceptually and in the type of projects undertaken. As these concern the socio-ecological perspective their exposition is reserved for Volume III.

It is postulated that networks of this kind will play an increasingly important role in the future development of fields concerned with the social engagement of social science.

General Outcomes

Type C Organizations

The experience of building the Tavistock seemed to be relevant to a number of organizations in one country or another that were engaged in pathfinding endeavors. The Institute, in fact, had become a member of a new class of organizations whose importance was increasing as the turbulent environment

TABLE I   International Network: Description of Nodes*

Node	Initiating individuals	Description
United Kingdom		
Scottish Institute of Human Relations	Jock Sutherland	When Sutherland returned to his native Edinburgh in the late 1960s, on retiring as Director of the Tavistock Clinic, he set up this independent center to deal with the range of activities covered by the School of Family Psychiatry and Community Mental Health.
Centre for Family and Environmental Research	Robert and Rhona Rapoport	This center was set up in London in the early 1970s when the Rapoports (both anthropologists and the latter also a psycho-analyst) moved their work on dual career families and related concerns with the family/work interface outside the Tavistock to establish an independent identity.
Department of Continuing Management Education, Loughborough University	Gurth Higgin	In 1974 Higgin was appointed to a new chair in this field and developed the first department of its kind in a British university with a new type of graduate diploma and strong links with industry in the region. There has been an emphasis on participatory methods.
Organisation for Promoting Understanding in Society (OPUS)	Eric Miller	This was set up in 1975 by Sir Charles Goodeve, the dean of British OR and a member of the Tavistock Council. It has an educational function, through which citizens can be helped to use their own "authority" more effectively. It seeks to investigate whether psycho-analytical understanding can be applied to society as a field of study in its own right.
Foundation for Adaptation in Changing Environments	Tony Ambrose Harold Bridger	This small Foundation concerned with projects in the socio-ecological field was set up in the early 1980s by Ambrose, originally a developmental psychologist, at the Tavistock's Department for Children and Parents. It has the form of a network organization, being without permanent staff. Originally at Minster Lovell, a village near Oxford, it has now moved to Geneva as so much of its work has become connected with the World Health Organization.

TABLE I   *Continued*

Node	Initiating individuals	Description
Europe		
Work Research Institute, Oslo, Norway	Einar Thorsrud Fred Emery David Herbst Eric Trist	This has become one of the principal institutions world-wide for the development of the socio-technical and socio-ecological perspectives. Thorsrud, its Director from 1962 until his untimely death in 1985, had been a frequent visitor at the Tavistock. Emery—and to some extent Trist—played a major role in its development during the 1960s. Herbst, also from the Tavistock, became a permanent staff member.
School of Business Administration, Erasmus University, Holland	Hans van Beinum	In 1971 van Beinum returned to Holland to set up a department of post-experience management education at Erasmus University. It has influenced the development of the socio-technical and socio-ecological fields in Europe.
Institute for Transitional Dynamics, Lucerne, Switzerland	Harold Bridger	This small but promising institute, set up by Bridger in the 1980s, focusses on organizational transitions. It is a network organization without permanent staff.
Australia		
Centre for Continuing Education, Australian National University	Fred and Merrelyn Emery	When Emery returned to Australia in 1969 as a Senior Fellow at the Research School for the Social Sciences at the Australian National University, he became associated with this center which is on the boundary between the academic and practical worlds. It has become a southern Tavistock in all three perspectives, being responsible for many of the key conceptual and methodological developments.
Canada		
Action Learning Group, Faculty of Environmental Studies, York University, Toronto	Eric Trist	In 1978 Trist joined the Faculty of Environmental Studies with which his relations had been growing for several years. The purpose was further to develop the socio-ecological perspective, especially in Third World projects, and to foster socio-technical projects throughout Can-

TABLE I   *Continued*

Node	Initiating individuals	Description
		ada. Search conferences have been introduced and teaching begun in futures studies. The center functions as a Canadian Tavistock.
Ontario Quality of Working Life Centre	Hans van Beinum	Toward the end of the 1970s the widespread interest in quality of working life (QWL) in Canada caused the Ontario government to set up a center for advancing this field, supported by employers and unions. Van Beinum resigned from his chair in Holland to become its executive director. Changes in the industrial and political climate in Canada have just recently prompted the Ontario government to close the Centre despite its considerable success.
India		
BM Institute, Ahmedabad	Kamalini Sarabhai Jock Sutherland	Kamalini Sarabhai, the wife of Gautam Sarabhai, head of Sarabhai Industries, one of the largest industrial concerns in India, came to the Tavistock for training in child development. On returning to India she and her husband set up what is called the BM Institute, very much along the lines of the Tavistock Clinic School of Family Psychiatry and Community Mental Health.
National Labour Institute and Punjab Institute for Public Administration	Nitish De Fred Emery	An unusual Indian social scientist, the late Nitish De, pioneered the socio-ecological and socio-technical approaches in the sub-continent. He had to move from one center to another because of political difficulties. He maintained strong relations with the Australian node.
United States		
Wright Institute, Berkeley, California	Nevitt Sanford Eric Trist	Sanford, a principal author of *The Authoritarian Personality* (1950), spent a sabbatical at the Tavistock in the early 1950s. Prevented by constraints at both Berkeley and Stanford from integrating

TABLE 1   *Continued*

Node	Initiating individuals	Description
		social and clinical psychology, he set up, during the 1960s, an independent organization modelled on the Tavistock. It has functioned as a U.S. Tavistock (West). Since Sanford's retirement, however, it has been principally concerned with training clinical psychologists.
A. K. Rice Institute	Margaret Rioch A. K. Rice	In 1964 Margaret Rioch from the Washington School of Psychiatry, with which the Tavistock had close connections, set up an American version of the Leicester Conference with the assistance of A. K. Rice. On his unexpected death in 1969 she named the American organization the A. K. Rice Institute. It has since developed chapters throughout the United States.
Center for Quality of Working Life, University of California, Los Angeles	Louis Davis Eric Trist	Davis, an engineer turned social scientist, had introduced the socio-technical study of job design in the United States. In 1965/66 he spent a sabbatical at the Tavistock. The next year Trist joined him at UCLA and together they developed the first graduate socio-technical program in a university at both the master's and doctoral levels.
Department of Social Systems Sciences, Wharton School, University of Pennsylvania	Russell Ackoff Eric Trist	Wishing to set up a new Department of Social Systems Sciences, Ackoff persuaded Trist, then at UCLA, to join him in 1969. A very large and successful Ph.D. program developed, beginning a U.S. Tavistock (East). However, many Wharton faculty have not been friendly towards a systems approach and recently the University has phased out the academic program. One of the two associated research centers has been absorbed into the Wharton Center for Applied Research. The other, with Ackoff, has become linked to the Union Graduate School, where doctoral and master's programs are about to begin again.

*In order of establishment

TABLE 2   International Networks: Interconnections and Perspectives

Node	People establishing			Perspectives of work*		
	Visitor to Tavistock	Visitor from Tavistock	Migration from Tavistock	sP	sT	sE
Centre for Family and Environmental Research			*	*		*
Scottish Institute of Human Relations			*	*		
Department of Continuing Management Education, Loughborough University			*	*	*	*
Organisation for Promoting Understanding in Society (OPUS)		*				*
Foundation for Adaptation in Changing Environments		*	*	*		*
Work Research Institute, Oslo, Norway	*	*	*		*	*
School of Business Administration, Erasmus University, Holland		*	*		*	*
Institute for Transitional Dynamics, Lucerne, Switzerland			*	*		*
Centre for Continuing Education, Australian National University			*	*	*	*
Action Learning Group, Faculty of Environmental Studies, York University, Toronto			*	*	*	*
Ontario Quality of Working Life Centre			*		*	
BM Institute, Ahmedabad	*	*		*		
National Labour Institute and Punjab Institute for Public Administration		*			*	*
Wright Institute, Berkeley, California	*	*		*		*
A. K. Rice Institute, Washington, D.C.	*	*		*		
Center for Quality of Working Life, University of California, Los Angeles	*		*		*	
Department of Social Systems Sciences, Wharton School, University of Pennsylvania	*	*	*	*	*	*

*The codes sP, sT and sE indicate in which of the three perspectives (socio-psychological, socio-technical, socio-ecological) work has been carried out in the new settings.

became more salient. In addition to university centers engaged in basic research, and consulting groups, whether inside or outside operating organizations, engaged in applied research, there is a third type of research organization whose mission is distinct from either and which requires a different kind of distinctive competence.

There has been a good deal of confusion about what this third type does—"problem-oriented research" has been a common label—and denigration of its worth. The Institute has had to work out its properties in order more fully to understand itself and to gain general recognition for the kind of work it undertakes (Trist, 1970).

The three types of organization, shown in Table 3, have distinctive patterns and may be described as follows:

Type A Centers of basic research associated with major teaching facilities, located within universities as autonomous departments undertaking both undergraduate and graduate teaching. Here, research problems are determined by the needs of theory and method, and express a research/teaching mix.

Type B Centers of professional social science activity that undertake work on immediate practical problems, located within user organizations or in external consulting groups. User organizations require a means of identifying areas of social science knowledge relevant to their interests and need social science professionals in continuous contact with administrators. In such centers research problems are determined by client needs. They express a research/service mix.

Type C Centers of applied research associated with advanced research training. They may be regarded as a resultant of Types A and B and supply the necessary link between them. They may be located either on the boundaries of universities or outside them as independent institutes. They are problem-centered and inter-disciplinary, but focus on generic rather than specific problems. They accept professional as well as scientific responsibility for the projects they undertake, and contribute both to the improvement of practice and to theoretical development. Their work expresses a research/action mix.

These three types of institution form an interdependent system. One type cannot be fully effective without the others since the feedback of each into the others is critical for the balanced development of the whole. The boundaries of A and B can easily extend into C, and those of C into either A or B.

The Institute is a Type C organization. It has had continually to face the dilemmas and conflicts of needing to be an innovative research body at the leading edge and an operational body to a considerable extent paying its own way. This has been a condition of preserving its independence. To accomplish

TABLE 3   Characteristics of Main Types of Research Organization

	University departments	User organizations	Special institutes
Source of problem	Needs of theory and method	Specific client needs	General "field" needs (meta-problems)
Level of problem	Abstract	Concrete	Generic
Activity mix	Research/teaching	Research/service	Research/action
Disciplinary mix	Single	Multiple	Interrelated
Overall pattern	Type A	Type B	Type C

both of these aims simultaneously constitutes a paradox fundamental to the existence of such bodies.

Type C institutes are not organized around disciplines but around generic problems (meta-problems or problématiques), which are field determined. They need the capacity to respond to emergent issues and to move rapidly into new areas. Sub-units need to be free to move in and out. So do staff.

The experience of fashioning the Institute showed that Type C organizational cultures need to be based on group creativeness. This contradicts the tradition of academic individualism. A group culture is inherent in projects that depend on collaboration for the achievement of inter-disciplinary endeavors. What gets done is more important than who does it. This affects questions of reward and recognition. A very strong tradition of group values had been inherited from the war-time Tavistock group. Appropriate ways had to be found of reaffirming them. These have not always been successful.

A difficult question arises regarding financial stability. The funding pattern described in the discussion of optimum balance is an ideal which the Institute succeeded in approximating only at certain times. Two organizations with which it has compared itself—the Institute for Social Research at the University of Michigan and the Work Research Institute in Oslo—have been able to achieve financial stability in ways unavailable to the Tavistock. In the first, the University allowed the Institute to retain overheads which would otherwise have gone to the University itself and staff to hold part-time faculty appointments which were not at risk. In Oslo, the Norwegian government provided for a certain number of senior appointments and assisted with overheads. The Tavistock has never attained such conditions. A priority for any Type C institute is continually to search for appropriate means of securing financial stability.

A structural necessity is to allow a very high degree of autonomy to sub-systems and to tolerate wide differences of viewpoint. This creates the need for a democratic system of governance such as that constituted by the pre-war

Tavistock organizational revolution that laid the basis for future developments. The form of organizational democracy that grew up after the war had become eroded when the division into two groups occurred.

This failure points to the need for a Type C institute to maintain the process side of its organizational life. In the rapidly changing conditions of a turbulent environment fresh appreciations have to be made frequently and staff conflicts worked through. If the organization is to remain an open system in its environment it has to maintain an open system within itself.

This concept of the Institute's basic organizational character was strengthened when it became a member of an international network. Beyond a certain stage innovative Type C organizations need such a network. They cannot go it alone.

Innovative organizations that come into existence in response to critical problems in their societies can usefully continue only so far as they remain capable of addressing further problems of this kind. Some of the organizations in the Tavistock network have already gone out of existence, but new ones have emerged. The London organization has survived several crises, but is still, after 40 years, a transitional organization. Though its member organizations may change, it is much less likely that the network itself will go out of existence. The evolution of the Tavistock enterprise has now reached a higher system level—that of the network. Yet in time, many of the nodes are likely to become more closely linked with other networks than the original set and to be absorbed in the more general stream of the social sciences.

Three Research Perspectives

As the matrix became established it became evident that most of the Institute's activities could be subsumed under three perspectives, called in these volumes the socio-psychological, the socio-technical and the socio-ecological perspectives. These emerged from each other in relation to changes taking place in the wider societal environment. One could not have been forecast from the others. Though interdependent, each has its own focus. Many of the more complex projects require all three perspectives.

The original perspective, which grew out of World War II, is called the socio-psychological rather than the psycho-social, as, in Institute projects, the psychological forces are directed towards the social field, whereas in the Clinic it is the other way around. The source concepts for this perspective are: the object relations approach, field theory, the personality-culture approach and systems theory, especially in its open system form. The Institute's contribution has been to bring them together in a new configuration, which it has made operational.

Experience during World War II had shown that psychoanalytic object relations theory could unify the psychological and social fields in a way that no other could. This was the reason for making psychoanalytic training an essential ingredient of the capabilities required to fulfill the post-war mission of the Institute. It soon led to entirely new concepts: those of Bion (1961) concerning basic unconscious assumptions in group life, which he linked to Melanie Klein's (1948) views on the paranoid-schizoid and depressive positions; and Jaques's (1953) theory on the use of social structure as a defense against anxiety.

Field theory appealed to several of the Tavistock psychiatrists who were impressed with Lewin's emphasis on the here-and-now, the Galilean as opposed to the Aristotelian philosophy of science and the theory of joint causation expressed in the formula $B = f(P,E)$. His work on group decision making and on the dynamics of social change, particularly as put forward in his two posthumous papers for the first issue of *Human Relations* (1947), were found to be most cogent. His dictum that the best way to understand a system is to change it gave prime importance to action research.

In 1933 Trist had attended Sapir's seminar, given to his graduate students at Yale, on the impact of culture on personality, the theme of his epoch-making international seminar the previous year. To link personality and culture was foreign to the structural approach in British social anthropology. While learning from the structural approach, Trist (Vol. I) was led to a concept of culture as a psycho-social process which could mediate between purely sociological and purely psychological frames of reference, a combination of which was needed in action research.

While on sabbatical at the Institute from Australia in 1951, Emery alerted his colleagues to the significance for social science of von Bertalanffy's (1950) notion of open systems. This provided a new way of considering individuals, groups and organizations in relation to their environments and foreshadowed the importance later to be attached to Sommerhoff's (1950, 1969) theory of directive correlation. As time went on the theoretical underpinnings of projects became an amalgam of these four conceptual traditions. The socio-psychological perspective (represented in Volume I) enables work at all system levels, from micro- to macro-, to be covered within a single framework.

The socio-technical perspective (represented in Volume II) was entirely novel. It originated in the early mining studies (Trist and Bamforth, 1951). Numerous projects have shown that the prevailing pattern of top-down bureaucracy is beginning to give way to an emergent non-linear paradigm. The new paradigm is based on discovering the best match between the social and technical systems of an organization, since called the principle of joint optimization (Emery, 1959). The notion of one narrowly skilled man doing one fractionated task was replaced by that of the multi-skilled work group that could exchange assignments in a whole task system. This led to the further formulation by Emery (1967) of the second design principle, the redundancy of functions, as contrasted with the redundancy of parts.

Efforts to bring about changes in this new direction have encountered resistances of profound cultural and psychological depth. These can be more readily understood when their basis in unconscious processes is recognized, for they disturb socially structured psychological defenses in management and worker alike, and threaten established identities. The loss of the familiar, even if beset with "bad" attributes, often entails mourning. The possibly "good" may threaten because it is untried. Change strategies have to allow for the fact that working through such difficulties takes time. Moreover, intensive socio-technical change threatens existing power systems and requires a redistribution of power.

The main developments as regards operational projects took place in the 1960s and 1970s and are still continuing. Until well into that latter decade the socio-technical field developed largely in terms of projects carried out by members of the Tavistock in a number of countries.

The importance of self-regulating organizations has become much greater in the context of the increasing levels of interdependence, complexity and uncertainty that characterize societies at the present time. Beyond certain thresholds the center/periphery model (Schon, 1971) no longer holds. There come into being far more complex interactive webs of relationship that cannot be handled in this way. These changes in the wider environment prompted the creation of the socio-ecological perspective (represented in Volume III).

The coming of the new information technologies and the signs of a transition to a post-industrial society pose new problems related to emergent values such as co-operation and nurturance. Competition and dominance are becoming dysfunctional as the main drivers of post-industrial society. The value dilemmas created are reflected in the conflicts experienced by client organizations and in higher levels of stress for the individual. A first attempt to conceptualize the new "problématique" was made by Emery and Trist (1965) in a paper entitled "The Causal Texture of Organizational Environments" (Vol. III). This introduces a new theory of environmental types which arranges environments in terms of their increasing complexity. The contemporary environment is said to be taking on the character of a "turbulent field" in which the amount of disorder is increasing. In the limit is a "vortical" state in which adaptation would be impossible.

Turbulence cannot be managed by top-down hierarchies of the kind exhibited in bureaucratic forms of organization. These are variety-reducing, so that there is not enough internal variety to manage the increase in external variety (Ashby, 1960). Needed are organizational forms that are variety-increasing. These are inherently participative and require a substantial degree of democratization in organizational life.

No organization, however large, can go it alone in a turbulent environment.

Dissimilar organizations become directively correlated. They need to become linked in networks. A new focus of the Institute's work has been, therefore, the development of collaborative modes of intervention for the reduction of turbulence and the building of inter-organizational networks that can address "meta-problems" at the "domain" level. Projects of this kind have led it into the field of futures studies—"the future in the context of the present" (Emery and Trist, 1972/73) and "ideal-seeking" systems (Emery, 1976). New process methodologies such as the "search conference" have been introduced (Emery and Emery, 1978) to solve multi-party conflicts, to improve social coherence and to envision more desirable futures.

The socio-ecological approach is linked to the socio-technical because of the critical importance of self-regulating organizations for turbulence reduction. It is further linked to the socio-psychological approach because of the need to reduce stress and prevent regression. Primitive levels of behavior can only too easily appear in face of higher levels of uncertainty. This is one of the greatest dangers facing the world as the present century draws to its close.

These three perspectives, all arising from field experience, would appear to have general significance for work concerned with the social engagement of social science.

References

Ackoff, R.L. and F.E. Emery. 1972. *On Purposeful Systems.* Chicago: Aldine-Atherton.

Adorno, T.W., E. Frenkel-Brunswick, D.J. Levinson and N. Sanford (Editors). 1950. *The Authoritarian Personality.* New York: Harper and Row.

Alcock, T. 1963. *The Rorschach in Practice.* London: Tavistock Publications.

Ashby, W.R. 1960. *Design for a Brain: The Origin of Adaptive Behavior.* Second Edition. New York: Wiley.

Balint, M. 1954. "Training General Practitioners in Psychotherapy." *British Medical Journal,* I:115–20.

Bion, W.R. 1948–51. "Experiences in Groups." *Human Relations,* 1:314–20, 487–96; 2:13–22, 295–303; 3:3–14, 395–402; 4:221–27.

———. 1961. *Experiences in Groups and Other Papers.* London: Tavistock Publications; New York: Basic Books.

Bott, E. 1955. "Conjugal Roles and Social Networks." *Human Relations,* 8:345–84. Vol. I, pp. 323–50.

———. 1957. *Family and Social Network: Roles, Norms and External Relationships in Ordinary Urban Families* (2nd edition, 1971). London: Tavistock Publications.

Bowlby, J. 1949. "The Study and Reduction of Group Tensions in the Family." *Human Relations,* 2:123–28. Vol. I, pp. 291–98.

Bridger, H. 1990. Vol I. "The Discovery of the Therapeutic Community: The Northfield Experiments," pp. 68–87.

Dicks, H.V. 1060. "Notes on the Russian National Character." In *The Transformation of Russian Society: Aspects of Social Change Since 1861,* edited by C.E. Black. Cambridge, Mass.: Harvard University Press. Vol. I, pp. 558–73.

————. 1970. *Fifty Years of the Tavistock Clinic*. London: Routledge and Kegan Paul.

————. 1972. *Licensed Mass Murder*. New York: Basic Books.

Emery, F.E. 1959. *Characteristics of Socio-Technical Systems*. London: Tavistock Institute Document 527. Revised in *The Emergence of a New Paradigm of Work*. Canberra: Centre for Continuing Education, Australian National University, 1978.

————. 1967. "The Next Thirty Years: Concepts, Methods and Anticipations." *Human Relations*, 20:199–237.

————. 1970. *Freedom and Justice Within Walls: The Bristol Prison Experiment*. London: Tavistock Publications. Vol. I, "Freedom and Justice Within Walls: The Bristol Prison Experiment and an Australian Sequel," pp. 511–32.

————. 1976. *Futures We Are In*. Leiden: Martinus Nijhoff. Chapter 4 reproduced in part, Vol. II, "The Second Design Principle: Participation and the Democratization of Work," pp. 214–33.

Emery, F.E., E.L. Hilgendorf and B.L. Irving. 1968. *The Psychological Dynamics of Smoking*. London: Tobacco Research Council.

Emery, F.E. and E. Thorsrud. 1969. *Form and Content in Industrial Democracy: Some Experiences from Norway and Other European Countries*. London: Tavistock Publications.

————. 1976. *Democracy at Work*. Leiden: Martinus Nijhoff.

Emery, F.E. and E.L. Trist. 1965. "The Causal Texture of Organizational Environments." *Human Relations*, 18:21–32.

————. 1972/73. *Towards a Social Ecology: Contextual Appreciation of the Future in the Present*. London/New York: Plenum Press.

Emery, M. and F.E. Emery. 1978. "Searching: For New Directions, In New Ways . . . For New Times." In *Management Handbook for Public Administrators*, edited by J.W. Sutherland. New York and London: Van Nostrand Reinhold.

Friend, J.K. and W.N. Jessop. 1969. *Local Government and Strategic Choice*. London: Tavistock Publications.

Friend, J.K., J.M. Power and C.J.L. Yewlett. 1974. *Public Planning: The Inter-Corporate Dimension*. London: Tavistock Publications.

Higgin, G.W. and G. Hjelholt, 1990. Vol. I, "Action Research in Minisocieties," pp. 246–58.

Higgin, G.W. and W.N. Jessop. 1963. *Communications in the Building Industry*. London: Tavistock Publications.

Hill, J.M.M. and E.L. Trist. 1955. "Changes in Accidents and Other Absences with Length of Service." *Human Relations*, 8:121–52. Vol. I, "Temporary Withdrawal from Work Under Full Employment: The Formation of an Absence Culture," pp. 494–510.

Hill, P. 1971. *Towards a New Philosophy of Management*. London: Gower Press.

Jaques, E. 1951. *The Changing Culture of a Factory*. London: Tavistock Publications. Reissued 1987, New York: Garland.

————. 1953. "On the Dynamics of Social Structure." *Human Relations*, 6:3–24. Vol. I, pp. 420–38.

Klein, M. 1948. *Contributions to Psycho-Analysis 1921–1945*. London: Hogarth Press.

Laing, R.D., H. Phillipson and A. Lee. 1966. *Interpersonal Perception: A Theory and a Method of Research*. London: Tavistock Publications.

Lewin, K. 1947. "Frontiers in Group Dynamics." *Human Relations*, 1:5–41, 143–53.

Menzies Lyth, I. and E. Trist. 1989. In I. Menzies Lyth, *The Dynamics of the Social*. London: Free Association Books.

Miller, E. 1990. Vol. I. "Experiential Learning in Groups, I: The Development of the

Leicester Model"; "II: Recent Developments in Dissemination and Applications," pp. 165–85; 186–98.

Miller, E.J. and A.K. Rice. 1967. *Systems of Organization: Task and Sentient Systems and Their Boundary Control.* London: Tavistock Publications.

Pincus, L. (Editor). 1960. *Marriage: Studies in Emotional Conflict and Growth.* London: Methuen.

Rice, A.K. 1965. *Learning for Leadership: Interpersonal and Intergroup Relations.* London: Tavistock Publications.

Schon, D. 1971. *Beyond the Stable State.* London: Temple Smith.

Sommerhoff, G. 1950. *Analytical Biology.* Oxford: Oxford University Press.

———. 1969. "The Abstract Characteristics of Living Systems." In *Systems Thinking: Selected Readings,* edited by F.E. Emery. Harmondsworth: Penguin Books.

Stringer, J. 1967. "Operational Research for Multi-Organizations." *Operational Research Quarterly,* 18:105–20.

Thorsrud, E. and F.E. Emery. 1964. *Industrielt Demokrati.* Oslo: Oslo University Press. Reissued in 1969 as Emery and Thorsrud, *Form and Content in Industrial Democracy.*

Tomkins, S. 1962. *Affect, Imagery, Consciousness.* New York: Springer.

Trist, E.L. 1970. "The Organization and Financing of Social Research." In *UNESCO: Main Trends of Research in the Social Sciences. Part I: Social Sciences.* Paris: Mouton.

———. 1990. Vol. I. "Culture as a Pycho-Social Process," pp. 539–45.

Trist, E.L. and K.W. Bamforth. 1951. "Some Social and Psychological Consequences of the Longwall Method of Coal-getting." *Human Relations,* 4:3–38.

Trist, E.L., G.W. Higgin, H. Murray and A.B. Pollock. 1963. *Organizational Choice: Capabilities of Groups at the Coal Face Under Changing Technologies: The Loss, Rediscovery and Transformation of a Work Tradition.* London: Tavistock Publications. Reissued 1987, New York: Garland. Chapters 19–22, Vol. I, "The Assumption of Ordinariness as a Denial Mechanism: Innovation and Conflict in a Coal Mine," pp. 476–93. Chapters 13, 14, Vol. II, "Alternative Work Organizations: An Exact Comparison," pp. 84–105.

von Bertalanffy, L. 1950. "The Theory of Open Systems in Physics and Biology." *Science,* 3:22–29.

Wilson, A.T.M. 1949. "Some Reflections and Suggestions on the Prevention and Treatment of Marital Problems." *Human Relations,* 2:233–52.

Winnicott, D.W. 1965. *The Maturational Process and the Facilitating Environment.* London: Hogarth.

Woodhouse, D. 1990. Vol. I. "Non-Medical Marital Therapy: The Growth of the Institute of Marital Studies," pp. 299–322.

Volume II

The Socio-Technical Perspective

Eric Trist

Introduction to Volume II[1]

Origin of the Concept

The socio-technical concept arose in conjunction with the first of several field projects undertaken by the Tavistock Institute in the coal-mining industry in Britain. The time (1949) was that of the postwar reconstruction of industry in relation to which the Institute had two action research projects.[2] One project was concerned with group relations in depth at all levels (including the management/labor interface) in a single organization—an engineering company in the private sector. The other project focused on the diffusion of innovative work practices and organizational arrangements that did not require major capital expenditure but which gave promise of raising productivity. The former project represented the first comprehensive application in an industrial setting of the socio-clinical ideas concerning groups being developed at the Tavistock. For this purpose a novel action research methodology was introduced. (The book describing the project became a classic [Jaques, 1951].) Nevertheless, the organization was approached exclusively as a social system. The second project was led, through the circumstances described below, to include the technical as well as the social system in the factors to be considered and to postulate that the relations between them should constitute *a new field of inquiry.*

Coal being then the chief source of power, much industrial reconstruction depended on there being a plentiful and cheap supply. But the newly nationalized industry was not doing well. Productivity failed to increase in step with increases in mechanization. Men were leaving the mines in large numbers for more attractive opportunities in the factories. Among those who remained, absenteeism averaged 20 percent. Labor disputes were frequent despite improved conditions of employment. Some time earlier the National Coal Board had asked the Institute to make a comparative study of a high producing, high

---

[1]This paper is taken from E.L. Trist, "The Evolution of Socio-Technical Systems," in *Perspectives on Organization Design and Behavior,* edited by A.H. Van de Ven and W.F. Joyce. New York: John Wiley, 1981.

[2]Through the Human Factors Panel of the then government's Productivity Committee on funds administered by the Medical Research Council.

morale mine and a low producing, low morale, but otherwise equivalent mine. Despite nationalization, however, our research team was not welcome at the coal face under the auspices of the Board.

There were at the Institute at that time six postgraduate Fellows being trained for industrial fieldwork. Among these, three had a trade union background and one had been a miner. After a year, the Fellows were encouraged to revisit their former industries and make a report on any new perceptions they might have. One of these Fellows, Ken Bamforth, returned with news of an innovation in work practice and organization which had occurred in a new seam in the colliery where he used to work in the South Yorkshire coalfield. The seam, the Haighmoor, had become possible to mine "shortwall" because of improved roof control. I can recall now the excitement with which I listened to him. No time was lost in my going up to visit this colliery where, since we were introduced by Ken, the local management and union readily agreed to our "researching" their innovation with a view to its diffusion to other mines. The area general manager (who had the oversight of some 20 mines) welcomed the idea. The technical conception of the new scheme was his, though the men, with union support, had proposed the manning arrangements.

The work organization of the new seam was, to us, a novel phenomenon consisting of relatively autonomous groups interchanging roles and shifts and regulating their affairs with a minimum of supervision. Cooperation between task groups was everywhere in evidence, personal commitment obvious, absenteeism low, accidents infrequent, productivity high. The contrast was large between the atmosphere and arrangements on these faces and those in the conventional areas of the pit, where the negative features characteristic of the industry were glaringly apparent. The men told us that in order to adapt with best advantage to the technical conditions in the new seam, they had evolved a form of work organization based on practices common in the unmechanized days when small groups, who took responsibility for the entire cycle, had worked autonomously. These practices had disappeared as the pits became progressively more mechanized in relation to the introduction of "longwall" working. This method had enlarged the scale of operations and led to aggregates of men of considerable size having their jobs broken down into one-man/one-task roles, while coordination and control were externalized in supervision, which became coercive. Now they had found a way, at a higher level of mechanization, of recovering the group cohesion and self-regulation they had lost and of advancing their power to participate in decisions concerning their work arrangements. For this reason, the book which overviewed the Tavistock mining studies was subtitled. *The Loss, Rediscovery and Transformation of a Work Tradition* (Trist et al., 1963). The transformation represented a change of direction in organizational design. For several decades the prevailing direction had been to increase bureaucratization with each increase in scale and level of mechanization. The organizational model that fused Weber's description of bureaucracy with Frederick Taylor's concept of scientific management had become pervasive. The Haighmoor innovation showed that there was an alternative.

Those concerned with it had made an *organizational choice* (Trist et al., 1963). They could, with minor modifications, have extended the prevailing mode of working. They chose instead to elaborate a major design alternative. It was not true that the only way of designing work organizations must conform to Tayloristic and bureaucratic principles. There were other ways, which represented a discontinuity with the prevailing mode. The technological imperative could be disobeyed with positive economic as well as human results. What happened in the Haighmoor seam gave to Bamforth and myself a first glimpse of the "emergence of a new paradigm of work" (Emery, 1978/Vol. II) in which the best match would be sought between the requirements of the social and technical systems.

Some of the principles involved were as follows:

- The *work system,* which comprised a set of activities that made up a functioning whole, now became the basic unit rather than the single jobs into which it was decomposable.
- Correspondingly, the *work group* became central rather than the individual jobholder.
- *Internal regulation* of the system by the group was thus rendered possible rather than the external regulation of individuals by supervisors.
- A design principle based on the *redundancy of functions*[3] rather than on the redundancy of parts (Emery, 1967) characterized the underlying organizational philosophy which tended to develop multiple skills in the individual and immensely increase the response repertoire of the group.
- This principle valued the *discretionary* rather than the prescribed part of work roles (Jaques, 1956).
- It treated the individual as *complementary* to the machine rather than as an extension of it (Jordan, 1963).
- It was *variety-increasing* for both the individual and the organization rather than variety-decreasing in the bureaucratic mode.

Conceptually, the new paradigm entailed a shift in the way work organizations were envisaged. Under the old paradigm, engineers, following the technological imperative, would design whatever organization the technology seemed to require. This was a rule accepted by all concerned (Davis et al., 1955).

The "people cost" of proceeding in this way was not considered. Any people cost, it was presumed, could be compensated for first by improving the

---

[3]This concept is explained on page 214 below.

socio-economic conditions of employment and then by improving "human relations." The movement under this latter title arose during the interwar period
when the model of the technocratic bureaucracy was becoming entrenched. It
failed to arrest the spread of work alienation after World War II (Baldamus,
1951, 1961; Walker and Guest, 1952). At the Glacier Metal Company where
Jaques (1951) carried out his research it was observed that, despite the progressive personnel policies adopted and the far-reaching changes made in the
character of management/labor relations, there was no reduction in the "split
at the bottom of the executive chain." Nothing had happened to change the
structure of jobs. There was no change in the nature of the immediate work
experience.

The idea of separate approaches to the social and the technical systems of an
organization could no longer suffice for one such as myself who had experienced the profound consequences of a change in social/technical relations such
as had occurred in the Haighmoor development. Work organizations exist to do
work—which involves people using technological artifacts (whether hard or
soft) to carry out sets of tasks related to specified overall purposes. Accordingly, a conceptual reframing was proposed in which work organizations were
envisaged as socio-technical systems rather than simply as social systems
(Trist, 1950a). The social and technical systems were the substantive factors—
the people and the equipment. Economic performance and job satisfaction
were outcomes, the level of which depended on the goodness of fit between the
substantive factors. The following research tasks emerged in the Tavistock
program:

- The theoretical development of the core concept.
- Development of methods for the analytical study of the relations of
  technologies and organizational forms in different settings.
- A search for criteria to obtain the best match between the technological
  and social components.
- Action research to improve the match.
- Finding ways to measure and evaluate outcomes through comparative and
  longitudinal studies.
- Finding ways to diffuse socio-technical improvements.

These tasks could not be carried out in a preplanned sequence. The research
team had first to make an extensive reconnaissance of the field to locate
relevant opportunities. It then had to become actively linked to them in ways
which would sanction their study in a collaborative mode. The idiom of inquiry
was action research (Trist, 1976b).

Socio-technical studies needed to be carried out at three broad levels—from
micro to macro—all of which are interrelated:

Primary work systems. These are the systems which carry out the set of
    activities involved in an identifiable and bounded subsystem of a whole

organization—such as a line department or a service unit (cf. Miller, 1959/Vol. II). They may consist of a single face-to-face group or a number of such groups, together with support and specialist personnel and representatives of management, plus the relevant equipment and other resources. They have a recognized purpose which unifies the people and the activities.

Whole organization systems. At one limit these would be plants or equivalent self-standing workplaces. At the other, they would be entire corporations or public agencies. They persist by maintaining a steady state with their environment.

Macrosocial systems. These include systems in communities and industrial sectors, and institutions operating at the overall level of a society. They constitute what I have called "domains" (Trist, 1976a; 1979a). One may regard media as socio-technical systems. McLuhan (1964) has shown that the technical character of different media has far-reaching effects on users. The same applies to architectural forms and the infrastructure of the built environment. Although these are not organizations, they are socio-technical phenomena. They are media in Heider's (1942) as well as McLuhan's sense.

As the historical process of a society unfolds, individuals change their values and expectations concerning work roles. This changes the parameters of organizational design. Conversely, changes in technology bring about changes in values, cognitive structures, life-styles, habitats and communications which profoundly alter a society and its chances of survival. Socio-technical phenomena are contextual as well as organizational.

Not all social systems are socio-technical. Emery (1959/Vol. II), following Nadel (1951), distinguished between "operative" and "regulative" institutions and proposed restricting the term "socio-technical" to the former. Regulative organizations are concerned directly with the psycho-social ends of their members and with instilling, maintaining or changing cultural values and norms; the power and the position of interest groups; or the social structure itself. Many such organizations employ technologies as adjuncts and have secondary instrumental systems which are socio-technical. By contrast, organizations which are primarily socio-technical are directly dependent on their material means and resources for their outputs. Their core interface consists of the relations between a nonhuman system and a human system.

There are mixed forms typified by the co-presence of psycho-social and socio-technical ends, which may be congruent or conflicting. An example of the latter would be a prison with both an electronic surveillance system and a therapeutic community. Hospitals are inherently socio-technical as well as psycho-social, which accounts for the complexity of some of their dilemmas.

From the beginning, the socio-technical concept has developed in terms of systems since it is concerned with interdependencies. It has also developed in terms of open system theory since it is concerned with the environment in which an organization must actively maintain a steady state. Von Bertalanffy's (1950) paper on "Open Systems in Physics and Biology" became available at the time that the socio-technical concept was being formulated. It influenced both theory-building and field projects, compelling attention alike to self-regulation and environmental relations. As regards the special role of technology, Emery put it as follows:

> The *technological component,* in converting inputs into outputs, *plays a major role in determining the self-regulating properties of an enterprise.* It functions as one of the major boundary conditions of the social system in mediating between the ends of an enterprise and the external environment. Because of this, the materials, machines and territory that go to making up the technological component are usually defined, in any modern society, as "belonging" to an enterprise, or are excluded from similar control by other enterprises. They represent, as it were, an "internal environment." This being the case, it is not possible to define the conditions under which such an open system achieves a steady state unless the mediating boundary conditions are in some way represented amongst the "system constants" [cf. von Bertalanffy, 1950]. The technological component has been found to play this mediating role and hence it follows that the open system concept, as applied to the enterprise, ought to be referred to the socio-technical system, not simply to the social system (Emery, 1959)

Source Influences

An interest in social and technical relations arose in my own thinking first at the macrosocial level, next at the whole organizational level and thence at the level of primary work systems. This last, however, became the crucial level as regards the initiation of field projects that provided the concrete route through which the broader levels could again be reached.

Lewis Mumford (1934) in *Technics and Civilization* had introduced me to the idea of linking the two. Anthropology and cultural history suggested that, if the material and symbolic cultures of a society were not connected by any simple principle of linear causality (as some interpreters of Marx have implied), they were nevertheless intertwined in a complex web of mutual causality (Trist, 1950b/Vol. I). In the language of E.A. Singer (1959) they were coproducers of each other. The technological choices made by a society are critical expressions of its world view. As new technologies develop, new societal possibilities may or may not be taken up. The mode of their elaboration may be constructive or destructive. There are unanticipated consequences. In the period following World War II the information technologies of the second industrial revolution were already beginning to make themselves felt. It seemed not unlikely that there would be as big a cultural shift associated with them as with the energy technologies of the first industrial revolution.

As regards the whole organization level, the first industrial project in which I was involved made it impossible not to look at the relations between technical and social systems. This encounter was with the jute industry in Dundee, Scotland, where in the late 1930s I was a member of an interdisciplinary research team studying unemployment. The spinning section of the industry was being "rationalized," causing not only more unemployment but a de-skilling of the remaining workers, along with an extension of managerial controls. As to alienation, workers in the interview sample would say that they might as well be unemployed, while the appearance of time-study personnel provoked a bitter reaction in the trade unions. In the changes taking place, the technical and social aspects were interactive. A new socio-technical system emerged—that of a more controlling "technocratic bureaucracy" with very different properties from the earlier system in terms of which jute spinning had been, and jute weaving still was, organized.

Then came World War II. A new military socio-technical system appeared in the form of the German Panzer Divisions, formidably competent in the way they linked men and machines to fit their purposes. The French army had failed to develop an equivalent system, despite de Gaulle's proposals. As the war proceeded, military technology gave increasing scope for, and prominence to, small group formations, recognizing their power to make flexible decisions and to remain cohesive under rapidly changing conditions. This led to a recasting of the role of junior officers and the kind of relations (more open and more democratic) best maintained between them and their men. In Britain the War Office Selection Boards to which I was attached were created to choose officers capable of behaving in this way (Murray, 1990/Vol. I). The Boards made extensive use of W.R. Bion's (1946) method of leaderless groups, which allowed leadership to emerge and rotate in a variety of group settings. All this opened up new areas of group dynamics—extended after the war when Bion (1950; 1961) introduced therapy groups at the Tavistock Clinic. A parallel influence was that of Lewin's (1939; 1951) experiments on group climates and group decision making, together with the beginnings of the National Training Laboratories at Bethel, Maine. These traditions became fused at the Tavistock. Bion focused on the unconscious factors obstructing the attainment of group purposes and on group creativeness; Lewin on the commitment to action consequent on participation and on the performance superiority of the democratic mode. Both emphasized the capacity of the small group for self-regulation, an aspect of systems theory which received increasing attention as cybernetics developed (Weiner, 1950).

Going Against the Grain of the 1950s

To a number of us at this time, and certainly to me, it seemed that the small self-regulating group held the clue to a very great deal that might be improved in work organizations. Knowledge about this allowed considerable advances during and immediately after World War II. Experiences in industry in the reconstruction period had shown that socio-technical relations were patterned on the breakdown of work into externally controlled one-person/one-job units and that top-down management hierarchies were being even more rigidly maintained than in the prewar period. The pattern of technocratic bureaucracy was increasing in strength.

Hence the interest of the Haighmoor development, which pointed to the existence of an alternative pattern going in the opposite direction to the prevailing mode. The Divisional Board, however, did not wish attention drawn to it. They feared the power change that would be consequent on allowing groups to become more autonomous at a time when they themselves were intent on intensifying managerial controls in order to accelerate the full mechanization of the mines. They refused to allow the research to continue and balked at Bamforth and myself referring to it in the paper that we published (Trist and Bamforth, 1951) on conventional longwall working. It would lead, they said, to expectations that could not be fulfilled; for, while autonomous groups might be successful on the Haighmoor shortwalls, they would not be feasible on the longwall layouts which represented the prevailing method of mining. Later, this opinion was found to be false, though widely held. The Divisional Board's reaction suggested that any attempt to reverse the prevailing mode would be met with very serious resistance. To move in the opposite direction meant going against the grain of a macro-social trend of institution-building in terms of the model of the technocratic bureaucracy, which had yet to reach its peak or disclose its dysfunctionality.

Several major pioneer studies were carried out during the decade. They established a number of research findings of key importance; however, their effect on industrial practice was negligible. Neither what happened nor what failed to happen is widely known. These studies are reviewed here to provide a short account of what turned out to be the latency decade of the socio-technical approach.

Continuation of the Mining Studies

If the Haighmoor development had general meaning, it was reasonable to assume that similar developments would occur elsewhere. In fact, a parallel development in a more advanced form and on a larger scale emerged in another Division of the National Coal Board (East Midlands), where one of the Area Managers, W.V. Sheppard (1949; 1951), was developing a method of continuous mining—a radical innovation designed on what appeared to be sociotechnical principles. There were two versions: the semi-mechanized (Wilson et al., 1951; Trist et al., 1963/Vol. II) and the fully mechanized (Trist, 1953a). The second was delayed because of teething troubles in an ingenious but somewhat underpowered cutter-loader invented by Sheppard. Faces were 100 and 120 yards in length, alternating advance with retreat and concentrated in one district so that only one main road needed to be maintained. Autonomous groups of 20 to 25 conducted all operations on one shift. There were three production shifts every 24 hours instead of one shift—the other two shifts had been concerned with coal face preparation and equipment shifting that were now done in parallel with coal getting. All members were multiskilled and were paid the same day wage, that was then judged more appropriate for continuous mining than a bonus. Productivity and work satisfaction were unusually and consistently high. A beginning was made in spreading the new system to six pits. Emery (1952), who was over at the Tavistock on sabbatical from Australia, made a study of this process, paying special attention to required changes in the supervisor's role. After Area-wide appreciation conferences had been held for managers and under-managers, an Area Training School was designed (Trist, 1953b) to which groups of eight (operators, foremen and mechanics) from each pit scheduled to go over to the new system came for a week (during which they visited the original mine). They had sessions with everyone concerned from the Area general manager to the face workers and the trade union secretary, who conducted the sessions in the new group organization. Members of these groups began to meet weekly to compare experiences. A kind of socio-technical development center was created in the Area workshops. This model was not picked up again for another 12 years, when something like it emerged both in the Norwegian Industrial Democracy Project (Thorsrud and Emery, 1964; Emery and Thorsrud, 1992/Vol. II) and the Shell Philosophy Project (Hill, 1971/Hill and Emery, Vol. II). It was a forerunner of "the deep slice" used by Emery (Emery, 1976) and by Emery and Emery (1974/Vol. II) in their method of Participant Design.

A study of overall Area organization was made (Trist, 1953c). The incoming technology, in association with autonomous work groups, reduced by one the number of management levels underground. Group Centres between collieries and the Area office were obviously redundant. Eventually, Divisional Boards between operating Areas and the national headquarters in London also seemed unnecessary. These superfluous levels of management were based on narrow spans of control which implied detailed supervision of subordinates at all levels rather than the socio-technical concept of boundary management which was congruent with maximizing the degree of self-regulation through an entire organizational system. In the course of time, these levels were in fact eliminated. This showed how the socio-technical concept could affect the organization as a whole and reduce the administrative overhead which has become so excessive in large technocratic and bureaucratic organizations.

Having reached the whole organization systems level, our research efforts (though on independent funds) were again stopped when a new Divisional Chairman took over. What had happened was seen in an entirely technological perspective—that of the new cutter-loader which had been introduced. Because machines of this type were judged not to be as good a bet for further mechanization as "shearing" machines, the whole project was regarded as not meriting continuation. Besides, granting more autonomy was not popular. The union regionally negotiated special pay for operators of new equipment. This broke up the unity of the face groups, which were further decimated when bonuses were introduced for various classes of workers. As time went on, the conventional system began to reinstate itself. Sociologically, this setback and the earlier one over the Haighmoor may be seen as examples of what Schon (1971) has called the "dynamic conservatism" of organizations.

A search of other coalfields produced only one, Durham, where the Divisional Board and the regional organization of the National Union of Mineworkers said they would like to proceed with social research into mining methods. Virtually all extant methods were available in the same low seam in a single area in the older part of the coalfield where customs were uniform and traditions common. Here, the research team found what the conventional wisdom had held to be impossible: the working of the conventional, semi-mechanized, three-shift longwall cycle by a set of autonomous work groups (locally known as "composite"). Groups of 40 to 50 men interchanged the various jobs required while alternating shifts in ways they felt best and evolved an innovative pay system that seemed equitable to them. Output was 25 percent higher with lower costs (40 percent) than on a comparison face similar in every respect (conditions, equipment, personnel) except that of work organization. Accidents, sickness and absenteeism were cut in half (Trist et al., 1963/Vol. II). Only one man left the composite faces in two years. Over the four-year period of the project, the conversion of an entire colliery with three seams from conventional to composite working was followed in detail. Much was learned about the conditions under which autonomous groups prosper and under which they fail. The potential of self-regulating groups in fully mechanized installations was studied and the research team began to collaborate in the design of socio-technical systems for the most advanced technology then available. A meticulous study of a single face team was made by Herbst (1962). It explored the mathematical relations between a number of key variables.

A report was submitted to the National Coal Board (Trist and Murray,

1958). The results were not disputed. But the Board's priorities were elsewhere—on the closing of uneconomical pits in the older coalfields and on carrying the union with it in implementing the national power-loading agreement, deemed critical for full mechanization. The Board was not willing to encourage anything new that might disturb the delicately balanced situation as the industry contracted in face of the greater use of oil. On the union side, the Durham Miners' Association sent the report to their National Executive. No reply was received at the Tavistock Institute.

Hugh Murray[4] has since made an archival study of composite agreements in various British coalfields. There were quite a few of these in the mid-1950s, but they were regarded simply as wage settlements. There was no understanding that they might have implications for work organization.

In the late 1960s Murray carried out an action-research study of layouts using very advanced technology. He found that the coincidence of specialized work roles and high absentee rates was giving rise to wide-scale disruption of production processes. Men were posted to places in their specialty all over the mine through a "pit market." There was little cohesion in work teams. Efforts to introduce multiskilling, which would have afforded the basis for greater team cohesion, met with little success (Murray and A. Trist, 1969).

During the 1970s an experimental section based on autonomous groups was tried out in a mine in the American coal industry with its room-and-pillar layouts and very different technology of roof bolting, continuous miners and shuttle cars. Positive results were obtained comparable to those obtained earlier in Britain, not only as regards productivity but also safety, which was the reason for union collaboration. Although a second autonomous section was started, an attempt to diffuse this form of work organization to the mine as a whole encountered insuperable difficulties which were not foreseen by members of the Labor/Management Steering Committee or the research team (Trist et al., 1977; Susman and Trist, 1977/Vol. II). This project has been independently evaluated by Goodman (1979).

The difficulties centered on the resentment of those not included in the experiment toward the privileges of those who were. This resentment would not have become acute had not expansion of the mine led to some inexperienced new recruits winning places (and hence the top wage rate) on the second autonomous section when experienced men withdrew their bids at the last moment in order to stay with a foreman (who then deserted them). There was no infringement of seniority rules, but the issue split the union.

The project shows in great detail how unanticipated and uncontrollable events in the broader, as well as the immediate, context can influence outcome in the later stages of an action-research undertaking. For example, the union's

[4]Personal communication, 1977.

national situation and leadership changed dramatically. The project also shows how the encapsulation of an innovation can prevent its diffusion and the dangers of applying classical experimental research design in the "moving ground" of a real-life field situation. Such a design was a condition of receiving initial support at the mine and from the sponsors of the national program of which it was a part.

Studies in Other Industries

Meanwhile, at the Tavistock, opportunities were sought in other industries. The first to arise was not only in another industry—textiles—but in another culture—India. In 1953 the late A.K. Rice (1958; 1963; 1953/Vol. II) paid his first visit to the Calico Mills in Ahmedabad during which time an automatic loom shed was converted from conventional to autonomous working, with results that surpassed expectations. Later, the change was diffused throughout the nonautomatic weaving sheds in this very large organization, which employed 9,000 people. Rice did no more than mention through an interpreter the idea of a group of workers becoming responsible for a group of looms. The loomshed employees took up the idea themselves, coming back the next day with a scheme that they asked management's permission to implement. Terms regarding a progressive payment scheme were negotiated and the first trials of the new system began. As with the mines, major initiatives were taken by the workers themselves. The depth of their commitment became apparent when the Communist Party of India (orthodox) took offense at the "Ahmedabad Experiment," since it involved collaboration, and drafted a number of their members from various parts of the country into the city, already swollen with refugees from West Pakistan, to agitate against it. Though their families were threatened and attempts were made to set Hindu and Muslim workers against each other, the Calico's employees stood by an innovation that was largely their own creation.

Yet the group method, as it was called, did not spread to other mills as originally expected. I asked Shankalal Banker, the venerable leader of the Ahmedabad Textiles Union, about this when I was in Ahmedabad in 1973. He replied that the other owners did not want to share their power. Also, as Miller (1975/Vol. II) reports, the nonautomatic loomsheds gradually regressed to conventional ways of working. Training was not kept up. New middle managers, who knew little of what had originally taken place, took over. Senior management became preoccupied with marketing and diversification. The automatic loom sheds, however, retained the group method and their high level of performance and satisfaction with it.

The Tavistock workers sought to discover how far alternative organizational patterns existed in service industries. An instance was found in a large retail chain consisting of small stores run by four to six employees with shared tasks and all-round skills; the "manager" was a working charge-hand (Pollock, 1954). When, however, this organization enlarged its stores and extended its lines of sale, specialized jobs with several different statuses and rewards appeared, along with formal control mechanisms.

At roughly the same time, opportunity arose to explore the possibility of an alternative organizational mode in a large teaching hospital. Advances in medical technology had turned the hospital into a "high pressure" center for intensive treatment, while reducing the length of patient stay and extending the range of diseases coped with. This had created severe problems in nurse training. The work system consisted of a set of tasks broken down into narrow jobs in a closely similar way to that in large-scale industry.

An attempt to introduce, in an experimental ward, the concept of a group of nurses becoming responsible for a group of patients met with both medical and administrative resistance, though much was learned about the embodiment in social structure and professional culture of psychological defenses against anxiety (Menzies, 1960/Vol. I). Integrated ward teams have since been developed in Australia by Stoelwinder (1978; Stoelwinder and Clayton, 1978).

As the last years of the immediate postwar period came to a close in the early 1950s, the mood of the society changed from collaboration, which had fostered local innovation, to competition and an adversarial climate in management/labor relations, which discouraged local innovation. No further instances of an alternative pattern were identified. Nevertheless, the mining and textile studies had suggested that continuous production industries which were advancing in automation might develop requirements which could eventually lead in a direction counter to the prevailing mode. Accordingly, analytic socio-technical studies were instituted in chemical plants and power stations (Murray, 1960; Emery and Marek, 1962). These studies disclosed a basic change in the core shop-floor tasks: workers were now outside the technology—adjusting, interpreting, monitoring, etc. They had become managers of work systems. They needed conceptual and perceptual skills rather than manipulative and physical skills. They usually worked interdependently with others because the essential task was to keep a complex system in a steady state. The opportunity to go over to an alternative pattern, however, did not seem to be under any "hot pursuit," though Bell (1956) had pointed to the possibility and Woodward (1958) noted the presence of fewer supervisors in continuous process than in mass production plants.

For a moment it looked as though a major action-research opportunity would be forthcoming in Britain. Richard Thomas and Baldwin (RTB), the largest complex in the British steel industry, were preparing to build the most modern steelworks in Europe. They wanted to break with many constraining precedents in management and with work practices that would inhibit taking full advantage of the most advanced equipment. The director of education and training invited the Tavistock to collaborate with him in evolving a new set of roles and decision rules, indeed a whole organizational structure, that would be a better match with the new technology. The method proposed was a series of participative workshops to be held in the RTB staff college, which would be attended by the different levels and functions of management, foremen, key operators and shop stewards. But there were delays in site construction—the ground proved more marshy than expected—and huge additional expenditures were incurred, which worried the Treasury. The participative workshops were never held. In the end, an organizational structure and the various associated appointees were crash-programmed, and all the old roles and practices were reinstated with (as time showed) negative consequences of a severe kind (Miller and Rice, 1967).

There was a rising interest in socio-technical relations among a number of social scientists concerned with industry in the British setting. In Scotland, Burns and Stalker (1961) observed a new management pattern, which they called "organismic" as contrasted with "mechanistic," in more technologically advanced industry. Woodward (1958) related changes in organizational structure to broad types of technology. Fensham and Hooper (1964) showed the increasing mismatch between conventional management and the requirements of a rationalized rayon industry. Such studies, however, were widely interpreted (not necessarily by their authors) as supporting a theory of technological determinism. There could be no organizational choice, as had been suggested by the Tavistock researchers.

In the United States[5] attention had been drawn to the counterproductive consequences of extreme job fractionalization (Walker and Guest, 1952). But concepts of job enlargement and rotation and, later, of job enrichment (Herzberg et al., 1959), though concerned with socio-technical relations, focused on the individual job rather than on the work system. In its orthodox form, job enrichment did not countenance participation but relied on experts brought in by management.

In continental Europe there were occasional signs of a concern with alternative organizational modes. Westerlund (1952) reported the introduction of small groups on the Stockholm telephone exchange. A similar transformation had been carried out in Glasgow by a telecommunications engineer (Smith, 1952). King (1964), from a training approach, had introduced groups with a good deal of scope for self-regulation in small textile firms in Norway. Van Beinum (1963) had completed his studies in the Dutch telecommunications industry. In the United States Davis (1957) introduced the concept of job

---

[5]No attempt has been made to cover the work of the many colleagues who became involved in this field, from its opening up in the decade of the 1970s, in the United States, Canada and many countries in Europe.

design. This constituted a basic critique of industrial engineering and opened the way for systems change which could involve groups and encourage participation. A working relationship between him and the Tavistock group was established.

An opportunity for stocktaking occurred at an International Conference on Workers' Participation in Management in Vienna (Trist, 1958). Interest centered on co-determination in Germany and on the Yugoslav workers councils. The idea of involving workers directly in decisions about what should best be done at their own level seemed strange to those concerned with industrial democracy. Only marginal attention was paid to the idea that an alternative pattern of work organization to that prevailing might be on the horizon. In the end, however, it was not entirely ignored (Clegg, 1960).

Confusion regarding the forms and meaning of industrial democracy has persisted. Four different forms may be distinguished, all of which represent modes of participation and the sharing of power. They are:

Interest group democracy, i.e., collective bargaining, through which organized labor gains power to take an independent role *vis-à-vis* management.

Representative democracy whereby those at the lower levels of an organization influence policies decided at higher levels (workers on boards, works councils).

Owner democracy as in employee-owned firms and cooperative establishments where there is participation in the equity.

Work-linked democracy whereby the participation is secured of those directly involved in decisions about how work shall be done at their own level.

These four forms may be found independently or together, in consonance or contradiction, and in different degrees in various contemporary industrial societies. The work-linked form has been the last to appear historically and is that with which the socio-technical restructuring of work is associated (Trist, 1979b). It is the only approach which positively changes the immediate quality of the work experience. The other approaches, which have their own merits, do not affect the basic problem of worker alienation. Increasing congruency may be hypothesized among the four factors in the longer run. Organizational democracy would be a preferable term to industrial democracy.

Conceptual Developments

A monograph by Emery (1959), who had returned to the Tavistock, put forward a first generalized model of the dimensions of social and technical systems, showing that, though they were multiple, they were not so numerous that analysis would become unmanageable. Eight dimensions were identified on the technical side, including level of mechanization/automation, unit operations, the temporo-spatial scale of the production process and so forth.[6] On the social side, rigorous attention had to be paid to occupational roles and their structure, methods of payment, the supervisory relationship, the work culture, etc.—all of which belong to the "socio" rather than the "psycho" group (Jennings, 1947). The psycho group, concerned with interpersonal relations and Bion-type "basic assumptions" regarding group behavior, however important, did not represent the starting point. Appropriate structural settings had to be created before desirable social climates and positive interpersonal relations would have the conditions in which to develop.

The original formulation of social and technical relations had been made in terms of obtaining the best match, or "goodness of fit," between the two. In conjunction with the Norwegian Industrial Democracy project (Emery and Thorsrud, 1992/Vol. II), Emery reformulated the matching process (in terms of the more advanced systems theory that had become available) as the *joint optimization of the social and technical systems*. The technical and social systems are *independent* of each other in the sense that the former follows the laws of the physical sciences, while the latter follows the laws of the human sciences and is a purposeful system. Yet they are *correlative* in that one requires the other for the *transformation* of an input into an output. This transformation comprises the functional task of a work system. Their relationship represents a *coupling* of dissimilars that can only be jointly optimized. Attempts to optimize for either the technical or social system alone will result in the suboptimization of the socio-technical whole.

In the language of Sommerhoff (1950; 1969), a work system depends on the social and technical components becoming *directively correlated* to produce a given goal state. They are *co-producers* of the outcome (Ackoff and Emery, 1972). The distinctive characteristics of each must be respected else their *contradictions* will intrude and their *complementarities* will remain unrealized (Trist, 1981/Vol. II).

This logic was held to underlie job and organizational design. Failure to build it into the primary work system would prevent it from becoming a property of the organization as a whole. Emery (1967; 1976/Vol. II) further proposed that, at the most general level, there are two basic organizational design principles. Paradigm I, based on the redundancy of parts, is represented in all forms of bureaucracy (from the pyramids onwards). Paradigm II, based on the redundancy of functions, is represented in self-managing groups leading to organizational democracy. This appears in emerging socio-technical forms.

The conceptual advances were "directively correlated" with the involvement of the Tavistock research team in the action-research opportunities which

---

[6]The others were the natural characteristics of the material, the degree of centrality of the various productive operations, the character of the maintenance and supply operations and that of the immediate physical work setting.

occurred as the decade of the 1960s unfolded. A further round of developments took place in 1965 (Davis et al., 1965). *On Purposeful Systems* (Ackoff and Emery, 1972) has had far-reaching conceptual influence on subsequent work.

The Pathfinding Role of the Norwegian Industrial Democracy Project

The hypothesis was made that no further advances could be expected until changes occurred in the "extended social field" of forces at the macrosocial level. Any happening of this kind would change the opportunities for, and meaning of, the efforts at the primary work system and whole organization levels. While no one could foretell where and when this might occur, such a happening could be expected from the increasing impact of the new information-based technologies.

The science-based industries were the "leading part" of the Western industrial system. They functioned as the principal change-generators and brought about many other changes, directly or indirectly (Emery and Trist, 1972/ 1973). Western societies were beginning what is often referred to as the second industrial revolution.

The anticipated happening occurred in 1962 in Norway where little modernization of industry had taken place in comparison with other Scandinavian countries. Economic growth had slowed down; the largest paper and pulp company went bankrupt; Norwegian firms were being taken over by multinationals. In many other respects this very small country began to feel it had lost control of its own destiny. Its environment had become what Emery and I (1963) have called "turbulent."

A sudden demand for workers' control erupted in the left wing of the trade union movement. Neither the Confederation of Employers nor the Confederation of Trade Unions felt they understood what it was about. Having set up an Institute for Industrial Social Research at the Technical University in Norway, they asked it to conduct an inquiry into the matter. Given the political pressures, Einar Thorsrud, the director, who had close contacts with the Tavistock Institute, felt that the inquiry would be better undertaken in association with a group outside Norway, which had accumulated relevant experience. Accordingly, he invited the Tavistock to collaborate. Very soon Emery and I became, with Thorsrud, part of a planning committee composed of representatives of the two Confederations. The task was to work out a jointly evolved research design. Involvement of the key stakeholders in each step was a basic principle of the design.

The first inquiry undertaken was into the role of the workers' directors, whose existence was mandated by law both in state-owned enterprises and in those where the state had some capital (former German capital given to Norway by the Allies after World War II). Various members of the board were interviewed, including the workers' directors, the principal members of management and of the trade union organization. It was found that, whether the workers' directors were outstanding performers or not, their presence, though valued as enhancing democratic control, had no effect on the feelings of alienation on the shop floor or on performance (Thorsrud and Emery, 1964; 1969). Accordingly, it was proposed that a complementary approach be tried— that of securing the direct participation of workers in decisions about what was done at their own level. These findings were widely discussed throughout the two Confederations and in the press. A consensus was reached that the mode of direct participation should be tried. The committee chose two sectors of industry that were not doing well and that were of strategic importance for the future of the economy (paper and pulp, and metal working). Criteria were established for selecting plants to conduct socio-technical field experiments that would serve as demonstration projects. Joint committees within these sectors then chose likely plants which the research team visited to test their suitability and to secure local participation.

The research team made a study of the culture and history of Norwegian society. Industrialization had been late and more benign than in those European countries (or the United States) where industrialization had occurred earlier. Industrial relations were stable at the national level where the two Confederations accepted their complementarity. Norway had not passed through a period during which patterns of deference to authority had become entrenched. Traditions of egalitarianism were deep and had been more continuously maintained than in most western societies. The hypothesis was made that this configuration would be favorable for the development of direct participation in the workplace. These favorable conditions were strengthened by the homogeneity of the society and by its small size. Members of key groups knew each other and overlapped. If they decided to move in a new direction, networks existed through which a wide support base could soon come into existence.

These contextual conditions permitted a series of four major socio-technical field experiments involving work restructuring not only to be launched but, in three cases, to be sustained (Thorsrud and Emery, 1964; 1969). Yet the hypothesis that widespread diffusion into Norwegian industry would occur from high-profile field sites turned out to be wrong. They became encapsulated (Herbst, 1976). The diffusion took place in Sweden at the end of the decade—when the Norwegian results created great interest in the Employers and Trade Union Associations. Thorsrud was invited to visit. By 1973, between 500 and 1,000 work-improvement projects of various kinds, small and large, were going on in many different industries. A new generation of Swedes (better educated and more affluent) refused (by absenteeism and turnover) to do the dullest and most menial jobs. The importation of Southern Europeans created social problems. Something had to be done. Managers and unions took up the Norwegian approach and adapted it to their own purposes.

After that, shifts in the macrosocial field in Scandinavia recentered attention on the representation of workers on boards of management just when, in Germany, some interest appeared in direct worker participation. A number of laws have been passed in Norway and Sweden. In both countries a third of the members of the boards have to be workers' representatives.

The Shell Philosophy Project

In Britain a large-scale socio-technical project, begun by Shell (UK) with the Tavistock Institute in 1965, showed the need to develop a new management philosophy to establish values and principles which could be seen by all to guide work redesign, if commitment was to be secured not only from the various levels of management but also from the work force (Hill, 1971/Hill and Emery, Vol. II). This project began with a three-and-a-half day off-site meeting with the 11 most senior managers, the internal consultants and four senior people from the Tavistock. It led to a whole series of two-and-a-half day, off-site residential conferences to discuss the original draft philosophy and to amend and ratify it. These conferences involved all levels of the organization from the Board to the shop floor and the outside trade union officials as well as the shop stewards.

After some four years, the advances brought about were arrested by an exceedingly complex situation within both the company and the industry. The ways in which the clock began to be turned back are described in Hill's (1971/Hill and Emery, Vol. II) book. The approach, however, was taken up by Shell in other countries—Australia, Holland and, more recently, Canada. It appears to be characteristic of innovative processes that after a certain time particular implementive sites reach their limit. The burden of trailblazing is then taken up by others where favorable conditions emerge.

Meanwhile, what had happened regarding work restructuring and participation, especially in Sweden, created interest in the United States. Though one or two pioneer socio-technical projects had been under way for some time in the United States, it was not until 1972 that wider public interest was awakened. Notions of work alienation were popularized by the media and associated with the threat of declining productivity in the face of Japanese and West German competition.

At an international conference held at Arden House in 1972, the term "quality of working life" (QWL) was introduced by Louis Davis. While "industrial democracy" fitted most European countries, the term had dangerous connotations in the United States at that time. Along with "Work in America" (Special Task Force, 1973; O'Toole, 1974), which extended consideration to the mental health aspects of the workplace and the work/family interface, this conference set the tone for further developments. In Bateson's (1972) sense, it repunctuated the field. The two volumes of papers emanating from it (Davis and Cherns, 1975) became its standard reference work. Since then socio-technical concepts and methods have become one input into a wider field concerned with changing social values and with studying the effects of values on organizations and their individual members. The age of resource scarcity coincided with increasing recognition that advanced industrial societies were producing conditions which were impoverishing the overall quality of life. The quality of life in the workplace is coming to be seen as a critical part of this overall quality. It is now less accepted that boredom and alienation are inherently a part of work life for the majority, or that they must perforce accept authoritarian control in narrow jobs. Examples can be pointed to in almost any industry of alternative forms of socio-technical relations where these negative features do not have to be endured. For individuals and organizations alike, there is a choice.

In the 1950s the societal climate was negative toward socio-technical innovation. Thirty years later, in the 1980s, the societal climate has become more positive (Walton, 1979). Nevertheless, in most Western countries the support base remains limited in face of the persisting power of the technocratic and bureaucratic mode. Yet this mode is being experienced as increasingly dysfunctional in the more complex and uncertain conditions of the wider environment. Emergent values are moving in the direction of regarding personal growth and empowerment as human rights. All who wish them should have the opportunity to cultivate them. The workplace constitutes a key setting for this purpose. A Norwegian law of 1976 gives workers the right to demand jobs conforming to Emery's six psychological principles that shaped the original socio-technical experiments of the Norwegian Industrial Democracy project:

- variety
- learning opportunity
- own decision power
- organizational support
- societal recognition
- a desirable future

In 1981 a second international conference was held, this time in Toronto, Canada. The 200 people attending the first conference in 1972 were almost entirely academics. In 1981, 1,700–1,800 people attended, most of whom were either managers or trade unionists. The real-world people were in the process of taking over. A large number of those present, including myself, expected a solid further development to take place during the 1980s. By and large, however, this has not happened. There has been much stagnation. Only in the last three or four years has the forward movement resumed. It cannot be said, even now, that it has become mainstream in any country. To make it so is the next task.

References

Ackoff, R.L. and F.E. Emery. 1972. *On Purposeful Systems*. Chicago: Aldine-Atherton.
Baldamus, W. 1951. "Types of Work and Motivation." *British Journal of Sociology,* 2:44–58.
————. 1961. *Efficiency and Effort: An Analysis of Industrial Administration*. London: Tavistock Publications.
Bateson, G. 1972. *Steps to an Ecology of Mind*. San Francisco: Chandler.
Bell, D. 1956. *Work and Its Discontents*. Boston: Beacon Press.
Bion, W.R. 1946. "The Leaderless Group Project." *Bulletin of the Menninger Clinic,* 10:77–81.
————. 1950. "Experiences in Groups V." *Human Relations,* 3:3–14.
————. 1961. *Experiences in Groups and Other Papers*. London: Tavistock Publications; New York: Basic Books.
Burns, T. and G.M. Stalker. 1961. *The Management of Innovation*. London: Tavistock Publications.
Clegg, H. 1960. *Industrial Democracy*. Oxford: Blackwell.
Davis, L.E. 1957. "Toward a Theory of Job Design." *Journal of Industrial Engineering,* 8:19–23.
Davis, L.E., R.R. Canter and J. Hoffman. 1955. "Current Job Design Criteria." *Journal of Industrial Engineering,* 6:5–11.
Davis, L.E. and A.B. Cherns. 1975. *The Quality of Work Life,* Vols. I and II. New York: Free Press.
Davis, L.E., F.E. Emery and P.G. Herbst. 1965. Papers from the Socio-Technical Theory Project. London: Tavistock Institute Document.
Emery, F.E. 1952. *The Deputy's Role in the Bolsover System of Continuous Mining*. London: Tavistock Institute Document 527.
————. 1959. *Characteristics of Socio-Technical Systems*. London: Tavistock Institute Document 527. Revised in *The New Paradigm of Work*. Canberra: Centre for Continuing Education, Australian National University, 1978. Also in *Design of Jobs*, edited by L.E. Davis and J.C. Taylor. Harmondsworth: Penguin Books, 1972. Vol II, pp. 157–86.
————. 1967. "The Next Thirty Years: Concepts, Methods and Anticipations." *Human Relations,* 20:199–237.
————. 1976. *Futures We Are In*. Leiden: Martinus Nijhoff. Chapter 4 reproduced in part, Vol. II, "The Second Design Principle: Participation and the Democratization of Work," pp. 214–33.
————. 1978. *The Emergence of a New Paradigm of Work*. Canberra: Centre for Continuing Education, Australian National University.
Emery, F.E. and M. Emery. 1974. *Participative Design: Work and Community Life*. Canberra: Centre for Continuing Education, Australian National University. Revised in Vol. II, "The Participative Design Workshop," pp. 599–613.

Emery, F.E. and J. Marek. 1962. "Some Socio-Technical Aspects of Automation." *Human Relations*, 15:17–26.

Emery, F.E. and E. Thorsrud. 1993. Vol. II. "The Norskhydro Fertilizer Plant," pp. 492–507.

Emery, F.E. and E.L. Trist. 1963. "The Causal Texture of Organizational Environments." Paper presented to the International Psychology Congress, Washington, D.C. Reprinted in *La Sociologie du Travail*, 1964, and in *Human Relations*, 18:21–32, 1965.

——. 1972/73. *Towards a Social Ecology: Contextual Appreciation of the Future in the Present.* London/New York: Plenum Press.

Fensham, F. and D. Hooper. 1964. *Changes in the British Rayon Industry.* London: Tavistock Publications.

Goodman, P.S. 1979. *Assessing Organizational Change: The Rushdon Quality of Work Experiment.* New York: Wiley.

Heider, F. 1942. "On Perception, Event Structure and Psychological Environment." *Psychological Issues*, 1, #2.

Herbst, P.G. 1962. *Autonomous Group Functioning: An Exploration in Behaviour Theory and Measurement.* London: Tavistock Publications.

——. 1976. *Alternatives to Hierarchies.* Leiden: Martinus Nijhoff.

Hertzberg, F., B. Mausner and B. Snyderman. 1959. *The Motivation to Work.* New York: John Wiley.

Hill, C.P. 1971. *Towards a New Philosophy of Management: The Company Development Programme of Shell U.K.* London: Gower Press. Excerpted, Vol. II, P. Hill and F. Emery, "Toward a New Philosophy of Management," pp. 259–82.

Jaques, E. 1951. *The Changing Culture of a Factory.* London: Tavistock Publications. Reissued 1987, New York: Garland.

——. 1956. *Measurement of Responsibility: A Study of Work, Payment and Individual Capacity.* New York: Dryden.

Jennings, H. 1947. "Leadership and Sociometric Choice." *Sociometry*, 10:32–49.

Jordan, N. 1963. "Allocation of Functions Between Men and Machines in Automated Systems." *Journal of Applied Psychology*, 47:161–65.

King, S.D.M. 1964. *Training Within the Organization: A Study of Company Policy and Procedures for the Systematic Training of Operators and Supervisors.* London: Tavistock Publications.

Lewin, K. 1939. "Patterns of Aggressive Behavior in Experimentally Created Social Climates." *Journal of Social Psychology*, 10:271–99.

——. 1951. *Field Theory in Social Science: Selected Theoretical Papers.* New York: Harper and Row.

McLuhan, M. 1964. *Understanding Media.* New York: McGraw-Hill.

Melman, S. 1958. *Decision-Making and Productivity.* Oxford: Blackwell.

Menzies, I.E.P. 1960. "A Case Study in the Functioning of Social Systems as a Defence Against Anxiety." *Human Relations*, 13:95–121. Vol. I, I. Menzies Lyth, "Social Systems as a Defense Against Anxiety: An Empirical Study of the Nursing Service of a General Hospital," pp. 439–62.

Miller, E.J. 1959. "Territory, Technology and Time: The Internal Differentiation of Complex Production Systems." *Human Relations*, 12:243–72; also Tavistock Institute Document 526. Vol. II, pp. 385–404.

——. 1975. "Socio-Technical Systems in Weaving, 1953–1970: A Follow-Up Study." *Human Relations*, 28:349–86. Revised, Vol. II, "The Ahmedabad Experiment Revisited: Work Organization in an Indian Weaving Shed, 1953–1970," pp. 130–56.

Miller, E.J. and A.K. Rice. 1967. *Systems of Organization*. London: Tavistock Publications.

Mumford, L. 1934. *Technics and Civilization*. Revised edition 1963. New York: Harcourt.

Murray, H. 1960. *Studies in Automated Technologies*. London: Tavistock Institute Document.

————. 1990. Vol. I, "The Transformation of Selection Procedures: The War Office Selection Boards," pp. 45–67.

Murray, H. and A.C. Trist. 1969. *Work Organization in the Doncaster Coal District*. London: Tavistock Institute Document.

Nadel, S.F. 1951. *The Foundations of Social Anthropology*. Glencoe, Ill.: Free Press.

O'Toole, J. (Editor). 1974. *Work and the Quality of Life: Resource Papers for "Work in America."* Cambridge, Mass.: MIT Press.

Pollock, A.B. 1954. *Retail Shop Organization*. London: Tavistock Institute Document.

Rice, A.K. 1953. "Productivity and Social Organization in an Indian Weaving Shed: An Examination of the Socio-Technical System of an Experimental Automatic Loomshed." *Human Relations*, 6:297–329. Condensed, Vol. II, "Productivity and Social Organization: An Indian Automated Weaving Shed," pp. 106–29.

————. 1958. *Productivity and Social Organization: The Ahmedabad Experiment: Technical Innovation, Work Organization and Management*. London: Tavistock Publications. Reissued 1987, New York: Garland.

————. 1963. *The Enterprise and Its Environment: A System Theory of Management Organization*. London: Tavistock Publications.

Schon, D. 1971. *Beyond the Stable State*. London: Temple Smith.

Sheppard, W.V. 1949. "Continuous Longwall Mining." *Colliery Guardian*, 178.

————. 1951. "Continuous Longwall Mining: Experiments at Bolsover Colliery." *Colliery Guardian*, 182.

Singer, E.A. 1959. *Experience and Reflection*, edited by C.W. Churchman. Philadelphia: University of Pennsylvania Press.

Smith, F. 1952. *Switchboard Reorganization*. London: General Post Office (unpublished monograph).

Sommerhoff, G. 1950. *Analytical Biology*. Oxford: Oxford University Press.

————. 1969. "The Abstract Characteristics of Living Systems." In *Systems Thinking: Selected Readings*, edited by F.E. Emery. Harmondsworth: Penguin Books.

Special Task Force. 1973. *Report to the Secretary of Health, Education and Welfare on Work in America*. Cambridge, Mass.: MIT Press.

Stoelwinder, J.U. 1978. *Ward Team Management: Five Years Later*. Philadelphia: University of Pennsylvania, Management and Behavioral Science Center, Wharton School.

Stoelwinder, J.U. and P.S. Clayton. 1978. "Hospital Organization Development: Changing the Focus from 'Better Management' to 'Better Patient Care'." *Journal of Applied Behavioral Science*, 14:400–414.

Susman, G. and E. Trist. 1977. "An Experiment in Autonomous Working in an American Underground Coalmine." *Human Relations*, 30:201–36. Revised and expanded, Vol. II, "Action Research in an American Underground Coal Mine," pp. 417–50.

Thorsrud, E. and F.E. Emery. 1964. *Industrielt Demokrati*. Oslo: Oslo University Press. Reissued in 1969 as F.E. Emery and E. Thorsrud, *Form and Content in Industrial Democracy: Some Experiences from Norway and Other European Countries*. London: Tavistock Publications.

————. 1969. *Mot en ny bedriftsorganisasjon*. Oslo: Tanum. Reissued in 1976 as F.E. Emery and E. Thorsrud, *Democracy at Work*. Leiden: Martinus Nijhoff.

Trist, E.L. 1950a. "The Relations of Social and Technical Systems in Coal-Mining." Paper presented to the British Psychological Society, Industrial Section.

————. 1950b. "Culture as a Psycho-Social Process." Paper presented to the Anthropological Section, British Association for the Advancement of Science. Vol. I, pp. 539–45.

————. 1953a. *Some Observations on the Machine Face as a Socio-Technical System*. London: Tavistock Institute Document 341.

————. 1953b. *An Area Training School in the National Coal Board*. London: Tavistock Institute Document.

————. 1953c. *Area Organization in the National Coal Board*. London: Tavistock Institute Document.

————. 1958. "Human Relations in Industry." Paper presented to the Seminar on Workers' Participation in Management, Congress for Cultural Freedom, Vienna.

————. 1976a. "A Concept of Organizational Ecology." *Bulletin of National Labour Institute* (New Delhi), 12:483–96 and *Australian Journal of Management*, 2:161–75.

————. 1976b. "Action Research and Adaptive Planning." In *Experimenting with Organizational Life: The Action Research Approach*, edited by A.W. Clark. London: Plenum.

————. 1979a. "Referent Organizations and the Development of Inter-Organizational Domains." Distinguished Lecture, Academy of Management 39th Annual Convention, Organization and Management Theory Division.

————. 1979b. "Adapting to a Changing World." In *Industrial Democracy Today*, edited by G. Sanderson. New York: McGraw-Hill-Ryerson.

————. 1981. "QWL and the '80s." Closing Address, International QWL Conference, Toronto. Vol. II, pp. 338–49.

Trist, E.L. and K.W. Bamforth. 1951. "Some Social and Psychological Consequences of the Longwall Method of Coal Getting." *Human Relations*, 4:3–38.

Trist, E.L., G.W. Higgin, H. Murray and A.B. Pollock. 1963. *Organizational Choice: Capabilities of Groups at the Coal Face Under Changing Technologies: The Loss, Rediscovery and Transformation of a Work Tradition*. London: Tavistock Publications. Reissued 1987, New York: Garland. Chapters 13, 14 revised, Vol. II, "Alternative Work Organizations: An Exact Comparison," pp. 84–105. Chapters 19–22, Vol. I, "The Assumption of Ordinariness as a Denial Mechanism: Innovation and Conflict in a Coal Mine," pp. 476–93.

Trist, E.L. and H. Murray. 1958. *Work Organization at the Coal Face: A Comparative Study of Mining Systems*. London: Tavistock Publications.

Trist, E.L., G.I. Susman and G.R. Brown. 1977. "An Experiment in Autonomous Working in an American Underground Coal Mine." *Human Relations*, 30:201–36.

van Beinum, H. 1963. *Een organisatie in beweging*. Leiden: Stanfert Kroese.

von Bertalanffy, L. 1950. "The Theory of Open Systems in Physics and Biology." *Science*, 3:23–29.

Walker, C.R. and H. Guest. 1952. *The Man on the Assembly Line*. Cambridge, Mass.: Harvard University Press.

Walton, R.E. 1979. "Work Innovations in the United States." *Harvard Business Review*, 57:88–98.

Weiner, N. 1950. *The Social Psychology of Organizing*. Reading, Mass.: Addison-Wesley.

Westerlund, G. 1952. *Group Leadership*. Stockholm: Nordisk Rotogravyr.
Wilson, A.T.M., E.L. Trist, F.E. Emery and K.W. Bamforth, 1951. *The Bolsover System of Continuous Mining*. London: Tavistock Institute Document.
Woodward, J. 1958. *Management and Technology*. London: Her Majesty's Stationery Office.

Shaping a New Field

F ormative projects of the 1950s will now be described—inevitably with hindsight—in terms of what happened and what did not happen. These projects led to a very large scale development in Norway that began in the early 1960s and that still continues. A large parallel project began in Shell Refineries in England and added to the conceptual input. By the 1970s the field was set for significant progress to take place in most Western industrial countries. A small beginning was made in one or two Third World countries.

By 1981, when the second international conference was held in Toronto, Canada, many of the fundamental concepts and methods now used in the field had been established. Most of these were originated by Emery, who remained at Tavistock until 1969 when he returned to Australia. Important additional concepts were introduced by Herbst.

The first international conference in New York in 1972 was attended by some 200 people, almost all of whom were academics. Nine years later, the second conference attracted 1,700 to 1,800 participants, most of whom were managers and trade unionists. Though the presentations were by academics who had a working record of projects in the field, the "real world" people were taking over.

The immediate step in the 1950s was to make detailed and precise analyses of work situations in terms which brought out the constraining effects of psychological and social factors in the ways in which technology was being utilized; therefore the need for changing these ways. An illustrative example was the filling shift in semi-mechanized longwall coal-mining studied by Trist and Bamforth. This was the first time such study was undertaken. Extracts from it are included here.

The next step was to ask about the implications of worker participation for organizational systems as a whole. This was examined in the Bolsover experiments in the East Midlands Division of the National Coal Board, where early experiments by Trist and his colleagues in continuous as distinct from cyclical mining were being carried out by an Area Manager, with union support.

Access to a different industry (textiles) was then found in India. Rice's project showed that the socio-technical approach could be transcultural. Though a follow-up study by Miller shows that the changes did not persist in nonautomatic looms, they were fully maintained in the automatic loom shed after 13 years.

In 1959, Emery made a general analysis of the characteristics of socio-technical systems that has remained the basis of a great deal in the field.

Eric Trist and Ken Bamforth

The Stress of Isolated Dependence[1]
The Filling Shift in the Semi-Mechanized Longwall Three-Shift Mining Cycle

Conventional semi-mechanized longwall coal-mining consisted of three shifts in the 24 hours. On the first shift, the coal was undercut by an electric coal cutter. On the second shift, it was hand-loaded onto the conveyor. In pre-conveyor days it was handfilled into tubs, and the men were still called fillers. On the third shift the equipment in the face and gates was moved forward. In other collieries where we worked, the filling shift was the middle shift of the cycle, which reduced the tension.

The Special Situation of the Filling Shift

Isolated Dependence

Relationships between members of the filling shift are characterized by an absence of functional interdependence that arises from the absence of role differentiation in the 20 identical tasks performed by the shift aggregate. The filler is the modern version of the second collier of the older hand-got systems, whose hewer has departed to the cutting shift. While his former mate has acquired a new partner in the back man on the coal cutter and is serviced by a new group of laborers who clear out the undercut—gummers—the filler is alone in his stint, the dimensions of which are those of the short face formerly worked in common. The advent of mechanization has changed but little the character of filling, except that the filler has, in his air pick, the assistance of one power-driven tool and, instead of a hand-pushed tub, a mechanically driven conveyor on which to load his coal.

The effect of the introduction of mechanized methods of face preparation and conveying, along with the retention of manual filling, has been not only to

[1]A shortened version of E.L. Trist and K.W. Bamforth, "Some Social and Psychological Consequences of the Longwall Method of Coal-Getting." *Human Relations*, 4:3–38, 1951.

isolate the filler from those with whom he formerly shared the coal getting task as a whole but to make him one of a large aggregate serviced by the same small group of preparation workers. In place of an actually present partner who belonged to him solely as the second member of an interdependent pair, he has acquired an "absent group," whom he must share with 19 others. The temporal distance separating him from this absent group is increased by the interval of the ripping shift.

The preparation group itself is so loosely organized that its boundaries are difficult to determine. The extent of the filler's dependence on earlier activities, if thought of as centered on the two cutters, is such that the cutting group must be expanded to include the two borers as well as the four gummers. Since, in addition, the filler is dependent on the belt-men, these latter, representing transformed but likewise absent versions of trammers formerly under his own eye, must also be included in his absent group. While, in the time perspective of the present, the filler has no relationships of functional interdependence with other fillers on his own shift, in the time perspective of the past, he must contend with a complex set of dependent relationships with the entire series of preparation workers who have preceded him in the face. These relationships are dependent rather than interdependent since, within a given cycle period, they operate only in one direction.

Though, from the filler's point of view, preparation personnel form a total group in virtue of their common relation to him, they do not constitute an organized group with respect to each other. The structure of their own relationships is that of a series of self-enclosed interdependent pairs whose connection with each other is small compared with their common connection with him. In this series the cutters form a pair of the extended type with the four gummers loosely attached. But gummings "left in" cause no difficulties for the cutters; and, though antecedent, the work on the borers also causes them no difficulties. On the next shift, the belt-builders complete the second part of an overall conveyor task begun by the breakers, but the work of this team is not affected by the level of performance of those who prepare the coal face. A series of absent pairs, on each and all of whom one is dependent but who themselves are not reciprocating this dependence and who remain relatively independent of each other, constitutes a difficult group with whom to enter into a working relationship. This difficulty is increased by the fact that their services have to be shared among 19 others, who are in the position of rivals for the receipt of preferential attention.

Difficulties are increased further by the fact that this succession of pairs pertains to the entire 180–200 yards of the face. For the pairs, the face is a single continuous region, whereas, for the fillers, it is differentiated into a series of short adjacent sections. For the individual filler it is the 8–10 yards of his own length. In the corner of this length the filler usually chalks up his name,

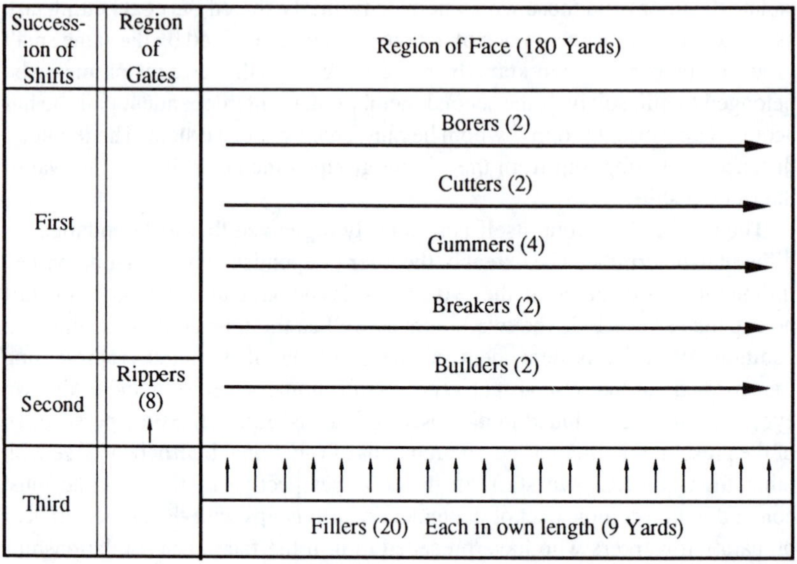

Succession of Shifts	Region of Gates	Region of Face (180 Yards)
First		Borers (2) ⟶
		Cutters (2) ⟶
		Gummers (4) ⟶
		Breakers (2) ⟶
Second	Rippers (8) ↑	Builders (2) ⟶
Third		↑↑↑↑↑↑↑↑↑↑↑↑↑↑↑↑↑↑↑↑↑↑↑↑↑↑↑↑↑
		Fillers (20) Each in own length (9 Yards)

Figure 1. Position and locomotion of successive groups of face workers on the longwall

but these chalk marks mean little more than just a name to traversing pairs. The structure of the preparation tasks as continuous activities covering the entire expanse of the face gives the succession of traversing pairs no functional relationship with the discrete tasks of individual fillers. The absent, internally disconnected group on which he is dependent takes no functional cognizance of the existence of the filler as an individual. In view of the far-reaching community—as well as work—separation that exists between the preparation and the filling shifts (produced by the time-table arrangements), actual cognizance tends also to be minimal. The pattern of these relationships is shown in Figure 1, where the picture presented is one in which, within the period of a given cycle, the fillers are left "alone with each other" and at the mercy of the rest.

UNEQUAL MEN WITH EQUAL STINTS UNDER UNEQUAL CONDITIONS

The fillers have no secure relationships in face of the differential incidence of the bad conditions they may encounter or of the bad work they may inherit from the preparation workers on whom they are dependent. The men who face these unequal conditions are themselves unequal, but the lengths of face they clear are the same. The detailed implications of this situation are set out in Table 1 where the differential incidence of some of the most common types of bad conditions and of bad work, in the different lengths of a typical face, is shown in relation to the variations in skill, conscientiousness and stamina in a typical set of fillers, fractionated into informal sub-groups interspersed with isolates.

The local arrival of certain types of bad conditions, such as rolls that move across the face (Table 2), can be anticipated, so that anxiety piles up. The passage across a face of a roll that continues for different periods of time in various lengths is shown in Figure 2. As regards bad work left by the other shifts, the filler is in the situation of never knowing what he may find, so that anxiety of a second kind arises that tends to produce chronic uncertainty and irritation. There is little doubt that these two circumstances contribute to the widespread incidence of psychosomatic and kindred neurotic disorders among those concerned.

Many instances were given of neurotic episodes occurring on shift—of men sitting in their lengths in stony silence, attacking their coal in a towering rage or leaving the face in panic. In a situation of dependent isolation, with the odds unequal as regards both his own resources and what is required of him, the individual inevitably erects protective defenses, which are elaborated and shared in the work group. These defenses are reactive rather than adaptive. Their effectiveness, therefore, is only partial. But without them life at the longwall would be intolerable for all but those whose level of personal adjustment is rather higher than that attained by most individuals in the course of their development.

In other coalfields in which we subsequently worked, and possibly also in parts of Yorkshire, the filling shift was placed in the middle of the cycle. This enabled more to be done in the last shift to prevent loss of the next cycle. In northwest Durham, not only were the two groups on either side of the main gate regarded as separate, but the six men next to the main gate and the six men next to the tail gate were supposed to help each other so that stress was greatly reduced in these small groups.

FOUR TYPES OF GROUP DEFENSE

INFORMAL ORGANIZATION

The functional isolation of the filler within his own group, which leaves him "officially" alone with his "coals," is met by an attempt to develop informal, small groups, of two, three or four, in which private arrangements to help each other out are made among neighbors. But these solely interpersonal arrange-

TABLE I Occupational Structure in the Longwall System

Shift sequence	Occupational roles	No. of men	Methods of payment	Group organization	Tasks	Skills	Status differences and ranking
First (usually called "cutting" shift). Either *night*, 8 p.m.–3.30 a.m., or *afternoon*, 12 noon–7.30 p.m. (borers start an hour earlier)	Borer	2	Per hole	Inter-dependent pair on same note.	Boring holes for shot-firer in each stint to depth of undercut.	Management of electric or pneumatic drills, placing of holes, judgment of roof, hardness of coal, etc.	4.5, equal in pair.
Though alternating between *night* and *afternoon*, personnel on the cutting shift are never on *days*.	Cutter	2	Per yard	Inter-dependent pair on same note, front man and back man.	Operating coal cutter to achieve even cut at assigned depth the entire length of the face; knocking out (front man), re-setting (back man) props as cutter passes. Back man inserts noggings.	Requires rather more "engineering" skill than other coal-face tasks. Mining skills in keeping cut even under changing conditions, watching roof control.	1, front man senior and responsible for cut; back man assists; cutting is the key preparation task.
	Gummer	4	Day wage	Loose group attached to cutters, though front man without supervisory authority.	Cleaning out undercut, so that clear space for coal to drop and level floor for filler. The coal between undercut and floor is called "the gummings."	Unskilled, heavy manual task, which unless conscientiously done creates difficulties for filler, for when gummings left in, the shot simply blows out and coal is left solid.	7, equal in group; some chance of promotion to cutter eventually.

Second (usually called the "ripping" shift). Either *night* or *after-noon* alternating with cutting shift. Rippers may start rather later than builders. None of these personnel go on *day* shift proper.

Role						
Belt-breaker	2	Per yard	Inter-dependent pair on same note.	Shifting belt-engine and tension-end into face clear of rippers; breaking up conveyor in old track, placing plates, etc., ready in new track, drawing off props in old creeping track; some packing as required.	Belt-breaking is a relatively simple task; engineering skill; engine shifting is awkward and heavy; drawing off and packing involve responsibility for roof control and require solid underground experience.	4.5, equal in pair.
Belt-builder	2	Per yard	Inter-dependent pair on same note.	Reassembling conveyor in new track; positioning belt-engine and tension-end in line with this; testing running of reassembled conveyor; placing chocks; packing as required.	As with breaking, the level of engineering skill is relatively simple; inconvenience caused to fillers if belt out of position. The roof control responsibilities demand solid underground experience.	4.5, equal in pair.
Ripper	8	Cubic measure	Cohesive functionally inter-related group on same note.	To "rip" "dirt" out of main and side gates to assigned heights; place cambers and build up roof into a solid, safe and durable structure; pack up the sides. The ripping team carries	This work requires the highest degree of building skill among coal face tasks. Some very heavy labor is entailed. Since the work is relatively permanent there is much pride	2, the status of the "main ripper" is next to that of the front man on the cutter, but he is not separately

TABLE I Continued

Shift sequence	Occupational roles	No. of men	Methods of payment	Group organization	Tasks	Skills	Status differences and ranking
					out all operations necessary to their task, doing their own boring. The task is a complete job in itself, seen through by the group within the compass of one shift.	of craft. On the ripper depends the safety of all gates and main ways.	paid. The group usually contains all degrees of experience and is egalitarian.
Third (usually called "filling" shift). Either *day*, 6 a.m.–1.30 p.m., or *afternoon*, 2 p.m.–9.30 p.m. Never *night*.	Filler	20	Weight—tonnage on conveyors	Aggregate of individuals with equal "stints"; all on same note; fractionated relationships and much isolation.	The length of the "stint" is determined by the depth of the cut and the thickness of the seam. Using hand or air pick and shovel, the filler "throws" the "shot" coal on to the conveyor until he has cleared his length, i.e. "filled off." He props up every 2 ft. 6 in. as he works in.	The filler remains in one work place while conditions change. Considerable underground experience is required to cope with bad conditions. Each man is responsible for his own section of roof. Bad work on other shifts makes the task harder. It is heavy in any case and varies in different parts of the wall.	4.5, equal throughout the group; "corner" men are envied; reputation of being good or bad workman is important.

| Total, 3 shifts | 7 roles | 40 men | 5 methods | 4 types | The common background of "underground" skill is more important than the task differences. | Differences in status and weekly earnings are small, apart from the case of the gummers. |

TABLE 2 Cumulative and Differential Incidence of Bad Conditions and Bad Work in the Filling Shift[a]

Types of adverse factor	Positions across the face of 20 fillers																			
	1	2	3	4	5	6	7	8	9	10	11	12	13	14	15	16	17	18	19	20
Loose roof—roof broken up by weight or natural "slips" (cracks) making it difficult to support; extra time required for timbering reduces that for filling.				x[b]	x	x				x				x	x	x				
Faults—sudden changes in slope of seam either up or down, producing bad conditions capable of anticipation, possibly lasting over a considerable period.	x	x																		x
Rolls—temporary unevenness in floor or roof reducing working height and producing severely cramped conditions in thin seams. As above for anticipation and duration.	x				x										x					
Roof weight—roof sagging down—especially in middle positions along the face where weight is greatest; not dissimilar to above in effect.					x	x	x							x	x	x	x			
Rising floor—from natural bad stone floor, or from the cut having been made into the coal so that the gas in the coal lifts up the floor, or from naturally inferior coal which is left down but which lifts (gas).				x		x								x	x					

Bad boring—holes bored short so that coal at the back of the undercut is unaffected by shot (hard backs); heavy extraction task with air pick at end of shift, when tired; or holes too low, so that shot leaves coal clinging to roof (sticky tops). Both these conditions tend to occur through naturally hard coal and certain types of roof.

Uneven cut—from the coal cutter having gone up into the coal. This reduces the filler's working height, cf. rolls, and the tonnage on which his wages depend. Also, as with rolls, faults, etc., it means that 3 ft. props have to be inserted in 2 ft. 6 in. height, which means sinking them in floor (dirting props) as an additional unremunerated task.

Gummings left in—failure on the part of the gummers to clear coal from undercut so that coal cannot drop and shot is wasted. The result is a solid mass of hard coal, requiring constant use of air pick and back-breaking effort. The amount left in varies.

Belt trouble—the belt may not have been set in a straight line, or bad joints may have been made, or it may not have been made tight enough. On top-delivery belts coal going back on the bottom belt very soon stops it. Belt stoppages may produce exceedingly awkward delays, especially if conditions are otherwise bad.

TABLE 2 Continued

Positions across the face of 20 fillers

Types of adverse factor	1	2	3	4	5	6	7	8	9	10	11	12	13	14	15	16	17	18	19	20
Total[c]	3	1	3	−	3	5	7	2	1	−	3	2	1	−	3	4	2	2	−	3
Skill[d]	+		+	+									−	+		−		−		+
Stamina[d]			+	+			−						−	−	−				+	
Conscientiousness[d]				−										+	+			−	+	
Sub-group membership[e]	a	a	a	I	b	b	I	c	c	c	d	d	I	e	e	e	e	I	f	f

[a] This table has been built up as a "model" of the situation from the experience of a group of face workers who acted as informants. It relates the effect of bad conditions and bad work, traversing the face unevenly, to the unequal personal and group qualities of the fillers.

[b] x indicates local distribution of difficulty in typical examples of different kinds of bad conditions and bad work.

[c] These numbers simply indicate the fact that several different kinds of things often go wrong in the same length. Severity varies. At one extreme there may be a series of minor nuisances, at the other one major interference. When conditions seriously deteriorate the interaction of factors and effects is such that some degree of disturbance is apt to be felt from most quarters at one or other point along the face.

[d] Plus or minus ratings have been given for supra- or infra-norm group status on the three attributes of skill, stamina and conscientiousness on the job, which represent the type of judgments of each other that men need to make, and do in fact make.

[e] Members of the same informal sub-group are indicated by the same letter; I = Isolate.

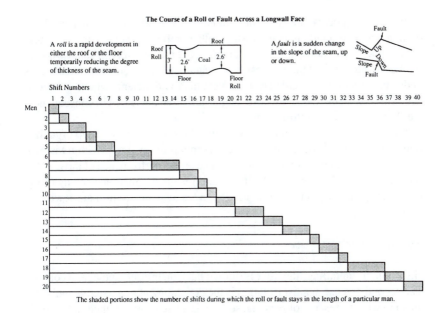

The Course of a Roll or Fault Across a Longwall Face

A *roll* is a rapid development in either the roof or the floor temporarily reducing the degree of thickness of the seam.

A *fault* is a sudden change in the slope of the seam, up or down.

The shaded portions show the number of shifts during which the roll or fault stays in the length of a particular man.

Figure 2. The course of a roll or fault across a longwall face

ments are undependable and open to manipulation for antisocial and competitive, as well as for mutually protective, ends. A number of isolates persist. The total face group is incapable, except defensively, of acting as a socially responsible whole since not even private allegiances are owed outside the small informal groups. These, in turn, are without responsible autonomy; the absence of institutionalized mutual obligation means that there are no statutory group tasks and each individual can be held ultimately responsible for clearing only his own length. Thus internal "rows" can easily break up the informal "coalitions," whose morale tends to be of the clique type.

Examples were, however, given to the writers of stable groups who stuck together and worked well over long periods. One informant said of these, "Here things are more like the old times in the pit." Groups of this kind were envied and also criticized for being "too close." They appeared sometimes to be held together by a natural leader and at other times to be made up of individuals of generally good personality. Most informants were agreed that there was a tendency for the extremes to sort themselves out; there were "good" and "bad" faces as well as "good" and "bad" cliques within a particular face aggregate. But all this happened as it might. There was no support from the system.

Isolates, it appears, are either individualists who "won't even share timber" or men with bad reputations with whom others refuse to work. Amongst these are the unconscientious who "won't help out at the end of shift" and who are frequently absent, and the helpless who "cannot learn to look after themselves under bad conditions." Others, whose stamina is deficient (whether through age, illness or neurosis) and whose lengths are often uncleared in consequence, are dropped from the informal groups.

Only to a very limited extent, therefore, does his informal group organization meet the filler's need for a secure role in a primary group within his own shift. In view of the extent of his dependence on the performance of those in the other two shifts, his need for this foundation is greater than that of any of the other occupational groups, while the resources available to him are fewer.

REACTIVE INDIVIDUALISM

His small group failing, the filler is thrown back on himself and against others. The second defense against isolation is the development of a reactive individualism in which a reserve of personal secrecy is apt to be maintained. Among his own shift mates there is competitive intrigue for the better places—middle positions are avoided (from these "it is a long way to creep")—and there is a scramble for jobs where conditions are good.

On some faces described to the writers, fear of victimization was rife, particularly in the form of being sent to work in a "bad place"; the deputy being more easily turned into a persecutor in view of the guilt arising from the intrigue and deception which the men practiced both against him and against each other. Against the deputy, advantage is taken of the scope afforded in the underground situation for petty deception over such matters as time of leaving the pit or the "measure that is sent up" (amount of coal filled onto the conveyor). With the deputy, however, men are also prepared to enter into alliance against each other, often for very good reasons—to stop mates from going absent and by so doing throwing more work onto the others who must then clear their lengths unless substitutes can be found.

As regards outside groups, practices of bribing members of the other shifts in the hope of getting a "good deal" in one's own length were mentioned by several informants. Tobacco is taken to the cutter; gummers are "stood a pint" on Sunday. These practices are to be regarded as symptoms of a state of affairs rather than as widespread in themselves. The effect of this defensive individualism is to reduce the sense of secure identification in the larger pit collectivity, which was the second principle on which the older equilibrium was based.

Nowhere is the distrust that shift mates have of each other more in evidence than in controversies over "bye-work" "slipping off the note." On what is referred to as the "big note" is entered all the contract and bye-work done during the week by the shift aggregate. This note is issued to the man called "the number man" since he is identified by his check number. In no sense is this individual a representative appointed by his mates. Only rarely is he an informal leader. Customarily he is a "corner man" whose length adjoins the main gate, i.e., the man most conveniently within reach of the deputy. When asked about bye-work, he does not always know what has been done at the far ends of the face, and he is under no obligation to stop his own work to find out. But though a number of men will grouse about their pay being short, mentioning this or that item as having slipped off the note, very few ever bother to check up. There are men who have worked on a face for three or four years and never once seen their own big note. Yet these are among the more ready to accuse the corner man or the deputy. The corner man is suspected at least of never forgetting to make the most of his own assignments. To the deputy is ascribed the intention of keeping the costs of his district down. Conspiracy between the two is often alleged. Only when a major rumpus occurs are such suspicions put to the test, but showdowns of this kind are avoided as they are apt to peter out in squabbles proving nothing.

The competition, intrigue, unwillingness to put allegations to the test and reserve of personal secrecy are parts of one pattern. Whatever their personal wishes, men feel under pressure to be out for themselves since the social structure in which they work denies them membership in any group that can legitimize interdependence. In this respect reactive individualism makes a basic interpretation of the social structure of the filling shift and is the only form of authorized behavior.

MUTUAL SCAPEGOATING

Fillers almost never see those who work on the "back shifts," and this absence of contact gives full scope for mutual and irresponsible scapegoating. When there is a crisis and the filling shift is unable to "fill off," the buck is passed to the other shifts—or vice versa if disorganization has occurred elsewhere. It is frequently also passed onto the deputy who is blamed for not finding substitutes and to repair men brought in but too old to stand the pace.

For these men to pass the buck back again to the fillers is fruitless. As the fillers do not exist as a responsible whole; they, as a group, are not there to take the blame, and the individual filler can always exempt himself. Since bad conditions and bad work interact so closely, it is usually difficult to pin blame specifically. Mutual scapegoating is a self-perpetuating system in which nothing is resolved and no one feels guilty. For all concerned to remain in collusion with such a system is a defense which allows each to make his "anonymous contribution" to the "group mentality" (Bion, 1949) which sabotages both the goal of cycle productivity and the needs of the individual for membership in a satisfying work group. So far as this pattern obtains, all strike at each other in a mock war in which no one is hurt yet all suffer.

This defense can also be seen as a backhanded attempt to recover the supportive unity lost through reactive individualism in a way that is consistent with it. For all to be "in the bad" together is at least a way of being together. If one's contribution to a group is to help carry the badness of others, the group's contribution to oneself is to allow one to leave some of one's own badness in the group by being granted the privilege of withdrawal so that one's absence is sanctioned on a fair share of occasions. This formula provides a workable scheme, since the tacit agreement is only too plausibly maintained that the badness both of the group and of the individual are exclusively effects of the system which the group is compelled to operate without having power to change, i.e., these effects are regarded as "induced" rather than as "own forces." The group and the individual can therefore deny and get rid of their own badness by ascribing it to the system. The alternative would be constructive limitation of its real deficiencies so that it might be operated with more productive results and a higher degree of mutual satisfaction.

Not that the system is felt as entirely bad since it is the means by which a living is earned. Moreover, under present economic conditions this living is a good one, both in terms of wages and of community status. But the benefits which these "goods" bring are not realized in the work activities of the group. They lie outside the work system, which is tolerated as a means to external ends rather than accepted also as an end in itself, worthy of wholehearted pursuit in virtue of the internal satisfactions it affords. When these different aspects of the matter are put together the expectation emerges of a balance being struck which would allow things to tick over, though with a degree of social illness costly alike to productivity and to personal well-being. This expectation accords with reality.

SELF-COMPENSATORY ABSENTEEISM

Withdrawal is the fourth form of defense, complementing mutual scapegoating, and absenteeism is to be regarded as a recognized social technique within this pattern. For example, one filler, returning from his week's paid vacation, complained that the first two shifts had "knocked it all out of him." The gummings had been left in. His coal was solid. He had had the air pick on all day. "I've tried cursing 'em but it's no use, and pleading with 'em but it's no use. I'll take a day off for this."

When conditions on a face deteriorate, especially in ways that are predictable, absenteeism among fillers sometimes piles up to a point where the remainder have to stay down an extra two or three hours in order to clear the face. Should this situation repeat itself for more than a day or two, those coming on shift often meet at the pit-head baths before presenting themselves for work. If fewer than a certain number arrive, all go home.

Absenteeism of this self-compensatory type, though carried out as an act of aggrieved defiance against a system felt in these circumstances as persecutory, is an attempt on the part of the individual to prolong his work life at the coal face. For, without the respite of occasional absences, he feels that he would soon become unable to carry on. In view of the accentuated differences both in wages and in status between face workers and repair, haulage or surface personnel, the goal of remaining at the coal face for as long as possible would appear to operate as a powerful motivational force in determining the behavior of the ordinary face worker.

The following is some of the material obtained in interviews and discussions. Fear of being "too old for the face at 40" or even at 35 was a frequently expressed anxiety, made more acute by personal experience of the painful tensions in miners' families where a father relegated to the surface at £5.19s.3d. a week must face a son, still in his early 20s, earning more than twice this wage. Instances were reported of quarrels between brothers, among whom long-standing but mild neurotic rivalries had existed, that severely disturbed the larger family when the older, through sickness (often of a psychosomatic kind), had been forced to leave the face. In the culture of the mining family a face worker husband is the object of special care on the part of his wife. There were men who felt that the privilege of this care, the emotional need for which was now stronger, was no longer merited once their elite position had been forfeited and their potency as breadwinners reduced. The dilemma of this situation is that fear of the loss of this care and acceptance of its continuing offer are both unbearable.

This self-compensatory absenteeism is a socially structured activity operated in accordance with a complex code that governs both the occasions and amounts regarded as permissible. It is a psycho-social defense motivated by the wish to remain at the coal face and is a species of "institutional" conduct with a functional role in the total social system in which the longwall method plays a central part.

This and the other three defenses discussed play a dynamically interrelated part in forming the culture (Trist, 1950/Vol. I) of the work group, though naturally the intensity to which the pattern is present varies widely and there are faces where the group atmosphere remains for long periods relatively immune from these influences. These are apt, however, to be "fair-weather" faces.

The danger is that habituation to working in a bad system has the compensation of enabling those concerned to leave too much both of their own and of their group's "badness" *in the system*. This built-in compensation ties them to the system despite their hatred of it. As well as its faults, it is their own hatred that they hate in the system, and there is usually stubborn refusal to recognize such projections in work groups not less than in therapy groups. A characteristic of faces with a bad group atmosphere is the protesting yet excited collusion of all concerned with the state of affairs. This is in contrast to the more independently critical and realistic attitude of those in groups where the pattern is less complete and less intense.

Some Problems of the Other Shifts

The Absence of Authority in the Cutting Team

As it is on this preparation group—containing the front and back man on the cutter and the four gummers—that the filling shift is most dependent, there is a special need for social organization to be sound at this point. But the cutting team does not exist officially as a group since the cutters are on their own note, responsible for and paid for their cutting alone. The gummers are not under their authority, and no one except the deputy can take responsibility for any tendency they may have to leave some or all of the gummings in in certain stints as they traverse the face. As they are on day wage, they have nothing to lose unless they go too far—so, at least, the fillers feel in their bitterness on this score.

As the lowest paid and lowest prestige group on the face, doing the least skilled task, gummers are both an outcast and a scapegoated group. Their work is arduous, dangerous, dusty—and awkward. Their hostility toward "the system" and toward other face workers is almost inevitable and is most easily displaced upon the fillers, whom they never see but can severely annoy—not necessarily with conscious malice—by leaving in some of the gummings under conditions of fatigue or difficulty. A system that puts this power of interference into the hands of a potentially disgruntled, scapegoated group, with no effective social means of controlling it, fosters the hostile tendencies almost inevitably present. These difficulties are increased by the fact that, among all face workers, status differences are greatest between cutters and gummers and by the fact that the cutters are a closed pair. Tensions within this ambiguously organized group are apt to be sharp.

There are, of course, instances where effective leadership is exercised over the gummers by the front man, and some of these were quoted by informants. But it was stressed at the same time that management could hold the cutters responsible only for the cut and that to exercise detailed supervision was an impossible task for a deputy, especially on back shifts where his territory of responsibility is apt to be more extensive than on day shift. In shift groups where a good spirit of cooperation obtains, the belt-breakers are often willing to help out the gummers. It was suggested that fewer lapses occurred when these interchanges took place. But the pattern of the cutting shift works against such cooperation, consisting as it does of four different categories of workers successively traversing the face with their own separately institutionalized component tasks, with no overall goal to bind them together and no functionally defined responsibilities to each other.

So closely tied, however, are the cutting and gumming operations that they cannot in practice be treated as separate. Hence arises the dilemma of the team that is at the same time not a team. Given a work system with a different type of culture there might be no problem but, given longwall separatism, there would appear to be no solution—until new conceptions of relationship emerge.

Some instances were quoted of gummers being paid by the front man, who could therefore be penalized for gummings left in by having money stopped out of his contract. But it was pointed out that this sanction could be applied only in cases of the grossest kind, which the deputy would in any case pick up, and that it tended to place cutters in the hands of their gummers. This suggests that the persistence or resuscitation of the old forms of contract are not in themselves enough to restore responsible autonomy.

THE SPLIT-OFF POSITION OF THE INTERDEPENDENT PAIRS

Superficially, borers, belt-builders and belt-breakers look like pair structures that echo those of pre-mechanized days. But, whereas the pairs of hand-got coal getting had craft status and an artisan type of independence in working their own face, with the satisfaction of seeing through the whole coal getting job, these longwall pairs are restricted to work tasks of a singularly narrow component character.

The borers are off by themselves; and, as regards the belt workers, since breakers and builders are on different shifts, neither can feel the satisfaction of accepting responsibility for the conveyor system as a whole.

The most fractionated tasks are therefore performed by those restricted to the narrowest relationships. It would be difficult to imagine a situation in which they were more completely split off from any sense of belonging to a shift or total production group. But they are at least responsible to each other and are based on a stable, if narrow, relationship.

The Social Viability of the Ripping Team

By contrast, the ripping team is a well-organized primary work group of seven or eight men with an intelligible total task, for which it carries complete responsibility. Rippers are frequently referred to by others as a "good crowd" who seldom "go absent on each other." Pride of craft is considerable. A main ripper and, usually, individuals of very varying experience compose the group, but it appears to manage its internal relationships without status difficulties. Here, responsible autonomy persists.

Unfortunately, like the other face-work groups, it is a group by itself, and there is no transfer of its more stable morale to other groups in the system. Working as it does in the main and side gates, it is felt to be a closed group very much apart from the interaction between the preparation and filling operations carried out in the face itself.

In all essential respects the ripping teams represent a survival of the hand-got past in the mechanical present. For the gates in which ripping parties of varying sizes operate are, as it were, their own "stalls," continuously and autonomously worked. All relevant operations are carried out within the group, which completes them within the compass of one shift. Rippers have escaped from, rather than become part of, the longwall system, retaining intact their total task, their multiple skills, their artisan independence and their small group organization. They work in the gates. Though part of the task remains small, the spatiotemporal structure is simple and methods are unmechanized. Changes consequent on the introduction of power-driven tools, or of steel replacing wood, have been assimilated without essential restructuring.

In the face, it was the introduction of machines (still foreign to the gates) that caused the appearance of a new order, changing the scale to mass production and bringing fractionation of tasks, extension of sequence, role and shift segregation, small group disorganization and inter-group dependence. In the gates the old order continues in a special setting. To compare the two, one needs only to step from gates to face. Those in the face once fared as well as those in the gates.

Conclusions

The fact that the desperate economic incentives of the between-war period no longer operate means a greater intolerance of unsatisfying or difficult working conditions, or systems of organization, among miners, even though they may not always be clear as to the exact nature of the resentment or hostility they often appear to feel. The persistence of socially ineffective structures at the coal face is likely to be a major factor in preventing a rise of morale, in discouraging recruitment and in increasing labor turnover.

The innovations in social organization of face-work groups that have begun to appear, and the success of some of those developments, suggest that the organizational changes brought about by nationalization provide a not inappropriate opportunity for the experimental working through of problems of the types that have been indicated. It can certainly be said with some confidence that within the industry there exist the necessary resources and creativity to allow widespread constructive developments to take place.

As regards the longwall system, the first need is for systematic study and evaluation of the changes so far tried.[2] It seems to the present writers, however, that a qualitative change will have to be effected in the general character of the method so that a social as well as a technological whole can come into existence. Only if this is achieved can the relationships of the cycle work group be successfully integrated and a new social balance created.

The immediate problems are to develop formal small-group organization on the filling shift and to work out an acceptable solution to the authority questions in the cutting team. But it is difficult to see how these problems can be solved effectively without restoring responsible autonomy to primary groups throughout the system and ensuring that each of these groups has a satisfying sub-whole as its work task and some scope for flexibility in work pace. Only if this is done will the stress of the deputy's role be reduced and his task of maintaining the cycle receive spontaneous support from the primary work groups.

It is likely that any attempts in this direction would need to take advantage of the recent trend of training face workers for more than one role so that interchangeability of tasks would be possible within work teams. Moreover, the problem of shift segregation will not be overcome until the situation is altered in which one large group is permanently organized round the day shift and the others round the back shifts. Some interchange between roles in preparation and filling tasks would seem worth consideration. Once preparation workers and fillers could experience each other's situation, mutual understanding and tolerance would be likely to increase.

It is to be borne in mind that developments in room-and-pillar methods appear to be stressing the value of the strongly knit primary work groups and that the most recent advances in mechanization, such as power loaders or strippers, both require work teams of this kind.

References

Bion, W.R. 1949. "Experiences in Groups III." *Human Relations*, 2:13–22.

Sheppard, W.V. 1951. "An Experiment in Continuous Longwall Mining at Bolsover Colliery." Paper presented at Institution of Mining Engineers, Annual General Meeting, January.

Trist, E.L. 1950. "Culture as a Psycho-Social Process." Paper presented to the Anthropological Section, British Association for the Advancement of Science. Vol. I, pp. 539–45.

[2]One of the most interesting of these changes is described in Sheppard (1951).

Eric Trist, Gurth Higgin, Hugh Murray and Alec Pollock

Alternative Work Organizations

An Exact Comparison[1]

A socio-psychological analysis of contrasting types of work organization on longwall faces in coal mines suggested that the composite form[2] was a better fit to the requirements of the mining system than the more widespread conventional form. To test this hypothesis, two comparative quantitative studies were made of ordinary coal production faces, geologically and technologically similar and not in any way experimental or otherwise atypical. The research design was based on a two-step comparison: the first, between two units with widely different sets of system characteristics, X (conventional) and Y (composite); the second, between two similar units, Y and Y(X), one of which had some of the X system characteristics. If the first comparison showed that Y was superior to X and the second that Y was superior to Y(X) then the hypothesis would be sustained.

Geological conditions in the seam were good, though minor differences existed in the seam section and in the amount of stone or dirt *bands* within it. A "longwall" unit (or panel) consisted of two 80 yard faces on either side of a main *gate* (tunnel). Face conveyor belts fed on to a main conveyor that discharged into a hopper from which tubs were filled. Face supports were wooden props and steel straps with collapsible steel chocks that reinforced the support system. (This was the customary setup before faces became completely mechanized.)

The coal was won by undercutting the face with electrical machines (driven

[1]This paper is a revised version of Chapters 13 and 14 in E.L. Trist, G.W. Higgin, H. Murray and A.B. Pollock, *Organizational Choice: Capabilities of Groups at the Coal Face Under Changing Technologies: The Loss, Rediscovery and Transformation of a Work Tradition.* London: Tavistock Publications, 1963. Reissued 1987, New York: Garland.

[2]In composite working all members are multiskilled; they can exchange shifts and deploy themselves as necessary to carry on with succeeding tasks (task continuity); they share equally in a common paynote. The teams are self-regulating and practice what we called responsible autonomy (Trist and Bamforth, 1951/Vol. II). The terms "autonomous" and "semi-autonomous" are used interchangeably in the literature.

by *cuttermen*) and clearing out the undercut (by *scufflers*) to allow the coal to be drilled and broken from the face with explosives. On the next shift *fillers* shoveled the coal on to the face conveyor and set roof supports as the face was cleared, and *hewers* removed coal at the head of the main gate with pneumatic picks. The fillers are followed on the next shift by the *pullers* who advance the face conveyors and the steel chocks. At the same time the *stonemen* enlarge and advance the three gateways between and at the end faces of the panel.

The primary task was the daily completion of a scheduled three-shift production cycle. Arrangements for winding filled tubs of coal up the pit shaft fixed the relationships of tasks to shifts, with coal being filled-off at specified times, alternating between *fore-* (first) and *back-* (second) shifts, with no winding taking place on the *night* (third) shift.

The division of the primary task into the familiar sequence of cutting, scuffling, filling, hewing, drilling, pulling and stonework meant that there was technical interdependence between the different main tasks. How any one task group carried out its activities affected, directly or indirectly, what had to be done by others, as was the case also with the way places were kept and equipment handled or repaired. A good deal of coordination was required if the continuity necessary for the smooth running of the cycle was to be achieved.

A Comparison of Organizational Extremes

CHARACTERISTICS OF TWO PANELS

The first comparison was between a longwall organized on conventional lines and one organized on composite principles, faces representing the most extreme forms of work group organization encountered in the research. Comparison was made at a macroscopic level since there was reason to believe that differences of a major order would be disclosed.

Both panels were in the same seam, at neighboring pits. Geological conditions were alike, the same cutting technology was used and the haulage was similar. The set of task roles were identical on the two panels. There were, however, slight differences in manning. The total cycle group on the conventional panel comprised 38 face workers, that on the composite 41, the difference reflecting minor geological differences, pit custom and also the somewhat increased task size on the composite panel.

The work force on the conventionally organized panel was divided into 14 separate groups, each on a different paynote. These groups were defined by their responsibility for one main task, which, drilling apart, was on only one face or in one gate. Beyond this territory and this activity they had neither responsibility nor rewards.

On the composite panel, the workers had formed themselves into one whole group on one equally shared paynote; all members were jointly responsible for all activities. Although manning the same set of roles, they had a system of rotation whereby they changed main tasks, shifts and activity groups in a way that they had prescribed for themselves.

The effects on face worker behavior of these two different forms of organization will now be examined in terms of approach to work, non-cycle activity, inter-group relations, face experience and absence. An assessment will then be made of their effects on cycle progress, regularity of production and level of productivity. Finally, their consequences for management will be discussed, taking into account the roles of deputy, overman and undermanager—those concerned with face and seam management.

DIFFERENCES IN FACE WORKER BEHAVIOR

As regards *approaches to work,* activities such as keeping the face in alignment and equipment in good running order, necessary to maintain the conditions for cycle completion, were of little concern to conventional work groups responsible only for one main task. Having no direct financial or group interest in the running of the cycle, they tended to be careless in these matters and not to mind how their way of doing their own main tasks might affect succeeding groups. Cuttermen, concentrating on yards cut, which is their basis of payment, did not bother if they cropped some of the coal and left it for the filler to dig out. Fillers, concentrating on tons filled, were not greatly worried by the consequences for the pullers of how they put in their supports. Pullers, in their turn, were not too careful about stacking withdrawn supports behind the belt and would leave them lying in the cutting track. All groups proceeded as though the cycle of operations were limited to their own task.

On the composite longwall, where there was only one team, all of whom shared a single primary task and a single paynote, groups anticipated the effects their activities might have on later shifts and anything likely to cause extra work was avoided. The standard of workmanship, therefore, was higher. The face was squared off and completely cleared, with no band or coal left lying; timber was in a straight line and gates and equipment were tidy. Quite different was the appearance of the conventional face, with spillage along the conveyor, timber badly set and gates and equipment in a rather neglected state.

These different approaches to work give rise to differences in the proportion of time spent on activities necessary for the progress of the cycle. Ideally, all work done by a face team is on main tasks and certain sub-tasks essential to their performance. To be contrasted is nonproductive ancillary work arising from disorganization or stoppages. Such *non-cycle activity* can never be en-

TABLE I   Non-Cycle Activity on a
Conventional Longwall

Task group	Percentage of face time
Pullers	62[a]
Cuttermen	45
Scufflers	45
Driller	45
Fillers	37
Hewers	16
Stonemen	8
Whole team	32

[a]Includes 43 percent arising from coal filling.

tirely eliminated, but time spent waiting-on, doing overtime or going on to other work is an index of the extent to which the cycle is disturbed. Table I sets out the proportion of face time spent on ancillary tasks by the various groups on the conventional longwall. One-third of all their activities was of such a kind, though the proportion varied considerably between different groups, as did the reasons for its occurrence. For the driller, cuttermen and scufflers, time became available for work away from the face because their main tasks did not occupy a whole shift. Non-cycle activity for the fillers arose from interruptions caused by conveyor belt breakages and tub shortages. For the pullers it was increased beyond that of any other group by the call made on them to overcome cycle lag by filling off coal left on the face; an average of 11 percent was left on by the fillers and clearing this before beginning their own tasks accounted for 43 percent of the pullers' additional work. Only the hewers and stonemen, whose tasks were on the whole independent of those of other groups, had relatively small amounts of non-cycle activity.

For no task group, however, was more than 11 percent of the time spent on ancillary work due to unavoidable causes. Over all the groups this proportion was 7 percent. The remaining 25 percent was additional work made for one group by another. Although such extra work was seen as an imposition, there was no objection to its inheritance, because it was paid for, so that no one was discouraged from carrying out his main task in a way that created work for others. This pattern is referred to as the institution of *made work* and is a latent effect of the division of the cycle aggregate into single task groups.

The common, equally shared paynote of the composite longwall was based on an inclusive fixed minimum, which covered sub-tasks as well as main tasks and any ancillary work created. In addition, there was a large piece-rate component, 42 percent of possible earnings being dependent on output. The men had an incentive, therefore, to complete the cycle without making unnecessary work. Main and sub-tasks accounted for virtually all time spent at the face, non-cycle activity being only half of 0.5 percent.

Inter-group relations on the conventional longwall were at one and the same time competitive and collusive. Men had two sorts of relationship according to whether other face workers were inside or outside their marrow group. The marrow relationship, confined to members of their own main task group, was a close, friendly relationship in which work and earnings were shared and members trusted and supported each other. But they had far fewer marrow than non-marrow relationships. These latter, which comprised their contacts with those in all other task groups, were competitive, suspicious and unsupportive, with a psychological flavor of tension rather than ease, and offered opportunities for collusion rather than cooperation. The basis of the competition, which was covert, was ultimately financial as each task group aimed to maximize its own earnings, while management aimed to hold total face costs within reasonable limits. There were, therefore, 14 different pressure points on the same budget. But separate advantage could not be too openly sought without endangering "worker solidarity," the traditional weapon against management. Collusion over made work provided a convenient way out of this dilemma, especially as it was largely unwitting. Men on the composite longwall had a common goal and only marrow relationships with all their fellow face workers. Problems of this kind could not arise.

Table 2 summarizes the main factors affecting day-to-day *experience of face work*. Men on the conventional longwall did their one main task on only the two shifts to which it was assigned and always with the same group of marrows. On the composite longwall, because of the rotation system, the scope of day-to-day experience was much more varied. Men rotated among several main tasks, shared all three shifts and moved from one activity group to another.

Face work places many stresses on the worker, particularly when things are not going well. One way of reducing these stresses is by making it possible for the worker to have a change of task, shift or workplace. When difficulties arise, one or two groups usually bear the brunt: if the roof is broken, the pullers and perhaps the fillers; if fragmentation in the gates is bad, the stonemen; if there is a small fault in the floor, the cutters. Seldom do all groups carry the burden of bad conditions equally. When difficulties occurred on the conventional long-

TABLE 2   Variety of Work Experience (averages for whole team)

Aspects of work experience	Conventional longwall	Composite longwall
Main tasks worked at	1.0	3.6
Different shifts worked on	2.0	2.9
Activity groups worked with	1.0	5.5

wall, the group with the extra load had no relief, but on the composite longwall the stress could be shared.

One effect of the differences in the scope of work experience and the possibility of sharing out the more stressful tasks can be seen in the *absence behavior* of the two teams. Men on the composite longwall had in their task/shift rotation system a means of relief if some of the face work became unduly heavy, whereas on the conventional longwall those who suffered from bad conditions had to put up with them. Their working life, therefore, was more stress-inducing and the needs and temptations to withdraw—to be absent—were greater. This expectation of a higher level of absence is supported by the figures for comparative absence set out in Table 3, the rate for all reasons being higher for the conventional longwall and that for voluntary absence over 10 times as great.

EFFECTS ON PRODUCTION

We now turn to the effect of face group organization on maintaining production. *Cycle progress* on the conventional longwall tended to be erratic since a good deal of time was lost on nonproductive ancillary work caused by internal

TABLE 3   Absence Rates (percent of possible shifts)

Reason for absence	Conventional longwall	Composite longwall
No reason given	4.3	0.4
Sickness and other	8.9	4.6
Accident	6.8	3.2
Total	20.0	8.2

and external interference. During this time the cycle stood still. The best that could be hoped for was that main tasks would be up to schedule. For the cycle to be in advance was impossible because, even if a group should finish its own task early, it could not go on to the next as this was the preserve of another group. Indeed, the figures given in Table 4 show that lag was usual on the conventional panel. There was a tendency for the fillers especially not to be able to finish so that management had to take counteractive measures—pay the pullers to complete the filling and send reinforcements to the face to complete the pulling. So usual was cycle lag on the conventional longwall that it required an average reinforcement of 6 percent per week. On the composite longwall the cycle usually ran schedule. It could, and often did, get ahead of itself. This was because of the task continuity which was practiced, each shift group going on to the next tasks of the cycle as soon as they finished their own work. When lag did occur, the face team increased its pace of work in order to catch up, or at least to gain enough control so that the next cycle could proceed. They would, for example, under severe pressure, concentrate on finishing the most crucial tasks, leaving other work to be completed later. In this way the composite longwall maintained itself without reinforcement. Counteraction was taken by the group itself, mainly through the practice of group continuity. This was something the formally segregated single task groups of the conventional face could not do. Only management was in a position to take counteraction.

As for *regularity of production* on the two faces during the period of observation, the conventional longwall, with conditions quite normal, ran for only 12 weeks before losing a cut and during these 12 weeks usually needed reinforcement to complete the cycle. The composite longwall, on the other hand, ran for 65 weeks without losing a cut and at no time needed reinforcement.

As regards *level of productivity,* the conventional longwall, in terms of output per manshift (oms) at the face, yielded 3.5 tons and the composite 5.3

TABLE 4   State of Cycle Progress at End of Filling Shift (percentage of cycles)

State of cycle progress	Conventional longwall	Composite longwall
In advance	0	22
Normal	31	73
Lagging	69	5
All cycles	100	100

TABLE 5   Productivity as Percentage of Estimated Face Potential

	Conventional longwall	Composite longwall
Without allowance for haulage system efficiency	67	95
With allowance	78	95

tons. The conventional was perceived as at the norm for the conditions and the composite as above it.

The seam sections, however, were different: the conventional face averaged 21″ of coal and 1½″ of band, the composite 26″ of coal and 6″ of band, so that the latter had the advantage of more coal height, together with the disadvantage of more band, while the conventional had the reverse conditions. The seam haulages, though similar in type, were not equally effective and the interference caused on the conventional face was greater. Comparison of the face oms was not, therefore, possible without adjustment of the figures, and each face was assessed against its own estimated potential. At 100 percent efficiency, 5.6 tons would have been expected from the composite panel and 4.5 tons from the conventional.

On this basis, and at first without any allowance being made for the greater amount of interference arising from its less efficient haulage, the conventional longwall was working at 67 percent of its potential (Table 5). In some measure this lesser efficiency of the haulage was due to poor maintenance resulting from back-bye labor being constantly drawn off to operating faces in order to cope with lagging cycles. It may therefore be regarded as a system defect. To some extent it was due also to the seam having been developed beyond the capacity of the haulage originally installed. A higher face productivity, however, would have increased the chances of something having been done about this when the working area was extended so that, once again, the effects of dysfunction cannot be entirely excluded.

If, however, in order to make the comparison more rigorous, full allowance is made for the higher level of external interference, the conventional face was working at 78 percent of its potential. The composite, by contrast, was working at 95 percent.

EFFECTS ON MANAGEMENT

Such different levels of effectiveness had very different consequences for face and seam management. On the conventional panel the entire burden of ensuring coordination of tasks and continuity of operations fell on officials. This entailed a great deal of effort, too much of which was expended on immediate measures necessary to counteract cycle dysfunction. With ancillary work at an overall level of 32 percent, the deputies (first-line supervisors) were heavily engaged in the detail of the ensuing complications, arguing with various task groups on precisely what needed doing and bargaining over amounts due and items eligible for payment. Apart from their statutory duties, such as patrolling their districts, testing for gas and ensuring application of support rules, the deputies' time was almost entirely absorbed in taking emergency action over technical breakdowns or tub shortages, events arising from system dysfunctioning, and in administering an itemized price list. Some idea of the demands of this latter activity can be gained from Table 6, which sets out the number of items involved in settling the pay of the different task groups on the conventional panel during an experimentally recorded quarter (13 weeks). Small opportunity was left to the deputies for attending to matters that, on a longer time span, would have reduced the level of interference.

The time and energy of the overmen (second-line officials responsible for the work of the shift) were similarly consumed in dealing with immediate problems. With six to eight faces operating in the seam, the overmen on the first and second shifts were obliged to give priority to getting as much coal out as possible from whichever faces were filling off, and most of these were usually to some degree lagging. They deployed men and tubs accordingly, improvising to secure maximum production for any given day. The overman coming in on the early nightshift had an even greater struggle, having first to eliminate whatever lag remained on all faces—with only limited winding time left—and then somehow to see that each face was advanced or cut so that the next day's cycles could proceed. What was intended as the principal maintenance and development shift became the principal troubleshooting shift, with men drawn off from repair and development work to reinforce lagging faces and those tasks falling behind which alone could maintain the level of seam functioning. To break the vicious circle at the overman level, however, was possible to no more than a limited extent since the greater part of the dysfunctioning was being generated anew every day within the face districts themselves—25 percent out of 32 percent on the face selected for detailed study.

The undermanager, the first official with overall responsibility for the cycle, was already three steps in managerial rank away from the coal face, a distance too great to exercise immediate control. He was more worried about keeping down costs than about raising productivity, tacitly accepting the latter as impossible without a degree of change outside his scope to initiate. Such an attitude, expressing a solely defensive strategy, is the natural corollary of being in a situation where no positive improvement is seriously hoped for. In keeping with this attitude, he saw his problems as arising more from the power of

TABLE 6 Items in the Price List of the Conventional Panel during One Quarter

Type of item	Task groups affected								All groups
	Pullers	Fillers	Cuttermen	Scufflers	Maingate stonemen	Driller	Hewers	Tailgate stonemen	
A	15	11	4	3	5	4	6	4	52
B	22	16	18	18	14	14	9	7	118
A + B	37	27	22	21	19	18	15	11	170

A: Items for which the rate (though not the amount in any instance) is fixed by agreements; B: Items for which neither the rate nor the amount is fixed by agreements (items covered by shift work)

task groups to bid up prices than from the inflation of face costs by system dysfunctioning.

Both he and the colliery manager had commended the seam as an example of a "very normal and well established" longwall operation—"a regular producer, pretty good conditions, a reasonable crowd of men though sharp about wages"—and this was also its reputation with higher management. The extent of cycle dysfunctioning was not perceived, the existing level of performance having come over the years to be accepted as the natural one. That the dysfunctioning might be due ultimately to the way the face team was organized was not believed when the present results were first discussed, though as time went on attitudes changed both at the colliery and in higher management. But initially an attempt was made to explain away as a special case what had been presented as typical. Several of the faces, it was said, were nearing the boundary so that only a limited investment in maintenance and new equipment had been justified; hopes were now placed in another group of faces soon to be opened out in a new area of the seam. When the research team visited these faces some months later, external interference was certainly reduced but coal was still being left on by the fillers, even if not so much or quite so often. The character of the disorganization, however, was unaltered, and over the course of time it would, in our opinion, have built up again toward its former level had not various technological changes ensued.

There was no greater contrast between the conventional and composite faces than in their management. As the composite organization was self-regulating, immediate cycle control was established by the group itself. The deputies needed neither to coerce, as it was in the interests of the men to get ahead, nor to bargain, as an allowance for an agreed range of sub- and ancillary tasks had been built into the Agreement. The comparable figure for the composite panel to the 170 items arising in the price list of the conventional panel was seven. Freed in this way, the deputies were able to give more time both to safety and to anticipating the needs of their districts. The center of gravity of their role changed from "propping up" a cycle always to some extent falling down on itself, to meeting the input and output needs of a going concern. To have the face cycle make demands on the deputies rather than the reverse was disconcerting at first, and a number of deputies felt their jobs had vanished. All but the most rigid, however, were able to readjust by taking a more active part in regulating the interactions of the face and the seam systems and to perceive the management of this "boundary zone" as their real task.

The existence of a self-regulating primary work group exerts an upward pressure in a managing system which affects all roles. With the elimination of made work by the face teams and with the deputies more active in seam liaison, one of the three overmen became superfluous. A single official, working a split shift, coped with both fore- and back-shift, establishing unified control over the production shifts at two rather than three levels from the coal face. This emergence of unified production control over an unlagging cycle enabled the overmen to maximize the maintenance function of the night shift so that almost all external interference was eliminated. The standard of maintenance in the entire seam system connected with these faces was of an altogether different order from that encountered elsewhere in the research.

All this allowed the undermanager to spread his attention to other seams which were more in need of it. He became more of an assistant manager. The extent to which a steady state had been reached may be gauged from the comment of the manager: "Now, I don't know that I have these faces in my pit." At the opposite extreme is the degree of involvement of this same manager in the panel described in Volume I (Trist et al., 1990/Vol. I), where the primary work group failed to become self-regulating. As the whole colliery was undergoing reorganization at this time, such involvement could be ill-afforded. The freedom needed higher up to manage change constructively is only won by establishing some freedom to manage at the bottom.

The emergence of a self-regulating primary work group undoes what Jaques (1951) has called the split at the bottom of the executive system, as there is no longer the same ultimate division into managers (of all ranks, including supervisors) and managed. Some of the managing has been taken over by the primary group—the part appropriate to its own task. Though this is what many in industry were allegedly seeking at this time and though a managerial philosophy was coming into existence which made this explicit (McGregor, 1960; Likert, 1961), such a development creates anxiety and produces resistance. In the present instance, the management/union negotiations went on for a year and might easily have broken down had not higher management lent support. The first difficulty is letting go of the traditional managerial controls over the primary group; the second is accepting the challenge of the consequent rise in the level of work now required within management. To surmount these difficulties, however, is to replace job alienation in the worker by task-oriented commitment; thence, by reducing the pressure of immediate troubleshooting, to increase the scope for creative problem-solving in management.

One qualification must be made to these conclusions. They have been drawn from comparison of only one conventional and one composite face. The two selected faces were as closely similar as field conditions would allow and where dissimilarities existed adjustments have been introduced. The aim has been to approximate in a fieldwork situation the design of a crucial experiment, the efficacy of the comparison depending on the identity of conditions rather than on the number of cases. Though complete identity cannot be claimed, the approximation obtained may be regarded as sufficient to establish the direction, if not the magnitude, of the result (cf. Lewin, 1935, Chapter 1). There are, of course, many conventional faces operating more efficiently than that studied and other composite faces operating less well than the example given. Indeed, an overlap is to be expected, with the better conventional faces having production records superior to those of the less effective composite faces. One comparison does not enable the performance range of the two systems to be investigated or estimates made of their mean levels of functional effectiveness. Such a qualification does not, however, invalidate the general conclusion concerning system characteristics: that the technical progress of the primary task is disrupted, in the conventional case, by disturbances induced by a fragmented social system; while, in the composite case, it is carried forward by the more continuous activity pattern arising from an integrated work group.

A Comparison of Partial and Fully Composite Working

Two Composite Organizations

The second comparison was between two composite longwalls, one of which was less composite than the other in the sense that its work organization had some features which were to be found on the conventional type of face. Since productivity differences were expected to be small, comparisons had to be carried out at a microscopic level. Placed on a scale of compositeness, the two longwalls just compared represent the extremes. A scale of compositeness would range from a strictly conventional organization with one-task/one-shift roles and no interchange between task groups to a fully composite organization with multi-task/multi-shift roles and completely free interchange between task groups. We shall now compare two composite longwalls, one of which—that used above—was closer to the composite end of the scale than the other.

Apart from the type of group organization that each developed for itself, these two panels were more alike than one would expect two longwalls to be, even in the same seam in the same pit. They were adjacent. They used exactly the same technology and worked to the same Agreement. Seam conditions were identical and the teams indistinguishable in qualifications and experience. They shared the same haulage and services. Both teams followed the composite work method as regards the practice of task continuity. The men were multiskilled workmen, all qualified for filling, drilling, pulling and stonework, and between one half and two thirds also for cutting. Both teams were self-selected and accepted complete responsibility for allocating themselves to the various jobs that management required them to fill. The method of payment was an all-in flat rate plus a piece-rate bonus, the common paynote being equally divided in each case among all team members.

This was the general form of the composite system originating in the seam. Nevertheless, over time the panels developed rather different ways of organizing themselves. The main differences (summarized in Table 7) were as follows.

TABLE 7   Differences between Panels in Face Group Organization

No. 1 Panel *(less composite organization)*	*No. 2 Panel* *(more composite organization)*
Face-wide: organized as two rather separate face teams.	Panel-wide: organized as two main alternating shift groups over the whole panel.
One-task jobs: men tend to work at only one main task.	Multi-task jobs: men rotate tasks systematically.
Each work place and task tied to a particular man.	Work places and tasks not tied to individuals.
Not customary for men to move from one work group to another.	Men move freely from one work group to another.

(1) The group on No. 1 Panel organized itself as two face teams, each taking responsibility for manning the three shifts on its particular face. This face-wide organization distinguishes it from the panel-wide organization on No. 2 Panel where no distinction between the two faces was made, the team dividing itself into two main shift groups, each with 20 men. Every fortnight the main shift groups alternated between the filling and pulling/stonework shifts and between them provided the men for the cutting shift, while the driller remained quasi-permanent.

(2) No. 1 Panel organized itself so that men tended to stick to one main task. For example, they would work as fillers or pullers, but not as both. In some ways this pattern is similar to that found on conventional longwalls but, since No. 1 Panel worked in the composite manner, all men became involved, in addition, in other tasks. Nevertheless, No. 1 Panel developed one-task roles. On No. 2 Panel, because men alternated between filling and pulling/stonework every fortnight and went on to cutting on a longer time basis, men carried out a range of different main tasks. They developed multi-task roles.

(3) On No. 1 Panel the team organized itself so that each specific job on the panel was the responsibility of a particular individual. The men tied themselves to work places and tasks. On No. 2 Panel, so long as all workplaces and tasks were manned by qualified team members, it was immaterial who they were. Jobs were not tied to individuals.

(4) No. 2 Panel team members moved freely from one activity group to another, not only from day to day but from week to week. A man could, for example, when filling, change from one face to the other. On No. 1 Panel there was little movement of this kind; men definitely tended to stick to one work place. It was not their custom to move, though movement was permissible.

These four differences in face group organization were not so extreme as indicated in that some of the features occurring on one panel were found on the other, especially as time went on. The differences, nevertheless, had consequences in three main areas—production performance, adaptation to changing conditions and effectiveness of cycle regulation.

Production Performance

It was planned that the two panels should produce half of the total pit output with a fifth of the face manpower. From the outset, the panels achieved this target. A face oms of the order of 5.3 tons was maintained without reinforcement of the 41-man teams throughout the 20 months of their operation. Both panels went for over 15 months before losing a cycle. In all they lost only 12.5 cycles out of 730 scheduled—1.5 percent.

Changes in conditions, however, must always be taken into account in assessing a performance record and to permit this, the concept of a *production phase* was introduced to indicate a period of time during which conditions in the task environment remained relatively constant. Data taken from pit records were analyzed to show what happened in four consecutive phases of production—A, B, C and D—each of which lasted some five months and between which there were identifiable differences. Figure 1 summarizes the results. Differences were greatest between D and the other three phases. This was the period when cuts were lost and at the end of which geological conditions had so far deteriorated that the faces were stopped.

The completeness index relates actual production per month to that estimated from coal height, face length and amount of advance. In phases A, B and C the completeness index was over 93 percent on No. 1 Panel and over 95 percent on No. 2 Panel, but in phase D it dropped to 87 percent on No. 1 and 90 percent on No. 2. The level of completeness on No. 2 Panel was always higher than on No. 1 Panel by 2 to 3 percent. In tonnage terms, this amounts to only 20 to 30 tons a week. It appears so regularly, however, that it cannot be regarded as due to chance. There is, therefore, a consistent difference between the panels in the extent to which they extracted all that coal be won by the given system of working. The seam was a particularly dirty one and from the outset it was recognized that to attempt a high degree of separation of band from coal would endanger cycle completion. The index for quality of performance shows both a low initial level and a marked downward trend, more and more band being filled off with the coal. As the panels advanced, the coal height fell steadily while the amount of stone-band increased, eventually to a point where, as has been mentioned, economic working was no longer possible. During the first three phases a high level of completeness was maintained, though quality

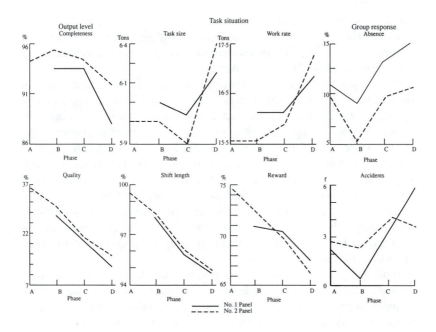

Figure I. Performance record of two composite longwalls

declined. Phase D saw not only a continued drop in quality but also a marked lowering in the level of completeness due to an increasing number of lost cuts. Throughout, however, No. 2 Panel did better than No. I Panel.

The declining height of the seam and the increasing proportion of band had two consequences. First, since band is almost twice as heavy as coal, the job became more onerous. Second, the falling coal height led management in phase D to increase the depth of undercut in order to maintain production. The gross effect was that a considerably heavier load of coal and band had to be handled by the team, as seen in the graph headed Task Size in Figure I. Although in phases A, B and C the task size decreased slightly, in phase D there was a very steep increase. As the panels advanced, the effective length of the shift available for work at the face decreased noticeably, the decrease shown in the graph headed Shift Length being equivalent, by the end of phase D, to a reduction of two manshifts per cycle—in a team of 41 men approximately 5 percent. The operations of the cycle had therefore to be compressed into shorter periods and the graphs for Quality and Shift Length follow a similar downward trend, showing that, with less time to do the job, quality suffered. With the increase in task size, and the decrease in time available, the teams had to work at a faster rate, as shown in the graph headed Work Rate. While the required rate was much the same in the first three phases, in phase D it increased greatly and for the fillers this meant handling 17.5 tons per manshift. Relating this to the drop in completeness, one may conclude that beyond such a limit cycle completion becomes endangered.

On both panels the piecework bonus was determined by the cubic yards of coal extracted. As coal height became less, so did possible earnings, since at that time the piece-rate did not take changes in coal height into account. Another way of looking at this situation is to consider what proportion of the effort expended during the shift was devoted to fill off coal as distinct from band. If 10 tons of coal and band had to be handled and 8 tons of this was coal, then 80 percent of the effort would be rewarded; on the other hand, if there were 12 tons of coal and band of which only 8 tons was coal, then no more than 66 percent of a man's work would be paid for. The graph headed Reward shows that, as the panels advanced, possible earnings bore less and less relation to the effort required. The similarity between the graphs for Quality and Reward shows one effect of this.

Though No. 2 Panel had a rather rougher time than No. 1 Panel, both followed a similar course, completeness of production falling sharply in the last phase when cycles were lost. This coincided with an increase in task size, a reduction in shift length, a faster work rate and a growing disparity between effort and reward. All these changes operated as a stress on the team who had, essentially, to deal with a bigger load. This may be referred to as *work load stress*.

ADAPTATION TO CHANGING CONDITIONS

One useful indicator of response to the stress of increased work load is provided by the absence record of the panels. During the period of the study, the face worker absence rate for the pit as a whole averaged 12 percent, but the panels themselves were below this level—10 percent for No. 1 and 8 percent for No. 2. The differences are significant not only between both panels and the rest of the pit, but also between the two panels themselves. Again, the trend favors No. 2. To investigate this more fully, absences during phase D—when the work load increased—have been compared with those in phase C, in which the work load was much the same as during the preceding phases.

The changes between these two phases produced striking differences of response from the two panels as may be seen on the graphs headed Absence and Accidents. On No. 1 Panel the absence rate increased with rising stress, on No. 2 Panel it remained unchanged. Figure 2 presents a fuller picture of these changes under Stress and Withdrawal (which gives the incidence trend in absences from all sources). On No. 1 Panel the rising absence rate was due largely to an increase in absences lasting only one day (cf. Hill and Trist,

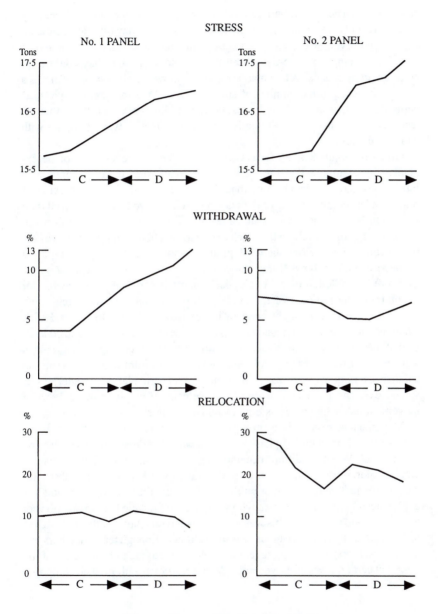

Figure 2. Stress, withdrawal and relocation

1955/Vol. I). There was, particularly, an increase in the incidence of one-day sicknesses and also an increase in accidents leading to a day off. No significant change, however, occurred in voluntary "no reason" absences. On No. 2 Panel, the changes in one-day absences were so small that they could have come about by chance. While increased stress showed itself on No. 1 Panel as a definite increase in the number of single days off, the incidence in phase D being double that in C, No. 2 Panel showed no difference. It follows that the team must have had some alternative and more effective way of coping with work load stress.

Given the equivalence of the two groups, the differences cannot be explained by assuming that the men on one panel were more susceptible to infection or more accident prone than those on the other. Rather, an explanation must be sought in terms of the way in which the two teams organized their work. On No. 1 Panel, where increased stress and absence go hand-in-hand, the team organized itself so that each man was tied to one main job. It was not the custom to move from one work group to another as the graph in Figure 2 headed Relocation shows. Since the wages of the team were dependent on the successful completion of the cycle, each man felt personally responsible for maintaining the progress of the cycle on his own shift and for coping with whatever interference might arise in his own workplace. On No. 2 Panel, where greater stress did not lead to increased absence, the team organized itself so that over a period of time each man carried out a wider range of tasks; men were not tied to a particular job and moved freely from one work group to another. Consequently excess load did not fall on particular men; rather, it was spread over the team as a whole. The Relocation graph shows a level of movement more than twice as high as on No. 1 Panel.

Movement across activity groups was, however, lower on No. 2 Panel during phase D than during phase C when it was over three times as high as on No. 1 Panel. When conditions became rougher the team saw to it that the most crucial roles were occupied only by the most experienced men. Substitutes were never sent on to cutting or pulling, or to where the roof was bad, and less experienced "regulars," or men who were not too fit, were kept in positions of less moment to the cycle. This was adaptive behavior, showing the realism and task-orientation characteristic of the group climate. Enough team members had the necessary experience to prevent any one from having to bear the brunt too long, but certain types of movement were not restricted to those who composed the informal "elite."

CYCLE REGULATION

In order to appreciate more fully the way in which the underlying differences in face group organization affected performance and adaptation to stress, it is necessary to examine how the two teams regulated cycle progress. Although composite teams spontaneously carry on with whatever job has next to be done, how far a shift can, or even should, proceed with the work of the cycle is governed by a very complex set of factors. Basically, it depends on what stage the cycle is at when the men come on shift. A quantitative study of the regulation of cycle progress during phase D, when the roughest conditions were experienced, was made by comparing, for each different beginning, the average state of the cycle at the end of the shift. For example, when the cycle is lagging because the cuttermen did not finish their work, the fillers manage to finish the cutting and also to complete their own work—they put a spurt on in order to eliminate the lag. When the cycle is normal, normal progress is made. When the cuttermen achieve a slight of medium advance and give the fillers a start, by the end of the shift the fillers have pushed the cycle a little further ahead. When, however, substantial advance is made by the cuttermen, the fillers aim simply to maintain it, there being no virtue in the team getting the cycle too far ahead, for the smooth running of the seam as a whole could be disrupted. The inference to be drawn for all shifts—cutting, filling, pulling and stonework—is that the teams were able to regulate their work to suit the varying conditions and to satisfy the requirements for optimum running of the seam system as a whole.

The panels differed considerably in their method of gaining control over cycle lag. On No. 1 Panel, lag of whatever degree—short of actual breakdown of the cycle—was eliminated during the shift that inherited it, whereas on No. 1 Panel two or three shifts would be allowed to elapse before the cycle was brought back into phase. The men on No. 1 Panel would not pass on any inherited lag to their marrows on the succeeding shift. Their attitude was that every shift should attempt to bring the cycle back into phase, regardless of whether control could be more economically achieved by passing on some of their work to the next shift. When the work load increased, each group, by attempting complete control over any lag it might inherit as well as aiming to finish its own job, raised still further the level of stress. In time, the greater strain which men experienced resulted in greater absence. Such were the consequences of a face group organization which tied men to particular jobs and limited interchange between work groups. On No. 2 Panel, by systematically rotating the various shifts, men came to know better what could be done under the conditions of each shift. They did not expect a particular shift to achieve complete control but accepted as quite reasonable that some of the consequences should be coped with by later shifts. With a span of three shifts as compared with one in which to eliminate lag, they therefore experienced less strain and no significant increase in absence occurred.

There was one other difference between the panels arising from the practice of having one face advanced by one cut ahead of the other (following) face. To ensure a smooth succession of cycles, operations on the advanced face needed to be slightly ahead of those on the following face, and close cooperation of the men working on the two faces was necessary for this optimum situation to be achieved. No. 2 Panel, which was organized on a panel-wide basis, always kept operations on its advanced face slightly ahead of those on the following face. When anyone was required for shift work in the gates, men were drawn from the following rather than the advanced face. The team also concentrated lost cuts on the following face—making the best of a bad job. No. 1 Panel, with its two rather separate face teams, operated quite differently. They kept operations on both the advanced and following faces closely in step. When men were required for shift work away from the face, they were drawn equally from both faces. Cuts were lost with the same frequency on both. This overall method of cycle regulation was suboptimum for the particular technology and the double-unit layout. The difference between panel-wide and face-wide organization had very real consequences for the regulation and progress of the cycle.

This comparative study indicates that one form of face group organization was a better fit than the other to the requirements of the situation in terms of

- The productivity of the faces—though there was little to choose between them, such differences as there were consistently favored the group organized on a panel-wide basis.
- Regulating cycle progress—though on both panels the practice of task continuity enabled the teams to get sufficiently ahead to cope with inevitable and unpredictable difficulties and interferences, the differences definitely favored the same panel.
- The social cost of maintaining a high production record—in sickness and accident absences, which arise from the way increased work load stress is coped with, there were considerable differences which again favored the same panel.

The face group organization that was panel-wide embodied systematic rotation of the various jobs among team members and did not tie a man to only one job, work group or face; it was the more effective in maintaining the smooth flow of the cycle and in coping with increased work load stress.

The differences in the operational records of these two composite longwalls are to be accounted for by the presence of certain "conventional" features in the face group organization of the less effective panel. The comparison of a conventional and a composite longwall showed that the superior production performance of composite organization stems from its more effective regulation of cycle progress. The second comparison is more stringent—that of two composite longwalls working under almost identical conditions though differing in their internal work organization. The results show unequivocally that the presence of conventional characteristics affected the way one of the panels regulated its work and caused a depression of its performance level, while increasing "casualties" in the face team. This two-step comparison leads to the general conclusion that, for workers carrying out a primary task comprising interdependent component activities interchangeable between group members, the composite form of organization has inherent characteristics more conducive to productive effectiveness, work satisfaction and social health than that based on separately treated single task groups.

References

Hill, J. and E. Trist. 1955. "Temporary Withdrawal from Work Under Full Employment." *Human Relations,* 8:121–52. Vol. I, "Temporary Withdrawal from Work Under Full Employment: The Formation of an Absence Culture," pp. 494–510.

Jaques, E. 1951. *The Changing Culture of a Factory.* London: Tavistock Publications. Reissued 1987, New York: Garland.

Lewin, K. 1935. *A Dynamic Theory of Personality: Selected Papers.* New York: McGraw-Hill.

Likert, R. 1961. *New Patterns of Management.* New York: McGraw-Hill.

McGregor, D. 1960. *The Human Side of Enterprise.* New York: McGraw-Hill.

Trist, E.L. and K.W. Bamforth. 1951. "Some Social and Psychological Consequences of the Longwall Method of Coal-Getting." *Human Relations,* 4:3–38. Shortened, Vol. II, "The Stress of Isolated Dependence: The Filling Shift in the Semi-Mechanized Longwall Three-Shift Mining Cycle," pp. 64–83.

Trist, E.L., G. Higgin, H. Murray and A. Pollock. 1990. Vol. I, "The Assumption of Ordinariness as a Denial Mechanism: Innovation and Conflict in a Coal Mine," pp. 476–93. (Shortened and rewritten version of chapters 19–22 in *Organizational Choice*; see Note 1.)

A.K. Rice

Productivity and Social Organization
An Indian Automated Weaving Shed[1]

The tendency to treat the technological and social organizations of an industrial unit as separate systems has sometimes led to difficulty when technological change has been introduced without adequate appreciation of its social repercussions. In their account of the Hawthorne Studies, Roethlisberger and Dickson (1939) described an industrial organization as a social system and drew attention to the interdependence of the technological and human organizations. In the human organization they included the formal and informal structures of groups. Trist and Bamforth (1951/Vol. II) showed that the introduction of the three-shift longwall cycle into British coal-mining resulted in the breakdown of an established social system and the formation of maladaptive mechanisms as defenses against the social and psychological consequences of the technological organization. Rice and Trist (1952), investigating change in labor turnover, used a method of analysis which suggested that an understanding of the whole system—the socio-technical system, containing both technical and social dimensions—was necessary to explain both the kind and the direction of change in labor turnover when either technological or social change occurred.[2]

This paper describes a preliminary analysis of the socio-technical system of an experimental automatic loom shed, weaving cotton cloth, on the basis of which the methods of working were reorganized and an increase in productivity achieved. The analysis was made during recent work by the Tavistock Institute in the Ahmedabad Manufacturing and Calico Printing Company Limited in Ahmedabad, India. The company, known more familiarly as the "Calico Mills," manufactures finished cloth from raw cotton and employs ap-

[1]This paper, condensed from "Productivity and Social Organization in an Indian Weaving Shed: An Examination of the Socio-Technical System of an Experimental Automatic Loomshed," *Human Relations*, 6:297–329, 1953, describes Rice's first experiment in designing a form of work organization to optimize the technical and social dimensions.

[2]Trist, who collaborated with the author in the writing of this paper, first used the concept of *socio-technical system* when studying the socio-psychological and technical problems of the introduction of increased mechanization in coal-mining. The term has since been extended to designate a general field of study concerned with the interrelations of the technical and socio-psychological organizations of production systems.

proximately 8,000 workers. The author visited the mills in the capacity of professional consultant. The purpose of his visit, which was exploratory, was to allow both the company and the Institute to discover whether it was possible to establish a collaborative relationship in which the Institute could make a contribution to the solution of the general social and production problems of the mills.

The analysis was made in collaboration with a development group in which the author worked with the chairman, mill manager and works manager of the company. (The works manager was the direct executive subordinate of the mill manager, who reported directly to the chairman. The works manager also acted, however, as technical staff officer to the chairman.) The members of this group collaborated closely, working as a group, in pairs or singly as the situation demanded, until each was satisfied of the validity of the analysis. They reported as a group to the other members of senior management at all stages. The decision to initiate the reorganization was taken by the chairman at a meeting which was attended by all senior managers. At that meeting the weaving master of the mill concerned was called in. He listened with evident enthusiasm to the proposals and began at once to produce from his own experience arguments in their favor. The works manager, as the senior executive responsible for the experimental loom shed, then discussed the proposals with the top supervisor of the shed. Thereafter, the supervisors and workers in the loom shed took over the proposals as their own; within a few hours, to the surprise of management, the workers had organized their own working groups. The chairman, mill manager, works manager and the author did not attend any of the discussions with supervisors or workers, nor did they visit the loom shed again until the reorganization had been implemented. The author returned to London on the seventh day of the experimental period and the results reported in this paper have been sent to him by the works manager. The paper was, however, discussed in detail with the chairman of the company, Gautam Sarabhai, when he was in England. His help with the paper and his permission to publish it are gratefully acknowledged.

The paper is in three parts. First, there is a brief description of the loom shed before reorganization; second, this organization is analyzed and the reorganization described; finally, the results of the reorganization are reported.

Experimental Automatic Loom Shed

ACTIVITIES OF THE LOOM SHED

Automatic looms had been introduced into one of the mills in June 1952. By March 1953, an experimental shed containing 224 looms had been set up. It was designed eventually to hold 304 looms but, at the time of reorganization, a part of the shed was still under construction.

The operations of automatic weaving are carried out by *bobbins* containing *weft* yarn (threads across the length of the cloth) and *beams* containing *warp* yarn (threads along the length of the cloth). An automatic loom is prepared for weaving by *loading*. A beam is *gated* into brackets at the back of a loom, and each warp thread is passed through the eye of a *heald*, then through a *reed*, or comb, to keep it in place and is finally connected to a roller on the front of the loom which takes the woven cloth. A bobbin containing weft yarn is placed in a *shuttle* from which it is automatically ejected when it is empty or when the weft thread breaks. Empty bobbins are automatically replaced by full bobbins stored in a *battery*. When the loom is weaving, the shuttle is knocked backward and forward through a *shed* formed by the separation of the warp threads by the rise of some healds and the fall of others. As the shuttle travels through the shed it leaves behind it a weft thread which is wound from the bobbin within the shuttle. Each weft thread so inserted is banged into place by the reed. The weaving ceases when the warp yarn on the beam has all been converted into cloth on the roller. The loom is then *unloaded,* the finished cloth is taken from the loom (this may occur at intervals during weaving by cutting off the finished cloth) and the empty beam is removed. During weaving, stops of short duration occur whenever a warp thread breaks. A loom is restarted when the broken ends have been joined together (knotted). The looms are fitted with mechanical stops which halt the loom automatically whenever a warp thread breaks.

The activities of a single loom are, therefore, cyclic—load, weave, unload. But since weaving time (including stops for yarn breaks) always greatly exceeds loading and unloading time, the total activities of a loom shed are continuous, only a small proportion of the looms being stopped for loading and unloading at any one time. During stops for the loading and unloading of looms, general loom maintenance, automatic device maintenance, tuning and oiling activities are carried out, and all accumulated fluff is removed from under the loom.

The length of yarn which can be wound on a beam or on a bobbin depends on the size of the beam or bobbin and on the fineness of the yarn (the *count*)—the finer the yarn, the higher the count. The kind of cloth woven (the *sort*) depends on the count of the yarn and on the number of threads to the inch in both warp and weft. The rate of weaving depends, therefore, on the speed and continuity of loom run and on the sort.

Under the climatic conditions in Ahmedabad, relative humidity in the loom shed has to be artificially maintained at 80 to 85 percent to enable yarn to stand up to the strain put on it in the weaving process. For this purpose, a humidification plant is installed which humidifies the whole shed.

Two eight-hour shifts were worked, the day shift from 7.00 a.m. to 3.30 p.m. and the night shift from 3.30 p.m. to midnight, with a half-hour break each in midshift.

Productivity is measured by two figures—efficiency and damage. Efficiency is the number of *picks* (weft threads) inserted in any shift expressed as a percentage of the number of picks which would have been inserted had the loom run continuously for the whole shift. No allowance is made for loading, unloading or for any other stops. Damage is the percentage of cloth not accepted as of standard quality by the inspectors and viewers after weaving. The higher the efficiency and the lower the damage, the greater the productivity.

OCCUPATIONAL ROLES AND TASKS

Current British and American practice had been followed in the organization of the shed. The total task of weaving had been broken down into component operations and each component was performed by different workers. The number of workers allocated to the various tasks had been based upon British, American and Japanese standards—the looms were of Japanese manufacture—modified by the time studies of work under Indian conditions and based on yarn breakage rates existing in the mill at the time of installation. The experimental shed started working when 12 looms had been installed. Neither management nor workers had had experience of modern working methods with automatic looms. During the first eight months looms were brought into production as they were erected and workers trained to use them. By March 1953, relatively stable conditions had been established with the 224 looms installed, and further loom erection had been halted pending the completion of the building.

At this point, the deployment of workers, with the number of workers per shift in each occupational role shown in parentheses, was as follows. A top supervisor was in overall charge of the two shifts. Responsible to him, on each shift, was a works supervisor. His command comprised all the shift workers except the humidification fitter (1), who reported directly to the top supervisor. Jobbers (2), whose task was mainly loom maintenance and adjustment, not only supervised the assistant jobbers (2) but also exercised some directive authority over all other workers. These included the feeler-motion maintenance fitter (1); weavers (8); gaters (2) who replaced empty beams; battery fillers (5) maintaining the supply of full bobbins; oiler (1); smash-hands (3) who joined broken ends of yarn after a major breakage and who were in training as weavers; cloth carrier (1); bobbin carriers (2); and sweeper (1). This complement of workers was considered to be adequate for up to 240 looms.

It is evident that, although all the tasks of the shed were interdependent, only the jobbers and assistant jobbers had any form of stable work group structure and that the other workers formed an aggregate of individuals some of whom were virtually independent of each other. The jobbers had some authority over most other workers, and weavers had some authority over smash-hands, but the lines of authority were confused and undefined. For example, the oiler could be directed by a jobber, but the relative authority of the two jobbers was not established. In the same way, the smash-hands could be given orders by a weaver, but the order in which the eight weavers could demand their services was not defined.

WORK ORGANIZATION

Because the production process of a loom shed, in contrast to that of a single loom, is continuous rather than cyclic, all activities in the shed were directed to maintaining the *steady state* of multiple loom weaving. Production in the shed, therefore, depended on the simultaneous execution of all activities. The activities were carried out by workers who performed tasks and took occupational roles. The tasks performed by the workers related their occupational roles to the activities of the shed. Because the activities of the shed had been broken down into their component tasks and the number of workers required to perform the tasks had been determined by work studies of the separate components, workers in different occupational roles worked on different numbers of looms.

There were eight loom groups of 24 to 32 looms manned by one weaver to each group; five loom groups of 40 to 60 looms manned by one battery filler to each; three loom groups of 60 to 80 manned by one smash-hand to each; two loom groups of 112 manned by one jobber, one assistant jobber, one gater and one bobbin carrier to each; and the total loom group of 224 manned by one feeler-motion fitter, one cloth carrier, one oiler, one sweeper and one humidification fitter. This method of determining the number of workers required to carry out a total production process is the normal production engineering corollary of job breakdown and work study. Katz and Kahn (1951) have included it as a major factor in their concept of the Machine Theory of Organization.

Altogether, therefore, there were 12 tasks performed by 29 workers, who among them took 12 occupational roles. Moreover, the looms in the shed were divided into five different kinds of loom groups which varied as to the number of looms, the number of tasks performed and the number of workers engaged in each group. Thus, the 12 tasks performed by 29 workers were performed in a total of 19 overlapping loom groups of five kinds.

MANAGEMENT HIERARCHY OF THE LOOM SHED

One consequence of the different kinds of loom groups and of the allocation of one component task to one occupational role was that the workers could not conveniently be grouped for supervision. Thus, in spite of the directive responsibility of the jobbers for all other workers and of the weavers for some, the work supervisor was directly responsible for 26 different individuals.

The overall picture of loom shed organization was a confused pattern of relationships among an aggregate of individuals for whom no stable internal group structure could be discerned. This picture may be both compared and contrasted with that found by Trist and Bamforth (1951/Vol. II) in the longwall system of coal-mining. The effect there of job breakdown and task allocation led, especially on the filling shift, to a similar aggregate of individuals with no discernible stable internal group structure; but the sequential nature of the process led to splitting and isolation and the segregation of those engaged on component tasks of the total process both between and within shifts. In the experimental automatic loom shed the continuous nature of the process and the simultaneous performance of all component tasks led to confusion.

CHANGE OF SORT

A change of sort—kind of cloth woven—may change the work load of some of the workers. Thus a change of sort involving a change to a higher reed (greater number of threads per inch in the warp) may require an increase in the number of weavers because the greater number of threads may cause more frequent breaks, but a change involving a yarn of finer count may require a decrease in the number of battery fillers, gaters and bobbin carriers because more yarn could be wound on bobbins and beams. Without necessarily requiring an alteration in the total number of workers, a change of sort involved, therefore, a change either in individual work loads or in the kinds of workers employed. Each change altered the relationships between interdependent tasks and re-structured some of the loom groups. Any change of sort was, therefore, likely to add to the confusion of task and worker relationships.

GOVERNMENT OF THE SHED

The work supervisor had so much to do in the handling of work allocations and of worker relationships that the top supervisor had to assist him by dealing directly with jobbers and other workers. Indeed, had not the top supervisor so helped the work supervisor, it is difficult to see how he could usefully have filled his time. In the same way, the jobbers' technological tasks were so many and their supervising responsibility so undefined that the work supervisor had to assist them by giving direct orders to their nominal subordinates.

This breakdown of the hierarchical structure placed a high premium on the quality of the relationships between the supervisors and between the work supervisor and the workers. That the breakdown had led to no overt relationship difficulties was undoubtedly due in part to the high quality of the relationships, but it was also due to the considerable attention which had been given to the experimental shed by the chairman, mill manager and works manager ever since its opening. The lack of internal structure had been counterbalanced by a strong management structure external to the workers. In practice, the *governing system* of the shed—the system, external to the production system, which services, coordinates and controls the production system (Rice and Trist, 1952)—included members of higher management in addition to those shown on the organization chart.

In spite of this strong governing system, however, the current figures for efficiency were lower and the percentage of damaged cloth higher than budgeted targets. Faced with this shortfall in expected productivity there were, apart from technological improvements, two possibilities: to further strengthen the external structure of the governing system by increasing the number of supervisors and tightening inspection or, by reorganization, to create and stabilize an internal structure of the working group. The danger of the former was that the workers would not only continue to experience the discomfort of the internally unstructured confusion but would feel further coerced and policed and, in consequence, might increase their resistance to greater effort and productivity. In addition, the presence of higher management in the governing system of the shed could only be temporary, and their withdrawal would leave gaps which would require more supervisors as replacements, thus enhancing any feelings the workers had of being regarded as untrustworthy.

The Socio-Technical System of the Loom Shed

INTERDEPENDENCE OF TASK AND INDEPENDENCE OF WORKERS

All tasks in the shed were interdependent, but many of the individual workers performing them were virtually independent in the sense that they were linked only through the work supervisor, while those who had interdependent relationships had varying degrees of interdependence in overlapping loom groups. Thus each weaver, depending on the sort on his looms, had on average the services of one quarter of the time of a dependent pair consisting of jobber and assistant jobber; five-eighths of that of a battery filler; three-eighths of that of a smash-hand; and so on. Any change of sort altered the proportions of the services he could command. Battery fillers each served, on average, one and three-eighths weavers; each smash-hand two and two-thirds weavers. With some sorts, the time of a particular battery filler might be completely consumed by serving the looms of two weavers and there was then opportunity for the two weavers and their battery filler to build interdependent relationships consistent with the interdependence of their tasks, but this was not a common pattern.

Generally, it may be said that the area of the shed and the number of workers were both too large and task relationships too confused for there to be much opportunity to build stable, cohesive relationships between the members of the total working group, and the confused loom groups precluded the formation of small, internally structured and internally led work groups consistent with task relatedness.

JOB BREAKDOWN, MULTIPLE GRADES AND WORKER MOBILITY

Job breakdown and consequent specialization had reduced the quality and range of skills required for performance of tasks in the loom shed. In contrast to conventional weaving, a weaver no longer had to service his looms, tune them, refill shuttles or stop the loom to prevent damage. Indeed, the loom itself had become the weaver and all the workers in the loom shed now serviced this mechanical weaver. In spite of the persistence of the title of weaver for one of the occupational roles, the weaver's task may be more accurately described as *loom-end-knotting*. (The similarity of this task to that of a *piecer* in ring spinning will be recognized by all who are familiar with the textile industry.)

In general, specialization of task had restricted the possibilities of task or role rotation. Because of low labor turnover, only the prospect of completion of the shed and the installation of more looms, an isolated event, held out any real hope of promotion or transfer. Even such an event only offered the opportunity of transfer from one specialized task to another.

Mobility was further restricted by the many different status grades which were allied to rate of pay. The rate of the jobber was 2.3 times that of the least skilled workers, and for the roles between these extremes there were seven other rates. Hence almost any exchange of tasks would have involved a change of pay—a change only easy to accomplish in one direction. In short, the workers were chained to their roles and tasks.

SMALL WORK GROUP ORGANIZATION

Six assumptions were made about work group organization:
When individual tasks are interdependent, the relationship between those performing the tasks will have important effects on productivity.

Groups of workers engaged in the same loom group are more likely to form internally structured stable and cohesive group relationships than those in overlapping groups.

Interchangeability of tasks (role rotation) gives greater freedom of movement to workers.

The coincidence of obvious physical and loom group boundaries enables a working group to realize itself and identify itself with its "territory."

The fewer differences there are in work group status (and pay) consistent with offering opportunities for promotion, the more likely is the internal structure of a group to stabilize itself and the more likely are its members to accept internal leadership.

If group stability is to be maintained, when individual members of small work groups become disaffected to the extent that they can no longer fit into their work group, they need to be able to move to other small work groups engaged on similar tasks.

None of the conditions in these assumptions was satisfied by the existing socio-technical system. The tasks of the loom shed were therefore reexamined. The smash-hands were already accepted as weavers-in-training, and the weaver depended to a considerable extent on the efficiency with which the battery filler performed his task. The battery fillers, in their turn, had aspirations to become weavers. Bobbin carriers fetched all bobbins from the spinning department for the battery fillers. Assistant jobbers were already members of a pair, and gaters sometimes assisted jobbers to get looms running after a stop to replace an empty beam. The feeler-motion maintenance fitter was responsible for a specialist part of general loom maintenance. The oiler was under the nominal control of both jobbers and, although the sweeper and the cloth carrier each had his special task and were not considered interchangeable, they and the oiler were all graded as unskilled.

Short and Long Loom Stops as a Basis for Analysis

Cloth is woven only when the loom is running; all tasks in the shed are, therefore, directed to keeping the loom weaving. Loom stops are of two kinds: *short stops* caused by simple yarn breaks (one-half to one minute) and *long stops* for gating (one to one-and-a-half hours), meal breaks (half an hour) and intervals between the second and first shifts (seven hours). During actual shift hours, workers could be divided into those whose tasks were directed to keeping the looms running through short stops and those whose tasks were to get the looms weaving again after a long stop. Thus, weavers, battery fillers, smash-hands and bobbin carriers were concerned with the weaving loom while gaters and cloth carriers were concerned when the loom was stopped for

TABLE 1   Temporal Analysis of Occupational Roles and Tasks

| | Tasks connected with | | | |
| | Short stops | Long stops | | |
Occupational roles	Weaving	Loading-unloading	Loom maintenance	Departmental duties
Weavers	x			
Battery fillers	x			
Smash-hands	x			
Bobbin carriers	x			
Gaters		x		
Cloth carriers		x		
Jobbers			x	
Assistant jobbers			x	
Feeler-motion fitters			x	
Oilers			x	
Sweepers			(x)	x
Humidification fitters				x

loading new beams at the back or for removing finished cloth from the front. At the same time, the jobber, assistant jobber, feeler-motion fitter and oiler had to use the opportunity of a long stop to obtain access to the loom for maintenance work. Even the sweeper had to use that time as his only opportunity to get under the loom to remove accumulated fluff. Only the humidification fitter was not concerned directly with looms and was, therefore, ignored in the subsequent analysis. The temporal analysis of the occupational roles and tasks in terms of short and long stops is shown in Table 1.

The reexamination of shed tasks and the temporal analysis of occupational roles and tasks suggested that two subgroupings were possible—a short stop sub-group and a long stop sub-group that would include those concerned with loading and unloading and with loom maintenance.

VARIATION IN NUMBERS REQUIRED WITH CHANGE OF SORT

Change of sort demanded substantial change in the number of battery fillers and gaters; some change in the number of cloth carriers and bobbin carriers; less change in the number of weavers; and virtually no change in the number of other workers. To examine the limits of the changes required, the theoretical number of looms which could be attended by weavers, battery fillers and gaters

TABLE 2   Varying Number of Weavers, Battery Fillers and Gaters Required for 960 Looms

Occupational roles	Numbers required for each main sort		
	Coarse	Medium	Fine
Weavers Battery fillers	60	42	38
Gaters	12	12	3
Total	72	54	41

TABLE 3   Number of Other Workers Required for 960 Looms

Occupational roles	Number required for all sorts
Jobbers	8
Assistant jobbers	8
Feeler-motion mechanics	4
Oilers	4
Sweepers	4
Bobbin carriers	4
Cloth carriers	8
Smash-hands	12
Total	52

was calculated for each of the 16 sorts likely to be woven in any loom shed in the mill. These were then converted to show the number of workers who would theoretically be required to work 960 looms for all varieties of sort. (The figure 960 was chosen arbitrarily to give a large enough number to avoid too much approximation.) The result showed that although there were considerable variations in the number of weavers, battery fillers and gaters over the whole range, they could be grouped into three main sorts in which comparatively little variation occurred in the total number of weavers and battery fillers or in the number of gaters. These main sorts corresponded to the coarse, medium and fine counts.

Variation in the numbers of cloth carriers and bobbin carriers with change of sort was found to be too small to merit consideration. It appeared, therefore, that, provided weavers and battery fillers could be regarded as having partly interchangeable tasks, two kinds of workers would be required, whose numbers would vary with change of sort. The figures are summarized in Table 2.

The numbers of other workers required for 960 looms based on the numbers in the shed are shown in Table 3.

Theoretical Work Group Organization

The results of these analyses were then combined with the results of the reexamination of related occupational roles. The combined result is shown in Table 4.

Inspection of the loom shed showed that the looms were installed in rows of 16 and that wide gangways separated off two blocks of 64. That is to say that a block of 64 looms was an easily recognizable territory separated from other looms by wide gangways and pillars. Further constructional work and the installation of more looms would turn two existing blocks of 24 into two more blocks of 64 looms.

It was therefore decided to start an experimental group on one block of 64 looms; to extend this, if successful, to the other block of 54 looms; and ultimately to use the block of 48 looms near the entrance of the shed as a training group. The figures for the theoretical number of workers required for 960 looms were, therefore, reduced to the number required for 64 looms and the results are given in Table 5.

Status Differences and Titles

An examination of the status grades showed that there appeared to be three natural grades, of which one would provide the group leader. These are shown

TABLE 4   Theoretical Numbers of Workers Required for 960
Looms

Sub-group	Occupational roles	Numbers required for each main sort		
		Coarse	Medium	Fine
Short stop	Weavers Battery fillers	60	42	38
	Smash-hands	12	12	12
	Bobbin carriers	4	4	4
	Total	76	58	54
Long stop	Jobbers and assistants Gaters Feeler-motion fitters	32	32	23
	Cloth carriers Oilers Sweepers	16	16	16
	Total	48	48	39
	Grand Total	124	106	93

in Table 6, together with the three proposed relative wage levels substituted for the nine current levels. For the group leader, the new grade involved a small rise in pay and for some previously designated "unskilled" the rise was larger. At the same time, whereas previously only jobbers and weavers were paid piece rates,[3] it was proposed that all members of the experimental group should participate. It was hoped that any increased cost incurred by these changes would be offset by eliminating the need for extra supervision and inspection and by greater efficiency.

The wide difference between grades B and D led to the interpolation of a sub-grade C (rank 1.6) for those who had earned promotion from grade D.

It was recognized that the current titles given to occupational roles would

[3]Piece rate was based on an average standard efficiency of 85 percent per month, higher or lower efficiencies resulting in proportional increase or decrease in the amount of pay, excluding "dearness" (cost of living) allowance which at that time was approximately 0.75 percent of the lowest wage. For an average monthly percentage efficiency of 87, the bonus equaled 2/85ths of the basic monthly rate (total pay less dearness allowance). For percentages over 92 the proportional increase was doubled, i.e., 93 was paid as 94, etc.

TABLE 5   Theoretical Numbers of Workers Required for 64 Looms

Sub-group	Occupational roles	Numbers required for each main sort		
		Coarse	Medium	Fine
Short stop	Weavers Battery fillers	4.0	2.8	2.5
	Smash-hands Bobbin carriers	1.1	1.1	1.1
	Total	5.1	3.9	3.6
Long stop	Jobbers and assistants Gaters Feeler-motion fitters	2.1	2.1	1.5
	Cloth carriers Oilers Sweepers	1.1	1.1	1.1
	Total	3.2	3.2	2.6
	Grand Total	8.3	7.1	6.2

TABLE 6   Status Grades for the Experimental Small Work Group

Grade	Status	Rank
A	Group leader who would also be the working head of the long stop sub-group	2.4
B	Fully experienced members of either the short stop sub-group or the long stop sub-group	2.0
D	Those engaged almost entirely on the "unskilled" jobs of battery filling, sweeping, oiling or carrying, but whose status should nevertheless be higher than that of a new unskilled entrant once they had been accepted as integral members of a working group	1.2

not necessarily be appropriate to any form of reorganized internally led small work group since more of the tasks would be interchangeable. Various possible titles were suggested but the danger of expressing, consciously or unconsciously, hopes or expectations led to a decision to await discussion with the supervisors and workers before trying to define either the new grades or the new roles.

The repeated examination of the occupational roles and tasks in the loom shed raised a number of other questions for which answers could not immediately be obtained or solutions, if obtainable, could not be immediately implemented. Some of these questions concerned the uniformity of the level of mechanization in the various shed operations; others would have involved analyses of other parts of the total textile manufacturing process. Time was not immediately available for the latter, and changing the level of mechanization in some operations required the solution of engineering problems and the invention or development of further mechanical devices. Some alterations—for example, those related to the removal of fluff—were awaiting the arrival of equipment already ordered.

One outstanding question was that of the long loom stops caused by meal breaks and by intervals between shifts. Apart from insisting that, in general, the purpose of an automatic machine was to run without attention, it was decided not to suggest at once any alteration in the current practice during meal breaks. The question of intervals between shifts was complicated by trade union agreements and Indian Industrial Court awards and was left for future consideration.

Results of the Experiment

SPONTANEOUS ACCEPTANCE OF REORGANIZATION

At a meeting of the chairman and the mill, works and personnel managers with the author, it was decided to discuss the analysis with the weaving master, the supervisors and the workers at once and, with their approval, to start an experimental group on the one block of 64 looms. The weaving master was called into the meeting, and as soon as he heard of the notion of *a group of workers for a group of looms,* he spontaneously accepted the proposed reorganization. His response provided for higher management a first validation of the "goodness of fit" of the proposed reorganization with the felt needs of those working in the experimental loom shed. The works manager started discussions with the supervisors on the same evening. It had been expected that it would probably take some time for the discussions to be held—first with the supervisors of each shift and then with the workers—and that the experimental group would then be chosen by the supervisors in consultation with the works manager and a suitable date for starting chosen. In the event, the supervisors and workers immediately took possession of the system and, by the next day, by a complex sociometric process which there was no time to investigate, the

TABLE 7   Composition of Each Experimental
Group

| | Number in each sub-group | | |
Grade	Short stop	Long stop	Total
A (leader)		1	1
B	2	1	3
D	2	1	3
Total	4	3	7

workers had themselves organized two experimental groups. By the following day, groups had been organized by the workers for the two blocks of 64 looms for both shifts, making four small work groups (experimental groups *a, b, c* and *d*). That the actual members of the groups so spontaneously chosen were not those who would have been picked by the works manager was considered (with some misgiving perhaps) less important than that the grouping was spontaneous and that the number in each group had been spontaneously fixed at seven. There were only medium counts on the particular looms and each work group consisted of a long stop sub-group of one grade A, one grade B and one grade D; a short stop sub-group of two grade B and two grade D. The composition is shown in Table 7.

It was decided to allow the groups so chosen to work for an experimental period whose length would be determined by events.

MANAGEMENT OF THE SHED AFTER REORGANIZATION

The immediate effect on management after the shed had settled down to this reorganization was that the number of individuals reporting directly to the work supervisor was reduced. Although those workers not included in the experimental groups still continued as before reorganization, those in the experimental groups were now responsible to their group leaders. In addition, workers requiring training, instead of being spread over the whole shed, could now be concentrated in one loom group of 48, where they could receive more direct attention from the supervisors. It was decided that, as soon as the building was completed and the full complement of 304 looms installed, the other two blocks of 64 looms would be organized in the same way as the experimental

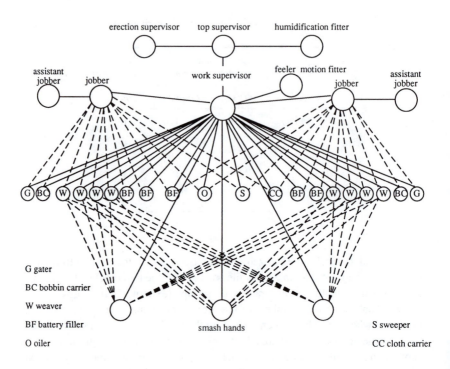

erection supervisor   top supervisor   humidification fitter

assistant
jobber   jobber   work supervisor   feeler motion fitter   assistant
jobber   jobber

G GC W W W W BF BF BF O S CC BF BF W W W W BC G

G gater

BC bobbin carrier

W weaver

BF battery filler   smash hands   S sweeper

O oiler   CC cloth carrier

Figure 1. Management hierarchy before change

groups. This organization would leave the work supervisor with four group leaders reporting directly to him and would free the top supervisor to give special attention to the training loom group. Instead of the shed's needing more supervision, it appeared that there was every chance that the present supervisors would be underemployed. Figures 1 and 2 represent the situation before and after change.

The sophistication of higher management in permitting the shed to reorganize itself was followed by the beginning of their withdrawal from the governing system of the shed, not so much as part of a consciously determined plan but as the result of increased confidence in the ability of those in the shed to solve their own problems. In August, the chairman of the company reported that, "Whereas I always spent some time in the experimental shed every time I went to the mill (on average twice a week), I don't think I've been in it more than two or three times since it was reorganized, not because I've lost any interest in it, but because I know it is going well."

So far as the group leaders and workers are concerned, there has been no noticeable change in their attitude to the reorganization since their first sponta-

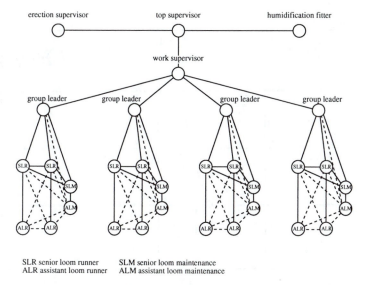

SLR senior loom runner   SLM senior loom maintenance
ALR assistant loom runner   ALM assistant loom maintenance

Figure 2. Management hierarchy after change

neous acceptance, and there have been requests from the workers not included in the experimental groups to be allowed to organize themselves in the same way. In discussion with the supervisors, the workers expressed a positive desire to avoid the old titles of their jobs but no enthusiasm for any other titles than the A, B and D grade designations. In August (the latest information), experimental group tasks were still known by all those in the shed as A, B and D jobs and those in occupational roles as A, B and D workers.

In general it can be said that, as far as can be ascertained, the assumptions made about small work group organization have been proved correct.

FOUR PHASES OF THE EXPERIMENTAL PERIOD

A detailed consideration of the experimental period shows that it may be described in four phases.

First Phase—the 11 working days immediately after reorganization. During this phase there was an increase in the efficiency of the experimental groups but at the cost of an increase in the percentage damage and of neglect of loom maintenance. (This was apart from a problem on the second day when a breakdown in the humidification plant flooded a part of the shed, spoiled 25 beams in the experimental groups and halted the whole shed for just over an hour.) This problem was discussed by the works manager with the supervisors,

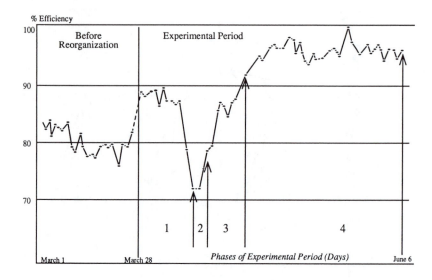

Figure 3. Percentage efficiency before and after reorganization

group leaders and workers who expressed themselves as willing to cooperate in the attempt to reduce the damage and improve maintenance but as unable adequately to keep down damage and keep up maintenance while maintaining the rate of working with short loom stops at 1.5 to 2.0 per hour.

Second Phase—three working days during which the top supervisor took over the group leadership of one of the groups to investigate the possibility of maintaining efficiency while avoiding increased damage and decreased maintenance. As a result of this investigation, during which efficiency fell considerably in all four groups, extra help at the rate of half an extra grade D worker was given to each group (based on theoretical needs with loom stops per hour of 1.75.)

Third Phase—eight working days of resettlement following the damage and maintenance investigation. In this phase efficiency climbed, damage remained less than it had been before the experiment started and loom maintenance was restored to its former level (Figures 3 and 4). Discussions took place among the works manager, supervisors, group leaders and workers about the running of looms during meal intervals.

Fourth Phase—the remaining 37 working days of the experimental period. As a result of discussions during the third phase, looms were not stopped by the workers at the beginning of the meal break but were allowed to run on until they stopped automatically when yarn broke. It was found possible to withdraw the extra help given in the third phase—notwithstanding the fact that the incidence of loom stops was still 1.6 per hour. After 37 days a partial third shift

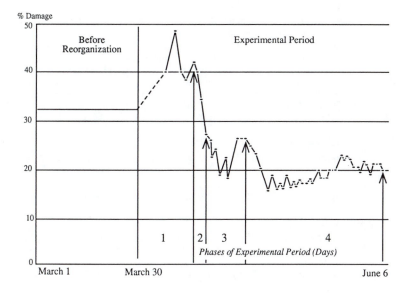

% Damage

Before
Reorganization

Experimental Period

1   2 3   4

Phases of Experimental Period (Days)

March 1   March 30   June 6

Figure 4. Percentage damage before and after reorganization

was started on one of the experimental blocks of 64 looms and on one of the groups of 48 looms. Results thereafter are not, therefore, strictly comparable with those of the experimental period.

FIGURES FOR EFFICIENCY AND DAMAGE

The results of the comparison of the mean percentage efficiencies of the experimental groups with the mean percentage efficiency of the shed before reorganization are given in Table 8 (figures are based on an eight-hour shift).

When the standard deviations of the distributions of percentage efficiencies were calculated, these confirmed a significant difference between the mean percentage efficiencies of each experimental group in the fourth phase and the shed efficiency before reorganization, and between the mean percentage efficiency of the combined groups in the fourth phase and the shed efficiency before reorganization. Except in the second phase (three days), they show no significant difference between the mean percentage efficiencies of the experimental groups or, in the fourth phase, between the standard deviations of the distributions of percentage efficiencies of the experimental groups. The standard deviations of the distributions of the experimental groups are less for each group than that of the distribution for the whole shed before reorganization.

The results of the comparison of mean percentage damage of the experimen-

TABLE 8   Mean Percentage Efficiencies of Four Experimental Groups Compared with Shed Efficiency before Reorganization

Phases of experimental period	Experimental group				Combined
	a	*b*	*c*	*d*	
1. March 30–April 10 11 working days	87.7	87.9	86.5	86.4	87.1
2. April 11–April 14 3 working days	67.7	69.6	73.2	79.8	72.6
3. April 15–April 23 8 working days	84.0	86.4	83.0	86.3	84.9
4. April 24–June 6 37 working days	95.9	96.2	94.0	94.1	95.0
Overall shed efficiency before reorganization[a] March 1–March 28 23 working days	(79.8)	(79.8)	(79.8)	(79.8)	79.8

[a]The range of individual weavers' efficiencies before reorganization was 74.4–85.0.

tal groups with the mean percentage damage of the shed before reorganization are given in Table 9. No daily damage figures were available for the period before reorganization or for the experimental groups for the first six days of the experimental period. Because there was no night shift in the inspection department, the damage of the experimental groups *a* and *b* and of *c* and *d* had to be combined.

The results show a significant difference between the mean percentage damage of each of the pairs of experimental groups and that of the shed before reorganization. They also show significant differences between the means of the experimental groups in all phases. The differences between the means of experimental groups can be accounted for by difficulties with humidification during construction, which affected the 64 looms near the new building more than the others. The boundary of the affected area was, however, difficult to define and other factors (at present unknown) may have affected performance.

It may also be noted that in the period before reorganization the proportion of looms to workers (excluding the humidification fitter) was 8:1; that if eventually the number of workers in the shed had been found adequate to handle 240 looms, the proportion would then be 8.6:1; and that in the experimental groups the proportion was 8.5:1 during the period when extra help was given and 9.1:1 after it was withdrawn.

TABLE 9   Mean Percentage Damage of Four Experimental Groups
Compared with Shed Damage before Reorganization

Phases of experimental period	Experimental group		
	a & b	*c & d*	*Combined*
1. April 6–April 10 5 working days	37.8	45.5	41.6
2. April 11–April 14 3 working days	31.2	36.2	33.7
3. April 15–April 23 8 working days	18.8	25.7	22.3
4. April 24–June 6 37 working days	17.8	21.9	19.9
Overall shed damage be- fore reorganization March 1–March 28 23 working days	(31.8)	(31.8)	31.8

LIMITATIONS OF THE FINDINGS

The findings of the experiment are those of operational research. It was not possible, within the circumstances of the experiment, to relate the findings to the ecological background of economic, industrial or cultural conditions in India nor, because of language difficulties, was it possible to relate them to the attitudes and relationships of the supervisors and workers of the loom shed itself. The only evidence of the "goodness of fit" of the analysis was its spontaneous acceptance, rapid implementation and continuity. It may, however, be inferred that, by being permitted to implement their own reorganization, the workers were given a first experience of their own capacity to create an internal structure; and that management, in its turn, was able to accept the internal structuring of small work groups as a method of management and as an alternative to additional imposed external structure.

An examination of the efficiency and damage results in the rest of the shed—that is, the looms other than those included in the experimental groups—strongly suggests the effects of forces of induction from the experimental groups. Theoretically, the rest of the shed continued with the previous form of organization during the experimental period. The formation of the experimental groups, however, had an inevitably disturbing effect on the whole shed and involved a reallocation of tasks and work loads among the rest of the workers.

TABLE 10   Efficiency and Damage Percentages for Rest of Loom
Shed during Experimental Period

Phases of experimental period	Efficiency	Damage
1. April 6–April 10 5 working days	71.0	42.7
2. April 11–April 14 3 working days	66.6	40.5
3. April 15–April 23 8 working days	68.9	26.6
4. April 25–June 6 37 working days	81.4	23.0
Shed before reorganization March 1–March 28 23 working days	79.8	31.8

This disturbance, apart from any of the effects of being left out of the experiment, would have led to the expectation of induced negative forces in the experimental period. These expectations were confirmed by the results, but only in the first three phases of the experimental period. During the fourth phase, the mean percentage efficiency of the rest of the shed was 81.4 (shed efficiency before reorganization was 79.8), and the mean percentage damage was 23.0 (shed damage before reorganization was 31.8). The full figures are given in Table 10.

The view that this improvement was a reflection of the success of the experimental groups was supported by a request from the workers in the rest of the shed to be allowed to reorganize themselves in the same way as had the experimental groups. Action was deferred until the end of the experimental period.

There is, as yet, no adequate information about the effects and repercussions in the rest of the mill. There have been no known adverse effects and some favorable interest has been shown. As far as can be ascertained, social, economic and technological conditions both outside and inside the mill and loom shed remained constant throughout the period for which results are reported in this paper. The only known change is that of weather, which grew steadily hotter from the beginning of March to the end of July.

On June 7 a partial third shift was started on one of the experimental groups of 64 looms and on one of the groups of 48 looms. The shift was started with new and comparatively inexperienced workers. It provided the opportunity for the upgrading of some of the members of the experimental groups and the reallocation of some tasks. The results since June 7 are not, therefore, comparable with those of the experimental period. The mean percentage efficiency of the whole shed for all shifts for the period June 8 to August 22 (the latest figures available) was, however, 90.3 (before reorganization, 79.8) and the mean percentage damage was 24.5 (before reorganization, 31.8). The works manager comments, "these results have coincided with the most difficult part of the year, working conditions are severe and absenteeism maximum."

Note. In the concluding sentence of his original paper, Rice says, "The exploration has led to arrangements for further collaboration. It is hoped, therefore, to follow up the experiment reported in this paper and to publish further reports as results become available." Such results were, in fact, published in his follow-up paper, "Productivity and Social Organization in an Indian Weaving Mill: II," *Human Relations,* 8:399–428, and further updated in his *The Enterprise and Its Environment* (London: Tavistock Publications, 1963).

References

Katz, D. and R.L. Kahn. 1951. "Human Organization and Worker Motivation." In *Industrial Productivity: A Social and Economic Analysis,* edited by L.R. Trip, Industrial Relations Research Association. Madison, Wis.: Solomon, Barkin.

Rice, A.K. and E.L. Trist. 1952. "Institutional and Sub-Institutional Determinants of Change in Labour Turnover." *Human Relations,* 5:347–71.

Roethlisberger, F.J. and W.J. Dickson. 1939. *Management and the Worker: An Account of a Research Program Conducted by the Western Electric Company.* Cambridge, Mass.: Harvard University Press.

Trist, E.L. and K.W. Bamforth. 1951. "Some Social and Psychological Consequences of the Longwall Method of Coal-Getting." *Human Relations,* 4:3–38. Shortened, Vol. II, "The Stress of Isolated Dependence: The Filling Shift in the Semi-Mechanized Longwall Three-Shift Mining Cycle," pp. 64–83.

Eric J. Miller

The Ahmedabad Experiment Revisited
Work Organization in an Indian Weaving Shed, 1953–1970[1]

A.K. Rice, in *Productivity and Social Organization: The Ahmedabad Experiment* (1958), described an experimental reorganization of weaving in an Indian textile company. In the experiments, which were carried out in 1953/54 and which involved both automatic and nonautomatic looms, semiautonomous work groups were formed with responsibility for production and routine maintenance on a group of looms. Rice's work was the first attempt to apply the concept of a socio-technical system to the design of a production process and the experimental changes resulted in substantial improvements in output, quality and work satisfaction. Rice and the author also worked with this company in implementing a set of changes in organization and management (cf. Rice, 1963). Subsequently, the experimental forms of group working were extended to other loom sheds in the company's mills.

In 1970, the author, with a colleague, undertook a follow-up study of this "group system" in four locations in the company. These included the two original sites and two other loom sheds in which this method of working had been introduced later. The study showed that the work organization and levels of performance in one of the original sites had remained virtually unchanged over the 16 years. In a newer automatic loom shed, group working had largely disappeared; regression had also occurred in both the other sheds studied. Explanations are offered for these differential outcomes and there is a discussion of resilience in systems of work organization.

The concept of the *socio-technical system* was developed at the Tavistock Institute nearly 40 years ago (Trist and Bamforth, 1951). Showing that a production system could be analyzed in terms of the symbiotic relationship of two systems, the technical and the social, the Institute began a productive

[1]The original version of this paper appeared as E. Miller, "Socio-Technical Systems in Weaving, 1953–1970: A Follow-up Study," in *Human Relations*, 28:349–86, 1975. A shortened and slightly revised version was reprinted in *Organizational Democracy and Political Processes*, edited by C. Crouch and F. Heller. Chichester: John Wiley & Sons, 1983. It is the latter, with slight editorial changes, that is reproduced in this volume.

search for "the 'right' organization that would satisfy both task and social needs"; somewhat later, however, it was recognized that "there are settings where elegant solutions of this kind cannot be found or where, if found, they introduce new and intractable constraints" (Miller and Rice, 1967:xii).

In Rice's work in 1953 at The Calico Mills, Ahmedabad, India,[2]

> Attempts were made to take into account both the independent and inter-dependent properties of the social, technological and economic dimensions of existing socio-technical systems, and to establish new systems in which all dimensions were more adequately inter-related than they had previously been. (Rice, 1958:4)

In three papers (1953, 1955a, 1955b) and in the book from which the above quotation is taken (*Productivity and Social Organization: The Ahmedabad Experiment*) he describes an experimental reorganization of weaving, first in an automatic loom shed and second on nonautomatic looms. In both instances, internally led groups of workers were formed, each group being responsible for production and line maintenance on a group of looms.

The book also describes concomitant changes in management organization that the company introduced while Rice was acting as consultant during the period from 1953 to 1956. The story of management reorganization up to 1961 is continued in Rice's second book, *The Enterprise and Its Environment* (1963), which also gives updated information on the two loom shed experiments.

This work of Rice's has been widely cited. For example, it is described by Katz and Kahn (1966:455) as "by and large . . . an amazing success story." McGregor (1960, 1966) refers to it as a case of collaboration leading to integration; Myers (1959) as an example of involving workers in shop-floor decision making; K. Davis (1962:497) as an example of a work situation promoting group cohesiveness; and Likert (1961:38–43) as illustrating how such cohesiveness can result in better performance figures. Building directly and indirectly on Rice's early experiments and the work of Trist and his research team, autonomous group working proliferated during the 1960s and 1970s in many different countries in a wide variety of factories and offices.

For the most part, Rice's methodology has been either accepted or actively praised, for example by L.E. Davis (1967). Vroom and Maier (1961:438) are more cautious, saying that it is "difficult to draw unequivocal conclusions concerning the underlying processes." One dissenting voice is that of Roy

---

[2]"Calico Mills" is the name by which the Ahmedabad Manufacturing and Calico Printing Company is generally known. In the rest of this paper we refer to it simply as "the company." This is to avoid confusion since one of the spinning and weaving units within the company's Textile Division carries the same name. This latter we call "Calico Mill " or "Calico." The other spinning and weaving unit with which this paper is concerned is "Jubilee Mill" or "Jubilee."

(1969), who criticizes the methodology and suggests that in his interpretation of the results he achieved Rice had greatly underestimated the extra cash incentive to the group workers.

Rice was to have revisited the company in his consultant role in 1969. Part of his task was to examine the implications for work organization of further technological change in the textile industry. This visit had to be abandoned because of an illness that led to Rice's premature death toward the end of 1969. The author, who had during 1956–58 worked for the company as an internal consultant in collaboration with Rice, went as a substitute for him for one month in July/August 1970. This seemed to be a good opportunity to review the present state of the socio-technical system that Rice had helped to introduce, to analyze changes that had occurred and to try to refine the assumptions on which the original system was designed. Permission was sought from the company to deploy a second Tavistock staff member, A.F. Shaw, in a research capacity.[3]

In addition to observation and study of performance records, individual interviews and group discussions were held with a substantial number of workers, both in the original experimental areas and in the loom sheds where forms of group working had been introduced later. (Other textile companies in Ahmedabad also adopted or adapted the Calico approach; but that experience has not been studied.) Our data spanned a period of 17 years.

The Experiments and the Outcomes

The site of Rice's first experiment was the automatic loom shed at Jubilee Mill (here called "Jubilee Auto"), which in 1953–54 contained 288 looms. After nine months a second experiment was initiated on 120 nonautomatic Lancashire looms at Calico Mill ("Calico Exp").

Graphs showing follow-up performance figures in both experiments during the period 1954–60 are given by Rice in his second book (1963:111–12). Higher levels of efficiency reached during the experimental phases were largely sustained and, in the case of the nonautomatic looms, even slightly improved during the subsequent six years. Similarly, the levels of damage went down and stayed down.

Comparisons of performance data need to be treated with a good deal of caution. It is virtually impossible to make precise comparisons between dif-

[3]A Social Science Research Council grant covered Shaw's travel to and from India and also salary costs; while in India Shaw stayed as a guest of the company. I would like to thank both these groups for making this work possible. I am also grateful to Shaw for his preliminary analysis and interpretation of the data.

ferent types of looms weaving different types of cloth. "Before and after" comparisons on the same looms weaving similar types of cloth are more reliable. Apart from minor changes that may be made in the methods of calculating efficiency and in inspection standards, however, a reduction in loom speeds can lead to improved efficiency figures but a decline in output. Efficiency is measured in terms of the number of "picks" (weft threads) inserted during a given period (usually a shift) expressed as a percentage of the number that would have been inserted if the loom had run continuously throughout the period. Speeds were adjusted during the first experiments but, so far as could be checked, not subsequently. The performance data therefore probably do show real trends. It has also to be noted that, although fluctuations in the quality of yarn can increase or decrease the work load on the looms, in the form of organization designed by the workers in consultation with Rice and agreed to by management, provision was made to increase or decrease the number of workers according to sample measurements of the number of breaks occurring in the warp and weft yarn. Thus, although labor productivity would change, the broad levels of efficiency and damage should remain substantially the same. Maintenance of the looms, which also affects both efficiency and damage, is the responsibility of the group in this type of work organization. There are, however, limitations on the extent to which the work group can offset the consequences for efficiency and damage of poor quality of supplies (such as shuttles) and spare parts (see below).

In 1956–57, group working was extended to the so-called Pit Shed at Calico (Calico Pit), which had 440 nonautomatic looms. During the 1960s, Jubilee Auto was enlarged, with the addition of 128 looms of a different type, and the company installed a large new automatic loom shed at Calico with 656 looms, on which group working was also introduced (Calico Auto).

Over these 17 years, progressive changes were occurring in the company's market and sources of supplies. Since the early 1950s it had been the avowed policy of the management to raise norms of productivity and quality, and Rice's experiments themselves were designed as a means to that end. The effects of this policy were reflected in the company's record of profitability, which was surpassed by few other mills in India (Rice, 1963:108). As the company enhanced its reputation for design and quality in the Indian markets and correspondingly was able to command a progressively higher average price per yard of cloth sold, its management aspired to becoming increasingly competitive in export markets, not only within the relatively less developed countries of the Far East, the Middle East and Africa but also in the more stringent markets of the West—for example, shirting for the mass-production garment industry, which demands continuous pieces of flawless cloth.

There were two significant constraints. First, there was a limited availability of the long staple cottons required for the finest and most profitable fabrics, since these had to be imported, mainly from Egypt, and India had maintained a tight control over imports for many years. To make full use of this raw material, high standards were demanded in spinning and weaving. Second, governmental regulations, imposed to protect the hand loom industry, prevented the installation of additional power looms. There was little scope for increasing profits through expansion and consequently greater emphasis on productivity and profit per loom. Top management pressures to maintain and improve quality and output were thus strong and persistent.

Import controls also restricted availability of loom spare parts and supplies. Domestically manufactured substitutes were often of low quality. This situation led to damage and reduced efficiency and to some deterioration in the general condition of the looms.

It is in this context that the developments in work organization have to be considered. For ease of presentation I shall depart from the chronological sequence and first discuss the experience with nonautomatic looms—Calico Exp and Calico Pit—before considering the automatic loom experiment and subsequent developments. My accounts of the original experiments are inevitably abbreviated and oversimplified. Readers are referred to Rice's publications for the detailed material.

Calico Exp

On the nonautomatic looms at Calico, the presenting problem was to improve quality. The looms were operated on two shifts; low output and high damage made three-shift working uneconomical.

In the conventional work system, each weaver operated two looms and was responsible for some ancillary activities such as collecting weft yarn and delivering woven cloth, other workers were also involved: jobbers (for loom maintenance and supervision of weavers), beam carriers, oilers. In the experimental shed set up in January 1954, small work groups were constituted to perform all the tasks of weaving and maintenance on groups of 40 looms, all of which wove the same kind of cloth continuously. Five natural grades within a work group were found: group leader, smash tenter/assistant group leader, front loom worker, back loom worker and helper. These group members performed interdependent tasks and formed interdependent relationships. An aggregate of 22 workers in the conventional system was replaced by an internally structured group of 11. Minimum basic rates were raised. Bonuses were paid for both quantity and quality and, at the workers' own request, reflected group rather than individual performance.

The experimental period lasted 10 months (January–November 1954), during which time both management and workers progressively "tested-out" each other's sincerity and willingness to cooperate. Gradually permissive and collaborative relationships were assisted by the institution of informal group meetings and of more formal conferences. In the conferences the whole executive chain responsible for production was present and, at the workers' request, all shifts attended the same conferences, some coming during their free time.

During the initial phase the quality of cloth actually declined, but then it steadily improved. By the end of the experimental period, both quality and efficiency had settled down at a significantly higher level than in other loom sheds. One factor in improved quality was a reduction in loom speeds of 11 percent. Despite efficiency increases, therefore, output per loom hour was actually reduced. On the other hand, labor productivity increased substantially and this, in conjunction with the higher average price per yard obtainable from the improved cloth, made three-shift working viable. Compared with the existing two-shift two-loom system, the experimental three-shift group system showed the following results: the mean earnings of the group were 55 percent higher; the cost per loom was 13 percent higher; the output was 21 percent higher; and the number of damages 59 percent less. These results were achieved on the most difficult sort[4] regularly woven in the mills.

Rice concluded:

> The immediate practical result of the experiment has been to demonstrate that in the Calico Mills the breakdown of the "whole" task of weaving into component operations, each performed by a different worker, and the re-integration of the workers into an internally structured work-group that performs the "whole" task on a group of looms, can be accomplished in one process provided that permissive and collaborative relationships can be built up between all those concerned.
>
> . . . The experimental system has established new norms of performance and earnings for nonautomatic weaving. The conclusion was reached that the acceptance of the new system and the determination to make it work were due to its providing more opportunities for effective task performance and for the building of more stable and secure small work-group relationships than those existing in the conventional system with which the traditional norms of performance and wages were associated. (1958:166)

The 1970 version of the group system conformed closely to that described by Rice (1958). The shed contained, as in 1954, three blocks of 40 looms, operated by nine work groups over the three shifts. Within each group there

---

[4]"Sorts" or types of cloth are classified by the "count" (thickness) of yarn and the number of warp and weft threads to the inch.

were five roles. The group leader (A), the assistant group leader (B+) and the sweeper/general assistant (E) comprised the gating[5] and maintenance sub-group. The weaving sub-group consisted of B workers operating on the fronts of the looms, shuttling and mending the front warp, and C workers on the backs, mending the back warp and engaging in fault prevention. The size of this sub-group depended on the work load as measured by the current rate of warp and weft breakages. At the time of the follow-up study the most usual numbers were four or five Bs and four Cs, giving an overall group size of 12 to 13. The range was 10 to 15.

Table 1 compares efficiency and damage in Calico Exp during 1969–70 with the last phase of the 1954 experimental period. On both indices, the 1969–70 performance is slightly better than that of 1954 and, indeed, for the whole period up to 1959, but not as good as that for 1959–60 (see Rice, 1963:112).

It seems safe to assume that no significant change had occurred in standards of performance over the 16-year period. Indeed, there is one quite remarkable piece of evidence indicating that they had remained unchanged. Rice noted that performance on one block of looms was consistently superior, in terms of efficiency and damage, but no reason for this could be discovered and "by the end of the experimental period there had been no conclusive explanation" (1958:114). Fifteen years later, the performance data for 1969–70 showed precisely the same pattern.

In general, not only the structure of the groups but also the method of working was hardly distinguishable from that which had been developing during 1954. During his observations, the field worker was impressed by the smooth rhythm of working. All members seemed to know exactly where and in what combination with others they could be most appropriately deployed at any given moment. Rice's description of a group culture of mutual helping between sub-groups and individuals still held true.

The fact that the group leader had a managerial as well as a maintenance role was accepted and sanctioned by group members generally. Group leaders saw the management of boundary transactions as their responsibility. They checked the group's inputs and outputs and mediated relations with the rest of the organization. Other group workers would not contact supervisors directly. Supervisors, on the other hand, felt it was their duty to approach workers directly if, for example, there were signs of slackness. Group leaders countered this by ignoring shift supervisors and the section head and going directly to the weaving master of Calico as a whole if they had problems. By doing this they were reasserting the historical privileged position of the experimental shed, for the weaving master had himself been a shift supervisor there in 1954.

[5]"Gating" is the installation of the beam of warp yarn and threading of yarn onto the loom.

TABLE 1   Calico Exp: Efficiency and Damage, 1954 and 1969–70

Period	Index of % efficiency	Index of damages per 1000 yards
July–Nov. 1954	100.0	100.0
Jan.–June 1969	101.0	79.7
July–Dec. 1969	101.1	82.3
Jan.–June 1970	100.3	96.9

In practice, supervisors seldom exercised their "right" to intervene within the groups.

Calico Pit

The nonautomatic looms in this shed had been converted to group working in 1956–57. In size and composition, the groups were identical to those in Calico Exp. In Calico Pit, however, there was a greater variation in deployment between one group and another. Although B workers were always held to be more skilled than C workers, the managerial view that B workers should operate at the fronts and C at the backs was not universally observed in practice. (Front work was theoretically held to be more responsible because it was from this position that the loom could be started and stopped, and also more skilled in terms of the type of mending required.) In a few groups B and C workers had the same roles but worked different numbers of looms. There were also differences between groups in the extent to which workers were rigidly allocated to a specific number of looms or allowed and encouraged to overlap with neighbors within a group. In general, there was more rigidity in Calico Pit than in Calico Exp. In one pattern observed in groups in Calico Pit, four B workers each worked front and back on six looms and four C workers each worked front and back on four looms.

In 1969–70, efficiencies in Calico Pit were 3.5 to 5 percentage points lower and damage rates 4 to 7 times higher than in Calico Exp. Performance in Calico Pit was said to have been always inferior, but in the absence of earlier records it is not possible to say whether the difference had remained stable or widened. According to managers, the only significant technical difference between the two sheds was that humidity in Calico Exp was somewhat more favorable for weaving; but this is insufficient to explain the persistent performance gap.

There were, however, notable differences in the role of the group leader and the relation of the groups to their environment. In some groups, as in Calico Exp, all official contact between group members and the rest of the mill was mediated through the group leader. In other cases group leaders seemed hardly aware of the input and output of their groups and would not be informed by group members of transactions with shift supervisors or with other sections of the weaving department.

Direct intervention by shift supervisors in the operation of the groups was much more common than in Calico Exp. Partly, as already noted, this was because Calico Exp group leaders had maintained the habit of approaching the weaving master directly if they had problems. Partly, too, it was because the supervisors felt it necessary to contact workers only when group performance was deemed to be poor and then, by their own accounts, they spent three-quarters of their time with the three or four groups that had the poorest production and quality figures. Since performance in the Calico Exp was seen as consistently satisfactory, there was no reason for supervisory intervention.

The working assumption of the supervisors in Calico Pit was that poor performance in the group was something to be remedied by intensive supervision of individuals within it; it was held to be a phenomenon for which the group, through its leader, could be held accountable and called upon to correct. Thus, the accepted mode of intervention undermined both the authority of the group leader and the possible collective responsibility of the group for its members' performance. It was certainly inconsistent with Rice's conception of the group system.

In terms of perception and attitudes there was a great deal of similarity between Calico Exp and Calico Pit. All the supervisors and group leaders and most of the workers described the group system as having two distinctive characteristics:

It required cooperation between group members.

There was a differentiation of the weaving task into work on the front and the back of the looms.

About half the workers regarded the former and half the latter as the most distinctive feature which marked off the group system from other working arrangements in weaving.

The group workers saw themselves as having higher status than those under conventional working arrangements. In Calico Exp this was linked especially with their historical success in increasing efficiency and quality compared with the previous system of working.

This feeling of higher status was evidently not linked to pay. The fact that they earned more money was perceived rather as something that bound them to the group system and prevented them from moving elsewhere, even though some of the older workers said they felt tired and overworked. There was a commonly held belief among workers on nonautomatic looms that work in the group system was so hard as to shorten one's life. It was also said that the higher work load led to a need for better quality food, which in turn offset some of the advantages of higher wages.

The idea of cooperation among group members was highly valued. Correspondingly, the major complaints about the system were that some or all workers did not cooperate and that the team spirit that was supposed to exist was sometimes not in evidence. Workers spoke of having to "carry" fellow group members who were slow, old, lazy or troublesome. For example, one group leader spent a large part of his working day resting outside the weaving shed. Members of his group were resigned to this but not resentful. The assistant group leader on whom a larger part of the work had fallen said, "We have been together a long time—he deserves a rest." Workers were reluctant to criticize unproductive fellow group members. This was thought to be a prerogative solely of the group leader.

In spite of complaints about diminishing team spirit, group identification appeared to be quite high. Differences between groups were readily observable in style and pace of working. Physical boundaries between groups were especially noticeable during the festivities of the Hindu New Year. Some looms had been decorated with flowers, leaves, colored paper and balloons and others had either remained undecorated or had been garlanded in distinctive styles. Group identification was encouraged by publication of monthly production figures, which seemed to promote a spirit of inter-group competition. Workers frequently used the words "we" and "us" in reference to their groups. They spoke of being especially friendly with fellow group members and of sitting together with them during rest breaks.

Jubilee Auto

The position in 1953 was that 224 (rising later to 288) automatic looms had been installed with an expectation of considerable improvements in output and quality; but actual performance was no better than with conventional looms.

Rice's analysis of the work organization showed that the weaving process had been broken down into component tasks and that the number of workers assigned to each component had been determined by work studies. The resultant pattern was of an aggregate of individuals with confused task and role relationships, ambiguities in accountability and no discernible internal group structure. Rice postulated that on automatic looms the title of "weaver" for an occupational role was no longer appropriate: the weaver was now the loom, and all workers, including "weavers," serviced machines. The tasks performed could be differentiated into two main types: those concerned with weaving and those concerned with gating and loom maintenance. There were, in addition, only minor ancillary services. Rice then proposed the idea of a group of workers for a group of looms. The theoretical numbers required for blocks of 654 looms were calculated. Three "natural" grades within a work group were identified, instead of the existing nine grades. These grades were designated by letters. Workers coming into these grades would be paid a slightly higher rate than before, and it was also decided to pay piece rates on the basis of the performance of the group as a whole.

Loom shed supervisors and workers spontaneously took possession of the reorganization, the workers themselves immediately organizing four experimental internally led small groups. This was in March 1953. These groups abandoned the old titles, using only the new letter grades. After an immediate increase in efficiency at the cost of increased damage and inadequate maintenance, they settled at a new level of performance in which efficiency had risen from just over 80 percent to around 90 percent, while the percentage of damage had improved from 40 percent before reorganization to an average of roughly 20 percent.

When the form of organization was extended to the rest of the shed, and a third shift started, the efficiency was maintained for several months, but in October and November of 1953 it dropped steeply over a period of five weeks. At the same time the figures for damage rose steadily. Investigation showed that each group had to contend with variations in the sort woven; there had been insufficient spare workers; training of new and existing workers in the new methods of organization had been neglected and also diffused throughout all groups; and the basis on which the original experimental groups had been formed had not allowed sufficient time for group leaders to perform the task of leading. As a result of the difficulties caused by these factors, group members had regressed to earlier working habits more appropriate to individual than to group working.

Various corrective measures were taken, including establishment of basic rates of pay, segregation of training from production and reduction of the variety of sorts in any one group. Recovery was rapid.

> It was concluded that the first spontaneous acceptance of the new system and the subsequent determination to make it work were due primarily to the workers' intuitive acceptance of it as one which would provide them with the security and protection of small group membership which they had lost by leaving their villages and their families to enter industry. At the same time the new system allowed them to perform their primary task effectively and thus provided them with an important source of satisfaction. (Rice, 1958:110)

In 1970, Jubilee Auto contained 240 "S"-type looms dating from the 1953 experiment and 128 "K"-type looms installed in the late 1960s. They were arranged in groups of 64 or 56 and all operated in three shifts. Most groups wove two sorts of cloth which were, on the whole, finer and more expensive than those produced on the Calico nonautomatic looms.

The 1969–70 performance figures for Jubilee Auto are given in Table 2, which suggests that on the "S"-type looms efficiency was slightly lower and quality higher than in 1954–55. It also points to a short-term decline in performance, in both efficiency and quality, in the "S" groups and to an opposite trend on the "K" looms, while the weighted average figures for Jubilee Auto as a whole, especially the figures for efficiency, remained remarkably steady over the 18 months. It is possible to surmise that Jubilee Auto was engaging in an unacknowledged process of setting new performance norms for the loom shed as a whole. This would be consistent with the fact that neither in methods of working nor in modes of supervisory intervention were the "S" and "K" groups observably different in behavior. They also had similar proportions of older and newer workers. However, it must be noted that the variation of the "S" groups was within the range of variation that occurred during 1955–60 when damage figures in particular showed marked cyclical rises and falls (Rice, 1963:111, Figure 19).

The original grades of workers in the experimental groups on automatic looms were described by Rice (1958:69) as follows:

A: Overall group leader, working head of gating and maintenance sub-group.

B: Fully skilled member of either weaving or gating and maintenance sub-group.

C: Not yet fully skilled member of sub-group but has acquired enough skill to help with main sub-group tasks.

D: Full members of group mainly engaged on less skilled jobs—battery filling, oiling, etc.

E: New unskilled entrants not yet accepted as group members.

A, B and D were the "natural" grades; C and E were transitional. Subsequently the B worker in the gating and maintenance sub-group had been reclassified as a B+ with a slightly higher rate of pay. This seems to have been a carryover from the grading on nonautomatic looms. The usual complement of workers in a group in 1970 was 1 A, 1 B+, 2 B, 2 C and 1 D—a total of seven—the Bs and Cs being members of the weaving sub-group. Moreover, C, instead of being transitional had become quasi-permanent; C workers were promoted to the B grade not when they had achieved the necessary skill but when vacancies occurred—and then on the basis of seniority.

In the experimental period of 1953, the group of 64 looms had been perceived as an entity for which the group as a whole was jointly responsible and where there had been a great deal of mutual helping among the various categories of workers—for example, members of the maintenance sub-group would help members of the weaving sub-group and vice versa. In 1970, the

TABLE 2   Jubilee Auto: Efficiency and Damage, 1954–55 and 1969–70

	"S"-type looms		"K"-type looms		All looms	
Period	Index of % efficiency	Index of % damage[a]	Index of % efficiency	Index of % damage[a]	Index of % efficiency	Index of % damage[a]
Dec. 1954–June 1955	100.0	100.0	—	—	—	—
Jan.–June 1969	97.8	67.8	88.1	125.5	94.6	87.1
July–Dec. 1969	96.9	78.7	89.9	122.0	94.7	93.0
Jan.–June 1970	95.2	91.8	91.6	109.3	94.1	97.8

[a]The damage index is calculated from the percentage of cloth classified by inspectors as below standard quality—a different measurement from that on the nonautomatic looms. Note that in the efficiency index higher is better and in the damage index higher is worse, compared with 1954–55.

group was typically operated in two halves, with one or two B workers and one C worker responsible for a set of 32 looms. Moreover, while supervisors and group leaders tended to regard the 32 looms as a block, for the operation of which the sub-group of two or three workers was responsible, in practice the workers themselves also tended to allocate specific looms among themselves so that each C worker, for example, might be regarded as totally responsible for 10 to 16 looms.

This situation is strikingly reminiscent of the regression during the experimental period when the B grade workers had begun to take the warp mending on 32 looms each.

> As the efficiency fell they expressed resentment about the group bonus and the participation in it of other group members. . . . The D grade workers, whose tasks included helping B grade workers by doing simple warp mending, reverted to battery filling only, each taking 32 looms. This left them underloaded despite the general overload. (Rice, 1958:94)

Rice indicates that as a result of steps taken during the follow-up period these regressive habits were corrected and the groups reverted to their previous cooperative methods of working. The actual methods of working observed in 1970, however, closely corresponded to those that Rice had described as regressed and, if anything, sub-tasks within the group were more sharply differentiated and there was less cooperation between different categories. For example, it now appeared exceptional for a group leader to help with weaving subtasks. Consistent with this change was the fact that group leaders were more often than not referred to by the preexperimental title of "jobber," implying a reversion to the traditional role predominantly concerned with maintenance.

While group leaders appeared, and felt themselves to be, so preoccupied by their maintenance responsibilities that they had little time left for the other activities of their role, supervisors in Jubilee Auto, especially those more recently recruited, were confused about the work system. They were told to operate "the group system," yet the nature of this system was not clearly defined to them. Their experience was of being pressed for more production, but encountering a collective resistance from the workers against any such increase. Some supervisors would respond by trying to work through the group leader. Others would go straight to individual workers. In this, too, there were echoes of the 1953 regression:

> Faced with the lack of group leadership and the regression to earlier work habits—the supervisors themselves tended to regress to earlier patterns of management behaviour. They by-passed the group leaders and dealt directly with workers. . . . The intervention by the supervisors in the organizing of group tasks

tended further to destroy the internally structured leadership of the groups. (Rice, 1958:94–95)

Workers were confused by the variation in supervisory styles. A typical statement was: "Each officer has his own ways; then the workers just have to follow." But some believed that at least part of the responsibility for the situation lay farther up in the hierarchy, stating that "supervisors are now under pressure from above for more production but they work less hard themselves and just put pressure on others."

Perhaps because of the combination of the arbitrariness of the supervisors and the relative impotence of the group leaders in facilitating the task, there was much greater use in Jubilee Auto of union representatives as an alternative channel of communication between group members and departmental management. It was through these representatives, for example, that complaints about shortages of supplies or about the quality of spare parts were often passed.

The Jubilee Auto supervisors also constantly intervened in the composition of groups. In the Calico nonautomatic loom shed, group membership was highly stable. In cases of absence or increased work load substitutes would be brought in from a pool. In Jubilee Auto, on the other hand, though a similar pool existed, an absence or a vacancy in one group tended to lead to a consequential series of transfers between groups based on seniority. The group, through its group leader, had no say over the qualifications of the workers allocated to it. Thus the supervisors' approach to the allocation of resources implied that the groups were no more than transient sets of interchangeable individuals.

A third of the workers interviewed in Jubilee Auto claimed to have belonged to the 1953 experimental groups. These workers and long-service supervisors spoke of a characteristic of the system being "the working together of men as in families," the group leader being like a father and the other members like sons. Post-1953 recruits were said to have had no training for group working as such. For example, the group leader of one group had been recruited directly into that position from another mill after only one day's tests of mechanical and maintenance skills. He had received no instruction about the characteristics of the particular work system he was to operate. The same applied to supervisors. Whether or not older employees were correct in saying that an increased work load over the past three years had inhibited cooperation and mutual helping, it was observable that the more recently recruited workers seemed most confused about what the group system involved. Although they were told that cooperation was the distinctive characteristic of the system, their experience was of taking responsibility for a specific number of looms and of neither giving nor receiving very much help. The unique characteristic, as many saw it, was that in this work system a group of workers operated 64 looms in two sets of 32, whereas in other mills a similar group would operate 48 looms in two sets of 24.

Some feeling of competition among groups and internally between half-groups was fostered by the posting of daily loom efficiencies on a notice board in the loom shed. When workers spoke about availability and quality of supplies it was also in terms of supplies for their own groups or half-groups. However, there was less identification with groups and competition between them than in Calico Exp,where those interviewed spoke a great deal about "our group"; in Jubilee Auto "we" referred as often as not to all the workers in the loom shed. They spoke of their friends as coming from throughout the shed and not specifically from their own groups. This may have been linked to the fact that, because of the policy for dealing with absences and vacancies, there was greater inter-group mobility. Although promotion based on seniority was recognized as being far from ideal because of the disruption it created, it was nevertheless held by management and unions to be the fairest and least corruptible.

Despite complaints about the group system, in particular about the "exploitation" of C workers, some of whom did the same work as Bs for less money, those interviewed generally expressed contentment with their jobs within Jubilee Mill. Jobs were held to be better there than in other mills, partly because wages were higher and were paid promptly; but greater emphasis was given to the belief that the mill had a good reputation, was free from corruption and offered safe employment. Group working as such was not cited as a distinctive source of satisfaction.

Calico Auto

The new automatic shed at the Calico Mill had been started in 1962 and at the time of the follow-up study accommodated 656 automatic looms of five different makes. These were intended to weave the finest, most expensive sorts in the company's range.

From the outset it had been planned to operate these new looms with the group system developed in Jubilee Auto. The looms were accordingly arranged in blocks of 64 or 48, and some Jubilee people were transferred to the new department. However, many new people also had to be recruited to the supervisory staff and work force. For the most part these recruits did not have prior experience of automatic looms, which were not then common in Ahmedabad, so the opportunity existed to train them in the desired methods of working.

Buildup to levels of efficiency and quality acceptable to management had been relatively slow, but by the time of the study Calico Auto was, with certain ill-defined reservations, regarded as a success. Productivity and quality were perceived as comparing favorably with those in other Indian mills, though they still fell somewhat short of the "best international standards" to which the company, in its efforts to become a major exporter of fine cloths, now aspired.

It became apparent during the research that the actual method of working in this loom shed was very different from the type of group system that management outside the loom shed believed to be in operation. Although the weaving master in charge of the department knew that he was supposed to be operating a "group system," he was also aware of strong pressure to keep up production. He felt, correctly, that he was judged primarily by his department's efficiency and quality figures which, in fact, he had been successful in improving. To do this he had used methods which he had found successful elsewhere, instituting many checks on performance and closely supervising individuals.

The supervisory staff in the department knew, or thought they knew, the way in which a "proper group system" should be operated. Like some of their counterparts in Jubilee Auto they had the mistaken belief that B and C workers were supposed to be differentiated between tasks on the front and back of the looms, and they had the added misconception that C workers were supposed to be on the front and B workers on the back—the opposite of the method of working on the nonautomatic looms where this differentiation was appropriate. The weaving master, conscious of the contradiction between senior management's view of the socio-technical system in the automatic shed and the system that was actually in operation, sought at first to hide the situation from us. During the first phase of Shaw's visits to the sheds, section heads and supervisors were ordering their men to patrol all the looms in set routes and had differentiated B and C workers in the way just indicated. Only when individual operatives were interviewed was this revealed. They had noticed the coincidence of Shaw's visits with the "new" work system. Since this method was so far removed from current work practices and also, one surmises, from the method of working introduced in the early days of this loom shed, it is hardly surprising that the short period of a few days in which this new system was in operation was reported to have been chaotic and, at least in retrospect, a matter of some amusement.

Formally, Calico Auto had the same five grades of workers as Jubilee Auto—A, B+, B, C and D, with A, B+ and D workers concerned primarily with gating and maintenance. However, these letters were seldom used; the terminology was that of other mills. A and B+ were "jobber" (or "tackler") and "assistant jobber"; B and C were "weavers"; D was a "helper." B and C workers were specifically assigned to a number of looms which were regarded as exclusively their responsibility. If, as was often the case, the allocation was of two Bs and two Cs to a group of 64 looms, each would be responsible for 16 looms. If, as sometimes happened, the work load required an additional C worker, he would be available to help the other "weavers" on "their" looms. The actual method of working, therefore, was little different from that in other automatic loom sheds in Ahmedabad. Managerial and supervisory staff in the department acknowledged that many, if not most, of the C workers were as competent and qualified as the B workers but saw themselves as having a limited establishment for B workers. It was small wonder, therefore, that many workers reported that the only distinctive feature of Calico's so-called group system compared with other mills' working arrangements was that some weavers (the Cs) were paid 25 rupees a month less than other weavers (the Bs) for doing the same job. This grievance was the basis for a demand from the union to do away with the C category as a permanent grade of workers throughout the group system. In this respect, the demand was consistent with Rice's original conception of the group system for automatic looms in which the C grade was, for the individual employee, essentially transitional; when the C worker obtained sufficient experience and competence he would be promoted to the B grade. The grievance, however, was somewhat less relevant to the Jubilee Auto situation and less relevant still to the Calico nonautomatic situation where there remained a genuine differentiation of task between the B front workers and the C back workers.

If in Jubilee Auto there was some ambiguity and discrepancy in supervisory behavior, in Calico Auto there was practically none. Here the principal discrepancy, as already noted, was between senior management's conception of the socio-technical system of the automatic shed and the system actually in operation. Within the department it was the individual and not the group that was the object of supervision. As in Jubilee, there were frequent moves from one group to another.

However, the philosophy of individual supervision obviously raised questions about the role of the group leader. This led to some friction between some supervisors and group leaders. Shift supervisors were often straight out of technical college, had no production experience before joining the company and their average age was about 23. Group leaders were on average some five years older and had the benefit of accumulated practical experience. In interviews, both described many of their duties in an almost identical way: to be responsible for the efficiency and quality of the group of looms and workers, to check the maintenance of the looms and to report each day on the number of looms idle and workers absent. Group leaders expressed frustration at what they regarded as the poaching of their task by supervisors and at the discrepancy between their officially stated leadership responsibilities and the only one that was exclusively theirs—the allocation of work on the looms during tea breaks. Supervisors for their part expressed annoyance at having to attend to the maintenance and tuning of looms because, they claimed, the group leaders were not doing this properly themselves. Essentially, therefore, the corollary of direct individual supervision by the supervisors was the limitation of the group leaders to their maintenance role.

Many of the workers interviewed in Calico Auto made the same point as some of those in Jubilee—that the only discriminating feature of the Calico work system was that the work load was higher than in other mills since it was usually based on 64 looms rather than 48. A few workers compared their work system with that of Calico Exp, which they saw as having the advantage of a lower work load and also cooperation between workers. Only one of those interviewed had previously worked in Calico Exp and his comment was, "I am not afraid of work but nobody helps me here."

As in Jubilee Auto, changes in work load and absenteeism led to frequent movements of manual operatives from one group to another. Identification tended to be with the automatic shed as a whole rather than with a specific work group. Operatives reported that their friends were scattered throughout the shed rather than confined to their own groups, and thus they would sometimes help friends in other groups with their work. Since by doing this they were boosting the earnings of friends at the expense of their own earnings and those of their fellow group workers, this is perhaps the clearest evidence that, although there was a singular lack of group feeling within Calico Auto, there was a felt need to engage in cooperative working arrangements.

Tension between the group leaders and shift supervisors has already been mentioned. Overall, operatives expressed considerable discontent with the work arrangement and repeatedly referred to it as a method by which management could underpay some weavers. There were reports that outside the mill supervisors had been assaulted and the weaving master threatened with physical violence.

Discussion

Between 1953 and 1956 Rice helped to introduce and develop two types of "group system" in automatic and nonautomatic weaving. There were differences between these two systems related to the technology of the two types of looms, but the underlying concept of work organization was the same for both: a small, internally led group of workers, responsible for the whole task of weaving on a group of looms.

By 1970, the so-called group system encompassed widely different methods of working.[6] The main common thread was that the individual's pay was to some extent affected by efficiency and damage on a group of looms.

The group system in Calico Exp in 1970 differed little from Rice's description of it some 15 years before. Group identification was high; members of the group cooperated with one another in their work; the group leader exercised a

---

[6]It is worth noting that the term "group system" has been taken over as an English word among Gujarati- and Hindi-speaking people in the mills, as not easily translated into these languages.

boundary function; and supervisors seldom intervened with individual group members. It is notable that this was still, in 1970, called the experimental shed, which emphasizes the strong link to the past. Slightly more than half the workers had belonged to the original experimental groups and associated what they felt to be their present high status with their historical achievements at the time of the experiment. The type of cloth woven was still the same and, as we have seen, norms of performance seemed to have persisted for 14 years. It was as though the shed had been held within a kind of stasis—a monument to the original experiment.

In Calico Pit, the group system in 1970 resembled that of Calico Exp though performance was significantly inferior and there was greater variation between groups in methods of working. Certainly in some there was more of a differentiation of function between group members with correspondingly less cooperation. Compared with Calico Exp there was somewhat less group identification and a tendency for the supervisors to take over boundary control functions that in the experimental shed belonged to the group leader.

In Jubilee Auto the shift in this direction was even more pronounced. Workers in many groups were held responsible for operating a specific subset of looms; there was little mutual help; identification with the group was limited; the group leader was preoccupied with his loom maintenance activities; and to a considerable extent the shift supervisor directly controlled the activities of individual workers. Efficiency and quality, however, were fairly close to levels attained during the original experiment.

Finally, in Calico Auto, except for the brief phase when the charade was put on for the benefit of the research worker, the method of working could scarcely be described as a group system at all. Group identification and internal cooperation were virtually lacking. The terminology to describe different categories of workers was much the same as in other mills. The group leader was effectively a jobber with maintenance responsibilities, though still somewhat resentful of the fact that supervisors were taking responsibility for internal management of the group and intervening with individual group members.

We therefore have to try to account for the persistence in Calico Exp of the socio-technical system developed by Rice, for the emergence of a discrepant system in Calico Auto and for the development in Calico Pit and in Jubilee Auto of systems appearing to be intermediate between these two extremes.

I have described two developments in the relation of the company to its environment that impinged on the loom sheds. First, the efforts to enter more lucrative markets led to pressure to maintain and improve output and quality; second, inability to procure spare parts and supplies of the appropriate standard increased both maintenance work load and the need for attention in weaving activities. The latter factor may have exacerbated the tendency of production incentive schemes in general, especially with three-shift working, to maximize production in the short term at the expense of maintenance of machines. Probably, therefore, the group leaders in 1970 were facing an accumulated legacy of sub-optimum loom maintenance.

The method of working had been designed so that each loom group, as a socio-technical system, had a certain amount of resilience to absorb and adjust to variations in its inputs without invoking regulatory interventions from outside. One feature was that the size of the weaving sub-group could be increased if yarn inputs were substandard. Apart from that, the main source of resilience was flexibility in task allocation in place of a rigid division of labor between categories of workers and between individuals. Rice went some way toward specifying the boundary conditions within which the systems could be expected to maintain a steady state: for this, the regression of late 1953 in Jubilee Auto provided illuminating data. The resilience of the groups was evidenced in Jubilee Auto, for example, by the fact that they were able to weave varieties of cloth that had previously been found "unweavable" on the looms concerned. The early evidence supported Rice's proposition that

> the performance of the primary task is supported by powerful social and psychological forces which ensure that a considerable capacity for cooperation is evoked among the members of the organization created to perform it. (Rice, 1958:33)

It suggested that the socio-technical systems that had evolved optimized task and "sentient" needs (cf. Miller and Rice, 1967, pp. xii–xv, 251–69/Vol. I).

Rice's discussion of the regression in Jubilee implies that a reversion to a more rigid differentiation of labor could be taken as a symptom that the group as a social system had exceeded the limits of its capacity to accommodate to external change. When such symptoms are observed, the sophisticated managerial response is to seek ways of (1) reducing the sources of disturbance in terms of variability of inputs; (2) increasing the resilience of the group—in other words, to adjust the technical and/or social system in such a way that optimization between them is restored.

The corrective measures taken during the first half of 1954 in Jubilee Auto had these characteristics. The boundaries of the groups were restored and they recovered their viability and resilience. The kinds of decisions required to achieve this, however, had in some cases to be made at a fairly high managerial level. This was possible while group methods of working were still in an experimental phase and while, correspondingly, senior managers were very directly concerned in monitoring the effectiveness of the experiment. Subsequently, as group working "settled down" as an established and less controversial form of work organization, top management involvement was gradually withdrawn.

The reorganization of management undertaken in the company between 1954 and 1960 (see Rice, 1958; 1963) involved the drawing of organizational boundaries around not merely these primary work groups but also around a series of progressively wider systems—the shift, the section, the loom shed, the mill—each of which was designed to have corresponding resilience. The role of a supervisor or manager was conceived in terms of regulating the boundary of the system for which he was responsible so as to maintain its internal resilience in the face of change; the corollary of this, of course, was that he was expected to draw the attention of his superior to sources of disturbance to which it was beyond the capacity of his own system to adjust. The position in the loom sheds in 1970 suggests that these successive boundaries had not effectively been controlled. Disturbances had been transmitted to and into the work groups themselves. The concept of boundary control, even if understood theoretically, had not been implemented in practice and, what is more, it had evidently not been considered important to ensure that supervisors understood its implications for their own jobs in relation to the groups. Consequently, by their direct internal interventions, supervisors further helped to destroy the resilience of the groups and to foster rigid differentiation of individual tasks.

One factor of possible relevance here was the progressively diminishing "bite" of the bonus system. The group worker's wage packet included three components—a rate for the category, a dearness allowance and a bonus calculated on the first rate. Between 1953 and 1970, basic rates had increased only marginally while the dearness allowance component had trebled. Thus, for example, for a B worker in Calico Exp in 1954, with a basic rate of 115 rupees a month and a dearness allowance of 62 rupees, the average bonus of 28 percent on the basic rate was 18 percent of total earnings. By 1970, when the figures were 125 and 180 rupees respectively, the 28 percent would have yielded a net bonus of only 11½ percent. This is an example of a factor that might have reduced—or more importantly have been held by supervisory staff to reduce—the capacity of groups to maintain their self-regulating capabilities. It may also be noted that the maintenance of high levels of performance in Calico Exp in spite of the fact that a reduction of effort and thus of efficiency would have led to only a marginal reduction of earnings indicated that the effects of the cash incentive may have been smaller than Roy (1969) suggests.

Therefore, between 1953 and 1970 the groups were faced with a constant series of minor readjustments. Some of these were recurrent since seasonal or fashion variables required cyclical changes from one sort or one pattern of cloth to another. However, the loom sheds were also having to adjust to the progressive attempts of the company's management to improve its overall position vis-à-vis a changing set of competitors. Therefore, it was not simply a question of maintaining an equilibrium within a broadly static range of possible steady states but of attaining an equilibrium within a constantly altering trajectory.

We still have to explain the differences between loom sheds observed in

1970. In fact, the nature of the pressures was such that they were likely to be experienced maximally in Calico Auto and minimally in Calico Exp. Calico Auto was weaving the finest and most expensive sorts with a high fashion component (thus implying the need for cyclical adjustment), and these were also the types of cloth most influenced by the company's search for new and profitable markets. It was in this shed that marginal improvements in production and quality would produce the greatest payoff as improved profits. In Calico Exp, on the other hand, although the type of cloth woven was by no means simple—in fact there had been a deliberate decision when the experimental shed was set up to select the most difficult sort commonly woven—it was a product for which there was a reliable market and in which few, if any, improvements in quality standards were required since the acceptably higher norms had been attained at the end of the experimental period in 1954. Here it had been possible to maintain a steady state. Jubilee Auto was in an intermediate position in that the fabrics woven were neither so fine nor so profitable as in Calico Auto, though at the same time there had been continuing pressure over the years to move to marginally more profitable, and correspondingly more difficult, sorts and to improve quality standards. In Calico Pit the evidence is less clear. It seems likely, however, that the process of extending the group system to this shed may have involved too inflexible a transfer of group structure, without giving the groups enough room or help to discover their own modes of working within the appropriate culture. Some found their own resilient modes; but in other instances they failed to develop adequate boundaries within which self-regulation could occur so that supervisory intervention became integral to the regulatory function within groups.

Problems of spares and supplies impinged differentially in the same directions. Closer tolerances are required for automatic than for nonautomatic looms and for finer than for coarser cloth.

Probably an additional factor for differences among loom sheds was the surviving proportion of original group members in each of the sheds. To the extent that group members had internalized a group method of working they could be expected to be better able to maintain resilience and to resist incoming disturbances.[7] As we have seen, more than half the workers in Calico Exp come into this category, a third in Jubilee Auto and a negligible number in Calico Auto. Thus, direct intervention by supervisors with individual workers, which would be regarded as abnormal in, for example, Calico Exp would be accepted as normal and natural by those who had experienced more conventional modes of work organization and supervision elsewhere.

This also suggests that the need for individual recognition by one's supe-

---

[7]In a British food factory I have seen group workers explicitly instructing a new supervisor on appropriate behavior.

riors, which is quite strong in the Indian culture, was not really provided for within Rice's concept of group organization. The individual was to derive satisfaction primarily from the respect of his colleagues within the group. It would seem that this need could remain submerged so long as the group as a whole could be perceived externally as being sufficiently successful—though our observations in 1970 suggest that the role of the group leader, even in Calico Exp, had been made more into that of a superior or boss and less of a *primus inter pares* than Rice had originally envisaged. One would therefore postulate that the diminishing experience of success, accompanied by a withdrawal of group leaders from the leadership aspects of their roles into a greater preoccupation with maintenance, would lead to the reactivation of the need for recognition from outside the group. This would increase individual workers' readiness to accept direct supervisory intervention from outside and correspondingly move the mode of intra-group relations away from cooperation.

Although Myers (1959) noted that Rice's innovations reflected a democratic, participative philosophy which was at variance with the paternalistic, authoritarian philosophy generally prevalent in Indian management, and Rice himself stressed the importance of developing "permissive and collaborative relationships" which brought workers, supervisors and managers together in problem-solving approaches, both these comments are more apposite to the process of introducing the experimental changes than to the nature of the ongoing socio-technical systems that emerged. The "permissive" element in these systems was the investment of authority and discretion within the group. Their built-in capability for self-regulation made them resilient over time within certain boundaries of stability.

Rice's application of systemic concepts to organization had been much influenced by the biologist von Bertalanffy (1950), who introduced the idea of a quasi-stationary equilibrium in an open system. Understanding of ecological systems has developed considerably in the last 20 years, and it is now well known that intervention in such systems needs to be circumspect if unanticipated side effects are to be avoided. Thus, direct attempts to raise crop yields by applying pesticides and/or fertilizers will probably produce short-term benefits, but consequential changes in the wider ecological system are problematic and may in the longer term cancel any gains and even lead to regression to lower productivity than had prevailed in the first instance. Loss of variability and a contraction of the boundaries of stability mean a loss in the system's capacity for self-regulation. The goal of maximizing productivity in ecological systems has therefore become suspect—unless a very long time scale is projected. Indeed, modern ecologists are suggesting that the appropriate "conceptual framework for man's intervention into ecological systems . . . changes the emphasis from maximizing the probability of success to minimizing the chance of disaster" (Holling and Goldberg, 1971:226). Nowadays some planners are learning this lesson as these authors and others (for example, Friend and Jessop, 1969) have indicated.

The analogy with industrial production systems is suggestive, even compelling. Single-minded pursuit of efficiency goals nevertheless dies hard in industry. (Here I am using "efficiency" in its more ordinary sense.) Rice's approach, insofar as he was building a new resilience into the experimental socio-technical systems, was entirely consistent with the goal of "minimizing the chance of disaster"; but in the prevailing industrial ethos it would have been difficult for him to claim this as his intention and still more difficult for others to perceive it. Paradoxically, because the prior pursuit of efficiency goals had resulted in a relatively unproductive work organization, Rice's efforts led to improved performance in the short term and could thus be interpreted as being in harmony with efficiency goals—for example, Likert (1961) saw Rice's experiments as confirming that group cohesiveness leads to higher performance. It is much more plausible to suggest that the effect on performance of introducing a socio-technical system designed for long-term viability will depend on whether preexisting levels of performance were high or low. Similarly, it can be postulated that performance of a system designed for minimizing disaster can almost always be improved by intervention designed to maximize efficiency. What is problematic is the length of time over which the improvement can be sustained. The most probable outcomes are a decline in performance, a multiplication of regulatory interventions, or both, and eventual loss of resilience. If this is so, then the most remarkable outcome of Rice's experiments is that the "group system" survived so completely in Calico Exp and, albeit to a lesser extent, in Jubilee Auto, during a period of considerable change and in a managerial environment in which efficiency goals largely prevailed.

This suggests that the goal of designing systems to minimize the chances of disaster may be more appropriate to industrial organization than is generally recognized. However much one may endorse the values attached to "participation," "permissive and collaborative relationships," "industrial democracy" and similar terms, they are too readily reducible to management styles and to modes of conducting interpersonal relationships. They do not call into question the *task* of management or the prevailing assumption that managing is the prerogative of people who carry the title and status of "manager." Rice's group members demonstrated that they could manage themselves. His achievement was in drawing the boundaries of the production system in such a way as to allow this to happen. The role that we conventionally think of as managerial then becomes a boundary function (cf. Miller and Rice, 1967/Vol. I). The task can be defined as: to provide the boundary conditions within which members of the organization manage their roles and relationships in such a way as to produce effective task performance (Miller, 1977). Likert was right in connecting group cohesiveness to task performance; whether the chosen task is one that the company would wish to see performed is another matter. Although now, 35 years after Rice's first experiment, the term "socio-technical system" is widely used, it is a pity that the concept of boundary management remains so little appreciated.

References

Davis, K. 1962. *Human Relations at Work* (2nd edition). New York: McGraw-Hill.

Davis, L.E. 1967. "Job Design and Productivity." In *Studies in Personnel and Industrial Psychology,* edited by E.A. Fleishman. Homewood, Ill.: Dorsey.

Friend, J.K. and W.N. Jessop. 1969. *Local Government and Strategic Choice: An Operational Research Approach to the Processes of Public Planning.* London: Tavistock Publications.

Holling, C.S. and M.A. Goldberg. 1971. "Ecology and Planning." *Journal of the American Institute of Planners,* 37:221–30.

Katz, D. and R.L. Kahn. 1966. *The Social Psychology of Organizations.* New York: Wiley.

Likert, R. 1961. *New Patterns of Management.* New York: McGraw-Hill.

McGregor, D. 1960. *The Human Side of Enterprise.* New York: McGraw-Hill.

———. 1966. "Why Not Exploit Behavioral Science?" In *Leadership and Motivation,* edited by W.G. Bennis and E.H. Schein. Cambridge, Mass.: MIT Press.

Miller, E.J. 1975. "Socio-Technical Systems in Weaving, 1953–1970: A Follow-Up Study." *Human Relations,* 28:349–86.

———. 1977. "Organizational Development and Industrial Democracy: A Current Case-Study." In *Organizational Development in the UK and USA: A Joint Evaluation,* edited by C.L. Cooper. London: Macmillan.

Miller, E.J. and A.K. Rice. 1967. *Systems of Organization: Task and Sentient Systems and Their Boundary Control.* London: Tavistock Publications. Portions also in Vol. I, "Task and Sentient Systems and Their Boundary Controls," pp. 259–83.

Myers, C.A. 1959. "Management in India." In *Management in the Industrial World: An International Analysis,* edited by F. Harbison and C.A. Myers. New York: McGraw-Hill.

Rice, A.K. 1953. "Productivity and Social Organization in an Indian Weaving Shed: An Examination of the Socio-Technical System of an Experimental Automatic Loomshed." *Human Relations,* 6:297–329. Condensed, Vol. II, "Productivity and Social Organization: An Indian Automated Weaving Shed," pp. 106–29.

———. 1955a. "The Experimental Reorganization of Non-Automatic Weaving in an Indian Mill: A Further Study of Productivity and Social Organization." *Human Relations,* 8:199–249.

———. 1955b. "Productivity and Social Organization in an Indian Weaving Mill II: A Follow-Up Study of the Experimental Reorganization of Automatic Weaving." *Human Relations,* 8:399–428.

———. 1958. *Productivity and Social Organization: The Ahmedabad Experiment: Technical Innovation, Work Organization, and Management.* London: Tavistock Publications. Reissued 1987, New York: Garland.

———. 1963. *The Enterprise and Its Environment: A System Theory of Management Organization.* London: Tavistock Publications.

Roy, S.K. 1969. "A Re-examination of the Methodology of A.K. Rice's Textile Mill Work Reorganization." *Indian Journal of Industrial Relations,* 5:170–91.

Trist, E.L. and K.W. Bamforth. 1951. "Some Social and Psychological Consequences of the Longwall Method of Coal-getting." *Human Relations,* 4:3–38.

von Bertalanffy, L. 1950. "The Theory of Open Systems in Physics and Biology." *Science,* 3:23–29.

Vroom, V.H. and N.R.F. Maier. 1961. "Industrial Social Psychology." *Annual Review of Psychology,* 12:413–46.

Fred Emery

Characteristics of Socio-Technical Systems[1]

Introduction to the Concept of Socio-Technical Systems

The main methodological questions that will be touched on are the need for
- some system concepts,
- the concept of "open system,"
- the concept of "socio-technical system" rather than simply "social system."

There exists a highly diverse body of scientific concepts and findings about work organizations and the people who operate them. This diversity reflects the many problems that modern industry and commerce present for scientific study. For both practical and scientific purposes it is often necessary to isolate problems such as design of machinery for human convenience, job evaluation, selection, incentive schemes, primary group organization, supervision and management organization. At the same time, most specialists agree that these problems are interrelated—beyond a certain point the solution of one kind of problem depends upon solving some of the others.

Problems of task performance, supervision, etc., have the character of part problems. Thus, the analysis of the characteristics of enterprises as systems has strategic significance for our understanding of many specific industrial problems. The more we know about these systems, the more we can identify what is relevant to a particular problem and detect problems missed by the conventional framework of problem analysis.

There remains an important question: should an enterprise be construed as a "closed" or an "open" system, i.e., relatively closed or open with respect to its external environment?

The "open systems" concept logically implies systems that spontaneously reorganize toward states of greater heterogeneity and complexity and achieve a "steady state" at a level where they can still do work. Enterprises appear to

[1]A revision of the original in *Design of Jobs,* edited by L.E. Davis and J.C. Taylor. Harmondsworth: Penguin Books, 1972. See also Emery (1959).

possess the characteristics of open systems. They grow by processes of internal elaboration (Herbst, 1954) and often manage to achieve a steady state while doing work, i.e., a state in which the enterprise maintains a continuous "throughput" despite numerous external changes—what Lewin (1951, ch.9) called "quasi-stationary equilibrium." The appropriateness of the open systems concept can be settled, however, only by examining in detail those relations between an enterprise and its external environment that are involved in achieving a steady state. Any enterprise exists through regular commerce in products or services with other enterprises, institutions and persons in its external social environment. The enterprise requires physical supports for its activities—a workplace, materials, tools and machines—and a stable organization of people able and willing to modify the material throughput or provide the requisite services.

An enterprise responds to the joint action of its immediate material and human resources and to a broader social environment. The form of wider environmental influence illustrated here pertains to its effects upon the ends of the enterprise. By changing the conditions of an enterprise's commerce, the environmental factors also change the ends it can pursue and make pursuit of other ends inimical to its survival. Thus, just as the immediate means and resources limit the sorts of commerce in which an enterprise can engage, so the wider factors impose new ends and changes in the enterprise's means and resources.

A characteristic of open systems is that, while in constant commerce with the environment, they are also *selective and, within limits, self-regulating.*

The *technological component,* in converting inputs into outputs, plays a major role in determining the self-regulating properties of an enterprise. It functions as a major boundary condition of the social system in mediating between the ends of an enterprise and the external environment. Because of this, the materials, machines and territory that make up the technological component are usually defined as "belonging" to an enterprise. They represent, as it were, an "internal environment."

Thus, it is not possible to define the conditions under which an open system achieves a steady state unless the "system constants" include mediating boundary conditions (cf. von Bertalanffy, 1950). The technological component has been found to play this mediating role. It follows that the open system concept, as applied to enterprises, ought to be referred to the socio-technical system, not simply to the social system.

Williams (1950) suggests that, at this level of generality, one should distinguish economic as well as social and technological systems; and also that "it might be convenient to define a political system" (p.9). This suggestion confuses concrete referents with analytical abstraction. An enterprise is a body of people and material means; analytically, one should abstract, from the concrete social relations existing between these things, aspects concerning allocation of limited resources for consumption or production, power and responsibility, etc. The first step in studying an enterprise is, however, to identify the characteristics of its substantive components. After this, one may fruitfully study the economic and political aspects.

It might be justifiable to exclude the technological component from the system concept if it played only a passive and intermittent role. However, it cannot be dismissed as simply a set of limits that influence an enterprise only in its initial stages and when it oversteps its limits. There is an almost constant accommodation of changes in the external environment, and the technological component not only sets limits upon what can be done but also creates demands that must be reflected in the internal organization and ends of an enterprise.

However, an enterprise can pursue other strategies that exploit the lesser, but still real, dependence of the environment upon the enterprise. Although dependence of an enterprise on its external environment is usually the most striking aspect, there is, inevitably, some interdependence. An enterprise can select from among the range of personnel, resources and technologies offered by its external environment and can develop new markets or transform old ones.

Because the enterprise is an open system, its management "manages" both an internal system and an external environment. To regard an enterprise as closed and to concentrate on management of the "internal system" would be to expose it to the full impact of the vagaries of the broader environment.

The Main Features of an Enterprise as a Socio-Technical System

The first function of a socio-technical systems concept is as a frame of reference—a general way of ordering the facts. It directs attention to the following groups of problems as the focus of three main stages in the analysis of the enterprise:

- The analysis of the component parts to reveal the way each contributes to the performance of the enterprise and creates or meets the requirements of other parts. The first components to analyze are (1) the technical and (2) the "work relationship structure" and its occupational roles.
- The analysis of the interrelation of these parts with particular reference to the problems of internal coordination and control thus created.
- The detection and analysis of the relevant external environment of the enterprise and the way the enterprise manages its relations to it.

The same frame of reference may well be applied to the study of parts of an enterprise. For primary work groups, the relevant environment is provided by the enterprise itself, since it defines the ends of these groups, controls the input of people and materials and constantly influences group performance. Analysis of parts of an enterprise also involves attention to details usually disregarded in analysis of the enterprise as a whole. To analyze structure, "no more is required than the whole from which the analysis starts and two levels of analysis" (Feibleman and Friend, 1945:42). In the study of a part-system, the roles and the interpersonal action constitute the two required levels of analysis. Both levels require decision taking—deciding overall objectives for the set of roles and deciding who should perform which roles at a given time.

In its second function, the concept of socio-technical systems invokes a body of subordinate concepts and hypotheses to describe and explain the behavior of enterprises and their members. This function is not strictly derived from the first. There is no single body of concepts that can claim to be *the* theory of socio-technical systems. Concepts in use range from highly abstract ones drawn from general system theory to descriptive ones, such as task interdependence and the primary work group.

THE TECHNOLOGICAL COMPONENT

Trist and Bamforth (1951:5), in the first public usage of the concept of "socio-technical system," made the common distinction between the "technological system" and the "social structure consisting of the occupational roles that have been institutionalized in its use." The next step in social scientific analysis is usually to seize upon some isolated aspects of the technological system, such as repetitive work, the coerciveness of the conveyor belt or the piecemeal tasks, and to relate these to the observed social life of the work group. Even a detailed study of the technology has not been treated as a basis for this next step but has been relegated, as in Warner and Low (1947), to an appendix. The same error occurs on the social side:

> It has been fashionable of late, particularly in the humans relations school, to assume that the actual job, its technology and its mechanical and physical requirements, are relatively unimportant compared to the social and psychological situation of men at work. (Drucker, 1952)

The Trist and Bamforth study broke with this tradition by treating the problem as one of relating two *systems,* both part of a more inclusive system:

> So close is the relationship between the various aspects that the social and the psychological can be understood only in terms of the detailed engineering facts and of the way the technological system as a whole behaves in the environment of the underground (mining) situation. (Trist and Bamforth, 1951:11)

They introduced a number of concepts to depict the interaction of the two systems and those characteristics of technological systems that are most relevant to the social system. To do that requires a detailed knowledge of the technological system and the descriptive terms used by engineers and operators. It results, however, in describing technology in significantly different terms from those used by engineers or operators. A social scientist's description of the technological system intimately portrays its demands on the social system, whereas an engineer describes what the machines, apparatus and materials require of each other for efficient coordinated operation.

At this point, the distinction may be made between purely technical requirements—e.g., the conveyor speeds required to feed a particular machine at optimum rate—and those that arise because machines cannot produce without human intervention. Both have to be taken into account by an enterprise, but the former is usually the province only of engineers. On the human side, there is an overlap in the professional interests of engineers and social scientists in the field of "human engineering"—the design of machines and their coordinate tasks for optimum fit between them and the skills of human operators. Beyond this are problems of relating technological requirements to people as purposeful beings, not simply as another kind of machine, and to groups of people, not simply to isolated individuals. It is these latter problems which will be considered here.

It is useful to identify the main technological dimensions that affect social systems. These can guide the analysis of a given technology and enable comparison of it with others. The following list includes those dimensions singled out by Tavistock researchers and also makes explicit others that have been implicit until now. The list is not exhaustive.

The natural characteristic of the material being worked upon insofar as it limits, assists or introduces uncontrolled variation into the labor requirements of the production process, for example, in coal-mining where the hardness and "grain" of the coal exert considerable influence on the strain experienced by individuals, work groups and management. Rice (1958; 1953/Vol. II) has indicated how the variation in tensile strength of cotton creates social and psychological problems in textile mills. The nature of the material may underlie such broad differences as those between agriculture and industry or, within industry, between process and fabrication. As with each dimension listed here, it is not possible to argue directly from these facts to the operators' behavior— how they will respond depends also upon other factors.

The level of mechanization (or automation). This dimension has been rightly considered the most important. Historically, changes in degree of mechanization have been more frequent and have shown a singleness of direction and a logic not apparent in changes that occur in the other dimensions. Changes in mechanization level will frequently effect changes in the other dimensions. A more powerful machine, for example, makes the difference in hardness of coal less relevant, or the inflexibility of a high speed spinning machine makes more necessary the uniformity of the cotton.

Degree of mechanization determines the relative contributions of machines and men to the production process, and the direction of development is to lessen the human contribution. More detailed criteria are needed to judge differences in mechanization among technological systems or even among parts of a single system. These criteria are now receiving attention in connection with what has been called "automation."

While the term automation has been used in a number of ways, all users seem to have in mind an ideal concept of a fully automatic factory or office. Thus, all technical developments in this direction and an emerging philosophy of management, production and design have tended to be gathered under the title of automation (Bright, 1955). We need to treat technical change as an independent variable if we are to trace its social and psychological effects on production systems. The term automation is thus restricted to *"the use of devices—mechanical, pneumatic, hydraulic, electrical and electronic—for making automatic decisions and efforts."*[2] So defined, automation includes what is commonly regarded as mechanization, i.e., "the use of mechanical techniques for performing automatic efforts, usually with pneumatic and hydraulic elements." This definition still does not clarify the concept. We need to specify at what point the term "automation" is warranted.

At a certain level in mechanizing a production system, there occurs a "recentering" of attention from the manual operator to the machine, from man-hours to machine-hours. "The provision of and maintenance of conditions which best allow the machine to operate and to continue operating, become the goal of the system" (Trist, 1953). It is only when the efficiency criterion of machine utilization replaces that of man-hours that it seems useful to refer to the ideal end point of full automation rather than, as with the term mechanization, to make comparison with the beginning point of manufacture. In the scale in Table 1, developed from Bright (1955) and Amber and Amber (1956), the "watershed" may be placed between levels 2 and 3. Much finer distinctions are possible than are made in the scale, and, as Bright has shown, are required to represent those higher levels of automation in which more and more of the calculation (conceptual skill) is embodied in the machine. Computers enable levels of calculation not economically feasible with human operators, even if humanly possible.

The unit operations required to complete the changes involved in production and the natural grouping of these units into *production phases* (as in the construction of a process chart by production engineers). The patterns of phases may be changed by changes in the machines or natural conditions, for

---

[2]This is the definition of automation that is given editorially in Emery (1957).

TABLE I Types of Human Activity Replaced by Machines at Different Technical Levels

Level	Power (gross motor action)		Control				Examples
	For basic function	For auxiliary function	Fine motor action for guidance & positioning	Perceptual skill (monitoring)	Conceptual skill (calculating)	Control characteristics	
0	—	—	—	—	—	—	hand tools
1	X	—	—	—	—	—	portable electric tools
2	X	X	—	—	—	—	bench lathes, power shovels
3	X	X	X	—	—	"open loop"	transfer machines
4	X	X	X	X	—	"closed loop" (pre-set limits)	chemical process plants
5	X	X	X	X	X	"closed loop" (variable limits)	computer-aided machines

While the general format is that of describing successive stages in replacing human labor and skills, it needs to be borne in mind that automation does more than this; it makes possible things that are not within human potentiality and would necessitate the introduction of further dimensions to represent higher levels—in particular the levels of computer functioning.

example, the way multi-jib cutters eliminated blasting operations in coal-mining, the effects of continuous casting in foundries and of the replacement of pressing by metal cutting in machine shops. A change from mechanical to hydraulic mining would produce even more drastic operations changes. New processes such as powder molding, extrusion and electric spark machining point to an important dimension of technological changes different from mechanization.

In some respects, this dimension reflects natural forces brought under human control by the expansion of scientific knowledge beyond mechanics and hydraulics into atomic and molecular physics, organic chemistry and biochemistry. In many new industrial processes no underlying similarity exists between machines and the worker-as-a-machine. New processes represent qualitatively new forces for production, and entail new demands for certain kinds of labor and coordination. The emergence of laboratories and work roles for scientifically trained personnel changes labor requirements and creates new problems of coordination. The new processes blur the distinction between "unit operations" and "phases," as operatives tend to be engaged not with the units of a phase but with controlling the conditions (e.g., temperature, acidity, pressure or flow) that permit the natural processes themselves to carry through the whole phase of the work. As these conditions are closely interdependent, operatives' work must be closely coordinated and there is not the same possibility for externalizing the coordination as exists when responsibility can be allocated for each of a number of separate unit operations.

The degree of centrality of the different production operations. It is also possible to distinguish differences in the degree to which various production processes command special attention, special effort or special skill. Thus in machining metal, it may be that only removing the final few thousandths of an inch requires high level skills; in coal-mining the filling operations will have a greater effect on the total process than will, for instance, speed and skill in shifting the gear head.

These activities are, by implicit definition, necessary to the productive process. But, from the point of view of the performance of the whole productive system (which includes the operators, etc.), it makes a considerable difference whether the organization of operative and supervisory roles reflects the centrality of key processes. A further distinction may sometimes be required between *necessary* but irregular and infrequent operations and *optional* ("ancillary" or "external") operations. These latter are not strictly necessary to a productive system's performance but still serve some real or presumed function.

The maintenance operations needed to maintain conditions required by the productive process. These "boundary conditions" of production concern some of the points at which the productive process interacts with, and is influenced by, the internal material environment, and they help protect the process from disruption or unpredictable fluctuation due to the latter. Such activities include repair and maintenance. Their relation to productive operations varies with differences in each dimension listed above and requires different roles and work relationship structures.

At low levels of mechanization, it may be tolerable to have a considerable social and organizational gap between production and maintenance workers. Skilled maintenance workers frequently live a life apart from the others and have a great deal of influence on the determination of maintenance priorities. However, with higher mechanization, the greater internal differentiation and rate of production of the technology make it much more sensitive to changes in its boundary conditions and impose heavier demands on maintenance. Reorganization of maintenance to meet these demands is influenced by two general requirements:

- Preventive maintenance to promote continuity of running and prevent faults and breakdowns in the machines.
- When breakdowns do occur, to keep loss of machine time down to a minimum. (Trist, 1953)

Production roles have been redefined to include responsibility for some running maintenance and initial diagnosis of machine breakdowns (cf. Trist, 1953 and Rice, 1958 for examples in mining and textile manufacture, respectively), and the performance of these roles has been strengthened by the introduction of "drills" (cf. Trist, 1953). In addition, maintenance organizations have been elaborated into sections responsible for on-the-spot repair, repair-without-replacement, repair-with-replacement, etc., to maximize machine utilization while keeping replacement costs within an economic limit.

Supply operations also set major boundary conditions for production as they seek to maintain a planned production rate despite unplanned variations in the import and export of materials from and to the external environment. They differ from maintenance both in their tasks and in the source of variability that they seek to offset. They are less difficult to coordinate with productive operations but, because of their externally directed activities, are more difficult to coordinate with the overall purpose of the enterprise. Thus, they frequently create demands that have to be handled at the managerial level of the social system.

Dependent in the first instance on the demands of the productive operations and the external environment, these supply operations in turn create specific demands on the social system for personnel and coordination. Like maintenance, the supply operations become more critical to efficient performance as mechanization increases. The greater rate of throughput raises the cost of stoppages due to failure of supplies and requires more effort to hold stocks within economic limits. These factors create a mechanized and automated supply technology commensurate with the new production technology (cf. recent "Just in Time" methods).

The spatiotemporal dimension of the production process. The spatial layout and the spread of the process over time (operations carried out simultaneously or sequentially, on one shift or across several shifts) influence coordination, mutual support and interpersonal contact. The spatiotemporal distribution of machines and of operatives tends to influence the ease with which interdependent activities are coordinated, supplied and maintained. It creates a specific human ecology by throwing some people together and separating others. Lombard (1955) shows that this independent effect of spatial location arises from a tendency of workers to value a stable territory and to interact more with those nearest to them.

These aspects of a technological system can sometimes be varied independently. Thus, although the Bolsover "handfilled" longwall mining system differed from the conventional longwall system only in its spatial scale, it made possible a greatly different "work relationship structure" and different occupational roles (Wilson et al., 1951). The temporal dimension changed as a result of the spatial change and, with the introduction of a continuous mining machine into the Bolsover system, the spatial dimension remained constant but the temporal dimension underwent great change and led to the emergence of a new set of requirements (Trist, 1953).

In analyzing the spatial and temporal dimensions, we need to consider the extent to which they make a real difference to communication and other social processes involved in operating the technology. Thus, the spatiotemporal concentration of production that occurs with increased mechanization and automation does not lead consistently to closer contact among operatives because there is often a thinning-out of labor, growth in the physical size of the plant and more multi-shift working. While a number of important generalizations can be made about the effects of the spatiotemporal dimension (Miller, 1959/Vol. II), these are usually complicated by the demands for cooperation that arise from the other dimension of the technology.

The immediate physical work setting. Many of the immediate conditions of temperature, light, noise, dust and dirt are broadly dependent upon the nature of the material and the level of mechanization. Certain working conditions are regarded as characteristic of foundries, ironworks, cotton mills, machine shops and mining. It is desirable to consider physical setting as a separate dimension because these conditions are, within broad limits, capable of considerable variation, and because they are related differently to the social system. As Walker (1957) has shown in his study of the Lorain Tube Mills, local variations in physical conditions may cause strife in the social system if "bad" conditions are attributed to managerial indifference. The classic Hawthorne study showed that the major effect of changing physical conditions may be that of convincing workers of management's concern for their welfare. In both cases, it is the relative independence of the work setting from other technological dimensions that underlies this influence on the social system.

The relative importance of these dimensions will vary with the purposes and objects of study. Unless these dimensions are considered, we cannot exclude the possibility that observed roles and role relations are a response to some undetected technological requirements.

Failure to consider these facts makes it difficult to assess the validity of many social scientific findings in this field, including many on the effects of "automation." In ignoring the technological variable, we run the risk of attributing causal effects to factors that are merely concomitant (cf. a case of "spurious correlation").

An analysis in these terms can yield a systematic picture of the human tasks and task interrelations required by a technological system. However, between these requirements and the social system there is not a strict one-to-one relation, but what is logically referred to as a correlative relation (cf. Feibleman and Friend, 1945, who observe that this is what one would expect to find between two separate systems or processes).

In a simple operation such as manually moving and stacking railway sleepers (ties) there may be only one single suitable work relationship structure, namely a cooperating pair, each worker taking an end of the sleeper and lifting, supporting, walking and throwing in close coordination with the other. The ordinary production process is much more complex, and it is unusual to find only one particular work relationship structure that can be fitted to these tasks.

Some technological features that increase the indeterminacy of the relation are:

- The variability in size of the tasks. They are not all one man-shift size.
- The spatial separation that often makes it difficult to group together interdependent tasks that ought to be brought together. The need to avoid lost time and effort in travel may dictate the grouping of unrelated tasks or concentration on tasks that are very similar.
- The simultaneity or temporal separation of tasks may likewise suggest, or even necessitate, different groupings of tasks from those indicated by task similarities and dependencies.

From the social system arise other equally potent influences. These may dictate quite different grouping of tasks to meet the real or presumed requirements of the social system.

Allowing for the "openness" of the relation between tasks and sets of roles, there is still a great deal to be gained from developing concepts that describe the different forms of task relations.

In the Tavistock Institute studies, there have occurred a number of such concepts (Herbst, 1959; 1976/Vol. II). The simplest conceptual distinction is between dependent and independent individual tasks. Independent tasks, by definition, do not require cooperation between workers, unless:

- They are dependent with respect to the supporting activities or conditions that they require.
- They are dependent with respect to some "end-condition" or goal.

These two cases permit considerable freedom of choice between different forms of work structure. Roles may be organized so that workers are unconcerned with the end result (defined as someone else's responsibility), so that they are competitive; or they create a group collectively concerned with the end result. Such groups have been found, experimentally, to yield positive effects on performance and morale (Deutsch, 1949; Coch and French 1948; Lawrence and Smith, 1955). Rather less freedom exists in the case of "dependence with respect to supports." There are dangers in having workers compete for things they need in order to carry out their task. The devices by which they secure these things may deprive others of "fair" access. On the other hand, a choice can be made between providing these things separately to each worker, which strengthens the supervisor's hand, or making a group of workers jointly responsible for results.

There are two kinds of dependent tasks. *Simultaneous interdependence* is characteristic of a task too large for an individual to perform in the required time and hence broken into individual part-tasks. At one extreme is "simple interdependence" in which similar part-tasks have to be performed together if they are to be effective. At the other extreme is "complex simultaneous interdependence" in which the essential factor is the presence of different and complementary actions executed simultaneously and with reference to each other (Asch, 1952:175). These systems of complex cooperation have the fundamental purpose of accomplishing a given task within a concentrated period of time. In composite mining systems, this form of cooperation has the important effect of guaranteeing continuity in the face of individual failure—a reliably performing group despite the failure of some individuals to come up to the mark.

Successional dependence is the most widespread form of task interdependence. It occurs in two main forms: the task may be such that, as in longwall coal-mining, only one set of operations can be carried out on each shift; or successive operations can be performed simultaneously, as on an assembly line. This difference affects coordination and group formation but not the classification of forms of dependency. The following appear to be the possible forms:

cyclic   abc, abc, etc. A chain of tasks is normally only a section of a
              cycle.

convergent   a & b to c
divergent   a to b & c

There is also a *part/whole* interdependence when an individual task is a minor part of a whole task for which another individual is responsible (e.g., the relation between the manual plugger and the operator of the piercer machine in the Lorain Tube Mill [Walker, 1957]).

There are many more possibilities. Task relations can vary in the *reciprocity* or *nonreciprocity* of dependence, direction of dependence and *degree of dependence,* which is partly determined by the time lag between the end of one task and the beginning of the next. In some cases there may be very little variation possible; in others a great deal. Automated production lines frequently allow little variation, and some form of "buffer" supplies have to be inserted to reduce the degree of dependence. Tasks may also be dependent upon the *quality* of work done in preceding tasks. This dependency may be lessened by inserting special inspection/rejection roles or devices.

A chain of sequential dependent tasks may be influenced by the location of the "pacesetters." Thus, in automated Tube Mills (cf. Walker, 1957) there is a chain of tasks, each dependent upon the preceding one for its supply of prepared materials. The pacesetter tends to be one of the middle tasks. This shifts dependencies so that previous tasks become interdependent and following tasks more dependent.

Another important feature is that in less rigidly dependent task structures (e.g., composite mining systems), role relations vary depending upon the need to lessen unnecessary travel (of workers or materials) and the "dead time" of waiting for the next task.

WORK RELATIONSHIP STRUCTURES AND OCCUPATIONAL ROLES

Trist and Bamforth (1951:9) have postulated that the demands created by a technological system are met first by "bringing into existence a *work relationship structure.*" This structure is related to *tasks and task-interdependencies* that, together with the machines and apparatus, constitute the *component operations* cycle required by the productive process under its particular conditions of mechanization, spatiotemporal scale, immediate environment, etc. A key concept, *occupational role,* served to identify the individual's location within the work relationship structure and in relation to the production process:

> Occupational roles express the relationship between a production process and the social organization of the group. In one direction they are related to tasks which

are related to each other; in the other, to people who are also related to each other. (Trist and Bamforth, 1951:14)

The role concept alone does not explain how individuals will experience tasks, nor does it explain the various interdependencies between tasks and between workers.

The concept of role does, however, lead one to expect workers to experience tasks not in isolation but as roles that generate a sense of dependency, subordination, self-worth, trust, isolation, etc. Thus, although individuals may find immediate tasks distasteful (probably most typical for operators in modern industry), they may gain compensatory satisfaction from other role aspects that concern relations with fellow workers, supervisors and the enterprise. Where the components of a role form a "weak gestalt," however, there would be more likelihood of "compensation" than where these components form a "strong gestalt." This problem can be explored further only through the second aspect of the role concept.

This aspect suggests that at the next level, task interdependencies are co-related primarily to role relationships rather than to interpersonal relations, i.e., social relations formed to cope with task demands rather than informal social relations serving individual ends.

E. Gross (1956) has aptly described the underlying processes as those of *symbiosis* and *consensus* respectively. The distinction draws attention to a further distinction among formally defined symbiotic role structure, informal symbiotic relations and informal consensual relations. In the informal symbiotic relations, the individuals remain oriented to the institutional goals, but in the consensual relations individuals are (according to our use of the terms) oriented toward personal goals that are not adequately catered for, or may even be threatened, by the formal organizational goals. These primary groups on a consensual basis will be functional to the extent that they save the organization the trouble of catering for these personal feelings and interests and prevent more extreme individual solutions of absenteeism and accidents (in military organizations these groups appear to lessen the chances of desertion and self-wounding). They will be dysfunctional if they can pursue their interests only at the expense of the organizational goals for, in this case, they will be more able to resist organizational pressures than they would be as isolated individuals (Collins et al., 1946; Roy, 1952, 1954; Dalton, 1948).

The formal and informal symbiotic ties may be regarded as two aspects of the role structure. "Informality" here implies that the traditions or sanctions are carried by peers and not explicitly recognized by management.

From the above discussion, it is clear that there is an acute problem in trying to "map" the task structure with a formal role structure. Reliance on informal mapping, even if immediately effective, reduces the control of the enterprise leadership and makes it more difficult for them to meet wider challenges. The evidence suggests that formal recognition of group responsibility may close the gap between the definition of roles and the wide range of task interdependencies that exist. A difficulty remains, however, in detecting within the total task structure a genuine basis for such groups.

The mapping problem is simplified by the recognition that there may often be groupings of production tasks that have "whole" characteristics. A qualitatively different relation of tasks and roles emerges when a set of *connected roles* is grouped around a whole task. This allows a closer coordination of role and task interdependencies than where these are mediated by the overall tasks alone. These connected sets of roles show greater autonomy and are less dependent upon external supervision and coordination (cf. Trist and Bamforth, 1951, on the longwall ripping team, and Rice, 1958, on the reorganized weaving teams). Individuals experience through group membership the satisfaction of completing a whole task that is denied them in doing individual tasks (Wilson et al., 1951, par. 38, give experimental evidence of this effect).

A group consisting of the smallest number that can perform a "whole" task and can satisfy the social and psychological needs of its members is, alike from the point of view of task performance and of those performing it, the most satisfactory and efficient group. (Rice, 1958:36)

We can assume that this phenomenon operates through the psychological identification of the individual with the other persons in the group rather than through the role definition of an individual's task as part of the whole task. Thus Rice (1958) discusses the optimum size of the group in terms of clinical experience (p.37) and Wilson et al. (1951:46) express surprise when they find this phenomenon in a group of 19:

We had thought that a group of 19 might be rather large, but experience of relations on the face has considerably reassured us on this point. (par. 46)

In a later mining study, this phenomenon was observed in a primary work group of over 40 members.

This question of group size has plagued attempts to analyze the relation between task and work relationship structures. I think it shows the extent to which the new notions of work groups remain entangled with the recent "human relations" concept. The assumption that "friendliness" is the critical factor in group cohesiveness has been at the center of the semi-ideological human relations movement. The implicit structure of the argument can be illustrated as shown in Figure 1.

The friendship theory of work relations rests on three propositions:

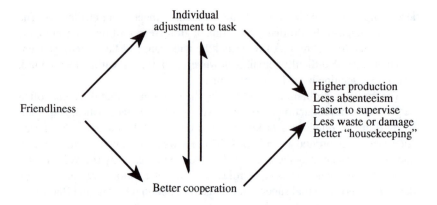

Figure 1. The premises of the human relations movement

- Friendliness on the job leads to better individual adjustment to the task.
- Friendliness leads to greater willingness to help.
- Interaction leads to greater "knowledge of others" and hence to more effective cooperation.

Our present concern is with the last two propositions. Jasinski's (1956) study of assembly-line groups provides a useful test in that the objective requirements for interdependence are very low. His study showed that workers who are adjusted to their task do not care whether or not they can talk to their fellow workers. However, among those not so task-oriented, the best adjusted are those who have friendly relations with other workers. Unfortunately, there is no indication of the strength of these friendships (whether, for instance, they carry over into private life). A more dramatic qualification is that friendships on the job may, in the absence of task orientation or organizational commitment, substantially increase the difficulty of enforcing task performance (cf. Roy, 1954).

In terms of the second proposition, the desirable work relationship structure could be achieved by:

- Organizing the workers into small groups. A large group inhibits stable interaction patterns. "With more than 12, the complexities of the multiple relationships to be maintained become too great to be carried by every member, and the group tends to be split into sub-groups" (Rice, 1958:37). Groups of six to 12 increase the possibilities of interaction and allow for group identification to develop and a heightened sense of belongingness.
- Increasing the likelihood of friendship by some sociometric self-selection of the group or, if this is not possible, selecting as group members those

who are most similar to each other on the grounds that interaction between similars leads more quickly to friendliness.

These measures have not been uniformly successful. There exist stable, effective groups too large for their behavior to be explained on these grounds. Extended investigation suggests that insofar as workers accept their work role, i.e., are task oriented, they prefer to work with others who are "psychologically distant" and "task-centered" (Fiedler, 1953).

What is required are relations in which workers see their task performances as mutually supporting. Supportive relations are not equivalent to, nor dependent upon, friendship and would tend to be disrupted by interpersonal hostility or intensive friendships. Several important facts point to the significance of "mutual support" in productive relations:

> An individual may not be willing to accept a task in the absence of support, even though able to perform it. (Marshall, 1947; Hughes, 1946)

If support is seen as coming, at least in part, from the group with whom the workers' tasks make them interdependent, then they will tend to value the group, to accept the group task in part as their own; as a corollary, they wish to be persons of significance for the group and to have their task performance accepted as a significant contribution to the group task.

No doubt some friendliness will develop under these circumstances, constrained by the task requirements and essentially a by-product of group formation, not in itself crucial for enhanced performances. From this viewpoint, friendship might occur with high performance even though it is not causally related to the latter, and one would expect to find it constrained to on-the-job relations.

It appears that support ought to be built into the organization of roles if task performance demands it—that with interdependent tasks the roles be so defined as to enhance mutual support and the task be so organized and rewarded as to facilitate identification of part-tasks with the whole.

Conversely, if tasks are interdependent and yet for managerial reasons group formation is not desired, then support must come from sources other than those sharing tasks and the rewards and penalties have to be related to performance of the part-tasks.

The interaction hypothesis (not to be confused with the interaction/friendship hypothesis) has undergone similar modification. Knowledge of others is not consistently found to be related to effective performance (Fiedler, 1953; Steiner, 1955). Only that knowledge is required that is relevant to the cooperative performance of the group task. In a stable socio-technical system, this knowledge tends to be incorporated into the role system. Knowledge of the role system informs each individual of what can be expected of whom and when.

> It is the advantage of role systems that behavior synthesis has been incorporated into the system itself, and that participants need not infer the strategies of their associates or improvise an effective synthesis as they engage in collective action. They need only to produce the behaviors which are situationally appropriate for members of their category. (Steiner, 1955:272)

The formal definition of a role system only encompasses one part of the role content. Every role system tends over time to accumulate and synthesize a wealth of knowledge about the role behaviors for various contingencies, whether from variations in the group task, the personalities entering the system or the system's environment. This important aspect is supported by the parallel emergence of role *standards* that enable members of a role system to classify variations from the "normal," based on what is relevant to the group's task performance rather than personal determinants (cf. Collins et al., 1946; Roy, 1952; 1954).

This suggests that the key interaction for a group is of a kind which permits development of a role culture and mutual testing out of the role-bearers (hence the significance of "drills" in breaking in a new ship crew). The same persons need not be kept in continuous interaction. Considerable role rotation is possible. In fact, knowledge of the role system is more likely to follow from rotation; harmful distortions can result from viewing a role system from just one position.

THE ENTERPRISE AS AN INTERNALLY DIFFERENTIATED ENTITY

In a mining system, the method of face work is the independent variable. Once this is changed, everything else has to come into line until a new internally self-consistent structure emerges which affects everything from the face to the surface (Wilson et al., 1951, par. 54).

In the coal-mining and textile studies, only a part of the enterprise was studied, and the work structures could be changed by executive action. Both studies insisted that changes in the work structure would set up forces toward change in the rest of the social system and, conversely, that the effects of changes in the social system would depend in part upon the character of the existing work structure.

Trist and Wilson traced this dynamic relation through the concepts of *coordination* and *control*. Required by all production systems, these become key "executive functions" of the management. Coordination and coercion come into sharp focus in the role of supervisor or foreman. Some of the supervisor's problems can be brought out by considering the effects of the different demands on the operatives in "isolated" work roles and in groups with a whole task.

So long as work roles center on isolated tasks, special roles are required to coordinate the different tasks. The more unpredictable the variation in the task/labor coordination and the greater the interdependence of the task phases, the greater the need for coordination. Conflicting production demands require, in addition, some form of scheduling.

Coordination may be provided by special supervisory roles and in part by the creation of primary work groups. The occupant of a special supervisory role is dependent upon all workers "doing their bit" for coordination of different tasks to be effective. Yet the supervisor can only influence a worker's behavior by threat of sanctions or promise of reward. Supervisors would be overwhelmed by work and anxiety if they tried to do each task whenever anything went wrong. Any unpredictable variation—changes in task orientation of workers, a move from male to female operatives, even decline in quality of raw materials—could increase the demand for external supervision and the use of coercive sanctions.

In this particular relation of worker to supervisor the "alienated" character of modern labor becomes most obvious. Management delegates the quality and rate of work to the supervisor, who entices or cajoles the worker into "accepting" a share of the responsibility. The "coercion" is unavoidable. Yet, without detailed controls, rewards and punishments, it undermines the operative's willingness to work. This is the classic dilemma of autocratic control, justified on the ground that within the supervisor/worker relation "persuasion or social influence to work harder would produce more work. In fact, this does not happen" (Argyle et al., 1958:36).

On the other hand, supervisors might minimize coercion and the consequent disruption of the task. The most important techniques are not those that manipulate personal relations with the workers, which would likely result in collusion to avoid their role obligations (Roy, 1954) or in undermining faith in the enterprise as promises remain unfulfilled.

Nevertheless, this "human relations" approach frequently appears in training courses for supervisors in industry, the armed services and other occupational fields (cf. National Institute of Industrial Psychology [NIIP], 1951; Zaleznik, 1951). It assumes "that job satisfaction and output are positively related. Not only is this not generally the case, but in some studies they have been found to be negatively related" (Argyle et al., 1958: 36). Appropriate supervisory actions seek to lessen the strain operatives experience in doing their tasks (cf. Lewin, 1951:202–7). Supervisors may lessen irritating "resistances in task-performance by providing 'know-how,' adequate maintenance and other support, and may spread the strain more evenly by programming work to match differences in machines and operatives." Such actions increase the control that individuals have over their tasks. Interactions with the supervisor are more likely to be in response to operator needs than supervisor's anxieties, and operators will see supervisors as more concerned with their needs. (Walker et al., 1956, gave much the same picture in their study of assembly-line foremen.)

Coordination may be more effective if work roles are embedded in a primary work group with its corresponding group task (cf. Trist, 1953, par. 69–73). By allowing a degree of self-government to such groups, first-level supervisors can focus on coordinating tasks between groups and with various service groups. Supervisors would be less concerned with wielding sanctions under these conditions. When internal group sanctions are inadequate, the matter would normally concern a level of management above the supervisor. The supervisory role would, however, require higher conceptual skills. Self-managed groups are more complex to supervise than individual roles. They do more over space and time that cannot be overseen directly, requiring a conceptual representation of what is going on. Effective supervision would entail planning further ahead so that the groups receive sufficient support and servicing to keep going. This orientation of first-level supervisors toward coordination is similar to that of upper management and less preoccupied with controlling the individual/task relation that is a prerequisite of functional supervision (cf. NIIP, 1951:2730). As a general proposition, *the primary task of the supervisor is to manage the immediate boundary conditions of the worker/task relation* and thus effectively relate them to the larger organizational structures.

It should also be clear that an enterprise is not completely free to choose between isolated and group organization of tasks:

> The degree to which a work group is capable of responsible autonomy is a function of the extent to which its work task is itself autonomous in the sense of being an independent and self-completing whole. (Wilson et al., 1951, par. 22)

The definition of group powers, and hence the delegation of responsibility, is easier to achieve when "tasks performed by individuals and groups can be performed within definable physical boundaries. Those responsible for the task can then 'own' their 'territory.' They can easily identify what is theirs and who belongs in it. They can raise questions about the right of others, not engaged on the task, to be there" (Rice, 1958:35; Miller, 1959/Vol. II).

There are other limits too—the kinds of persons in the group, and the group's ability to control the task and to take responsibility. If these conditions are not present, merely dictating that such-and-such operatives shall constitute a group would not make any difference to the supervisory requirements.

The effects of high mechanization and automation on supervision will vary with the requirements for coordination and the possibilities for "positive" supervisory practices that these technologies create. Regarding the different forms of high mechanization, it is only possible to make limited generalizations. Their common characteristics suggest that a higher level of coordination will be required to offset the greater rate of production, the greater potential loss of production and cost of damage due to errors. These conditions, plus the "sensitive" nature of the individual operative's contribution, make it even more necessary to reduce any feeling of coercion. This is obviously so for operatives employing conceptual skills who are responsible for relatively complex judgments and decisions.

The Psychological Requirements of the Individual

The preceding outline of socio-technical theory revealed several weak points— matters that are given empirical attention but that have not been developed theoretically beyond a few isolated hypotheses:

- The burdens, satisfactions and individual experiences in carrying out various tasks, including the problem of "alienation."
- The "recalcitrance" of individuals and social groups in the face of the overall requirements of the enterprise (particularly as it creates control mechanisms based on coercion and manipulation).
- The emergence within an enterprise of purposes other than those expressed in, or supportive of, its goals.

The immediate impression is that these are all "dysfunctional" aspects of enterprise life, and hence that the theory is a species of "managerial sociology" (Friedman, 1955). However, there are reasons for regarding this as a superficial explanation—as noted above, these matters are given empirical attention in the studies of the Tavistock Institute of Human Relations and of the other "system theorists." The lack of theoretical development seems consistent with a justifiable emphasis upon first clarifying the requirements of socio-technical systems up to, and including, whole enterprises. At the level of analyzing individual enterprises, the conditions basically contributing to the above phenomena must be regarded as "givens"; they are rooted in the broader human, social, cultural and economic context of the enterprise. Theoretically, they present the same sort of problem that Chein (1954) raises in his study of environmental determinants of individual behavior; i.e., these are systematically conditioned by facts lying outside the immediately relevant frame of reference. Thus, while it is correct to say that failure to consider these environmental encroachments will lead to certain kinds of errors (Wilensky, 1957), it would be incorrect to damn socio-technical or related system theories for their failure theoretically to encompass such problems. What this criticism does validly entail is that socio-technical analysis must draw heavily upon other areas of social science, as we found necessary in clarifying what was "human relations" and what was "autonomous group functioning."

THE INDIVIDUAL AND THE TASK

Individuals in an enterprise perform at least those tasks dictated by the technological requirements. It is necessary that the tasks and persons be so matched that it is physically possible for the persons to keep on performing them. This matching process may involve job analysis, selection, training and job re-design. If this process deals only with what is physically possible, it refers to what the task requires of the individual, not what the individual requires of the task. However, as soon as the problem is raised of making it likely that employees will, in fact, perform their tasks, then the enterprise must take account of the psychological properties of its employees and modify its structure beyond what is dictated by technological requirements alone. The dependence of an enterprise upon persons to operate its technology constitutes an inescapable dilemma. It is frequently possible for a "hard-headed" leadership to deny the reality of the problem, but it is extremely doubtful if any institution can persist without accommodating to the fact that whole persons are employed, not just the psychological bits that fit the technological requirements.

> The whole individual raises new problems for the organization, partly because of the needs of his own personality and partly because he brings with him a set of established habits as well, perhaps, as commitments to special groups outside of the organization. (Selznick, 1948:26)

For individuals to perform certain tasks, one or more of the following general psychological conditions must exist:
- Performance of the task itself satisfies some psychological needs of the individual.
- Performance of the task is not in itself satisfying but it is an unavoidable prerequisite to achieving other psychological satisfactions (i.e., it has means-characteristics) or avoiding other more unpleasant conditions.
- Performance is induced by demands perceived to arise from the task itself (i.e., it arises from "task orientation").

Only the first and last conditions refer to intrinsic satisfactions of the task. These suggest some ways that tasks may be modified to meet the psychological requirements of workers and align their activities and their interests more closely to the purposes of the enterprise. The second condition covers the typical extrinsic rewards and punishments and the inherent dilemmas (cf.

Lewin, 1935, chap. 4). If this is the dominant way of relating workers to tasks, then:

Much of the enterprise's effort must be devoted to constraints that prevent "unearned" rewards or avoidance of "earned" penalties.

The enterprise's attempts to meet the worker's other psychological requirements (e.g., for satisfying interpersonal relations and for a meaningful relation to society) will be negated in part by unsatisfying task relations. Nor does attaching incentives to task performance necessarily mean that tasks can be designed solely to meet technological requirements. Close control of the effort/reward relation exerts pressure toward ever greater fragmenting of tasks into measurable individual performance units. This process often goes beyond technological requirements.

Perhaps, despite its drawbacks, this is the only practicable method of relating workers to tasks in modern industry, but it is desirable to consider alternative possibilities.

Both specialist and generalist writings on industry tend to evade the unpleasant side of this problem by assuming that work, at the operative level, is, or could be, a source of immediate psychological satisfaction. The evidence from many occupations and from clinical study raises strong doubts that this is the case. The work of most operatives yields little opportunity for libidinal satisfaction. Only a favored few engage in creative work or work according to their inclinations. For many more there is a sort of satisfaction gained from a habitual work habit formed over the years that Baldamus (1951) has called a "dull contentment." It is a sort of borderline satisfaction, quite distinct from the experience of pleasurable activities or the quieter satisfaction of an engaging task, but quite prevalent in industry.

The third condition under which we might expect people to perform work—task orientation—seems to be the only viable alternative to the "stick and carrot." It points in a very different direction, namely, to the specific features of tasks that lead workers to experience different satisfactions in different jobs, even though the money and conditions may be no better. Consideration of workers' task preferences reveals two major factors. One is a preference for tasks that induce strong forces within the individual to complete or continue them, and the other a preference for tasks over which the individual has considerable personal control. These factors contribute to the development of task orientation—a state in which the individual's interest is aroused, engaged and directed by the character of the task.

While it is difficult to imagine in modern industry much increase in creative or libidinally satisfying tasks (despite a reduction of working hours and an increase in time available for libidinal satisfaction), it is possible to conceive of a great reduction in alienating work. If this can be achieved by creating the conditions for task orientation, it need not negate the technological requirements of an enterprise nor seriously modify its primary task or purpose. It is not suggested that these modifications could make work so satisfying as to eliminate the distinction between work and leisure (cf. Curle, 1949). No modification discussed here is likely to lessen the pressure for shorter working hours.

Now let us turn to the conditions under which task orientation will tend to emerge and the effects it is likely to have. The two prerequisites seem to be:

- The individual should have control over the materials and processes of the task.
- The task should be structured to induce forces on the individual toward aiding its completion or continuation.

Both aspects are often ignored by experimental psychologists because of their assumption that an individual will be motivated to work only when impelled by his or her own internal forces. The present distinction arises from recent efforts to understand those instances in which "there is activity growing out of interest in the task itself, in the problems and challenges it offers. The task guides the person, steers his action, becomes the center of concern" (Asch, 1952:303). This distinction does not imply that personal motivations are absent but asks "whether the ego can lend itself to a task or whether it remains the center of reference" (Asch, 1952:304).

Lacking control over the task, an individual will find himself split between a concern for the task and a constant "looking over the shoulder" at the alien source of control, namely, supervision.

A study of classroom behavior reveals situations so similar as to warrant quoting:

> The child's relation to the learning material is given little opportunity to develop into a spontaneous interest relation because it is overshadowed by the teacher-child relationship. The teacher generally decides what material should be worked on, the relative importance of the different aspects, how it should be worked, the standards of achievement and when work should cease. It is only rarely that the child's behavior is spontaneously oriented towards problems posed by the material itself or guided by the demands implicit in the structure of the material. Because the initiative and guidance come from *the teacher, the behavior of the child is oriented primarily towards the teacher and not towards the material to be learnt.* (Oeser and Emery, 1954:132)

This similarity enables schools to make a major contribution to the work discipline of society. The concept of work as necessary even if not pleasant and the norms supporting alienated labor will tend to be inculcated during these middle childhood years of socialization (cf. Baldamus, 1957:199–200). Failure of the schools to bring about this resignation to alienated labor could undermine the efficacy of industrial incentives and throw considerable strain on family, work and other institutions that deal with the adolescents.

People alienated from work may identify with and take over the standards of supervisors, but it is also likely that many will "stand outside" the work relation and seek to "get by" with various techniques of ingratiation or evasion. Outright hostility and refusal to work may also be produced:

> By decreasing the child's possibilities of developing an intrinsic interest in the learning materials the possibility of an actual conflict between the child's own forces and those of the teacher is also increased. That is, it becomes more likely that the child will perceive the situation as *coercive* and will attempt to leave it in pursuit of his own interest, or, failing in this, will restructure it to suit his own ends by destroying the learning materials or challenging the authority of the teacher. (Oeser and Emery, 1954)

The degree of control possessed by an individual will depend on the nature of the task or the authority that is delegated and on the knowledge and skill brought to the task. Thus, the knowledge that a skilled worker brings to a job enables choices of modes and rates of operation not obvious to the unskilled. As pointed out by Jaques these aspects refer to the *discretionary content* of a task:

> all those elements in which choice of how to do a job was left to the person doing it . . . having to choose the best feeds and speeds or an impoverished job on a machine; having to decide whether the finish on a piece of work would satisfy some particular customer; . . . having to plan and organize one's work in order to get it done within a prescribed time. (1956:34)

Degree of control also depends on the extent to which an individual is free from inspection or supervisory checkup—what Jaques (1956) has termed the *time span of responsibility.*

The second set of conditions affecting task orientation are structural characteristics of the tasks. Experimental work on learning has amply proven that degree of task structure has considerable psychological influence. If the task is too complicated, an individual, if motivated to learn, will display vicarious trial and error activity. If the task is so simple as to appear "structureless," learning will again only occur if rewarded or punished in a strictly scheduled fashion—a form of blind conditioning. Between these limits is a range of meaningful structure in which the individual learns by varying degrees of insight and, significantly, without extrinsic reward or punishment.

The effect of structure on performance has been less studied. It has, however been demonstrated that

- There can be psychological forces toward performance of a task other than those arising from preexistent needs within the person (cf. Asch, 1952:308–10; Henle and Aull, 1953; Lewis, 1944).

- To the extent that the individual grasps the task and his function, he paces himself within the demands of the system, the needs of the task become *the environment of requirements* to which he subordinates his action (Asch, 1952:175).
- Repetitive performance of a task leads more quickly to satiation, the smaller and simpler the task (Lewin, 1951:283–84).

Visual attention is similarly influenced by the pattern of changes in the perceptual field (Dember and Earl, 1957). The most general statement of the relation between structure of a task and activity has come from Peak:

> The condition of maximum duration of activity is to be expected, therefore, at some distance-between-parts which is great enough to prevent immediate onset of decrement and yet small enough to provide relatively high probability of continuing transmission of activation from one part of the structure to another. (1958:831)

This principle of optimum structure does not indicate the structural forms most conducive to performance. Baldamus (1951) has done much to bring together the available industrial data. He postulates several forms of "traction" and sources of resistance that commonly arise in modern industry. He distinguishes reactions "according to the external objective cause which tends to bind successive cycles into a continuous flow of activity" (p.48), e.g., fine traction, process traction, batch traction (cf. Smith and Lem, 1955) and object traction (corresponding to the oft observed tendency to complete a whole object). The sources of resistance are located primarily in things that break the continuity of work, e.g., poor tools and materials, brief work cycles. Tasks vary with respect to these features and such variations make it more or less easy for a worker to become absorbed in the task.

Where the definition of the work role and the nature of the task permit the development of task orientation, the following differences tend to emerge between behavior in these conditions and that in conditions of "ego orientation." Ego orientation is assumed to exist when the task provides a means toward achieving a personal goal, e.g., a noxious task performed for substitute or compensating satisfaction. To quote Asch (1952):

> . . . task-orientation frees one for seeing and understanding situations in their own terms. In contrast, focusing on the self may interfere with giving oneself to the task, it may restrict or narrow the outlook by introducing directions alien to the task and deprive the person of freedom to abandon predetermined paths and follow in new directions. (p. 311)

> The attitude of intrinsic interest may produce a more serene relation to the task. (p.311)

Whether a person can command a sustained interest in a given direction may depend on the nature of his relation to it; if the interests of the ego are no longer served by a given activity, the ground for its pursuit will vanish . . . we would expect the dynamics of task-oriented interests to be different, that the activity itself would provide a force for its continuation and proper completion. In general, we would expect a task-oriented person to be more steady and reliable. (p.312)

. . . the important possibility must be considered that the ego may simply not be able to furnish the forces for dealing with certain situations no matter how strong the ego forces may be. (p.312)

Unfortunately, many industrial tasks lack the structural characteristics required for task orientation, and the demand for close coordination makes intolerable the discontinuity and variation that arise from delegating responsibility for the task to the individual.

There is much greater scope in the development of group responsibility for group tasks. If the individual's tasks are genuinely interdependent with the group task, then it is possible for the individual to relate meaningfully to his personal activity through this group task (cf. Deutsch, 1949; Horwitz, 1954). A group task, with its greater size and complexity, is more likely to provide structural conditions conducive to goal-setting and striving.

With some autonomy and a wide sharing of the needed skills, a group can provide continuity in task performance unlikely to be achieved by individuals alone or under supervisory control.

Such work groups also counter one undesirable by-product of the individual's alienation from productive activity: his estrangement from his fellow workers. If workers dislike their tasks, they are less likely to maintain relations with others that arise from task interdependence. Attempts by others to get or offer help are likely to be regarded as attempts at manipulation for their own ends. If workers find that participation in the group gives meaning to their activity, their task-mediated relations are likely to become satisfying. Offers or requests for help will tend to be accepted as shared goals and norms, not interpreted as condescension or manipulation.

THE INDIVIDUAL AND THE ENTERPRISE

The discussion so far has concerned one aspect of alienation—of a person from his or her productive activity. Equally significant for the individual, and for the enterprise, is alienation from the product of labor. In modern industry individuals do not claim the product of their labors. Nevertheless, there are good psychological grounds for considering the possibility that an individual may relate to the product that embodies his efforts. Whereas an individual's alienation from activity relates to the task and his work roles, alienation from the product can be considered only in terms of relation to the enterprise; society initially attributes the rights to the product to the enterprise alone. Workers who see this relation isolated from its social context are likely to consider the appropriation of their products as a relative weakening of their position and regard the enterprise's interest in greater production, better quality and less waste as, at best, no concern of theirs (Walker, 1957). Nor is this effect eliminated if workers do not have, or desire, personal access to these products. Only by meaningfully relating an individual to his society can an enterprise hope to minimize this form of alienation (Gross, 1953). If an enterprise demonstrates distinctive competence in the marketplace, it enhances the possibility that its members will see themselves as meaningfully related to their society through the product of their activities. Neither competence nor market are sufficient in themselves; distinctive competence and market demand are both required.

In summary, the movement toward humanizing industry needs to be refocused from supporting informal defense mechanisms within enterprises to exploring the possibilities of basic, though limited, structural changes.

References

Amber, C.H. and P.S. Amber. 1956. "A Yardstick for Automation." *American Machinist* (August).

Argyle, M., G. Gardner and F. Cioffi. 1958. "Supervisory Methods Related to Productivity, Absenteeism and Labour Turnover." *Human Relations,* 11:23–40.

Asch, S.E. 1952. *Social Psychology.* New York: Prentice-Hall.

Baldamus, W. 1951. "Types of Work and Motivation." *British Journal of Sociology,* 2:44–58.

———. 1957. "The Relationship Between Wage and Effort." *Journal of Industrial Economics,* 5:192–201.

Bright, J.R. 1955. "How to Evaluate Automation." *Harvard Business Review* (July/ August).

Chein, I. 1954. "The Environment as a Determinant of Behavior." *Journal of Social Psychology,* 39:115–27.

Coch, L. and J.R.P. French. 1948. "Overcoming Resistance to Change." *Human Relations,* 1:512–32.

Collins, D., M. Dalton and D.M. Roy. 1946. "Restriction of Output and Social Cleavage in Industry." *Applied Anthropology,* 5:1–14.

Curle, A. 1949. "Incentives to Work: An Anthropological Appraisal." *Human Relations,* 2:41–48.

Dalton, M. 1948. "The Industrial 'Rate-Buster': A Characterization." *Applied Anthropology,* 1:5–18.

Dember, W.N. and R.W. Earl. 1957. "Analysis of Exploratory, Manipulatory and Curiosity Behaviors." *Psychological Review,* 64:91–96.

Deutsch, M. 1949. "An Experimental Study of the Effects of Cooperation and Competition upon Group Processes." *Human Relations,* 2:199–231.

Drucker, P.F. 1952. "The Employee Society." *American Journal of Sociology,* 58:358–63.

Emery, F.E. 1957. Editorial in *Instruments and Automation,* 30:1475–78.

———. 1959. *Characteristics of Socio-Technical Systems.* London: Tavistock Institute Document 527. Revised in *The Emergence of a New Paradigm of Work.* Canberra: Centre for Continuing Education, Australian National University, 1978. Also in *Design of Jobs,* edited by L.E. Davis and J.C. Taylor. Harmondsworth: Penguin Books, 1972. Vol. II, pp. 157–86.

Feibleman, J. and J.W. Friend. 1945. "The Structure and Function of Organization." *Philosophical Review,* 54:19–44.

Fiedler, F.E. 1953. "The Psychological-Distance Dimension in Interpersonal Relations." *Journal of Personality,* 22:142–50.

Friedmann, G. 1955. *Industrial Society: The Emergence of the Human Problems of Automation.* Glencoe, Ill.: Free Press.

Gross, E. 1953. "Some Functional Consequences of Primary Controls in Formal Work Organizations." *American Sociological Review,* 18:368–73.

———. 1956. "Symbiosis and Consensus as Integrative Factors in Small Groups." *American Sociological Review,* 21:174–79.

Henle, M. and G. Aull. 1953. "Factors Decisive for Resumption of Interrupted Activities: The Question Reopened." *Psychological Review,* 60:81–88.

Herbst, P.G. 1954. "The Analyses of Social Flow Systems." *Human Relations,* 7:327–36.

———. 1959. *Task Structure and Work Relations.* London: Tavistock Institute Document 528.

———. 1976. *Alternatives to Hierarchies.* Leiden: Martinus Nijhoff. Chapter 3, Vol. II, pp. 283–93.

Horwitz, M. 1954. "The Recall of Interrupted Group Tasks: An Experimental Study of Individual Motivation in Relation to Group Goals." *Human Relations,* 7:3–38.

Hughes, E. C. 1946. "The Knitting of Racial Groups in Industry." *American Sociological Review,* 11:512–19.

Jaques, E. 1956. *Measurement of Responsibility: A Study of Work, Payment, and Industrial Capacity.* London: Tavistock Publications.

Jasinski, F.J. 1956. "Technological Delimitation of Reciprocal Relationships: A Study of Interaction Patterns in Industry." *Human Organization,* 15:24–28.

Lawrence, L.C. and P.C. Smith. 1955. "Group Decision and Employee Participation." *Journal of Applied Psychology,* 39:334–37.

Lewin, K. 1935. *A Dynamic Theory of Personality: Selected Papers.* New York: McGraw-Hill.

———. 1951. *Field Theory in Social Science: Selected Theoretical Papers.* New York: Harper and Row.

Lewis, H.B. 1944. "An Experimental Study of the Role of the Ego in Work. I: The Role of the Ego in Cooperative Work." *Journal of Experimental Psychology,* 34:113–26.

Lombard, G.F.F. 1955. *Behavior in a Selling Group: A Case Study of Inter-Personal Relations in a Department Store.* Boston: Harvard University Graduate School of Business Administration.

Marshall, S.L.A. 1947. *Men Under Fire.* New York: Morrow.

Miller, E.J. 1959. *Technology, Territory and Time: The Internal Differentiation of Complex Production Systems.* London: Tavistock Institute Document 526; *Human Relations,* 12:243–72. Vol. II, pp. 385–404.

National Institute of Industrial Psychology (NIIP). 1951. *The Foreman*. London: Staples Press.

Oeser, O.A. and F.E. Emery. 1954. *Social Structure and Personality in a Rural Community*. London: Routledge and Kegan Paul.

Peak, H. 1958. "Psychological Structure and Psychological Activity." *Psychological Review*, 65:325–47.

Rice, A.K. 1953. "Productivity and Social Organisation in an Indian Automated Weaving Shed." *Human Relations*, 6:297–329. Condensed in Vol. II, pp. 106–129.

―――. 1958. *Productivity and Social Organization: The Ahmedabad Experiment*. London: Tavistock Publications. Reissued 1987, New York: Garland.

Roy, D. 1952. "Quota Restriction and Goldbricking in a Machine Shop." *American Journal of Sociology*, 57:427–42.

―――. 1954. "Efficiency and 'The Fix': Informal Intergroup Relations in a Piecework Machine Shop." *American Journal of Sociology*, 60:255–66.

Selznick, P. 1948. "Foundations of the Theory of Organization." *American Sociological Review*, 13:25–35.

Smith, P.C. and C. Lem. 1955. "Positive Aspects of Motivation in Repetitive Work: Effects of Lot Size upon Spacing of Voluntary Work Stoppages." *Journal of Applied Psychology*, 39:330–33.

Steiner, I.D. 1955. "Interpersonal Behavior as Influenced by Accuracy of Social Perception." *Psychological Review*, 62:268–74.

Trist, E.L. 1953. *Some Observations on the Machine Face as a Socio-Technical System*. London: Tavistock Institute Document 341.

Trist, E.L. and K.W. Bamforth. 1951. "Some Social and Psychological Consequences of the Longwall Method of Coal-Getting." *Human Relations*, 4:3–38. Shortened, Vol. II, "The Stress of Isolated Dependence: The Filling Shift in the Semi-Mechanized Longwall Three-Shift Mining Cycle," pp. 64–83.

von Bertalanffy, L. 1950. "The Theory of Open Systems in Physics and Biology." *Science*, 3:23–29.

Walker, C.R. 1957. *Toward the Automatic Factory: A Case Study of Men and Machines*. New Haven, Conn.: Yale University Press.

Walker, C.R., R.H. Guest and A.N. Turner. 1956. *The Foreman on the Assembly Line*. Cambridge, Mass.: Harvard University Press.

Warner, W.L. and J.O. Low. 1947. *The Social System of the Modern Factory: The Strike, a Social Analysis*. New Haven, Conn.: Yale University Press.

Wilensky, H.L. 1957. "Human Relations in the Workplace: An Appraisal of Some Recent Research." In *Research in Industrial Human Relations: A Critical Appraisal*, edited by C.M. Arensberg et al. New York: Harper.

Williams, R.H. 1950. *The Theory of Action in Operations Research and in Social Sciences*. Baltimore: Johns Hopkins University, Operations Research Office, T-13.

Wilson, A.T.M., E.L. Trist, F.E. Emery and K.W. Bamforth. 1951. *The Bolsover System of Continuous Mining*. London: Tavistock Institute Document 290.

Zaleznik, A. 1951. *Foreman Training in a Growing Enterprise*. Boston: Boston University Graduate School of Business Administration.

Conceptual Developments

During the 1960s and 1970s a number of conceptual advances were made, largely by Fred Emery and one or two associates. Little of this was published until the late 1970s. The first concept had to do with building new plants on greenfield sites, which offer immense opportunities to try out new principles. Failure to take such opportunities may delay significant advances for years. Emery's analysis of the assembly line draws attention to Volvo's decision to break with the assembly line in its new plant at Kalmar. The design presented by the original team was too conventional for the managing director, who extended the range of expertise and brought in people from outside so that an innovative second look might produce basic reconsiderations. The assembly line is the hallmark of the old paradigm, though the controversies over the success of Volvo's alternative at Kalmar have been considerable. The European Economic Community recommended the abolition of the assembly line, asking for the exploration of human and economically effective alternatives.

A formulation of far-reaching importance was Emery's distinction, as early as 1967, between the first and second design principles. The *second design principle* represented, in an operational form, the full generalization of the socio-technical idea as an organizational principle based on the "redundancy of functions" as opposed to the "redundancy of parts" as in the *first design principle*. It was concerned with organizations in a Type IV (turbulent) environment and had inherent tendencies toward participative (nonhierarchical) orders and evolutionary democratic principles. As such, it is distinct from, and opposed to, all forms of bureaucracy. It empowers the individual through including his or her participation and in so doing democratizes the organization. Emery goes on to show that it can become the basis of a new social order in which the work experience of the many, as compared with the few, may be changed from negative to positive.

In discussion with Norwegian students, Emery affirms that socio-technical ideas are not marginal as the Marxists among them maintained but are independent of socialism and capitalism, offering a new way to find an acceptable and sustainable society.

Characteristic of the socio-technical field is that the main concepts that guided its development arose in conjunction with the key projects that provided new empirical opportunity. The first of these was the Norwegian Industrial Democracy project which began in 1962, in which members of the Tavistock Institute worked with members of the Norwegian Institute of Industrial Social

Research at Trondheim University and with key members of the Employers and Trade Union joint committee, government representatives joining later.

The first phase of the project was concerned with the role of boards, and particularly the role of workers' directors, which the government required in state enterprises and also in enterprises where the government had taken over capital in private firms which were German-funded before World War II. The joint committee found that Worker Directors, while being valued for creating a democratic atmosphere, did nothing to relieve the alienation present at the level of the workers.

To discover a feasible and effective mode of personal participation therefore became the next theme of the project. Workers were involved in direct participation in changes in work practices at their own level. This had the sought-after effect.

In the second of the four field experiments, at Hunsfoss pulp and paper mill, it was found that task forces of workers, technicians and supervisors could solve hitherto unsolved problems. The new chemical technology required a much cleaner separation of bark before the wood entered the mill. The remedies introduced to secure this greatly increased productivity. These, and remedies introduced for other problems, prevented the mill from closing; the local community dependent on it survived.

When Shell brought the question of the need for a new managerial philosophy to the Tavistock Institute, Emery showed that its logic involved the underlying acceptance of a key new idea: that the resources of a company were also the resources of society and that the position one took on this was fundamental. Such a concept could secure the full support of both management and unions. The philosophy was accepted by the top board and then offered for discussion by all levels of the company, including the workers.

The next major contributor was Herbst, who formulated the concept of minimal critical specifications in design. In a rapidly changing environment such as that now obtaining, over-specified designs became obsolete before they were finished. The new way was to design in only those items which had to be dealt with immediately and to leave all else to be determined when more of the future environment became known. This open system approach involved continuous re-appreciation and learning.

Herbst also produced a theory of alternatives to hierarchies. This involved, at the primary work level, work groups, matrices and networks. Primary work groups exist where the tasks are such that all members of the group can learn them. Where some of the tasks are too complex for this, matrices develop in which some tasks are done by everyone but others require full or partial specialists. In networks the people do not all know each other and may be physically distant, yet they can work interdependently over long time periods.

A network is not an overall entity like a group—it is an open structure of varying size and composition.

Since bureaucratic organizations cannot cope with turbulent environments, Davis envisioned that a crisis was growing in production management. Cherns made a summary of socio-technical concepts which many people have found useful.

There remained to be discovered how all this appears at different levels of the organization, though both Emery and Beer had made beginnings. Herbst was continuing his work on this problem at the time of his unexpected death.

Trist outlined the key ideas which had become current at the beginning of the 1980s and gave his forecast of developments as the closing address to the second International Conference in Toronto in 1981.

Fred Emery

Designing Socio-Technical Systems for Greenfield Sites[1]

In the arguments that are going on about the democratization of work, we can see people talking past each other because they have fundamentally different models or paradigms of what work is all about. These paradigms are consistent within themselves but quite irreconcilable with each other. If you are looking at work through one paradigm you cannot see what is seen through another.

At the heart of the traditional paradigm of work is the master/servant relation. Logically, this is a relation of asymmetrical dependence: the servant is dependent on the master for the job. As far as the master is concerned the servant is a redundant, replaceable part. From this relation the notions of managerial prerogatives and the right to hire-and-fire flow naturally.

Over the past 15 to 20 years a new paradigm has emerged (cf. Emery and Thorsrud, 1976). It is a relation of symmetrical dependence, a relation of cooperation within work. It expresses a refusal to accept the role of servant in a master/servant relation. It accepts, however, that workers are often able to do their work better with good management and that management can do nothing without workers.

The conflict between these paradigms comes to a focus on the role of the foreman. In the old paradigm the foreman/first-line supervisors are the essential link between managerial decision making and shop floor activity but are not themselves part of management. Neither, of course, are they accepted as workers. They are in the unenviable role of being the meat in the sandwich.

In the new model of work there is no place for the role of foreman. Such a role is quite antithetical to the notion of there being cooperation on the job. It implies that the workers are not being trusted to keep up their end of a relation of symmetrical dependence.

The role of the foreman is so central to the traditional authoritarian system that the first question to ask of any proposed scheme for democratization of work is: what does it do to the foreman's role? If it leaves that role intact then the scheme is fraudulent—at best mere icing on the cake. Most representative

[1]Slightly revised from the original in *Journal of Occupational Behaviour*, 1:19–27, 1980.

schemes are of this nature. While the elected representatives are off at their council meetings, the foreman continues to rule the roost. Similarly, most of the job enrichment, job enlargement schemes put forward by Herzberg, Scott-Myers and Ford leave the foreman's role quite untouched. For those who see the world of work through the traditional paradigm these schemes have an attraction. They can accept that happier workers could be more docile, maybe even produce more. They can accept that dull, meaningless and repetitive work activities make for unhappy workers and hence that there is some value in rewriting the individual job specifications to put more meaning in the task and provide more variety. What they simply cannot accept is that people would better perform even these improved jobs, and better coordinate them, if the foreman was not standing over them. Their implicit assumption about "the psychology of the worker" is obvious from the argument that is usually thrown in to clinch the case: "If the foreman was not there a natural leader would emerge and probably be even harder on them."

When people have had years to build a work culture on a different and opposing paradigm, it is painfully difficult to change the situation by mere scientific argument. One is inclined, in fact, to the pessimistic view that the great physicist Max Born expressed in looking back over the turbulent history of quantum physics:

> A new scientific truth does not triumph by convincing its opponents and making them see the light, but rather because its opponents eventually die, and a new generation grows up that is familiar with it. (quoted by Kuhn, 1962, p. 150)

We have experienced many difficulties in introducing the new paradigm into established workplaces. It has been like trying to fight one's way through a World War I defense system. The first line of trenches is occupied by the trade union officials and can be negotiated beforehand. Behind this is a second line of trenches that arises from the formulation of on-the-job customs and pro-cedures. This second line is held by the rank and file of workers. These defenses are specific to the workplace and protect individual workers from abuse even when their trade union officials desert them or are powerless to intervene. Working people have no alternative to developing this second line of defense: the law of the land or the powers of the unions usually do not reach far enough into the workplace to prevent abuse of managerial prerogatives. How-ever, these defenses can readily blind workers to changes that serve their interests. The defenses have usually emerged for good reasons that are now buried in the past, the occasions and the authors forgotten. That they emerged for some good reason is the reason for their being sacrosanct and the reason for their being extremely difficult to negotiate. In fact, any attempt to negotiate them is seen, ipso facto, as proof of evil managerial intentions. Sophisticated socio-technical analysis that proves the existence of joint benefits to workers and management helps, but not much in these circumstances.

Greenfield sites offer a good chance for a socio-technical analysis to make a contribution because in such cases a second line of defense has not emerged and most matters can be negotiated beforehand with trade union officials (and laid down for the new management). The workers and management can start from the beginning in conditions that allow for cooperation or open confrontation.

If socio-technical analysis is to play its part then:

• It must be involved in the planning process before technical planning has preempted too many options with regard to who is to be employed and how they are to be organized. This is contrary to common practice where the technical designers are guided only by such simple-minded criteria as minimal manning.

• It must be concerned with creating those interfaces between the technical and the social system that allow for the fulfillment of the human requirements of a job and an organization of people around the work which is maximally self-governing.

The first requirement can be met only by the relevant decision makers becoming more conscious of their social responsibility. Social scientists, or engineers-cum-social scientists, have the responsibility for identifying what has to be taken into account in order to design effective socio-technical systems; systems that are rewarding to all that take part in them.

In "Some Characteristics of Socio-Technical Systems" (1959, rev. 1978/ Vol. II) I tried to spell out what we knew about these desiderata. A lot of discussion has taken place since that was written. The need for greenfield site design has become more critical as more and more organizations find that they are incapable of undoing the exploitative and defensive systems built into their existing plants. There is, furthermore, the chance that by demonstrating what can be done at a new plant, the management and workers in the old plants will be inspired to follow suit.

In designing a social system to operate efficiently a modern capital intensive plant, the key problem is that of creating *self-managing groups* to man the interface with the technical system. The term "self-managing group" deserves comment as it highlights why I should want to talk about the groups' management problems. Through the 1950s and 1960s it was common to refer to democratized work groups as "semiautonomous groups." Only in the 1970s was it felt that the idea was more clearly conveyed by the concept of self-managing groups. I do not think that the shift in terminology was accidental or arbitrary.

The first studies of democratized work groups were in traditional work settings, e.g., coal-mining faces, textiles and metal fabrication. In each of these cases the most serious problem was that of how much autonomy work groups could have which would be consonant with company production plans, maintenance procedures, safety rules and personnel practices. Cooperation within the groups was no real problem, as most people could easily master the tasks done by others and hence help out or relieve others as the need arose. Control over each others' contribution to the group task was also of little problem. The workplaces were intimate enough to enable each to see what the others were doing or not doing. All of the tasks were well enough understood to enable others to judge whether the workmanship was up to standard, and the constant face-to-face interaction made it reasonably easy to generate group pressure on those not pulling their weight. This last comment should not be taken to imply that these groups pressure everyone to keep up with the best and fastest workers. (In my experience the bull-gang atmosphere has only emerged when a group's reward was based on a simple index of quantity produced.) Typically, these groups are far more conscious of, and responsive to, variations in skill, intelligence, age, etc., including daily variation due to health, than any foreman could be expected to be no matter how well versed in human relations theory. People in relatively stable groups, even up to platoon size, seem to be remarkably adept at keeping books on favors given and debts due, and yet not at all impatient about balancing the books.

Thus it was that in these kinds of work settings we had simply to work out beforehand what was going to be the group territory, what were adequate performance levels and rewards and what limits to group autonomy had to be observed. That done, it could be left to the group to learn how they would manage themselves. In the case of our first Norwegian experiment—in the wiredrawing department of the Oslo Iron and Steel Works—I do recall very serious discussions about whether the groups should first be taught the art of group self-management. The previous mode of individual working had, as our interviews had shown, completely inhibited any sense of group identity, mutual respect or cooperativeness. We decided that such teaching would be a bit too insulting to the self-respect of the workers. After both shifts had been working for several weeks it was obvious that we need not have worried.

This emphasis on degrees of autonomy started to change with our very first case of a continuously operating process plant—the chemical pulp department of the Hunsfoss Pulp and Paper Company in 1964. Although we did not appreciate it at the time, we were probably fortunate that there was a further complication. At the heart of the production of chemical pulp was a batch method of digesting the wood chips. Each batch took approximately 16 hours in the cooker and there was no way of knowing how successfully the process was going until it emerged from the cooker. Thus each batch was started on one shift and finished on another (even two shifts later). Responsibility could not be located within a shift group; it had somehow to be located within the ensemble of four shifts that provided the continuous manning. The conditions of an open workshop and face-to-face interaction were not present (cf. Miller, 1959/Vol. II). There also seemed to be restrictions on the degree of multiskilling; a person from another section of the department could be trained to take an assistant's role in a particular section but the prospect of one person being thoroughly versed in more than one section seemed to be well in the future. Even within a shift, the operators were so widely scattered that there was little chance of them overseeing each other.

Under the conditions found at Hunsfoss, it became clear that autonomy was critically dependent on the cross-shift group evolving forms of effective self-management. Intuition and common sense could not suffice when the people whose tasks were interdependent were in no position to see what the others were doing; when the effectiveness of group pressures was grossly attenuated; and when it was very difficult to judge what had contributed what to any result.

Subsequently it became clear that, if work was to be democratized for interdependent workers who are widely separated by their skills or by space and time, the critical problem was not that of deciding on the degree of autonomy that should be allowed but of devising information systems that enable effective self-management. To allow any degree of autonomy in the absence of an effective information system would be simply to induce anarchy, a laissez-faire situation where each of the interdependent parts went its own way. In describing this matter I have used the notion of an "information system" as a piece of shorthand to refer to an information system that is about agreed objectives and review of performances. An information system that simply reported on what each interdependent part had performed would degenerate into an unhelpful exercise in one-upmanship and scapegoating.

My basic proposition in this paper is that under such conditions, self-managing groups have problems with controlling and coordinating their efforts that are much greater than would be the case if they were bureaucratically organized, as is the case similarly with the setting of their objectives.

Let us look first at how control and coordination are achieved in a bureaucratic section. The fundamental premise of bureaucratic organization is that each individual is allotted a personal task that must be performed and is usually allotted workplace and working hours. The more these matters are laid down in rules, regulations and job specifications, the easier it is to pinpoint movements that are out of control. In the absence of such fine controls, supervision usually requires strong rewards and penalties. Control is then simply a matter of supervisors overseeing the individuals in their sections to make sure that they are at their allotted workplaces during the specified working hours and performing their allotted tasks. Coordination is simplified because in overseeing for purposes of control supervisors have, or think they have, knowledge of which workers are behind with their task, which ahead and what shuffling of people between jobs needs to be done to catch up on the backlog. If no one is ahead supervisors may decide that some work is less urgent and may be allowed to lag; alternatively, reserves held by superiors may be called on. Such reserve forces are commonplace as the individual workers in this system are motivated to pretend that they are fully occupied with their allotted tasks, even when they are not, and to cry "overload" when, with a bit of extra effort, they could cope. The reserves are not always designated as such. They usually accrue through an incremental process of overmanning. When the work being done by one person regularly piles up to what the supervisor takes to be one-and-a-half manshift loads, another person is sought to split the work. It will be noted that the problems of coordination tend to be solved by evasion—"delegating" them up the chain of command—rather than by trying to get a better grip on the actual work situation.

The setting of objectives is also much easier for the supervisor or superintendent in a bureaucracy. It is enough if supervisors know the order of importance that their direct superintendent places on the different tasks to be performed by their sections. It is no concern of theirs if the superintendent has got it wrong from the organization's point of view. In matters to which the superintendent is indifferent, supervisors are free to order them according to their personal preferences and feelings. Even if they get this wrong, they can escape blame by pointing to the lack of explicit orders from above.

At a theoretical level we can note that control in a bureaucracy is made easier by familiarity with the myriad rules, regulations and job specifications and by familiarity with the dodges the workers are likely to employ. Coordination is made easier by familiarity with what the boss wants and a personal style of management that gets the job done. Supervisors will not seek efficiency in the use of their resources if that is likely to lead to some resources being taken away or to the weakening of their case for additional resources. The setting of objectives is a similar mixture of familiarity and personal preference (the dimension of Probability of Choice [Ackoff and Emery, 1972]) and of effectiveness (the dimension of Probable Effectiveness). The dimension of organizational choice that is absent is that of Relative Value or Intention. In its absence the question of efficiency can be of only academic interest.

We need to note also that any attempt to run a bureaucracy by "management by objectives" is fundamentally flawed by the fact that the objectives of supervisors for their sections are not the objectives of any one of their subordinates whose objectives are limited to their own allotted subtask. The same lack of identity holds between superintendents and the supervisors reporting to them.

So far I have discussed a bureaucratic section as if it were working at one place and time and was not beyond the ability of the supervisor to supervise. What special difficulties are posed for a bureaucratic organization when the section task is performed on different shifts, in separate workplaces or when the task involves several specialist skills in the work force? The bureaucratic form of organization copes with this problem with the greatest of ease, although with a further loss of efficiency—it simply throws up another level of traditional supervisory roles. As most organizations in real life are of this complex type it is not difficult to see why the overwhelming majority of schemes to introduce management by objectives and integrated information systems fail to get off the ground.

Let us now turn to the difficulties that self-managing groups face in controlling and coordinating their activities and in setting their objectives. Some of the difficulties are obvious. Control is more difficult because no one is so free of other duties that they can, at practically any time of their choosing, make an overall inspection and no individual has formal authority over any of the others. Coordination is difficult for much the same reason: no one can spend much of their time seeing how work is going with the other sub-groups, and no one can command help from others, they can only request help. Nor can they so readily request extra resources from the next line of command. The supervisor has usually been told, "This is the job for your section and these are the resources you will have at your command." It is not his or her fault if there turns out to be a mismatch, although he or she will probably justify the request on the grounds that things have changed rather than suggest that the superiors made a misjudgment or are incompetent. A self-managing group, on the other hand, will have started with a negotiated agreement about the resources they needed to perform their task. They will need hard evidence in order to renegotiate the agreement.

To add to these difficulties, no one in an extended or multiply skilled group will know at any one time who is doing what and where. Hence it can be difficult to know who best to seek immediate help from or who needs help. This is far more confusing than in a bureaucratically organized section. In such a section, one can count on each person being engaged with the subtask spelled out in the job specification at the work station allotted.

The situation is not all negative. Members of a self-managing group are in a position to subject each other to fairly continuous and close scrutiny, even when they are split into subgroups through which they rotate. This can be a direct scrutiny when one is helping another by sharing the same subtask or by just assisting with a less skilled part of the task. It can be indirect evaluation *if* the group members understand the technical interdependencies within the total group task. Thus, there is a considerable potential for exercising intra-group controls in a realistic and sensitive manner. They are not likely to be misled by the face a worker would show to a supervisor. Furthermore, the relation among members of such a group is a relation among "us," and hence requests for assistance are going to be very much more powerful than requests made in a "them-and-us" context.

These potentialities are not going to be realized in an extended group, let alone sustained, unless the difficulties discussed above are overcome.

The face-to-face semiautonomous group can take its own ongoing activity as a common reference for its constituent members. Seeing what is going on around them, the group can decide what they should be doing next, or be seen by others to be defaulting. In a bureaucratic section, extended or face-to-face, they have only to look over their shoulders to see the common reference—the supervisor. For the extended self-managing group, relations have to be mediated by reference to the group task as it is reflected in symbols that are free of temporal and spatial limitations and free of professional jargon.

Thus it is that self-managing groups require an *integrated information system*. It is not something imposed to enable someone in higher authority to keep track of the groups and the resources they use but a requirement that is intrinsic to their self-management. In the Hunsfoss example mentioned earlier, this was reflected in the demand for a central information center, continuously updated throughout each shift and across shifts by the operators themselves, to keep track of what was in the "pipeline" and to measure progress against targets. All parameters that could be significant for any part of the group task were recorded, not just those that, in the past, some supervisor or superintendent had a fad about. By the same token, standing rules and regulations for plant operation were gradually replaced by standard operating procedures that evolved with accumulating empirical evidence. I do not know how far the latter continued to evolve, but eight years after moving toward this form of organization I was able to observe that the information center was still the hub of operator activity and still growing in its comprehensiveness.

In discussing the need for an integrated information system that will allow group members to know what is happening in other parts of their system, I have been guilty of putting the cart before the horse for ease of exposition.

No integrated information system is of use unless there is:

• a need to know;
• an ability to understand what is conveyed;
• an ability to learn from what is understood.

The need to know will be felt by group members only if they accept responsibility for the achievement of group objectives. Many things, such as potential reward and trust of management, will affect the acceptance of responsibility. One thing is sure, however, and that is that a group will not accept responsibility, or will quickly regret accepting responsibility, for an open-ended commitment. Setting group goals as moving from output level A percent to output level A + 10 percent is one such open-ended commitment. It does not delimit the responsibilities of the group to the organization because it does not specify the inputs that are allowable and necessary. Appropriate objectives must so specify inputs and outputs that a group can demand to be judged on "value added" (or saved).

In bureaucratically organized systems hardly any supervisors or superintendents have any notion of the value added by their area of command. In a system of self-managing groups such information is mandatory, and hence it is necessary conscientiously to apply the tools of the management sciences. To seek to continue to manage by the seat of one's pants is to court disaster in one's industrial relations.

It will be obvious that input/output analysis at this level throughout an organization is going to provide an unusually high level of organizational self-consciousness, but only at the expense of considerable instrumentation and logging and the discomfort of considerable reorganization of those many support services that seem to defy objective evaluation.

Generation of this sort of information is of little use if it is understood by only a few in the group. Under those circumstances knowledge becomes power. By implication, this takes us beyond training for doing a specified job to education in what is involved in the total group task. Insofar as the task reaches from material inputs to a product, we are referring to polytechnical education. In bringing on-line a new fertilizer plant in Norway in 1967, we thought it revolutionary to provide a theoretical course of 200 hours for operators. To do the same thing in a highly capital intensive mining and milling operation in 1978, we have had to specify more than 500 hours of formal classroom education for operators.

Effective use of this knowledge and information cannot be taken for granted, nor can one place too much responsibility for combining these factors on experts outside the group. It becomes necessary for the group to have the means and the skill to monitor what it does with at least the proficiency that in past decades was shown by quality control engineers and production planners. Fortunately, the growth in computer assisted analyzers has made this possible.

Where these three conditions are met, a viable integrated information system is possible. Not only does this ensure that the operators are alert to what is going on in the process they are operating and hence able quickly to take appropriate action; it also provides the means for continuously learning how better to do their job, which, in my experience, is the critical criterion. If, at any point in the life of a plant, the learning curve plateaus, there is reason to believe that the management of the self-managing groups has gone bad.

This brings me to my last point. How does one manage an organization where the interface with the technical system is primarily controlled by self-managing groups of operatives? Not only has the foreman gone, but also the whole layer of production planners, quality controllers, etc., that Frederick

Taylor so fervently espoused. Even the role of departmental and shift superintendents is cast into doubt.

It seems to me that the primary tool of management is the negotiated agreement on group objectives. I have already alluded to the destructive nature of agreements that simply define outputs. Clearly, the agreement must cover the "minimum critical specifications" (to use Herbst's 1974/Vol. II phrase) for economic transformation of the inputs to the product, within legal limits imposed for such things as human safety and health. This should not be difficult for management who, after all, have skilled resources at their command, or on call. Since the negotiations are about the operation of a technical system that has some unifying character, this should be a much easier problem than carving a group task up into individual work stations and manshift units (on spurious estimates of "norms"; cf. Baldamus, 1961). It needs only to be added that the negotiations are about a *socio*-technical system, and hence among the minimum critical specifications to be negotiated are the selection of group members, their training and their access to other skilled personnel.

The point I have wished to make in this paper is that the move toward self-management in complex organizations is going to mean more conscious management, not more of the laissez-faire, seat of the pants management which is the bread and butter of the bureaucracies.

References

Ackoff, R.L. and F.E. Emery. 1972. *On Purposeful Systems*. Chicago: Aldine-Atherton.

Baldamus, W. 1961. *Efficiency and Effort: An Analysis of Industrial Administration*. London: Tavistock Publications.

Emery, F.E. 1959. *Characteristics of Socio-Technical Systems*. London: Tavistock Institute Document 527. Revised in *The Emergence of a New Paradigm of Work*. Canberra: Centre for Continuing Education, Australian National University, 1978; also in *Design of Jobs*, edited by L.E. Davis and J.C. Taylor. Harmondsworth: Penguin Books, 1972. Vol. II, pp. 157–86.

Emery, F.E. and E. Thorsrud. 1976. *Democracy at Work*. Leiden: Martinus Nijhoff.

Herbst, P.G. 1974. *Socio-Technical Design: Strategies in Multidisciplinary Research*. London: Tavistock Publications. Revised version of Chapter 2 in Vol. II, "Designing with Minimal Critical Specifications," pp. 294–302.

Kuhn, T.S. 1962. *The Structure of Scientific Revolutions*. Chicago: Phoenix.

Miller, E.J. 1959. "Technology, Territory and Time: The Internal Differentiation of Complex Production Systems." *Human Relations*, 12:243–72; London: Tavistock Institute Document 526. Vol. II, pp. 385–404.

Fred Emery

The Assembly Line
Its Logic and Our Future[1]

Nowhere do the issues involved in the democratization of work come so sharply into focus as in discussion of the future of the assembly line.

The principles of the assembly line seem to be the basis on which Western affluence is built, and yet it creates a multitude of inhumane, degrading jobs, jobs that increasingly have to be filled by second-class citizens. The challenge is to achieve the low cost of mass-produced goods without creating the human cost. Two facts have led me to choose the automobile assembly line as an example within which to spell out the general principles.

First, Henry Ford's introduction of the continuous flow conveyor to the assembly of automobiles was the apogee of a modern mode of human management, a mode that started to emerge with Frederick Taylor and Gilbreth in the late nineteenth century. The much publicized fiasco of the General Motors Lordstown plant in 1972 seemed to mark the end of that era. Volvo's announcement, within the following months, of the radically new concept for its Kalmar assembly plant seemed to herald the beginning of a new era of human management.

Second, the logic of human management that was enshrined by the car makers became the logic that was worshiped by practically all other large scale manufacturers. It came to be seen by the 1940s and 1950s as the only *sure* way of manufacturing increasingly complex products at a cost that could serve a mass market. As the real cost of labor has increased through the twentieth century, it has been seen as the *only possible* way of creating mass markets or of meeting the demands these mass markets make for industrial inputs. So it was not too surprising to find a process industry like ICI (UK) as the leading proponent in Britain, in the postwar years, of the philosophy of Henry Ford.

What I am suggesting is that the logic of the car assembly line is a keystone—probably *the* keystone—to prevailing twentieth-century concepts of human management. The logic of production by a continuous flow line was

[1]Excerpted from *Futures We Are In*. Leiden: Martinus Nijhoff, 1976.

well understood in the early phases of industrialization. Both Charles Babbage and Karl Marx spelled out this logic. The logic was an "if X then Y" logic. If a complex production task was broken down into a set of constituent tasks, then the level of craft skills required was lowered and hence the cost of labor was lowered. At the extreme, a class of unskilled labor emerged to perform the very elementary tasks that practically always remain after a complex task has been broken down to its minimum skill requirements. Such unskilled laborers would have no part to play in craft production. There is another valuable side of this coin that was not obvious until a much later date: if one lowers the level of craft skill needed for a product, it becomes much easier to switch to production of major variations of that product, e.g., from swords to ploughshares. Massive reskilling of craftsmen is not needed.

Once the partition of a task had been successful in reducing the necessary level of craft skills, it was only natural that further partitions leading to even broader and cheaper labor markets should be sought. World War II gave a further great stimulus to this approach. The military demanded large scale production of very complex machines when often the only available labor force was that conscripted from outside the traditional industrial work force, e.g., women, pensioners and peasants. The know-how flowed over from blue collar work to the organization of offices. Insurance offices, taxation offices, etc., organized for mass flow production of documents.

However, to realize the economic advantages of task segmentation it was necessary to cope with several sources of cost *inherent* in the method:
- transfer costs,
- standardization,
- "balancing the line,"
- external supervision and "pacing."

Transfer Costs

Individual craft production requires a minimum movement of the object under production. Partitioning of production requires transport of the object between each of the work stations at which someone is performing a different subtask. The costs are those of sheer physical movement, of repositioning so that the next operation can proceed and "waiting time" when valuable semi-products are, as it were, simply in storage. Henry Ford's introduction of conveyor belts to car assembly seemed to be the natural outcome of the attempt to reduce these transport costs. Conveyor chains had already transformed the Chicago slaughterhouses. Palletization and fork-lift trucks continue to reduce these costs in assembly areas where continuous belts or chains are not justifiable.

Standardization

Partitioning of a production process was simply not an economic proposition unless there was a fair probability that the separately produced parts could be reconstituted to yield a workable version of the final product. It would not have to be as good as the craft-produced product if its cost was sufficiently lower. This was obvious enough with the eighteenth-century flow-line production of pully blocks at the Woolwich Naval Arsenal and the early nineteenth-century production of Whitney's muskets. Reduction of this inherent cost has a long history. From Maudslay's slide rest onward there has been a continuous evolution in specialized tools, machine, jigs and fixtures to enable relatively unskilled labor continuously to replicate relatively skilled operations to a higher degree of standardization. The aim throughout was that expressed by Whitney:

> To form the tools so that the tools themselves shall fashion the work and give to every part its just proportion—which when once accomplished, will give expedition, uniformity and exactness to the whole.

The most radical developments emerged in the second quarter of this century with metrology, the sophisticated concept of tolerance levels, expressed in statistical quality control and national standards authorities. The difficult emergence of this latter revolution in Australian industry is well documented in chapter 7 of Mellor's (1958) volume of the history of World War II.

"Balancing the Line"

This is a problem that does not arise with the individual craftsman. Whatever the problems with a given phase of production on a particular lot of raw materials, one can proceed immediately to the next phase as soon as one is satisfied with what has been done. One does not have to wait to catch up with oneself. When the task is partitioned that is not possible. Each set of workers are skilled or, rather, semiskilled in only their own subtask. They are not skilled to help clear any bottleneck or make up any shortfall in other parts of the line. They can simply stand idle and wait. Theoretically, there is in a flow line an *iron law of proportionality* such as Marx writes about. Theoretically, it should be like the recipe for a cake: so many hours of this kind of labor, so many of that kind of labor, etc., and, presto, the final product. Unfortunately for the application of the theory, it is not as simple as making cakes.

Balancing the line to reduce downtime was an on-the-line art of observation until Taylor and Gilbreth came on the scene. Their contribution was Methods,

Time, Management (MTM). At last the balancing of a line seemed to be a science. Controlled observation and measurements seemed to offer a way of not just balancing the labor requirements of the major segments of a line, but of scientifically planning the work load and skill level of each and every individual work station. Planning and measuring costs money, but there has seemed no other way to reduce the downtime losses inherent in the original fractionation of production.

Let us now look briefly at the fourth major source of costs inherent in line assembly. Then we can ask what all this means.

External Supervision and "Pacing"

So long as the individual craftsman produced the whole product, control and coordination of work on the various subtasks was no problem. The workers managed that themselves. With the fractionation of production a special class of work emerged, the work of supervision. Each person on the assembly line has to attend to his or her own piece of the work, and hence someone else must coordinate what is happening at the different work stations, reallocate work when the line becomes unbalanced and re-enforce work standards when individual performance drifts away from them. A major headache has been the near universal tendency of workers on fractionated tasks to depart from planned work times. The self-pacing that enables the craftsperson/producer to vary the work pace and yet maintain good targets for overall production times appears to be absent from small fractionated tasks that are repeated endlessly. Tighter supervision and incentive payment schemes seemed appropriate forms of the carrot and stick procedure to replace this element of self-pacing.

The moving line emerged as the major innovation. Once properly manned for a given speed, it seemed that this speed had only to be maintained by the supervisors to ensure that planned work times would be maintained. Dawdling at any work station would quickly reveal itself in persons moving off station to try to finish their parts. However, it is not quite so simple as that. It is possible on some work stations to let unfinished work go down the line with a chance of its not being detected until the product is in the consumer's hands. The main point was readily learned. The conveyor was a means not just of lowering transfer costs but also of reducing supervisory costs. At certain tempos the line even gave operators a satisfactory sense of work rhythm, a feeling of being drawn along by the work. Davis's (1966) study even suggests that the contribution to control may often be the main justification of the conveyor.

What I have spelled out is old hat to any production engineer. Nevertheless, it prepares the ground for the point of what follows.

We have heard a great deal lately about the demise of the automobile assembly line. The Volvo plant at Kalmar (opened in 1974) does not even have conveyor belts. The European Economic Community pronounced in 1973 that the assembly line would have to be abolished in the European car industry.

I suggest that the Kalmar plant does not represent any departure from the basic principles of mass flow-line production. In the first place, decision makers there are still seeking the maximum economic advantages to be gained from fractionation of the overall task. In the second place, the plant and its organization have been designed to reduce the same inherent costs of mass flow production, i.e., costs of transfer, standardization, balancing, coordination and pacing. Kalmar is designed as a mass-production flow-line to produce an economically competitive product. There is no radical departure from the principles of flow-line production, only from its practice.

Note, however, that I previously stressed that their aim was "maximum economic advantage from fractionation," *not* maximum fractionation. What they have done is to recognize that the costs we have discussed are inherent in production based on fractionated tasks. The further one pushes fractionation, the greater these costs become, particularly the costs other than transfer because they are more related to human responsiveness. *The objective of gaining maximum economic advantage from fractionation cannot be the objective of maximum fractionation.* There is some *optimal* level to be sought at a point before the gains are whittled away by rising costs.

Why has this logic been so obvious to the Kalmar designers and yet has appeared to escape other car plant designers? I do not think it is just because MTM, quality control, production supervision, designers, etc., operate in separate boxes with their own departmental goals. After all, at the plant design phase there are usually opportunities for the various specialties to come together. I think the reason lies deeper. If we look at the traditional practices in designing a mass flow line, we find that a critical assumption has slipped in and been reinforced by the widespread reliance on MTM, as a planning tool and as a control tool. This assumption is that it must be possible for each individual worker to be held responsible by an external supervisor for individual performance. On this assumption MTM goes beyond being a planning tool to determine or redetermine the probable labor requirements of sections of the line. It becomes part of the detailed day-to-day supervisory control over production. Under this impetus fractionation heads down to the lowest common denominator (lcd) of the labor on the line.

The same assumption that a line must be built up from the individually supervised one worker/one shift unit has gone into the design of algorithms to determine line balance. Ingall (1965) has reviewed 10 or so of the major algorithms. They all embody the same assumption. They go further along with MTM to assert that this is a firm building block by assuming that, on average, different operators work at the same pace; on average, an individual operator works at the same pace throughout a shift; on average, cycle time of the operation is irrelevant; on average, learning on the job can be ignored; on average, variations in parts and equipment can be ignored.

An average is just that, an average. It represents the mean value of a set of different observed states of a system parameter. It does not even tell us whether the exact average state has ever occurred. One thing is pretty sure: at any one time on a line it is most improbable that all aspects are operating at their average value. Typically, something is always non-average—wrong—and when one thing is wrong so are half a dozen other things.

The practical problems of balancing a line simply cannot be solved by abstracting this aspect from the total system of potential gains and inherent costs of flow production. As Ingall (1965) concludes in his review of assembly line balancing:

> Knowing whether these problems occur together is important because analysing them separately is not sufficient if they do. Using the "sum" of the results obtained by analysing each problem separately as the procedure for the combined problem can be a dangerous pastime. (1965:4)

The practical significance of the balancing problem may be gauged from the finding of Kilbridge and Wester (1963) that the U.S. automobile industry wasted about 25 percent of assembly-line workers' time through uneven work assignment. No doubt this figure had been reduced at Lordstown in 1972.

I have wandered a little afield because I wished to stress how far this assumption about the individual building block has unquestionably grown into the professional ways of looking at the assembly line. It is this, I suggest, which has prevented others from seeing the obvious logic of the line as did the Kalmar designers. This hidden assumption has, I think, had a further distorting effect on thinking about the line.

Some people in the car industry during the 1950s and 1960s became sensitive to the fact that pursuit of maximum fractionation was self-defeating. They realized it was not at all like the engineering problem of pursuing maximum aircraft speed by reducing friction and drag. They realized it was not a problem to be solved by the grease of yet higher relative pay, by "featherbedding" or by any of those things that Walter Reuther of the U.S. Automobile Workers' Union bitterly referred to as "gold-plating the sweat-shop."

The response of these people to these critical insights was to look again at the building block, the one-worker/one-shift unit, to see what could be done about that. They did not question whether the individual was the appropriate block for building on.

One proposal to arise from this was to employ on the line only people who were at, or very close to, the lowest common denominator used by the MTM and the planners, i.e., donkeys for donkey work. This proposal does not look so good now as the international pool of cheap migrant labor dries up. In any case, there was little future in this proposal. Provided the line designers pursued the same twisted logic of maximum fractionation, they would inevitably design around an even lower, cheaper common denominator and the other costs would rise again.

The other proposal was to discard the concept of an lcd and accept job enlargement or enrichment up to a point which would come closest to the optimal fractionation for a majority of the people on the line. Imposing such enrichment on the minority whose optimum was below this level was an immediately obvious practical flaw. A more deep-seated flaw was that this job-enrichment approach argued from consideration of only one aspect of the system: task fractionation. It did not simultaneously confront the other parameters of the system: balancing, pacing, etc.

These parameters constitute a *system* of production. If some people on the line are responsible for only one parameter and someone else has the problem of looking after the other parameters, inefficiency and trouble have been designed in (Ackoff and Emery, 1972:222–27). No designers in their right senses would design a purely technical system in that way unless there were a very considerable lag time between changes on that parameter and changes on the other system parameters. I think I am safe in saying that no such protective lag time exists for the parameter of degree of task fractionation in a mass flow line. If something goes wrong with, for instance, the line balance or pace, the operator can very quickly become frustrated by a stoppage and consequent break in the rhythm of work or be temporarily slotted into some other station on the line.

An organization like this is basically unstable and is rendered even more so when the other party (or parties) looking after the other parameters live in the more powerful world of management, i.e., when communications are subject to the constant distortion of messages going between "them" and "us." Inevitably, the supervisors, MTM, work programmers, etc., respond to the predictable system problems by pushing for more fractionation and tighter controls.

The instability I am referring to is not that of the technical system of mass flow production. The instability is that of a superimposed organization which has very different roots in history. This organizational instability has very serious practical consequences. First, it makes it pretty well impossible to enrich individual jobs, either by a formal program or informally by supervisors who have taken to heart their exposure to courses on human relations in industry. As the pressures build up, the screws are back on again. Second, it is not just on the line that the pressures are experienced. As the instabilities accumulate to their recurrent crises on the line, all levels of staff are sucked down to coping with deficiencies in performance of the levels below them. Even the plant manager lives by the hour-to-hour performance of the line. Third, the almost universal experience of these phenomena of instability has created a sustained history of, almost an addiction to, technical solutions that would design people out of the system, or at least "fool-proof" technologies.

It is in looking at the mass flow production line as a *socio-technical system* that we come to what is really radical about the Kalmar design. The designers approached their task with an awareness that the problems of flow-line production could be theoretically approached in different organizational designs. At one extreme they literally examined the old cottage industry. More seriously, they compared the Norwegian experiences (Thorsrud and Emery, 1969; Emery and Thorsrud, Vol. II) with the semiautonomous work group as the building unit, as against the traditional individual/shift/work station unit.

The most striking outcome was the discovery that, in an appropriately skilled and sized work group, all the key parameters of mass flow production could come together and be controlled vis-à-vis each other at that level. Picturesquely, this was labeled "a lot of little factories within a factory." In terms of how we picture a factory, this the groups are not. Walk around Kalmar and you see nothing that even looks like a lot of little workshops producing their own cars. In system terms, however, it is a very apt description, a very valid design criterion.

This becomes more apparent if we look at the production groups formed at Kalmar. The first effects are rather like those some farmers have gained from cooperation. Individually, their resources gave them little or no freedom of movement, and they had to ride with a market that was basically out of their control. Collectively, they have found new degrees of freedom and have started to shape their markets to allow even more freedom.

Formation of semiautonomous groups on the Kalmar assembly line has given workers a cycle time and buffers that would be negligible if split up for individual work stations. Split up in this way, no one could take an untimed coffee break; grouped together, everyone can, without increasing overall downtime. On individual work stations, everyone has to meet the standard work on that particular job, minute by minute; in the group setting, variations in individual levels of optimal performance can be met hour by hour. Those who prefer repetitive tasks can get them; those that need to be told what to do will be told by others in the group. Within the range of their task, the group can balance their work without outside assistance. If quality control is among the group's responsibilities and they are given time allowance for this, it can be within their capabilities.

Now we come to the fundamental matter of coordination, control and pacing.[2] If a semiautonomous work group is not willing to exercise control and coordination over its members, then the design flow lines must go back to the traditional model. At this point, I must rely on experience, not theory. The experience, over more than 20 years with a wide range of technologies and societies, is simply this: *if reasonably sized groups have accepted a set of production targets and have the resources to pursue them at reasonable reward to themselves, they will better achieve those targets than they would if each person was under external supervisory control.* If a theory is required, then I think it need be no more than that spelled out in the six psychological requirements defined in 1964 (Thorsrud and Emery). In groups that have sufficient autonomy and are sufficiently small to allow face-to-face learning, these criteria can be maximally realized. It has been the realization of these individual human requirements that has enabled semiautonomous group working of mass flow lines to do what could not be done by MTM and algorithms for balancing the lines. There is also no economic way in which the individual psychological requirements could be maximally recognized by psychological testing procedures to fit individuals to the individual/shift slots of MTM.

I have suggested that the revolution at Kalmar has not been that of throwing out the assembly line. The revolutionary change began with the eradication of an organizational principle of one worker/one shift/one station; a principle that had no intrinsic relation to the design of assembly lines. Further, I have suggested that the payoff in the change began with selecting as the building block a socio-technical unit—an appropriately skilled and sized semiautonomous group—that had the potential of simultaneously controlling, from their own immediate experience, the basic set of parameters of gain and cost in the total system.

It might be excusable to expand a little on this last point. Just as in scientific fields one of the most critical strategic breakthroughs is discovery of the appropriate "unit of analysis," so in production systems it is discovery of the basic "unit of design." Identifying "unit operations" was a classic break-through in the tremendously complex problems of chemical engineering. With this in mind, the British Social Science Research Council funded an international, interdisciplinary team "to devise a conceptual scheme for the analysis of men-machine-equipment relations with the more common unit operations" (Emery, 1966). The conclusion of this study was that *the basic unit for design of socio-technical systems must itself be a socio-technical unit* and *have the characteristics of an open system.*

---

[2]Volvo engineers came up with an ingenious technical solution to the transfer problems: the individual self-propelled carriage. This allows the groups to vary the times put into each car while maintaining average flow on to the next groups.

In design terms, this represents the lowest level at which it is possible to optimize jointly the human and technical with respect to environmental requirements (the overall system inputs and outputs). Failure to recognize this may lead to design decisions being made solely on technical and economic cost criteria with consequent inefficiencies from:
- excess operating costs,
- maintenance difficulties,
- lack of growth in system performance,
- high overheads for control and supervision,
- lack of adaptability to market shifts (Emery, 1966).

Now, after nearly 10 years of living with this conclusion, I think I am prepared to argue even more strongly for a further conclusion unanimously arrived at by the study team: the best designs will be those that make the most use of the highest human potentials one could expect to find in any average group of eight to 10 human beings. My argument is this: first, there is a basic fact about systems that is simply ducked by the current plethora of so-called systems theoreticians, that "it is not simply the fact of linkages but rather the principle according to which all linkages fall together in *one controlling order* which makes an organization" (Feibleman and Friend, 1969). "Every system has one and only one construction principle . . . *unitas multiplex*" (Angyal, 1941). The overriding principle of the mass flow production lines we are talking about is "economically productive." Any designer who creates a section which was itself unconcerned about being an economically productive part of the total system has created a "tool," not a genuine part of the system. As a tool it may be good or bad, sharp or blunt, but it is still a dull, nonadapting thing; it does not respond to changes in circumstances, it does not learn, it simply wears in and wears out. A genuine part of a system embodies in its own *modus operandi* the same governing principle as the overall system. In adapting it draws closer to the principle of the system.

The second aspect of systems design goes one significant step further to note that "systems are specific forms of the distribution of members in a dimensional domain. . . . In aggregates it is significant that the parts are added; in a system it is significant that the parts are arranged" (Angyal, 1941).

The usual design of an assembly line does nothing to create system properties in any section of the line. It simply adds more of this or that quanta of labor to the section. In practice, it sets up an inexorable demand for labor once the designed line comes into operation. When reality inevitably departs from theory there is a buildup of pressure on some individual work stations. Everyone else insists that their work station is a full house and hence additional work stations have to be squeezed in to cope with the peak points. That is, the original design predicates a creep to overmanning. Adaptive rearrangement, which would be the first response of a system design, comes a very poor second in these designs.

It is easy to fob off responsibility for this trend to trade union pressures. It is not primarily due to this. It is primarily the result of the original engineering design. There is sufficient evidence that unions would agree to different designs that offer real advantages to their members. If what the unions are offered are aggregative designs from which the employers hope to maximize their economic gains through maximizing fractionation, then the unions must exploit this game to the maximum of their ability. Until recently, the unions have not had the alternative possibility of sending the employers back to the drawing board. They have not had this possibility because they have not had the knowledge of alternatives that enabled Gyllenhamer of Volvo to send his designers back and back again to the drawing boards until they got a really new concept for the Kalmar plant. The Kalmar design finished up as a genuine systems design. By the first criterion, the groups were enabled to confront, and take responsibility for, the basic parameters that determined whether they were an economically productive section. By the second criterion, the groups were enabled and encouraged to meet variance in their circumstances by rearrangement of their own efforts. Adding further permanent members was very much a last resort, to be used only after making-do by rearranging themselves or temporarily borrowing labor from neighboring groups. As we had seen from the earliest coal-mining studies, there was a marked reluctance of groups to accept any change of group membership until they had done their best to cope with their work problem on their own.

There is a third and last step in systems thinking that is, I believe, important to the design of productive systems. In the statement of the first two principles I may have appeared to play down the characteristics of the human beings that are the indispensable elements of socio-technical systems.

I have spoken simply of "overriding principles" and the priority of "positions of parts and the arrangement and rearrangement of the parts." The third principle is, however, that "the more the inherent properties of parts are utilized as codeterminants of positional values . . . the greater the organisation of the whole" (Angyal, 1941:27). It states that higher levels of organization can be achieved only by the fuller use of the inherent properties of parts as codeterminants of positional values. "The human organism, for example, is highly economical in this respect: it carries a minimal load of irrelevant properties of parts; most of the properties are 'utilized,' that is, are codeterminants of the positional value of the part" (Angyal, 1941). This principle means, quite simply, that the best design for any productive system will be that which not only allows that the goals of any subsystem, any part, embody in some manner the overall system goals (Principle I) but allows any such part to be self-managing to the point that it will seek to cope with external variances in the first instance by rearranging its own use of resources (Principle II). The best design will be that which also recruits or develops its constituent parts so that they have the intrinsic properties suited to the demands on the position they occupy. At the simplest level, the third principle would indicate designing-in a degree of multiskilling that would meet the probable rearrangements of the section about its tasks. At a more sophisticated level of design, account would be taken of the human potentialities for reasoning, creativity and leadership that might be expected in any group of 8 or 10 human beings. This would mean designing the social system of the small group so that it becomes an instrument for its members—something they largely manage themselves—not vice versa. Then it becomes *variety increasing* for them, and they are enabled to pursue not only production goals but also purposes and even ideals that pertain to themselves.

References

Ackoff, R.L. and F.E. Emery. 1972. *On Purposeful Systems*. Chicago: Aldine-Atherton.

Angyal, A. 1941. *Foundations for a Science of Personality*. New York: The Commonwealth Fund. Reprinted as "A Logic of Systems," in *Systems Thinking: Selected Readings*, Vol. 1, edited by F.E. Emery, Harmondsworth: Penguin Books, 1969.

Davis, L.E. 1966. "The Design of Jobs." *Industrial Relations*, 6:21–45.

Emery, F.E. 1966. " 'Unit Operations' as a Unit of Analysis" in *The Emergence of a New Paradigm of Work*, edited by F.E. Emery. Canberra: Centre for Continuing Education, Australian National University.

Emery, F.E. and E. Thorsrud. 1992. "The Norskhydro Fertilizer Plant." Vol. II, pp. 492–507.

Feibleman, J. and J.W. Friend. 1969. "The Structure and Function of Organization." In *Systems Thinking: Selected Readings*, Vol. 1, edited by F.E. Emery. Harmondsworth: Penguin Books.

Ingall, E.J. 1965. "Review of Assembly Line Balancing." *Journal of Industrial Engineering*, 16.

Kilbridge, M.N. and L. Wester. 1963. "The Assembly Line Model-Mix Sequencing Problem." *Proceedings of the Third International Conference on Operations Research*. Oslo.

Mellor, D.P. 1958. *The Role of Science and Industry*, Volume 5, Series 4 of *Australia in the War of 1939–45*. Canberra: Australian War Memorial.

Thorsrud, E. and F.E. Emery. 1964. *Industrielt Demokrati*. Oslo: Oslo University Press. Reissued in 1969 as F.E. Emery and E. Thorsrud, *Form and Content in Industrial Democracy: Some Experiences from Norway and Other European Countries*. London: Tavistock Publications.

———. 1969. *Mot en ny bedriftsorganisasjon*. Oslo: Tanum. Reissued in 1976 as F.E. Emery and E. Thorsrud, *Democracy at Work*. Leiden: Martinus Nijhoff.

Fred Emery

The Second Design Principle
Participation and the Democratization of Work[1]

Two Basic Organizational Designs

In choosing their organizational designs, people do not confront an infinite range of choice. Far from it. If their organizations are to be purposive, they have to be adaptive over a wide range of evolving circumstances. The alternative is some sort of servomechanism with a fixed repertoire of responses, capable of surviving only within a very narrow range of foreseeable conditions. To achieve wide adaptiveness redundancy has to be built into the system. This is an important property, as with each arithmetic increase in redundancy the reliability of the system tends to increase exponentially (Pierce, 1964).

There are two basic ways that redundancy can be built in:

By adding redundant parts to the system. Each part is replaceable; as and when one part fails, another takes over.

By adding redundant functions to the parts. At any one time some of the functions of any part will be redundant to the role it is playing at the time; as and when a part fails in the function it is performing, other parts can assume the function; so long as a part retains any of its functional capabilities (i.e., functional relative to system requirements) it is of some value to the system.

The first design of redundant parts has been described by Mumford (1967) as the *megamachine,* and he has traced its long Asian history and more recent Western debut. Feibleman and Friend (1969) characterized the logical properties of the first design as *subjective seriality* in which "the governing relation is *asymmetrical* dependence. The sharing of parts is necessary to one of the parts but not to both" (p.36). The second design is characterized by them as *complementary seriality,* in which "the governing relation is *symmetrical* dependence. The sharing of parts is necessary to both of the parts. Neither part can survive separation" (p.36), " . . . parts are on a parity with respect to their relations with others parts, and each is dependent upon the other" (p.38). It is of interest

[1]A reproduction of part of Chapter 4 of *Futures We Are In.* Leiden: Martinus Nijhoff, 1976.

that their analysis of *the structure and function of organization* revealed no more than just these two basic designs at the level of purposeful systems.

If redundancy is sought by having redundant parts, then there must be special control mechanisms (specialized parts) to determine which parts are failing and have to be rendered redundant and which have to be activated for any particular response to be adaptive. If the control is to be reliable it, too, must have redundant parts, and hence the question of yet another level of control emerges. The more difficult it becomes to determine the failure of dependent parts in time to make adaptive replacements, the more the levels of control tend to proliferate (compare the many levels of control to be found in an army or an oil refinery with the few that are found necessary in a car assembly plant).

One can expect a bias toward choosing the first design if
• the costs of the individual parts are low,
• there are long lead times available for the organization to learn new modes of response.

Certainly, once this first basic design is chosen, efforts will be made to keep down the cost of the individual part by sustaining a pool of unemployed, obtaining access to pools of poor and preferably dispossessed peasantry (e.g., the *Gastarbeiter* of Germany and Australia's postwar migration scheme) or specializing and standardizing the function of the individual parts to minimize costs of training and retraining (Taylorism).

Regarding the second source of bias toward the megamachine it is worth starting our considerations from the often made observation that this is a great way to run a railway or an army:

> There are irrefutable advantages to this kind of organisation. Discipline is good, errors in routine procedures rarely go unchecked, and if the very top man is an exceedingly able executive he can usually make the whole organisation jump to his command very quickly. It usually takes a long time to build, and it is at its most successful when the function of the organisation is to control a very large number of people all doing more or less the same thing. It is the way most armies are organised—platoon, company, battalion, brigade, division, corps, army— and if you want to make a million men advance or retreat at a few hours notice it is hard to think of a better system. (Jay, 1970:73)

Armies fight for short periods of their life under conditions of great uncertainty, great turbulence. Hence it is hard to reconcile Jay's enthusiasm for organizing armies in this way with the contention that they are only adaptive when allowed "long lead times for learning." It is also hard to reconcile with the organizational logic that underlies the contention that *this type of system is inherently error-amplifying*. The governing principle of asymmetrical dependence means that errors will leak in from the environment like water from a sieve. It is in no one's interest to be rendered redundant because of association with an error or failure. Even without that psychological weakness, the relation of asymmetrical dependence will ensure that the flow upward of information from one level of control to the next will take the following form:

$$T = (1-F)^n \quad .$$

If there were five good people reporting to a manager, people who were truthful (T) eight times out of ten, i.e.,

$$T = (1.0-0.2)^5 \quad .$$

then there would be, on average, only one in three occasions when it could be said that this must be sound advice because they are unanimous. However, the same principle applies at all levels. If this manager and five others at the same level have been well chosen and hence are right nine times out of ten, then the chances of their superior getting such a good straight message through them from the level below are, by the same arithmetic, 0.002—twice in a thousand such communications! (Beer, 1972). This very disturbing property of error-amplification arises in a system based on asymmetrical dependence because each manager must seek to maintain the asymmetrical dependence of subordinates. Hence managers will seek to ensure that their subordinates each give *independent* judgments and that they cannot go into collusion to influence decisions. But the mathematics of this are inexorable. The more this aim of controlling subordinates is achieved, the greater the error; even if the subordinates are not psychologically motivated to protect themselves by hiding their errors.

Given this inherent weakness, a major part of the effort of utilizing cheap dependent labor by this first design has gone into control systems that will minimize the weakness. Thus Jay, in the above quote, says that in these types of organizations discipline is usually good. I suggest that in these types of organizations one usually finds good discipline not because they naturally create good discipline but because they cannot function without imposing good discipline. That they cannot function unless their individual parts are not only replaceable but are also so threatened by punishment or withdrawal of rewards that they will behave in a preprogrammed manner regardless of the evidence of their senses or their common sense. Lewis Mumford has documented the vicious practices of torture and maiming that were introduced with the earliest emergence of the megamachine. Poet laureate Masefield has documented the inhuman disciplinary practices of the Royal Navy up to the age of steam.

Taylor and his contemporaries simply devised new "sticks and carrots" so that this organizational design could function within societies like the United States of America where the Constitution forbids "cruel and unusual punishment." There was no change in the aim; the aim remained that of blocking the holes of the sieve, preventing error getting into the system. By elaborate preprogramming of the parts at the work face and of the control systems, expected contingencies could be met and failure of a part quickly identified. As Jay (1970) observed, such an organization "usually takes a long time to build." Standard operating procedures, rules and regulations and training manuals have to be multiplied to meet the ever emerging contingencies. They can rarely be wiped off the book because there can rarely be agreement among the control agencies that such contingencies might not occur again. New contingencies are slow to be recognized because of the possibility that they are inventions of subordinates trying to cover up mistakes that might lead to their redundancy.

I can now summarize the learning properties of an organizational design based on redundant parts. There is an optimal amount of error that is necessary for learning by any type of system. The error-amplifying characteristic of this type of system threatens to swamp it with so much error that it is reduced to the response strategy of an addictive gambler (or a cat in a Thorndike puzzle box), i.e., to stick rigidly to a system, right or wrong. The major active response to error—even those errors that are necessary for learning—is to prevent it from getting into the system and to eliminate or send to limbo any part that appears to be associated with the intake of error or its perpetuation. With this kind of learning where is the adaptiveness?

Jay is undoubtedly correct in stating that with this sort of system it is hard to think of a better one "if you want to make a million men advance or retreat at a few hours notice." It is possible, with months of work, to preprogram so many to start to advance or to start to retreat within hours of the starter's gun. Adaptive control, however, more or less finishes after that point, unless one has preprogrammed reserve forces to be fed into the subsequent action. Field Marshal Haig released a vast preprogrammed army across the front at the Somme at 7.30 a.m. on July 1, 1916. At 3.00 p.m. that day, he had precious little idea of where his many divisions were or what they were doing, although none of them had gone more than a mile or so from where they were at dawn. They had disappeared into the fog of war. This sort of information flow hardly augurs well for adaptability. When the Passchendaele offensive opened on July 31, 1917, there was little evidence that learning had occurred in the previous year. As I said earlier, this type of organization needs a long lead time for learning. So long, indeed, that Liddell-Hart (1944) said that armies normally prepare themselves to fight their last war.

The criterion of survival can be somewhat misleading in circumstances where the competing parties are all organized on the first design principle. The big battalions win the wars but lose the peace because of the price they pay for victory.

It should be clear by now that choice of the design principle of redundant parts predetermines the ideals that such a society will pursue.[2] Person will be set against person in the asymmetrical master/servant relation to ensure that their collectivized labor will produce *Plenty* in the form of pyramids, skyscrapers or other such indicators of the greatness of their masters. Better ways to ensure increased productivity will evolve and, when evolved, be widely adopted. But, more and more, people will doubt whether these means of increasing plenty are reconcilable with the quality of human life. *Truth* will be a precious commodity in an environment where it decays so quickly in transmission to the key decision makers. Every effort will be made to arrive at better ways to establish the truth and to disseminate such methods when they emerge. The good will be an ideal of high standing, as befits an ideal. Science becomes the new fountain of wisdom and becomes increasingly mistrusted in societies based on this first design principle. The concept of the "good Samaritan" evolves into the Welfare State. Good deeds are increasingly done by numbers, and the poor, deserving or not, wonder whether they are not just replaceable ciphers in a code that they cannot break.

The ideal of *Beauty,* an ideal which should move all people, suffers a particularly cruel fate in systems designed on this principle. The ideal becomes embodied in that which is biggest, whitest and most durable, and capable of demolition tomorrow. The criteria of beauty—those which attract patronage— are grandeur and being esoteric. Both place beauty beyond what might be aspired to by a servant in a system based on master/servant relations, i.e., subjective seriality. The alternative design based on redundant functions (multifunctional parts) has been the favored design in the Western cultural tradition, if not always in practice. It also appears to have been the general preference in human societies up to the point where swidden agriculture gave way to societies based primarily on sedentary cultivation and the use of metals.

The basic conditions favoring the alternative design are

- The individual parts are costly (e.g., well educated or skilled) or highly valued.
- Adaptation has to be to a highly variable, complexly intercorrelated environment, i.e., one in which a great deal of potential error is present and is not randomized.

In contrast to the first design, this one is essentially *error attenuating.* The

---

[2]The following three criteria for identifying an ideal are taken from Churchman and Ackoff (1949).

system, by its own functioning, tends to suppress errors that come into the system. The formula given by Beer is

$$T = (1-F^n) .$$

Thus, if, as in the first example, five people reporting to a manager are each usually right in their judgment eight times out of ten, then

$$T = (1.0-(0.2)^5) .$$

Only about three times in 10,000 will they unanimously give him the wrong advice. The relation of symmetrical dependence means that they will check with each other as to the quality of the advice they were thinking of giving. We have assumed that they are no better as individual managers than those in the first example and no better than each other. Each is assumed fallible on two occasions out of ten. They will not, however, be fallible in the same ways and hence by working via this second design they help in suppressing each other's tendency to err.

With this quality a great deal of error can be accepted into the system and learned from. Rigid barriers of standing operating procedures and manuals do not have to be defensively manned as in the first design. Error is coped with by continuous learning and rearrangement of functions, not by prescription and rearrangement of parts. In this system advantage can be taken of the principle that the total sum of error in the system is equivalent to the square root of the sum of the square of the errors in each part. Attention can be directed to the weakest link and not to the specialized controlling parts as required in the first system. A further distinction between the two designs arises when the sources of error in the environment are to some extent correlated: "it never rains but it pours." The first design is at its best when the sources of error are independent and only randomly occur together. Where this is not naturally the case, special efforts are devoted to approximate this condition, e.g., keeping external relations in special compartments and being very secretive about what is going on in those compartments. The second design learns improved adaptation by exposing itself to the difficulties arising from these external interdependencies.

A striking difference between the two systems occurs in the switching mechanisms. In the first design the critical decision is switching some parts to redundancy and activating others. The individual parts are probably not keen to be rendered redundant and not even very enthusiastic about being activated. These decisions are for the special control parts and it is irrelevant to their function whether the parts know *why* they are switched. In fact, anything that psychologically separates the special control parts from the others would help to ensure that proper decision rules are followed and are not obfuscated by *merely* human considerations. In the second design, with its governing principle of symmetrical dependency, the switching is governed by the conditions of mutual help. The problem is that all parts, or enough parts, need to be alert and willing to bring their unused capabilities into action when the shared task demands it. *Without considerable sharing of values and objectives, the potential of this design may not be realized,* which may be one reason why Taylor (1911) turned to revamping the first design for the utilization of the multinational work force pouring into United States industry in his day.

One other property of these systems was noted by Feibleman and Friend (1969) and has frequently been observed. Organizations based on redundancy of parts constantly strive to accumulate a superfluity of parts to ensure that at any one time they have more parts than they actually need for what they are doing. These reserves of duplicated parts are essential to ordinary day-to-day operation and are the major insurance against the unexpected. This superfluity of manning is sought at all levels except the very top. By contrast, organizations based on redundancy of functions (capabilities) find their optimal level at a point where undermanning stretches their joint resources and frequently challenges them to reallocate functions.

In choosing this second design for their organizations, people are implicitly making choices among ideals—for homonomy rather than self-seeking, self-serving autonomous strivings; for mutual help and nurturance rather than their own survival in the system; for inclusion of the criterion of humaneness along with the usual decision rules of effectiveness and efficiency. It may be difficult to grasp, but the emergence of a rich complex field of directive correlations within such organizations would even make them seem to be more beautiful settings to be in.[3]

I do not think that we can hope actively to adapt to turbulent environments without restructuring major institutions along the lines of the second design principle, redundancy of the functions of individual parts. As noted above, bureaucracies are based on the first principle and the individual is an instrument of the system. *An instrument functions as a lower order system than the system that uses it* (Ackoff and Emery, 1972:31–32). Quite simply, using an analogy from mathematical statistics, an instrument is always going to operate with one degree of freedom less than the system using it. Thus, although a social system is a purposeful system whose members are purposeful, there is a constant

---

[3]In *Logic of the Living Brain* (1972) Sommerhoff tried to identify models that would explain the uniquely adaptive characteristics of that organ and still do justice to the knowledge we have of its structure and functioning. He was led to reject the design based on redundant parts and to postulate two variants based on redundant functions. These two variants closely parallel the two discussed by Emery and Emery (1973).

tendency toward *increasing* or *decreasing variety* in the range and level of the behavior of the individual members. In systems based on the first principle, the tendency will be toward *variety decreasing;* the range of purposeful behavior will be restricted and increasingly behavior will be at a lower level of multi-goal-seeking or goal-seeking behavior. The assembly line has been the epitome of this process but the same phenomenon appears in the bureaucratic organization of even scientific and engineering work (Burns and Stalker, 1961).

Systems designed on the second principle will tend to be *variety increasing;* to maintain and extend the multifunctionality of their members, they will seek to extend the range of their purposeful behavior and increase the opportunities and support for ideal-seeking behavior. That is, such systems will be founded on the assumption that they are best served by serving as an instrument to the potentially higher system capabilities of their individual members.

Democratization of Work

As mentioned earlier, the choice of organizational design is simply twofold. In a turbulent environment only the choice of the second principle is potentially adaptive. Only organizations based on this principle can be expected to develop and nurture ideal-seeking individuals. Only a sufficiency of ideal-seeking individuals can offer the choice of bringing turbulent social fields under control (Winnicott, 1950).

Work, and the organization of people around work, is the "leading part" of Western societies. What happens at work tends to determine what can and does happen in the areas of family life, education, leisure, etc. This is not to deny that these other areas of living have their own history and their own self-determining characteristics.

Bureaucratization of work in Western society has been a major contributor to the present social turbulence both in negating Western values and in creating monolithic organizations whose decisions could set off autochthonous processes in their environments.

It might seem that people could meet part of their present needs by simply debureaucratizing their organizations. This is not a viable solution as is well demonstrated by the anemic failure of such movements to change the nature of industrial life. Examples are the human relations movement of the 1940s and 1950s and job enrichment of the 1960s. The efficiency of an organization can only be reduced if its various parts or aspects are designed according to contradictory design principles. There must be interfaces between such aspects or parts, and at these interfaces the conflict in principles undermines coordination. In discussing how the U.S. aerospace industry was forced by environmental pressures toward the second design principle in their research and development work but were, overall, hung up on the first principle, Kingdon (1973:18) observes:

> Of course these two principles, or organizational purposes, may not always be in accord with each other. In fact, it is more nearly the case that the two are in conflict with one another and that conflict resolution is a necessary part of the matrix organizational form. (cf. Burns and Stalker, 1961)

The target that people will increasingly set for themselves is not just debureaucratization but the positive target of redesigning their work organizations on the second principle, the target of democratizing work.

The movement to do just this can be clearly traced from the first experiment in the Bolsover coal mine in 1952 (Trist et al., 1963/Vol. II) through Emery and Emery (1973/Vol. II) and Davis (1971) to the work of O'Toole (1974) in relation to the Report of a Special Task Force (1973) to the Secretary of Health, Education and Welfare of the United States on *Work in America.*

Before examining in detail what is entailed in the notion of democratization of work, let us note two general features.

First, the essential change in the design of work organizations is that the "building block" is changed from the unit of one worker/one job under direct supervisory control to the semiautonomous group of people carrying responsibility for a unitary task. In this latter type of organization, the interface between the individual and the organization, no matter how large, is the face-to-face group.

The success that has arisen from reorganizing work around small, relatively autonomous groups would seem to follow from the shift in instrumentality. When the small social system becomes an instrument for its members there is a tendency for it to become *variety increasing;* they are able to pursue not only production goals but also purposes and even ideals that pertain to themselves— the ideals of homonomy, nurturance, humanity and beauty (see Ackoff and Emery, 1972, for these key ideals). This possibility emerges only when they have the responsibility for managing how they will relate to each other and what responsibilities they will assume toward each other.

Second, the starting points of this movement give some explanation of why I think it will become the dominant trend in Western industry. The first moves were in the science-based industries, particularly the process industries. The very nature of their technologies challenged the rationality of bureaucratic organization. Only in the 1970s did the assembly line become a key focus. This time it came as a revulsion against the tool-like use of human beings. This general revulsion has already spread to challenge most forms of bureaucratized work, mental as well as manual, professional as well as nonprofessional. The first and deepest commitments to change came from Scandinavia. I believe that it was easier to start there not only because of the socially advanced nature of Norwegian and Swedish society, but also because they were smallish, culturally homogeneous societies. Their industrialization had started late and had neither created deep divisive class hatreds nor removed them far from their preindustrial culture. It is probably only by their example that they have been given that the other larger countries have felt able to grasp the nettle.

Matrix Organizations

The vertically and horizontally monopolistic organization is an adaptive product of the disturbed reactive environment. I do not believe that there is any way in which such structures can adapt as individuals do to turbulent environments (despite Terrebury, 1968). They cannot themselves be ideal-seeking, and hence their chances for survival are dependent upon creating organizational environments within which enough of their members will be ideal-seeking. These organizational environments cannot be created by individual organizations.

I see two organizational tendencies emerging as potentially effective responses to turbulence: one with regard to relations between organizations, including those between national parts of the so-called multinationals; the other with regard to "corporate planning."

Whereas disturbed, reactive environments require one or other form of accommodation between similar but competitive organizations (whose fates are to a degree negatively correlated), turbulent environments require some relationship between dissimilar organizations whose fates are basically positively correlated; that is, relationships that will maximize cooperation while still recognizing that no one organization could take over the role of the other. I am inclined to speak of this type of relationship as an organizational matrix; it delimits the shape of things within the field it covers but at the same time, because it delimits, it enables some definable shape to be achieved. While one aspect of the matrix provides for evolution of ground rules, another independent but related aspect must provide for broader social sanctioning. Insofar as the sanctioning processes can be concretized in an institutional form, it should be possible for the component organizations to retain an effective degree of autonomy *and* to engage in effective joint search for the ground rules. Within the domain covered by such a matrix, there need to be further sanctioning processes to control the diffusion of values throughout the member organizations. Outstanding examples of such organizational matrices are those that have emerged to cover international communication.

It should be noted that in referring to the matrix type of organizations as one possible way of coping with turbulent fields, we are not suggesting that the higher level of sanctioning can be given by state controlled bodies, nor are we suggesting that the functioning of these matrices would eliminate the need for other measures to achieve stability. Matrix organizations, even if successful, would only help stability by helping to transform turbulent environments into the kinds of environments that I have described as clustered-placid (Type 2) and disturbed-reactive (Type 3). Within the environments thus created, an organization could hope to achieve stability through its strategies and tactics. However, the transformed environments can no longer be described in terms of optimal location (as in Type 2) or capabilities (as in Type 3). The strategic objective has to be formulated in terms of institutionalization. As Selznick (1957) states in his analysis of the leadership of modern American corporations,

> the default of leadership shows itself in an acute form when organizational achievement or survival is confounded with institutional success. . . . the executive becomes a statesman as he makes the transition from administrative management to institutional leadership.

This transition will probably be rendered easier as the current attempts to redefine property rights clarify the relations between the technologically productive area and the total social system. Private property rights are being increasingly treated as simply rights of privileged access to resources that still remain the resources of the total society. To that extent, the social value concerning the protection and development of those resources becomes an intrinsic part of the framework of management objectives and a basis for matrix organizations (Hill, 1971/Hill and Emery, Vol. II).

It is of interest that May's (1972) mathematical modeling of large complex systems suggested a similar strategy for avoiding instability. Referring to Gardner and Ashby's (1970) computations, he notes that

> 12-species communities with 15 percent connectance have probability essentially zero of being stable, whereas if the interactions be organized into three separate 4 X 4 blocks of 4-species communities, each with a consequent 45 percent connectance, the "organized" 12-species models will be stable with probability 34 percent. . . . Such examples suggest that our model multi-species communities, for given average interaction strength and web connectance, will do better if the interactions tend to be arranged in "blocks"—again a feature observed in many natural ecosystems. (1972:414)

For passively adaptive systems (Principle 1), this would mean no more than the strategy of segmentation discussed earlier. For actively adaptive systems (Principle 2), we are suggesting that matrix type organizations will, like the logic of cluster sampling, maximize the variance within their particular matrices and hence lessen the variance and difficulties of the ends they agree upon as being related to other such matrices. This is opposed to the logic of strata sampling and the strategy of segmentation, which seem to minimize the variance within strata and consequently maximize that between them. When one considers the interpenetration of sources of variance in a turbulent social field, it is not surprising that the logic of matrix organization so closely approximates that of cluster sampling.

Adaptive Planning

The processes of strategic planning are also modified. Insofar as institutionalization becomes a prerequisite for stability, the setting of subordinate goals will necessitate a bias toward those goals that are in character with the organization and a selecting of the goal paths that offer a maximum convergence about ideals held in common with other parties (Simmonds, 1975).

I have already referred to the technology of planning that emerged in the disturbed-reactive environment (Type 3). I think that this style of planning for optimization will be not just ineffective but maladaptive: the pattern of active maladaption response described as "synoptic idealism." Ackoff (1970) has identified the emerging pattern of "adaptive planning."

This notion of active planning may be compared with Lindblom and Hirschman's "disjointed incrementalism." The convergence is not surprising, as disjointed incrementalism was identified as the type of planning required in the face of gross complexity, future uncertainty and the difficulty in mobilizing human potential for implementation. At the same time, active adaptive planning lays a stress on the conscious identification of shared values or shared perspectives, past or present, that is absent from disjointed incrementalism. Of the 10 characteristics associated with disjointed incrementalism (Hirschman and Lindblom, 1969:358–59) at least four—1, 2, 3 and 8—are essentially in the satisficing mode. As a result, this way runs the risk of degenerating into the passive adaptation of parish pump politics. Active adaptation requires some sense of desirable futures as a deliberate step to avoid entrapment in the past.

Notions of planning are so central to current concepts of how society will deal with its future that I think the whole concept needs to be rethought. It is not simply a matter of "corporate planning" but of planning for cities, leisure, social welfare, economic growth, etc. The extended treatment by Hirschman and Lindblom seems faulty; that of Ackoff was only meant to suggest what is needed.

The decision to plan implies some commitment to bring into being a state of affairs that does not presently exist and is not expected to occur naturally within the desired time. The kind of planning we expect to emerge is that which will produce plans that will *probably* come to pass. It is not enough to have one of the optimizer's *feasible* plans. We need plans which will probably come to pass because the people involved in or served by their implementation want them to succeed. The hard-won agreements that the optimizer has for the initial, hard-nosed definition of objectives are no guarantee of active support when it comes to implementation. On the contrary, I think that these agreements carry within them the seed of subsequent subversion (as insistence on doctrinal purity in other fields of human endeavor carry the seeds of deviationism and heresy). Nor can the optimizer carry the day with his arrays of fact, statistical forecasts and impartial, objective calculations of the cost-effectiveness of alternative paths. These things do carry weight and may silence overt opposition, but, where there is a feeling that justice is not being done, facts will not convince otherwise. One has only to recall the instances where the nagging doubts of one individual have eventually led to a murder case being reopened. The apparent dilemma in "modern" planning is *how does the expert make a contribution of planning without alienating people?* This almost has the making of a paradox for social planners: the more knowledge experts accumulate, the greater the gap in understanding between them and the people and the less likely they are to go along with their plans for implementation or, to put it otherwise, the more we know, the less we can do. In his own context Mao posed it as the problem of "Red or Expert."

I do not think we can suggest any way to resolve this dilemma unless we confront, simultaneously, another dilemma. Planning to produce a new state of affairs seems to presuppose that we know where we want to go, we know where we are now, we know what paths will take us from here to there and we know what means we have for traversing those paths. For turbulent social environments this presumes an awful lot of knowledge. When the social setting and the human instruments of change are both changing, the knowledge we have today is increasingly less relevant. The dilemma is *how can we expect to improve our planning in the face of relatively decreasing knowledge?* Again, we come close to a paradox: the more society changes, the more we need to be able to plan but the less we have the knowledge with which to plan.

The common element in the two dilemmas is the notion of "expert knowledge." If we are to resolve these dilemmas, we will have to ask whether what we understand by expert knowledge is the kind of knowledge required for planning social changes in a changing society. I think there is room for doubt on at least three scores.

First, decision makers mistake the nature of the situations for which they are seeking a planning solution. Even the optimizers seem to think they are engaged in problem-solving. They think they know the problem and simply have to search through existing knowledge in order to come up with a range of probable solutions which they can then compare. Social planning has, however, come to be more like puzzle-solving than problem-solving. Each situation is so complex and unpredictable that one has to learn each unique set of steps that leads to a solution. In problem-solving it is typical to have the insightful "eureka" experience when a solution suddenly becomes apparent and after that it is just a matter of work to put the pieces together. In a puzzle one does not have this experience. The relation between the pieces is very much a matter of local determination. One can determine what is required for the piece to fit but, until that piece is found one has very little idea of what is going to be required of the piece after that. Previous experience or training cannot enrich the repertoire of solutions; at best they may help a person "learn how to learn." This does not sound like our expert. The expert is usually chock-a-block full of knowledge about what solutions will solve a given class of problem.

Not surprisingly, the *Oxford English Dictionary* (OED) helps to clarify the distinction I have tried to make. A problem is literally "a thing thrown or put forward." The implication is that when faced with a problem we are also given a knowledge from whence it arose, was thrown from or put forward by. This implication is enhanced when the OED states that, in logic, "a problem can be that of arriving at the conclusion in a syllogism"; in geometry, "a proposition in which something (further) is required to be done"; in physics and mathematics, "a question or inquiry which *starting from some given conditions*[4] investigates some fact, result or law." Chess "problems" are similarly defined by the OED as deriving from a given arrangement of pieces and set of rules. Beyond this, the OED does indicate that the word was once upon a time used to indicate that something was puzzling, enigmatic, a riddle; their last quote for this usage is dated A.D. 1602.

A puzzle is not defined by the OED in terms of what is out there that indicates and may assist what the person does by way of producing a solution. A puzzle is defined as simply a state of mind—"the state of being puzzled or bewildered; bewilderment; confusion; perplexity how to act or decide." What is "out there" in the case of a puzzle is indicated by a discussion of Chinese puzzles. Essentially, it is a matter of a person being expected to achieve a result that seems impossible to achieve, e.g., "to remove a piece of string from an object without untying it." Interestingly, the word puzzle (unlike "problem") has also readily assumed the form of a verb, e.g., "to search in a bewildered or perplexed way; to fumble, grope for something; to get through by perplexed searching"; "to puzzle out: to make out by the exercise of ingenuity and patience."

Second, the experts in this field have tended to act on a faulty model of so-called rational decision making. They theorize and write as if decision making

---

[4]Author's italics.

was explicable in terms of only two dimensions: probable efficiency of different paths and relative value of the outcomes. Another dimension is necessary (Heider, 1946; Jordan, 1968; Ackoff and Emery, 1972). This other dimension is the probability of choice and reflects the *intrinsic* value of a course of action to the chooser as distinct from its *extrinsic* or means/end value. This human dimension is reflected in the old folk wisdom of "better the devil you know," "furthest hills are greenest," "a bird in hand." The persistent and pervasive role of these nonrational factors has been explicated by Heider (1946) and unwittingly demonstrated in the "uncooperativeness" of humans in the recent rash of experimental studies of decision making. Similarly, established organizations show their own style in nonrational preference for ways of acting, particularly those that have had a special significance in their past, e.g., Rolls-Royce.

Third, people have tended to assume that what we need to know are more and more facts, when what is needed is knowledge of human ideals. This had come up very strongly with so-called enlightened operations researchers. Faced with the sorts of difficulties outlined above, they have sought for yet more knowledge: knowledge about people's motivations and how they can be managed to bring about predictable changes. I suggest that they are not about to get this knowledge from the social sciences (despite the pretensions of some social scientists) and that, even if they did, they would still be in a puzzle situation. The situational features to which the people respond would still be emerging in unpredictable ways. Where people are expected to go from *A* to *B* in ways that can be determined only as they proceed, it becomes more important that *they* must have a bit more knowledge about some of the paths; they must themselves be able to learn so that they can evaluate.

If one were to take seriously these strictures, the role of the planners would be no longer that of the experts riding with the powers that be. Instead the planning functions would be seen to involve:

- Conducting some search process whereby the main parties to the proposed change can clearly identify and agree about the *ideals* the change is supposed to serve and the kinds of paths most in character with them.
- Designing a change process that will enable relevant learning to take place at rates appropriate to the demands of time—this being the time within which change must occur to avoid intolerable costs of not changing and the time by which decisions need to be made if adequate resources are to be mobilized.
- Devising social mechanisms for participation whereby the choice of paths will reflect the intrinsic value of these paths for those who will have to traverse them.

There are many considerations that lead one to regard identification of ideals as the first requirement for planning social change. Only ideals seem to have the necessary breadth and stretch in social space and time. Motivations, attitudes and social objectives may well change as planning and implementation proceed, but human ideals do not appear to change so rapidly. This is not to say that the relative weightings of the ideals might not change[5] but even here we tend to have storm warnings well before the shifts become socially relevant (e.g., the shifts in "the Protestant ethic" which have only now become broadly relevant but which were heralded many years ago by the Beat generation of Kerouac). Similarly, only ideals seem to have the breadth of influence to encompass the range of contesting interests that can be expected in an area ripe for planned change. Ideals do not ordinarily have the same urgency in human affairs as motivations, but what they lack in this respect may be more than compensated for if their identification recenters a zero-sum conflict to pursuit of common interests.

Ideals have the further advantage that they are not esoteric. Certainly, social scientists can lay no claims to expertise in deciding these matters. If a planned change is supposed to serve certain ideals then the layperson can, and will, understand the criteria for judging the planning process before being confronted by the final, and possibly irreversible, outcome. That judgment may not extend to a learned appraisal of why things are going wrong or what action should be taken, but at least the alarm may be sounded in time for something useful to be done.

One special property of ideals needs to be noted because of the damage it does to the optimizer's claim to "planning excellence." The ideals that influence the behavior of people cannot be subsumed under a single ideal. Omnipotence, which is the one ideal that if achieved would permit the achievement of all other ideals, is only directly and single-mindedly pursued by infants and some sick, dependent people. Identification of the ideals involved in planned social change is almost certain to identify more than one noncomparable ideal, e.g., homonomy, nurturance, humanity and beauty. In such a context of multiple ideals, the skills of the optimizer cannot yield *the* plan. Hopefully, they may still be utilized for tactical problems.

The other direction in which it was suggested that planning might change was toward designing ways of "learning to learn." Clearly, this cannot be just a matter of pushing people in at the deep end. There must be some way of using accumulated experience and expertise to advantage.

In this mode of planning, the main cognitive searching shifts from search for means to search for ends. The search for means becomes less of a cognitive activity and more that of field experimentation. By such intervention one may get some sense of emerging possibilities and difficulties; what resources are

---

[5]In my experience differences in relative weighting have not been a serious obstacle to cooperation, providing valuation has been uniformly positive or negative.

actually needed; what resources, including human commitment and innovations, can be generated in the process of change; what shifts in emphases or changes in time taken are needed. In a situation of social change this kind of intervention can give us information for the choice of paths that we cannot expect to get from the massive cross-sectional surveys favored by the engineers-cum-urban planners. These surveys give us little more than history. By intervention, by pushing, tugging and tearing at the causal strands, we start to get some idea of the changing texture of the social field in which change is planned.

It will be noted that in this mode of planning, the "logical" order of planning activities becomes somewhat confused. Implementation and the selection of courses of action become inextricably involved with each other. Similarly, the allocation of resources becomes a means of encouraging the finding and selection of the best path(s). Resources do not automatically flow to those courses of action that, on previous cognitive analysis, have been determined to be "the best." Instead, resources flow toward those areas of implementation that show the most promise. Nor can one expect clear decision rules to decide what shows the most promise. The very notion of "showing promise" involves what is hoped for but not really expected. An initially disastrous experiment may be regarded as a place to channel resources if it shows that a lesson has been learned and local commitment created.

Planning in this mode must upset the optimizer. Where, it will be asked, is the control that will ensure that each part of the plan is enacted in a way and at a time that will ensure optimal use of resources? Where are the objective, impartial decision rules (and protective departmentalization of *the* planning function) that will ensure that politically and personally motivated choices do not subvert the planned ends? These features are, in fact, absent and their absence could be critical to the optimizer's plans and planning. Our point is that in a rapidly changing society, the optimizing mode of planning for social change is about as adaptive as a pig in water—the more the pig tries to swim, the more it slashes its own throat.

The optimizer tends to assume that plans are being prepared for a uninodal organization that will have the authority and power to command, through existing channels of coordination and control, that the plan be translated into reality. The new mode of planning assumes that there will be a multiplicity of nodes of power and that only a measure of cooperation between them will produce change in the desired direction. Consequently, in this new mode, the planners create the basis for control that emerges from a shared sense of ideals and present requirements and creates channels of communication and irritation appropriate to the shared needs for coordination.

In a very real sense, the most important product of this style of active adaptive planning is not the plan but the *community-in-planning*. The process creates the conditions for learning to learn, affirms the overriding significance of shared ideals and reduces the need for planning as a separate organizational activity. We can expect that this style of planning will generate an institutional form that will be as much part of our emerging societies as the campfire was to the aborigines, namely, the "search conference" (M. Emery and F.E. Emery, 1978/Vol. III). When new "matrix" formations seem necessary or old ones need to be discarded, we can expect those with potentially relevant *operational* responsibilities to come together for a brief span of days and nights to search jointly for the implications of sensed changes in their shared environments. Thus, for instance, union leaders and leaders of productive enterprises will seek such opportunities to share their understanding of how the "rules of the game" are changing. They will not relegate this task to "research officers"; they will not risk waiting to infer it from changes in each other's tactics and strategies; they will not attempt to deal with such matters in committee. In committee, it is necessary to stick with that which is *significantly* probable and trade from unchangeable corners. A good chairperson is one who rules out discussion of matters of mere possibility or low probability. Likewise, if a committee member is suspected of switching hats during a discussion, a good chairperson will insist on that member explicitly identifying the position he or she is taking.

In "search" even the improbable must be considered as a possible key to the future. Existing bodies of data and current notions of what is relevant can be no substitute for people's own sense of what is coming over the horizon. The reason for this great openness is simply that today's probabilities are not a sure guide to the future, but the future is likely to emerge from some of the possibilities that now exist. However, most people abhor such a degree of openness and are not likely to put up with it unless given ample time in which to search, freedom from the compulsion to arrive at explicit decisions and free- dom from the outside interruptions of work and family.

It is this latter point that has led to the use of "social islands." The participants are brought together to form an isolated community for as many days and nights as seem necessary for their work. This temporary community not only reifies the overriding purposes but provides psychological support to the individual. It represents a return to the older wisdom of the Persian tribes, reported by Herodotus, that no group decision reached at night was binding unless reaffirmed by daylight, and vice versa.

It may seem that an undue conservatism is built in by the stress on partici- pants including "the persons with the highest operational responsibilities." However, if the search process is to issue forth into a wide range of experimen- tal interventions, it must have the sanctioning of the existing powers and it must have the active support of those who control the operational units. If this support is not forthcoming, the matter is one for a power solution, not a planning solution. One further matter offsets the conservative bias. In a rapidly changing social setting, the greatest resistances to planned change are likely to arise from fear of change rather than from vested interests. Vested interests can be identified, calculated and negotiated as part of the price of change. Fear of change cannot; hence the great value of winning the hard core of professional leadership.

To identify the ideal goals that will be relevant to the planning process, the participants will tend to build up a shared picture of where the system has come from, as well as a shared picture of its likely futures. Beyond this, they will evolve guiding strategies for change that will bring others into the planning process and win their commitment to the ideal goals. As is stressed by Ackoff and by Schon, this means the emergence of broadly participative social systems that will "learn to learn" these systems will not just create mechanisms whereby they are fed knowledge accumulated by experts.

References

Ackoff, R.L. 1970. *A Concept of Corporate Planning.* New York: Wiley.

Ackoff, R.L. and F.E. Emery. 1972. *On Purposeful Systems.* Chicago: Aldine-Atherton.

Beer, S. 1972. *The Brain of the Firm: A Development in Management Cybernetics.* New York: Herder and Herder.

Burns, T. and G.M. Stalker. 1961. *The Management of Innovation.* London: Tavistock Publications.

Churchman, C.W. and R.L. Ackoff. 1949. "The Democratization of Philosophy." *Science and Society,* 13:327–39.

Davis, L.E. 1966. "Pacing Effects on Manned Assembly Lines." *International Journal of Industrial Engineering,* 4:171–77.

———. 1971. "The Coming Crisis for Production Management." *International Journal of Production Research,* 9:65–82.

Emery, F.E. and M. Emery. 1973. *Participative Design: Work and Community Life.* Canberra: Centre for Continuing Education, Australian National University Press. Revised, Vol. II, "The Participative Design Workshop," pp. 599–613.

———. 1978. "Searching: For New Directions, In New Ways . . . For New Times." In *Management Handbook for Public Administrators,* edited by J.W. Sutherland. New York and London: Van Nostrand.

Feibleman, J. and J.W. Friend. 1969. "The Structure and Function of Organization." In *Systems Thinking: Selected Readings,* Vol. 1, edited by F.E. Emery. Harmondsworth: Penguin Books.

Gardner, M.R. and W.R. Ashby. 1970. "Connectance of Large Dynamic (Cybernetic) Systems: Critical Values for Stability." *Nature,* 228:748.

Heider, F. 1946. "Attitudes and Cognitive Organization." *Journal of Psychology,* 21:107–12.

Hill, P. 1971. *Towards a New Philosophy of Management: The Company Development*

Programme of Shell U.K. London: Gower Press. Excerpted in Vol. II as P. Hill and F. Emery, "Toward a New Philosophy of Management," pp. 259–82.

Hirschman, A.O. and C.C. Lindblom. 1969. "Economic Development, Research and Development, Policy Making: Some Converging Views." In *Systems Thinking: Selected Readings,* Vol. 1, edited by F.E. Emery. Harmondsworth: Penguin Books.

Jay, A. 1970. *Management and Machiavelli: An Inquiry into the Politics of Corporate Life.* Harmondsworth: Penguin Books.

Jordan, N. 1968. *Themes in Speculative Psychology.* London: Tavistock Publications.

Kingdon, D.R. 1973. *Matrix Organization: Managing Information Technologies.* London: Tavistock Publications.

Liddell-Hart, B.H. 1944. *Thoughts on War.* London: Faber.

May, R.M. 1972. "Will a Large Complex System be Stable?" *Nature,* 238:413–14.

Mellor, D.P. 1958. *The Role of Science and Industry.* Volume 5, Series Four of *Australia in the War of 1939–45.* Canberra: Australian War Memorial.

Mumford, L. 1967. *The Myth of the Machine: Technics and Human Development.* London: Secker and Warburg.

O'Toole, J. (Editor) 1974. *Work and the Quality of Life: Resource Papers for "Work in America."* Cambridge, Mass.: MIT Press.

Pierce, W.H. 1964. "Redundancy in Computers." *Scientific American* (February).

Selznick, P. 1957. *Leadership in Administration: A Sociological Interpretation.* Evanston, Ill.: Row Peterson.

Simmonds, W.H.C. 1975. "Planning and R&D in a Turbulent Environment." *Research Management* (November): 17–21.

Sommerhoff, G. 1972. *Logic of the Living Brain.* Oxford: Oxford University Press.

Special Task Force. 1973. *Report to the Secretary of Health, Education and Welfare on Work in America.* Cambridge, Mass.: MIT Press.

Taylor, F.W. 1911. *The Principles of Scientific Management.* New York: Harper and Row.

Terrebury, S. 1968. "The Evolution of Organizational Environments." *Administrative Science Quarterly,* 12:590–613.

Trist, E.L., G.W. Higgin, H. Murray and A.B. Pollock. 1963. *Organizational Choice: Capabilities of Groups at the Coal Face Under Changing Technologies: The Loss, Rediscovery and Transformation of a Work Tradition.* London: Tavistock Publications. Reissued 1987, New York: Garland. Chapters 13, 14 revised, Vol. II, "Alternative Work Organizations: An Exact Comparison," pp. 84–105. Chapters 19–22, Vol. I, "The Assumption of Ordinariness as a Denial Mechanism: Innovation and Conflict in a Coal Mine," pp. 476–93.

Winnicott, D.W. 1950. "Some Thoughts on the Meaning of the Word Democracy." *Human Relations,* 3:175–86.

Fred Emery

Socio-Technical Foundations for a New Social Order?[1]

> The myth of the machine and the cult of divine kingship rose together.
> Lewis Mumford, *The Myth of the Machine.*

There are reasons to believe that the world economy is once again in the throes of a phase change. There are also reasons to believe that this phase change, like the preceding ones, will involve a paradigmatic shift in the organization of people around their work. If this is so, then our perceptions of what has happened in the past decade or more in the world of work may need to be modified; likewise our perceptions of where those changes are leading us.

I do not wish to dwell on the first proposition but will have to comment on it in order to give sufficient reason for us to take seriously the second proposition about the paradigmatic shift.

It was only in early 1978 that I was alerted to the possibility that the Kondratiev (1935) hypothesis[2] might have to be taken seriously. Since G. Garry's critique in 1943, I had regarded that hypothesis as "unproven." Since about 1950 I had fully accepted the economists' claim that Keynes had advanced their science to the point that only governmental mismanagement could precipitate another depression, and that the Bretton Woods Agreements would enable any such outbreak to be confined to the mismanaged nation.

It has not been difficult to establish that Garry was wrong. Kondratiev's historical statistical series were certainly incomplete and inconclusive, but the trends he detected were fully validated by our analysis of the comprehensive series of historical statistics that were now available (Banks and Textor, 1971; Mitchell, 1975). Blainey's (1970; 1973) and Singer and Small's (1972) historical studies of gold discoveries and of wars had disposed of Garry's argument that "even if the K-cycles of activity/depression in the world economy did

[1]Revised slightly from the original in *Human Relations*, 35:1095–1122, 1982. The second part will be incorporated in a wider paper on educational paradigms in Volume III.

[2]Kondratiev suggested that economic depressions occurred in capitalistic economies on a cycle of approximately 50 years.

occur they were explained in terms of the *exogenous* factors of gold discoveries and wars; hence they did not indicate any inherent and predictably recurrent instability in the world economic system." Garry seized on one further weakness in Kondratiev's position, namely that he had not suggested a dynamic that might explain how the international system could generate such serious instabilities at approximately 50-year intervals. So long as this elaboration was absent, the Kondratiev hypothesis had doubtful scientific status; one did not know whether it belonged to meteorology, economics or psycho-cultural cycles.

The Massachusetts Institute of Technology computer simulation of a national economy has resolved this last problem in Kondratiev's favor (Forrester, 1976). Our national economies run in a way that generates the K-cycles. I might note in passing that the centrally planned economies have the same fundamental difficulty in correlating the production of consumer and producer goods. On the historical facts, the political revolution of 1917 did nothing to protect the Union of Soviet Socialist Republics from the 1930s depression and is doing nothing for the Soviet Bloc members now.

Granted the scientific status of the Kondratiev hypothesis, there is still the practical question. Is the depression now on us; is this just another business cycle with the depression likely in the late 1980s; or is Walt Rostow (1978) right in his amazing suggestion that we went into the depression in late 1972 and are now on another long upswing? The facts only permit one of the first two answers. There could be some sort of brief recovery as in 1976–79, but that is unlikely to restore the so-called propensity to invest or effective demand.

I have come this far along this line of discussion because I think there is a relation between these developments and the seriousness with which employers pursue the quality of working life (QWL). I will go further to suggest that in periods of growth employers will toy with QWL in order to accommodate to cultural changes and will temporarily suspend such games during a downturn in the business cycle. However, in struggling to get out of a prolonged depression they will not be just playing. Let me now go back to the second proposition presented in my opening remarks—that these depressions are phase changes in the world system involving the ruling paradigm of work.

I concluded in 1979 that the Kondratiev hypothesis had to be taken seriously (for the reasons given above). It seemed obvious that each of the depression periods, the 1830–40s, 1880–90s, the later 1920s and the 1930s, should be studied for clues as to the nature and effects of this class of system crises. No national statistical series were available to me that would pinpoint the economic crisis of around 1790, and hence that critical period in modern history was left as a relatively shadowy thing compared to the interpretation of the other periods. (Phyllis Deane, in the second [1978] edition of her *The First*

Industrial Revolution, has presented statistical evidence that Britain suffered a deep economic depression in the 1780s and also in the 1740s [pp. 109–11, particularly Figure 1].)

Certain common features stand out. The emergence of the world economy (circa 1780) and its regular breakdown at long intervals introduced a new element into social life. Prosperity, change and continual improvement in the conditions of life came to be seen as the normal way of things. After a generation and more of this, the proof of the social system does indeed appear to be in the eating.

The onset of a great depression is inevitably seen against such an historical background of progress. The social system that has come to be taken for granted by the general populace itself becomes the object of attention and questioning as people's expectations are dashed. The questioning is all the more critical because the economic setback does not at all seem like the result of crop failures, or the hand of God. What a depression challenges is not just a mass of individual expectations but a socially dominant worldview that has given sanction to many of the central institutions of the society and to their relations of mutual support or condescension.

It is this that makes every great depression a *potential* producer of social evolution. Close study of modern revolutions has led scholars to the same conclusion.

> Revolutions are most likely to occur when a prolonged period of objective economic and social development is followed by a short period of sharp reversal. The all-important effect on the minds of people in a particular society is to produce, during the former period, an expectation of a continued ability to satisfy needs—which continue to rise—and during the latter, a mental state of anxiety and frustration when manifest reality breaks away from anticipated reality. The actual state of socio-economic development is less significant than the expectation that past progress, now blocked, can and must continue in the future. . . . The crucial factor is the vague or specific fear that ground gained over a long period of time will be quickly lost. (Davies, 1962:6–7)

Before the emergence of the world economy the persistence of poverty and the frequent recurrence of starvation due to crop failures and wars did not bring about social revolution. At most, the sporadic uprisings confirmed that there was no alternative to the existing order but disorder, pillaging and brigandage. At best, the hope was for some justice within the traditional order, not a reordering that might free people from their traditional roles.

The social instability induced by the long waves in the world economy can be observed in each of the great depressions. The potential for social revolution is, however, as much manifested by counterrevolution as by revolutionary action. The potential is far more widely manifested in the ferment of revolutionary ideas that appears to affect all areas of human endeavor in these periods and have passionate sway over the masses of people, not just the intelligentsia whose business it is to trade in ideas.

The ideas that come to have such a sway on popular thinking do not usually emerge in the period of economic crisis itself. Typically, they have gained intellectual currency in the period of economic slowdown before the depression. This makes it easier to discern which of the many ideas in this preceding period of intellectual (not social) ferment are likely to take hold. Similarly, the institutional changes that are closely tied to these new ideas are as likely to appear in the last days before the economic depression as in the period of depression itself. So in this respect also there should be some clues.

Some implications seem clear from the past history of depression periods. Thus we would expect that the onset of a great depression in the 1980s would change the tempo and direction of the trends observed in the 1950s and 1960s:

- greater tension in the work force and in industrial relations;
- predatory behavior among corporations (corporate cannibalism);
- shrinkage of governmental budgets;
- renewed social polarization of haves and have-nots;
- *popular* challenge to the prevailing institutional myths about governance, the economy, religion, education, family and human ideals;
- a reversal of the movement to liberalize trade between nations (increasing autarchy).

In short, all the contracts between people, their neighbors, their masters and their gods are likely to be called into question.

Each *recovery* from economic depression also had certain common economic and technical features. Each time, recovery has been marked by:

- the adoption, on a large scale, of *new technologies* that created new markets and greatly enhanced investment possibilities (Schumpeter, 1939);
- the adoption of new forms of distribution to serve wider and more scattered markets;
- the emergence of new forms of energy that were cheaper, simpler to exploit and more flexible (from water power to coal, to electricity, to oil, to gas);
- a step-wise expansion of use of sources of raw materials and labor (for example, the opening of the prairies and tropical plantations and the great waves of internal and international migration);
- emergence of new forms of business organization (Aglietta, 1979).

It was some time before I realized that there was in all of this a critical integrating factor. It was apparently not enough for new investments and new corporate forms to bring together new technologies, new forms of energy and new supplies of labor. New forms of labor organization appeared. Nor apparently was it enough for each management and plant to find its own best solution. At each crisis a generalized solution appears to have emerged. Each time it was as if a new generation of labor was being subjected to a new form of industrial discipline.

Let us examine those statements.

From Subjective to Objective Division of Labor

The first phase of industrialization did not emerge on the back of any particular technological revolution and certainly not on the back of the steam engine. Von Tunzelbaum (1978) has amply documented the fact that the steam engine and steam driven machines only became a significant factor in the textile industry of Britain in the recovery from the depression of the 1830s and 1840s.

The industrial system emerged on the basis of the "factory system," a form of work organization, *not* a new technology. At the heart of the factory system were the following features:

- the centralization of workplaces "under a single roof"—the physical definition of a factory;
- the fencing in of the factory and imposition of control over access or departure at the factory gate;
- the imposition of a strict working day and working week;
- the allocation, where possible, of work stations with fixed locations;
- a detailed division of labor that enhanced the role of semiskilled workers at the expense of the multiskilled craftsmen;
- the creation of a class of unskilled labor to enable the semiskilled operatives to devote themselves to their allotted tasks and provide a reserve force against daily fluctuations in attendance. In the cottage craft system only those in formal or informal apprenticeship were unskilled;
- the creation of a class of workers whose established and exclusive function is the supervision of the work of others—foremen.

Within the factories no one person produces a marketable product; he or she contributes to just a part or facet of the product. This focusing on details does not equip the workers to enter commodity markets as private producers. None of these essential features of the early system of manufacturing rests on the introduction of more efficient technologies, although hand tools went through a very rapid evolution to meet the requirements of specialized detail laborers.

The governing principle of the system of manufacture was the *subjective division of labor* within a master/servant relation. It contrasted markedly with the putting-out system. The putting-out system was still basically a free market in which cottage craftsmen negotiated the value they added to the merchants' material through the equipment and labor they had at their own disposal. It was a relation of symmetrical dependence, not the asymmetrical dependence of a master/servant relation. The efficiency of cottage-based production rested on the flexibility of multiskilling, not on division of labor.

With the wisdom of hindsight we can see that the economic viability of the early system of manufacturing did not arise from greater productive efficiency. It certainly increased the rate of circulation of the merchants' capital and reduced transport costs, but it did not get more output from the same labor inputs. It was more *effective* in getting more work out of people, however, and hence more production. It was able to do this because, for the relatively free market of the putting-out system, it was possible to substitute the very unfree labor market of that era. That labor market was unorganized, except for the minority of key craftsmen and their apprentices.

It was also a market in which there were no customs, norms and traditions such as gave the servant some rights in the more personalized asymmetrical dependency of feudalism, and no legislative controls other than the existing criminal and property laws. The cottage craftsmen were under the constraints of community and kin to maintain some standards of civilized existence. The manufacturers were under no such constraint (Marcus, 1974). It is little wonder that the cottage craftsmen, for the most part, preferred slowly to starve to death rather than submit themselves or their family members to the tyranny and indignity of factory employment. It is little wonder either that they attributed their difficulties, first and foremost, to unfair competition arising from the unfree labor market of dispossessed people. Despite the myth that has arisen, the prime object of the Luddite movement was undercutting the manufacturer not the newfangled machines. Breaking up the machines had much the same significance as the traditional burning of the wicked landowners' hay ricks— striking at the hip-pocket nerve. In the first instance the manufacturer's capital was rendered unproductive until the machines were replaced, a lengthy process in those days, and in the latter instance the landowner was disabled from carrying stock through the winter.

Andrew Ure, who was writing at a time much closer to those events, was in no two minds about what was the central integrating feature of emergent industrialism. We remember Richard Arkwright as the inventor of the spinning frame. Maybe he just stole the idea for his invention as he subsequently stole so many other ideas, but Ure could see that

The main difficulty . . . lay . . . above all in training human beings to renounce their desultory habits of work, and to identify themselves with the unvarying regularity of the complex automation. To devise and administer a successful code of factory discipline, suited to the necessities of factory diligence, was the Herculean endeavour and achievement of Arkwright! Even at the present day . . . it is found nearly impossible to convert persons past the age of puberty into useful factory hands. (quoted by Marx, 1906, vol.1, p.463)

The principles of factory discipline had to be learned again when the Lowells founded the textile industry of New England (Kasson, 1977).

I have dwelt on this first phase of industrialism because it so clearly illustrates the central integrating role of principles of work organization. The early factory system of organization made it possible to adopt and successfully exploit existing inventions such as Arkwright's spinning frame and the over-shot water wheel, inventions that quite likely would not have found a role in the putting-out system. Contrary to Schumpeter's thesis (1939), the factory system did not emerge just because those technologies existed.

We can see also that this first phase provided a fertile seedbed for the technological developments that were to be so eagerly seized upon in the next phase, *after* a needed principle of work organization had appeared.

The transition to the second phase of industrialism is important to our understanding of industrialism. It is important because we have tended to fuse the first and second phases and to see the factory system as the natural consequence of the invention of steam-driven machinery. The machinery available at the emergence of the second phase offered a great increase in efficiency, provided it could be powered by steam and located near sources of coal. This combination would have to provide an irresistible reason for centralizing labor in factories; this at least is such a rational explanation that we assume that it is what happened. Such is our myth of the birth of industrialism; and it remains a potent and persistent source of distortion in our attempts to understand what is happening in industry today. We even persist in using the term "manufacturing" when it properly relates only to the first phase before the emergence of "machinofacture."

The second phase emerges with the acceptance of an organizing principle that underlies all succeeding phases, at least until now. This is what Marx called the *objective* division of labor. The factory adopted machines to further reduce dependence on the small but critical group of craftsmen and to achieve the efficiencies that steam-powered machinery was beginning to demonstrate. With this development it no longer made sense to allocate people to work with those tools and tasks for which they were subjectively best fitted. People had to be allocated to whatever tasks were needed to keep the machines producing. These tasks were dictated by the design of the particular machines, but general classes of jobs emerged: for example, the attendants who watched the machines for signs of malfunctioning, the feeders and off-loaders, the sweepers, the oilers and greasers, the maintenance mechanics, the millwrights, the boilermen, the shifters and the storemen.

This process constitutes a very significant step in the regression of the product. Under subjective division of labor the product moves out of reach of its producer to a commodity market that cannot be entered as a producer-seller. However, the detail laborer still contributes something of the product itself, even if it is only stitching a collar to a shirt. With machinofacture the operator is simply feeding and maintaining the beast: the beast takes the raw materials and makes the product. This is a figure/ground reversal. In manufacture the worker dictated what the tools did and apparently contributed greatly to the design and evolution of those tools. In machinofacture the machine dictated what the worker did, and factory workers contributed very little to machine design.

In reviewing this transition it might appear that, although we had misjudged the nature of the first phase of industrialism, here at last were the real beginnings of industrial society. At least, we might argue, from about the 1840s technology came into dominance and began to dictate the pace of growth and the forms of industrial organization. Certainly the growth of industrial civilization between the world economic crisis of the 1830s and 1840s and the next great crisis of the 1880s and early 1890s was like nothing that could be recalled. The great industrial exhibitions of London and Paris in the 1850s were paeans of praise for the revolution wrought by the dominance of technology in the first age of machinofacture. Haeckel and many many others were preaching a new religion—scientific materialism. God was irrelevant and the day of doom put off forever as the marriage of science, technology and industry guaranteed a prospect of boundless progress. Looking back, it is easy to understand and forgive this short-sighted ebullience.

Of more significance for understanding how that second phase of industrialism continues to color our present thinking is the fact that two such incompatible social philosophers as Max Weber and Frederick Engels arrived at this same conclusion, despite the "great depression" of the 1880s and early 1890s. Max Weber foresaw the bureaucratization of all walks of society, because this was the rational and predictable way of achieving efficiency in the allocation of resources to create reward. As Frederick Engels put it more eloquently, in terms that read like the Old Testament,

> If man by dint of his knowledge and inventive genius, has subdued the forces of nature, the latter avenge themselves upon him by subjecting him insofar as he employs them, to a veritable despotism *independent of all social organization.* (1894)

It was Lewis Mumford (1967) who so succinctly labeled this as the "myth of the machine." He thus identified a prime case of misplaced concreteness.

Machinofacture emerged from the womb of manufacturing. Machines were being designed for the factory market, not for the poverty stricken and nearly defunct cottage industries. Industry was dividing into the now traditional departments of producer goods and consumer goods, and the "foolproof" machine was coming into its own. The point is this: insofar as technology after the 1840s appeared to set the pace for economic growth and to dictate the forms of industrial organization, it did so on the basis of the assumptions already established within the system of manufacturing. It completed the process of getting the craftsman out of the direct processes of production (not, however, out of the tool room and boiler room or out of maintenance).

Now let us stand back from the details of the first and second phases of industrialism.

A New Paradigm of Work

Taking a broader historical perspective, we notice that these earlier phases were of only academic interest so long as we, in the 1970s and 1980s, thought that we were now confronted with the emergence of just another phase in the series. When it appeared that we might possibly be confronted with a *system change,* not just a phase change, a reconsideration of these early periods became imperative. Such reconsideration became imperative because it was necessary to identify the principles governing the *whole* system of industrialism through all of its phases, not just the specific principles governing the phase we are in and the phase from which it immediately arose.

In *Futures We Are In* (Emery, 1976), I thought it sufficient to tackle the latter task. I tried to spell out the paradigm of scientific management that Frederick Taylor devised to lead the way out of the economic crisis of the 1880s and 1890s. I also tried to spell out the paradigm of the assembly line, the paradigm that has dominated the post-1930s depression phase. I do not think it is difficult to deduce from that book what I thought would happen next in industrial organization. I clearly believed that a new paradigm of work was emerging and hence at least a new phase of industrialism. I do not think that I rated the change higher than that. My expectation was that the general adoption of the principle of "self-managing production groups" (semi-autonomous groups) would domesticate industrialism and promote changes in nonwork areas.

Within the new paradigm the foreman and the unskilled laborer would start to disappear, and the worker would gain the dignity of deciding what was to be done and what was meaningful work. At the same time, the product was tending to recede further as computer tape-instructed machines, microprocessors, diagnosed faults and physical sensors replaced human attendants. Self-managing groups and quality control circles reverse this tendency. As groups they can map a production line and identify something that is *their* product.

Kumar (1978) and Aglietta (1979) have confirmed what Marx and, 130 years later, von Tunzelbaum had asserted. Recovery from the deep crises of industrialism has always depended upon the emergence of a more effective *social* form for eliciting productivity. No technology was sufficient in itself to create such a growth in productivity. At this point in time, we have to consider whether the new paradigm of work is just a reaction to the increase in automation of productive activities. Certainly, we find once again that the leadership in adopting the new paradigm of work comes from those that stand to gain most from the new technologies. But, yet once again, the widespread adoption of the technologies follows from and does not precede and determine the organization of work. It is within the context of self-managing work groups and quality control circles that major corporations are seeking the adoption of new technology (*Business Week,* May 11, 1981). In such a context a technological change is significantly less threatening to workers (Emery and Thorsrud, 1976).

I think I have been wrong in thinking that all that will happen this time will be a replay of Schumpeter's scenario—a massive shift of capital into a new branch of industry. If that were so, then it would be easy to identify the microprocessor as the steam engine of the next phase of growth (Emery, 1978). Aglietta's arguments (1979:385–86) have convinced me that the critical growth must come from achieving greatly increased productivity in the infrastructure areas of health, education and welfare. This growth will come from opening these fields to private enterprise, as is implicit in the welfare scheme of guaranteed minimum incomes, and the widespread replacement of those bureaucracies by democratization of the workplace in hospitals, schools, prisons and the like. In this setting consumerism will sprout new wings.

The first four paradigms of work can each be identified as members of a series. They all presuppose asymmetrical dependence and the correlative sanctity of managerial prerogatives. The generative principle of the series was that of maximizing the proportion of the working day that each worker actually spent on working. With the assembly line, the last excuse for taking a bit of a break from the job was eliminated; there was no longer any excuse for walking away to pick up something. Note, however, that the currently emerging paradigm is a break with that series. It presupposes relations that are more nearly those of symmetrical dependence as the production goals and membership of the self-managing groups become the subject of negotiation and the concept of managerial prerogatives becomes secularized. The generative principle is no longer that of extracting a high proportion of labor time from the working day. Efficiency of production is the generative principle for both work groups and managers. In this context individual workers regain some time of their own during the shift and an ability to pursue some purposes of their own. It is not quite as good as getting time off for golf, but it is a reversal of a 200-year trend that ended only with Lordstown in 1972.

This new paradigm does not fit into the historical series that I have outlined. It would have to constitute a system change, not just a phase change within the old system. A system change in the nature of the wage relation could not stop short of a massive change in the social infrastructure creating the next generations of workers.

Emerging Characteristics of a New Social Order

With each of the phase changes in the socio-technical basis of industrial civilization we have seen something of the massive changes required in the associated social infrastructure. It has taken the wide-sweeping minds of people like Siegfried Giedion (1948), Lewis Mumford (1967), R.J. Forbes (1971) and Carlo Cipolla (1962) to reveal this to us. Because of the work of such people we have some sense of the great waves of migration, urbanism, secular education, artistic innovation, scientific discovery and so forth that have periodically convulsed industrial society. Now that we seem to be confronted with a system change and not just a phase change we must be prepared to confront even more radical convulsions.

There are any number of threads that one might pick up to trace out how our social infrastructure might evolve. I have chosen to pursue the educational thread. Education is the factor that became dominant in the motif woven by the last phase of industrialism and, in these last years of crisis, it has become the "whipping boy" for the collapse of personal and social expectations.

If this is the beginning of the end of the master/servant relationship, then what do we do with a system that has, since compulsory, secular education emerged in the 1880s and 1890s, educated young people to serve in the master/servant relationship? If industry and its administrative systems have had to move toward a self-governing paradigm of symmetrical dependence rather than asymmetrical dependence, then for whom are the educational institutions producing the old product? Producing people for mature industries and civil services locked into the backwaters of tradition must fail and cause dependent clients similarly to fail. Those industries are, of course, extremely vociferous in defense of their conservatism. Typically, they are the industries that find most comfort in avoiding change and are most able to get tariff protection by joining employers' federations, chambers of commerce and the like. It is second nature to them to get governments to provide them with what they need—including the kind of employees they need. The big powerful corporations in the science-based industries do not typically work through these bodies. They are, however, the pacesetters in employee practices. They are the ones the educationists must watch. The modern trend in education toward producing more independent and emotionally mature students would seem to be in keeping with the advanced personnel practices of the modern corporations.

At the same time the greater emphasis on education on the job calls into question the massive investment we have made in higher education. The excessive division of labor that justified the mass production of experts has had its day. The higher degree will have about the same relevance to economic recovery as the V-8 car engine.

On the basis of the matters I have discussed, I cannot see how we can recover to take up the economic growth path we were on in the 1960s, nor can I see any hope of reestablishing autocracy as the norm of employment. If recovery is not likely to conform to tradition, if we must think along new lines, then we must try to see what are the most probable strands that will interweave to give us some sort of new system.

The major reason for the system change is a shift in values in the community profound enough to be referred to as a cultural revolution, rather than any shortage of resources. This effect has spread into the workplace and makes it impossible to recover productivity in the way that we did before. We cannot get the productivity out of our workers or managers in the traditional manner, not even with microprocessing. I have identified what I think are five salient strands for the making of a new system, four of which would be on anyone's collection of starters. They are arranged in Figure 1 in an order that depicts the extremes: the pressure for a low energy, high equity society on the one side and, on the other, the pressure for a high technology society.

I am not alone in thinking a low energy, more equitable society to be a very probable future for Australia. In 1978 the Sentry Insurance Company commissioned Roger and Merrelyn Layton, of the University of New South Wales, to do a survey of the Australian work force. In that survey, alternative scenarios of the future were put to people, asking them which they thought was *most probable* and which they thought *most desirable*. About one third of the sample of Australian workers, trade union leaders, managers and public administrators, when asked about the *most probable futures,* replied that they could not see past a continuing depression scenario. Of the two thirds who could see past a depression scenario, half saw a normal recovery to a 1960 type society of high energy usage and inevitable social inequity (although few thought it "most desirable"). The other half, however, reckoned that the most probable future was "small-is-beautiful"—"low energy" and "social equity." I was very surprised at this finding because I thought that this scenario would be known only to college educated people and middle-class trendies. The mass media in Australia had given this scenario no serious attention, so we have to assume that people had worked it out for themselves.

One can, of course, ask one question beyond that: even if people think that the small-is-beautiful scenario is the most probable future, do they understand enough about the way the economy works? Are they being realistic? One answer was given by a group in Argentina who modeled the major regions of

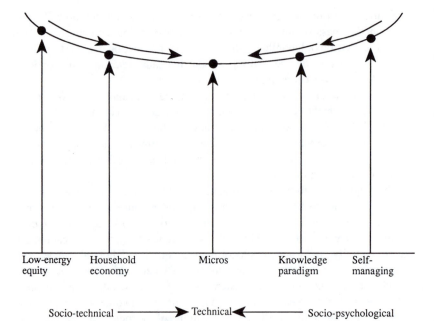

Figure 1. The clustering of emerging strands

the world economy in order to see what changes would have to take place to enable South America, Central America, South East Asia, India and Australasia to provide for the basic needs of their people in the year 2000 (Herrara, 1976). When they modeled these economies they tested the implications of two different optimization criteria. One was the classical capitalist system, where resources are allocated so as to maximize growth in the Gross Domestic Product (GDP). The other criterion was the allocation of resources so as to maximize the average life span of the population. They inferred, for a number of reasons, that optimizing to increase the average life span of a population was the best way to ensure movement toward a more equitable society. The first criterion corresponds to the Laytons' high energy, social inequity scenario and the second to their low energy, social equity scenario.

The Argentinian study then posed the question as to what growth rates would be needed under these different conditions to eliminate poverty by the year 2000. By their figures, Australia would need an average growth rate of 15 percent per annum to achieve this goal if resources were allocated in the usual fashion. The Australian economy has never sustained anything like this rate of growth for any past stretch of 20 years. I have already noted that even a 3 percent growth rate has had to be discarded as over optimistic (Emery, 1978). We must also note that nowhere in sight are the energy resources that would be needed to fuel such growth rates. By comparison, this target of no poverty in the year 2000 would be achieved by an average 2 percent growth rate if resources were allocated on the criteria of maximizing average life span. Put that way, the low energy, high equity scenario does not seem nearly as unrealistic as attempting to recover along the 1960s path of high energy, low equity.

I can keep my comments brief on two of the threads presented in Figure 1. The microprocessor revolution has been widely discussed, and we are beginning to realize that it is not just another technological step forward in the long series from water-powered looms and steam-driven hammers. In conjunction with electronic sensors and "chip memories," the microprocessor will inevitably revolutionize the interface between workers and machines, people and knowledge. The vast hordes of workers pouring in and out of mass-assembly plants, department stores and huge office blocks will become a thing of the past. Equally, the long, lifetime commitment to a job will also disappear. We have adjusted to this sort of problem in the past by formally recognizing all sorts of claims on the national wealth other than that of engaging in paid employment (for example, pensions, scholarships, fellowships, long service leave).

Gershuny (1978) and Scott Burns (1975) have pointed to a related phenomenon: the rapid growth of various forms of self-employment and pursuit of ways of reducing dependence on salaried wages. The evidence they have adduced suggests that this is no passing fad. It is a trend, furthermore, that should be considerably strengthened by the spread of the microprocessors into household equipment. As with Singers' new sewing machine, the microprocessor overcomes skill barriers that previously gave home-produced products a bad name.

Just as I have suggested that the human energy crisis has been more critical for industry than the fuel crisis, so now I am going a step further to suggest that *the knowledge revolution may consist in the release of human capabilities rather than in microprocessors, optic fibers and satellites.*

Surpassing the Traditional Barrier Between Intellectual and Manual Labor

The massive growth of higher education and science-based technologies has served only to reinforce the historical antithesis between intellectual and manual labor. In a seminal monograph, Alfred Sohn-Rethel (1978) has spelled out in detail how profound and persistent is that antithesis. It emerged with Plato's philosophy, Euclid's geometry and Aristotle's formal logic. These unique, unprecedented and unparalleled concatenations of intellectual explosions all took place in the fourth century B.C. and, to all intents and purposes, rose in one tiny geographical spot, the grove of Academus, one mile northwest of Athens. It is said that when Plato opened his think tank there in 387 B.C., he inscribed over the entrance, "Let no man ignorant of geometry enter here." In that one brief historical moment, intellectual labor proved that it could create a product incommensurably superior to any product of manual labor or the senses. They had produced truths that were timeless and universal. No such intellectual explosion occurred in any other culture, and nothing like it was to be seen until the seventeenth century in Europe. In that century the potential uniqueness of the product of intellectual labor was reasserted in the theoretical inventions of Galileo and Newton and Cartesian geometry. The precarious claims that the Aristotelians had for producing a unique and superior intellectual product by logical induction from the observed facts were gradually surpassed by the claims of science. After Einstein there was no doubt about what were the strongest grounds for defending the claim of the uniqueness of the product of intellectual labor. Those grounds were in science, not in law and theology.

If we are going to gain an understanding of the antithesis between intellectual and manual labor then we have to understand the nature of intellectual labor. No one, I suggest, is going to understand the nature of intellectual labor until they grasp what was done by Euclid, Galileo, Newton and Einstein. Nor will they understand the sacrifices that modern societies will undergo while they wait for another such genius. All the rest—the technicians, technologists and scientists—are but the army of ants who labor in vain if the queen ant does not turn up. The unique intellectual product cannot be produced by educating people in the sciences or any other body of scholarly knowledge. The facts are against any such idea. In each of the cases mentioned above there was a step forward in timeless, universal theory. Each step forward was a great step toward the understanding and control of natural forces. Each step was also a miracle. They were miracles because there was no apparent way in which these great advances in systematic theory could have emerged from just seeing something that others had not noticed, for example, an apple falling on one's head. They could not have arisen in the way that a recipe is discovered by a very perceptive cook or in the way that Edison contributed so much to our technical know-how. The theoretical advances we are talking about could only be the work of human geniuses, although that explanation tells us nothing about how to invent theory.

The division we observe today between scientists and technologists, the experts, and the ordinary workers at bench and desk is located quite precisely in the historical events that I have outlined. The division is first and foremost a division between those who can, alone or through their community, trace the logical proof of their ideas back to the great systemic structures erected by

Euclid, Newton, Einstein and so forth and those who cannot. Years of graduate education are seen as necessary before people can be expected to be able to logically relate, through their disciplinary community, its textbooks, hand-books and professional journals, to these unquestionable systemic founda-tions. More than that, the "science of psychology" postulates that only a few people have the innate ability to grasp these systemic concepts. Piaget's scheme of the psychological maturation of human intellect ends with the achievement of "propositional operations" at adolescence. Very few people mature to the point where they can grasp the higher levels of abstraction. It was said, perhaps for effect, that at any one time there were only four or five people who really understood Einstein's theory of relativity. The implication was clear: intellectual knowledge had become so esoteric that there could be no question of participative management of that knowledge. And this was not trivial knowledge; it was the knowledge that built the bomb and offered the solution to energy shortages.

The few who can grasp and work with such "fourth order" concepts are at the peak of academic excellence and constitute the high priests of the scientific and technical establishments. The nearest parallel in the field of manual labor would be the inventors, and they rarely command social respect or support.

In the process of democratizing work we have not squarely confronted this historical division of intellectual and manual labor. The removal of the fore-man and first-line supervisors only affected the source of know-how, not the locus of expert knowledge. Democratizing the workplace has certainly created greater openness at the boundary between expert and operative personnel, but the polarity persists. It persists even when direct forms of participation in departmental management have been devised; for example, the "jury" system (Emery, 1981). In a sense, all of the forms of participation in management decision making must seem somewhat suspect when the experts employed by management constitute a special source of authority.

This is not just a theoretical possibility. Quite early in the Norwegian Industrial Democracy Program we identified two "black belts" of resistance to democratization. We were already very familiar with one. Beyond the reach of trade union agreements and the power of trade union officials there was a whole defense system based on local custom and usage and the assumption that any management-inspired change had to be a change for the worse. The second black belt had not been foreseen, or at least had only appeared as a shade of grey. We had thought of the engineers, chemical technologists and the like as simply part of middle management who would fall in line with the wishes of top management. We had not anticipated the extent to which they would feel threatened by the release of knowledge to the shop floor and had not realized the extent to which these experts had their own managers "blinded by science."

The "deep slice" technique of participative design (F.E. Emery and M. Emery, 1976; 1974/Vol. II) was a partial answer to this source of resistance. At least it gave the experts a chance to negotiate directly with operatives about their new boundaries. Beyond that I blithely thought that this problem of "Red or Expert," as Mao Tse-Tung had phrased it, would be resolved by democratization of the educational process in the colleges and universities.

Having now gone over a draft of Trevor Williams's new book (1982), I think I have been glossing over a much deeper historical conflict between education and democracy. It is not simply a matter of debureaucratizing universities. My earlier confidence had come from a number of educational experiments that I had carried out in universities in the postwar decade.

Compared with traditional programs it seemed well proven that *most* people benefited from controlling their own learning and their use of resources, including the negotiation of staff time and efforts. These experiments never ran longer than three years, never involved more than one class at a time and all included a good proportion of mature ex-servicemen. I was not particularly concerned that some students did not take kindly to such democratization, even though these exceptions included potential scholars who eventually made the professorial ranks. Equally, I was little concerned that these experiments were aborted as soon as I moved on. These seemed to be the usual preliminary reactions to new ideas.

The experiments reported by Trevor Williams have for me effectively reversed the figure/ground relation. He reports on experiments with undergraduate and postgraduate courses in management that have been under his control for the greater part of the 1970s. He reports also on a massive in-house educational program with the managers and technologists of Telecommunication Australia. On the surface the results are simply a repeat of what I and many others have demonstrated, that is, that *most* people do obviously benefit from the democratization of their learning. But this time there was a difference. Williams's work was on a scale that could not be ignored by the parent institution, and he stayed around long enough to "cop the flak."

There was one other matter contributing to the reversal of my perceptual field. I had been very closely involved with Trevor Williams in the designing and redesigning of his experiments without realizing that any radical shift in meaning was involved. However, with Merrelyn Emery I had been intensively engaged in studying the future of communications technologies and had been forced by the evidence to conclusions that converged on those arising from Williams's work. In the older technologies of the telephone exchange and the architecture of main-frame computers, it was sufficient to identify the way that designers had, without thinking, followed the same design principle as that embedded in bureaucratic organizations—reliability through building in redundant parts (Emery, 1967). In the newer technologies involving the electronic handling of visual information, we were finding that the most fundamental assumptions were ones that concerned not these organizational alternatives but epistemological assumptions about the sheer physiological ability of people to gain information from the world around them. Wilbur Schramm, the international salesman for Education Tele-Vision for some two decades, has once again demonstrated that there is a fundamental mismatch between what television should be able to do, on those epistemological assumptions, and what it actually achieves (Schramm, 1960).

What Williams has done, in an eminently practical and constructive way, is to show us that as the outer layer of bureaucratic assumptions is peeled away, the underlying assumptions about the incompetence of people to learn from their experience are evoked. As these deeper assumptions are evoked, the achievements of democratization are first challenged and then *destroyed or encapsulated*. Such a process of encapsulation was observed in Norway in the 1970s after the successes of the 1960s. Historically, the negating processes have been found after most radical and popular revolutions (Marcuse, 1966). In this case such destruction is not in the cards because there is no other way that offers comparable growth in productivity. Encapsulation is in the cards. Quality of working life could become a management tool that creates an elite of multiskilled highly rewarded employees against a backdrop of large-scale unemployment and a multitude of short-term, part-time jobs in service industries. Note, however, that an encapsulation that preserves some of the critical managerial prerogatives within the corporation still does not seal off the enriching effects on the community of such multiskilled, self-respecting workers.

The major service that Williams has done for us is to identify the fact that democratization of an area as significant as work cannot evade encapsulation unless the educational process is radically changed. This is not a new problem, but then I, and I guess many others, have not been looking back at the history of leaps and tumbles whereby we got to the spectacular period of growth in the years 1955 to 1972. I use Williams's work as a vehicle to identify the emerging challenges in the process of democratizing work. There is now little that is scientifically challenging in confronting autocracy in the workplace. I find that there is a great deal in confronting the "meritocracy."

It would appear that whenever industrial society is in one of its recurrent periods of economic downturn and social turmoil, as in the 1960s, the relationship of education and democracy becomes a leading question.

Author's note, 1991

The concern expressed at the end of this 1982 paper was not misplaced. In 1988 Shoshana Zuboff published her perceptive case studies of "informated" technologies—*In the Age of the Smart Machines*. By informated technologies she means computerized, automated technologies that not only operate according to pre-determined programs but also record and analyze what the program, equipment and operator are doing during the operation and, if necessary, some of the changing states of the operational environment. It is the world of the microprocessor-controlled operations that informs at the same time as it instructs. The productive capabilities of these informating technologies can be realized only by operators who have the conceptual skills required for diagnosis and optimization of system performance; or by managers replacing operators at the workface. As Zuboff evidences, there are some plants where both operators and managers have realized what they are confronted with. Some operators find it hard, if not impossible, to cope with the change from manual labor to intellectual labor. Many more managers find it difficult to accept that their status as *the* intellectual workers in the plant is being undermined. The informating technologies challenge the boundaries between intellectual and manual labor. That is a challenge that has to be understood in psycho-social terms.

References

Aglietta, M. 1979. *A Theory of Capitalist Regulation: The U.S. Experience.* New York: New Left Books.

Banks, A.S. and R.B. Textor. 1971. *Cross Polity Time Series Data.* Cambridge, Mass.: MIT Press.

Blainey, G. 1970. "A Theory of Mineral Discoveries." *Economic History Review,* 23:298–313.

———. 1973. *The Causes of War.* London: Macmillan.

Burns, S. 1975. *Home Inc.* Garden City, N.Y.: Doubleday.

Business Week. 1981. "The New Industrial Relations." Special Report, May 11.

Cipolla, C. 1962. *The Economic History of World Population.* Harmondsworth: Penguin Books. Seventh edition, 1978.

Davies, J.C. 1962. "Toward a Theory of Revolution." *American Sociological Review,* 27:6–7.

Deane, P. 1978. *The First Industrial Revolution* (second edition). Cambridge: Cambridge University Press.

Emery, F.E. 1967. "The Next Thirty Years: Concepts, Methods and Anticipations." *Human Relations,* 20:199–237.

———. 1976. *Futures We Are In.* Leiden: Martinus Nijhoff. Chapter 4 reproduced in part, Vol. II, "The Second Design Principle: Participation and the Democratization of Work," pp. 214–33.

———. 1978. "The Fifth Wave." In *Limits to Choice,* edited by F.E. Emery. Canberra: Centre for Continuing Education, Australian National University.

———. 1981. "Educational Paradigms." *Human Futures* (Spring): 1–17.

Emery, F.E. and M. Emery. 1974. *Participatory Design: Work and Community Life.* Canberra: Centre for Continuing Education, Australian National University. Revised version, Vol. II, "The Participative Design Workshop," pp. 599–613.

————. 1976. *A Choice of Futures*. Leiden: Martinus Nijhoff.

Emery, F.E. and E. Thorsrud. 1976. *Democracy at Work*. Leiden: Martinus Nijhoff.

Engels, F. 1894. "On Authority." In *Selected Works*, Vol. 1. Moscow: Foreign Languages Publishing House, 1952.

Forbes, R.J. 1971. *The Conquest of Nature: Technology and Its Consequences*. Harmondsworth: Penguin Books.

Forrester, J.W. 1976. "Business Structure, Economic Cycles and National Policy." *Futures* (June).

Garry, G. 1943. "Kondratiev's Theory of Long Cycles." *Review of Economic Statistics*, 23:203–20.

Gershuny, F. 1978. *After Industrial Society? The Emerging Self-Service Economy*. Atlantic Highlands, N.J.: Humanities Press.

Giedion, S. 1948. *Mechanization Takes Command: A Contribution to Anonymous History*. New York: Oxford University Press.

Herrara, A.D. 1976. *Catastrophe or New Society?* Toronto: Institute for International Development.

Kasson, J.F. 1977. *Technology and Republican Values in America, 1778–1900*. Harmondsworth: Penguin Books.

Kondratiev, M.D. 1935. "The Long Waves in Economic Life." *Review of Economic Statistics*, 17:105–15.

Kumar, K. 1978. *Prophecy and Progress: The Sociology of Industrial and Post-Industrial Society*. Harmondsworth: Penguin Books.

Marcus, S. 1974. *Engels, Manchester and the Working Class*. London: Weidenfeld and Nicholson.

Marcuse, H. 1966. "Political Preface 1966" to *Eros and Civilization: A Philosophical Inquiry into Freud* (second edition). London: Routledge and Kegan Paul.

Marx, K. 1906. *Capital*. Chicago: Charles Kerr.

Mitchell, B.R. 1975. *European Historical Statistics 1750–1970*. New York: Columbia University Press.

Mumford, L. 1967. *The Myth of the Machine: Technics and Human Development*. London: Secker and Warburg.

Rostow, W.W. 1978. *The World Economy: History and Prospect*. London: Macmillan.

Schramm, W. (Editor). 1960. *The Impact of Educational T.V.* Urbana: University of Illinois Press.

Schumpeter, J.A. 1939. *Business Cycles*. New York: McGraw-Hill.

Singer, J.D. and M. Small. 1972. *The Wages of War, 1816–1965: A Statistical Handbook*. New York: Wiley.

Sohn-Rethel, A. 1978. *Intellectual and Manual Labour: A Critique of Epistemology*. London: Macmillan.

von Tunzelbaum, G.N. 1978. *Steam and British Industrialization to 1860*. Oxford: Clarendon Press.

Williams, T. 1982. *Learning to Manage Our Futures: The Participative Redesign of Societies in Turbulent Transition*. New York: Wiley.

Zuboff, S. 1988. *In the Age of the Smart Machine: The Future of Work and Power*. Oxford: Heinemann.

Fred Emery

The Historical Validity of the Norwegian Industrial Democracy Project[1]

A new line in radical social criticism has emerged among the university students of Norway. It is not unique to Norwegian students.

Insofar as we have believed the Industrial Democracy project to be a radical, scientifically based response to the central human and organizational dilemmas of modern industry, it behooves us to consider the criticisms of the students.

Essentially, their criticism is that the Industrial Democracy project is too late and, in any case, has been too limited in its aims. Because of these faults, it draws attention from the need for a total social transformation and beguiles the working people into hoping for gradual reform when only a violent break with the past can possibly be liberating. This appears to differ from the traditional Marxist critique only in its insistence on total transformation. The Marxists believed that transformation of the class relations in the productive process had to precede transformation of society at large. Our own position would seem to differ from both in three assumptions we make:

(a) The class relations in the productive process have evolved to such a stage of socialization (in the separation of ownership and management, the definition of the social character of capital and the professionalization of management) that it is possible to strive realistically for a revolutionary improvement in the concrete productive relations of workers and management. We note, in passing, that the Bolshevik revolution of 1917 left this problem untouched and for the next 50 years the conditions for tackling it did not apparently exist. Similarly, the piecemeal transformations in class relations in the advanced Western societies produced by nationalization of coal mining, etc., appeared to have no radical effect on the concrete day-to-day relations of managers and workers.

(b) The transformation of these concrete productive relations does not necessarily involve a conflict in class interests (given the "socialization of industry" mentioned above and the current level of technological development).

[1]Revised slightly from Tavistock Document HRC 210, 1975.

(c) The transformation of the concrete day-to-day relations in production is the key to transforming, or restoring, the other personal, social and institutional relations into which people enter.

The last of these beliefs was not a prerequisite to our engaging in this project. This would still have been justified in its own right provided it was not going to precipitate undue trouble or disproportionately reduce the choices people would have to determine their future.

These three basic assumptions are all subject to historical validation.

To my mind, the Norwegian experience already validates our first two assumptions that the Marxist contradiction is dépassé. Of course, it is reassuring to see the way the British are starting to follow the Norwegian example, but the essential point is that the class structure of Norwegian industry did not constitute a major obstacle to the realization of the project. The major obstacle to its acceptance has been the cultural and personality syndrome that Fromm (1950) called "the fear of freedom." The major obstacles to its spread to other larger capitalist countries would appear to be their complexity and cultural heterogeneity.

This should not surprise us. The fantastic growth in our productive capabilities has confronted us with the elimination of the domination of person over person, not simply a change in the form of domination. To confront successfully the cultures that have emerged over the past centuries as people sought to live with slavery, feudalism and capitalism, it is necessary for them to find common ground in deeper cultural roots. In some societies this will be harder to do than in others and in some, such as the United States, it may well be that it is impossible to confront this task without the guidance of some contemporary examples, such as Scandinavia.

Our last assumption was that the concrete day-to-day relations of production are the keystone to modern societies. This is becoming our most central concern, and yet it is the assumption for which we have the least direct evidence of what it means to a community when its working people are generally engaged in meaningful and challenging tasks.

There is, however, a lot of indirect evidence for making this assumption. Consider, first, the main contemporary arguments against it.

1. The student radicals have, on occasion, argued that it is the struggle against the universities which is the leading force for social transformation; that it is they who will lead the workers out of industrial bondage. The facts suggest that they are simply reacting to the industrialization of the universities. Admittedly, their reaction is informed with a perspective of the future which was inconceivable to earlier generations, but it is still only a reaction, a riot, not a revolutionary movement. The students suffer from the existing produc-

tive relations and may drop out in large numbers but are in no position to transform them from without. Their experience to date only confirms our assumption.

2. McLuhan appears to be arguing that it is the direct effects of the technology of electronic communication which are currently transforming all social relations, including the productive relations. He sees little choice for us in all of this, except perhaps that by gaining conscious insight we may lessen the pain of accepting the changes. Active determination of our future is, according to him, precluded by the numbness, the Narcissus narcosis, that characterizes social relations in general. Marcuse (1968:25), on balance, agrees with this pessimistic doctrine since he refers to it as the general replacement of psychological identification by primitive mimesis. Contrary to this, we think there is still a point of leverage for change. We maintain that it is by creating meaningful and challenging productive relations that people will be able and willing to put new content into the web of electronic communication. Insofar as daily work gives a sense of personal worth, identity and growth, people will enter into the web of general social relations as conscious individuals.

Against these alternative perspectives, we are arguing that while they correctly perceive the demise of the old dynamic of the class relation in production, they fail to see that this has laid bare the more fundamental and pernicious contradiction within the concrete relations of production. Labor and the technological progress that is meant to liberate us from poverty and drudgery is still being carried out in the stultifying and degrading traditional mode of domination and subordination. If anything, the scientific rationalization of the traditional mode is intensifying the contradiction between the possibilities for free development of human potentialities and the actualities of daily life in the work force.

The revolutionary content of our project rests on the realization that this contradiction can be resolved only by changes in the techniques of production and that the techniques of production include not only the tools but the concepts for their use; thus a lathe with the concept of tolerance limits is a different technology from one without the concept. Techniques of production that include concepts of personal interest, learning, innovation and decision making have been successfully evolved for a number of branches of industry. These efforts are in line with Marcuse's (1968:31) observation that "as all freedom depends on the conquest of alien necessity, the realization of freedom depends on the *techniques* of this conquest." These efforts are contrary to the ideological movements of the human relations schools which see the techniques of management as something distinct from the techniques of production and hence readily susceptible to human manipulation and the eventual masking of the contradiction to which we have drawn attention.

Let us now speculate about our third assumption, namely that the concrete relations in production are the leading part, the key link, in the transformation of society. We have discussed this so-called Phase C of the project for many years but have kept these discussions to ourselves and sought not to raise such questions in public. We neither wished to appear as dreamers nor to discourage people by pointing to the enormity of the tasks that lay ahead. Insofar as the proposed industrial changes could only increase the power of people freely to determine their future, we felt no guilt in hiding our personal thoughts.

What is likely to happen in other areas of social life as the industrial democracy project takes root? The effects on education are perhaps easiest to surmise because we are already involved in the education of managers and others for roles in the new socio-technical systems. Education for production by autonomous groups clearly requires an educational process in which autonomous groups are a basic element; the ability to use experts as resources presupposes experience with using academic staff as resource people; a naturally curious and creative response to the work situation presupposes that these potentialities are not stultified in educational processes; technical and social innovation and creativity presuppose a genuine polytechnic education and a grounding in the basic facts of people/task dynamics and of group dynamics. If such education is required in the reeducation of today's managers, foremen and workers, can we avoid making similar changes in higher, secondary and even primary education?

Similar considerations arise if we consider the quality of community life, leisure, the fate of the Welfare State and, hopefully, the quality of family life. Rather than dwell on what is patently obvious, let me proceed to my last point.

I have so far concentrated on the comparison of our project with current alternatives. Marcuse (1968:175) has gone beyond this to postulate criteria for testing the historical validity of any project that seeks to transcend the status quo. Following is a brief examination of my projections against his criteria.

1. The transcendent project must be in accordance with the real possibilities open at the attained level of the material and intellectual culture.

As argued in discussion of our assumptions (a) and (b), the Industrial Democracy project appears to meet this criterion.

2. The transcendent project, in order to falsify the established totality, must demonstrate higher rationality in the threefold sense that

(a) it offers the prospect of preserving and improving the productive achievements of civilization;

Our experiments to date show that we have every reason to expect that the democratization of work will do just this.

(b) it defines the established totality in its very structure, basic tendencies and relations;

As Marcuse (1968:23) himself points out, "stupefying work where it is no longer a real necessity" is the tap root of the "established totality." The tendencies and relations that arise from this have been partly spelled out in the early papers on socio-technical systems (Emery, 1977), but more has become apparent only in the course of our field experiments.

> (c) its realization offers a greater chance for the pacification of exis-
> tence, within the framework of institutions which offer a greater
> chance for the free development of human needs and faculties.

The democratization of work should very materially contribute to the "pacification of existence" and be a major force in the remolding of the "framework of institutions" to better aid the release and development of human potentialities. This effect is not dependent on most work in society having been redesigned. People will almost certainly wish to tackle these other tasks as soon as they are convinced that accomplishment of the industrial phase is only a matter of time.

Marcuse's analysis is so similar to mine that it is necessary to ask how he came to the pessimistic conclusion that the only possibility for change, and that dubious, lay with those social fragments that lie outside the productive process.

The answer is that he came right up to the door we are forcing. For example, in writing of the Soviet experiment, Marcuse stated that "if it could lead to self-determination at the very base of human existence, namely in the dimension of necessary labour it would be the most radical and most complete revolution in history" (p.49). Having come this far, he had no key to the door. The thin red thread that runs from the early Lewinian experiments (1936) on the dynamics of person/task relations (e.g., satiation, Zeigarnick effect, substitution, level of aspiration) to the "social climates" experiments and hence to the socio-technical experiments was outside his vision.

These very general thoughts may make it easier for us to formulate the tasks for Phase C of the Industrial Democracy project. There seems to be some urgency about this since people will almost certainly wish to tackle these tasks as soon as they are convinced that accomplishment of the industrial phase is only a matter of time.

References

Emery, F.E. 1977. *Futures We Are In*. Leiden: Martinus Nijhoff. Chapter 4 reproduced in part, Vol. II, "The Second Design Principle: Participation and the Democratization of Work," pp. 214–33.

Fromm, E. 1950. *The Fear of Freedom*. London: Kegan Paul, Trench, Trubner.

Lewin, K. 1936. *A Dynamic Theory of Personality: Selected Theoretical Papers*. New York: McGraw-Hill.

Marcuse, H. 1968. *One Dimensional Man: Studies in the Ideology of Advanced Industrial Society*. London: Sphere Books.

Paul Hill and Fred Emery

Toward a New Philosophy of Management[1]

Acceptance of Proposals

Shell (UK), an autonomous company in the Royal Dutch Shell Group, had become very seriously concerned with the alienation and poor performance of its hourly employees and also of a good many of its supervisors and managers. It was essential that a change be made to commitment and productive initiative as it was necessary to automate the refineries fully and this immense task could not succeed without the cooperation of all. A small group of three, called Employee Relations Planning (ERP), headed by Paul Hill, had been formed to study the long range problems involved and to suggest remedies. These remedies had included the devising of a new management philosophy which could be accepted from the boardroom to the shop floor. At a two-day conference in 1965 with the managing director and his full senior management team, it was agreed that ERP should proceed with the task of working out a draft document and that they should seek social science advice. This decision resulted in the Tavistock's Human Resource Centre being consulted.

This was the first of three critical decision-making meetings that the company's top management team was to hold within the space of 12 months to determine whether the development program should be planned and launched and, if so, the way it should grow. In the course of the meeting, which had been highly structured with a detailed agenda indicating all the points on which decisions were needed, there was ample opportunity for examination of both diagnosis and action plans. One statement in the ERP report that caused some managers concern was: "Effective management in modern industry can only be practised by consent of those managed." It was explained that this did not mean or imply that, in order to get anything done, managers must request the consent of each individual to carry out a particular instruction. It simply meant that unless there was a general acceptance of management's right to give instructions in any area, such instructions would not be carried out effectively.

[1]Excerpted with minor changes from Paul Hill, *Towards a New Philosophy of Management: The Company Development Programme of Shell U.K.* London: Gower Press, 1971.

At worst, there could be open rejection of the instructions, for example through a withdrawal of labor. At best, people would go through the motions but the work would not get done effectively.

The outcome of the meeting was a general acceptance of ERP's diagnosis of the problem and the endorsement of all the proposals for action. Specifically, the meeting decided that

- It should be a long-term objective of the company to secure an improvement in attitudes.
- Changes in management attitudes were necessary and should be initiated without delay.
- A participative management philosophy and style, as advocated in the report, should be introduced into all managerial and supervisory ranks, starting at the top.
- ERP should produce a detailed statement of objectives and management philosophy for discussion by the management team.
- ERP should find themselves appropriate social science assistance for the drafting of the document. The question of social science help in subsequent phases of the program was left open for future consideration.
- Detailed proposals should be drawn up for a system of target-setting and performance review, which would be agreed upon in principle.
- ERP should prepare detailed terms of reference for the proposed study teams which would be making exploratory studies of the areas likely to be affected by productivity bargaining.

The first critical step had been taken and the next management decision point had been delineated. That decision point would be taken up after discussion of the statement of objectives and philosophy which ERP were now required to produce.

Also as a result of this meeting, the management of Shell Chemical Company Limited decided that they would like their employees at Stanlow and Shell Haven chemical plants to participate fully in the program. They reserved their judgment about including the remainder of their organizations.

Securing Social Science Assistance

After the meeting ERP produced a work program showing the tasks envisaged over the following 12 months. On the one hand, the program called for the drafting of a statement of objectives and philosophy and its dissemination through a series of conferences resulting in a start on implementation measures, as yet unspecified. On the other hand, it called for the establishment of study teams, for which terms of reference were now laid down, leading to the beginning of joint discussions with union representatives.

In parallel with seeking social science help, a first attempt was made to draft the philosophy statement. The team members were forced to admit to themselves, however, that their efforts amounted to no more than a reasonably elegant piece of exhortation: a plea for a participative management style which lacked rational foundation and logical structure. It was clear that the statement would need to be more firmly based on reason and logic if it were to stand up to the rigorous testing it would undoubtedly be submitted to by managers throughout the company. The exercise served, therefore, to reinforce the need for outside assistance with this task.

While fully convinced of the need for help, ERP and others in the company found themselves rather ignorant about how to engage appropriate social science assistance. There appeared to be no register of resources available in the field. They decided, therefore, to make individual approaches to a number of prominent social scientists in Britain, sending each a copy of the ERP report and work program. Meetings were then arranged.

In each case the outcome of these discussions was similar. The company's intentions were approved, with varying degrees of enthusiasm, but none of the social scientists approached had sufficient time available to assist with the project. In spite of this, the discussions were valuable. In addition to a specific recommendation to approach the Tavistock Institute, they provided an opportunity to expose the proposed change program to a range of informed social science opinion, and confirmation that the proposals made sense. They also gave ERP a clearer recognition of the scale of social science help which would be needed for a project of the complexity envisaged.

The Tavistock Institute Human Resources Centre

An approach was duly made to the Tavistock Institute. The Institute was composed of five Centres whose domains ranged from family and community psychiatry to operational research. The company approached the Human Resources Centre group whose chairman was Eric Trist. Future use of the term "Tavistock" will refer specifically to this group.

A meeting with Trist and his colleagues in May 1965 showed a high degree of mutual interest and compatibility of objectives. Tavistock were impressed with the scope of the company's plans and with their relevance to their own previous work in this field. They felt they could contribute theoretically to the launching and development of the project and, on the basis of their practical knowledge and experience, lend support at times of setback and disappointment which, they warned, would inevitably arise in the course of such a large-scale undertaking. Furthermore, they could make sufficient resources immediately available to work on it.

Trial Period

At the suggestion of Tavistock it was agreed that the company would engage their services for a trial period of three to four months, beginning in July 1965. This would allow sufficient time for an orientation program, the drafting of the statement of objectives and philosophy and its acceptance or rejection by the company's management team.

The working arrangements would be flexible. Four senior members of the Tavistock would make themselves available whenever they were needed. They were Eric Trist (the leader), Fred Emery, Gurth Higgin and Harold Bridger. At the end of the trial period the company and the Tavistock would be in a position to decide whether they wished to continue the collaboration.

Orientation

The first concern of Trist and his colleagues was to explore for themselves the company's organization and technical system, its objectives, its boundaries and its links with the outside world. Higgin made a visit to Shell's Pernis refinery in the Netherlands in order to get a firsthand impression of the technology of which, as yet, Tavistock had no intimate knowledge. It was better that they should learn about this technology from a location independent of those in the UK where they were to be involved.

Their normal link with the company was the ERP team. By channeling all contacts and communications through ERP it was possible to coordinate activities and plot the movement of the project. Moreover, Tavistock saw it as an important task not only to feed in to the company as much of their own knowledge and experience as possible but also to help people inside the company acquire social science skills and expertise. The ERP team were the logical people with whom to start this process, and Tavistock set out to build a close collaborative relationship with them. From the beginning, therefore, Tavistock and ERP established a pattern of joint discussions and planning meetings which was to continue throughout the project.

Tavistock members visited each of the refineries and met all the senior executives in the company's head office. In addition to carrying out their own appreciation of the company's situation, they were concerned with assessing the validity of the problem diagnosis on which ERP had based its action proposals.

ERP's assumptions about the level of morale and motivation among shop floor people, for example, had been based on its members' own working experience and their extensive contacts with hourly paid employees. The possibility of conducting an attitude survey to get some objective data on the subject had been considered in 1964 but had been rejected because it was feared the results would have been unduly influenced by the decrease in employees imposed by the company in that year.

By the end of their orientation program, Tavistock were satisfied that the diagnosis appeared to be valid. The next task was to produce a draft of the objectives and philosophy statement.

The Statement of Objectives and Philosophy

The statement was to be the focal point of the whole development program. It was to set out exactly what the objectives of the company were and the philosophy, or principles, which would serve as guidelines to managers when making decisions. This was felt to be essential if the long-term aim of changing unfavorable attitudes and securing a higher level of commitment to the company's objectives was to be achieved. It was also necessary to give employees the opportunity to discuss the statement so that they could either accept or reject the objectives and principles it set out. It was hoped that both would be endorsed by employees at all levels and that, as a result, they would in time be encouraged and motivated to devote their energies to putting the philosophy into practice. Acceptance would imply, in broad terms, consent to manage and be managed in accordance with the principles set out in the statement and in pursuit of the stated objectives.

Drafting the Statement

Although it was not immediately apparent, the theories and concepts which Tavistock had developed fitted exactly into the picture the company wished to create. Moreover, they provided the firm logical structure which the statement needed and which had been lacking from ERP's own first efforts at drafting.

The statement was drafted by a small team: Emery of Tavistock and two members of ERP. They had available to them a set of company objectives which had recently been drawn up by the management team. They also had available the experience that all the Tavistock members had gained as a result of the orientation program and their own analysis of the company system. Working only part of the time, they completed the task within a month.

Purpose and Criteria

The drafting team first established for themselves the purpose the statement was to serve and the criteria its contents would have to meet.

It was agreed that the statement was not intended to serve as a public relations document for use outside the company, nor was it in any way to be used for industrial relations purposes or to replace existing agreements with the trade unions. It was intended to be a working document which would provide practical guidance in the management and operation of the company. Two main drafting criteria were established:

Validity. The contents of the statement would have to be seen as valid by all employees and have some relevance to the actual performance of tasks in the various areas of the company's activity. Furthermore, its contents should continue to be valid and relevant over a reasonable span of time—five to ten years—by taking into account any developments such as those in technology which could be foreseen within that time span.

Appropriateness. The principles, or values, written into the statement would have to be appropriate to the nature of the company's main activities—that is, refining.

Jargon

The first draft was tested out informally with a number of people at various levels and in different functions. First reactions to the document were often doubtful since the concepts embodied in it were new to people and some of the wording caused problems. However, after a process of discussion and clarification and some minor modification of the text, everyone consulted was satisfied that the contents were both valid and appropriate.

Tavistock and ERP agreed that no attempt should be made to "simplify" the document by eliminating or paraphrasing the jargon. Such an attempt would, they felt, result in a loss of some of the statement's meaning and power. Furthermore, it was not intended that the document be used as a "hand-out" for employees to read without the opportunity for debate and discussion. Experience had shown that discussion was essential to bring out its full meaning and implications and that in the course of this process the jargon usually ceased to be a problem.

Summary of the Statement's Contents

The full statement is reproduced later in this paper. Before reading it, however, it will be helpful to look at its structure (Figure 1) in conjunction with the summary of its contents which follows and which highlights the major concepts involved. The statement consisted of the seven main sections shown in Figure 1.

1. *Primary objective.* The company's primary objective is expressed in terms of maximizing its contribution to the Group's long term profitability

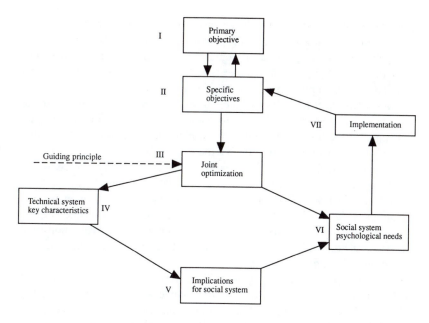

Figure 1. Logical structure of the statement of objectives and philosophy

insofar as this arises from the efficient use of resources. There follows what could be termed the company's social objective, involving commitment to two key concepts:

(a) That all the resources it uses are "social resources" (that is, are in the last analysis resources of the community) and must be protected and developed as such.

(b) That the resources must be used to contribute to the satisfaction of the community's needs for products and services.

Thus the company commits itself to seeking improved profitability and the creation of new wealth only in ways which will also benefit society—through meeting community needs efficiently and through protecting and developing the social resources it uses.

2. *Specific objectives.* Six specific objectives are spelled out within the overall framework of the primary objective. Two are operational objectives concerned with meeting present and future market requirements. The third is related to the company's position in the Group. The last three derive from the commitment to protect and develop resources and are concerned with the development of people, safety and the need to minimize pollution of the environment.

3. *The principle of joint optimization as a guide to implementation.* The guiding principle to assist the company in pursuing its objectives is the joint

optimization of the social and technical systems. Joint optimization means the best possible matching together of the people in any unit and the way their jobs are organized, with the physical equipment and material resources in that unit. The statement of this principle here leads on to an examination of the technical system and of its implications for the design of the social system.

4. *Key characteristics of the evolving technical system*. Seven fundamental characteristics of the technical system are identified which are likely to remain unchanged in the foreseeable future and which must therefore be taken into account in deciding how best to design the social system.

5. *Implications for the social system*. By considering the implications of the key technical characteristics, the most appropriate matching human characteristics are suggested. The most important human task in running process operations is identified as information handling. As this is a skill which cannot be controlled by external supervision, employees must be internally motivated to carry it out efficiently. It follows that the key human characteristics required are responsibility and commitment.

6. *Responsibility and commitment*. This section is concerned with what must be done to create conditions in which people will develop responsibility and commitment to their tasks. It is suggested that two things are necessary:

(a) Satisfactory terms and conditions of employment.
(b) Jobs which enable them to satisfy the basic psychological needs of human beings in their work.

What are considered to be the main psychological needs are then set out, together with some general principles to be taken into account in redesigning jobs.

7. *Principle of implementation of the philosophy*. The philosophy must be tested in the company through all employees having the opportunity to relate its implications to their own situation. Senior managers have a special responsibility for leading the process of testing and dissemination, and for implementation.

Text of the Statement

The version of the statement quoted below is dated May 1966 and incorporates a number of additions and improvements that resulted from the first wave of dissemination conferences for senior managers. The key concepts and framework, however, survived intact from the original draft.

STATEMENT OF OBJECTIVES AND MANAGEMENT PHILOSOPHY

1. *Primary objective*. The company is primarily concerned to maximise its contribution to the long-term profitability of the Shell Group insofar as this arises

from the efficiency with which it uses the Group's resources of men, money and material.

The resources to which it has legal rights of privileged access are nonetheless part of the total resources of society as a whole and are, in this sense, social resources; the company believes that they must be protected, developed and managed as such. It furthermore believes that its use of these resources must be such as to contribute to meeting society's requirements for products and services.

The company recognises, however, that ultimate discretion for what can be done to maximise Group profitability cannot properly be exercised without having a total picture of the exploration, production, transportation, manufacturing, marketing and research functions. Since the activities of the company lie mainly within the manufacturing function, this makes necessary the statement of its specific objectives in terms of the minimum expenditure of resources appropriate to the discharge of its responsibilities to the Group.

2. *Specific objectives.* Specifically this commits the company to:

1. Meeting the current market requirements for refined petroleum products with minimum expenditure of total resources per unit of quantity of given quality.

2. Ensuring the company's ability to meet emerging market requirements with decreasing expenditure of total resources per unit of quantity of specified quality.

An essential task of management is to seek at all times optimal solutions to 1 and 2.

In addition, the company is specifically committed by its position in the Group to:

3. Seeking continually from the Group the power and the information necessary to enable it to meet its responsibilities. In certain circumstances it may be necessary to seek a redefinition of its responsibilities in order that the company's capabilities may be best used on behalf of the Group.

Implicit in these three specific objectives and in the fact that the company's resources are part of the total resources of society are the following additional specific objectives:

4. Creating conditions in which employees at all levels will be encouraged and enabled to develop and to realise their potentialities while contributing towards the company's objectives.

5. Carrying out its productive and other operations in such a way as to safeguard the health and safety of its employees and the public.

6. Seeking to reduce any interference that may be caused by its activities to the amenities of the community, accepting the measures practised under comparable conditions in British industry as a minimum standard and making use of the expertise and knowledge available within the Group.

3. *The principle of joint optimisation as a guide to implementation.* The com-

pany must manage both a social system, of people and their organisation, and a technical system, of physical equipment and resources. Optimisation of its overall operations can be achieved only by jointly optimising the operation of these two systems; attempts to optimise the two independently of each other, or undue emphasis upon one of them at the expense or the neglect of the other, must fail to achieve optimisation for the company as a whole.

4. *Key characteristics of the evolving technical system.* In order to create appropriate conditions for the optimisation of the overall system, it is necessary to design the social system jointly with the technical system recognising that the latter has certain key persistent characteristics which must be taken into account. These characteristics are:

1. The company forms part of a complex, science-based industry subject to rapid technical change. This rate of change can be expected to increase in the future.

2. There is a wide measure of flexibility available in all the main processes involved in oil refining, i.e., distillation, conversion and blending. The added value which results from refining operations depends to a high degree upon the skillful use of this flexibility in plant design and operation and the programming of refinery and overall company operations in order to meet variable market requirements from given and variable inputs.

3. The company is capital-intensive and it follows that adequate criteria of overall company performance must be sought mainly in measures of efficiency of plant utilisation. The importance to overall company performance of efficient plant utilisation makes necessary a high degree of plant reliability.

4. The company's refineries are already highly involved with automation and instrumentation. Pressure for a very much higher level of automation and instrumentation arises from the development of new processes and the drive towards optimal use of flexibility described in 2 above and the need to improve the ability to control, identify and account for the large number of movements through the technical system at any one time.

5. There is considerable variation in the degree of automation of different operations in the company. Labour-intensive activities exist side by side with highly automated ones. Despite the trends noted in 1 and 4 above, some variation is likely to persist.

6. The company's process operations are carried out on a continuous twenty-four hours per day, seven-day week basis, by a number of shift teams, while many associated service activities are carried out discontinuously on a day working basis.

7. The refineries and head office are geographically widely separated and within refineries there is considerable dispersion of the various activities. For economic and technical reasons this characteristic is likely to persist.

5. *Implications for the social system*. The rapid and increasing rate of change in the technical system defined in characteristic 1 creates a special need for new expertise, skills and knowledge at all levels, and new forms of organisation to cope with changing requirements. It also increases the rate at which skills and knowledge are rendered obsolete. The company believes that its objectives in relation to the social nature of its resources commit it to train its employees in new skills and new knowledge where obsolescence of skills and knowledge has resulted from its own or the industry's technical development. These effects require the company to plan for the development of appropriate skills and forms of organisation in parallel with the planning of technical change.

The most significant consequence of characteristics 2, 3, 4, 6 and 7 is that economic production within our process technology is critically dependent upon people effectively dealing with information yielded by the technical system and contributing the most appropriate information to the control and guidance of that system. Some of these informational flows are confined to individuals who take information from the technical system and feed back guidance directly into it. Other informational flows must be carried at any one time by a network of many people at many different organisational levels. The effectiveness of this social informational network depends upon the recognition by all those involved in its design and operation that it is made up of people and is therefore affected by the factors that influence human behaviour.

The wide geographical dispersion of the refineries and the extensive layout within the refineries themselves present an impediment to effective communications. This makes it even more necessary for the company to design efficient informational flows.

A further consequence of characteristic 3, namely the need for a high degree of plant reliability, is that economic production is also highly dependent upon the application of craft skills and knowledge.

In information handling, and to a large degree in the exercise of craft skills, the problem is to avoid lapses of attention and errors in observing, diagnosing and communicating or acting upon information. Information-handling work in the refining industry is such that lapses and errors are likely to result in heavy costs, both from delay in recognising errors and taking corrective action and from the nature of the equipment and the processes involved. The only promising way of avoiding these faults is for the individual to be internally motivated to exercise responsibility and initiative. Any external control can only act after the error has occurred or had its effect.

In contrast, in those jobs where the main human contribution is manual labour, there is some choice as to how control may be achieved. Although optimal control requires internal motivation, the shortcomings associated with mainly manual tasks do not result in heavy costs and it is possible to achieve an economic degree of control by external incentives and supervision. For these reasons the exercise of personal responsibility and initiative in such work, although desirable, may be considered less significant.

However, the manual jobs in the refineries (characteristic 5) exist mainly amongst service activities ancillary to the operating and engineering activities which are central to the task of oil refining. It is considered essential that the company's philosophy should be appropriate to the nature of these central activities. For those activities of a different nature it may be necessary to modify them through technical developments, e.g., the introduction of mechanisation or automation, or to develop other social systems appropriate to them, in keeping with the values of the company's philosophy.

Despite the complication arising from characteristic 5 therefore, the major implication of this group of technical characteristics emerges as the need to develop a high level of personal responsibility and initiative.

6. *Responsibility and commitment.* People cannot be expected to develop within themselves and to exercise the level of responsibility and initiative that is required unless they can be involved in their task and unless, in the long run, it is possible to develop commitment to the objectives served by their task.

The company recognises that it cannot expect its employees at all levels to develop adequate involvement and commitment spontaneously or in response to mere exhortation. It must set out to create the conditions under which such commitment may develop.

The work of social scientists has shown that the creation of such conditions cannot be achieved simply by the provision of satisfactory terms of service, including remuneration. The provision of such terms of service is essential, but is not in itself sufficient; for involvement and commitment at all levels it is necessary to go beyond this, to meet the general psychological requirements that men have of their work.

The following are some of the psychological requirements that relate to the content of a job:

1. The need for the content of the work to be reasonably demanding of the individual in terms other than those of sheer endurance, and for it to provide some variety.

2. The need for an individual to know what his job is and how he is performing in it.

3. The need to be able to learn on the job and go on learning.

4. The need for some area of decision making where the individual can exercise his discretion.

5. The need for some degree of social support and recognition within the organisation.

6. The need for an individual to be able to relate what he does and what he produces to the objectives of the company and to his life in the community.

7. The need to feel that the job leads to some sort of desirable future which does not necessarily imply promotion.

These requirements exist in some form for the large majority of men and at all levels of employment. Their relative significance, however, will clearly vary from individual to individual and it is not possible to provide for their fulfilment in the same way for all kinds of people. Similarly, different jobs will provide varying degrees of opportunity for the fulfilment of particular requirements.

They cannot generally be met, however, simply by redesigning individual jobs. Most tasks involve more than one person and, in any case, all jobs must be organisationally related to the company's objectives. If the efforts to meet the above requirements for individuals are not to be frustrated, the company must observe certain principles in developing its organisational form. Thus, the individual must know not only what he is required to do, but also the way in which his work ties in with what others are doing, the part he plays in the communications network and the limits within which he has genuine discretionary powers. Furthermore, the individual's responsibilities should be defined in terms of objectives to be pursued; although procedural rules are necessary for coordination, they must be reviewed regularly in the light of experience gained in pursuing these objectives.

Responsibility and authority must go hand in hand in order to avoid situations in which people are delegated responsibility but do not have the means to exercise it. Likewise, the company must be ready to redefine responsibilities where there are capabilities which are unused.

Not least, the company must seek to ensure that the distribution of status and reward is consistent with the level of responsibility carried by the individual.

In following this course the company will seek the fullest involvement of all employees and will make the best use of available knowledge and experience of the social sciences.

7. *Principle of implementation of the philosophy.* The effective implementation and communication of the philosophy throughout the company can be achieved only if its mode of implementation manifests the spirit of the philosophy. Verbal or written communication alone will not suffice; it is essential that all employees be enabled to relate the philosophy to themselves by participating in the implementation of the philosophy in their particular parts of the company.

A special burden of responsibility must rest with the senior managers, who alone are in a position to exercise the leadership and provide the necessary impetus to translate the philosophy into a living reality. Starting with their commitment, it will be possible to involve progressively the other levels of the employees in searching out the implications for themselves. As the philosophy begins to shape the activities of the company it will be able more effectively to pursue its objectives.

Management Reactions to the Statement

The most important test the draft statement had to face was the detailed examination it received from the company's top management team. Unless the document was accepted by them the attitude-change program would clearly not be launched. For this purpose a three-day residential conference was arranged in October, 1965 at the Selsdon Park Hotel near London. Present were the managing director, his functional heads of departments and the general managers and their deputies from the refineries. Tavistock and ERP were there as advisers. With the managing director in the chair, the group worked through the document sentence by sentence, testing its validity and appropriateness to the company. Afternoons were free on the first two days, with working sessions before and after the evening meal. Informal discussions then carried on until late in the night.

The whole of the document provoked intensive discussion. It raised some new issues, and it focused a new light on old issues.

Primary Objective

Most important of all was the discussion on the formulation of the company's primary objective, since the concept of social resources and the idea of interdependent and complementary economic and social objectives lent cohesion to the rest of the statement.

The concept of social resources itself and the notion that the company had legal rights only of privileged access to its resources rather than outright ownership was different from the traditional concept of property. Also unfamiliar was the notion that employees are social resources to be protected and developed rather than "commodities," however well they might be treated. Yet the concept was accepted without much argument. While the idea came initially as a shock, the oil industry is sufficiently familiar with practical examples of the right of access to resources being withdrawn from companies by some societies through nationalization or expropriation for the concept to be recognized as relevant. Most of those present had worked in many parts of the world, and there was a fund of experience in dealing with the problems of setting up a new refinery—finding, recruiting and training people from the local communities. It was not difficult to perceive of such people as social resources.

There was, however, strong argument about the use of the term "profitability" in preference to "profits." The latter represented finite sums of money, the former a state of affairs which had continuously to be maintained if the enterprise was to survive. A vast concern like Shell was in business "for keeps"; it was not expendable and was intimately involved in many critical ways with the societies in which it operated. That it should continue to succeed and how it used its power were important issues to many people beyond itself.

The main debate concerned the validity of extending the scope of the primary objective beyond the commitment to maximize contributions to the group's long term profitability. It was considered by some that the inclusion of the words "long term" automatically ruled out any undesirable or antisocial methods of making profit, since such activity would inevitably have adverse repercussions on the company's reputation and its long-term prospects. In response to this argument, it was agreed that senior managers would to varying degrees carry in their minds the complex implications attaching to the phrase "long term profitability." They were relatively well equipped from their privileged position in the company to be able to commit themselves to work toward such a complex overall objective. It was unlikely, however, that those on the shop floor would carry a similar set of implications in their minds. Their set of implications would tend to be quite different, particularly if they—and others—interpreted the word "profitability" to mean simply the profits distributed annually to shareholders, the dividends always being made as large as possible at their expense. What the company was now seeking was an overall objective which all employees in the organization could understand in the same way and to which they could all commit themselves. It was therefore essential to spell out exactly what it should be and not to rely on implications which could differ between individuals or which might not be recognized at all.

There were three possible formulations of the primary objective the drafters could have used. They were referred to as positions 1, 2 and 3, the latter corresponding to the formulation used in the statement although for the purpose of this explication it was put in a simpler form. They were:

Position 1. The company is primarily concerned to maximize its contribution to the long term profitability of the Group.

Position 2. The company is primarily concerned to maximize its contribution to the long term profitability of the Group, with due regard for its social obligations for the welfare of its employees and the community.

Position 3. The company is primarily concerned to maximize its contribution to the long term profitability of the Group insofar as this arises from the efficiency with which it uses the Group's resources of men, money and material, accepting that these are social resources to be used for meeting society's requirements.

Discussion

POSITION 1

It was argued that position 1 represents profit maximization without any qualification. It corresponded to the objectives which had been drafted by the top management team after their meeting in March 1965, of which the primary objective was: "To maximize the return on capital employed for the company, having due regard for manufacturing costs." This may be the conventional way of stating the objective of a business, but individuals working in an organization strictly guided by such a primary objective would tend to adopt a similar self-seeking attitude and would strive simply to maximize their own personal gain. Unions would see no reason why they should not struggle to get the biggest possible share of the cake. If profit maximization was the rule of the game, it was their job to learn to play it as well as they could. The example was quoted of the explicit adoption of just such a philosophy by unions in the United States after the Second World War (in place of the class struggle), and this had now crossed the Atlantic. Such a philosophy also told managers that their primary objective was their own career interests and that to be over-concerned about the good of the company was irrational.

POSITION 2

Position 2 recognized that the company had some social obligations which are seen as constraints on profit maximization. While legal constraints are normally observed, and while the company may choose on occasion to go beyond legal requirements, it reserves the right to cut back whenever it feels it necessary to do so. Thus the choice as to the degree of social obligation that should be recognized in any particular situation is left entirely up to the company, which retains complete control in its own hands. Employees in an organization guided by a Position 2 objective would be unlikely to trust the management always to exercise its discretion in a fair and consistent manner. They may see it as a technique to buy off individual self-seeking. Such distrust would be confirmed and strengthened if the company chose to revert to Position 1 in hard times, which Position 2 leaves it free to do. At such times, paternalism would be replaced by the hard line. Employees would find their suspicions justified and would become angry and cynical. The way the recent reductions in manning levels had been carried out had led to serious repercussions and had caused a marked degree of alienation within the ranks of management itself.

POSITION 3

Position 3 differs from Position 2 in that it builds in an amalgamation of economic and social values and a criterion for their reconciliation: the commitment to efficient use of social resources. It openly commits the company to observe the amalgamation. It does not allow a reversion to Position 1. It lays the foundations for company objectives to which it would be hoped the commitment of all employees could in the long run be secured. An attitude of trust would be built up.

During the discussion there was some initial support from a few of the managers for the Position 1 approach. Although they agreed the company did not operate in that way, they were reluctant to commit to paper any constraints on profit maximization (beyond those implied by "long term") when they had no clear and rational criteria for doing so. It was generally felt that in the past the company's position had been that described in Position 2. It was recognized, however, that there had on occasions been swings back to Position 1, with apparent disregard of social obligations, and that this oscillation between 2 and 1 had undoubtedly contributed a great deal to the high level of distrust of management's intentions, not only among shop floor employees but also among supervisors and managers. A simpler example of such oscillation than the 1964 rundown was the extension of facilities for part-time studies enjoyed by staff workers to the hourly paid employees in the early 1960s and the subsequent withdrawal of these facilities a year or two later. Such pinpricks not only annoyed—they were symbolic.

It was finally agreed by everyone that Position 3 most appropriately described what the company was now setting out to do. It was particularly necessary to move in this direction in view of the accelerating rate of technological change and the higher level of uncertainty this brought about for all. Position 3 offered the prospect of establishing a positive and consistent pattern of management, a stable anchor in an unstable world. The conjunction of the economic objective and the social objective was felt to be valid and acceptable. Moreover, it was considered that far from being a constraint on profitability, the recognition of the need to protect and develop social resources would, in the long term, prove to be contributing to the company's profitability. To treat employees as resources and to develop their talents would be more than ever necessary in the more automated and changing world of the future. The two parts of the primary objective were not opposed but complementary.

IMPLICATIONS OF POSITION 3

Some of the implications of accepting Position 3 as the primary objective were explored in depth. For example, it meant that profit could be sought only through the efficient use of resources: profit from exploitation or degrading of resources would be contrary to the objective. This applied equally to the treatment of people, raw material, equipment, money or the environment. It ruled out such activities as the crude use of market power, or price fixing, as a substitute for the continuing search for improved competence in the manufacture of competitive products of quality. By committing themselves explicitly to this social objective of protecting and developing resources, managers would be open to question by employees if their decisions appeared to be inconsistent with it. Further, in establishing social objectives down the line, alongside operational objectives, it would become necessary to give greater recognition to social costs, whether these were borne by employees in terms of stress or obsolescence or by the community in terms of nuisance or pollution.

Clearly, however, some limits had to be set. The commitment to protect and develop resources could not be open-ended. The principle was accordingly established that the commitment should apply only to those resources which the company used. It was not committing itself to expenditure on community resources which it did not itself use. Further, the level to which it should protect and develop its resources was to be interpreted in accordance with the prevailing standards and values of society.

To take a practical example, the company could not unilaterally be committed to eliminate all pollution resulting from its operations regardless of cost. Yet some managers felt the company should undertake some measure of leadership in this respect. Taking a leadership role meant anticipating the future; it meant seeking improved solutions by setting its own reasonable example and by using its influence to secure the cooperation of others. As a result a guideline was built into the document by an addition to specific objective 2:6 which then read: "seeking to reduce any interference that may be caused by its activities to the amenities of the community, accepting the measures practised under comparable conditions in British industry as a minimum standard and making use of the expertise and knowledge available within the Group."

The Company's Position Within the Group

Discussion of the third paragraph of section 1 of the statement, which describes the implications of the company's relationship with the Group, served to reinforce several already recognized needs. Separated from the market at both the crude input and the product output ends, the company had no meaningful profit indicators by which to measure its own efficiency. In their early visits to the refineries, the Tavistock team had found this to be a cause of great anxiety among manufacturing people, allied with feelings of inferiority to and resentment of marketing people. It encouraged misleading beliefs about profit centers in manufacturing locations, beliefs which were particularly unsuited to Group balancing refineries. The company's specific objectives had, therefore, to be framed in terms of meeting the requirements put upon it with the minimum expenditure of resources. This did not equate with cost-cutting. It meant meeting market requirements in a way which "used up" the minimum of its total resources and which was compatible with protecting and developing them.

This led to the underlining of the need for the company to generate more effective yardsticks of its own performance. Also underlined was the need for better communication channels across the company boundary with the Group central supply unit and with the marketing organization. This would permit more information to flow into the company and provide greater opportunity for the company to challenge decisions affecting its operations. As the potential benefits this would bring were perceived at company level, so it was recognized that people at the refineries would have similar needs and similar potential benefits at their level.

A new specific objective, 2:3, was in due course added to the statement. It read: "In addition, the company is specifically committed to: seeking continually from the Group the power and information necessary to enable it to meet its responsibilities. In certain circumstances it may be necessary to seek a redefinition of its responsibilities in order that the company's capabilities may be best used on behalf of the Group."

Joint Optimization as a Guide to Implementation

While it was conceded that the use of jargon should be minimized, the terminology of the statement was defended by Tavistock on the grounds that every branch of knowledge has its own set of concepts which people have to learn if they want to understand what it has to offer. Furthermore, an advantage of the use of the appropriate terminology was that it ensured that important points would be adequately discussed and explored. A danger inherent in the use of paraphrase was that people would tend to accept points as obvious, without considering their implications. Thus while "joint optimization of the socio-technical system" at first gave people pause and demanded explanations, a paraphrase such as "the best matching of the people and the equipment in the organization" might be accepted as reasonable or self-evident and passed over without challenge.

The conference members accepted without difficulty the notion that any production system consists of two parts: the social system, made up of people, with their physical and psychological requirements and characteristics, and the way they are organized, both formally and informally, in the work situation; and the technical system, comprising the equipment and plant with its particular characteristics and requirements and the way it is laid out. The idea of joint optimization was that these two subsystems should be matched together in the most appropriate and effective way.

The main difficulty shared by most managers was, however, to imagine that there could be any better or significantly different way of organizing people to operate a process unit, or any other piece of equipment, than the traditional way. Until it was accepted that there was, in fact, a wide range of choice in the way the social and the technical systems could be matched together, the real significance of the concept of joint optimization was not apparent. What served to bring home to the conference members the meaning of organizational choice was a graphic description by one of the Tavistock team of the contrast in effectiveness between two methods of operation of longwall coal faces (Trist et al., 1963/Vol. II). From this point on, the possibility of applying the concept within the refinery situation became more real.

The socio-technical approach to designing jobs and organizations was seen as striking a balance between the two main theories which had previously governed—and mostly still do govern—the way jobs are set up.

The most common approach to job design has always been machine-dominated. This is the mechanistic or "scientific management" approach (Taylor, 1911), which regards the people who must operate equipment virtually as extensions of the machinery. Time and motion study, payment by results schemes and much of current industrial engineering have derived from this traditional mechanistic approach to job design. In a situation where the work force is willing to submit to boring, tiring, repetitive jobs, the approach produces results. In a situation, however, where the work force becomes frustrated and antagonized by the nature of their tasks, the system can easily be disrupted if they behave in ways other than those laid down.

If the scientific management approach concerns itself mainly with the technical system, the second major approach—the human relations school—is concerned almost entirely with the social system. The human relations school sprang from the work of Elton Mayo, who, through his studies at the Hawthorne works of the Western Electric Company over the years 1927–33, demonstrated that the social system in an organization had very distinctive characteristics of its own (Roethlisberger and Dickson, 1939).

The human relations approach with its stress on the individual's attitude, role in the group and status in the social system undoubtedly led to improvements in working conditions, welfare arrangements and employee services. But it focused exclusively on the social system with virtually no regard to the effect the technical system had on people's actual tasks. Its usefulness has accordingly tended to be limited.

The new feature of Tavistock's socio-technical approach to job design was the recognition that, because of their interdependence, the social and the technical systems had to be considered together. As the coal mine studies had clearly demonstrated, it was necessary to analyze exactly what requirements the technical system imposed upon the people who operated it. Only then was it possible to organize the tasks in a way which both satisfied the technical requirements and made the best use of the properties of the social system itself.

The scientific management approach required people to carry out simple, repetitive tasks in a consistent manner over long periods of time. Machines are eminently suited to this type of task—people are not. The socio-technical approach, by contrast, seeks to utilize those capabilities of the social system which are distinctively human, for example, the ability to be flexible and adaptive, to make judgments and decisions. Only by matching these human capabilities with the complementary characteristics of the technology can the best overall result be obtained.

Furthermore, by arranging tasks in a way which enables people to utilize their distinctive capabilities, the socio-technical approach opens up the possibility of motivating people through their interest in, and commitment to, their work rather than simply through financial rewards, as in the scientific management approach.

That people should be interested in and committed to their work becomes particularly necessary in advanced and changing technologies. The statement's examination of the key characteristics of the company's refining technology brought out the fact that the basic skills required were perceptual and cognitive. People had to use good judgment and make good decisions. This could not be secured by external supervision. Hence the importance of involvement and commitment. To correct errors after they had occurred was too late and too costly. Workers had to be self-regulating and internally motivated to anticipate events. This was not simply desirable, it was essential for the efficient operation of the system.

Practical Implications

The outcome of this discussion was general agreement that the concept of joint optimization was highly relevant to the company's situation. The technical manager present said the company had concentrated very much on optimizing the technical system. Only after the design of a new technical system was complete would the question of manning it normally be considered. The concept of joint optimization implied the need to plan technical and social systems together if the best results were to be achieved. The new refinery at Teesport provided an opportunity to do this.

Another major implication of acceptance of this concept, and one which was to be discussed again at many location conferences, was that the manager of a department must be responsible for the entire socio-technical system and not only for meeting operational targets. The tendency in the past had often been for the manager to concentrate attention on the problems of the technical system and to pass problems arising in the social system to the personnel department.

Psychological Needs

Section 6 of the statement, dealing with the conditions which have to be provided if people are to develop responsibility and commitment to their tasks, was accepted by the management team as relevant to the refinery situation. There was general agreement that in many parts of the organization the company was not fully utilizing its human capabilities. There were also doubts, however, about the extent to which it would be possible in practice to establish appropriate conditions for some sections of the work force, but there again the limits of what might be feasible were not known.

Results of the Conference

During the concluding session on the third day, each manager gave his personal reactions to the contents of the draft statement. The managing director reserved his own views until last.

The outcome was that each manager accepted the document as valid and appropriate to the company's needs. Each gave his commitment to manage in accordance with its principles. The level of enthusiasm varied and some reservations were expressed but overall there was strong support for the statement. One manager believed that this event could well prove to be the most important management conference the company had ever held. The managing director made clear his own support of the principles and said that the three days' testing of the statement had dispelled some initial skepticism. He then stated his personal commitment.

The reservations expressed were concerned mainly with the difficulty foreseen in getting the statement widely disseminated and understood throughout the company and uncertainty, at this stage, about how the ideas in the philosophy could be put into practice. Conference members themselves would need more time to consider fully the implications of the statement for their own roles and their own departments. It was also felt necessary to see how senior managers in the refineries reacted to the philosophy before it was transmitted down the line, and certainly before the trade unions were involved.

Action Items

The following decisions were taken:

- In view of the successful outcome of the trial period and the acceptance of the draft statement, the action research relationship with Tavistock would be extended so that they could help with the dissemination process and with the development of the program. It was recognized that their participation in the Selsdon Park conference had been a critical factor in its success.
- Each refinery, and head office, would hold its own conferences to discuss the statement with their own senior staff. Tavistock and ERP would be available to help if requested.
- When all senior staff in the company had had the opportunity to work through the statement, a further conference of the top management team would be held early in 1966 to review progress and decide what further steps to take.
- The Statement of Objectives and Philosophy would continue to be regarded as a draft. It was anticipated that additional modifications and improvements would be proposed from staff at the refineries. ERP was to be the custodian of the draft, responsible for collecting and coordinating all suggested amendments.
- Until the statement had proved acceptable to refinery senior staff and the program was more firmly established, it should be given minimum publicity in order to avoid undesirable rumors. At the refineries, where the absence at conferences of numbers of senior staff could hardly go unnoticed, it should be stated simply that the company was studying in depth its objectives and method of operating. If and when there was anything further to communicate, it would be done.
- Location managements should begin to consider what were the implications of the statement within their commands, in terms of action to be taken, both at their own level and at less senior levels in the organization, and eventually on the shop floor and in the unions.

The refinery conferences at all levels, including the unions, were held in residential settings and lasted two-and-a-half days. The general manager was in the chair and his deputy was with him. ERP and the Tavistock were present. There were 20 to 30 refinery people each time, working sometimes as a whole group and sometimes in small groups. A number of modifications and amendments were introduced, but the basic philosophy emerging from the top management conference was accepted by all groups, though the degree of commitment varied. The next step was to create implementive projects that would put the philosophy into action and involve the managers and workers immediately concerned in carrying them out.

References

Roethlisberger, F.J. and W.J. Dickson. 1939. *Management and the Worker: An Account of a Research Program Conducted by the Western Electric Company, Hawthorne Works, Chicago.* Cambridge, Mass.: Harvard University Press.

Taylor, F.W. 1911. *The Principles and Methods of Scientific Management.* New York: Harper and Row.

Trist, E.L., G.W. Higgin, H. Murray and A.B. Pollock. 1963. *Organizational Choice: Capabilities of Groups at the Coal Face Under Changing Technologies: The Loss, Rediscovery and Transformation of a Work Tradition.* London: Tavistock Publications. Reissued 1987, New York: Garland. Chapters 13, 14 revised, Vol. II, "Alternative Work Organizations: An Exact Comparison," pp. 84–105. Chapters 19–22, Vol. I, "The Assumption of Ordinariness as a Denial Mechanism: Innovation and Conflict in a Coal Mine," pp. 476–93.

David (P.G.) Herbst

Alternatives to Hierarchies[1]

Processes of social change often move from a given state to its opposite or to its converse. Moving in either of these directions, the transformations achieved remain contained within the logic of the given.

Moving out of an authoritarian structure which has become discredited, obsolescent or inefficient, a transition may occur to a converse authoritarian form. Alternatively, if an authoritarian structure becomes simply eroded, as happened in the Victorian middle class structure of parent/child relationship, then a transition may go to its opposite—a laissez-faire relationship. From here a transition may occur at the next stage to an authoritarian form in new institutional settings such as paramilitary youth movements. Changes of this type are shifts within an essentially one-dimensional conception of society. It is more difficult to find and achieve a fourth alternative that is neither authoritarian nor laissez-faire and that lies outside the logic which generates this type of process cycle (Figure I). In much the same way, transition from a pattern of competitive individualism within an academic community may take the form of establishing the opposite—making group decisions on all issues.

In the case of bureaucratic hierarchical organizations, an attempt to move out of this system may be perceived as going in the direction of the opposite, that is, a chaotic unstructured state. Alternatively, transition from, say, a centralized to a decentralized system produces the converse without necessarily changing the basic mode of operation of the organization.

There has been a view that a hierarchical organization is the only possible form of organization. This would be true if each of the component parts were restricted to a specialized function. In this case a single structure of hierarchical levels is generated to coordinate the functioning of the specialized parts.

The alternative argument has been that since each element is part of a larger whole, which is again part of a larger whole, and so on, a pattern of hierarchical domination is inevitable. This assumes that development of part/whole relationships is the only way in which elements can be related to one another.

Here again, the process of social change can become locked within, and

[1]Slightly revised from Chapter 3 in *Alternatives to Hierarchies*. Leiden: Martinus Nijhoff, 1976.

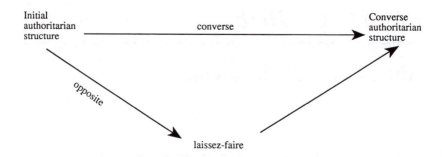

Figure 1. Locked-in authoritarian and laissez-faire logics

unable to go beyond, the inherent organizational logic. The steps required to find a way out are to

• Identify the basic assumptions which generate the organizational logic.
• Search for an alternative set of assumptions.
• Derive the characteristics of alternative types of organization.

The basic assumption which generates bureaucratic hierarchical structures is that each member is restricted to a single specialized task. As a result, a single structure of hierarchical linking relationships is established within which the functioning of each level is controlled by the next higher level.

If the one person/one task principle is abandoned, then the requirement for a hierarchical organization disappears and organizations result which, instead of having a single rigid structure of relationships, have the capacity for multi-structured functioning (Figure 2).

The first case of an alternative type of organization which was studied in some detail is the composite autonomous group. This is based on the principle that each member is able to carry out all, or at least most, tasks. More recently it was discovered that if the principle is adopted that each member has a specialist function, but at the same time an overlapping competence with other members, then what is generated is a matrix organization. Figure 3 shows the type of organization generated by each of these design principles.

The study of nonhierarchical organizations of this type shows that these have the capacity for functioning by way of directive correlation of the activities of members who may be working independently or in smaller subsets. That is, although members may work independently for shorter or longer periods, the work of each supports and facilitates the work of others in the direction of the achievements of a joint aim.[2] This makes it possible to identify

---

[2]The concept of directive correlation was formulated by Sommerhoff (1950). Its relevance to the study of social systems was pointed out by F. Emery (1967).

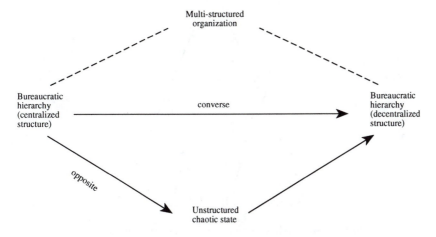

Figure 2. Identification of a fourth alternative

the operating principle of a network in which members may be geographically dispersed and have no form of direct control over one another.

In the following we shall discuss the characteristics of composite autonomous, matrix and network organizations, first at the level of small groups, and then consider the feasibility of these types of organization at the level of larger social units.

The common characteristics of each of the different types of nonhierarchical organization are

- The capacity for multistructured function.
- The capacity for achieving and maintaining directive correlation of ongoing activities.

Each of the nonhierarchical types of organization points to the possibility for developing organizational relationships which not only permit but also support the individual autonomous development of members, going beyond the choice between the Scylla of competitive individualism and the Charybdis of collectivist and authoritarian solutions, thus avoiding the sacrifice of the individual to the overriding needs and demands of a social system.

Historically, the first nonhierarchical type of organization which was discovered and described in some detail was the *composite autonomous group*. Within this type of group all members are capable of carrying out all, or at least most, tasks. The members of the group being equipotential, none has a special leadership function. The special characteristic of this type of organization is that it has no specific structure but can adopt any temporary structure that is judged by the members to be appropriate at any one time. Thus, there is no

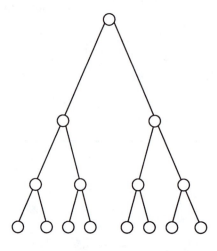

One person/one task, generates a single structure of hierarchical levels.

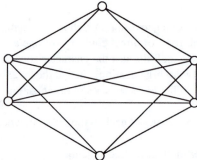

Each person/all tasks, provides the conditions for a composite autonomous group, and allows any structure of work relationships to be utilized.

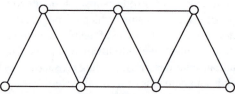

Each person has an overlapping competence with other members, provides the conditions for a matrix organization. In the above case, each person is capable of carrying out two to four tasks. This type or organization has a basic structure, but at the same time allows a variety of possible work relationships to be utilized.

Figure 3. Alternative types of task allocation leading to different types of organizational structures

necessary requirement for all members to work together on any task or to make group decisions. They may at any one time each work individually or in subsets. However, the requirement in this case is that the activities of individual subsets of the group remain directively correlated toward the joint achievement of a specified aim. The requirement that all members are able to carry out all tasks has a consequence that the required competence range for the total task will need to be within a feasible range. The size of the group is generally relatively small. However, there are examples of linked sets of autonomous groups which can operate as a unit of up to 40 persons.

In a *matrix group* each member has a specialist function but each has an overlapping competence with some other group members. In this case there is a structural constraint. At the same time a large variety of alternative structures can be generated and utilized depending on task requirements. The special characteristic of the matrix group is that, as far as the design principle is concerned, there is no necessary limit to the size of the group. However, there is no practical experience so far which might indicate the approximate limits to a viable group size. The design principles for this type of organization were initially theoretically formulated, and it is only quite recently that an implementation has been carried out on board a ship (Herbst, 1974/Vol. II). This does not mean that matrix groups have not existed in the past without having been recognized. A recent study has shown that some of the characteristics of a matrix organization have been traditionally evolved in some banking organizations.

A *network group* can be described as the converse of an autonomous group. The members of a network are normally dispersed individually or in small subsets. It is only infrequently that they come together as a joint group in a work session and for direct communication. In an autonomous group, on the other hand, the members normally work in close association with one another and network type properties emerge in the work situation only temporarily and for shorter periods, whenever the group splits into smaller subsets in carrying out its task.

The basic characteristic of a network is the maintenance of long term directive correlations, mutually facilitating the achievement of a jointly recognized aim. The purpose of this type of organization is typically to find ways of going beyond the established given. As an organization it provides the maximum autonomy of individual members consistent with, and under some conditions optimally suitable for, the achievement of a joint aim.

There are several reasons why organizations of this type tend to remain relatively unrecognized for long periods. To take the case of a network of scientists as an example,

> Communications may be in the available literature but their significance may initially only be visible to, and actively responded to by, relatively few others.

The aim may be only vaguely specifiable at first, and possible means of implementation may be quite tentative and unclear to the network members themselves. The joint task and commitment of network members becomes that of working toward the clarification of both the aim and the means of implementation.

A web of directive correlation is scarcely ever visible to the outsider and may also become recognizable to the participants only in retrospect. It is not simply a matter of information flowing more easily within the network.

The type of process which occurs is that the contribution of member A may be recognized as an innovative step by member B, who may be able to take this further in his own work. This again may help A to see further implications. In this way a cumulative process within the network may lead to a new approach to a problem which is a joint product of the group. At the same time, approaches which show themselves to be inadequate can be rapidly modified or abandoned. The absence of status striving by individual members is a critical factor in being able to abandon or modify unproductive approaches. In this way the primary function of a network is the development and maintenance of a joint learning process, and its productivity depends on the actual or evolving complementary skills of its members. In the nature of its task, its mode of organization and its process of functioning, a network is possibly as far removed from a bureaucratic hierarchical organization as it is possible to get.

Although network groups may maintain their existence over some decades, they are in principle temporary systems. As such, members will normally maintain their role in more conventional institutional settings. In this case the linkage between different institutions may become a correlated function, which at the next stage points in the direction of a network organization in which the nodes are institutions. A network group, as its task becomes completed, that is as its approach becomes converted into a new established given, may become institutionalized as some kind of professional society or the members may disband and move toward new fields.

Each of the types of organization discussed has existed for some time; however, they have generally been either unrecognized or exceptional. Known actual cases at this time, whether discovered as naturally evolved forms or achieved by design implementation, are on a small scale. A study of cases of this type was essential to developing, gradually, an understanding of both the basic design principle and the mode of functioning of organizations of this type. Table 1 gives a tentative overview of the characteristics of nonhierarchical organizations at the group size level. One of the basic differences between bureaucratic hierarchical and nonhierarchical forms of organization will be seen to lie in the fact that bureaucratic hierarchical organizations are based on the principle of a single rigid structure, while each nonhierarchical form of organization has the capacity for multistructured functioning.

The problem at present is that of investigating the relevance and feasibility of the design principles for larger social units. There are at least two ways of proceeding:

- If a change of scale occurs due to growth then, just as it is possible to develop larger bureaucratic hierarchical organizations with organizations of the same type as components, so it may be possible to develop a network of networks.
- The constituents of a matrix or network, instead of being individuals, may be organizational units of different types.

There is insufficient experience so far with the utilization of autonomous groups as building blocks for larger units. There appear to be two possible problems:

- The requirement that members be capable of carrying out all or most tasks restricts the size of individual units.
- Autonomous type groups have, for the most part, been implemented within the structure of existing hierarchical type organizations, specifically in bottom-up change strategies, and thus have been built at least temporarily into a partially inconsistent context.

The approach which has been found specifically appropriate for large-scale units is the network organization. This type of approach was, in fact, utilized from the beginning in the Norwegian Work Democratization Project (Emery and Thorsrud, Vol. II). To see its significance what is needed is a figure/ground reversal.

Organizational networks may, in much the same way as project groups, be utilized to implement changes somewhere else. In this case they function as adaptations of a fundamentally bureaucratic structure. Their mode of functioning as nonhierarchical organizations is quite different.

An example is the type of enterprise that has evolved in a project concerned with working toward a new form or organization on merchant ships, which initially was concerned with developing an autonomous type group for the subordinate crew and more recently with developing a matrix group of officers (Herbst, 1974/Vol. II). As it proceeded, the project required a change in headquarters organization, a change in maritime schools that involved the Ministry of Education, changes in certification and regulation, changes in trade union structure and functioning, changes in the process and direction of technological and architectural design and changes also in the role of the researchers involved.

The implementation process that involves changes in the mode of functioning of each of the constituent organizations and also changes in their relation-

TABLE 1 Types of Group Organization

	Bureaucratic hierarchical	Composite autonomous	Matrix	Network
Task structure	Product (P) procedures (π) and input state (I) are given by specification $\pi(I) \to P$ or assumed to be reducible to this form in terms of given norms and rules.	Product is specified. Input states are specifiable but procedures are not, or a requisite choice exists. $?(I) \to P$	There may be a variety of products. $?(I) \to P$ or $?(?) \to P$ Procedures and possibly input requirements are not specified.	Neither initial nor outcome state are specified in operational terms $?(?) \to ?$ The task is to achieve a more specifiable task structure.
Task competence range of members	One person/one specialized task.	Each person/all tasks.	Each person has a specialized task together with overlapping competence with other members	Overlapping competence range of members.
Organizational structure	A single specified structure of relationships.	Can adopt any type of temporary structure depending on recognized task requirements.	A basic structure is given by the pattern of overlapping competencies but within this a variety of structures may be adopted.	Sets of members may, and generally do, engage in joint project work for shorter or longer periods. The structure is given by the web of directive correlations.
Basic principle of organization	Parallel and independent activity of contiguous members. Regulated by specified activity programs and normative rules.	Mutual facilitation of contiguous members in direct interaction with one another. Joined and shared responsibility. Short-term directive correlation when members work in smaller subsets.	Intermediate between composite group and network. Members work predominantly in smaller subsets and the pattern of all working together on a task is less frequently adopted.	Long-term directive correlation of dispersed members. Selective interdependence.

Feasible size	No apparent limitation to the subordination of parts.	Sets of autonomous groups linked by rotation of members are possible. The use of this type of organization for larger scale units needs to be further investigated.	In principle there is no limit to the size of a matrix. However, the problem of viability has not yet been investigated. At the next level a matrix in which organizational units are components appears to be possible.	Network groups are limited in size. A network of networks appears to be possible. The main utilization of this type of organization lies in the development and maintenance of directive correlations of organizations involved in a long-term change process.
Environmental suitability	The assumption is that the environment, including human beings, both can and should be converted to and maintained in a highly predictable form.	While means/ends relationships may remain basically predictable, operational conditions may be subject to marked variations. At the same time autonomous groups have a capacity for both technical and organizational learning.	The conditions may be such that a number of aims need to be achieved in a coordinated way. At the same time a shift of aims can lie within, or not too far beyond, the adaptability range without requiring basic change of the organizational form. The matrix organization provides this case a balance between structural constraints and flexibility	In their original form network groups were established to tackle problems outside the established given. At present their relevance lies in respect to mildly turbulent environments. Their stabilizing structure lies in the fabric of directive correlations. Matrix organizations are appropriate for production tasks. Network organizations are appropriate when a number of different organizations become involved in a relatively continuous and long-term change process. Their basic characteristic is that the research function becomes incorporated and dispersed within the organization. It is at this stage that the traditional role of academic and research institutes with exclusive property rights to the research function is no longer appropriate.

ships to one another is almost precisely the same as that described previously for the little network group. The project is to go beyond the established given system. The aim to be achieved finally cannot initially be specified in detail. The initial time horizon may be 10 to 15 years. The project is such that no organization by itself can go ahead very far since it is linked to the other organizations involved by interdependence and complementarity relationships, which become manifest in the change process. The major difference as compared to the informal network group is that, while interdependence relationships of the latter are a result of selective interdependence, the initial structure of interdependence relationships is given by the nature and scope of the change process.

In the present case, given a joint commitment of the organizations concerned for initial exploratory steps in the accepted direction of change, a representative committee was formed, which then constituted the formal core of an evolving network group. Taking exploratory steps for changing the organization on board project ships, provisional facilities for additional education of officers for a matrix organization were required. With the agreement to go further, a new structure for maritime education has been established which affects both career paths and certification requirements. What becomes visible now is that while previously the captain had to be recruited via the deck department, he can now be recruited from any part of the matrix group. To implement an extension of the new form of organization what needed to be explored at the next stage were requisite changes in the organization at head office and the development of new types of relationship between head office and ships. At the same time, ship personnel have been involved in the design of new living quarters, providing lounges and restaurants for the total crew and an equalization of cabin facilities, thus removing one of the traditional supports of the earlier segmented, hierarchical status structure. The extension of the number of project ships has at the same time led to a diffusion network between different shipping companies. At a later stage, a need for the change of trade unions, which are at present based on the traditional work roles, may become recognized.

What is meant by a figure/ground reversal in the present case is that the initial object of change becomes at the next stage a means for the transformation of the larger social system. Within this process, each of the participant organizations is able to change itself adaptively in relationship to other participant organizations. Within the organizational network, the process of change moves along the lines of a gradually evolving fabric of directive correlations. Each implementation step becomes subject to evaluation, and after each step new steps forward may become visible and subject to exploration. In this way a continuous learning process is developed and maintained within which theories and guiding hypotheses become evolved and modified in a constant confrontation with the empirical results obtained. What is found here is a possible alternative to traditional ways of achieving social change which, whatever the ostensible and often idealistic aims, may by their mode of implementation maintain the established given and at worst add momentum to the extension and preservation of bureaucratic or authoritarian social orders.

An extension of a matrix structure to the next higher level becomes possible if we have a set of organizations each with a specialist task but with some overlapping competence, which can link smaller and shifting subsets in carrying out their tasks. It would appear that within a matrix organization autonomous type groups will have a more appropriate context, given that they are able at this stage to take an active participant role within a larger organizational context.

References

Emery, F. 1967. "The Next Thirty Years: Concepts, Methods and Anticipations." *Human Relations,* 20:199–237.
Emery, F. and E. Thorsrud. 1992. "The Norskhydro Fertilizer Plant." Vol. II, pp. 492–507.
Herbst, P.G. 1974. *Socio-Technical Design: Strategies in Multi-Disciplinary Research.* London: Tavistock Publications. Excerpted in Vol. II, "A Learning Organization in Practice: M/S *Balao,*" pp. 409–16.
Sommerhoff, G. 1950. *Analytical Biology.* Oxford: Oxford University Press.

David (P.G.) Herbst

Designing with Minimal Critical Specifications[1]

Critical Specification Design

There are a number of recent developments in molecular engineering, in biosimulation and in the study of socio-technical systems that point to the emergence of new design principles.

Early engineering techniques were based on the method of building up increasingly complex machine structures that produced simple components which were then assembled to produce a final product.

In molecular engineering the structure of material itself, either as it exists or as it can be produced to specified criteria, is used to effect required transformations. Further, since many materials have metastable states, their structural form can change in response to signals, in the form of heat, pressure or light, so that the same material can operate as a different machine depending on environmental conditions (von Hippel, 1965). This points to the emergence of new forms of production engineering which are no longer based on the principle of successive decomposition, linkage of components and hierarchical control structure.

From the point of view of production design, the key development lies in the study and design of autonomous systems. Here we find two lines of development, one from biophysics and the other in the socio-technical study of work organization.

The last few decades have seen the emergence of cybernetics (Wiener, 1961), showing that self-adjustment requires the existence of cyclic feedback processes; of communication theory (Shannon and Weaver, 1949), which provides measures of structure and error variance of discrete processes; and of open-system theory (von Bertalanffy, 1950), which demonstrates that open systems can maintain steady-state functioning without the use of a separate control mechanism.

An interesting point of departure is the non-specification technique de-

[1]A shortened and revised version of Chapter 2 in P.G. Herbst, *Socio-Technical Design: Strategies in Multi-Disciplinary Research*. London: Tavistock Publications, 1974.

scribed by Beurle (1962) in a paper on the properties of random nets. These are generally a set of elements with random connections. Beurle argues that the nervous system may initially be somewhat like this but that later, in response to transactions with an already structured environment, an internal adjusted structure which corresponds to a biased network structure should gradually emerge. Clearly, a random network can learn practically any desired response, but something has to be added to get to a workable model.[2] Without going into the detail of recent, more sophisticated, work, what we find here is a new approach to the problem of design which is no longer concerned with complete detailed specification but with *minimal critical specifications*.

The main reason for this approach was a concern with systems that can learn and that can adjust themselves to environmental changes. Adjustment, learning and creative and intelligent behavior minimally require:

- internal variability to create alternative response patterns;
- the testing of alternative response patterns and evaluation of the outcome;
- selection of the most appropriate response.

This is one of the lines of development that led to the study of autonomous systems. What was made clear at this stage was that variability, and thus making errors, was not a bad thing and that, on the contrary, systems must have sufficient potential and mobilizable internal variability and mechanisms for the self-correction of error in order to be able to adjust to a variable environment.

The third, and to some extent parallel, line of development is more directly relevant to the design of production systems. Before the Second World War, the problem of optimizing the functioning of industrial and work organizations was looked at either from a techno-economic point of view or in terms of improving the social organization and human relations. What was left out of account was that the social organization is not independent of the technical production system. It is possible, as has been done in the past, to look for an optimal technical solution. However, if the correlated social system required is inferior then the total production system may be far short of the optimal. A series of studies of socio-technical systems undertaken in the coal-mining industry showed that this was indeed the case and demonstrated further that a given technological system can be operated by several different types of work organization. The variables that may remain to some extent free are the pattern of task allocation, the allocation of task responsibility and the method of payment.

What emerged at this stage was the concept of autonomous work groups that would overcome the dysfunctional properties of fractionated work organizations (Trist and Bamforth, 1951/Vol. II; Wilson, 1951; Rice, 1958; Emery and

---

[2]The simplest model of this type is found in stochastic learning theory which is based on a single type of response element that can change its probability of response. What is lacking here is the possibility of structural growth.

Trist, 1960; Herbst, 1962; Trist et al., 1963). This work converged with new principles that were being developed in the field of job design (Davis, 1962; 1966).

The principle of minimal critical specification design can be stated as that of identifying the minimal set of conditions required to create visible self-maintaining and self-adjusting production units. An optimal solution is obtained if the unit requires no external supervision and control of its internal functioning and no internal staff concerned with supervision, control or work coordination. The management function should primarily be supportive and concerned with mediating the relationship of the unit to its environment.

There is consistent evidence that work systems of this type are superior in terms of relevant social and psychological criteria. Chronic conflict between workers, and between workers and management, disappears. For individual members, the task provides the opportunity for learning and for participating in technical and organizational problem-solving. The group as a whole can learn on the basis of its experience and becomes able to utilize experts as consultants. Conditions are created for the development of mutual trust and respect and thus also of self-respect. Just as internal conflicts and warring factions export their conflict into their environment, cooperative relationships can now be developed with the environment. At the same time, a considerable reduction of unproductive overhead and management costs can be achieved.

It cannot be expected that social organizations of this type will be ideal for and attractive to everyone. Since human beings differ in their emotional and social maturity, and human needs change in the course of development and growth, no single type of social system can be optimal. If in the case of autonomous groups there is less of a problem, this is because such groups cannot be imposed but depend for their development and maintenance on the consent of all involved. At the same time, a significant point about self-maintaining systems is that they do not possess a single rigid structure but have the characteristics of a matrix organization that can adapt its internal structure to meet internal and external task demands.

There are two problems that will need to be considered in more detail:

What are the critical conditions for the operation of self-maintaining socio-technical units? What we are looking for here is a minimal set of necessary and sufficient conditions. It should be noted that, insofar as we are dealing with a set of interdependent variables, there will be more than one possible set of critical conditions. We shall in that case need to find a set of variables that can be included in the set of design criteria.

Given this, we need new design techniques based not on the iteration of techno-economic variables only but on the joint iteration of techno-economic and socio-psychological variables.

Supporting conditions for a viable self-maintaining production unit are the following:

A clearly definable total task with an, as far as possible, easily measurable outcome state that may be in the form of the quantity and quality of a product and also an easily measurable set of relevant input states. These provide the necessarily information both for evaluation of the system's performance and for maintenance and adjustment of the internal process.

A single social system responsible for the total production unit. The unit should include, as far as possible, all the equipment and skills required for process control and technical maintenance.

Given that the functional elements of the production process are interdependent with respect to the achievement of the outcome state, the social organization should be such that individual members do not establish primary commitment to any part function—that is, do not lay claim to ownership of, or preferential access to, any task or equipment—but are jointly committed to optimizing the functioning of the unit with the outcome state as the primary focal goal.

In traditional types of work organization, doing and deciding tend to be split and decision-making functions are allocated to higher levels of the hierarchy. Self-maintenance requires that relevant decision-making functions be brought down to the lowest possible level and reintegrated into the operational work organization. This becomes of particular importance where the decision-making content of component tasks has become depleted by means of computer programming and automation.

Responsible autonomy cannot generally be established and maintained unless the available tasks require personal responsibility based on some degree of competence, judgment and skill. Similarly, unless the total task allocated to a production unit requires the development and use of personal competence, acceptance of joint responsibility for the organization and functioning of the unit may not be achievable.

Emery and Thorsrud (1969) have formulated relevant criteria for job design in the form of hypotheses about the way in which tasks may be more effectively put together to make jobs and at the same time to satisfy general psychological requirements.

Any new design technique will need to incorporate the basic set of techno-economic variables. However, instead of providing a detailed specification of all variables, the critical specification technique requires the identification of a minimal set of variables that have to be specified and the identification of other variables that have to be left free. The free variables are those that are required if the system is to achieve self-maintaining properties. The initial set of variables that require specification and are thus turned into fixed structural parameters may later be even further reducible since, given system properties, the specification of a given set of characteristics may lead to the emergence of steady-state properties of other system characteristics.

The existing production design technique is based on the successive decomposition of the total production process into part-product processes; these are then decomposed into operational units; and these are finally decomposed into elementary person/machine operations. At each level there is an iteration cycle which provides the specification for the next lower unit until, ideally, every movement of operators and machine operation is rigidly specified (Figure 1).

What is produced in the end is not a functioning unit. In order to coordinate the often thousands of split-off process elements, to counter the variances that arise in each processing and transport segment and also the variance produced by the social-organizational links created by workers and finally to adjust the system to variances in input and changing product specifications, a superstructure of work is required in the form of supervision, inspection, control, planning, scheduling and personnel work. This additional system again requires coordination and produces variances for which a next higher level has to be provided, and so on. Insofar as the system finally produces more variance than it can control at any level, it exports the unmanageable surplus variance to the environment wherever it can be absorbed, compensated for or simply got rid of. Both the rapidly growing rate of environmental pollution and the increasing incidence of chronic mental health disorders show that the problems exported can no longer be absorbed by the environment or effectively compensated for by the social and professional organizations created for this purpose.

The creation of viable systems at the production-process level is aimed at:
- avoiding the production of variance due to incompatible technical-process requirements and social-organizational requirements;
- providing the conditions, where possible, for variance to be controlled *within* the unit itself.

An alternative design procedure will therefore need to include, at each iteration level, the corresponding set of social-system variables. This will require, at each level, methods for studying the social-organizational implications of technical decisions. The critical level for viable system construction is Level 4, which is concerned with the selection and linkage of operational units. While at this point the design problem is made more complex, this should be more than compensated for by cutting off fixed specification at this level since Levels 5 and 6 contain variables that should almost all remain free in order to provide the necessary conditions for the production unit to operate as a self-maintaining socio-technical unit. The design process would in this case take the form shown in Figure 2.

Design techniques require
- definition of the relevant social-organizational variables;
- socio-technical methods for inferring the organizational implications of a given technical-process structure;
- construction of a feasible joint iteration procedure.

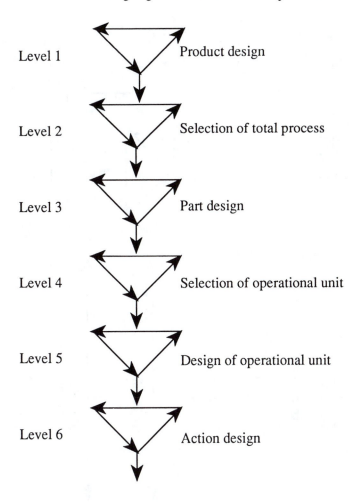

Figure 1. Technical unit design

Evolutionary System Design

Nature does not create in the way in which factories do. A seed does not contain a complete specification of the organism, and the information given by the genes does not provide for one-step implementation. Yet, in spite of the fact that the information given by the gene structure is quite limited, the growth process proceeds with self-maintenance properties at each stage until a viable

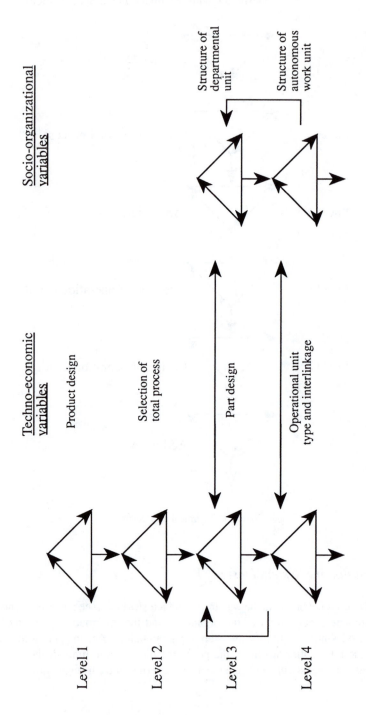

Figure 2. Socio-technical unit design

organism is completed that structurally reproduces the original one with a very high degree of reliability.

Let us simply note at this stage that:

Reliable production does not require a complete specification of either the production process or the final product.

The creation of a complex structure does not require the initial production of elements which are later connected to produce the final product.

The production process is not one step from specification of structure to structural implementation, but always goes through successive growth stages.

It is not simply the final product that is a viable system, but a viable system exists at every stage of growth.

It appears likely that production processes incorporating these principles will eventually be developed.

However that may be, an understanding of growth principles is necessary for an understanding of the conditions for psychological and organizational development. A technological system can be designed and implemented by construction. A social organization cannot be created in the same way. The conditions for both psychological and organizational growth are more similar to biological growth, as against the mechanical construction type. This means that:

If we want to implement viable autonomous social systems, the design will not consist of a specification of the final system (although the characteristics of this system which are aimed at will have to be defined and accepted); rather, what has to be specified and implemented are the conditions that make it possible for a system of this type to develop.

The social system aimed at can rarely be implemented in one step but will need to go through successive stages of growth. The technical design should, in this case, be such that a viable socio-technical system exists at each stage. Thus if a system is designed for composite group operation there should also be provision for the possibility of more fractionated operation during the initial learning stage, and also for the possibility of regression to a more primitive organizational form.

References

Beurle, R.L. 1962. "Functional Organization in Random Networks." In *Principles of Self-Organization*, edited by H. von Foerster and G.W. Zopf. Oxford: Pergamon Press.

Davis, L.E. 1962. "The Effects of Automation on Job Design." *Industrial Relations*, 2:53–71.

———. 1966. "The Design of Jobs." London: Tavistock Document; *Industrial Rela-*

tions, 6:21–45. Revised in *Design of Jobs*, edited by L.E. Davis and J.C. Taylor. Harmondsworth: Penguin Books, 1972.

Emery, F.E. and E. Thorsrud. 1969. *Form and Content in Industrial Democracy: Some Experiences from Norway and Other European Countries*. London: Tavistock Publications.

Emery, F.E. and E.L. Trist. 1960. "Socio-Technical Systems." In *Management Sciences, Models and Techniques*, Vol. 2, edited by C.W. Churchman and M. Verhulst. Oxford: Pergamon Press.

Herbst, P.G. 1962. *Autonomous Group Functioning: An Exploration in Behaviour Theory and Measurement*. London: Tavistock Publications.

Rice, A.K. 1958. *Productivity and Social Organization: The Ahmedabad Experiment*. London: Tavistock Publications. Reissued 1987, New York: Garland.

Shannon, C.E. and W. Weaver. 1949. *The Mathematical Theory of Communication*. Urbana: University of Illinois Press. Reprinted 1962.

Trist, E.L. and K.W. Bamforth. 1951. "Some Social and Psychological Consequences of the Longwall Method of Coal-Getting." *Human Relations*, 4:3–38. Shortened version, Vol. II, "The Stress of Isolated Dependence: The Filling Shift in the Semi-Mechanized Longwall Three-Shift Mining Cycle," pp. 64–83.

Trist, E.L., G.W. Higgin, H. Murray and A.B. Pollock. 1963. *Organizational Choice: Capabilities of Groups at the Coal Face Under Changing Technologies: The Loss, Rediscovery and Transformation of a Work Tradition*. London: Tavistock Publications. Reissued 1987, New York: Garland. Chapters 13, 14 revised, Vol. II, "Alternative Work Organizations: An Exact Comparison," pp. 84–105. Chapters 19–22, Vol I, "The Assumption of Ordinariness as a Denial Mechanism: Innovation and Conflict in a Coal Mine," pp. 476–93.

von Bertalanffy, L. 1950. "The Theory of Open Systems in Physics and Biology." *Science*, 3:23–29.

von Hippel, A.R. (Editor) 1965. *The Molecular Designing of Materials and Devices*. Cambridge, Mass.: MIT Press.

Wiener, N. 1961. *Cybernetics: Control and Communication in the Animal and the Machine*. Second edition. Cambridge, Mass.: MIT Press.

Wilson, A.T.M. 1951. "Some Aspects of Social Process: Lewin Memorial Award Lecture." *Journal of Social Issues*, Supplement No. 5.

Louis Davis

The Coming Crisis for Production Management[1]

Events cast their shadows before them. Already we can discern changes in our environment more than sufficient to show that Western industrial society is in transition from one historical era to another. It is the purpose of this paper to indicate that the environmental characteristics of the post-industrial era will lead to crisis and massive dislocation unless adaptation occurs. The anticipated consequences will be greatest, at first, for the production industries because they stand at the confluence of changes involving technology, social values, the economic environment, organizational design, job design and the practice of management.

Managers, as rational leaders, will seek to avoid these consequences by altering the forms of institutional regulation and control. It is a secondary purpose to describe some ways in which managers are already beginning this process. Specifically, examples will be given from the research results and organizational experiments of an international coalition of English, American and Norwegian researchers.

The Post-Industrial Challenge

CHANGES IN SOCIETY

In recent years, changes in Western societal environments have been reflective of a rising level of expectations concerning material, social and personal needs. The seeming ease with which new (automated) technology satisfies material needs, coupled with the provision of subsistence-level support for its citizens by society, has stimulated a growing concern on the part of individuals over their relationship to work, its meaningfulness and its value, i.e., a concern for the quality of work life (Davis, 1970). In the United States, questioning of

[1]Excerpted from *International Journal of Production Research*, 9:65–82, 1971, based on "The Coming Crisis in Production Management Technology and Organization," International Conference on Production Research, University of Birmingham, 1971.

the relationship between work and satisfaction of material needs is widespread through the ranks of university students, industrial workers and minority unemployed. The viability of the belief that individuals may be used to satisfy the economic goals of organizations is being seriously questioned. It appears that people may no longer let themselves be used; they wish to see some relationship between their own work and the social life around them, and they wish some desirable future for themselves in their continuing relationship with organizations. No longer will workers patiently endure dehumanized work roles in order to achieve increased material rewards.

Among university students these expectations are leading to refusals to accept jobs with major corporations in favor of more "socially oriented" institutions—an unfortunate loss of talented people. Even the unemployed are refusing to accept dead-end, demeaning jobs (Doeringer, 1969), appearing to be as selective about accepting jobs as are the employed about changing jobs. There appear to be means, partly provided by society, for subsisting in minority ghettos without entering the industrial world. For industrial workers there is a revival of concern with the once-buried questions of alienation from work, job satisfaction, personal freedom and initiative and the dignity of the individual in the workplace. Although, on the surface, the expressed concern is over the effects of automation on job availability and greater sharing in wealth produced, restlessness in unions, their failure to grow in the nonindustrial sectors and the frequent overthrow of union leaders are all indicators, in the United States, of a changing field that stems from the increasingly tenuous relationship between work and satisfaction of material needs.

Another factor impelling social change is the continuously rising level of education that Western countries provide, which is changing the attitudes, the aspirations and the expectations of major segments of society (Bell, 1967). Future trends are already visible in California, where almost half of young people of college and university age are in school and where one third of all the scientists and engineers in the United States are employed. One of the forces driving the transition into the post-industrial era is the growing application of automated, computer-aided production systems. This development is bringing about crucial changes in the relationship between technology and the social organization of production—changes of such magnitude that the displacement of workers and skills by computers is reduced to the status of a relatively minor effect.

The most striking characteristic of sophisticated, automated technology is that it absorbs routine activities into the machines, creating a new relationship between the technology and its embedded social system. The humans in automated systems are interdependent components required to respond to *stochastic,* not deterministic, conditions, i.e., they operate in an environment where "important events" are randomly occurring and unpredictable. Sophisticated skills must be maintained, though they may be called into use only very occasionally. This technological shift disturbs long-established boundaries between jobs and skills and between operations and maintenance. It has also contributed to a shift in the working population from providing goods to providing personal and societal services. As may be expected, there is a shift from blue-collar to white-collar work in clerical, technical and service jobs. At all levels of society, individuals find that they must change their careers or jobs over time.

Still further, the new technology requires a high degree of commitment and autonomy on the part of workers in the automated production process (Davis, 1970). The required degree of autonomy is likely to be in serious conflict with the assumptions and values held within the bureaucratic technostructure (Galbraith, 1967).

Another feature is that there are, in effect, two intertwined technologies. The primary technology contains the transformations needed to produce the desired output. It is machine- and capital-intensive. The secondary technology contains the support and service activities, such as loading and unloading materials, tools, etc. It is labor-intensive and its variances are capable of stopping or reducing throughput; but enhancing the secondary technology will not enhance the primary technology and its throughputs.

Although it poses new problems, highly sophisticated technology possesses an unrecognized flexibility in relation to social systems. There exists an extensive array of configurations of the technology that can, within limits, be designed to suit the social systems desired. This property disaffirms the notion of the "technological imperative" widely held by both engineers and social scientists. It places the burden on managers, hopefully aided by social scientists, to elucidate the characteristics of their particular social system suitable to the evolving post-industrial era.

In production systems, stochastic events have two characteristics: unpredictability as to time and unpredictability as to nature. For economic reasons, they must be overcome as rapidly as possible, which imposes certain requirements on those who do the work. First, the workers must have a large repertoire of responses because the specific intervention that will be required is not known. Second, they cannot depend on supervision because they must respond immediately to events that occur irregularly and without warning. Third, they must be committed to undertaking the necessary tasks on their own initiative.

This makes for a very different world in which the organization is far more dependent on the individual, although there may be fewer individuals. From the point of view of the organization, the chain of causation is:

- If the production process collapses, the economic goals of the organization will not be met.
- If appropriate responses are not taken to stochastic events, the production process will collapse.

- If the organization's members are not committed to their functions, the appropriate responses will not be made. (Davis, 1966)

Commitment cannot be forced or bought; it can only arise out of the experiences of the individual with the quality of life in the working situation, i.e., with the job. Therefore, automated industries seek to build into jobs the characteristics that will develop commitment on the part of the individual. The major characteristics are those of planning, self-control and self-regulation, i.e., of autonomy.

A comparison between an industry that is highly automated and one that is not demonstrates these differences very clearly. In the oil-refining industry, the tasks that remain to be performed pertain almost entirely to control and regulation, and the line between supervisor and worker is tenuous. The construction industry, on the other hand, still retains prominent roles for workers as a source of energy and tool guidance, and supervision (often at several levels) mediates all system actions. Industrial relations officers in the oil industry are proud of their "advanced and enlightened" personnel practices. And, indeed, these practices may be accurately described as enlightened. But they were not adopted for the sake of their enlightenment. They were adopted because they are a necessary functional response to the demands of process technology.

Here is the point at which both the social and the technological forces can be seen working toward the same end, for "job characteristics that develop commitment" and thus promote the economic goals of the highly automated organization are exactly those that are beginning to emerge as demands for "meaningfulness" from the social environment—participation and control, personal freedom and initiative.

Nor is this linking of the two forces confined to industries that are as highly automated as oil and chemicals. Most industries are neither all automated nor all conventional; they utilize a mix of the two modes of production. If an industry has some employees whose jobs are designed to meet the requirements of automated technology, then the enhanced quality of their work life is visible to all the employees of the organization, creating demands by all for better, more meaningful jobs. It becomes very difficult to maintain a distinction in job design solely on the basis of a distinction in technological base.

CHANGES IN ECONOMIC ORGANIZATION

Developments in technology are interrelated with changes in economic organization. The scale of economic units is growing, stimulated by the developments of sophisticated production technology and organized knowledge leading to new products. In turn, this is leading to new arrangements in the market, stimulating the development of higher-order interactions.

The organized use of knowledge brings about constant product innovation and, for firms in electronics, aerospace, computers, information processing, etc., a new phenomenon in market relationships appears. Such firms are continually in the process of redefining their products and their futures—an exercise that reflects back on their internal organization structures and on the response flexibility of their members. Within these companies, there is an observable shift to high-talent personnel and to the development of strategies of distinctive competence, stores of experience and built-in redundancy of response capabilities.

THE CONSEQUENCES OF THESE CHANGES

A pervasive feature of the post-industrial environment is that it is taking on the quality of a turbulent field (Emery and Trist, 1965). Turbulence arises from increased complexity and from the size of the total environment. It is compounded by increased interdependence of the environment's parts and the unpredictable connections arising among them as a result of accelerating but uneven change. The area of relevant uncertainty for individuals and organizations increases and tests the limits of human adaptability; earlier forms of adaptation, developed in response to a simpler environment, appear to suffice no longer. The turbulent environment requires that boundaries of organizations be extended into their technological, social and economic environments. The organization needs to identify the causal characteristics of the environments so that it can develop response strategies. The production organization, in particular, must provide a structure, a style of management and jobs so designed that adaptation can take place without massive dislocation.

The Post-Industrial Opportunity

Although the presence of the features outlined in the previous section indicates that we are already well launched into the post-industrial era, Trist (1968) finds that we suffer from a cultural lag—the absence of a culture congruent with the identifiable needs of post-industrialism. Furthermore, in the turbulent environmental texture of the post-industrial era, the individual organization, city, state or even nation—acting alone—may be unable to meet the demands of increasing levels of complexity. Resources will have to be pooled; there will be a need for more sharing, more trust and more cooperation.

Seldom does society have a second chance to redress deep-seated errors in social organization and members' roles; however, the opportunity may now be at hand to overcome alienation and provide humanly meaningful work in socio-technical institutions (Fromm, 1968; Emery, 1967a). The development, over a period of nearly 20 years, of a body of theory (Emery, 1969) concerned with the analysis and design of interacting technological and social systems has furthered the examination of questions of organization and job design in complex environments, too long considered to be exclusively an art form. The diffusion of knowledge about applications of these theories is itself changing the environment of other organizations. The concepts were first developed in Britain (Emery and Trist, 1960) and followed up by developments in the United States and in Norway, Canada and Sweden. They are far from having come into common practice. Their most comprehensive application is taking place in Norway, on a national scale, as a basis for developing organizational and job design strategies suitable to a democratic society.

Briefly, socio-technical systems theory rests on two essential premises. The first is that in any purposive organization in which workers are required to perform the organization's activities, there is a joint system operating—a *socio-technical* system. When work is to be done, and when human beings are required actors in the performance of this work, then the desired output is achieved through the actions of a social system as well as a technological system. Further, these systems so interlock that the achievement of the output becomes a function of the appropriate joint operation of both systems. The operative word is "joint" for it is here that the socio-technical idea departs from more widely held views—those in which the social system is thought to be completely dependent on the technical system. The concept of joint optimization (Emery, 1967b/Vol. II) is proposed, which states that it is impossible to optimize for overall performance without seeking to optimize jointly the correlative independent social and technological systems.

The second premise is that every socio-technical system is embedded in an environment—an environment that is influenced by a culture and its values, an environment that is influenced by a set of generally acceptable practices, an environment that permits certain roles for the organisms in it. To understand a work system or an organization, one must understand the environmental forces that are operating on it. Without this understanding, it is impossible to develop an effective job or organization. This emphasis on environmental forces suggests, correctly, that the socio-technical systems idea falls within the larger body of "open system" theories. What does this mean? Simply, that there is a constant interchange between what goes on in a work system or an organization and what goes on in the environment. The boundaries between the environment and the system are highly permeable and what goes on outside affects what goes on inside. When something occurs in the general society, it will inevitably affect what occurs in organizations. There may be a period of cultural lag but, sooner or later, the societal tremor will register on the organizational seismographs.

Significantly, socio-technical systems theory provides a basis for analysis and design overcoming the greatest inhibition to development of organization and job strategies in a growing turbulent environment. It breaks through the long-existing tight compartments between the worlds of those who plan, study and manage social systems and those who do so for technological systems. At once it makes nonsensical the existing positions of psychologists and sociologists that in purposive organizations the technology is unalterable and must be accepted as a given requirement. Most frequently, therefore, only variables and relationships not influenced by technology are examined and altered. Without inclusion of technology, which considerably determines what work is about and what demands exist for the individual and the organization, not only are peripheral relations examined but they tend to become disproportionately magnified, making interpretation and use of findings difficult, if not impossible. Similarly, it makes nonsensical the "technological imperative" position of engineers, economists and managers who consider psychological and social requirements as constraints and at best as boundary conditions of technological systems. That a substantial part of technological system design includes social system design is neither understood nor appreciated. Frightful assumptions, supported by societal values, are made, and people and groups become built into machines and processes as requirements.

Socio-technical systems analysis provides a basis for determining appropriate boundaries of systems containing people, machines, materials and information. It considers the operation of such systems within the framework of an environment that is made an overt and specific object of the socio-technical study. It concerns itself with spontaneous reorganization or adaptation, with control of system variance, with growth, self-regulation, etc. These are aspects of system study that will become increasingly important as organizations in the post-industrial era are required to develop strategies that focus on adaptability and commitment. For these reasons, socio-technical systems analysis is felt to offer one of the best current approaches to meeting the post-industrial challenge.

The final section of this paper presents some selective aspects of socio-technical theory and application in greater detail.

Results of Organizational and Job Design Research

A number of developments, including on-site organizational experiments, lend strong support to the prospects of successfully developing suitable strategies of organization for the post-industrial era. In general, successful outcomes are measured by various objective criteria dependent on the finding of an accommodation between the demands of the organization and the technology on the one hand, and the needs and desires of people on the other, so that the needs of both are provided for. A summary report of the U.S. and British empirical studies appeared in "The Design of Jobs" (Davis, 1966).

The studies sought to find conditions in organization structure and job contents leading to cooperation, commitment, learning and growth, ability to change and improved performance. The findings can be summarized under four categories of requirements: responsible autonomy, adaptability, variety and participation. When these factors were present, they led to learnings and behaviors that seemed to provide the sought-for organization and job response qualities. These studies lend support to the general model of responsible autonomous job and group behavior as a key factor in socio-technical relationships in production organizations.

By autonomous is meant that the content, structure and organization of jobs are such that individuals or groups performing those jobs can plan, regulate and control their own worlds.

When the attributes and characteristics of jobs were such that the individual or group became largely autonomous in the working situation, then meaningfulness, satisfaction and learning increased significantly, as did wide knowledge of process, identification with product, commitment to desired action and responsibility for outcomes. These supported the development of a job structure that permitted social interaction among job-holders and communication with peers and supervisors, particularly when the maintenance of continuity of operation was required. Simultaneously, high performance in quantity and quality of product or service outcomes was achieved. This has been demonstrated in such widely different settings as the mining of coal (Trist et al., 1963), the maintenance of a chemical refinery and the manufacture of aircraft instruments (Davis and Werling, 1960; Davis and Valfer, 1966).

The second requirements category, which has been mainly the province of psychologists, is concerned with "adaptation." The contents of the job have to be such that the individual can learn from what is going on around him, can grow, can develop, can adjust. Slighted, but not overlooked, is the psychological concept of self-actualization or personal growth, which appears to be central to the development of motivation and commitment through satisfaction of higher-order intrinsic needs of individuals. The most potent way of satisfying intrinsic needs may well be through job design (Lawler, 1969). Too often jobs in conventional industrial organizations have simply required people to adapt to restricted, fractionated activities, overlooking their enormous capacity to learn and adapt to complexity.

Where the socio-technical system was so designed that the necessary adaptive behavior was facilitated, positive results in economic performance and in job satisfaction occurred at all levels in the organization, as demonstrated in studies in oil refineries, automated chemical plants, pulp and paper plants (Thorsrud and Emery, 1969) and aircraft instrument plants (Davis, 1966).

The third category is concerned with variety. It has, surely, always been known, but only lately has it been demonstrated, that part of what a living organism requires to function effectively is a variety of experiences. If people are to be alert and responsive to their working environments, they need variety in the work situation. Routine, repetitious tasks tend to extinguish the individual, who is there physically but not in any other way—who has "disappeared" from the scene. Psychologists have also studied this phenomenon in various "deprived environments." Adult humans confined to "stimulus-free" environments begin to hallucinate. Workers may respond to the deprived work situation in much the same way—by disappearing. Getting them back is another issue. Variety in industrial work has been the subject of study and controversy for 50 years. Recently, considerable attention has focused on the benefits to the individual and the organization of enlarging jobs to add variety (Herzberg, 1966; Davis, 1957).

There is another aspect of the need for variety that is less well recognized in the industrial setting today, but that will become increasingly important in the emergent technological environment. The cyberneticist Ashby (1960) has described this aspect of variety as a general criterion for intelligent behavior of any kind. To Ashby, adequate adaptation is only possible if an organism already has a stored set of responses of the requisite variety. This implies that in the work situation where unexpected things will happen, the task content of a job and the training for that job should match this potential variability.

The last category concerns participation of individuals in the decisions affecting their work. Participation in development of job content and organizational relations, as well as in planning of changes, was fundamental to the outcomes achieved by the studies in Norway (Thorsrud and Emery, 1969) and in the aircraft instrument industry (Davis, 1962; 1966). Participation plays a role in learning and growth and permits those affected by changes in their roles and environments to develop assessments of the effects. An extensive literature on the process and dynamics of change (Bennis, 1966) supports the findings of the field studies.

In a pioneering study, Lawrence and Lorsch (1967) examined the effects of uncertainty in technology and markets on the structure, relationship and performance of organizations. They found that where uncertainty is high, influence is high, i.e., if the situation becomes increasingly unpredictable, decision making is forced down into the organization where the requisite expertise for daily decisions resides. Under environments of uncertainty, influence and authority are more evenly distributed; organizations become "polyarchic." Under environments of certainty or stability, organizations tend to be relatively less democratic, with influence, authority and responsibility centralized. These findings were derived from studies of firms in contrasting certain and uncertain environments.

Another category, which goes beyond the four mentioned and is implicit in them, concerns the total system of work. In the field studies, if tasks and activities within jobs fell into meaningful patterns, reflecting the interdependence between the individual job and the larger production system, then enhanced performance satisfaction and learning took place. In socio-technical terms, this interdependence is most closely associated with the points at which variance is introduced from one production process into another. When necessary skills, tasks and information were incorporated into individual or group jobs, adjustments could be made to handle error and exceptions within the affected subsystem; failing that, the variances were exported to other interconnecting systems. (In "deterministic" systems, the layer upon layer of supervisors, buttressed by inspectors, utility men, repairmen, etc., absorb the variances exported from the workplace.)

These organizational experiments indicate that individuals and organizations can change and adapt to turbulent environments. Nonetheless, in moving into the post-industrial era, considerable learning is still needed about building into the organizational milieu the capability for continuing change. A number of studies have indicated that, if spontaneous and innovative behaviors are to result, conditions will have to be developed to bring about internalization of organizational goals (Katz and Kahn, 1966). Such internalization exists at the upper levels of organizations but, except in the Norwegian experiments, is found in the lower levels only in voluntary organizations.

In the postindustrial era, current organizational structures will become increasingly dysfunctional. If strategies of survival are to be developed, advanced societies and particularly the managers of their industrial and business organizations will have to accept the obligation to examine existing assumptions and to face the value issues regarding workers and technology raised by the evolving environments. Existing jobs and organizations will have to undergo reorganization to meet the requirement for a continuing high rate of change, new technologies and changing aspirations and expectations. These undertakings will be wrenching for institutions and individuals. Providing prescriptions would be presumptuous, but some organizations, joined by socio-technical research/consultants, seem to be well into the process.

References

Ashby, W.R. 1960. *Design for a Brain: The Origin of Adaptive Behavior*. Second Edition. New York: Wiley (first edition 1952). London: Chapman and Hall.

Bell, D. 1967. "Notes on the Post-Industrial Society: I and II." *Public Interest*, nos. 6 & 7.

Bennis, W.G. 1966. *Changing Organizations: Essays on the Development and Evolution of Human Organization*. New York: McGraw-Hill.

Davis, L.E. 1957. "Toward a Theory of Job Design." *Journal of Industrial Engineering*, 8:19–23.

———. 1962. "The Effects of Automation on Job Design." *Industrial Relations*, 2:53–71.

———. 1966. "The Design of Jobs." London: Tavistock Institute Document; *Industrial Relations*, 6:21–45. Revised in *Design of Jobs*, edited by L.E. Davis and J.C. Taylor. Harmondsworth: Penguin Books, 1972.

———. 1970. "Restructuring Jobs for Social Goals." *Manpower*, 2:2–5.

———. 1971. "Job Satisfaction Research: The Post-Industrial View." *Industrial Relations*, 10:176–93.

Davis, L.E. and E.S. Valfer. 1966. "Studies in Supervisory Job Design." *Human Relations*, 17:339–52.

Davis, L.E. and R. Werling. 1960. "Job Design Factors." *Occupational Psychology*, 34:109–32.

Doeringer, P.B. 1969. "Ghetto Labor Markets and Manpower." *Monthly Labor Review*, 92:55–56.

Emery, F.E. 1967a. "The Next Thirty Years: Concepts, Methods and Anticipations." *Human Relations*, 20:199–237.

———. 1967b. "The Nine-Step Model." Presented to an International Meeting on Socio-Technical Systems, Lincoln, England. Vol. II, pp. 569–79.

———. 1969. *Systems Thinking: Selected Readings*. Harmondsworth: Penguin Books.

Emery, F.E. and E.L. Trist. 1960. "Socio-Technical Systems." In *Management Sciences, Models and Techniques*, Vol. 2, edited by C.W. Churchman and M. Verhulst. Oxford: Pergamon Press.

———. 1965. "The Causal Texture of Organizational Environments." *Human Relations*, 18:21–32.

Fromm, E. 1968. *The Revolution of Hope: Toward a Humanized Technology*. New York: Harper and Row.

Galbraith, J.K. 1967. *The New Industrial State*. New York: Houghton Mifflin. Fourth edition 1985.

Herzberg, F. 1966. *Work and the Nature of Man*. Cleveland: World Publishing.

Katz, D. and R.L. Kahn. 1966. *The Social Psychology of Organizations*. New York: Wiley.

Lawler, E.E. 1969. "Job Design and Employee Motivation." *Personnel Psychology*, 22:426–43.

Lawrence, P.R. and J.H. Lorsch. 1967. *Organization and Environment: Managing Differentiation and Integration*. Cambridge, Mass.: Harvard University Press.

Thorsrud, E. and F.E. Emery. 1969. *Mot en ny bedriftsorganisasjon*. Oslo: Tanum. Reissued 1976 as F.E. Emery and E. Thorsrud, *Democracy at Work*. Leiden: Martinus Nijhoff.

Trist, E.L. 1968. *Urban North America: The Challenge of the Next Thirty Years—A Social Psychological Viewpoint*. Town Planning Institute of Canada.

Trist, E.L., G.W. Higgin, H. Murray and A.B. Pollock. 1963. *Organizational Choice: Capabilities of Groups at the Coal Face Under Changing Technologies: The Loss, Rediscovery and Transformation of a Work Tradition*. London: Tavistock Publications.

Albert Cherns

Principles of Socio-Technical Design[1,2]

The art of organization design is simultaneously esoteric and poorly developed. Most existing organizations were not born but "just growed." Many bear the recognizable stigmata of the operations of various well-known consultancy groups. There is, of course, no lack of available models, and no one seeking to set up an organization need reinvent the wheel. But organization design is generally an outcome, not an input. The input in manufacturing organizations is provided by the engineers, both those who design machines and equipment and those who design work methods and layout—the industrial engineers. Increasingly, operations researchers, systems analysts, the designers of computerized information systems, and the providers of "management services" of all kinds are having their say. In non-manufacturing work organizations, it is the latter who are most influential. And all of them, whether they recognize it or not, bring assumptions about people into their operations and their design. Most simply put, these assumptions can generally be described as Taylorist or System X—people are unpredictable; if they are not stopped by the system design, they will screw things up; it would be best to eliminate them completely but, since this is not possible, we must anticipate all the eventualities and then program them into the machines. The outcome is the familiar pattern of hierarchies of supervision and control to make sure that people do what is required of them, and departments of specialists to inject the "expert" knowledge that may be required by the complexities of manufacturing, marketing and allied processes but is equally often required to make the elaborate control, measurement and information systems work.

We have found in our own work, in both teaching and consulting, that engineers readily perceive that they are involved in organization design and that what they are designing is a socio-technical system built around much knowledge and thought on the technical, and little on the social, side of the system. There is, of course, the danger that the term *socio-technical system* very rapidly becomes a shibboleth, the mere pronouncing of which distin-

[1]Slightly revised from a paper in *Human Relations*, 29:783–92, 1976.

[2]I am indebted to Louis E. Davis, on whose work in designing new organizations I have drawn heavily in this article, which arises out of the courses we have given together at UCLA and elsewhere.

guishes the *cognoscenti* from the ignorant and uninitiated. But recognizing that a production system requires a social system to integrate the activities of the people who operate, maintain and renew it; account for it and keep it fed with the resources it requires and dispose of the products does nothing by itself to improve the design. And while discussion of the characteristics of social systems is helpful, that still leaves us with the problem that there are many ways of achieving their essential objectives.

We teach engineers that any social system must, if it is to survive, perform the function of Parsons's (1951) four subsystems. As we present them, these functions are:

- attainment of the goals of the organization;
- adaptation to the environment;
- integration of the activities of the people in the organization, including the resolution of conflict, whether task-based, organization-based or interpersonally-based;
- providing for the continued occupation of the essential roles through recruitment and socialization.

The advantage of this analysis is that it tells designers that if they do not take these absolute requirements of a social system into account, they will find that they will be met in some way or other, quite probably in ways that will do as much to thwart as to facilitate the functions for which the designers plan. But it still leaves wide open the question of how to design a social system or, more fundamental, how much a social system should be designed. That there is a choice in such matters can be as much a revelation to the engineer as the fact that there is a choice of technology to achieve production objectives is to the social scientist.

How, then, do you design a socio-technical system? Can we communicate any principles of socio-technical design? The first thing to be said is that a lot depends upon your objectives. All organizations are socio-technical systems; that is no more than a definition, a tautology. But the phrase was first used with, and has acquired, the connotation that organizational objectives are best met not by the optimization of the technical system and the adaptation of a social system to it, but by the joint optimization (Emery, 1967/Vol. II) of the technical and the social aspects, thus exploiting the adaptability and innovativeness of people in attaining goals instead of over-determining technically the manner in which these goals should be attained.

It is an obvious corollary that such design requires knowledge of the way machines and technical systems behave and of the way people and groups behave. Unless a designer is an engineer and a social scientist, both are required, which means engineers discussing alternative technical ways of attaining objectives with social scientists. This is not easy unless social scientists will take the trouble to learn enough about technology to understand the kinds of options that are open to engineers. The design team has indeed to be a multifunctional one as we have described elsewhere (Cherns, 1973).

In the process of designing ideas, no doubt the constant interchange among engineer, manager, social scientist, financial controller, personnel specialist and so on can do much to ensure that all aspects are considered, but the socio-technical concepts involved need not be hammered out afresh every time. They can be collected and presented in such a way as to ensure that they are taken account of without straitjacketing the designer. To this end, we have described nine principles, which we offer as a checklist, not a blueprint. They represent a distillation of experience and owe more to the writings of others (Emery, 1967/Vol. II; Emery and Trist, 1972/73; Herbst, 1974/Vol. II) than to our own originality. They have not, however, previously been systematized.

Principle 1: Compatibility

The process of design must be compatible with its objectives. A camel has been defined as a horse designed by a committee, and that joke unkindly incorporates negative evaluations of camels and committees. Camels certainly have minds of their own, but perhaps any attempt to draw more parallels between a camel and a social system would be unduly fanciful. Would a horse be more acceptable to a despot and a camel to a democrat? The point to be made, however, is that a participative social system cannot be created by fiat.

If the objective of design is a system capable of self-modification, of adapting to change and of making the most use of the creative capacities of the individual, then a constructively participative organization is needed. A necessary condition for this to occur is that people be given the opportunity to participate in the design of the jobs they are to perform. In a redesign of an existing organization, the people are already there. A design for a new organization has, however, to be undertaken before most of the people are hired. To some extent their jobs will have been designed for them in advance but this extent can be kept to a minimum. In one case (Davis and Cherns, 1975), the design team took the view that they would not design other people's lives. Having defined what were to be the objectives to be met and the competencies required to meet them, they deferred, until the individual was appointed, any discussion of how the job was to be performed. As in most cases "job" was not defined, this meant involving the people appointed as a team. Clearly some decisions had and have to be taken in advance; there has to be a pretty firm notion of how many people will be required and of what kinds of competence must be sought, but this is governed by the second principle.

Principle 2: Minimal Critical Specification

This principle has two aspects, negative and positive. The negative simply states that no more should be specified than is absolutely essential; the positive requires that we identify what is essential. It is of wide application and implies the minimal critical specification of tasks, the minimal critical allocation of tasks to jobs or jobs to roles and the specification of objectives with minimal critical specification of methods of obtaining them. While it may be necessary to be quite precise about what has to be done, it is rarely necessary to be precise about how it is to be done. In most organizations there is far too much specificity about how and, indeed, about what. Any careful observer of people in their work situation will learn how people contrive to get the job done despite the rules. As the railwaymen in Britain have demonstrated, the whole system can be brought to a grinding halt by "working to rule." Many of the rules are there to provide protection when things go wrong for those who imposed them; strictly applied, they totally inhibit adaptation and even effective action.

In any case, it is a mistake to specify more than is needed because by doing so options are closed that could be kept open. This premature closing of options is a pervasive fault in design; it arises not only because of the desire to reduce uncertainty, but also because it helps designers to get their own way. We measure our success and effectiveness less by the quality of the ultimate design than by the quantity of our ideas and preferences that have been incorporated into it.

One way of dealing with the cavalier treatment of options is to challenge each design decision and demand that alternatives always be offered. This may result in claims that the design process is being expensively delayed. Design proposals may also be defended on the ground that any other choice will run up against some obstacle, such as a company practice, a trade union agreement or a manning problem. These obstacles can then be regarded and logged as constraints upon a better socio-technical solution. When they have all been logged, each can be examined to estimate the cost of removing it. The cost may sometimes be prohibitive but frequently turns out to be less formidable than supposed or than the engineer has presented it to be.

Principle 3: The Socio-Technical Criterion

This principle states that variances, if they cannot be eliminated, must be controlled as near to their point of origin as possible. We need here to define *variance,* a word much used in socio-technical literature. Variance is any unprogrammed event; a key variance is one which critically affects outcome. This might be a deviation in quality of raw material, the failure to take action at a critical time, a machine failure and so on. Much of the elaboration of supervision, inspection and management is the effort to control variance, typically by action that does less to prevent variance than to try to correct its consequences. The most obvious example is the inspection function. Inspecting a product, the outcome of any activity, does not make right what is wrong. And if this inspection is carried out in a separate department some time after the event, the correction of the variance becomes a long loop, which is a poor design for learning. The socio-technical criterion requires that inspection be incorporated with production where possible, thus allowing people to inspect their own work and learn from their mistakes. This also reduces the number of communication links across departmental boundaries (see also Principle 5). The fewer the variances that are exported from the place where they arise, the fewer the levels of supervision and control that are required and the more "complete" the jobs of the people concerned to whom it now becomes possible to allocate an objective and the resources necessary to attain it. Frequently what is required to attain this objective turns out to be the supply of the appropriate information (see Principle 6).

Identifying variances and determining the key variances is a process often requiring lengthy analysis, and from time to time efforts have been made to codify it. One version, known as the nine-step analysis, has been developed by Davis and Cherns (1975). It has been used in enough organizations to give us some assurance that it can be adapted to use with any type of work organization, not just with manufacturing industry.

Principle 4: The Multifunctionality Principle—Organism vs. Mechanism

The traditional form of organization relies very heavily on the redundancy of parts. It requires people to perform highly specialized, fractionated tasks. There is often a rapid turnover of such people, but they are comparatively easily replaced. Each is treated as a replaceable part. Simple mechanisms are constructed on the same principle. Disadvantages arise when a range of responses is required, that is, when a large repertoire of performances is required from the mechanism or the organization. This usually occurs if the environmental demands vary. It then becomes more adaptive and less wasteful for each element to possess more than one function. The same function can be performed in different ways by using different combinations of elements. There are several routes to the same goal—the principle sometimes described as equifinality. Complex organisms have all gone this route of development. The computer, for example, is a typical multifunctional mechanism. The principle of minimal critical specification permits the organization to adopt this principle also.

Principle 5: Boundary Location

In any organization, departmental boundaries have to be drawn somewhere. Miller (1959/Vol. II) has shown that such boundaries are usually drawn so as to group people and activities on the basis of one or more of three criteria: technology, territory and time. Grouping by technology is typically seen in machine shops, where all the grinding machines are in one room, the Grinding Department; the milling machines in another, the Milling Department; and so on, with each department under the supervision of a specialist, a foreman grinder, etc. The consequences of this for the scheduling of work has been well described by Williamson (1972). A part in construction may be for months shuffled between departments, spending 1 percent of that time actually in contact with the machines. The consequent excessive cost of such work has been one of the stimuli to "group technology," the establishment of departments which each contain a variety of machines so that a part can be completed within one department. This corresponds to a grouping on the basis of time; the contiguity in time of operations indicates that they may well be organized together. Group technology also has consequences for the operation of the department as a team, with its members taking responsibility for the scheduling of operations and possibly the rotation of jobs.

Other examples of grouping on the basis of technology but not, of course, group technology, are the typing pool and the telephone switchboard. The switchboard may also be an example of the criterion of territory. Switchboard operators are bound together by the design of the machine. But the territorial principle can operate on the basis of little other than spatial contiguity. If the engineers have, for convenience, located different activities in the same area, the maintenance of control over the people working there suggests that they be made answerable to the same supervision. Retail trade organization is often of this kind with a floor supervisor. Organizations of this kind give rise to "dotted-line" relationships of functional responsibility.

All these criteria are pragmatic and defensible up to a point. But they possess notable disadvantages. They tend to erect boundaries which interfere with the desirable sharing of knowledge and experience. A simple example may suffice. In an organization concerned with the distribution of petroleum products studied by Cherns and Taylor (unpublished), the clerks who collected customers' orders were organized in a department separate from that of the drivers for whom schedules were worked out. A driver would pick up a schedule allocating him a vehicle and a route. Frequently the receipt of the routing would stimulate a string of expletives from the driver: "If I did what this *** has told me to do, I should not be able to do half the job. I would arrive at customer B just after 12 o'clock when the only man with the key to the pumps has gone off on his lunch break. And it's no use my turning up to customer P until I have discharged enough of my load for his short pipe to reach my tank. And finally I would end up on the *** road just in the middle of the rush hour. It would serve him right if I followed these instructions. I would run out of time [exceed the permitted number of consecutive driving hours] right in the middle of a throughway." There was no doubt pardonable exaggeration in all this; the point is that the drivers had acquired a great deal of knowledge about customers, routes, etc., but being organized into a separate department, they shared very little of this knowledge with the routing clerks who, however, received the customers' complaints before the drivers.

The principle has certain corollaries. A very important one concerns the management of the boundaries between department and department, between department and the organization as whole and between the organization and the outside world. The more the control of activities within the department becomes the responsibility of the members, the more the role of the supervisor/foreman/manager is concentrated on the boundary activities—ensuring that the team has adequate resources to carry out its functions, coordinating activities with those of other departments and foreseeing the changes likely to impinge upon them. This boundary maintenance role is precisely the requirement of the supervisor in a well-designed system.

Under favorable circumstances, working groups can acquire and handle a greater degree of autonomy and learn to manage their own boundaries. This implies locating responsibility for coordination clearly and firmly with those whose efforts require coordination if the common objectives are to be achieved. The role of supervisor now becomes that of a "resource" to the working group.

Principle 6: Information Flow

This principle states that information systems should be designed to provide information *in the first place* to the point where action on the basis of it will be needed. Information systems are not typically so designed. The capacity of computer-controlled systems to provide information about the state of the system, both totally and in great detail, to any organizational point has been used to supply to the top echelons of the organization information that is really useful only at lower levels and that acts as an incitement to the top management to intervene in the conduct of operations for which their subordinates are and should be responsible. The designer of the information system is naturally concerned to demonstrate its potentialities and is hard to convince that certain kinds of information can be potentially harmful when presented to high organizational levels. Properly directed, sophisticated information systems can, however, supply a work team with exactly the right type and amount of feedback to enable them to learn to control the variances which occur within the scope of their spheres of responsibility and competence and to anticipate events which are likely to have a bearing on their performance.

Principle 7: Support Congruence

This principle states that the systems of social support should be designed so as to reinforce the behaviors that the organization structure is designed to elicit. If, for example, the organization is designed on the basis of group or team operation with team responsibility, a payment system incorporating individual members would be incongruent with these objectives. Not only payment systems, but systems of selection, training, conflict resolution, work measurement, performance assessment, timekeeping, leave allocation, promotion and separation can all reinforce or contradict the behaviors which are desired. This is to say that the management philosophy should be consistent and that management's actions should be consistent with its expressed philosophy. Not infrequently, a management committed to philosophies of participation simultaneously adopts systems of work measurement, for example, which are in gross contradiction. Even management as progressive and committed to the humanization of work as that of Volvo's Kalmar plant has retained a commitment to a system of payment based on MTM, a technique of work measurement utilizing time and method study. Until replaced, this may pose an obstacle to the further humanization of work at Kalmar to which the management is committed.

Principle 8: Design and Human Values

This principle states that an objective of organizational design should be to provide a high quality of work. We recognize that quality is a subjective phenomenon and that everyone wants to have responsibility, variety, involvement, growth, etc. The objective is to provide these for those who do want them without subjecting those who do not to the tyranny of peer control. In this regard, we are obliged to recognize that all desirable objectives may not be achievable simultaneously.

What constitutes human work is a matter again of subjective judgment based on certain psychological assumptions. Thorsrud (1972) has identified six characteristics of a good job which can be striven for in the design of organizations and jobs:

- The need for the content of a job to be reasonably demanding of the worker in terms other than sheer endurance, and yet to provide a minimum of variety (not necessarily novelty).
- The need to be able to learn on the job and to go on learning (again, it is a question of neither too much nor too little).
- The need for some minimal area of decision making that individuals can call their own.
- The need for some minimal degree of social support and recognition in the workplace.
- The need for individuals to be able to relate what they do and what they produce to their social life.
- The need to feel that the job leads to some sort of desirable future (not necessarily promotion).

Principle 9: Incompletion

Design is a reiterative process. The closure of options opens new ones. At the end we are back at the beginning. The Forth Bridge, in its day an outstanding example of iron technology, required painting to fend off the rust. Starting at the Midlothian end, a posse of painters no sooner reached the Fife end than the Midlothian end required painting again. Varying the image, Jewish tradition prescribes that one brick be omitted in the construction of a dwelling lest the jealousy of God's angels be excited. Disregarding the superstition, the message is acceptable. As soon as design is implemented, its consequences indicate the need for redesign. The multifunctional, multilevel, multidisciplinary team required for design is needed for its evaluation and review.

Concluding Remarks

Who is the socio-technical designer to whom this paper is especially addressed? The analysis, preparation and implementation of a socio-technical design is the property of no individual or set of individuals; it belongs to the members of the organization whose working lives are being designed. Special skills and knowledge may well be, and often are, required, and these are provided as a resource by socio-technical consultants or action researchers.

But participation by employees in the design of their organizations may imply that they accept, or show readiness to accept, work roles which go beyond the agreements and constraints evolved by negotiation between management and union on their behalf. Unions are thus inevitably involved in the process, whether in a collaborative, neutral or antagonistic role. Can they be partners in design? This is a role which has seldom been offered to, and even more rarely accepted by, unions. It is not a role for which they have prepared themselves, and it is one which could easily blur their primary responsibilities to their members. Yet without them the viability of the design must be in some doubt. And the design of a social support system implies designing the functions of the shop steward, if not the union official. Our first principle, compatibility, requires that the unions be brought into the design if that is at all possible. But if they are to come in, they, too, will need to acquire new competencies.

References

Cherns, A.B. 1973. "Helping Managers: What the Social Scientist Needs to Know." *Organizational Dynamics* (Autumn): 51–67.

Davis, L.E. and A.B. Cherns. 1975. *The Quality of Working Life*, Vols. 1 and 2. New York: Free Press.

Emery, F.E. 1967. "The Nine-Step Model." Presented to an International Meeting on Socio-Technical Systems, Lincoln, England. Vol. II, pp. 569–79.

Emery, F.E. and E.L. Trist. 1972/73. *Towards a Social Ecology: Contextual Appreciation of the Future in the Present*. London/New York: Plenum Press.

Herbst, P.G. 1974. *Socio-Technical Design: Strategies in Multi-Disciplinary Research*. London: Tavistock Publications. Chapter 2 shortened and revised, Vol. II, "Designing with Minimal Critical Specifications," pp. 294–302.

Miller, E.J. 1959. "Technology, Territory and Time: The Internal Differentiation of Complex Production Systems." *Human Relations*, 12:243–72. Vol. II, pp. 385–404.

Parsons, T. 1951. *The Social System*. London: Routledge and Kegan Paul.

Thorsrud, E. 1972. "Policy Making as a Learning Process." In *Social Science and Government: Policies and Problems*, edited by A.B. Cherns, R. Sinclair and W.I. Jenkins. London: Tavistock Publications.

Williamson, D.T.N. 1972. "The Anachronistic Factory." *Proceedings of the Royal Society*, A331:139–60.

Eric Trist

Socio-Technical Ideas at the End of the '70s[1]

This paper will describe, in the briefest possible compass, what is meant by *quality of working life,* a relatively new approach to work and organizational improvement. The term itself, QWL as it has come to be called for short, was coined at a small international conference held at Columbia University's conference center (Arden House) in September 1972.

Available terms such as "industrial democracy," with its European connotation, did not suit North American conditions, while "job enrichment" and "job design" were too narrow. A new general term, politically neutral but indicating the direction that future development would likely take, seemed to be required. QWL proved the most acceptable among the suggestions made.

The purpose of the Arden House meeting was to obtain a better understanding of the frustrations and maladies of the workplace that were occasioning poor morale and poor performance and to identify approaches that would lead to positive outcomes. The most promising way forward seemed to lie in an increasing number of innovative work improvement projects undertaken in organizations of widely different kinds in most Western countries. A few pioneer studies in the 1950s had led to some quite large scale, well-sustained endeavors during the 1960s. These, in turn, had stimulated a much wider field of activities as the decade of the 1970s opened up. These projects have been based on participative decision making and work restructuring. Most of them have been able, simultaneously, to increase both job satisfaction and organizational performance, even though quite a number of them petered out, either through mistakes made by those immediately concerned or, more often, through lack of support in the wider organization, where most people did not understand what was being attempted and where many felt threatened by it. What the new designs did accomplish was to improve the quality of work experience of those directly involved and show that this could pay off.

Though these projects began in manufacturing industry, they have since been carried out in service industries, in the public as well as the private sector,

[1]Revised from a paper in *Adapting to a Changing World.* Ottawa: Labour Canada, 1981.

and in hospitals and educational establishments. The principles have been discovered to be quite general. They apply, moreover, to all levels and functions. Nevertheless, special attention has been paid to the lower levels that had been neglected in earlier approaches to organizational development that had focused on management.

The Basic Concept

Concern with improving the quality of life is increasing in all Western countries. To improve the quality of life in the workplace, where we spend half of our waking time, is a central part of this concern which represents an emergent value as Western societies pass from the industrial to the post-industrial era. This latter is usually defined as a state reached when manufacturing industry, because of its capital intensive and advanced technical condition, employs less than a half—perhaps no more than a third or a quarter—of the working population.

Though the problem of a new form of scarcity regarding the depletion of nonrenewable resources has now appeared, this does not mean that the old form of economic scarcity need return. Technology has developed to a point where enough can be produced to provide for the basic needs of all at a level considerably above that of mere subsistence. (At least this is so in the advanced countries, and this paper is concerned with Canada as an advanced country.)

The post-scarcity situation is changing the underlying attitude of people to work. A survey carried out in 1974 for the Federal Government of Canada showed that, while 97 percent of Canadians preferred being employed to being unemployed, only 67 percent were willing to take the meanest and dullest type of job at the minimum wage; 33 percent said they would sooner be on welfare. Though commitment to work is still central to people's lives, this commitment is becoming conditional on the quality of the work experience rather than remaining a compulsion of dire necessity. While 85 percent of respondents felt "satisfied" with their jobs in a vague and general way, only 50 percent would take the same job again, and only 30 percent felt seriously committed and involved in what they were doing (Table 1).

Canadians (in the same survey) put the following features at the top of a long list of desirable job requirements: interesting work; the means to do it; a piece of the action; dignity. Only then came good pay and job security. Though these two economic factors were placed first by the unskilled group, this group also included the four noneconomic factors in their top six factors (Table 2). Similar results have been obtained in a number of Western countries. In the post-scarcity situation, an increasing number of people (though not, of course, everyone) are seeking, over and above a reasonable and reasonably secure

TABLE 1   Job Satisfaction

Survey response	Percent
My job is o.k.	85
Take same job again	50
Involved and committed	30
Rather be employed	97
Rather be unemployed	3
Take dull job at minimum wage	67
Sooner be on welfare	33

TABLE 2   Most Desirable Features of Jobs

Interesting work

Means to do it

Piece of the action

Dignity

Good pay

Job security

More skilled emphasize human factors

Less skilled emphasize economic factors

Both include all six among most desirable factors

standard of living, an opportunity both to develop themselves and to contribute to society. One would expect to find a higher proportion of such people in technologically advanced rather than in less advanced industries because of the sophistication and challenging character of many of the core jobs. To enhance the opportunities presented and the wish to respond to them is what is meant by improving the quality of life in the workplace.

The majority of jobs, however, in most manufacturing and service industries have been designed in a narrow and circumscribed fashion that yields a low quality of working life for the many as distinct from a high quality of life for the privileged few. These jobs are monotonous and uninteresting for large numbers of white-collar as well as blue-collar workers. They give little scope for personal fulfillment or accomplishment. They are associated with high turnover and absenteeism; with grievances and labor disputes; with unnecessary downtime; with bad work leading to costly rework; with increased alcoholism, drug abuse and psychological stress. All these are symptoms of what is often referred to as *alienation*. Directly and indirectly, they all tend to increase production costs.

Yet it is not necessary for most ordinary jobs to be designed in this way. Experience is now available from projects undertaken in most Western countries to show that many such jobs can be designed or redesigned so that they do give rise to interesting work; do afford means over which people can exercise considerable control; do give people more of the action and do enable them to recover a sense of human dignity. When work is restructured along these lines, two results usually follow: higher job satisfaction is experienced and a higher level of performance is achieved. Quality of working life and productivity are positively associated.

When this is not the case, enough experience is now on hand to enable us to point to the reasons. Most commonly the dissociation arises because the deeper values and wider organizational issues involved are not understood by those concerned. The restructuring of work in what may be called the new design idiom cannot for long yield positive results if it is confined merely to one or two small areas of an organization. Under these conditions, innovative projects tend to fade out. Disappointment ensues; one is worse off than before. To obtain lasting benefits, the new idiom has to be diffused through an entire work establishment, such as an operating plant, and supported by management above this level in multi-plant concerns.

The Underlying Philosophy

The transformation involved requires a new philosophy that regards work as a factor fundamental to human development rather than simply as a means of earning a living. Such a philosophy entails designing work organizations to this end. The new design idiom depends on the primacy of collaboration over competition inside the organization, so that it may become more competitive outside in the marketplace and hence survive and hence increase job security. This requires a participant management style, nonbureaucratic organizational forms and new principles of work restructuring. Together these factors can create jobs worth doing for their own sake for everyone in the organization.

They permit a new work ethic to develop which recognizes the importance of the quality of working life as a way to personal growth and as a central part of the quality of life as a whole.

As much as goods and services, the product of work is people. There is growing evidence that those with a higher QWL have more to offer at home and become more active in the community. A society can be no better than the quality of its people. This depends to an important extent on how far work experience over the years fosters or prevents personal development.

Advanced industrial societies have reached a critical point regarding the choices that must be made on this issue. Economic growth has slowed down. Inflation has become persistent. The rising standard of living experienced since World War II has depended on the continuance of high economic growth and the containment of inflation. With slower economic growth and uncontained inflation, the prevention of income erosion, not to speak of the achievement of income gain, depends more than ever on increasing productivity (Table 3). But nowhere is productivity increasing sufficiently for this purpose. Too often it is stationary, and there are many instances of decline.

With the passing of the age of scarcity (that is, the old scarcity) the carrot and stick have lost their former powers of persuasion. Paradoxically, the maintenance of our material well-being now depends on our making advances on the nonmaterial plane. Whether the level of technology is high or low, simple or complex, actual, as compared with possible, performance is a function of the involvement in, and commitment to, what workers are doing by those directly concerned. Involvement and commitment cannot be imposed. They can only be given, and are given only when they arise naturally from the intrinsic value of job experience. To improve the quality of working life for its own sake has paradoxically become the main way now available to get the best out of increasingly sophisticated technology and to improve the bottom line.

Industrial advance has produced a world in which the levels of interdependence and complexity, and hence of uncertainty, have become higher than any previously experienced. The environment has become *turbulent*. Change has become continuous. We have "lost the stable state." Under these conditions, conventional bureaucratic and technocratic organizations are too inflexible and non-innovative to retain competitive advantage. Organizations moving into the new idiom have the resourcefulness to develop in alternative directions. Their members, at all levels, are more willing to take risks. They are future-oriented, a quality that has become mandatory (for survival) in a rapidly changing environment in which competition is worldwide (Table 4).

Industry in the advanced countries is becoming information-dependent. The complex information handling, which characterizes the core jobs both in the office and on the shop floor in such industries, requires the sophisticated interpretation of data and the anticipation and prevention of error. Workers

TABLE 3   New Economic Situation

Slower growth

Inflation

Lower profit levels

Wage increases more difficult

Needed: higher level of organization performance

Depending on: higher job satisfaction
              more collaboration
              doing more with less

TABLE 4   World Environment

Change rate
   Interdependence
   Complexity
   Uncertainty

Loss of stable state

Turbulence
   Conventional organizations not coping as well
   Innovative organizations doing better

have become managers of job systems. To a large extent they supervise themselves. Correction that mainly depends on external supervision is too frequently too late. The science-based industries, particularly, cannot, without self-damage, produce jobs which are the extreme as regards narrowness and repetitiousness. But traditional approaches to job design are resulting in just such jobs at a time when the microelectronics revolution is getting underway. This has particularly serious implications for continuous process industries and those concerned with computer-aided assembly and fabrication.

All in all, concern with QWL is to be seen as an emergent value arising in advanced industrial societies as they pass into the post-industrial era. With the old scarcity dynamic no longer operative, the attitudes, especially among younger (and more educated) workers, have changed. A job which allows personal fulfillment rather than one which simply enables a living to be earned is increasingly expected, except among those who seem irreversibly alienated and parasitical. The design of jobs in the new idiom has become the best way to secure higher productivity, more than ever necessary in face of slower economic growth and persistent inflation. Such job designs form the basis of a process of organizational transformation from bureaucratic and technocratic forms which are rigid and non-innovative to more flexible, innovative forms founded on participation rather than authoritarianism. These emerging forms are more able to maintain competitive advantage in fast changing environments. They give scope for a higher quality of working life for the many rather than for merely the privileged few. In so doing, they contribute to human betterment and reduce the divisions and tensions in the wider society.

Principles

We must now ask how the basic concept and underlying philosophy can be translated into practice. For this purpose a set of principles and strategies has gradually evolved from the experience of the large number of QWL projects which have now been undertaken. They are, however, no more than guidelines. Every project must be custom-built by those directly concerned who must themselves discover what is best for them through their own learning. Each QWL project is a unique process. Nevertheless, it must embody certain fundamentals, else it will no longer be QWL. These fundamentals are described in what follows.

The new idiom of job design entails abandoning what has become known as the technological imperative (that the requirements of the technology must be met whatever the cost to people). To be abandoned also is the notion that improving "human relations" will, by itself, compensate for modes of job structuring that unduly limit the scope of the human individual through the extreme application of the principles of a "scientific management." Machines and people are different. Work systems need to be designed so that the best match is obtained between the two, which are complementary. This principle has become known as the *joint optimization* of the social and technical system. A work organization is a *socio-technical* system (Table 5).

Jobs have two sets of properties: extrinsic and intrinsic (Table 6). The extrinsic are familiar: fair and adequate pay; job security; benefits such as vacations and pensions; safe and healthy conditions in the work environment; due process regarding grievance, dismissal, etc. The intrinsic properties constitute a newly recognized dimension: tasks which offer variety and challenge (elbow room); opportunities to go on learning on the job; to make some decisions oneself, to have some autonomy, some piece of the action which is one's own; to experience group belongingness with recognition and support from superiors, colleagues and subordinates; to feel that what one does is making an identifiable and meaningful contribution to the overall outcome and

TABLE 5   Joint Optimization of Technical and Human Resources

Industrial engineering, operations research and management science approaches

Human relations approaches

The systemic, socio-technical approach

TABLE 6   Properties of Jobs

Extrinsic	Intrinsic
Fair and adequate pay	Variety and challenge
Job security	Continuous learning
Benefits	Discretion, autonomy
Safety	Recognition and support
Health	Meaningful social contribution
Due process	Desirable future
Conditions of employment	The job itself
Socio-economic	Psycho-social

gives one an acceptable occupational identity; to believe one's work life contains some promise of a desirable future (not necessarily promotion but additional experience; for example, further training, redeployment, wider responsibility, etc.).

In the new design idiom, the preferred way to redesign jobs is to involve the people who actually do them, and who have the most intimate knowledge of them, in the redesign process. They can begin by rating their present jobs on the criteria given in Table 6. They then learn to analyze their work systematically and to identify what needs changing. Then one or two operators (office personnel if the unit is administrative or sales clerks if it is retail), along with a supervisor and staff specialist, can make change proposals and test out their acceptability to the work group and to management. This is known as *participant design* (Emery and Emery, 1974/Vol. II). Beginning in limited areas with trial projects, participant design gradually extends to the whole organization. Some of the best successes have been obtained in designing new establishments in this way involving both current employees with relevant experience and the first groups of employees who will actually work in these establishments. A principle of *minimum critical specification* (Herbst, 1974/ Vol. II) is followed, which means that much is left open to be decided as operating experience is gained. Any unions concerned are involved from the beginning. If the organization is nonunion, other ways have to be found through which employees can express their views about what concerns them as a group.

Participation is the basis of the new idiom. One must distinguish, however, between direct or work-linked participation in decision making at one's own level and representative participation through having workers on Boards or Works Councils. Only the former can directly improve the quality of work experience. The latter is concerned with problems of governance: who is to have a voice in deciding the nature of the businesses to be engaged in, the broad strategies followed, the distribution of profits, etc. In some countries the two go together; in others one is preferred, the other avoided. Either or both may be deemed incompatible with free collective bargaining as they may compromise union independence (Table 7). Some unions, however, see advantages in participating in both, as in Scandinavia, or more particularly in the representative form, as in West Germany. In North America most unions have held themselves aloof from participating in either, though one or two unions in the United States and Canada have begun to engage in the work-linked form. In Table 8, the situation as regards the strength of collective bargaining, representative and work-linked democracy is summarized using a five point scale (0–4). In several countries the situation is in transition.

The range of QWL activities is very broad. Joint labor-management steering committees may be formed to decide on and monitor acceptable projects and action groups to carry them out. The projects themselves may involve the introduction of flextime, gain sharing plans such as Scanlon or payment for what one knows rather than for what one does; work restructuring, involving workers in the process of product improvement or in redesigning layouts; evolving schemes of job progression so that skills are widened and taking more responsibility in self-managing semiautonomous work groups that absorb some maintenance, quality control and planning tasks (Table 9).

Quality of working life activities usually lead to a number of concrete results. The literature is agreed that an improvement in product quality is almost always achieved. Usually, there is a reduction in costs through such factors as less downtime. Often, too, the levels of labor turnover, absenteeism and sickness become markedly less. There are fewer grievances and labor disputes (Table 10). Attainment of these results, however, depends on QWL endeavors being supported by all levels of management and, in unionized plants, on the cooperation of the union(s) being secured.

Activities of the above kind cannot be successfully undertaken unless the

TABLE 7   Forms of Industrial Democracy

Representative	Workers on Boards, Works Councils
Work-linked	Participant design of the workplace
Interest group	Collective bargaining, binding contracts

TABLE 8   Levels of Industrial Democracy in Selected Western Countries, 1978

Country	Collective bargaining	Representative democracy	Work-linked democracy
Norway	4	3–4	2–3
Sweden	4	3–4	2–3
Holland	3	2	1–2
Germany	2	4	0–1
France	2	1	0–1
U.K.	4	0–?	0–1
U.S.	2–3	0	0–1
Canada	2–3	0	0–1
Australia	2–3	0–1	1–2
Yugoslavia	0	4	0–?

TABLE 9   QWL Activities

Redesign of jobs	More work group autonomy
Layout redesign	Wider organizational changes
Product improvements	New roles for supervisors
Process improvements	Problem solving training
Changes in information flows	Interpersonal, group skills training
Changes in support services	Management development

TABLE 10   QWL Results

Improvement in quality

Reduction in costs

Increase in output

Reduced turnover

Less absenteeism

Less sickness

Fewer grievances

Fewer strikes

role of the supervisor is changed from that of an old style boss to that of a facilitator. Such facilitators will now need interpersonal and group skills, training ability, capacity for forward planning on a longer time horizon and will need to negotiate priorities on behalf of their groups with other departments. This requires a considerable training investment. The work force also requires training in additional skills and wider responsibilities.

These activities will sooner or later entail a change in the character of the organization. This transformation involves a shift from one basic pattern to another. A basic pattern of this kind that contains many components all consistent with each other is often referred to as a *paradigm*. The old organizational paradigm constitutes a rigid technocratic bureaucracy. The new constitutes a much more flexible and adaptive modality based on participation and joint optimization (see Trist, 1981/Vol. II, Table 2).

The old paradigm is based on the technological imperative; people are viewed simply as extensions of the machine, as expendable spare parts; work is simplified on the one worker/one job principle; controls are externalized in supervision, functional staff and precise work rules and administrative procedures; management is authoritarian; the pyramid is tall; the climate is one of internal competition and gamesmanship; risks are avoided; innovation is low.

The new paradigm is based on joint optimization; people are viewed as complementary to the machine and are to be developed for their own sake and as key organizational assets; jobs are grouped into operational subsystems with skills being broadened and controls internalized as far as possible in the primary work group; management style is participative; the pyramid becomes flatter; the climate is one of openness and cooperation; risk-taking is encouraged and the level of innovation goes up.

In the old paradigm, the organization pursues only its own interests. In the new paradigm, externally, the organization recognizes its interdependence with the wider environment, both social and physical, so that some of the externalities begin to be internalized. Within itself, it recognizes the need continuously to improve the QWL of its members—to produce high quality people as well as goods or services of high quality. On both counts, the organization accepts *social responsibility* as a condition of continuing its market thrust.

Organizations belonging to the new paradigm are not "feather-bedded." They are much "leaner" than those belonging to the old. Manning levels in both the blue- and white-collar work force are lower, often a third lower. There are fewer supervisors and junior staff members. Fewer specialist departments are required, so there are also fewer middle managers. There are far fewer work interruptions. Absenteeism, turnover and grievances are lower. Any of the new plants or administrative establishments designed on the new principles will demonstrate these features. In established organizations, great consideration and care need to be given to all those, at whatever level, who are likely, or believe they are likely, to be adversely affected by the very substantial changes involved in making the transition. Particularly important is the involvement, in the preparatory as well as the later stages, of middle management and supervision and the hourly employees (the union[s], if there are any). Any attempts for the sake of short run economic gains to make changes in ways which contravene the basic commitment to participation and the determination to secure win/win outcomes for all (whatever compromises have to be made) will create distrust and will discredit QWL as a philosophy of work.

Strategies

Four main options are available at the overall corporate level as regards QWL change strategies (Table 11). The first is to reject QWL, at least for the foreseeable future: to wait until many more organizations have gone this route and to reconsider when the new paradigm has become a generally accepted mode and when the main "do's and don'ts" have become well established. The next is to adopt a laissez-faire posture. If one or two managers here and there want to try something, let them. If they fall on their face, too bad; if they succeed, the brownie points are theirs. But there is no support from the wider organizational system. Projects undertaken in these circumstances tend to fade out when the initiators are transferred, promoted or when they leave. The

TABLE 11   Four Options

Rejection

Laissez-faire

Selective development

Corporate-wide commitment

negative aftermath militates against further developments (Trist and Dwyer, 1982/Vol. II).

The third option may be called *selective development* (Table 12). Top management is not prepared to make an unqualified commitment to the new idiom and to make public a statement of management philosophy that fully embraces QWL in its widest implications. It is, however, willing to give corporate support to QWL projects in carefully selected establishments where local management and workers are interested, the local union is supportive and there is a reasonable chance not only of initial gains but of self-sustaining success.

Finally, in some corporations, or indeed public agencies, top management may judge that enough experience has been gained and benefits proven that an overall public commitment can be made and continuous efforts undertaken in all parts of the organization. A few organizations (in several countries) have made such commitments and are following them through in practice. Nothing, however, is more likely to turn the clock back than a declaration which turns out to be largely rhetorical. In any case, such a declaration would be premature with regard to the current beliefs and attitudes in most sections and levels of the organization, or unwise because it would conflict with immediate priorities so that the necessary attention could not be given.

Selective development seems to be the course increasingly favored by organizations embarking on long range QWL programs, especially when they are large and diversified. This entails being clear about the nature of the likely benefits and taking into account the interests of all parties involved, given the rapidly changing environment and the changing character of the work force. The risks and costs of *not* embarking on long range QWL programs need to be weighed no less carefully than the risks and costs of going forward. In the longer term, the penalties of inaction can be very great, but too much in the way of immediate disturbance can be self-defeating.

In conclusion, QWL opens up a set of very basic issues. Deep questions of value are involved, of organizational purpose and of the type of society one

TABLE 12   Selective Development

Benefits of selective development
Risks and costs of selective development
Risks and costs of not pursuing selective development

regards as constituting a desirable future. If one wants a more human and a more democratic world rather than a more inhuman and a more totalitarian world, one is likely to conclude that QWL will contribute to realizing it. One may, in addition, believe that advanced industrial societies cannot persist unmodified too many decades longer in their prevailing mode without producing severe dysfunction and unacceptable suffering, and that what the private sector chooses to do in initiating change will be critical in avoiding negative outcomes. In this case, one is still more likely to conclude that improving the quality of life in the workplace, as part of increasing the quality of life as a whole, has become one of the central issues of our times. The scale of effort required, the determination necessary to sustain programs in the face of resistance and setbacks will then—but only then—seem worthwhile.

The benefits of QWL are essentially long term. They have implications for the wider society and for the development of the individual as well as for the organization itself. They provide one of the critical ways of reducing social conflict in the decades immediately ahead.

In organizational life, we are entering an era in which QWL is to be regarded as a main means of maintaining, and very often increasing, the level of performance in face of rapid change and unforeseeable events.

References

Emery, F. and M. Emery. 1974. *Participative Design: Work and Community Life.* Canberra: Centre for Continuing Education, Australian National University. Revised version, Vol. II, "The Participative Design Workshop," pp. 599–613.

Herbst, D. (P.G.). 1974. *Socio-Technical Design: Strategies in Multi-Disciplinary Research.* London: Tavistock Publications. Revised version of Chapter 2, Vol. II, "Designing with Minimal Critical Specifications," pp. 294–302.

Trist, E. 1981. "QWL and the '80s." Closing address, International Conference on QWL and the '80s, Toronto. Vol. II, pp. 338–49.

Trist, E. and C. Dwyer. 1982. "The Limits of Laissez-Faire as a Socio-Technical Change Strategy." Chapter 8 in *The Innovative Organization: Productivity Programs in Action,* edited by R. Zager and M. Rosow. New York and Oxford: Pergamon. Revised version, Vol. II, pp. 451–73.

Eric Trist

QWL and the '80s[1]

In thinking out what I might say at our last lunch—if not our last supper—I reluctantly concluded that I had better write it out as, in my case, the constraint of time is compounded by a tendency to run out of control very soon after I have opened my mouth. Therefore, I will read this address, accepting that it is better to be dull but brief than to aspire to be more lively but take longer. I also felt I would be incomprehensible without visual support. The choice lay between transparencies and handouts. I have chosen handouts, as transparencies, even with generous projection, would not easily be seen except by those favorably placed in a room of this size.[2] I hope you will allow, therefore, that my choice of technology has taken the "socio-" into account and that we may begin in a state of joint optimization.

Whatever the tasks of QWL in the '80s, they will take place in an environment of increasing turbulence, a term which I will explain in a few moments. The degree of societal change at present taking place is very great, at least as great as that accompanying the first industrial revolution. We are now well into the second industrial revolution based on information, rather than simply energy, technologies (Ackoff, 1974). The second industrial revolution is being led by the microprocessor, and still newer technologies will doubtless follow, with far-reaching effects on social relations and institutions throughout our societies. We shall, for example, have to give up the idea of full employment, at least as traditionally understood. The recent youth riots in Britain by those of all colors exemplify our unpreparedness to deal with the problems of a partially employed society.

Quality of working life as an international enterprise arose in the early '70s when the assumption of full employment was still valid. We must continue, indeed intensify and accelerate, all we have been doing since then and are preparing to do now; but during the '80s we must, in addition, discover the tasks of QWL in a partially employed society. I will return to this theme toward the end of my presentation.

The societal transition we are in is often referred to as a transition from an

---

[1]Closing address to the International Conference on QWL and the '80s, Toronto, 1981.
[2]Two very large connecting ballrooms were filled for this address.

TABLE I   Change in Organizational Paradigm

From	Toward
A disturbed-reactive environment	A turbulent environment
The redundancy of parts	The redundancy of functions
The old organizational paradigm	The new organizational paradigm
Low QWL for the many	High QWL for the many

industrial to a post-industrial order, though the meaning of post-industrial is far from clear and there is more than one version of it. But, for organizational life, it entails in any case moving away from a departing (old) paradigm, with *low* QWL for the many, toward an emergent (new) paradigm, with *high* QWL for the many.

Looking at the increasing rate of change, even as far back as the '60s, Fred Emery and I (1965) distinguished four types of environment. The first two, where the change rate was slow, need not be discussed in the present context. The third environmental type, called the *disturbed-reactive,* reflects an accelerating change rate and became increasingly salient as the industrial revolution progressed (Table 1). It zenithed some time after World War II when the science-based industries rose to prominence in the wake of the knowledge and information explosions. The best chances of survival in this world went to large scale organizations with the capacity to make formidable competitive change through amassed expertise. This enabled them to maximize their independent power. The organizational form they perfected was the competitive and singular technocratic bureaucracy in which the ideas of Weber and Frederick Taylor were matched and operationalized to fit the requirements of the disturbed-reactive environment.

The very success of the technocratic bureaucracy has increased the salience of another type of environment, very different from the disturbed-reactive, which is mismatched with technocratic bureaucracy. The new environment is called the *turbulent field* in which large competing organizations, all acting independently in diverse directions, produce unanticipated and dissonant consequences. The result is a contextual commotion that makes it seem as if the "ground" were moving as well as the organizational actors. This is what is meant by turbulence. Subjectively, it is experienced as a "loss of the stable state" as Schon (1971) has put it.

As compared with the disturbed-reactive environment, the turbulent field is characterized by a higher level of interdependence and a higher level of complexity. Together, these generate a much higher level of uncertainty. The higher levels of interdependence, complexity and uncertainty now to be found in the world environment pass the limits within which technocratic bureaucracies were designed to cope.

This means that we must search for an alternative based on a different design principle. Emery (1967) has shown that there are two basic organizational design principles, both of which display "redundancy" in the sense of reserve capacity, as any system must. In the first, the *redundancy* is of *parts* and is mechanistic. The parts are broken down so that the ultimate elements are as simple and inexpensive as possible, as with the unskilled worker in a narrow job who is cheap to replace and who takes little time to train. The technocratic bureaucracy is founded on this type of design.

In the second design principle, the *redundancy* is of *functions* and is organic. Any component system has a repertoire that can be put to many uses, so that increased adaptive flexibility is acquired. While redundancy of functions holds at the biological level, as for example in the human body, it becomes far more critical at the organizational level where the components—individual humans and groups of humans—are themselves purposeful systems. Humans have the capacity for self-regulation so that control may become internal rather than external. Only organizations based on the redundancy of functions have the flexibility and innovative potential to give the possibility of adaptation to a rapid change rate, increasing complexity and environmental uncertainty.

This capability makes it imperative to move operationally from the old organizational paradigm toward the new, while the changes taking place in the attitudes and values of the younger generations now in, or soon to enter, the workplace make it additionally necessary that a high QWL be available for the many rather than the privileged few. This the second design principle makes possible. These changes are mandatory to ensure our survival at any reasonable economic standard. For we already know that at any given technological level the maintenance of, let alone any increase in, productivity is dependent on scope for human development. This is the central message of QWL.

The shift from the old to the new organizational paradigm represents a discontinuity—a shift in the underlying pattern of social values and relations from competition to collaboration. The nature of this shift is shown in Figure 1, which is drawn from the work of Calvin Pava (1980). In the departing paradigm the overriding governing value is competition: factional warfare of varying degrees limits and constrains collaborative relations. Collaboration is required but is only a subordinate value. In the emerging paradigm collaboration becomes the governing value, which limits and constrains factional competition. Competition is still required, but it now expresses the subordinate value. This is what I mean by a discontinuity.

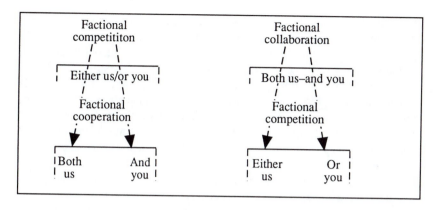

Figure 1. Reversal of competitive and collaborative relations

In a turbulent environment, no organization is powerful enough, however large, to go it entirely alone or to force its will on others solely by coercion. The interdependencies in which it is implicated are too many. It has to surrender some sovereignty, to share some power. It has to work out with others what I like to refer to as a *negotiated order.*

In the field of industrial relations this means that labor and management cannot continue in an exclusively adversarial posture in the win/lose mode. Several modes of labor/management collaboration, including QWL, have been accepted for some time in Scandinavia, and co-determination has become the built-in way in countries such as Germany; but during the '70s a collaborative mode began to appear alongside the adversarial mode in countries such as the United States and Canada, where adversarial postures have been a religion—not without some very good reasons. This new collaborative mode has been growing in relation to QWL.

A fundamental condition must be satisfied to permit the growth of collaboration in labor-management relations; the power of labor has to increase vis-à-vis that of management. The more the power balance of the two independent parties approaches equality, the greater the likelihood of their working collaboratively on the unsolved emergent issues on which the welfare of both depends and on which progress to a more democratic form of society also depends. This is a very different story from unions getting in bed with management; or putting QWL in to keep the unions out. That sort of behavior belongs to the old paradigm.

An example of an early step being taken toward the new paradigm is Doug Fraser, the UAW chief, going on the Board of Chrysler. Another is the alternative corporate plan put up by the Combined Shop Stewards Committee of Lucas Aerospace in Britain. Despite stormy initial rejection, this plan not only won some eventual acceptance but lit fires in other prominent British companies that were not doing well, such as Vickers and Parsons where many of the stewards' proposals were accepted (Coates and Topham, 1980). If one can imagine what would happen much further down the road, it is not entirely fanciful to think that, even in North America, collaboration might become primary in labor/management relations, while competition would be reserved for more familiar contract issues. In a turbulent environment, the finding of common ground provides the basis of survival for both management and labor; thence of the wider society.

Survival in a turbulent environment depends on human development because it requires innovation. Innovation is necessary to meet the rapid change rate and the rising complexity and uncertainty. QWL operates in the direction of making workers more resourceful and more innovative, therefore more capable and more powerful. Management depends on the increased capability of the workforce for the success of the enterprise from which the workforce also benefits. This is to put in first place a win/win mode based on collaboration rather than a win/lose mode based on adversarial competition. This competition is still present but now recedes to second place. So long as a disturbed-reactive environment remained salient, the win/lose adversarial mode appropriately took first place. Given the salience of a turbulent field, it can no longer remain in first place, which belongs to collaboration.

Let me now look at the attributes of the old and new organizational paradigms as related to QWL. They are summarized in Table 2. As we have been discussing these issues throughout the Conference and as an account of them is given in my paper, "The Evolution of Socio-Technical Systems," made available by the Ontario QWL Centre (Trist, 1981a/Vol. II), I need not dwell on them but will simply note that a change in these attributes from the old paradigm to the new brings into being conditions that allow commitment to grow and alienation to decrease. Equally important is the replacement of a climate of low risk-taking with one of innovation. This depends on high trust and openness in relations between management and labor and within both. These qualities are mandatory if we are to transform traditional technocratic bureaucracies into continuous adaptive learning systems.

This transformation is imperative for survival in a fast-changing environment. It involves nothing less than the working out of a new organizational philosophy which all the principal stakeholders, including the unions, can voluntarily accept. The transition from old to new will be a slow and difficult evolution as those holding on to the old are going to resist. They will counter-attack. They will sabotage. Some of this destructiveness will be unconscious as well as conscious, and therefore more difficult to get at.

A key implication of the list is that QWL projects have to be multidimen-

TABLE 2   Attributes of the Two Paradigms

Old Paradigm	New Paradigm
The technological imperative	Joint optimization
Worker as an extension of the machine	Worker as complementary to the machine
Worker as an expendable spare part	Worker as a resource to be developed
Maximum task breakdown, simple narrow skills	Optimum task grouping, multiple broad skills
External controls (supervisors, specialist staffs, procedures)	Internal controls (self-regulating subsystems)
Tall organization chart, autocratic style	Flat organization chart, participative style
Competition, gamesmanship	Collaboration, collegiality
Organization's purposes only	Members' and society's purposes also
Alienation	Commitment
Low risk-taking	Innovation

TABLE 3   Four Options for QWL

Rejection

Laissez-faire

Selective development

Corporate-wide commitment

sional. They cannot remain limited to one or two aspects only of organizational life.

Table 3 shows four main strategic options regarding QWL (Trist, 1981b). Outright *rejection* is becoming less common and is infeasible as a long-range position in a turbulent environment. *Laissez-faire* was the most common option during the '70s. Innovative managers were allowed to go ahead without organizational support. Many projects faded out as a result. *Selective development* exists in two versions. In the first, there is no overall corporate commitment to QWL, but top management discerns certain work establishments in its purview where it actively encourages QWL projects because it considers success likely and the need significant. This is a pragmatic approach of considerable relevance to large heterogeneous organizations in which different managers and unions espouse different values and have different outlooks. In the second, selective development goes along with the overall *corporate-wide commitment*. A QWL philosophy has been arrived at after much consideration, and public commitment to it has been obtained from the principal stakeholders including the union(s). Even with this done, QWL projects cannot be started up simultaneously across the board so that the question of site selection again arises. Corporate commitment in conjunction with selective development gives the best chance for QWL projects to endure. This approach is being adopted by such corporations as General Motors and American Telephone and Telegraph. It will, I believe, spread during the '80s.

Let me now list some of the main tasks that QWL faces in the '80s:

- To make more completely the shift toward the new paradigm in established as well as new work organizations (where we have been rather successful during the '70s); to go system-wide in these organizations and to learn better how to do this; to find ways of accomplishing diffusion faster. We need more than ever to use the introduction of advanced technology as a lever.
- To encourage independent union initiatives. It is essential that many more unions than the few who have so far done so should take up QWL on their own terms for their own sake, as unions, and press management to move in the QWL direction—as the UAW did with General Motors in 1973. Otherwise there will be fewer unions around by the year 2000.
- There is a great need to extend community-based QWL as this makes for synergy and not only yields strong network effects but relates work to other areas of life. Similarly, there is need to extend QWL to the sectoral level, as Einar Thorsrud (1981) has done with the Norwegian Merchant Navy and as the steel industry is doing in the United States, so that wider problématiques are addressed that cannot be dealt with at the level of the single organization.
- We need to make greater use of the capabilities of women,who are more experienced than men in the intuitive and holistic thinking required to deal with many emergent problems and in the development of nurturant climates necessary to advance our response-capability in turbulent environments.
- We need to learn to work far more with small businesses. This was a priority in projects such as Jamestown (Trist, Vol. III).
- We need to assist Third World countries in skipping from prebureaucratic to postbureaucratic organizational modes. There is no need for these countries to go through several decades of bureaucratic regimentation.

- There is great scope for developing the use of media such as videotape and film to accelerate diffusion and provide widespread learning opportunities. More communication can become two-way and very large numbers of people can be reached.

Quality of working life needs to become related to other forms of organizational democracy. These are shown in Table 4 as at present distributed among selected countries (Trist, 1981a). These forms all represent modes of participation; they all involve power sharing. Power sharing is at the heart of QWL.

Historically, collective bargaining was the first to emerge; employee ownership, often in the form of cooperatives or (more recently) of firms divested from conglomerates followed; then came representative democracy with workers on boards, though not sharing in the equity. The work-linked form has been the last to appear. It is concerned with work restructuring and participation at one's own level of decision making and is that with which QWL has been most closely associated as it directly affects the quality of work experience. The four forms have evolved independently. Some of them are regarded as contradictory in certain countries.

In what may be called the Scandinavian pattern, which Holland and Australia approximate, there is a trend to *confluence*. I would expect the work-linked form, as the only form directly affecting the texture of immediate work experience, to spread in combination with other forms. Combinations of three, if not four (foursomes are beginning to occur in smaller firms), are likely to

TABLE 4   Distribution of Forms of Organizational Democracy in Selected Countries, 1980[a]

Country[b]	Collective bargaining	Representative	Owner	Work-linked
Norway	4	3½	1½	2½
Sweden	4	3½	1½	2½
Holland	3	2	1	1½
Australia	2½	1	1	1½
Germany	2½	4	−1	−1
France	2½	1	−1	−1
Britain	4	0	1	0+
U.S.	2	0+	1	1½
Canada	2½	0+	1½	−1
Yugoslavia	0	4	4	0+

[a]Ratings, on a scale 0–4, are personal estimates of the author (Trist, 1981a).
[b]Norway and Sweden exemplify a congruent Scandinavian pattern which Holland and Australia approximate. The larger European countries show no consistency. The U.S. and Canada express a North American form. Yugoslavia is very different with no independent unions.

become more common in more countries during the '80s. Workers will tend to demand a greater share in the strategic decisions of their organizations as they become more self-managing. The means will vary; there is room for pluralism. In the uncertainty of a turbulent environment, people become increasingly uneasy when they are without any degree of control over large decisions that affect their main life chances. The spread of unemployment and the increasing number of mergers and of plant locations overseas will increase these feelings. More workers may, therefore, be expected to seek representation on boards and participation in the equity of their firms, while advancing union strength and restructuring their jobs. Nevertheless, many will remain content with the last two and others will not press even for these.

All the tasks I have mentioned so far are underway to some extent and will proceed during the '80s in the teeth of opposition from the old paradigm which still has hold on most of the world. But there is a new task: to establish a dissociation between the concept of employment and the concept of work—a consequence of the microprocessor and related technological revolutions. This makes it incumbent upon us to bring into being *a partially employed yet fully engaged society*. As yet, we do not know how to do this. It is a task which requires fresh appreciations. We must legitimate and respect the work that people do when they are not in places of paid employment. We must eliminate their shame and their guilt over not being in such a place. We must assure them a standard of living sufficient for them to take their full place as members of society. We shall have to find some new words, new generative metaphors as Don Schon (1981) calls them, to express the reframing required.

Simplifications and cost reduction are possible in some sections of the engineering industry where layoffs have been estimated at over 50 percent. Word processing is likely to occasion similar personnel shrinkages in many white collar occupations, which will not be able to absorb those made redundant from manufacturing as they did during the first round of automation. Jenkins and Sherman (1979) forecast an overall reduction of 23.2 percent in the British labor force by the year 2000 and identify high risk jobs and sectors. They titled their book *The Collapse of Work*. The senior author is a major trade union leader. His would appear to be the most comprehensive statement on the issue from a union standpoint. If the present economic slowdown continues, the level of employment forecast will be reached by the early '90s, with women being disproportionately affected.

Simply to shorten the work week by a day or to propose some equivalent device, such as work sharing or a new norm of working part time, is necessary but not sufficient to provide a solution to unemployment on the scale anticipated, particularly when, in addition to microprocessors and industrial robots, further displacement of older industry to the Third World is taken into account. The meaning of work itself will need reconsideration. Sachs, the development economist, has suggested (1980) that work in the sense of paid employment will have to be rationed—though it would presumably be possible for the work addicted to purchase work stamps from the less addicted! In addition to his or her paid work, an individual would have an occupation in what Sachs calls the "civil society," the community. This concept is consonant with that of the dual economy in which gift and barter arrangements grow up in a "social economy" that exists in parallel with the market economy (Robertson, 1981). Transactions in this nonmarket domain may come to equal those in the market domain.

The social economy includes activities which people undertake for themselves by way of self-reliance. They may involve community workshops and many new types of social arrangement. "Jobs" in this area tend to be of high quality and to promote personal growth. They are likely to make the ordinary world of work less central and to make ambition or status in it less preoccupying than it is at present, at least for some kinds of people. There will be more choices in lifestyles, more types of career paths open. Allied to this is a reassessment of the household as a work field that reflects the changing roles of men and women in the domestic socio-technical system and the links of this system with outside employment. The divorce between home and work, which has been so complete in industrial societies, may be less complete in the post-industrial order.

I will not attempt to go into the question of the decentralization, not only of organizations but of society, which microelectronic technologies make possible. They could, of course, also take us toward greater centralization—to the end of the pier that George Orwell called "1984." The choice is ours. There is no doubt regarding which road QWL bids us take.

I would like to close by briefly mentioning a project in a district of Edinburgh, to which I have been going as research adviser during the last five years, as this experience has greatly influenced my search for alternatives (Trist and Burgess, 1979/Vol. III). The district is called Craigmillar; it has its own castle where the haggis was invented. Nevertheless, it is a low income public housing estate where some 25,000 people have lived without amenities in an isolated area on the edge of the city. Industry has gone: the two mines are long closed; the breweries, except one bottling and distribution plant, have gone elsewhere. Unemployment of young adult males varies between 20 and 30 percent; for women, unemployment is far higher and too few adolescents have known what it is like to work. Yet this community is at the leading edge of post-industrial innovation and does an enormous amount of work without much in the way of employment.

Some years ago a mother and housewife called Helen Crummy was annoyed because her son, who had some talent for music, could not get music lessons at school. There was no music in the curriculum in such a place as Craigmillar. She got music lessons going and, with others, held a small festival at which local talent could perform. They found they were as good as many other folks. This has led in time to a vast development in community arts that has now become internationally famous. They write and produce musicals and dramas on social issues arising locally and take them touring in the rest of Scotland and in continental Europe.

Their organization is called the Craigmillar Festival Society and Mrs. Crummy is Organizing Secretary. Their activities, under local resident control, have transformed a once negative identity into a positive identity. They have gone on to undertake many forms of social service using neighborhood workers, again local residents, who give better attention at lower cost than official departments. They have, with the support of a grant from the European Economic Community, developed a comprehensive action plan for the future of Craigmillar. They have won acceptance for many of their proposals from local, regional and national authorities, often after severe conflict (which still goes on), although their aim for the Festival Society is shared government, not the replacement of statutory bodies. They have won a high school and a community center and have stopped the planning authority from driving a freeway through the middle of their community.

They have turned a dilapidated church into a community arts center and other buildings into community workshops and meeting places for youth. They have constructed play sculptures for children and have painted bright murals (which have remained unvandalized) in several dull public places.

The jobs in the establishments that have created these amenities, indeed in all Festival Society activities, have high QWL. I have seen many ordinary people grow amazingly in the last few years. Many hundreds have been involved in one way or another, at any given time, in making constructive use of government schemes.

All this is work but not employment. What is it if not QWL? The Craigmillar way is one way toward a fully engaged, if partially employed, society. Moreover, the Festival Society has won the cooperation of several large firms in Edinburgh, who have taken on Craigmillar people because they have become resourceful and committed. A way back to the market place has been opened for quite a few.

The QWL mission is to foster human development through work that is better and more economically executed as a result. The QWL mission can be carried out beyond employment as well as within it. Each can reinforce the other.

We must continue to create jobs of high quality and bring into being organizations and communities through the new paradigm that provide the enabling conditions for such jobs to come into existence in both the market and social economies. Otherwise we are not likely to fare too well in countervailing the turbulent environment that increasingly surrounds us.

References

Ackoff, R.L. 1974. *Redesigning the Future: A Systems Approach to Societal Problems.* New York: John Wiley.

Coates, K. and T. Topham. 1980. "Workers' Control and Self-Management in Great Britain." *Human Futures,* 3:127–41.

Emery, F.E. 1967. "The Next Thirty Years: Concepts, Methods and Anticipations." *Human Relations,* 20:199–237.

Emery, F.E. and E.L. Trist. 1965. "The Causal Texture of Organizational Environments." *Human Relations,* 18:21–32.

Jenkins, C. and B. Sherman. 1979. *The Collapse of Work.* London: Eyre Methuen.

Pava, C. 1980. "Normative Incrementalism." Ph.D. dissertation, University of Pennsylvania.

Robertson, J. 1981. *The Redistribution of Work.* Turning Point Paper No. 1. Spring Cottage, Ironbridge, Shropshire, England.

Sachs, I. 1980. *Development and Maldevelopment.* IFDA Dossier No. 2. iFDA, 4 Place du Marché, 1260 Nyon, Switzerland.

Schon, D.A. 1971. *Beyond the Stable State.* London: Temple Smith.

———. 1981. "Framing and Reframing the Problems of Cities." In *Making Cities Work: The Dynamics of Urban Innovation,* edited by D. Morley, S. Proudfoot and T. Burns. London: Croom Helm.

Thorsrud, E. 1981. *Work, Home and Education—A New Career Pattern in the Norwegian Merchant Navy.* Paper presented to Plenary Session on QWL, Conference of the American Sociological Association, Toronto.

Trist, E.L. 1981a. "The Evolution of Socio-Technical Systems." In *Perspectives on Organization Design and Behavior,* edited by A.H. Van de Ven and W.F. Joyce. New York: John Wiley; and as an Occasional Paper, Ontario Quality of Working Life Centre, Toronto. Reprinted, Vol. II, pp. 36–59.

———. 1981b. "The Quality of Working Life and Work Improvement." In *A Reader in the Quality of Working Life.* Ottawa: Labour Canada.

Trist, E.L. and S. Burgess. 1979. "Multiple Deprivation: A Human and Economic Approach." *Linkage,* 3:8–9.

Associated Studies

While the above topics are of basic importance, others have yet to be explored and some have not yet been formulated. One promising line would be to examine the relevance of recent advances in the philosophy of science.

Morgan explores the relevance of Prigogine's ideas of the whole being contained in the part, fluctuation at a distance from equilibrium and dissipative structure. Klein takes up the question of the far-reaching effects of the different training of engineers and social scientists. Finally, Miller examines questions of technology, territory and time in complex production systems.

Gareth Morgan

Organizational Choice and the New Technology[1]

Eric Trist has had an immense impact on modern social science and is well known for many different contributions. Three of these have had a particular impact on my own development. First is the idea that organizations are not subject to forces of blind determinism and that those who design and manage organizations always face a choice in deciding how organizations are to operate in practice. Second is the strong emphasis on the social aspect of organization expressed most vividly in the idea that organizations are socio-technical systems that can be designed in ways that tap, enhance and develop human potentialities. Third is the idea that organizations can become open-ended evolving systems that learn and change along with the wider social ecology.

In this paper I want to explore the implications of these ideas with reference to the challenges and opportunities posed by development in microprocessing technology.

Organization and Technology: A Question of Choice

As is well known, Trist's ideas on the relation between organization and technology were first addressed in his seminal paper with Ken Bamforth on the introduction of the "longwall" method of coal getting in British mines (Trist and Bamforth, 1951/Vol. II). This method of mining introduced a type of assembly-line technology to the coal face and was accompanied by an in-creasingly mechanistic and bureaucratic style of work organization. In com-mon with so much technological and organizational change occurring at the time, the quest for organizational efficiency in the mines was associated with a raw determinism that simultaneously mechanized production methods *and* the web of human relations through which they were organized. Trist and Bam-

[1]This paper first appeared in *Learning Works: Searching for Organizational Futures*, edited by S. Wright and D. Morley. Toronto: Adapting by Learning Group, Faculty of Environmental Studies, York University, 1989.

forth's article highlighted the problems of this determinism, showing that the mechanization of work relations often had adverse human, social and organizational consequences and that any particular technology could usually be used within the context of a variety of organizational forms. Trist demonstrated that the advantages of technological developments could be harnessed within the context of work systems that were self-organizing rather than rigidly organized; social and organic rather than mechanistic and bureaucratic; and open and evolving rather than closed. In this 1951 article and subsequent writings (e.g., Trist et al., 1963) he stressed that there was no deterministic link between technology and organization and that the introduction of new technologies always presents an occasion for organizational choice.

Organizational Choice and Microprocessing Technology

Recent developments in microprocessing technology make it helpful to remember the lessons to be drawn from this early work, for we are in danger of making exactly the same mistakes that were made in adapting organizations to machine technology. Many applications of the new technology are still accompanied by determinism and attitudes that harness the power of the technology within the context of old and narrow concepts of organizations—particularly the bureaucratic. For example, many managers and systems designers, who view "organization" as synonymous with "bureaucratic control," merely use the new technology to enhance productive efficiency or to implement the idea of the centrally controlled organization in which almost every action and decision can be monitored and influenced by those in control. New wine is poured into old bottles: the immense capacities offered by the new technology are merely channeled into old and established ways of doing things rather than used as a transformative influence capable of changing how we organize in ways that we may never have thought possible. More than any other development of the twentieth century, the new technology offers a means of transforming organizations in a way that simultaneously makes them effective, efficient, humane and intelligent. In short, it offers a means of realizing the human and organizational values and capacities that Trist and his Tavistock colleagues have espoused over the years. But for these values and capacities to be realized in practice, it is important that those who use and implement the technologies are aware of the choices they face.

The New Technology Can be Used to Transform Organization

Three characteristics of microprocessing technology seem particularly important in appreciating its transformative potential:

- its multifunctionality;
- its ability to create an identity between organization and information;
- its ability to redefine and restructure part/whole relations.

MULTIFUNCTIONALITY

Microprocessors are multipurpose tools. They create capacities. Microprocessors are much more flexible than conventional machines that are designed to perform highly specific functions and to achieve predetermined goals. They create means rather than promote ends, and they promote generalizability rather than narrow specialism.

However, whether this capacity for multifunctionality is realized in practice depends on the way the technology is used. It is a matter of choice. Consider, for example, the contrasting ways in which the technology has been used in both manufacturing and office applications. In some manufacturing firms, robots and other microprocessing systems have merely been used to promote the efficiency of existing modes of work organization. They are frequently used in automobile manufacture to replace people on the assembly line as efficient single-purpose machines. In other applications, however, they are used to transform work systems to promote multifunctionality and thus to increase the flexibility of systems. A good example, again drawn from the automobile industry, is found in the flexibility of those systems of car production where variations in the model being produced can be made on an ongoing basis. Under the so-called *kanban* (signpost) system, certain Japanese manufacturers can produce different cars in whatever sequence is desired on the very same assembly line because the technology has been designed so that it can serve many ends at once.

In many offices the new technology is often used just to streamline existing bureaucratic arrangements rather than to transform the organization of work by utilizing the technology to diffuse information and control and thus to promote more generalized, holistic forms of organization. The former tends to produce new kinds of bureaucratic organization where the computer, rather than specific line-managers, is in control of a fairly static organizational design. Use in the latter way tends to create organizational arrangements where people possess a greater ability to process and interpret information and thus to extend capacities for intelligent, adaptive action. In the former case, the office becomes a more efficient quasi-bureaucratic machine that is able to perform predefined tasks in an optimal way. In the latter case the office becomes more like a self-organizing entity that can learn and evolve as it negotiates new challenges, opportunities and insights. Developments in information-processing technology, particularly in allowing multiple points of entry to central data systems and the use of decentralized "local" systems and developments in audiovisual communications technology (e.g., telephone, satellite, facsimile transmission), enhance capacities for multifunctional organization to an extraordinary degree.

THE IDENTITY BETWEEN ORGANIZATION AND INFORMATION

The new technology is by nature an information-processing technology and, like no other technology before it, has a capacity to create an identity between information and organization. The use of microprocessing facilities allows organizations to become more and more like information systems. Consider, for example, how whole offices and departments are being replaced by computers. Organized relations between people become replaced by relations within and between computer programs. The form and structure of an organization increasingly becomes synonymous with the design of these programs and other information processing capacities.

The identity of organization is being transformed by this development. Face-to-face interactions between people are increasingly being replaced by interactions with an information system. In the process, the idea of an organization as a spatial domain is being replaced with the idea that organizations are networks of information. And, as microprocessing technology continues to develop our capacities for information processing and general communications, we may expect organizations to become much more decentralized and less visible than they are now, with people working and interacting from their homes rather than their offices, engaging in televised transactions rather than flying across continents, and so on. All this has enormous transformative potential, changing our very conception of what organization is all about and opening the way to many new forms of organization in practice.

THE REDEFINITION AND RESTRUCTURING OF PART/WHOLE RELATIONS

All the above developments have important implications for the way we understand part/whole relations. Traditionally, organizations have been viewed as composites of separate parts, whether of people, machines, resources or knowledge. Developments in the new technology have a capacity to undermine and restructure this distinction between part and whole, for in multifunctional systems that are spatially separate rather than integrated, organizations need no longer be just the sum of their parts. They can develop in ways that allow each part to approximate and develop capacities that formerly could only be realized through the activities of the whole, or major sections of the whole. Consider, for example, how the new technology allows people to develop and design their own "user-drive" information systems or to examine and manipulate centralized data banks in ways that allow them to set their own bounds on the contributions they are able to make to their organizations. Formerly, such contributions would require coordinated activities from quite separate parts of the organization, e.g., the information users, systems designers and others involved in the general control and management of the organization.

The user-driven potential of the new technology provides a means of creating organizations where loosely coupled parts set the pace and direction of the organization as a whole. The new technology creates a potential for creating organizations possessing very different kinds of part/whole relations in which different "parts" are in a position to take initiatives and assume leadership roles. A prototype of this model of organization is found in systems employing autonomous work groups where each group strives to achieve the character of a complete system of organization and where each member of the group attempts to possess the skills and abilities required by the whole. This kind of organization is based on a system of relations where the distinctions between part and whole are very blurred. The whole is encoded and active in each and every part. The new technology creates a means of developing these kinds of relationships to an extent that has not really been possible before.

Realizing Transformative Potential in Practice

Whether organizations are able to develop and utilize these aspects of the new technology to their full extent will depend on the kind of organizational choices that are made. In particular, choice will depend on the ability of those making decisions relating to the use and design of the new technology (especially software applications) to appreciate that there are alternatives to the bureaucratic concept of organization and that we need not limit our use of the technology to re-creating bureaucracies in a streamlined and high-tech form.

Thus, to break free of the bureaucratic concept, new ideas about organization are necessary. We need ways of thinking that will allow us to promote multifunctionality rather than narrow specialization, that allow us to create organizations that are more like open-ended networks than closed physical entities and that permit initiative and direction that are decentralized and heterarchical rather than invested in a narrow group of individuals. We need, in short, a way of organizing that can make organizations as flexible and adaptive as the new technology they are now in a position to use.

As a way of developing this kind of organizational capacity, colleagues working with Trist at York University have been experimenting with the image of a holographic system as an organizational design.

The Holograph as a New Metaphor for Organization

A holograph is a photograph taken with a lensless camera using laser beams, where approximations of the whole image are stored in all the parts. Thus, if the photographic plate is broken, an approximation of the entire image can be reconstituted from any of the parts.

Although holography originally developed as a rather abstract aspect of laser science, holographic principles are now being used to explain many aspects of the world around us. Neuro-scientists like Karl Pribram of Stanford University have suggested that the brain may operate in accordance with holographic principles and that holography may be demonstrating basic organizing principles that pervade the whole universe (Pribram, 1975, 1979; Bohm, 1978, 1980).

For our purposes here the main point about research on holography is that it identifies a new organizing principle that has close affinity with the capacities created by microprocessing technology. Microelectronics is an information processing technology that creates the kind of self-organizing ability demonstrated in the way a holographic image can be reconstituted from any of its parts. By using holographic imagery as a means of thinking about how the new technology can be used in practice, we have a means of creating organizations that depart from bureaucratic principles on almost every count.

Facilitating Holographic Organization

As I have suggested at much greater length elsewhere (Morgan and Ramirez, 1984; Morgan, 1986), it is possible to build organizations that have holographic, brainlike capacities by developing the implications of four interrelated principles (Figure 1). Collectively, these principles provide a means of designing organizational forms so that each part of the system strives to embrace the qualities of the whole and to self-organize in an ongoing way. The principle of *redundant functions* shows a means of building wholes into parts by creating redundancy, connectivity and simultaneous specialization and generalization. The principle of *requisite variety* helps to provide practical guidelines in the design of part/whole relations by showing exactly how much of the whole needs to be built into a given part. And the principles of *learning to learn* and *minimum critical specification* show how we can enhance capacities for self-organization.

Any system with an ability to self-organize must have an element of redundancy in internal design because without redundancy capacities for action are completely determined. Redundancy represents a form of excess that allows the system some room to maneuver. Without such redundancy, a system

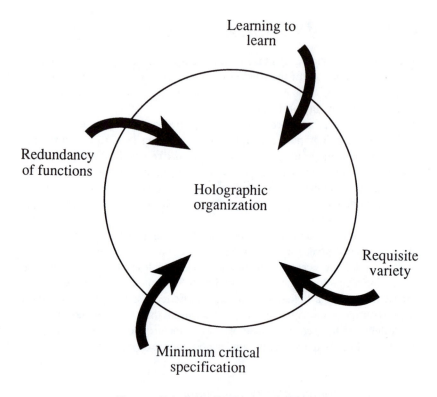

Figure 1. Principles of holographic design

has no real capacity to reflect on and question how it is operating and hence to change its mode of functioning in constructive ways. In other words, it has no capacity for intelligent action in the sense of being able to adjust action to take account of changes in the nature of relations within which the action is set.

Fred Emery (1967) has suggested that there are two design methods for building redundancy into a system. The first concerns a strategy involving a *redundancy of parts*, where each part is precisely designed to perform a specific function, special parts being added to the system for the purpose of control and to back up or replace operating parts whenever they fail. Redundancy here is built into "spare parts." The design principle is mechanistic and is clearly reflected in the bureaucratic form of organization, where the primary concern is to design a structure of precisely defined jobs (parts) that fit together to form a coherent whole. Special procedures are introduced to ensure that the parts function in accordance with the original design in the form of rules, controls and supervision. The result is typically a hierarchical structure where one part is responsible for controlling another.

If we look around the organizational world, it is easy to see evidence of this kind of redundancy; the supervisor or manager who spends his or her time ensuring that *others* are working; the troubleshooter or maintenance team that "stands by" waiting for problems to arise; the employee reading a newspaper or idly passing time because there is no work to do; employees passing a request or problem to colleague Y "because that's his job, not mine"; the quality controller searching for mistakes and defects that, under different conditions, could much more easily be spotted and rectified by those who produced them. Under this design principle, the capacity for redesign and change of the system rests with the parts assigned this function—for example, production engineers, planning teams and systems designers. Such systems are organized, and can be reorganized, but they have little capacity to self-organize.

The second design method proceeds by incorporating a *redundancy of functions*. Instead of adding spare parts to a system, extra functions are added to each of the operating parts so that each part is able to engage in a range of functions rather than perform a single specialized activity. The system is thus specialized and generalized at one and the same time. An example of this design principle is found in organizations employing autonomous work groups where members acquire multiple skills so that they are able to perform each other's jobs and to substitute for each other as the need arises. At any one time, each member possesses skills or functions that are redundant in the sense that they are not being used for the job at hand. However, this organizational design possesses flexibility and a capacity for reorganization within each and every part of the system which is absent from systems of fixed functional design.

Systems based on redundant functions are holographic in that capacities relevant for the functioning of the whole are built into the parts, creating a completely new relationship between part and whole. In a design based on redundant parts, e.g., an assembly line where production workers, supervisors, efficiency experts and quality controllers have fixed roles to perform, the whole is the sum of predesigned parts. In the holographic design, in contrast, the parts are a reflection of the nature of the whole, since they take their specific shape at any one time in relation to the contingencies and problems arising in the total situation. Under this design principle, roles and activities can be changed in an ongoing manner to meet and solve problems that arise, with a minimum of external help. This contrasts with situations based on redundant parts where problems typically activate a hierarchy of authority and control. When a problem arises on an assembly line it is typically viewed as "someone else's problem," since those operating the line often do not know, care about or have the authority to deal with the problems posed. Problems lie outside the domain of one's normal job, and remedial action has to be initiated and controlled from elsewhere. A degree of passivity and neglect is thus built into the system. In systems based on redundant functions, the nature of one's job is set by the changing pattern of demands with which one is dealing. Needless to say, the two design principles create qualitatively different relationships between people and their work. Under a system of redundant parts, involvement is partial and instrumental; under the principle of redundant functions, involvement is more holistic and absorbing.

Implementing holographic organizational design inevitably raises the question of how much redundancy should be built into any given part. While the holographic principle suggests that we should try to build everything into everything else, in many human systems this is an impossible ideal. In many modern organizations the range of knowledge and skills required is such that it is impossible for everybody to become skilled in everything. So what do we do?

It is here that the idea of *requisite variety* becomes important. This principle, originally formulated by W. Ross Ashby (1952, 1956), suggests that the internal diversity of any self-regulating system must match the complexity of its environment if it is to deal with the challenges posed by that environment. Or, to put the matter differently, any control system must be as varied and complex as the environment being controlled. Used within the context of holographic design, this means that all elements of an organization should embody critical dimensions of the environment with which they have to deal so that they can self-organize to cope with the demands they are likely to face.

The principle of requisite variety thus gives clear guidelines as to how the principle of redundant functions should be applied. It suggests that redundancy (variety) should always be built into a system where it is *directly* needed, rather than at a distance. This means that close attention must be paid to the "boundary relations" between organizational units and their environments to ensure that requisite variety always falls within the unit in question. Design must proceed from questions such as: What is the nature of the environment being faced? Can all the skills for dealing with this environment be possessed by every individual? If they can, then build around multifunctional people, as in the model of the autonomous work group discussed earlier. If not, then build around multifunctioned teams that collectively possess the requisite skills and abilities and where each individual member is as generalized as possible, creating a pattern of overlapping skills and knowledge bases in the team overall. It is here that we find a means of coping with the problem that everybody can not be skilled in everything; by recognizing that, when this is the case, the multidisciplined team or work group becomes the basic unit around which the organization is built. Organization can thus be developed in a cellular manner around self-organizing groups that have the requisite skills and abilities to deal with the environment in a holistic and integrated way.

The principle of requisite variety thus has important implications for the design of almost every aspect of organization. Whether we are talking about the creation of a corporate planning group, research department or work group in a factory, it argues in favor of a proactive embracing of the environment in all its diversity. Very often managers create the reverse circumstance, reducing variety in order to achieve greater internal consensus. Corporate planning teams are often built around people who think along the same lines rather than around a diverse set of stakeholders who can actually represent the complexity of the problems with which the team ultimately has to deal.

The principles of redundant functions and requisite variety create systems that have a capacity for self-organization. For this capacity to be realized and to assume coherent direction the two further organizing principles also have to be kept in mind: *minimum critical specification* and *learning to learn.*

The first of these principles reverses the bureaucratic principle that organizational arrangements need to be defined as clearly and as precisely as possible. In attempting to organize in this way, one eliminates the capacity for self-organization. The principle of minimum critical specification (Herbst, 1974/Vol. II) suggests that managers and organizational designers should primarily adopt a facilitating or orchestrating role, creating "enabling conditions" that allow a system to find its own form. One of the advantages of the principle of redundant functions is that it creates a great deal of internal flexibility. In autonomous work groups, for example, every member is usually capable of substituting for every other member, creating numerous *potential* forms of organization. The more one attempts to specify or predesign what should occur, the more one erodes this flexibility. The principle of minimum critical specification thus attempts to preserve flexibility by suggesting that, in general, one should specify no more than is absolutely necessary for a particular activity to occur.

In running a meeting, it may be necessary to have someone to chair the meeting and to take notes, but it is not necessary to institutionalize the process and have a chairperson and a secretary. Roles can be allowed to change and evolve according to circumstances. In running a group or project, bureaucratic patterns of fixed hierarchical leadership can be replaced by a heterarchical pattern where there is no leading element and where the dominant element at any given time depends on the total situation. Different people can take the initiative on different occasions according to the contribution they are able to make. Instead of making roles clear and separate, they can be left deliberately vague, ambiguous and overlapping so that they can be formulated and clarified through practice and inquiry. The basic idea is to create a situation in which inquiry rather than predesign provides the main driving force, encouraging organization members to reflect on what they are doing and to take appropriate action. This style helps to promote forms of questioning and conflict between competing ideas that can keep organizations flexible and diversified while remaining capable of evolving sufficient and appropriate structure to deal with the problems that arise.

The principle of minimum critical specification thus helps to preserve the capacities for self-organization that bureaucratic principles usually erode. The danger of such flexibility is that it has the potential to become chaotic. This is why the principle of *learning to learn* must be developed as a fourth element of holographic design.

A system's capacity for coherent self-regulation and control depends on its ability to engage in processes of single- and double-loop learning (Bateson, 1972; Argyris and Schon, 1978). These two levels of learning allow a system to guide itself with reference to a set of coherent values or norms, while questioning whether these norms provide an appropriate basis for guiding behavior. For a holographic system to acquire integration and coherence and to evolve in response to changing demands, these learning capacities must be actively encouraged. The members of such a system must share some sense of collective identity while being prepared to question, challenge and change this identity as circumstances require. In an autonomous work group, for example, it is necessary that members find a sense of value in the kind of activities in which they are engaged and in the products that they produce. They should be open to the kinds of learning that allow them to contribute to changes in the design of these activities and products in an active way. Given that there are so few predetermined rules for guiding behavior, direction and coherence must come from the group members themselves as they set and honor shared values and norms that are allowed to evolve along with changing circumstances.

One of the most important functions of those responsible for designing and managing the kind of "enabling conditions" referred to earlier is that of helping to create a context or ethos that fosters this kind of shared identity and learning orientation.

Holographic Organization and the New Technology

There are many aspects of microprocessing technology that facilitate this kind of holographic organization. This technology can diffuse information, communications and control in a way that has not really been possible up to now. It has an important decentralizing potential and, as Pava (1983) has noted, can promote many transformations in existing organizational arrangements that are highly consistent with a general move towards a more holographic style of organization. The technology

- allows tools, machines and human beings to be endowed with an information-processing capacity that enables increased "intelligence," adaptability and self-direction;
- allows for the linking and meshing of people and machines to increase communication, adaptability and self-direction;
- dissolves the need for hierarchy and command as a primary mode of communication and coordination;
- diffuses information-processing capacities by allowing multiple points of entry to central data systems and by creating the capacity for developing on-the-spot local information systems;
- provides the possibility of many people, not merely the top management, being able to acquire an overall view of an organization and its work and thus to evolve decisions and policies relevant to the whole;
- reduces the transaction costs in the process of communication and decision making;
- transforms traditional skills and knowledge bases, making them widely rather than narrowly available—and more accessible—thus reducing the need for experts and other professionals;
- increases the possibility of self-sufficiency and thus the capacities for self-organization;
- dissolves the need for proximity as a basis for interaction, creating new possibilities for communication and coordination;
- increases in general the scope for user-driven systems of work design and organization.

Interestingly, the holographic style of organization is highly consistent with certain lines of advanced computer systems design that are moving toward the development of relational data bases with multiple points of access and potential patterns of interaction and toward the development of fully integrated user-driven systems. In many applications (e.g., Tapscott et al., 1985) it is being learned that such systems tend to be most effective when they are designed and driven by the people that ultimately have to use them. Computer systems that are imposed on organizations by external consultants, remote systems designers or top management appear to be nowhere near as successful as those that are designed in conjunction with those who are closest to knowing what information and designs are required and who ultimately have to use them—that is, the users.

The principles of holographic design provide a coherent frame of reference for guiding the way microprocessing technology is introduced into an organization and how it is allowed to evolve. In contrast with bureaucratic approaches, which tend to favor top-down styles of design and implementation, the holographic model favors bottom-up approaches where the required degree of integration and balance between central and local information systems, mainframes, personal computers, etc., is established through a system where the parts (users) are allowed to shape the nature and direction of the whole. Of course, trade-offs and hard decisions have to be made. Duplication and redundancy have to be constrained by economic and other realities with which an organization is dealing but there are always holographic means of dealing with these issues. Use can be made of "technology" or "systems development" teams that reflect the range of interests represented in the organization in accordance with the principle of requisite variety. These teams can formulate policy and establish appropriate degrees of integration in a way that allows the developing use of the technology to exert a transformative influence on the organization as a whole. Ideas on organizational design that emphasize the importance of decentralization over centralization—as in the principles underlying autonomous work groups (Susman, 1976; Herbst, 1962); organic networks (Burns and Stalker, 1961; Kingdon, 1973); and the concept of the multidivisional "M-form society" (Ouchi, 1984)—all have an important role to play. The key to such designs is to create systems that allow the parts of an organization, whether individuals or groups, to remain separate yet integrated.

The thrust of this kind of approach is to create user-driven styles of organization where people occupy the foreground and where the technology (powerful though it may be) occupies a supporting role. This approach requires appreciation of the essential interdependence between people and technology and of the fact that technological change, on the scale made possible by the microelectronics revolution, may require extensive organizational transformation. The potential of the technology rests not just in changing the way we do things, but in changing what we actually do.

In arguing that a new mind-set is required to deal with the implications of the new technology, my intention is not to replace one kind of determinism with another. I have advocated a holographic style of organization to harness the potential of the technology that may be viewed as a new imperative. I have chosen to develop the argument in stark terms because I feel that the bureaucratic attitude is so entrenched in the way most of us think about organization that we often need this kind of stark argument in order to have any chance of breaking free of traditional practice.

In adopting and developing the implications of the technology, we do face a choice. And, starkly presented, it is a choice between approaches that reflect the traditional bureaucratic values, or more democratic, holographic values. The power of the bureaucratic mode of thought, and the substantive interests that it sustains, leaves little room for anyone to expect that managers and others with the power to change prevailing modes of organization will do so overnight. The move from bureaucratic to more holographic styles of organization inevitably has an impact on power relations within an organization and is often constrained by existing power structures. As many others have noted, developments in the new technology are a double-edged sword in this regard; they simultaneously increase the potential for centralization *and* decentralization according to the organizational choices that are made. My real hope is that by achieving an understanding of the holographic model of organization, we may have a better means of realizing the decentralizing, democratic potential of the new technology and thus of moving organizations closer toward the humanistic vision that Eric Trist has always thought realizable, and which he has spent so much time and energy trying to achieve in practice.

References

Argyris, C. and D. Schon. 1978. *Organizational Learning: A Theory of Action Perspective.* Reading, Mass.: Addison-Wesley.

Ashby, W.R. 1952. *Design for a Brain.* London: Chapman and Hall.

———. 1956. *An Introduction to Cybernetics.* London: Chapman and Hall.

Bateson, G. 1972. *Steps to an Ecology of Mind: Collected Essays in Anthropology, Psychiatry, Evolution and Epistemology.* San Francisco: Chandler.

Bohm, D. 1978. "The Implicate Order: A New Order of Physics." *Process Studies,* 8:73–102.

———. 1980. *Wholeness and the Implicate Order.* London: Routledge and Kegan Paul.

Burns, T. and G.M. Stalker. 1961. *The Management of Innovation.* London: Tavistock Publications; Chicago: Quadrangle Books.

Emery, F.E. 1967. "The Next Thirty Years: Concepts, Methods and Anticipations." *Human Relations,* 20:199–237.

Herbst, P.G. 1962. *Autonomous Group Functioning: An Exploration in Behavior Theory and Measurement.* London: Tavistock Publications. Revised version of Chapter 2, Vol. II, "Designing with Minimal Critical Specifications," pp. 294–302.

———. 1974. *Socio-Technical Design: Strategies in Multi-Disciplinary Research.* London: Tavistock Publications.

Kingdon, D.R. 1973. *Matrix Organization: Managing Information Technologies.* London: Tavistock Publications.

Morgan, G. 1986. *Images of Organization.* Beverly Hills, Calif.: Sage.

Morgan, G. and R. Ramirez. 1984. "Action Learning: A Holographic Metaphor for Guiding Social Change." *Human Relations,* 20:199–237.

Ouchi, W.G. 1984. *The M-Form Society: How American Teamwork Can Recapture the Competitive Edge.* Reading, Mass.: Addison-Wesley.

Pava, C. 1983. *Managing New Office Technology: An Organizational Strategy.* New York: Free Press.

Pribram, K. 1975. "The Holographic Hypothesis of Memory Structure in Brain Function and Perception." In *Contemporary Developments in Mathematical Psychology,* edited by D. Krantz. San Francisco: Freeman.

———. 1979. "Holographic Memory." *Psychology Today* (February): 71–84.

Susman, G.I. 1976. *Autonomy of Work.* New York: Praeger.

Tapscott, D., D. Henderson and M. Greenberg. 1985. *Planning for Integrated Systems.* Toronto: Holt, Rinehart and Winston.

Trist, E.L. and K.W. Bamforth. 1951. "Some Social and Psychological Consequences of the Longwall Method of Coal-getting." *Human Relations,* 4:3–38. Revised version, Vol. II, "The Stress of Isolated Dependence: The Filling Shift in the Semi-Mechanized Longwall Three-Shift Mining Cycle," pp. 64–73.

Trist, E.L., G.W. Higgin, H. Murray and A.B. Pollock. 1963. *Organizational Choice: Capabilities of Groups at the Coal Face Under Changing Technologies: The Loss, Rediscovery and Transformation of a Work Tradition.* London: Tavistock Publications. Reissued 1987, New York: Garland. Chapters 13, 14 revised, Vol. II, "Alternative Work Organizations: An Exact Comparison," pp. 84–105. Chapters 19–22, Vol. I, "The Assumption of Ordinariness as a Denial Mechanism: Innovation and Conflict in a Coal Mine," pp. 476–93.

Lisl Klein

On the Collaboration Between Social Scientists and Engineers[1]

Dynamics and Models

THE DYNAMICS

The very term "socio-technical," used to characterize work systems, implies that there has been a process of splitting which needs to be rectified. Splitting is a process of psychic economy whereby people tend to simplify a complex situation by attributing all its X characteristics to one of a pair and all its Y characteristics to the other. The goodies are all-good and wear white hats, and the baddies are all-bad and wear black hats and possibly also black moustaches. Splitting means that one is most unlikely to be presented with a black moustache under a white hat.

Splitting is very pervasive. In its simplest form people identify one football team, one political party, one nation as all-good and others as all-bad; scientists are supposed to be all-rational; artists all-intuitive; industrialists concerned with money and nothing else; academics with knowledge and nothing else; etc. Although many people know with a part of their mind that things are really not like that, once splitting is established and becomes institutionalized, those involved get caught up in it, and it becomes very hard to break out of. Companies seem obliged to encapsulate their "soft" aspects in personnel departments or donations to ballet companies in order to maintain their required "toughness" intact. Politicians are unable to say *anything* good about the policies of their opponents. In turn, people and institutions begin to live up to what is apparently expected of them.

Something like this has happened in relation to technology and its human inputs and outputs. Clearly, they are interdependent: on the one hand, the

[1]Adapted from Chapter 6 in *Designing Human Centred Technology: A Cross-Disciplinary Project in Computer-Aided Manufacturing,* edited by H.H. Rosenbrook. London: Springer-Verlag, 1989.

inputs to design decisions in manufacturing systems are not only knowledge about the properties of materials and the dynamics of machining. They are also, first, factors affecting the individual designer, such as values and assumptions about how people function and about what is really economic and, second, organizational factors affecting design processes such as pressures on a team from outside, status differences when alternatives have to be selected, career development issues, etc.

On the other hand, the *outputs* from design decisions in manufacturing systems include effects on the perceptions, attitudes, skill repertoire and behavior of individuals, on organization and therefore also on society. The consequences for the people who work with and around the technology are, in turn, that technology is often not operated in the ways in which its designers—from a split position which blanks out the human and social aspects—intended. A split position would lead one to conclude from this that people should be eliminated from the system, not that they should be taken into account more realistically.

The most important aspect of all this is that the social and technical aspects of technology are split off. This splitting, against which are attempts to work in an integrated way is deeply institutionalized. It permeates professional institutions and their literature. There are populations whose horizons are dominated by the one and populations whose horizons are dominated by the other. Social scientists read what social scientists have written; engineers read what engineers have written.

The perpetuation of splitting by institutionalization is illustrated by my experience as a member of the steering committee of a project concerned with designing a flexible manufacturing system such that the operator would stay in control (Rosenbrock, 1989). I considered that I was not being as useful as I might because I did not understand the technology well enough. I asked for some teaching about metal cutting. Among other things, I was shown a video used in teaching first-year engineering students. It was an excellent teaching aid, but within the first five minutes two factors emerged:

• The operator was referred to as a constraint—a cost. He was never mentioned again.
• The content itself—the engineering—was very fascinating and absorbing.

These two things together would, of course, help to set a student's attitudes for life and be very difficult to counteract later.

Engineers and social scientists in the present age are to a considerable extent products of this deeply institutionalized splitting. So powerful is it that large parts of both professions see no relevance in collaborating with the other at all. Some social scientists are afraid of technology, and some engineers are afraid of getting into the human area.[2] These fears are difficult to acknowledge and, from such fears, the human aspect may take on a pseudo-mechanical form such as "the Man-Machine-Interface" or "the Human Factor."

There is also a substantial history of mutual criticism. On the side of the social sciences, more precisely of sociology, criticism has its roots in studies of the human and social consequences of production technology and was originally not directed at engineering design but at the economic framework within which it was taking place. Marx's original analysis of the societal consequences of trends in manufacturing technology contained much of what a present-day social scientist would call socio-technical understanding, i.e., understanding of the interplay between human and technical aspects of technology. The following is an example from Marx (1887):

> In the English letter-press printing trade, for example, there existed formerly a system, corresponding to that in manufactures and handicrafts, of advancing the apprentices from easy to more and more difficult work. They went through a course of teaching till they were finished printers. To be able to read and write was for every one of them a requirement of their trade. All this was changed by the printing machine. It employs two sorts of labourers, one grown up, tenters, the other, boys mostly from 11 to 17 years of age whose sole business is either to spread the sheets of paper under the machine, or to take from it the printed sheets. . . . A great part of them cannot read, and they are, as a rule, utter savages and very extraordinary creatures. To qualify them for the work they have to do, they require no intellectual training; there is little room in it for skill, and less for judgement; their wages, though rather high for boys, do not increase proportionately as they grow up, and the majority of them cannot look for advancement to the better paid and more responsible post of machine minder, because while each machine has but one minder, it has at least two, and often four boys attached to it. As soon as they get too old for such child's work, that is about 17 at the latest, they are discharged from the printing establishments. They become recruits of crime. Several attempts to procure them employment elsewhere were rendered of no avail by their ignorance and brutality.

However, Marx did not draw socio-technical conclusions, i.e., he did not conclude that social aspects should therefore feature in engineering design. He attributed the problems he saw to the ownership of private capital and to the drive to create surplus value. He did not take seriously, as an independent

---

[2]The term "socio-technical" has recently acquired some popularity, but activities going on under that label are frequently still confined to working only with the social system. "We are not here to discuss technology," said a consultant introducing a training course on socio-technical systems.

contributing factor, the human need to reduce complexity that results in splitting and allows for these models of man in the minds of engineering designers. Since designers were generally working for the owners of capital, the omission is understandable. But we know today that trends in design do not automatically change when ownership changes, as in nationalized industries or in socialist societies, or when the need for economy abates, e.g., during phases of subsidy. Splitting and its consequences are powerful independent contributing factors.

In the 1920s, 1930s and 1950s in Britain, a range of researches and other activities of social scientists began to elucidate specific rather than global problems. For example, empirical research showed that, given the opportunity, people varied their working pace in the course of the day without loss of output (Harding, 1931). This fact has never found its way into the kind of "knowledge" that is explicitly used in design. (In a recent project, the managing director of a company in the domestic electrical appliance industry commented that he was "amazed" at how miraculously their industrial relations improved when they took the mechanical drive off their assembly line.) What happened instead was a split development. Production engineers continued to work on the assumption that controllability and predictability required evenly spaced, i.e., mechanical, pacing. Then, in the 1950s, when basic standards of living were regained after the war, the motor industry began to suffer from waves of strikes, most of which were unofficial and short. It was not recognized that the main function of a short strike is simply to create a break, an interruption from work, and that the strikes were taking place in situations where work was machine-paced.

Again, research showed that, if the work system did not provide feedback (knowledge of results), people would insert a way to get such feedback informally (Wyatt and Fraser, 1928). And again empirical research showed that, if people's actions were closely controlled, as in work study systems, they would react by inserting controls of their own. "Fiddling" in work-studied incentive schemes had the function of exercising creativity and regaining control over one's work situation, which the formal system did not permit (Klein, 1964).

The coal-mining studies of the Tavistock Institute conceptualized much of this in a cumulative way. They showed that, given experience of a job and some flexibility, people would find the optimum way of doing the job for themselves. Conversely, if a new technology did not take account of their experience, its productivity potential was not realized. The technical system and the social system were truly interdependent (Trist et al., 1963).

In the 1960s, some engineers and their institutions began to be interested in the findings of empirical social research. With increasing frequency, social scientists were invited to take part in the conferences of engineering institutions. However, before a move toward integration in design could get very far, a second trend within the social sciences was making itself felt. The expansion of social science teaching and writing in the 1960s brought with it the re-emergence of critique as the dominant mode. This time it tended to be *mere* critique, on the basis of a preexisting formal theoretical framework, rather than empirical and grounded investigation as had been the case before and was, indeed, the case with Marx. Given that the frame of reference for critique was well established and that frames of reference for synthesis and contribution were only beginning to be worked out, critique was simply an easier option and many social scientists chose it. The two trends, sociological critique and socio-technical design, to some extent came into conflict. The difference between them is a fundamental one.

At that time, public awareness of a need to bring social science and engineering together was growing. But it has turned out that, where arrangements were made for social scientists to make a contribution to the education of engineers, they tended to do it from a split position, i.e., they tended to teach elements of social or psychological theory, not to help engineers incorporate human and social factors into their engineering.

Engineers, in turn, insofar as they have been aware at all of what social scientists were doing, have resented being forever criticized. They notice that social scientists are not given to studying the ways in which human life has been made easier by the products of engineering. They consider the social sciences to offer little in the way of positive contribution and find social scientists unwilling to dig in and help instead of criticizing. And, if they experience resentment, engineers can get their own back. It is easy to trap a social scientist with questions that are not only unanswerable but that serve to block the contribution that might be made. The following are two examples from experience:

> The first concerned the design of a new plant. "We want to design this plant so that the operators will be happy. What we need from you is advice on what colour to paint the walls to achieve this."
>
> The second concerned the design of equipment.
> Social scientist: "We need to keep options open for the operator."
> Engineer (after doing a quick calculation): "I reckon there are about four billion options. Which ones do you mean?"

This combination of recognizing the value of the other and resentment of the other is the dynamic of ambivalence. Both the habit of critique and the habit of resentment are sufficiently well established to have some of the characteristics of cultures, affecting to some extent even those, in both professions, who do wish to collaborate. It is against this background that attempts to work together take place.

MODELS OF SCIENCE

This discussion of the practical aspects of collaboration will now be confined to the concepts, methods and experience of those social scientists and those engineers who do wish to engage in collaborative work. For even where there is a wish to collaborate, there are still considerable handicaps. The phrase "multidisciplinary work" trips from the tongue more easily than it is realized in practice.

It is possible to postulate two models of science in approaching the topic of job design and work organization. In one model, a high value is placed on measurement and quantification in the search for precise guidelines. The other model accepts ambiguity and conflict of interest as part of the reality being dealt with. It is salutary to remember that "scientific management" was to a large extent motivated by a wish to take conflict out of the situation by developing "objective" standards that would be self-evidently correct and that would therefore be accepted by both management and workers. It has been one of the main causes of conflict ever since.

It would certainly not be true to say that engineers necessarily adhere to the first model and social scientists to the second. Much of engineering is still empirical (though that "still" shows the power of the stereotype), and there is much room for debate among engineers. On the other hand, a good deal of social science research is conducted within the natural science model.

There are also cultural influences at work. In Germany, for example, a clause in the Company Law of 1972 requires that "proven scientific findings about the workplace must be applied." This sounds strange to British ears. In Britain research involving people at work has been very context-specific, and the emphasis on application has been on cases and experiments rather than on the broad application of generalized "knowledge." The clause in Company Law has, in turn, had considerable influence both on the sponsorship and on the nature of research carried out since it was passed. For example, a piece of social science research was used to test what level of buffer stock on an assembly line would be optimal in freeing the operator from machine pacing. As part of a complex research program, a "job satisfaction index" was compiled from the views operators expressed about a range of things connected with their work. This index was then correlated with the buffers related to particular workplaces, and it was found that the bigger the buffer, the greater (for whatever reason) was the job satisfaction. Far from indicating an optimal level to which the law might then be applied, this brought the issue back into the arena of negotiation, and the social scientists, no less than the engineers, were disconcerted.

THE DISCIPLINES IN RELATION TO OUTPUTS

As a group of professionals, engineers have, of course, been evolving their methods and developing their products for much longer than have the social scientists. Social reflection about the output of technology is as old as technology itself. (Certainly the authors of Genesis had a view about the condition of man once he had to labor, and saw even God as needing a rest.) But as disciplines that attempt to aggregate the outputs at a societal level or to study them systematically at the individual level, and thus to verify social reflection empirically and systematically, the social sciences are young by comparison. And as professions which attempt to contribute the resulting knowledge and methods to a variety of spheres and to the design of plants and equipment, the social sciences are very much younger still. The very process of studying and commenting, by bringing gaps to light, has led social scientists into the habit of critique and has contributed to splitting, and has thus hindered the development of their contribution.

Nor do the social sciences have much to show in the way of products, at least as products are understood by engineers. By definition, where an idea or a finding in social science is accepted as valid, it becomes incorporated into the general body of common sense. Mothers are encouraged to stay in the hospital with their small children as a matter of common sense, not as a consequence of the research (Bowlby et al., 1952) that demonstrated the effects of this not being allowed. Thus the useful products of social science are likely to be in the form of understandings, methods, practices and institutions. Sometimes they may be standards, but where standards are applied, the processes of developing them, which social scientists may sometimes consider more valuable than the outcomes because of the learning involved, will have been bypassed. Engineers, on the other hand, are likely to want outputs in engineering terms, i.e., at least in the form of standards.

Standards which social scientists can formulate with confidence and without an empirical "research loop " are likely to concern processes, not outcomes; for example, "no installation without a transitional system involving proto-typing," rather than "no cycle time less than X seconds"; "operators should have some say in shaping their environment," rather than "the walls should be blue." This kind of advice may be experienced by engineers as especially unhelpful at the design stage of plant or equipment when the particular population of operators does not yet exist. To interpret and operationalize the general principle of "minimum critical specification" (Herbst, 1962; 1974/Vol. II) demands a great deal of work in particular situations.

The Disciplines in Relation to Methods

The social sciences may be weak on products, but they are strong on methods. First, it is possible to make values explicit, to get members of organizations to express them in terms of design criteria and to prioritize these and make them operational by getting them incorporated in design (Klein and Eason, 1990). But splitting affects preferences and expectations about methods, and such a systematic approach to design may not be what engineers look to social scientists for. The element that has been split off not only gets projected onto the other, it exists in oneself in an unintegrated way. I have been surprised in more than one situation when people who would not dream of making decisions about materials, or temperatures or surface finishes, without some kind of systematic trials, insist on either making, or asking for, decisions about people by some kind of inspired guesswork. For example,

> In a shipping organisation, a number of policies including 'integrated crewing' were introduced, designed to encourage seafarers to identify with the particular employer rather than with seafaring as a whole. It seemed at least possible that people who go to sea do not want to identify with a particular organisation; but when questioned why he was so sure that they would want to if given the opportunity, the manager concerned put his hand on his heart and said, "because I feel it here." (Klein, 1976)

One is somehow reminded of how Italians describe the behavior of foreign tourists in the face of Rome traffic. It is said that some foreigners, no doubt otherwise quite rational people, faced with the need to cross a busy street, put up one hand to stop the traffic, hold the other tightly over their eyes, and plunge. Like manufacturing design, it quite often works.

Secondly, the social sciences have a methodological concern for the links between process and outcomes. The dynamics at the input end of design have direct consequences for the output end; in fact, that is often where the origins of poor design decisions are to be found. If design decisions are made for reasons other than design needs, the outcome is bound to be problematic.

> A fierce argument about which of two layouts to adopt in a new plant was conducted on cost grounds (which were considered acceptable grounds for debate). It was in fact about the competition between the company's and its

parent company's engineering departments (which was not acceptable). The costs could not be assessed in their own right unless the dynamics could be worked through. (Klein and Eason, 1990)

Operational Issues and Institutionalization

Considering how long the concept of socio-technical interdependence has been around, critical mass for these ideas remains a very long way off. One of the reasons for this seems likely to be that discussion and development have focused too exclusively on the values and paradigms, to the neglect of the operational issues involved in turning them into practice, and to the neglect of institutionalization.

The joining of the two perspectives can take many forms. Engineers may internalize the concepts. In one such case, the project engineer began to write job descriptions in terms of the experiences and relationships involved as well as the activities to be carried out. Human aspects which are predictable, such as selection and training, may be incorporated in planning systems such as Critical Path Methods. But many issues cannot be anticipated in such a structured way. The design of transitional systems such as prototyping, simulations and the systematic testing of alternatives may be a particularly fruitful area for collaboration.

The following are some of the issues that arise in the course of operationalizing integrated work.

PHASING

When engineers and social scientists work together, many of the issues may be thought of as differences in values and often emerge operationally as problems of phasing. Putting the disciplines and their concerns together does not automatically lead to integration; the consequences of the original splitting still have to be worked through. Otherwise, if a project or development process has been designed with the assumptions of one discipline, the contributions of the other may appear as things that will hold it up. (There are, of course, differences within the two perspectives as well as between them: within social science approaches, strategies which rely wholly on the participation of those affected can perforce only involve those who are immediately present.) Representation of the two perspectives generally does not start at the same time or equally influence time estimates. The social perspective may be represented by philosophy statements for a long time before it is turned into implementation strategies; decision sequences may be seen as linear rather than cyclical, etc. The following are some illustrations of problems of phasing.

Company A was an oil company engaged in building a new fuel-oil pipeline from one of its refineries to a major distribution terminal. Fuel-oil facilities would need to be built at the terminal that until then had been engaged in the storage and distribution of other products.

One decision which had to be taken concerned the site of the control room. One alternative was to build a new control center at the entrance to the site so that truck drivers would be given instructions as they drove out and could hand in documents as they drove in. This would also have the effect of geographically separating the control of loading from the physical operation of loading. The alternative was to extend the present loading and transport control room at the center of the site. The engineer in charge of the construction asked what the difference would be in terms of the social organization and attitudes of the drivers. It was a very perceptive question; getting an answer would involve doing some work with the drivers.

An answer could be available within three weeks but the engineer could not wait. Major consequences for work roles and group relations were, of course, implied in the decision and the engineer realized this. But he was locked into a schedule for linking the design and construction of the new building with the opening of the pipeline and could not create a three-week delay. He had assumed that there might be a ready-made answer (Klein, 1976).

Company B was engaged in building a new high-speed canning plant. It was to be built on a site where the company already had some other operations so that, while the operators who would be staffing the plant were not yet available, there was a trade union organization. A Job Design Committee was established for a time to consider the nature of the jobs being created in the canner.

Two control systems engineers were involved in the planning of the cannery. They became interested in the idea of job design and, after some preliminary induction to the topic, one of them gave a presentation to the Job Design Committee. He said that, at that stage, the control systems could still be designed in almost any way the Committee wanted. He liked the idea of working as a service to the operators who would later be doing the jobs. But once the floors were laid, with channels for cables, it would be very difficult to change. The trade union representatives at that stage did not have enough knowledge of the process to be able to be very specific about what they would want. The technology was very new and advanced and the engineers had about two years' start on them in thinking and learning (Klein and Eason, 1990).

The problem of participants, or social science professionals, being out of phase with engineering designers in their absorption of the necessary know-how is very general (Eason, 1982). Unless arrangements can be made to deal with this discrepancy, contributions from social scientists are likely to be limited to general statements and "participation" is likely to be superficial and unreal.

Company C was also building a new plant, this time for the manufacture of confectionery. Much of the production machinery was to be transferred from an existing older building, and the job design contribution concerned the organization of work around existing equipment rather than the design of new equipment.

The prospect of an entirely new factory, an opportunity which people have only very rarely, was acting as a focus for a powerful vein of idealism in the company. Not only did the company want the jobs in the new factory to be satisfying for the people working there; they wanted the architecture to be innovative, to be human in scale and to make a distinct contribution to the built environment. This position had involved a good deal of discussion about company philosophy. At the time I joined the group, two concepts for the new factory were being debated: on the one hand, the concept of a large, hangarlike structure, within which there would be freedom and flexibility to arrange and rearrange things; and, on the other, something like a village street with small production units as well as social facilities such as a tea bar, a bank, possibly one or two stores. The result would give the "feel" of a varied and small-scale, village-like environment where people moving from one unit to another would inevitably meet each other. This would be far removed from the conventional idea of a factory.

Within a few minutes of joining the group, I was confronted with the question, "What do you think—large hangar or village street?" I had, of course, no basis for an opinion and realized the dilemma they were in. The company felt that they could not even begin to talk to architects until they had some idea of the basic shape of the building they wanted; one could not sensibly discuss the shape of the building without some idea of the production layout; and I could not contribute to discussion about the layout from the job design point of view without some socio-technical analysis of the production process, which required time. At that stage I had not even seen the production process.

Two meetings and some familiarization later, we achieved a breakthrough. The first of the products to be manufactured on the new site consisted almost entirely of crushed sugar with some additives, which was then compressed into a tablet and packaged. Groping for a more detailed understanding, I said, "Look, I still haven't understood the process properly. Suppose I'm a piece of sugar. I've just been delivered. What happens to me?" Somebody said, "Well, the first thing that happens to you is that you get blown along a tube. But there is a physical limit to how far you can be blown." I said, "OK, what happens next?" And somebody said, "Next, you get crushed into a powder." In this way I talked my way through the process in very great detail, role-playing the product. For example, I heard myself saying,

"All right, so now I'm a granule. What happens next?"
"Next, we drop mint oil on your head."
"Might you miss?"
"Yes, we might."
"How would that be discovered?" And so on.

The product was a fairly simple one which the company had been making for a long time, and ways of thinking about it had become rather set. In the transitional system established through role-playing the product, these ways of thinking began to unfreeze, and the participants began to discover alternatives and to say to each other, "It doesn't have to be like that. It could be like this if such-and-such conditions are met." In particular, some things which they had been used to thinking of in sequence could, it was found, be done in parallel. That meant that the logic of the production process was not necessarily a straight line, and this, in turn, meant that one could think in terms of a short, squat building. This was the eventual shape of the "product house" which emerged from this process.

In terms of work design, I realized afterward that my strategy had been about leaving options open. Once the factory was staffed and experience of the work system was beginning to accumulate, there was more chance of reviewing and revising the work design in a short, squat building than in one where the logic of the layout led to long, straight lines. In these, more things would be irrevocably fixed. From the socio-technical point of view, the short, square product house should have three functions: the opportunity to identify with the product; the opportunity for people to relate to each other; and the opportunity to keep design and organizational options open.

Architecturally, the product house turned out to be a kind of compromise between the aircraft hangar and the village street ideas—smaller than a hanger but larger than the cottages envisaged along the village street. With this concept the company then went in search of architects.

SYSTEMS BOUNDARIES—THE MEANING OF "HUMAN-CENTERED"

This set of issues is particularly relevant in the design of new technology. Within the human and social sciences there is a longstanding debate about how criteria that make a piece of equipment easy to use relate to criteria that make the work being done meaningful and that are conducive to the development of the person. In some instances they are simply different. For instance, the operator's autonomy does not generally feature among the usability criteria which "Human Factors" professionals apply. But in some instances the criteria can be in opposition. The usability criteria of Human Factors specialists usually include short learning times, while developmental criteria give a high value to opportunities for learning.

These differences are, then, sometimes debated as differences in values. They may also be seen as differences about systems boundaries, i.e., what is considered to be within the system and susceptible to design and change; and what is outside the system and part of the environment, i.e., to be taken as given. It is an issue that is likely to crop up within multidisciplinary design teams.

It may be useful to think of this problem in terms of a typology of products. In equipment design there is a crucial boundary between design decisions that are within the design project and those that are in the hands of the purchaser of the resulting product. Where a product is a *tool,* a means of doing something else, or where it creates a *task* which is only a part of a role so that the configuration of the role itself is out of the hands of the product designer, the aims of good integrated design may properly be in the direction of "usable." Where a product or system creates *roles,* and where the configuration of the role itself is therefore in the hands of the product or system designer, usability should be a minimum baseline, and the aim of good integrated design must be more in the direction of "developmental." At any rate, in such a situation the issue cannot be ignored. Product or systems designers cannot help influencing long-term consequences such as future organization or industrial relations, whether they want to or not.

There are, in fact, several scales, and the boundary will not be in the same place on all of them. It may be useful to draw a profile across them for a particular project (see table). The nearer a product profile is to the left-hand column, the more appropriate are usability criteria by themselves. The nearer it is to the right, the more do developmental criteria need to feature as well. This approach would by no means eliminate value-based debates, for instance on the question of safety and responsibility, but it should help to clarify them.

From	*To*
affects task	affects role
tool	system

INSTITUTIONALIZATION

Where the idea of the collaboration between social scientists and engineers is new to people, they are likely to become preoccupied with what this will actually mean in practice and how to set about it; they are much less likely to worry about longer-term considerations. However, this kind of work has now been going on long enough for some long-term issues to become clear—not so much how to make it start as how to make it stick!

The issue is institutionalization. To institutionalize something is to build it in, and it has already been pointed out how the problem is not so much that the technical and social aspects of engineering design have become split off from each other as that the split is deeply institutionalized. This means, for example, that every time membership of a design team or steering committee changes, the socio-technical perspective may need to be reasserted.

To make something stick requires a surprising range of interacting and mutually supporting institutions. This may be illustrated by the institutions supporting the simple decision to restrict driving to one side of the road. The assumption that it will happen is built in to the *design* of vehicles. It is built in to the *training* of drivers as well as in to their *legitimization*. It is built in to the formulation of *codes* and *standards* (the Highway Code, standards about the width and layout of roads, etc.). Then there is the *continual reinforcement* of seeing that others do it and, finally, *sanctions* if it does not happen. These institutions, in turn, are supported by *funds, training establishments, staffing* and *monitoring* (traffic police). It is the combination that makes these institutions, together, powerful and effective. In addition, a breach of the decision is generally clearly visible and unambiguous. As a result, the decision is mostly carried out; drivers are not continually deciding on which side of the road to drive.

Social aspects of work systems are, of course, not often so unambiguous. But it must be remembered that this is partly a matter of local tradition. In Germany, as has been stated, it is the law, with its accompanying sanctions, that says that "scientific findings about the workplace must be applied." In Germany, also, Human Factors methods and findings form part of the substance of some trade union agreements.

Where something can be formulated as a standard, that is a form of institutionalization. Where it can be integrated into the technology, such as dialogues that provide genuine options, or indicators on a machine that provide feedback or buffers that mitigate pacing, that is a more powerful form.

But to ensure that such structural influences are taken seriously in the first place, and for situations that cannot be formulated in these ways, the need is to achieve a degree of culture change. To attain this, it is not a matter of one or more social scientists joining a team; the socio-technical viewpoint must be represented powerfully enough, early enough and consistently enough, as a matter of routine. It must feature in the syllabuses of engineering students, in the appropriation for capital investments, in R&D budgets, in the qualifications and experience required of systems designers and in the assessment and emoluments of technical directors.

Collaboration between individual professionals is not enough. First, social scientists working as individual members of an engineering activity are likely to be exposed to projections of all the ambivalence, the hopes, anxieties and resentments that have accumulated in relation to the social sciences. If the things social scientists say are unwelcome, these may be seen as personal rather than professional contributions. Secondly, they will not have at their fingertips all the substantive and methodological contributions of all the social sciences. And thirdly, the number of things they have time to deal with will be very limited.

This is so even within a small team working on the development of a piece of equipment. It is much more so in the design and development of a large-scale plant, where there are so many things going on at the same time that it is hopelessly optimistic to see them all as consistent and rational tributaries of the mainstream. In the confectionery factory cited earlier, for example, it was not possible to keep alive the idea of keeping options open for three turbulent years between the decision concerning the shape of the building and the start of production in the new plant.

Some of many uncontrollable events may be:
- Market changes during the design and building process that influence the production capacity that is needed, leading to decisions outside the design teams.
- The purchase of off-the-shelf equipment that cannot be influenced unless this influence is exerted long before actual orders are placed, i.e., unless the culture of the equipment manufacturers can be influenced as well.
- Management development moves, which may not coincide with project needs, in which members of design teams as well as key people in the organizational context are moved around.

All these instances illustrate that the system which is carrying the design and development processes is an open and not a closed one. In these circumstances, mere collaboration between social scientists and engineers as professionals is not enough. Mere collaboration, however well it may be working, is too weak a mechanism to cope with open systems characteristics. On the other hand, mere infrastructure is not enough either, and formal guidelines circumvent the necessary processes of development and mutual learning. What is needed is collaboration supported by institutions and infrastructure.

References

Bowlby, J., J. Robertson and D. Rosenbluth. 1952. "A Two-Year-Old Goes to Hospital." *Psychoanalytic Study of the Child,* 7:82–94.

Eason, K. 1982. "The Process of Introducing Information Technology." *Behaviour and Information Technology,* I:197–213.

Harding, D.W. 1931. "A Note on the Sub-Division of Assembly Work." *Journal of the National Institute of Industrial Psychology,* 5:261–64.

Herbst, P.G. 1962. *Autonomous Group Functioning: An Exploration in Behaviour Theory and Measurement.* London: Tavistock Publications.

————. 1974. *Socio-Technical Design: Strategies in Multi-Disciplinary Research.* London: Tavistock Publications. Revised version of Chapter 2, Vol. II, "Designing with Minimal Critical Specifications," pp. 294–302.

Klein, L. 1964. *Multiproducts Ltd.: A Case Study on the Social Effects of Rationalised Production.* London: Her Majesty's Stationery Office.

————. 1976. *A Social Scientist in Industry.* London: Gower Press.

Klein, L. and K. Eason. 1990. *Social Science in Practice.* Cambridge: Cambridge University Press.

Marx, K. 1887. *Capital.* (English translation 1958. London: Lawrence and Wishart.)

Rosenbrock, H.H. (Editor). 1989. *Designing Human-Centred Technology: A Cross-Disciplinary Project in Computer-Aided Manufacturing.* London: Springer-Verlag.

Trist, E.L., G.W. Higgin, H. Murray and A.B. Pollock. 1963. *Organizational Choice: Capabilities of Groups at the Coal Face Under Changing Technologies: The Loss, Rediscovery and Transformation of a Work Tradition.* London: Tavistock Publications. Reissued 1987, New York: Garland.

Wyatt, S. and J.A. Fraser, assisted by F.G.L. Stock. 1928. *The Comparative Effects of Variety and Uniformity in Work.* London: Her Majesty's Stationery Office, Industrial Fatigue Research Board Report No. 52.

Eric J. Miller

Technology, Territory and Time
The Internal Differentiation of Complex Production Systems[1]

The concept of a production system as a socio-technical system (Trist and Bamforth, 1951/Vol. II) was further developed by Rice (1958) who developed a conceptual framework for the analysis of complex production systems. He argued that "any production system may be defined by reference to what is imported into and exported from it. . . . The [conversion] process of changing import into export may require the carrying out of either sequential or simultaneous operations, or of both. When different operations are carried out discretely, a production system may be differentiated into *operating systems*." In that case, the management of the production system "cannot be contained in any one operating system, and a system external to the operating systems is required to control and service their activities. This is the *managing system*" (Rice 1958:41–42). The present paper explores the principles of differentiation of operating units within a complex system.

The Transition from Simple to Complex System

The typical simple production system in industry is the primary work group. Elsewhere it appears in the small workshop, the retail store, the service station, etc.

The essential feature of such a system is that management is inherent in relationships within the group: either there is no recognized leader at all, as is the case in some mining groups (Trist et al., 1963), or, if there is one, all or most of the time is spent working alongside the other members of the group on tasks comparable to theirs. The leader's contribution to the output of the group tends to be directly productive rather than indirect and facilitative.

Herbst (1957) has described certain characteristics of simple and complex

---

[1]A condensation of a paper published in *Human Relations*, 12:243–72, 1959. References in the original to then unpublished papers are here replaced by later published versions.

behavior systems. He finds that one significant criterion of a simple system is that the relationship between input, size and output is linear. (Input and output are here measured in money rather than in goods). In small retail stores, for example, the total amount paid in wages (input) increases at a linear rate with sales turnover (output) achieved, while sales turnover increases at a linear rate with the size of the store, measured by the number of persons employed. In a complex system the relationship is nonlinear: "The presence of an administrative unit concerned with ongoing activities increases the rate at which sales turnover increases with size of the organization, and . . . the loss incurred by withdrawing personnel from production tasks decreases as the organization becomes larger" (Herbst, 1957:344). Herbst (1957:337–38) has this to say about the transition from a simple to a complex system:

> As the size of the simple system increases, and depending also on the extent of both its internal and external linkages, more and more work has to be carried out on the co-ordination of component functioning, so that a critical boundary value with respect to size is reached, beyond which intrinsic regulation breaks down. An increase in size beyond this point will become possible by differentiating out a separate integrating unit, which takes over the function of both control and coordinating of component units, thus leading to a transition from a simple to a complex system. The point at which intrinsic regulation breaks down will be determined by the effectiveness of the organizational structure. The less efficient the organizational structure happens to be, the earlier the point at which intrinsic regulation breaks down.

In other words, three critical factors in the transition are size, complexity and efficiency. Herbst here seems to be implying that the efficiency of a simple system is measured by the extent to which the system can tolerate increased size and complexity without throwing up a differentiated management function. However, if efficiency is measured by the ratio of output to size—a ratio that Herbst himself uses elsewhere in the same paper—then it would appear that this assumption might not always be justifiable. If, for example, a simple system of given size could secure a greater output by becoming reorganized as a complex system of the same size, then its persistence as a simple system would be relatively inefficient. "Resilience" might therefore be a more appropriate term than "efficiency" to describe the capacity of a simple system to withstand pressures, both external and internal, toward transformation into a complex system. This would be an omnibus term embracing a number of factors of small group functioning that counter the effects of increased size and complexity. Some of these factors are considered later in this section.

Size by itself is not a critical factor. Apart from the pair, groups of six to 12 are often said to be the most stable, in both psychotherapeutic and other situations (Rice, 1958:36–37). Fissiparous forces tend to develop in groups outside this optimum range, but there is no known maximum number beyond which the emergence of a full-time management function is inevitable. Much depends on the need for differentiation that is intrinsic to the task of the group and in the way the task has to be, or is being, performed. Herbst notes, for example, that in independent retail stores, a differentiated administrative function tends to appear when the staff numbers around five, whereas stores that belong to a retail chain retain the characteristics of simple systems until the size reaches about nine. Certain services are supplied to the latter by the large organizations to which they belong. In the Durham coalfield, autonomous groups of 41 have been shown to be effective (Trist et al., 1963). They have internally structured controls and services and lack any overtly recognized and titled leader. These groups are further discussed below.

Complexity may be considered in terms of Rice's import-conversion-export formulation. Imports into the system and exports from it may become more diverse. Complexity of the conversion process is likely to increase through diversification of input or output, or both, or through a change in the techniques or rates of production (Rice and Trist, 1952).

Before considering these factors of size and complexity in more detail, it seems necessary to stress that *an essential preliminary to differentiation of a managing system is the formation of subsystems with discrete subtasks within the simple system.* Role relationships cluster around the subtasks; such clusters of relationships become potential subsystems; and areas of less intensive relationships become potential boundaries between subsystems. Clustering may be functional for subtask performance, but the associated discontinuities between clusters may be dysfunctional for integrated performance of the total task. It becomes a function of a differentiated managing system to compensate for these discontinuities. Management mediates relationships among the lower-order systems that constitute the higher-order system in such a way as to ensure that the subtasks performed by the subunits add up to the total task of the whole unit.

If the principles of differentiation of subsystems can be identified, then the effects of changes of size and complexity can be more clearly understood; furthermore, the notion of "resilience"—the capacity to withstand, without sacrifice of efficiency, the pressures toward creation of a differentiated managing systems—will become less vague.

It is postulated here that there are three possible bases for clustering of role relationships and thus for the internal differentiation of a production system. These are technology, territory and time. Whenever forces toward differentiation operate upon a simple production system, it is one or more of these dimensions that will form the boundaries of the emergent subsystems and will provide the basis for the internal solidarity of the groups associated with them.

"Technology" here is given a broad meaning. It refers to the material means, techniques and skills required for the performance of a given task.

Differentiation of the input, conversion and export systems (the purchasing, manufacturing and selling of an industrial unit) is in this sense a technological differentiation; so also is differentiation of phases of the conversion operation (successive manufacturing processes) or specialization in buying or selling particular commodities. The greater the diversity of technologies used within a group, the stronger the forces toward differentiation of fully fledged subsystems, especially when the skills of some members are so specialized that others cannot aspire to have them or even to comprehend them and when interchange of roles between members of the total group becomes impracticable.[2] Increase in technological complexity or diversity tends to have this effect even though the quantum of input and output remains unchanged. It may even occur where the size of the system, in terms of the number of roles, is reduced.[3]

The dimension of territory is straightforward: it relates to the geography of task performance. An increase in the staff of a retail store from three persons to five may not precipitate formation of a differentiated management function. If, however, the two extra persons are employed to start a branch store—if, in other words, two potential subsystems are formed, spatially separated from one another—then the forces toward differentiation will be greatly increased. Physical separation is not essential to produce this result, but a sharp physical boundary of some kind is probably necessary before territory by itself can become a basis of subsystem differentiation within a simple production system. Identification of the group with its territory is, of course, a basic feature of all human societies and is also found among many of the higher mammals. Even boundaries that are imperceptible to an external observer may have highly charged emotional significance for the members of the groups they divide—especially when territorial differentiation is reinforced by technological differentiation. Technology, indeed, seems to seek the support of territory and only seldom stands by itself as a differentiating factor. (In many parts of India, castes differentiated from one another by their traditional occupations are also segregated spatially, living in different parts of the village or in different villages [Miller, 1954].)

The third dimension, time, is more commonly relevant to increasing the levels of differentiation in an already differentiated complex system, but it may also reinforce an increase in size in bringing about the transition from a simple system to a complex one. Forces toward differentiation probably begin to

---

[2]The obverse point was made by Rice (1958:37–39), who postulated that small work groups in modern mechanized industry usually require sufficient variety of roles (implying some technological differentiation) as to need some internal structuring, but should not have so much specialization as would lead to formation of inflexible subgroups.

[3]In her study of industrial firms in south Essex, Joan Woodward (1958:16) noted that "the number of levels of authority in the management hierarchy increased with technical complexity," while "the span of control of the first-line supervisor decreased."

develop when the requirements of task performance are such that the length of the working day or working week of the group exceeds the working period of any individual member. This factor of time is, of course, most pronounced in multi-shift systems. As in the case of territorial separation, subsystems tend to emerge with well-defined boundaries which, in this case, are based on time separation.

The subsystems and associated groupings described in the preceding paragraphs are those that are intrinsic to the structure of the task. Task structure is assumed to be inseparable from the type of technology and specialization involved, from the geography of the territory in which the task is performed and from the time scale of task performance—though within these limiting factors alternative structures may be possible.

Among the persons filling the roles of a production system, other groupings may occur based on propinquity, sex, age, religion, race and many other principles of association, and on occasion these groupings and related cleavages, perhaps by their coincidence with task-oriented groupings, may accelerate differentiation; or, if they cut across these groupings, they may retard it. It is the task-oriented subsystems themselves, however, which are relevant to task performance. These seem invariably to be differentiated by technology, territory, time or some combination of these. Production systems can probably not be satisfactorily broken down into subsystems on any other basis.

If territory, technology and time, singly or in combination, provide the basis for differentiation into task-relevant subsystems, the capacity of a simple system to tolerate growth and remain efficient without becoming transformed into a complex system is apparently related to two main factors: *mobility or fluidity* and *subsystem interdependence*. If individual members move frequently from one subsystem to another, so that there are no permanent subgroups of workers coinciding with the task subsystems, then the simple system will have greater capacity to tolerate an increase in size or complexity. Such movement compensates for discontinuities between subsystems. Secondly, the more immediately and directly performance of the task of each subsystem depends upon the performance of all the other subsystems, the more likely is the total simple system to remain viable in the face of forces toward differentiation. (Without some task interdependence it is, of course, not a production system but an assembly or aggregate of individuals.)

Exceptionally large simple production systems occur in longwall coal-mining, in a form of composite working described by Trist et al. (1963). As mentioned earlier, some of the composite groups have 41 members, working over three shifts. Both "resilience" factors operate strongly in these groups, which are internally differentiated by both technology and time. Although the individual subsystems have well-defined tasks, mobility between the subsystems allows many or all of the members to view inter-subsystem relationships from the perspective of the total system rather than from that of the subsystem they happen to belong to at any one time. Close reciprocal interdependence, necessary in these mining groups for achieving the total task, evidently helps to reinforce this global perspective.

It may well be that it is not the number of persons that limits the maximum size of a simple production system, but the number of subsystems. (A subsystem may consist of either an individual or a sub-group.) Certainly, complexity in task structuring can actually contribute to the cohesion of large simple systems. Where there are a number of subsystems interdependent in more than one direction, the complex conditions of equilibrium can be a substitute for a differentiated management function. It is the very lack of such complexity built in to the task that helps to lower the threshold of resilience in less structured simple production systems. Internal structuring for which the primary task does not cater is sought in other groupings (based on age, sex, etc.), implying involvement in other tasks that to a greater or lesser extent conflict with the primary task for which the system was constituted. In some cases it may be possible to use these factors of resilience and to restructure roles in such a way as to postpone the emergence of a differentiated managing system.

It can be inferred that, in any expanding or changing system in which no such restructuring has occurred, there is an optimum or "natural" stage for creating a new level of management. This is applicable equally to the initial transition from a simple system to a complex system and to the addition of a new level to an already complex hierarchical system.

Premature differentiation is uneconomic because the cost of adding a specialized administrative function is greater than the gain from any increase in efficiency that results. As subsystems have not been crystallized by task differentiation, government is more efficiently contained as an undifferentiated internal function. Indeed, extrinsic government, if imposed prematurely, may tend to be more destructive than integrative. This is the kind of situation in which the internal collaborative relationships, which before the change have been used constructively for task performance, are likely to be mobilized destructively against the imposed external management (cf. Trist and Bamforth, 1951/Vol. II).

Postponement of differentiation of the management function beyond the optimum stage also leads to a decline in the efficiency of the system, but for a different reason. The energies of group members, instead of being devoted to the primary task, are increasingly diverted to the task of holding the group together in the face of the fissiparous forces of sub-group formation and of differentiation. This is especially likely to happen if there is imbalance in the pattern of subsystem interdependence. Individuals experience conflict between identification with an emergent sub-group and identification with the total group. Only the creation of a new level of management, which allows the subsystems to become fully explicit simple systems and which reintegrates them as parts of a higher order system, permits the energies of the members to revert to primary task performance.

Herbst (1957) used the input-size-output relationship as an index for measuring the level of behavior systems and for diagnosing whether a given system is simple or complex. The reverse approach may also be useful. If a production system known to have the structural characteristics of a simple system increases in size, and if this expansion is unaccompanied by a linear increase in output, then (other things being equal) it is worth investigating whether the system has passed the optimum stage for differentiation—either because the subsystems are in a stage of disequilibrium or because of emergence of subgroups unrelated to the primary task of the system. The same possibility may exist if a simple system, remaining constant in size, shows over a period of time a declining output. Equally, if a structural transition from a simple to a complex system is not accompanied by the kind of change in size/output ratio predictable from a Herbst-type formula for systems of that kind, then it is possible that differentiation of the managing system has been premature.

Structure of Complex Production Systems

The forces toward transforming a simple system into a complex system, or toward increasing the levels of differentiation in a system that is already complex, are not only of theoretical interest to social scientists but also of practical interest to those concerned with management. It has already been suggested, for instance, that working efficiency and cost are likely to be adversely affected if the timing of a change in response to the accumulating forces toward differentiation is not opportune. A second cause of inefficiency may lie in an inappropriate choice of the basis of differentiation into subunits.

In the initial transition from a simple to a complex system, the basis of differentiation is usually directly traceable to the forces leading to differentiation. Consider the example of a small privately owned workshop that manufactures simple components, all of the same kind, for the automobile industry. Raw materials are delivered and the finished products removed by the company it supplies. Administration takes up little time of the owner, who works at a bench alongside the employees. This is the typical simple production system. Let us imagine that demand grows and, because of lack of space for expansion, the owner acquires two more workshops in the vicinity. If the three workshops are sufficiently far apart, the owner is likely to spend less time on the bench and to take a nearly full-time managerial role. The three workshops then become three simple operating systems within a complex production system. In other words, territorial expansion has led to differentiation, and it is territorially demarcated subunits that are explicitly recognized.

Alternatively, the expansion might have been achieved by adding two more shifts in the original workshop. The shifts would then become the recognized subunits and, because of the need for control and coordination over the 24 hours, the owner would again take a full-time managerial role.

We now have to consider what happens when additional forces toward differentiation operate on a production system that has already become complex and there is the prospect of extending the hierarchy by further differentiation. Here again, the forces themselves will dictate the new basis for differentiation, but not necessarily the level at which this will occur.

Reverting to our example, let us now suppose that further expansion requires all three workshops to run on three shifts. Each shift in each workshop is now likely to develop into a simple subsystem, and sooner or later the owner-manager will be compelled to realize that there are nine workshop shifts to be managed, instead of merely three workshops on one shift, or three shifts in one workshop (Table 1).

Increase in the number of subunits does not, of course, necessarily lead to further differentiation and to an increase in the number of levels. If, for example, output had been tripled by expanding from three workshops to nine, instead of by adding more shifts, the additional simple production systems so created could have become explicit without necessarily overextending the span of the overall manager's command. Even in the present example, it might be practicable to maintain direct control of the nine subunits, perhaps by employing additional staff for time keeping and recording production—that is, by increasing the size of the managing system without adding to the number of levels in the hierarchy. However, since the subsystems in this case are differentiated and interdependent along two dimensions (territory and time) that cut across each other, and therefore have to be coordinated along these two dimensions, it is likely that an additional level of management will be interposed.

The owner is now faced with a choice. He may introduce the new level by managing the three territories (workshops) through three foremen, delegating to the foreman in each workshop the task of coordinating the three shifts within it. Alternatively, he may elect to undertake coordination of the three shifts himself by appointing three shift foremen, each of whom is responsible for the work on one shift in all three workshops.[4] The fact that territorial differentiation preceded the addition of shifts by no means presupposes that, in the

---

[4]It was Rice who first drew my attention to this kind of choice, to which he also refers in Rice, 1958:177, 200–201.

TABLE I   Subunits Differentiated by Both Territory and Time

	Time Differentiation		
Territorial Differentiation	Workshop A Shift I	Workshop A Shift II	Workshop A Shift III
	Workshop B Shift I	Workshop B Shift II	Workshop B Shift III
	Workshop C Shift I	Workshop C Shift II	Workshop C Shift III

management hierarchy, territorial differentiation need occur at a higher level than differentiation by time.

It is now necessary to consider this choice in more detail. In fact, it is a real choice only insofar as territory and time are equally salient in differentiating the nine simple systems from one another. In terms of task relationships, this is so only when one shift in one workshop is equally interdependent with other shifts in the same workshop and with the corresponding shift in other workshops. Workshop A Shift I (A I) belongs then to two larger systems: it is part of the "A" system, within which the other systems are A II and A III, and it is part of the "I" system, within which the other systems are B I and C I (cf. Table I). In the situation of equal interdependence

$$R(A\ I,\ A\ II,\ A\ III) = R(A\ I,\ B\ I,\ C\ I)$$

where R is a measure of task interrelatedness between the simple systems. Such an equilibrium may make it possible for the nine workshop shifts to be managed directly without interposing a new level of differentiation.

We have seen that the formation of subsystems with discrete subtasks is a necessary preliminary to transition from a simple to a complex system. Similarly, in an expanding complex system, the clustering of subsystems precipitates an additional level of differentiation in which the clusters are acknowledged as explicit systems of a higher order than the constituent subsystems.

When two dimensions of differentiation are involved, with two implicit sets of systems cutting across one another, it is seldom that they actually have equal salience. Task relationships generally draw the basic units into the orbit of one system more strongly than into the other and so dictate the lines of higher order and lower order differentiation. Furthermore, even if task-oriented interrelations themselves do have equal salience, other factors may tend to tilt the balance one way or the other. Persons who share a compact territory over three shifts, for example, may feel more strongly identified than those who share the same shift-timing over dispersed territories. Alternatively, if the dispersal is limited, going to work at the same time, and hence sharing free time, may lead to closer identification.

Failure to differentiate on the appropriate basis will create stress in relationships, because the natural groupings inherent in the structure of task performance will run counter to the groupings dictated by the formal organization. Formal boundaries will cut through these natural groupings. This will inhibit development of solidarity in the formal units, with consequent lowering of work satisfaction and morale. In general, we can suggest that, to the extent that the formal structuring deviates from the reality of the task situation, whether in the basis for differentiation or in the boundaries of the formal subunits, to that extent will the management function itself have to multiply and become "top-heavy" in order to deal with the resultant dysphoria. Additional controls will have to be imposed. This tendency will increase in proportion to the interdependence of the formal units. If, on the other hand, a unit is appropriately subdivided in relation to total task performance—if it is cut, so to speak, with the grain and not against it—both the internal management of the constituent subunits and the overall integration of the total task are likely to require less effort.

Flexibility is not entirely lacking. Imposition of a managing system helps to crystallize the selected basis and boundaries of differentiation of operating systems. Therefore, provided that the salience of two dimensions is not too unequal, differentiation at the higher level along the dimension of lower salience may increase the salience of that dimension to a point where it exceeds that of the other. This would not appreciably increase the difficulties of management. Similarly, if prior clustering of subunits is not too strong, the emergent boundaries can be supplanted by formal boundaries that do not necessarily coincide with them. Such flexibility, however, occurs only in marginal cases.

So far, instances of only two orders of differentiation have been discussed—by territory and time. We have seen that there is, subject to certain limiting factors, a choice between

- first-order differentiation by territory and second-order differentiation by time; and
- first-order differentiation by time and second-order differentiation by territory.

A third possibility, provided the salience of the two dimensions is roughly equal, is to accept only one order of differentiation, operating systems being differentiated simultaneously by the time dimension in one direction and by the territorial dimension in the other. This is illustrated in Table 1, which shows three time subdivisions and three territorial subdivisions, making nine subunits in all.

Theoretically, there is yet another way of compressing differentiation by two dimensions into one level. This occurs when the two dimensions, instead of operating at right angles, coincide and reinforce one another. Time and territory coincide in this way when shift working is used in highly mechanized road construction. A piece of mobile equipment—the common technology—is operated by one team on one stretch of road in Shift I, by a second team on a fresh territory in Shift II, and so on. In longwall coal getting, time and technology coincide as differentiating dimensions, territory being undifferentiated: a different technology is used on each of three different shifts on one coal face. Both these combinations are fairly rare in industry, where it is territory and technology that most frequently coincide as reinforcing dimensions: in manufacturing operations, more often than not, each of a group of technologically differentiated subunits has its own discrete territory of task performance as well.

When all three dimensions of differentiation occur (if, in the example of the workshop, several products are manufactured in each of the three workshops on three shifts), the theoretical choice of order of differentiation is greatly increased. Assuming that differentiation occurs only once along each dimension, there are six combinations of three levels of differentiation, six more of two and one of one level. It should be noted that in the seven combinations involving differentiation by more than one dimension at one level, the simultaneous differentiation may be either *cross-cutting* or *coincident and reinforcing*.

When there are more than three levels, at least one dimension will become the basis of differentiation at more than one level. In a large manufacturing concern, for example, there may be first-order differentiation into purchasing, manufacturing and sales (technology); second-order differentiation of manufacturing into product units (technology, probably reinforced by territory); third-order differentiation of the product units into departments responsible for various phases of the process (again technology plus territory); and so forth. Time differentiation will occur in a multi-shift concern, but a 24-hour command is narrowed down into eight-hour commands at only one level in any segment of a hierarchy. It may nonetheless occur at different levels in different segments of the same total hierarchy.

Very often the internal structure of a large organization is the cumulative result of many small local changes. Adherence to a particular pattern of differentiation adopted in response to one change may limit the possible responses to subsequent changes. Insofar as the enterprise is a system, a change in one area will affect other areas. Accordingly, any organizational change must be planned in the context of the total structure, to ensure that it provides for the most efficient performance of the primary task of the enterprise.

To sum up, therefore, any production system, complex or simple, can be defined along the dimensions of territory, technology and time. A large system is broken down into progressively smaller systems along one or more of these dimensions at each level. The smallest systems are sometimes coextensive along one or even two dimensions with the overall system, but more often in a manufacturing organization they are shorter along all three dimensions. Each component system, however, has boundaries that serve to separate it from parallel systems and also boundaries that form part of the higher-order system's boundaries. Work-oriented relations crossing the former boundaries should be more intensive than those that cross the latter; if not, it can be inferred that an inappropriate basis of differentiation has been adopted and that the efficiency of the total system is less than optimal.

Internal Differentiation and Problems of Management

Where a complex production system is differentiated into subsystems, the total task is also broken down into subtasks associated with these subsystems. As Rice (1958:228) has pointed out, such a hierarchy of tasks may often lead to situations where "decisions taken within one component system which are consistent with its primary task may appear irrelevant or even harmful in a system of a different order." Differentiation into subsystems therefore throws up a managing system which has the reintegrative function of seeing that the constituent tasks of the subsystems are so performed that they add up to the overall task of the system as a whole.

It is suggested here that the way in which a task is broken down—in terms of the dimensions along which the subsystems are differentiated and in terms of the intrinsic interdependence between them—is a major determinant of the kind and quality of management required, including the kinds of control mechanism that will be appropriate. Fundamentally, of course, the dimension along which the system is differentiated at a given level is the dimension along which the major controls have to be exercised to secure reintegration.

Differentiation by territory, technology and time, singly and in combination, can at any one level take on seven different forms—three one-dimensional, three two-dimensional and one three-dimensional. These are set out in Table 2.

Multidimensional differentiation can be reinforcing, crosscutting or mixed, though the examples given in Table 2 are all of reinforcing differentiation: that is, at the level of differentiation in question, each component system is differentiated from every other along both the named dimensions. Examples of cross-cutting and mixed differentiation could also be added.

Types of task dependence have been classified in some detail by Herbst (1961) and Emery (1959/Vol. II). For present purposes it is relevant to consider the extent to which, at a given level of differentiation, the component systems

TABLE 2   The Seven Basic Forms of Differentiation at One Organizational Level

Differentiated dimensions	Undifferentiated dimensions	Examples	
1. Territory	Technology and time	(a)	Separate sections within a factory, or separate factories making same product
		(b)	Marketing organization; chain of retail stores
2. Technology	Time and territory	Shipbuilding	
3. Time	Territory and technology	Typical multi-shift structure in process and other industries	
4. Territory and technology	Time	(a)	Quasi-independent product units
		(b)	Consecutive manufacturing operations
5. Technology	Territory	Longwall coal-mining	
6. Time and territory	Technology	Mechanized road making with shiftworking	
7. Territory, technology and time		Milk: collection, processing and bottling, delivery	

(Note: The examples of two- and three-dimensional differentiation given are of a "reinforcing" type. Brief notes on these examples are given in the text.)

of a larger system are *co-dependent* on supplies, equipment and services, and interdependent for the attainment of the end result or goal of the larger system. One or both of these types of dependence may be present. Emery points out that interdependence may be further classified as cyclic, convergent or divergent. Distinctions can also be drawn between simple and complex dependence and between reciprocal and nonreciprocal dependence.

If the differentiation variables were separately considered in relation to all the dependency variables, the resultant number of combinations would be enormous. Here it will be sufficient to examine the three basic differentiation variables in a little more detail and to discuss a few models that occur fairly frequently in industry. From these the implications of other models can be inferred.

There is one other respect in which the present discussion is restricted. While the basis on which subsystems are differentiated and the nature of their dependencies are the internal system elements that create a particular pattern of demands on management, it is also a function of management to mediate in certain ways between the system and its environment (which may include successively larger systems of which it is a part), and environmental factors will inevitably impose certain other demands. Such factors, for example, may call for additional control mechanisms within the system. The more complex and diverse these environmental factors are, the greater the number and variety of control and service functions likely to be differentiated within the managing system, and the greater the consequent complexity of intra-system relationships. Here, however, environmental factors are held constant and attention is focused on internal factors relevant to the relations of a manager with his or her immediate subordinate group.

DIFFERENTIATION BY TERRITORY

It is characteristic of operating systems differentiated from one another only along the territorial dimension that the output of the total system to which they belong is the added sum of the outputs of the constituent systems. Output from one system can be high, low or even absent without directly affecting output from the others. In other words, where differentiation is only territorial, interdependence is minimal.

The extent to which the systems are co-dependent, on a single source of supplies, for example, or on centralized service functions, can vary considerably. Spatial segregation can be an important factor here, though not necessarily a determining one. To take the examples given in Table 2, if the territorially differentiated units are neighboring sections in the same factory, for example, the series of groups of workers on groups of looms in the textile mills described by Rice (1958), they are likely to draw their input from the same source and to be jointly dependent on a number of centralized services. If, however, the units are separate factories making identical products in different parts of the country, their co-dependence may well be less. Canneries and other food-processing plants are often dispersed in this way in order to be close to agricultural sources of supply. Decentralized control over input is practicable in such cases but is less appropriate where the factories (perhaps dispersed to be close to their markets) share a common and limited source of supply. Co-dependence may also extend to output: the smaller the fluctuations of output permissible in the total system, the greater the centralized control over the outputs of the constituent systems.

Putting it another way, we can say that where a unit is differentiated into territorial subunits, the individual subunits and the total unit are the same "length" along the input/output dimension. The constraints on procurement of input and on disposal of output that operate on the whole unit will place upper limits on the autonomy that can be given to the subunits. The stronger these external constraints, the greater the co-dependence of the subunits.

Problems may arise when territorially differentiated subunits have had to be created only because of the size of the total command. For example, in large sales organizations it is common to find one or more interposed levels of management that are unrelated to task boundaries. The commands for which such managers are responsible are not "systems" at all, but aggregates, with boundaries determined by administrative convenience and no unique "whole" task to integrate them. Those managers whose authority is inevitably constricted tend to be seen by their subordinates as a barrier between themselves and their "real" boss, and vice versa.

However, in other cases, so long as the territorial boundaries conform to the reality of the task structure and so long as subunit performance can be measured separately, this is one of the easiest kinds of command to manage, especially if the subunits are roughly equal in size. Because the operations of his or her subordinates are not interdependent, the superior is not concerned with maintaining collaborative relations between them. Indeed, competitive relations are often more appropriate. Their homogeneity makes comparisons straightforward, and a highly productive subunit can be used as an example and pacesetter for the others. Subject to the external constraints on autonomy, substantial delegation is possible, which means that a fairly large number of units can be included in one command, producing a flat hierarchy.

One practical difficulty that sometimes arises in such a command, however, is that the competitive situation gets out of hand. The superior may become so involved in resolving problems of real or imagined incomparability between the subordinates that he or she loses sight of the primary task of the system. The subordinates, for their part, are liable to seek short-term competitive advantages that may be detrimental in the long run; or alternatively they may go into collusion to protect themselves from competitive stress by establishing safely attainable norms. The common restrictive practices in industry and commerce are special cases of this form of organization.

There is another management problem that may occur in manufacturing units. This is the tendency for the subunits to develop an "individuality" that is based on more than their territorial differentiation from one another. Here we are not concerned with the general tendency of groups to develop a structure and culture that apparently transcend what is needed for attainment of their overt goals. We are concerned more specifically with a tendency to supplement territorial differentiation by technological differentiation. This is pacesetting of a special kind. In a manufacturing operation such as weaving, identical machinery may be used to turn out several varieties of one product. Even though all varieties are spread equitably among all subunits, individual subunits may develop a special proficiency in some. They acquire what Selznick (1957) called a "distinctive competence." This distinctive competence may be encouraged, perhaps almost accidentally, by assigning more of these varieties to the subunits in question. Such specialization is the beginning of technological differentiation. Management needs to be alert to such incipient changes and to recognize their implications. It is not simply a question of deciding whether the gains from specialization—probably in improved efficiency and quality—outweigh the disadvantages of reduced flexibility in production planning. Different methods of management are required: competition ceases to be an appropriate control mechanism when the subunits become heterogeneous. In the extreme situation, the varieties, by ceasing to be interchangeable, acquire the status of separate products, and the territorial differentiation becomes secondary to what is, in effect, technological differentiation between product units. Management of such units is discussed in the next section.

DIFFERENTIATION BY TECHNOLOGY

In cases of differentiation by technology, the notion of distinctive competence is very much present. The organization is built up around clusters of specialized skills and often specialized equipment, too. Members of a subunit that is differentiated from others along the technological dimension derive solidarity from their distinctive competence, often by exaggerating its distinctiveness. Preservation of that distinctiveness may become the primary task of the subunit. Management of a unit in which the subunits are differentiated (and therefore have to be reintegrated) along the technological dimension involves using the specialized contributions of the subunits to perform the primary task of the whole. To achieve this, the solidarity that the subunits derive from distinctive skills should be sufficient for them to maintain their viability as separate systems, but not so great that they lose sight of the total task of the larger unit. To strike such a balance is no easy task. Perceived threats to the integrity and distinctiveness of subunit skills mobilize the energies of subunit members toward preservation of the subunit at the expense of the unit as a whole. Closed-shop movements in departments of automobile factories and demarcation disputes in shipyards are familiar examples.

Operating systems are seldom differentiated from one another by technology alone. Perhaps the nearest approximation to this is in enterprises such as shipbuilding, where what is being made is also the territory of task performance. Even in shipbuilding, however, there is some supplementary differentiation by territory and time: certain jobs have to be done elsewhere in the yard and certain jobs on the ship itself cannot be started until preceding jobs are complete. The occupational groups at work on the ship at any one time have shifting and overlapping territorial boundaries, and it is along the technological dimension that they have primarily to be coordinated. Conventional longwall goal getting involves differentiation by both technology and time (Trist et al., 1963). The team working on a particular section of the coal face over a 24-hour period is subdivided into shifts where workers are distinguished from one another both by the times they work and by the kinds of tasks they do. Reinforcing differentiation by technology, territory and time may occur in a milk business: milk is collected from the farms in the afternoon and evening and brought to the central depot; there it is processed and bottled during the night; and next morning it goes out on the delivery rounds.

In industry, technological differentiation is commonly accompanied by territorial differentiation. The word "department," for example, often carries both connotations. Where the two are combined in this way, the former distinction always seems to be primary: territorial differentiation supplements and reinforces the technological. To some extent the combination also facilitates coordination by giving the technological groupings the security of a clear-cut physical boundary—contrasted with the vague and shifting boundaries of the shipyards.

DIFFERENTIATION BY TIME

In the ordinary multi-shift situation, where the subunits are differentiated from one another only by time and share a common territory and a common technology, their co-dependence is considerable. For example, maintenance failures on one shift affect the others. Generally this co-dependence is accompanied by a circular form of successional interdependence: each shift not only completes certain operations, exporting the material outside the total unit, but it also passes on some semi-finished material to the next shift for completion. Throughput time is a major determinant of interdependence. The longer the throughput time, the higher the proportion of semi-finished to finished material at the end of each shift; also, the less likely it is that individual shift performance, in terms of quantity and quality, can be measured precisely. Continuous operations of process industries provide an obvious example, but the production lines of the engineering industry also contain at any one time components in various stages of completion. Another factor that reduces the clear-cut self-containment of the shifts in the most highly automated industries, where shift working is most prevalent, is that the functions of so-called production workers have increasingly been taken over by the machines themselves. The task of the workers is to monitor and maintain, and the consequences of things they do or fail to do are often not immediately and clearly visible: the benefits or otherwise may fall upon succeeding shifts.

Furthermore, in most industries—indeed, in the society at large—night work is considered unnatural; a certain stigma is attached to it. Those who work while the rest of the world is asleep tend to feel cut off from society—and no doubt some select nightwork for this reason and may even become neurotically addicted to it. This is not the place for a discussion of the psychology of shift work: the point to be emphasized is that nightshifts often have a distinctive "atmosphere" of their own.[5] This is particularly true where a group of workers is permanently on nightshift. Nightshifts are less differentiated in this particular respect in enterprises such as chemical plants, steel plants or power stations, where continuous operations are dictated by the basic nature of the technology, and also where all shifts rotate.

It is clear that differentiation by time calls for positive managing skills to maintain the tempo and quality of work and to prevent the circular dependence from becoming a deteriorating cycle. The managerial problems inherent in this model make it important to eliminate avoidable complexities. Many of these stem from a failure on the part of management to conceptualize second and third shifts as discrete systems. Outside the industries where continuous operations are intrinsic to the technology, the second and third shifts have generally been introduced in order to supplement production from single-shift working without increasing capital investment; the notion that they are supplementary tends to be perpetuated not only in management attitudes but also in organization. Rice (1958) has given a good example of this kind of situation in a textile mill and also indicated that acceptance of the organizational consequences of three-shift working can lead to higher productivity and improved quality.

An avoidable complication occurs when the overall head of the three shifts also has the additional role of first-shift supervisor. The 24-hour responsibility of the overall head naturally cannot be discharged if he or she is regularly tied for eight hours to one shift only. A separate first-shift supervisor is therefore necessary. Related to this is a tendency to confuse first-shift control and service functions with headquarters functions, usually because office hours more nearly coincide with first-shift hours than with those of other shifts. The first-shift supervisor may be given responsibility for such functions as pertain to all shifts, or alternatively—and less frequently—certain services that are decentralized to the second- and third-shift supervisors are, for the first shift, retained under headquarters control. It is appropriate either to centralize such functions fully under the head of the total command or to decentralize them equally to the three subordinates, but not to delegate them to one or two subordinates only (cf. Rice, 1958:46). Difficulties of coordination are also increased if one shift supervisor—commonly on the third shift—has an operat-

[5]Often, too, the level of attention is lower and mistakes are more numerous (cf. Hill and Trist, 1955).

ing command that is smaller than the other two. Equalization of shift commands, by allowing the heads of the three shifts to collaborate as equals, may reduce the load on the managing system to an extent that more than offsets the cost of increased third-shift working. (This is not possible, of course, where there are wide fluctuations in the load, for example, in some engineering firms, and a "spill-over" nightshift is required irregularly in order to absorb these fluctuations and to maintain a steady dayshift load.)

The head of this kind of command therefore has to take specific precautions appropriate to the pattern of differentiation and interdependence: he or she needs to be aware of this 24-hour responsibility, to attend shift hand-overs as often as possible, to avoid delegating either too much or too little to the first-shift head and to avoid giving too small a command to the third-shift head. Meetings of the superior with his or her subordinates as a group help to emphasize the complementary contributions of the shifts to the total task of the command. Meeting the subordinates only individually makes it more difficult to ensure that all three shifts work together coherently. There are possibly advantages in a form of shift rotation that periodically alters the order of dependence of the shifts.

Where there are only two shifts, although the general problems are very much the same as in the three-shift situation—especially the sharing of territory and equipment—the reciprocity makes equilibrium easier to sustain because dependence and power balance each other. There is one drawback in having only two shift heads reporting to one superior: it is too small a command. Coordination and control of two subordinates generally give the superiors too little to do. They may tend to bypass their immediate subordinates, withdrawing authority and responsibility from them. Consequently it may prove desirable to combine, at the same level, differentiation by time with crosscutting differentiation by territory and/or technology. As was pointed out earlier, however, it is unlikely that the task structure will be such that interrelatedness along the time dimension will be equal to interrelatedness along the territorial/technological dimension.

In all cases of crosscutting differentiation, where two dimensions of differentiation are compressed into one level, formation of subgroups is to be expected along one dimension or the other. It has to be realized, however, that such groupings have no formal identity in this kind of structure, so that controls and services must be either fully centralized or else fully decentralized to the individual subunits.

Though the few models discussed here touch only the fringe of all the possible variations, they serve to indicate the different kinds of demand placed on management according to the types of boundary that separate the subunits and according to the type and degree of dependence between them. Consideration of these factors may be relevant to the selection, training and placement of managers. Though it is probably a little far-fetched to suggest that management of territorially differentiated units requires a special kind of person, it is certainly clear that techniques of management appropriate in that situation cannot effectively be transplanted into a situation where the units are differentiated along other dimensions and the patterns of co-dependence and interdependence are more complex.

References

Emery, F.E. 1959. *Characteristics of Socio-Technical Systems*. London: Tavistock Institute Document 527. Revised in *The Emergence of a New Paradigm of Work*. Canberra: Centre for Continuing Education, Australian National University, 1978. Also in *Design of Jobs*, edited by L.E. Davis and J.C. Taylor. Harmondsworth: Penguin Books, 1972; Vol. II, "Characteristics of Socio-Technical Systems," pp. 157–86.

Gulick, L. 1937. "Notes on the Theory of Organization, with Special Reference to Government in the United States." In *Papers on the Science of Administration*, edited by L. Gulick and L. Urwick. New York: Institute of Public Administration.

Herbst, P.G. 1957. "Management of Behaviour Structures by Means of Input-Output Data." *Human Relations,* 10:335–46.

Hill, J.M.M. and E.L. Trist. 1955. "Changes in Accidents and Other Absences with Length of Service." *Human Relations,* 8:121–52.

March, J.G. and H.A. Simon. 1958. *Organizations*. New York: Wiley; London: Chapman and Hall.

Miller, E.J. 1954. "Caste and Territory in Malabar." *American Anthropologist,* 56:410–20.

Rice, A.K. 1958. *Productivity and Social Organization: The Ahmedabad Experiment.* London: Tavistock Publications. Reissued 1987, New York: Garland.

Rice, A.K. and E.L. Trist. 1952. "Institutional and Sub-Institutional Determinants of Change in Labour Turnover." *Human Relations,* 5:347–71.

Selznick, P. 1957. *Leadership in Administration: A Sociological Interpretation*. Evanston, Ill.: Row, Peterson.

Trist, E.L. and K.W. Bamforth. 1951. "Some Social and Psychological Consequences of the Longwall Method of Coal-getting." *Human Relations,* 4:3–38. Revised, Vol. II, "The Stress of Isolated Dependence: The Filling Shift in the Semi-Mechanized Longwall Three-Shift Mining Cycle," pp. 64–83.

Trist, E.L., G.W. Higgin, H. Murray and A.B. Pollock. 1963. *Organizational Choice: Capabilities of Groups at the Coal Face Under Changing Technologies: The Loss, Rediscovery and Transformation of a Work Tradition.* London: Tavistock Publications. Reissued 1987, New York: Garland. Chapters 13, 14 revised, Vol. II, "Alternative Work Organizations: An Exact Comparison," pp. 84–105. Chapters 19–22, Vol. I, "The Assumption of Ordinariness as a Denial Mechanism: Innovation and Conflict in a Coal Mine," pp. 476–93.

Woodward, J. 1958. *Management and Technology*. Department of Scientific and Industrial Research: Problems of Progress in Industry, No.3. London: Her Majesty's Stationery Office.

Strategic Projects

The projects in this section illustrate the variety of socio-technical field projects and their various degrees of success and failure. Herbst's account of the voyage of the *Balao* describes the new form of organization that developed on the key Norwegian merchant ship, through which the Norwegian merchant navy has, along socio-technical lines, transformed a conventional form of ship design into an innovative form.

In the 1970s in the United States, the government supported a number of national projects. These had to be sanctioned by top management and the union(s) involved; by the corporation as well as those involved at the plant level, where there was a joint labor/management steering committee. Funding was half by the government and half by the company. External social science consultants were employed. The results were evaluated by an independent team on a common plan developed by the University of Michigan, which covered the first 18 months of each project. The analysis by Susman and Trist of the project at Rushton coal mine, which was both a success and a failure, brings into focus the complexities and the unpredictable changes in the factors influencing outcome in such undertakings.

The paper by Trist and Dwyer analyzes the phenomena of fade-out in projects in a very large multinational firm. They show that the projects were initiated by local management but were unknown at the corporate level; many locally successful endeavors failed through lack of higher level support. Experience of fade-out suggested that strategies of "periphery-in" should be replaced by strategies of "center-out" (Ketchum and Trist, 1992), which are exceedingly difficult to secure.

In the Canadian Federal Public Service, the pattern of change is assessed by Westley and Trist and shows the complexity of basic organizational change in large organizations. A few departments initiated further change, but no general change has taken place.

A special opportunity arose in the work at Norsk Hydro, the largest firm in Norway, when they decided to build a new fertilizer plant and invited the collaboration of Thorsrud and Emery. It became possible to study the plant's evolution and also to compare it with an existing fertilizer plant. The jobs in the new plant were designed on socio-technical principles with the full participation of those concerned. The results showed that 30 percent less people were required. This was the first occasion where a method of payment for overall capacity was used instead of the traditional method of payment for the particular part of that capacity actually being used.

In a parallel project in a new refinery in Shell, UK, tanker captains objected to bills of lading being signed by workers, and British Rail blamed the incidence of a fire on board a Shell rail tanker on the absence of a foreman in Shell's loading group. Key customer organizations could force an innovating organization back to conformity.

Williams shows how socio-technical principles reduced "repetition strain injury" in the Australian public service, which has gone further than those in other countries toward wide-scale application of socio-technical principles.

One of the most notable projects was that carried out at Sarnia, a new Shell chemical plant in western Ontario. The consultants were Davis, one of the leading social scientists in the field, and Sullivan, a leading official of the Energy and Chemical Workers Union. Entirely new ground was broken in a number of matters, including the fashioning of a contract. Through the acquisition of ancillary skills in lab work, maintenance and administration, production workers were able to secure more time on day shifts. Despite the progress made in the first two years, the project has hung fire in the 12 or so years since then.

Microprocessor technology and the big changes it implies are considered in the next section.

Reference

Ketchum, L.D. and E.L. Trist. 1992. *All Teams Are Not Created Equal: How Employee Empowerment Really Works*. Newbury Park, Ca.: Sage Publications.

David (P.G.) Herbst

A Learning Organization in Practice
M/S *Balao*[1]

Captain: When we started off, we were doubtful, but now we know—the way we work is right.

A/B Sailor: I know you won't believe me when I tell you this, but this is the best ship in the Norwegian fleet.

The field trip on M/S *Balao* from Sicily to the Black Sea port of Novoryssisk recorded in this paper was undertaken together with Ragnar Johansen in 1977. The new form of ship organization described was developed by Captain Egil Samuelsen with Johansen as his adviser. M/S *Balao* had been architecturally designed and equipped to function as an experimental development ship. A first socio-technical design was implemented at the time the ship was taken over by its crew. The initial design was evaluated by the crew, a process which took a period of two years, before the form of organization described in this paper was finally achieved.

The ship is no longer in service. All that is left today is one of the cabins of the crew, which stands on display at the Oslo Maritime Museum next to a cabin from the days of sailing vessels.

However, the ship had fulfilled its function as what Fred Emery, years earlier, had described as a "demonstration experiment." This was not an experiment in the laboratory sense, but a practical experiment to show that what was previously thought to be impossible actually could be done. The experiment was also a necessary way of providing the data needed for formulating more general principles.

A demonstration experiment is not a way of studying the world that is, but of the world that can be. A demonstration experiment allows a choice, not between what is and what might be theoretically, which is not a realistic choice, but between alternative possibilities that are demonstrable in practice. At the time, M/S *Balao* seemed to those who manned it like a solitary swallow. It was

---

[1] A new paper.

both an adventure and a cost for those who set out to explore the unknown in human and social capabilities.

Today, the experiment has become the model that provides the principles Norwegian shipping is seeking to implement over the next 10 to 15 years and that, together with the earlier M/S *Multina* experiment, also provides a guiding model in the development of new forms of ship organization in other European countries including Holland, Germany and England.

One of the innovative and significant developments is the method of participant work planning carried out by the crew with officers functioning in a supportive role. A more systematic account of participative work planning, and the onboard method of socio-technical task structure analysis employed, is in preparation. Both now form part of the curriculum for maritime school education in Norway.

The way in which *Balao* is organized is very simple and obvious when one is on board and yet so difficult to describe in any simple and systematic way. One has to unlearn almost everything one has learned from conventional ship organization. It is not just different in particular characteristics that can be pointed to. It differs qualitatively and totally. Within the new structural context, almost every element found in the conventional organization functions in a different way. The theories and principles which were useful for understanding conventional ship organization no longer apply.

In conventional organizations the role and status of individuals and of departments are the primary concern, and the task as such tends to become a secondary and sometimes almost irrelevant issue. Here the opposite is the case. The nature of the task is the primary concern and the question of roles and status a secondary issue. This is just one example of the kinds of structure reversal which are found. Five characteristics related to the work organization appear to be of particular significance.

Total crew involvement in organization of change. What has changed is not just a part of the organization but the total organization from top to bottom. The successful involvement at an early stage of the total crew in the process of change, which has been maintained for most of the period of over two years, has played a major role. At the same time, the sharing of dining, service and leisure facilities by the whole crew has led to a consistent change in the social life on board.

Organizational change as a learning process. What has been achieved is not just a new system of organization. From the start, steps taken to implement increased autonomy and active involvement in work planning of the crew were evaluated. Both negative and positive consequences were reviewed. By means of needed changes in the pay system and in the relationships to head office, further steps in organizational change became possible, which were again evaluated. In this way successive phases of change have occurred. What has been achieved is policy making as a learning process, that is, a process of action research which has made minimal use of outsiders as temporary resource persons. It is of some importance that no outsider has, at any time, attempted or been allowed to take over a directive role in the process.

Participative work planning. What has aided this process is the fact that the nature of the tasks on board changes week by week. Every planning session has presented new problems, in the course of which the competence of individuals has steadily increased and new work planning techniques have been developed and improved further. As a result, for example, cleaning and painting, which on a conventional ship are the most unskilled tasks with practically no learning potential, have become transformed into highly sophisticated opportunities for technical and organizational learning. Even if a task comes around again at a later stage, it may no longer be the same. Possible new technical procedures become apparent and, as both the number of competent persons and the level of competence increases, new work organizational solutions become possible.

What has evolved here is not simply job enlargement or job enrichment. A key characteristic of the new organizational context is that those who are going to do the task engage in preplanning meetings to map out work methods and technical requirements. This leads to the determination of boundary conditions; that is, the dependence of the task to be carried out on other tasks and other persons who may be affected. One of the officers will generally be asked to participate as a resource person. After the task is completed, more information will be available to provide a revised task analysis and, at a later stage, when new and better approaches to the task are developed and tested in practice, the task description will be updated. The material which becomes available in this way, specifically with respect to the number of persons and the approximate time required, can then be used to improve the joint planning carried out in weekly conferences.

Development of a learning community. What has evolved in this way is a learning community in which practically everyone is involved in one way or another. In a conventional organization, superiors instruct subordinates. Here, instruction has regained its original sense. Those who are formally superior instruct those who are formally subordinate but, in addition, colleagues instruct colleagues, and those who are formally subordinates instruct those who are their formal superiors. The relationship is more like that of seniors and juniors who have developed mutual respect. Coming out of the conference room after a weekly planning meeting, the captain commented that the work methods arrived at by the ratings turned out to have been better than the proposals made by the officers.

Looking back, my impression is that there was more learning going on aboard this ship than in almost any school I have visited. The reasons for this phenomenon are that learning was going on at so many different levels simultaneously. There is

- organizational learning;

- collegial learning on the job;
- instruction given by seniors to juniors in navigation, machine maintenance, crane operation and tool use;
- learning in the course of detailed work planning;
- learning of work planning in discussions of work allocation to new tasks.

There is also school-type learning, when twice a week a group of ratings come together for several hours in the conference room to work on textbook problems in physics and mathematics for their maritime certificate examinations. One of the officers helps them when they have difficulties and checks their solutions to the problems. When I asked whether officers asked for extra pay for teaching juniors, I found the question was not appropriate. The relevance of the new payment system that was introduced will be discussed later.

All this provides an organizational context within which people can find mutual support and help and are able to develop both their human qualities and their technical competence.

Open and joint territory. As a result of all the characteristics discussed so far, the rigid, almost impermeable compartmentalized boundaries, behind which crew members on conventional ships isolate themselves and which they utilize to play out their stagelike antipathies and ritualized conflicts, have practically disappeared. On conventional ships the norm is closure and exclusive control of territories. Here the norm is openness. A necessary exception is the privacy of personal cabins.

Entering the superstructure at the back of the ship, one comes directly into the coffee lounge. This adjoins the dining room. There is also a duty mess, convenient for use during working hours. From the coffee lounge, a stair up, one comes into the dayroom and bar. This adjoins the swimming pool and a library which can also be used as a small conference room. On the other side of the corridor there is a large L-shaped room that contains the offices of the chief officer, machine chief and captain. The captain's section opens into a large conference room. All the cabins are on successive levels of the superstructure. The navigation bridge is on the top level.

The standard cabin is about 17 square meters, consisting of a sitting room, a bathroom with toilet and shower and a small bedroom which also has a writing desk and stool.[2] Chief Officers have somewhat larger cabins. There is enough and suitable accommodation available to allow any crew member to bring his wife and children along, which they do usually in the summer months.

The machine room is painted in cool, beautiful colors and looks spotlessly clean. For awhile, one does not notice the heat. However, it is very noisy. In the control room it is cooler and the noise is no longer noticeable. From the

---

[2]Mrs. Schjetlin, an architect who collaborates with the Institute, participated in the design of the living quarters.

lower deck a stair leads down to a set of storerooms for equipment and material and a small but well-equipped machine shop. There is no bosun here to lock the stores and keep the key. After the work planning sessions, the team members responsible for jobs just go to the stores and fetch whatever material, equipment and tools are needed. The ship's budget provides for all the best and most suitable equipment to be available.

The automated machine room has made a considerable difference. Only the three navigation officers and three ratings are on a four-hour shift cycle. Since the ratings rotate their tasks after some time, and shift-over coincides with meal times, almost everyone is able to participate in the social life on board.

Passing to the coffee lounge after dinner, large groups form around the tables. From there, people move to the dayroom where, in the comfortable, closer and more informal layout, a more open pattern of shifting groups emerges. Some crew members wander into the library and others join for a game of table tennis. The bar is open all day until midnight, both at sea and in port. There are soft drinks and beer in the refrigerator and strong drinks on the shelf. No one sits at the bar. People just go and fetch what they need and note down in a book on the counter what they have taken. There is scarcely any consumption of alcohol. A few of the chief officers take a whisky in the evening. Some drop in during working hours to get themselves a cold drink. On the bridge, which is some distance away, there is always coffee brewing.

On conventional ships, status differences and boundaries are built into the layout. Changing the architectural design by itself may not be sufficient. At the same time, without this change it would not have been possible to go very far in the development of a more cooperative and equalitarian work and social organization.

So far, an outline has been given of what appear to be significant characteristics of the work and social organization on board. These are summarized below.

The change process has not been limited to any part of the organization but has affected the total work and social organization on board.

It has not been simply a changeover to a new system. The ship has gone through successive phases of organizational change that was evolved, tested and implemented by the people on board themselves.

This process has been aided by the fact that the nature and pattern of tasks change from week to week. At the same time, the steadily growing competence of crew members provides new organizational possibilities.

This has led to a continuously evolving work and learning community in which, in one way or another, practically everyone is involved. A crew member may, in one situation, be a learner and, in others, contribute to the teaching of others.

While there is a distinction between seniors and juniors both in terms of competence and ultimate responsibility, the rigid vertical, horizontal and territorial boundaries have disappeared. This development has been aided by the new layout and design of the office and living quarters and by the fact that work stores and service facilities are open to everyone. What has evolved is a ship in which the crew have accepted and taken joint responsibility for the running of the ship.

The central elements of the new structure are shown in Figure 1. The core of the new structure is the joint planning procedure that has evolved. This takes into account both the work requirements and the individual training needs of the crew. What is achieved is essentially a joint optimization of work and training requirements.

On a conventional type of ship where role and task specialization are given, planning tends to be little more than a mechanical job. This is not the case here. From week to week different autonomous-type task groups are formed based on the shifting sets of tasks. However, this does not entirely describe the actual work organization since, within the cooperative culture, others may join in informally to lend a hand. An officer on an inspection round, instead of noting some minor job that needs to be done, may just do it himself. The shifting set of autonomous work groups constitute a matrix organization. It is within this context of active involvement both in overall and detailed task planning, together with the work carried out within the structure of a matrix organization, that a continuous process of learning is maintained at the organizational, interpersonal and individual levels.

At present, the matrix organization encompasses most of the junior crew, together with the electrician and the repair man and to some extent the machine engineers. Most of the ratings and trainees are being brought up to the newly established level of ship technicians approaching a joint competence on deck and machine at the junior officer level. From there, the next step planned is the implementation of overlapping skills of deck and machine officers, thus arriving at a matrix organization which, apart from the steward department, will encompass practically the total crew. The bottom-up strategy of change is here on the way to being successfully implemented. If it is so implemented, then this is because, in the course of the change process, the squeeze on—and resulting opposition of—the middle management level has been largely avoided by the development of consensus at each significant step of the change process and by the development of mutual trust. As a result, also, those who at a given stage were not primarily and directly involved in the change process did not feel that other crew members might be engaged in actions which were counter to their interests.

So far only the organization on board a ship has been considered. However, the changes would not have been possible without requisite and critical changes

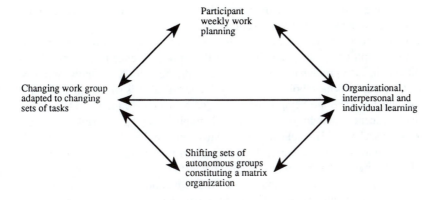

Figure 1. Central elements of the joint planning structure

in boundary conditions. These have altered to some extent the relationship between the ship and head office.

A major aim was to provide the conditions for achieving increased stability of the crew. The following operating principles have been implemented:

Flexible crew size. The size of the crew can vary over time between 19 and 26. An average of 23 is to be maintained.

Vacation plan. Each crew member is entitled to three months vacation. Vacation absences are planned on a yearly basis.

Both the above provide the conditions for personnel planning, a function which has increasingly been taken over by the ship.

Inclusive overtime payment. The monthly pay includes a fixed overtime payment for 14 hours a week.

Balao went through a difficult period in 1974. While a stable nucleus of persons has continued on board from the start, the haphazard "normal" replacement sent by the personnel department caused considerable problems. Two steps were taken: the planning conference was reorganized to provide more active involvement by the junior crew and more control was taken by the ship over personnel and replacement planning. A critical condition is that junior crew members be, as far as possible, willing and able to work both on deck and in the machine room and that they have, if possible, some technical school training. Over time, practically all the junior crew would be replaced by the new level of combined ship technicians (*skipsmekanikere*), who would effectively function as officer candidates. Stable vacation replacements were available for key ship's officers, including the captain.

Coming into the dock at Novoryssisk in the evening, one sees that everyone working on deck has the same yellow boiler suit. There is no way of seeing who are officers and who are crew. Both are working together on the ropes to get the ship tied up alongside the dock. The only difference is that one of the officers in each group has a walkie-talkie. Both the radio-telegraphist and one of the mess-girls have boiler suits as well, and the latter is shown how to work the winches. The job being finished, we go to the coffee lounge. One of the deck officers comes to join the radio-telegraphist, saying, "Thanks a lot for giving us a hand." He replies, "No need to thank me. I enjoyed it. It was fun."

Next day a staff member of the Russian Maritime Agency and a uniformed official come to pick me up by car. On the way to the local airport we pass rows and rows of newly built apartment blocks. I mention that we have just the same. The Maritime Agency official looks at me and asks: "Do you know what is the most important thing in the world?" I ask, "What is it?" He says, "The most important thing is humanization."

Gerald Susman and Eric Trist

Action Research in an American Underground Coal Mine[1]

Laying the Groundwork for an Experiment: May to November 1973

CONDITIONS LEADING TO AN AGREEMENT

In May 1973, Warren Hinks, president of Rushton Mining Company, and Arnold Miller, president of the United Mine Workers of America (UMWA), signed an agreement to undertake an experiment to create opportunities for autonomy and participation for workers within an operating face section of a coal mine. An operating face section rather than a mine as a whole was chosen as the unit of change because there was no previous experience in the U.S. mining industry with an innovation with such far reaching implications. The change was labeled "experimental" to give all interested parties an opportunity to assess its consequences before making a formal commitment to it. It was thought unlikely in 1973 that any management or local union would commit to a change of this kind without such provisions or commit to changing an entire mine at one time.

Several converging factors made such an agreement feasible at that time. In late 1972, the UMWA ousted a corrupt and scandal-ridden administration and elected a new reform-minded president whose campaign platform included a major focus on safety. The newly elected president appointed several young staff members who were interested and knowledgeable about worker participation in decision making and aware of the positive results of the pioneering work on autonomous work groups undertaken by the Tavistock Institute in the British coal industry (Trist et al., 1963).

The president of Rushton was also concerned about coal mine safety. He felt that more was required than was provided for by the provisions of the recently

[1] A revised and expanded version of the original, E.L. Trist, G.I. Susman and G.R. Brown, "An Experiment in Autonomous Working in an American Underground Coalmine." *Human Relations*, 30:201–36, 1977.

enacted Coal Mine Health and Safety Act and that greater external inspection and sanctioning, although necessary, could only be partially effective and that full effectiveness required more intensive training of foreman and workers. He also believed that the increasing rate of absenteeism in the industry (then about 13 percent) was a safety hazard. Workers who have been rescheduled by management to fill critical vacant positions perform tasks they do not regularly do and perform them with workers with whose habits and skills they are unfamiliar. Hinks also expressed concern about a new generation of miners who were younger, better educated and more militant than past generations. He was willing to explore any organizational innovations that would curb the increasing number of wildcat strikes and improve industrial relations in general. Hinks was receptive to the idea that increased involvement of workers in decision making and an overall improvement in work quality through the use of autonomous work groups might be a means to improve safety as well as increase productivity. He was thus willing to give the concept a try.

The research team received funding from the National Commission on Productivity and Work Quality and subsequently from the National Quality of Work Center (NQWC), affiliated with the Institute for Social Research, University of Michigan. These two agencies, federal and quasi-public respectively, were perceived as neutral third parties by management and the UMWA. Other relevant governmental sources were rejected due to suspicion by either management or the union. The agencies established the following guidelines for support of the experiment:

Funding would cover an 18-month period. Complete funding would be provided for the initial six months. During this time, management and the union would develop conditions under which an experiment would proceed. Half funding would be provided for the next 12 months, during which the actual experiment would be conducted. Management and the union would make up the other half in proportions to be decided. These funds were only to cover the research team's daily rates and travel expenses.

Management and the union must agree to develop a formula for sharing any gains resulting from improvements in performance.

A separately funded evaluation team would collect attitudinal and performance-related data and provide these to all parties by the end of the 18-month experimental period.[2]

A further evaluation would take place at the end of three years to see if the experiment and its outcomes were self-maintaining. The view of the

[2]The evaluation team was headed by Paul Goodman, Carnegie-Mellon University, on contract to the Institute for Social Research of the University of Michigan, which is responsible for the evaluation of all NQWC projects on a common model and is funded by the Ford Foundation.

funding agencies was that wider acceptance of the results would be assured if the larger publics concerned knew that the evaluation was done by an independent group with no vested interest in the program's outcome.

DEVELOPMENT OF THE "DOCUMENT"

A mechanism had to be developed to assure management and the union that both would retain joint ownership of the project as well as an equitable distribution of gain-sharing. The mechanism was a labor-management steering committee consisting of nearly all mine management above the foreman level (plus some foremen) as well as the local union officers and members of the Health and Safety and Mine (grievance) Committees. The steering committee met throughout the summer of 1973 and developed what became known as the "document." The document laid out the terms and conditions under which the experiment would proceed and be evaluated. Highlights of the document included selection of men, selection of the experimental section, new duties of the foreman, etc. There was agreement on modifying four basic provisions of the contract then in effect.

Elimination of pay differences on the experimental section for different job classifications. Mine management agreed to pay all members of the crew the top rate of $50.00 per day as the contract stood at the program's commencement.

Bypassing of the grievance mechanism and establishment of a joint committee at the mine site to oversee the experimental section and to handle all grievances that arose from it.

Freedom for crew members to learn new jobs within their section without these jobs having to be bid or posted minewide.

Relinquishment of management's right to direct the crew members at the work site.

The document was taken to the local union for membership vote in October 1973 and was accepted.

Selection, Orientation and Training of Volunteers: December 1973 to March 1974

SELECTION OF VOLUNTEERS

Twenty-four bids were posted (three eight-man crews), and the steering committee reviewed volunteers on the basis of seniority and job qualifications. The mechanics on the section did not volunteer but were assigned by the maintenance foreman. Two support positions were added to the section for reasons explained below. Under the existing union contract, miner operators and mechanics earned the top rate of $50.00 per day, miner helpers and roof bolters earned $47.25 per day, shuttle car operators earned $43.25 per day and support men earned $42.75 per day. Volunteers, their number given in parentheses, gave the following reasons for wishing to become members of the newly designated section (each worker was allowed to cite more than one reason): more money (7); better physical conditions (4); be my own boss (2); assigned by maintenance supervisor (2); learn more about mining (1); car pool buddy on section (1); get away from foreman who pushes for production (1); do my own thing (1). The age distribution of volunteers was 20–29 (12); 30–39 (7); 40–49 (3); 50–65 (5).

ORIENTATION PERIOD

A six-session orientation period began in December 1973; each session lasted for a full day in the mine classroom. There was a Monday and a Friday meeting for each of three weeks. Tuesdays, Wednesdays, and Thursdays were regular working days on the new section. During orientation meetings, the document was reviewed, autonomous work group concepts explained and all job tasks reviewed. The men received a job safety analysis program and a review of the state and federal safety laws. In addition, experiential exercises in group relations and problem solving were given, generally within the context of issues that the steering committee had not foreseen and which required resolution. The men were all experienced miners who claimed to know and to have sometimes done all the face jobs. Hence, it was proper that all should receive the top rate from the beginning.

TRAINING AND ADJUSTMENT PERIOD

A six-week period then followed during which the men worked at the jobs they initially bid on, but were encouraged to relearn as many of the other jobs as possible. They were to familiarize themselves with state and federal laws and begin to learn to manage their section. As the primary focus during this period was on training and learning, management agreed to a moratorium on pressure for production. In February 1974, the section elected one man from each crew to be a representative to the joint committee and also elected two representatives from the local union leadership. Management appointed five members. Thereafter, the labor-management steering committee declared the section autonomous and withdrew from active involvement in the project. The steering committee was to be reconvened to evaluate the project at a later date and to decide if additional sections should be initiated.

Socio-Technical Analysis: March 1974 to April 1975

The original experimental "year" was extended to 13 months due to the month-long national strike of November 1974. The research team's contributions over the next thirteen months can be divided into two basic categories:

- a socio-technical analysis of the room-and-pillar method of coal-mining when utilizing continuous mining equipment;
- introduction of several mechanisms for training and development as well as for conflict resolution, but most importantly for encouraging continuous planning and problem solving at several levels of the mine organization.

These contributions were not independent of each other; they proceeded in tandem and each influenced the conceptualization as well as the form in which concrete proposals of either category were offered. The contributions of the research team during this period were continuous rather than in the form of reports at specified intervals to the steering committee. Such an approach was compatible with the role the research team had conceived for itself, that of collaborator in a joint learning venture in which management and the union would develop and evaluate new methods.

THE TECHNICAL SYSTEM

In the continuous mining of coal by the room-and-pillar method (Cassidy, 1973), coal is cut at the face by a large machine with a continuously rotating drum studded with sharp bits. Below the drum, coal is gathered by large crablike arms and dumped onto one of two shuttle cars that are alternately filled and then driven down a pathway to a feeder, where the coal is emptied onto a continuously moving belt conveying the coal to the surface. Each time the face is cut 20 feet wide and 18 feet deep, the mining machine (the continuous miner) is withdrawn to a new face, leaving space for the newly exposed roof to be first timbered and then bolted. This sequence of activities constitutes the basic conversion process in development of a section. What remains after a section has been developed gives a checkerboard appearance of alternating open rooms and solid pillars. Following section development, the coal is removed from the pillars, causing a controlled collapse of the roof that is preceded by retreat of the mining equipment to a new pillar further from the original working face.

Against this "figure" of activities is the "ground" consisting of prepara-tory/maintenance tasks, e.g., repairs, moving supplies. All preparatory/main-tenance tasks are essential to continuance of the basic conversion process.

The seven men on each shift of a typical face section include the miner operator, who runs the continuous miner; the miner helper, who places timber at the freshly cut face, hangs ventilation curtains, moves power cables that energize the continuous miner, etc.; two shuttle-car operators; two roof bolters; and the mechanic. Support work, including maintenance of conveyor belts, building "brattices" (permanent ventilation stoppings), laying tracks, hauling supplies to the face, etc., is typically carried out by the general underground work force.

Analysis begins with recognition that conversion by the coal-mining indus-try from conventional (low mechanization) to continuous (high mechanization) methods fundamentally altered the nature of the technical system. The essen-tial feature of this conversion was to change the key contribution of humans from coal getting (a large machine now cuts the coal) to assuring that maximum use is made of the equipment and that breakdowns are minimized. There is, at the present stage of technological development, a significant discontinuity between the technical system's basic components. The productive capacity of the equipment far exceeds the capacity of the rest of the system to effectively and efficiently move coal from the mining equipment to the surface. If the continuous mining equipment were to run continuously, as its name implies, it would be capable of cutting up to 4,000 tons per shift (Faltenmayer, 1974); however, due to time consumed in moving the continuous miner from one cutting face to another, waiting time between shuttle cars, delays due to mechanical breakdowns, poor communication, unnecessary or poorly timed moves, etc., the continuous miner cuts only 350 to 400 tons per shift. The continuous miner can be used more effectively if the focus of human contribu-tions shifts from coal getting toward eliminating problems such as those discussed below.

Psycho-Social Consequences of the Technical System

ISOLATION OF THE MEN DURING WORK PERFORMANCE

During an eight-hour shift, effective operation of the mining system requires that there be a shared understanding among shift members and between them-selves and the foreman concerning what is required to minimize delays and shutdowns. Yet, because of the nature of underground mining, once work has begun, communication and coordination on a real-time basis is inhibited by distance between work sites as well as by darkness. Coordination improves when consensus is established before the shift begins so that everyone has a shared "map" of what is required and when. Current management practice places the entire responsibility for coordination on the foreman. He is the "glue" that pulls all the tasks together. Yet underground conditions make it very difficult to carry out this responsibility effectively.

CONTINUITY BETWEEN SHIFTS

The manner in which each shift performs its tasks and the conditions in which it leaves the section significantly influence the performance of the next shift. Current management practice considers the shift and the individual foreman as the primary production unit. This encourages competition between shifts where cooperation is vital. The consequence of this competition is gamesman-ship, in which winners get high tonnage and losers are left with bad conditions and, consequently, lower tonnage. Instead of planning to set up the next shift so that maximum coal will be mined across three shifts, the foreman and shift members use their planning abilities to thwart the other crews.

UNCERTAINTY OF CONDITIONS

About every 10 days, the mining system is literally picked up and moved 180 feet forward. With every such move, crew members must cope with new geological conditions and, as progress is made toward the next move, shuttle-car paths lengthen and the distance between support and facemen increases. Furthermore, even with the most diligent efforts at preventive maintenance, equipment breakdowns occur. These and other similar contingencies make it difficult to anticipate the conditions under which work and its coordination take place.

The traditional factory, facing relatively constant conditions, may be able to cope with its production system by assigning to each worker a set of tasks that only he or she is permitted to perform. This method of job assignment is prevalent in the mining industry today but is inappropriate to the conditions of uncertainty with which crew members and their foremen must cope.

CONCEPTS CONTRIBUTED BY THE RESEARCH TEAM

DOUBLE BIND ON FOREMEN FOR PRODUCTION AND SAFETY

Current management practice places foremen in a double-bind conflict in that higher management holds them solely responsible for both production and safety. Foremen are the repository of an industrywide conflict, the burden of which they must bear internally. If production is lower than expected, they are held accountable. If an accident or violation occurs on their section, they are held accountable both to management and to state and federal regulatory agencies. This conflict prevents them from giving primary attention to either and tempts them to vacillate between meeting one goal or the other.

THE BEST MATCH BETWEEN THE SOCIAL AND TECHNICAL SYSTEMS

The design process is a search for the best solution to a set of conflicting requirements. The best solution is necessarily an innovation as well as a work of art in the broadest sense of the term. If the solution were obvious, it would be merely calculated; there would be no design problem as such (Alexander, 1964). Additionally, the research team believes that it is neither necessary nor desirable that they be the innovators while management and the union are solely the consumers. The ultimate design that evolves requires the resources of the men, the union and the management. While no clear-cut division of labor exists among these contributors, the research team viewed itself as a catalyst and facilitator of problem solving by the other parties. The team's role was to introduce concepts and encourage discussion. Those who use the design must believe in it and "own" it. The final form it takes must, therefore, be the result of the efforts of all.

REDEFINITION OF THE PRIMARY TASK

When the social system members' definition of their primary task is congruent with what the technical system is designed to do, both systems can be more effectively utilized. Acceptance by management and section members of the definition of continuous mining as a transport system rather than as a production system will encourage both to be alert to key variables that affect the performance of a transport system. For example, search is likely to intensify on how to maximize use of the continuous miner while at the cutting face as well as to minimize delays and shutdowns.

PERFORMANCE AND MEASUREMENT OF THE PRIMARY TASK

The primary task may have a "pull" of its own if performance is evaluated per belt move (approximately every 10 days) in the context of the type of mining (e.g., development vs. pillars) and conditions faced, costs incurred, etc. If performance is fed back to section members in units such as these rather than in units that are accounting conveniences, the units will "stand by themselves" as bases around which activities are organized.

Performance data should be evaluated according to social units containing those members whose activities are most interdependent in pursuit of the primary task. In continuous mining the section of three shifts, not the single shift, is the natural unit containing those men and tasks that are most interdependent in operating and maintaining the transport system.

DEALING WITH UNCERTAINTY

Technical and geological conditions creating high uncertainty and task interdependence are best dealt with if several group members possess the necessary skills to deploy when unanticipated events arise. Delays will be minimized if corrective action is taken by those located closest to the events rather than by relying exclusively on those who claim a specific job title. A reward structure that minimizes status differences between crew members will encourage the learning of more than one job.

Additionally, more effective deployment of the group's skills should result when all group members are familiar with prevailing physical conditions as well as with each other's skill capacities and work habits. Therefore, containment within the work group of sufficient skills to carry out all relevant tasks should reduce the need to employ nongroup members to handle peripheral group activities as well as to substitute for absent group members. In contrast to the six-man shift utilized by other face sections where support work is done by the general underground work force, autonomous sections should have two additional members to perform the section's support work and fill in for vacant face positions. This arrangement is no more than a reassignment of manpower from one organizational unit, namely, the general underground, to another unit, a face section. No increase in overall manning is required.

THE SHIFT FOREMAN'S ROLE

The social system that approaches the best match with the technical system of continuous mining contains a redistribution of responsibilities between the foreman and crew members. Crew members should be made responsible for coordination of daily activities both within the crew and between crews. They are closer to the work than the foreman and can effectively coordinate their immediate activities. The foreman, being relieved of day-to-day production responsibilities, is freed to study the law and ensure its enforcement. Freedom from day-to-day responsibilities should provide the foreman an opportunity to develop a longer time horizon: for example, to learn to plan better for supply requirements, to see potential breakdowns before they occur and to plan for their systematic repair in conjunction with the maintenance department. Furthermore, a longer time horizon will permit foremen to place daily production within the context of the overall mine development plan. Instead of directing the crew, they can use the knowledge they gain from the above activities to become "resource" persons to crew members. Their contribution to production will be to provide information to crew members, to help them to use that information most effectively and, in discussion sessions, to facilitate the development of a consensus concerning activities to be carried out during the shift. The latter involves skills that most middle and upper level managers are encouraged to learn early in their careers. Although no less important at the foreman level, the learning of these skills has been neglected.

INSTITUTION BUILDING

Throughout the next 10 months the research team concentrated on the building of several mechanisms for training and development as well as for conflict resolution.

SECTION CONFERENCES

At approximately six-week intervals the entire 27 members of the section and the three foremen met in an aboveground classroom where events of the last six weeks were reviewed and the next six weeks planned. During these meetings the men were paid their regular daily rate. This time for review and planning was considered by the men and by management as of no less importance than time on the job. Each believed it would pay off in more effective performance in the long run. After each six-week interval, the research team systematically gathered data on absenteeism, productivity, supply costs and delays for feedback and discussion at section conferences.

UNDERGROUND VISITS

Twice a week during these 10 months two graduate assistants (doctoral candidates), Melvin Blumberg and James Thurman, made underground visits. They were instructed to reinforce the concepts discussed in the classroom meetings, to follow up on ambiguities and to collect information to discuss at the next section conference. Grant Brown, a mining engineer on the staff of the Mines and Minerals Department, Pennsylvania State University, was originally to spend considerable time with each section at the coal face. However, a new department chairman at his university refused to let him be away this much, which seriously limited what was accomplished in developing new work methods and understanding.

JOINT COMMITTEE MEETINGS

The joint committee met at irregular intervals throughout the spring to settle disputes that had arisen on the autonomous section. Beginning in September 1974 the joint committee began to meet regularly to discuss gain-sharing issues. Issues raised included how gains would be measured and divided, among whom the gains would be divided, etc. The research team considered it important in social dynamic terms that these issues be thoroughly explored before it was determined whether or not any gains might exist.

FOREMEN MEETINGS

Beginning in January 1974 the three foremen and other members of management met approximately every two weeks with the research team to discuss issues related to their own development and training. A four-point agenda was developed:

Safety. What unsafe acts did you stop crew members from doing since our last meeting? What violations did you observe and what corrective actions did you take?

Training. Who in the section has learned a new job or task?

Inside-outside relations. Issues related to supply ordering, preventive maintenance and development decisions were discussed with appropriate members of management who were asked to attend these meetings.

Planning and consensus building skills. Experiential exercises were given concerning problem-solving skills, conflict resolution, etc.

MANAGEMENT MEETINGS

Beginning in December 1974 these meetings, consisting of the highest levels of mine management, took place irregularly with overlapping sets of participants. The purpose of these meetings has been to discuss ad hoc problems as they emerged. It was agreed that these meetings occur more regularly for the purpose of dealing with interpersonal relations as well as to develop a problem-solving and planning culture.

CREATION OF A SECOND AUTONOMOUS SECTION

In August 1974 management was planning to create a fourth operating face section. Such planning had not yet begun in the summer of 1973, when the steering committee was developing the conditions for undertaking the original experiment. The question now arose as to whether this new section should be started as a conventional or as an autonomous section. The research team was accumulating evidence that weighed in favor of choosing the latter alternative. There were signs that many members of management were hostile to the experiment and related to section members with indifference or disdain. Such behavior resulted in part from the fact that section members began to initiate requests for more effective scheduling of supplies, tools, maintenance, etc. This reversal of the direction in which initiatives for action had flowed was in sharp contrast to previous management practice and produced hostile reactions among those middle-level managers to whom such flows were directed.

The research team believed that unless undeniable improvements in performance resulted, management would probably reject the experiment at the end of the experimental year. Such improvement was unlikely unless they could develop a philosophy and style of management that were compatible with autonomous group working. The likelihood was remote that they would make a commitment to adopting such a philosophy and style when there was only one autonomous section to deal with. The introduction of a second autonomous section was considered an event of sufficient significance to "unfreeze" the mine's social system and establish a new direction for learning.

The union members of the steering committee requested a local union vote on creating a second autonomous section. A "special" meeting was convened in September and was attended by 17 of the 27 members of the autonomous section. The composition of the group attending was highly atypical, as it included many members of the autonomous section who had not been to a local union meeting in years and excluded many of those who attended regularly scheduled meetings held at the beginning of each month. This unusual turnout of autonomous section members underscores the concern they felt about the future of the project. The local members voted affirmatively (26 to 5) and the second autonomous section began operations in October. The immediate reaction of the original autonomous section members confirmed the research team's view that an "encapsulation" and "rejection" process had been developing among middle management. Until this time many section members expressed the view that management would soon terminate the project and had felt tentative in their commitment to an endeavor that appeared destined to have a short life. The introduction of the second section produced a resurgence of enthusiasm among the original autonomous section members and a will to make the experiment a success. It was also at this time that the management meetings referred to in the previous section began to take place.

REPORT TO THE STEERING COMMITTEE

The research team presented a report to the steering committee in March 1975 in which the actions undertaken over the previous year were summarized and preliminary results presented. The separately funded evaluation team independently collected data for a more systematic analysis, but such results would not be available for some time (see Goodman, 1979).

Comparisons

The second autonomous section, having commenced in October 1974, had not been in operation for a sufficient period of time by March 1975 to provide any useful data. The last three months of 1974 included a month-long national strike and several holidays. Furthermore, caution is advised in comparing the autonomous section with the two remaining nonautonomous sections operating at the beginning of the experimental year. Direct comparisons are difficult because, for example, Nonautonomous section A had better conditions for most of 1974 than did the autonomous section as well as more "backup" equipment, making delays less frequent and prolonged. By contrast, Non-autonomous section B had a great deal of water and generally poor physical conditions throughout 1974. Nonautonomous A had four "ram cars" compared to two "shuttle cars" on Autonomous A. Ram cars, being battery operated, carry their power supply with them. Shuttle cars, connected by cables to a central power station, must be operated more carefully and, at times, more slowly to prevent the tangling, running over and damaging of cables.

Data for 1973 are presented for suggestive purposes only, because any comparisons with 1974 must be interpreted very cautiously, as the composition of the crews on each section changed when the experimental section was created. Furthermore, in a small mine, it was virtually impossible to "seal off" interaction between personnel of the various sections. For example, autonomous section foremen told the other foremen of their activities and training experiences, which some of the latter began to adopt on their own. All miners belong to the same local union and share their experiences at union meetings and at shift changes. Also, training and development activities for middle and upper management personnel who make minewide decisions were bound to have an impact across all three mining sections.

The research team has considered the mine as a whole as the proper unit of analysis, recognizing that "contamination" effects themselves are important data in their own right. Progress on the autonomous section would have to be measured in a longitudinal record of the section against its own past performance. This would show its capacity to learn. Comparisons with other sections have restricted use, though they can be illuminating. All numbers in the tables below are to be treated as descriptive statements. No attempts are made in terms of analytical statistics to infer what might be generalizable to other mines or to form a reliable basis for prediction.

HEALTH AND SAFETY VIOLATIONS

Table 1 shows federal violations assessed against each of the three sections for 1973 and 1974. The reduction in violations for the autonomous section is quite dramatic. This reduction, to about half the number in 1973, occurred in spite of an overall increase in violations for the mine as a whole. The increased number of violations on the other two sections can be attributed to the increased number of visits by federal inspectors to the mine, especially following a fatal accident on Nonautonomous section A in September. The autonomous section had fewer violations in 1974 even with more visits by federal inspectors.

ACCIDENTS

The figures in Table 2 are for all reported accidents and those that were lost-time accidents. The total reported accident rate and the lost-time accident rate for the autonomous section are superior to those of the other two sections for 1974. The fact that the autonomous section had eight members, compared to six members on the other two sections, works slightly to the former's disadvantage in such comparisons. The higher incidence of reported accidents for the mine as a whole in 1974 may be due in part to more stringent reporting requirements requested during the year by governmental agencies. Minor accidents such as cut fingers, bruises, etc., were not reported in 1973. The research team also was informed that conditions in the mine were generally more difficult in 1974 than 1973. If so, the lower overall incidence of reported accidents on the autonomous section is impressive, as this section maintained its overall 1973 record, while that on the other sections increased.

TABLE 1   Federal Violations, 1973 and 1974

	Autonomous	Nonautonomous A	Nonautonomous B	Total
1973	18	19	10	47
1974	7	37	17	61

TABLE 2   Total Reported Accidents and Lost-Time Accidents, 1973 and 1974

	Autonomous	Nonautonomous A	Nonautonomous B	Total
1973				
reported	6	5	4	15
lost-time	2	3	2	7
1974				
reported	7	14	11	32
lost-time	1	3	2	6

ABSENCES

Table 3 shows the number of absences (excused and unexcused) for each section in 1974. Because of the changes in section membership resulting from the experiment, the research team decided not to compare 1974 absenteeism data with 1973 data. The assumption of similar worker performance that was applied when comparing sections on other performance measures did not apply in this case, as only a few individuals contribute to most of the absenteeism. The evaluation team is expected to compile data that adjust for such changes in membership between sections.

The rates of absenteeism on all sections are low for the mining industry—those for the autonomous and Nonautonomous B sections being exceptionally low. The 1974 national average was 12.8 percent of man-days worked. There is no obvious explanation why Nonautonomous B had a consistently low absentee rate. This section experienced particularly bad conditions in 1974 and it might be that under such conditions the crew members did not want to let each other down; they share the bad as a way of enduring it and, of course, in so doing create safer conditions for themselves. For more positive reasons, also, the members of the autonomous section appear not to want to let each other down.

TABLE 3   Absenteeism by Sections, 1974

	Autonomous	Nonautonomous A	Nonautonomous B
Average crew size	(8)	(6.1)	(6.3)
Total man-days absent	135	187	112
Percentage absent per man-day	2.5	4.4	2.4

Costs

On the experimental section it was expected that a more positive attitude would mean that men would be less wasteful of supplies and take better care of equipment. As learning proceeded, the costs of supplies and maintenance should decrease. Table 4 shows direct inside costs (production and maintenance) per ton per quarter of 1974 for each of the three sections. (The whole cost of new equipment parts was charged to the autonomous section in the first quarter and to Nonautonomous A in the fourth quarter. This exaggerates the costs to these sections in these quarters.)

A number of factors must be taken into consideration before a final determination of actual costs is made. There was substantial inflation in the costs of some supplies, e.g., roof bolts, for which corrections must be calculated. Also, the type of mining that predominated throughout the year on each section must be controlled for. For example, fewer supplies are generally used for pillar work than for development. However, these corrections are unlikely to alter the basic differences in trends even after a discount is made for the first quarter. The autonomous section shows a downward trend, while this is not the case for the other two sections. This pattern appears to have been maintained early in 1975. January 1975 figures show costs on the autonomous section at $1.16 per ton compared to $1.85 on Nonautonomous A and $2.75 on Nonautonomous B.

Productivity

In the March 1975 report, the research team was not willing to state conclusively that the autonomous section showed higher productivity than the other two sections if comparisons were made between calendar years 1973 and 1974, though there was a management impression that it did so towards the end of 1974. At that time, the only statement that could be made with assurance

TABLE 4   Direct Inside Production and Maintenance Costs per Ton, 1974

	Autonomous	Nonautonomous A	Nonautonomous B
First quarter[a]	$1.58	$ .84	$1.56
Second quarter	1.40	1.12	1.73
Third quarter	1.24	1.05	1.38
Fourth quarter	1.13	3.56	1.41

[a]First quarter figures on all sections exclude January. Costs not calculated by sections until February 1974.

was that production had not decreased as a consequence of the program's introduction, nor as a cost of improving the safety level. It is a currently accepted belief in the coal industry that one of these goals—production or safety—must be sacrificed for the other.

The research team previously presented a field theoretical analysis of the social and technical forces that facilitated or inhibited productivity in the autonomous section. This analysis suggested that productivity in the autonomous section was inhibited for several months because members of the section were concerned that the experiment might end before completion of the one-year trial period. They had to deal with the hostilities of middle management, the derision of several members of other sections who saw in the new way of working a questioning of the value of their experience and skill (the epithet most frequently hurled in a sarcastic tone to autonomous section members was "Hey, superminer") and, finally and perhaps most importantly, they had to deal with the internal doubt and anxiety that are associated with being the sole carriers of an innovation.

The creation of the second autonomous section (B) reduced the strength of these inhibiting forces. During the last quarter of 1974 and the first nine months of 1975, Autonomous A was the highest producer among the four operating sections. With the exception of the months of March and April, the newly created Autonomous B was the second highest producer in the first nine months of 1975. Autonomous B may have performed so well because it did not have to carry the burden of innovation as did the first autonomous section, with all the inhibiting forces this created for it. The second section could mobilize its energies immediately toward improving production and safety. Autonomous B began operations with fewer experienced men than did Autonomous A. Virtually all the members of Autonomous A were very experienced miners. Autonomous B had a "core" of experienced miners doing face work, support work being done by men with very little mining experience. The inexperienced miners were thus deployed in a manner to minimize any negative effect they might have had on production and yet to provide them with a very effective means to learn about face work. They substituted for face workers who were absent and supplemented at the face when they could be helpful. The research team and several members of management noted that members of the second autonomous section seemed to adapt more rapidly than the first section to the new way of working, e.g., switching jobs, helping each other, etc. Section productivity is compared in Table 5.

The critical period for comparing production between sections begins in December 1974 after the month-long national strike and after state mine officials required all four sections in the mine to adopt a more complicated and time-consuming timbering plan following the fatality in Nonautonomous A the previous September. The change contributes to the overall lower production totals in 1975 as compared to 1974.

Another factor that may have contributed to lower 1975 totals, although its effect probably began some time in 1974, was the systematic effort by management to reduce "ghost coal." Ghost coal is the difference between the amount of coal that is measured on the surface coal pile compared with that recorded in the foremen's daily records (it has been as high as 20 to 25 percent of total production). The system of monitoring and rewarding (or criticizing) performance by foreman rather than by section encourages ghost coal, as the foremen stand a good chance of appearing to produce more than they actually do with a low probability of the discrepancy being traced directly to them (it can generally be traced to the section). One by-product of the experiment has been more accurate measurement of tonnage through more frequent visits by surveyors who measure cubic feet of coal extracted to cross-check foreman reports. Management reported an overall decrease in ghost coal after 1973. More than once, Autonomous A has been "right on the nose" in their monthly tonnage

TABLE 5   Tons of Clean Coal Produced per Day

	Autonomous A	Nonautonomous A	Nonautonomous B	Autonomous B
1974	756.3	805.8	562.2	449.3
1975	701.2	618.5	619.4	650.4
Critical period (Dec. 1974– Sept. 1975)	738.0	591.0	612.0	651.0

figures, while other sections have not. Efforts to persuade management to emphasize section performance were only partially successful before 1976 but, until then, foreman performance received more emphasis on the two non-autonomous sections than on the two autonomous ones. Such organizational practices may have worked to the disadvantage of the autonomous sections in productivity comparisons between 1973 and 1975.

Corrected for days in which sections (all three shifts) spent the entire day in the classroom, Autonomous A produced 25 percent more coal than Non-autonomous A (738 tons per day vs. 591 tons per day) and 21 percent more coal than Nonautonomous B (738 tons per day vs. 612 tons per day). Autonomous B was the second-highest producer in the mine (651 tons per day) during the same time period, December 1974 to September 1975. In spite of the constraints imposed on all four sections by the introduction of a more difficult (and safer) timbering plan, Autonomous A was much more able to maintain its former productivity level than was Nonautonomous A. Autonomous A's production dropped 2.4 percent after introduction of the new timbering plan compared with a drop of 26.6 percent on Nonautonomous A (see special case for Nonautonomous B in next paragraph). Trist et al. (1963) and Herbst (1962) offer evidence that autonomous work groups can adapt more readily to the introduction of such task constraints and to "disturbances" in general through their superior capability to deploy flexibly their human and technical resources.

It is difficult to dismiss these results as solely an artifact of changing physical conditions, for Autonomous A produced more coal each and every month for 10 months, during which all phases of mining should have been "evened out" between sections. More particularly, this would be the case between Autonomous A and Nonautonomous A (some minor correction for seam height may be required) than between the former and Nonautonomous B, although conditions on the latter were considerably better during the 10 months under consideration than they were in 1974. Furthermore, Nonautonomous A had four ram cars vs. Autonomous A's two shuttle cars (in order to run three ram cars, one of the mechanics or general underground crew members filled in as an "unofficial" seventh face-crew member; the fourth ram car functioned as a backup resource to minimize delay time); Nonautonomous A had five full-time mechanics vs. three mechanics on Autonomous A. Additionally, there were six belts between the surface and Autonomous A's face belt compared to three belts for Nonautonomous A. While the former was directly responsible for only the two belts closest to the face, there were still six potential sources of delay compared to three such sources on Nonautonomous A. One would reasonably expect Nonautonomous A to produce more coal than Autonomous A, considering all of the former's resource advantages. This would not be so in comparing Autonomous A to Nonautonomous B, which was prevented from doing any pillaring work (a considerably more productive phase of mining) because of bad physical conditions and because of restrictions imposed by federal and state safety laws.

Most members of management considered Nonautonomous A as the section against which to test the merits of the innovation. Progress on Autonomous A could hardly be mentioned without someone comparing its production to that of Nonautonomous A. One foreman on Nonautonomous A considered the introduction of the experimental section to be "throwing down the gauntlet," saying, "I'll be damned if I'll let [Autonomous A] beat us!"

The 10 month pattern ended one month after the local union voted in August 1975 to reject the document the steering committee had developed. By the end of September, three men had bid out of Autonomous A and several others on both autonomous sections were attempting to do the same. This was due to uncertainty over whether support men and shuttle-car operators on the two autonomous sections would return permanently to contract pay rates (they were paid contract rates from August 25 to September 29, when postvote initiatives went into effect). Several support men and several shuttle-car operators (mostly on Autonomous A) were now qualified by training to perform jobs paying top rates but their contract job classification pay rate was lower than what they had been earning in the autonomous sections. The performance of Autonomous A, hampered by a partially reconstituted membership and by difficult physical conditions, became progressively poorer. In December, it was the lowest producer among the four operating sections. The decreased productivity among members of both autonomous sections, but in particular Autonomous A, can be partly explained as a reconfiguration of field forces, a weakening of facilitating forces and strengthening of inhibiting ones. However, this does not convey the shattering of morale and the depth of disappointment expressed to the research team by members of the autonomous section following the negative August vote.

ATTITUDES

The evaluation team interviewed all the men working at the mine in December 1973, and again in June and October 1974. Preliminary data from the experimental section suggest that the following changes had taken place. The men
- perceived themselves as making more decisions concerning how the work is divided, what they should do, and how to do it;
- recognized the interdependence they had with each other and believed that their coworkers had many good ideas to contribute to improved performance:
- saw their supervisors as making fewer decisions affecting how they should perform their work.

In September 1974, members of the experimental section had a private meeting with officers of the international and district unions. The latter reported what they had been told to a meeting of the steering committee. The men had said they felt themselves respected by management as never before. They no longer felt tired when they got home from work. There was no longer the same stress, as the bosses were off their backs. They did not quarrel as much and did not leave things in a mess for the next shift.

Representatives of the section reported these attitudes publicly when they were on the same panel with management at conferences on work quality at Cleveland, Ohio, Buffalo, New York; and Washington, DC. The effects on audiences of some 100 people (managers, trade union officials from many industries and key staff from federal and state agencies) were very great.

Extending Autonomy to the Mine as a Whole: April to August 1975

The steering committee was pleased with the results reported above and was interested in expanding the experiment to the mine as a whole. Initial plans were for a different area of the mine to begin an orientation and training period every three months until all areas worked under autonomous conditions. However, the local union, realizing that the initial experimental year was drawing to a close, passed a motion at its March meeting calling for the entire mine to become autonomous at once or to drop the program completely. A number of union members considered it unacceptable for some areas of the mine to receive the program's benefits and privileges while others did not. Conversations with union members suggested that the vote did not so much reflect an understanding of the concept of autonomous working and a desire to try it as an attempt to reestablish equity within the mine, one way or the other. The company president was unwilling to accept the "at once" proposal, as he did not believe he had the management and training resources to carry out such massive change instantly. However, he was willing to discuss new alternatives with the union members of the steering committee. The steering committee, as a whole, subsequently decided that the proper way to proceed was to write a new document in which provisions would be developed for implementing autonomy in all areas of the mine. The local union accepted this procedure at its May meeting on the condition that the document be submitted to a union vote no later than the end of the summer vacation period in early August.

Although the steering committee would actually write the document in conjunction with the research team, procedures were planned for consultation with all members of the work force. Consequently, two rounds of three-hour meetings were held in May and June, each consisting of some 30 to 40 workers drawn from each area of the mine (four face sections, general underground, maintenance, surface, and preparation plant). At these meetings, members of management and the research team were present. Suggestions were offered by the workers and most were incorporated into the document. As the document neared completion, at the suggestion of the steering committee management agreed to allow the union members of the steering committee to meet alone on company time with each of the areas of the mine. The men had been somewhat inhibited in the presence of management and the research team. Such meetings took place during July and early August. During this time, district and international representatives of the UMWA attended meetings of the steering committee and contributed provisions to the document. Such representatives also attended a local union meeting in August and endorsed the principles of autonomous working. In mid-August, the document was placed before the local union membership for vote by secret ballot. The document failed to pass by a vote of 79 to 75. There was enormous confusion about the meeting as regards time and need for attendance. But the union would not hold a second ballot.

REASONS FOR A NEGATIVE UNION VOTE

Traditionally, a no-vote could be taken as a signal of the end of the experiment; that is, the no-vote was the outcome. However, in the view of the research team the vote was an event embedded in a process that could still be influenced, if the event itself were properly understood in terms of what yes-votes or no-votes meant to those who cast them. The steering committee, believing that the concept of autonomous working was too attractive to abandon easily and encouraged by the initial results, met during September and October to analyze the reasons why the vote went the way it did. After thorough discussions among themselves and with a large number of individuals in the work force, the steering committee found the following reasons for many of the no-votes cast. They can be grouped into four basic categories.

PERCEIVED INEQUITIES

The document upon which the union members voted provided that all who wished to participate in the program could earn the top rate within their respective areas of the mine for 90 man-production days (about four months). At the end of this period, a qualification committee made up of various management personnel would determine whether an individual had satisfactorily learned the job or jobs that the document had outlined for earning the top rate. (The union did not wish to participate in these assessments. If it had, the members of the mine committee would be placed in a "double bind," as they might have to present a grievance on behalf of a worker who was dissatisfied with a decision concerning his qualifications for a bidded job.) Several members perceived these provisions as inequitable because some members of the experimental groups received higher than contract rates for their job classifications for an entire year without having to demonstrate qualifications to a committee. Additionally, the prospect of taking any kind of test was threatening to some of the older workers and perceived as "undignifying" to many who felt that working in the mines for 20 to 40 years in some cases was qualification enough. The steering committee members stated in several of the communication meetings held before the vote that 90 percent of the men were already judged by a joint management-research team survey to be qualified for the jobs in question as based on observation over several years and that no tests were required of them. Of the remainder, most were expected to pass within the training period; a very few would be safety risks—this was public knowledge. The qualification provisions were to be applied mainly to new workers hired in the future. This point was not widely understood in spite of several efforts to clarify it. Feelings of inequity and of threat were too powerful for it to be heard.

A second issue arose among surface workers who disliked the document's provisions that excluded them from trading jobs with workers in the preparation plant. One of the jobs in the preparation plant paid a higher pay rate than any jobs that could be learned within the surface area.

A third source of perceived inequity demonstrates all too well that a planned intervention into a social process may produce unintended consequences. When the steering committee approved of the idea to start the fourth operating section as an autonomous one, it saw no reason at that time to discontinue the policy of paying all who volunteered to work on an autonomous section the top rate for face work. This was believed to be justified because all members of the first autonomous section were requested to perform or to learn to perform all of the jobs on the section, some of which normally paid the top rate. The common top rate for all would weaken the present "one man/one job" thinking that was prevalent and strengthen each member's identity with the primary task of the group as a whole. It was anticipated that senior, well-experienced miners would be the ones to bid into the new autonomous section, as had been the case with the first section.

In the event, only a limited number of the senior and experienced miners bid into the new section, because they had already established personal relationships in their present crews with their buddies and/or their foremen and didn't wish to sacrifice this for the uncertainties of working with new men and a new foreman under unfamiliar conditions. This was especially so on the section that had developed a tight in-group mentality through having had to face prolonged bad conditions. Two of the three foremen chose to go to the new autonomous section, partly to escape the bad physical conditions on the old section. Though abandoned, their crew members (with more years of mining experience than the mine average) stayed where they were. Several of the men on the third crew had signed the bid sheet to go to the new section but withdrew their names when they heard that their foreman would refuse to go with them. The unanticipated result was that many jobs on the new section were filled by apprentices with little more than 90 days of mining experience, who otherwise would have been outbid by more senior, qualified men. The inequity created by "green" miners receiving higher pay than some men with many years of experience outraged the sense of distributive justice of, perhaps, the majority of those outside the two autonomous sections, especially those on the other two face sections.

CHANGES IN THE NATIONAL CONTRACT

The national contract negotiated in late 1974 between the UMWA and the Bituminous Coal Operators Association (BCOA) altered the distribution of pay grades among underground face workers. In contrast to the 1971 contract in effect when the experiment began, roof bolters and miner helpers as well as miner operators and mechanics were now to receive the top rate paid for underground face working ($55.00 per day in the first year of a three-year contract). This contract change shifted the distribution of those men who would now earn the top rate according to their present job classification regardless of whether they participated in the autonomous program or not. Of the 54 workers in the two autonomous sections, 30 men now earned the top rate, that is, 56 percent of the workers on the two sections. On the other two sections with only 21 workers in each of the two sections (in the conventional manning pattern they did not have their own support men), 30 out of a total of 42 also earned the top rate, that is, 71 percent of the workers on these two sections. It is believed that this distribution shift influenced the August vote as some of the workers (particularly those in the two nonautonomous sections where no firsthand knowledge of the program existed) felt they had nothing to gain by voting "yes." More workers were now in a position of consolidating gains made through the national contract, and some expressed hostility toward those who could earn more money without having to "do it the hard way."

"UNION BUSTING" FEARS

Quite a number of union members, including some of the most influential older workers, expressed the view that the autonomous experiment was a plot to break the local union. Despite the fact that most of the workers knew that the experiment in autonomous working was jointly initiated by the union and management and that several international and district officers had endorsed the program, historical factors undoubtedly contributed to the fears expressed. First, the mine is located in a region of central Pennsylvania where the percentage of unionized mines is low and where several local coal managements were known to have attempted to blunt union organizing efforts by paying wages above the contract level. Credence was added to the belief that the experiment was an antiunion tactic by the fact that the program permitted some of the workers to earn higher pay than was provided by the national contract.

A second factor was that the current company president had bitterly opposed the successful union organizing effort that had taken place at the mine nearly a decade earlier. Many of the older miners had taken part in the organizing effort and had little faith that the company president had altered his position on unions. This was the case despite the fact that the president had publicly stated on repeated occasions that he now accepted the legitimacy of unions—otherwise he would not have accepted a joint labor-management committee—and that he did not oppose and, in fact, encouraged a union organizing effort at a new mine that he owned. Also, he no longer owned the mine under discussion, having sold it to a large public utility that had a good reputation for industrial relations.

A third factor was the knowledge among some workers that a mine in West Virginia had considered undertaking the same experiment as Rushton but had voted not to do so. It was widely explained that the vote at that mine had nothing to do with evaluation of the merits of autonomous work, but suspicions were aroused among many. Considering these circumstances, it is indeed difficult for members of a small local union at a relatively small mine in a relatively isolated region to carry such a burden of innovation by itself.

RESENTMENT AROUSED BY PRIVILEGES ENJOYED BY AUTONOMOUS SECTION MEMBERS

The proper unit of analysis in any effort at organizational change ought to contain those subunits that are either socially or technically affected by the change effort, in this case, the mine as a whole. The tactical considerations for beginning the experiment in one and subsequently two sections of the mine have already been discussed. Whether or not these tactics were the most feasible at the time can be debated. The research team believed that they were; the likelihood that the privileges enjoyed by the autonomous section members would be resented by members of other sections was anticipated, but not the strength or pervasiveness of these feelings.

Apart from the fact that all members of the autonomous sections were on the top rate, feelings of envy were aggravated by some of the following events or practices:

Members of nonautonomous sections greatly resented the absence of members of one or the other autonomous section on Sunday midnight shifts. The latter, when scheduled for Sunday midnight work, stayed home from work until Monday mornings to attend day-long section conferences.

Trips taken by autonomous section members to appear on panels at several conferences were resented.

Some members of the autonomous sections displayed elitist attitudes toward other workers in the mine due to the additional technical training the experiment had offered them.

Foremen and members of the nonautonomous sections resented the additional manpower resources provided to the autonomous sections in the form of two additional support men per shift. Each of the other two sections had two support men on the day shift only, but additional personnel were available to them on request as they were needed.

Resentment over the latter was exacerbated when management made comparisons between sections on productivity, accidents, violations, etc. Such comparisons were judged as unfair by nonautonomous section members, because they had less control over their manpower and fewer training opportunities.

Expression of sentiments over matters such as these was given wide circulation by some foremen on the nonautonomous sections and certain members of middle management who, before the vote, campaigned against extending autonomous working to other areas of the mine.

Initiatives After the Postvote Analysis: September to December 1975

The president of the company felt sufficient commitment to the values supporting greater decision-making opportunities for workers as well as sufficient encouragement from the initial results to make provisions for going ahead, subject to any limitations arising as a consequence of the negative union vote. He considered it a management prerogative to train his own managers in a style compatible with allowing workers greater participation in decision making. The 1974 national contract had already obligated management to provide more training to workers than any previous contract had required. However, the president did not perceive this obligation as a "concession" to the union but considered training as the most effective means to increase both productivity and safety. There were also no provisions in the contract prohibiting management from paying workers above the contract pay rate for any job classification, provided that the means for doing so did not discriminate against anyone who currently held that job classification.

As a result of the negative vote and the subsequent analysis by the steering committee that took the president's views into account, the initial experiment was declared terminated. The steering committee was abolished as the primary function mandated to it by the original document of October 1973 was to monitor and evaluate the original experiment. However, before taking such action, the steering committee sought guidance from the 1974 national contract to see if it provided for the legitimate existence of a forum within which both labor and management could discuss matters of mutual interest. One particular section of the contract provides that "Appropriate local and district officers of the union (including the Mine Health and Safety Committee) shall have the opportunity to review each training program and make comments and suggestions prior to its implementation." Accordingly, the union officers and management agreed to create a training and development committee to guide the training efforts to be undertaken within the mine.

The president of the company agreed to accept the principle of equity affirmed by the local union officers that members of all other areas of the mine be given the same provisions for training and the same time period for qualification as offered to the original two autonomous sections, that is, the top rate within their respective areas of the mine without having to take any qualification tests for a period of one year. The president accepted this principle for reestablishing equity among areas of the mine, but on the condition that all who receive these benefits should demonstrate good faith by making an effort to learn new jobs (by switching jobs, etc.) within the next 60 working days, and that the provision not apply to anyone who started working at the mine after October 1975, unless he qualified for top-rate pay by previous experience and qualification. All new, inexperienced "hires" would have to be qualified by management after learning one of the jobs already paying the top rate or by learning a combination of jobs deemed deserving of top-rate pay.

The decision was made to begin orientation and training periods immediately for all areas of the mine. Instead of the "massed" six-session training period provided to the original autonomous sections, the six remaining areas of the mine would rotate their classroom sessions between them (one session per area every six weeks). Plans also were made to begin a six-session management training program in January 1976 that would include management personnel from every level and area of the mine. Each session would be for the entire day on alternate Saturdays.

By December 1975, sentiments and beliefs had changed sufficiently for the local union to vote to allow its officers to sit down again with management and develop a new document which would be submitted to the membership for a vote. New proposals were developed to deal with the imbalance that had emerged after the introduction of the second autonomous section. It was no longer considered appropriate, however, to develop a comprehensive document for minewide autonomy, as had been done in response to the local union's "all or nothing" resolution. A comprehensive document offering a complete program was too complex and confusing for those who did not participate in writing it. This, no doubt, contributed to misunderstandings concerning specific provisions of the rejected document. It appeared that there was more merit in presenting proposals for innovation serially. Before any votes could take place, however, the union president was voted out of office by a candidate who opposed any further discussion with management about revival of the program. The research team stopped visiting the mine shortly after this but stayed in touch with some union members and managers on a periodic basis.

Rushton Revisited: April 1989

The first author invited seven participants in the original experiment to a luncheon meeting in April 1989. Three of the men had recently retired. Three of the remaining four held management positions. These men could provide information on developments at the mine over the past twelve years and offer clues to any lasting effects the experiment had on mine management and on the miners who worked in the autonomous sections. They also could provide explanations for any decline of autonomous practices over the intervening years.

The opportunities for learning provided to members of the autonomous sections had produced a "flowering" of talent and initiative. Among the members of the two autonomous sections, four became foremen and a fifth became a shift foreman. Four became local union officers; one became the president and the other three became members of the Health and Safety Committee. One of the original foremen is now the safety director, and another is a shift foreman.

These men continued their autonomous practices long after the experiment ended and had tried to influence newcomers to work in a similar way. They believed that everyone who participated in the experiment retained a favorable view of it. One man recalled that foremen did not have to tell members of an autonomous section what to do and that many knew more about mining practices and state and federal mining regulations than the foremen did. Another man said that his crew continued to work autonomously as long as it remained intact. He found it difficult to explain to replacement workers what autonomous work meant but had tried to demonstrate it by example.

The mining industry has been in a recession since oil prices declined dramatically in the early 1980s. As a result, several mines in the area have closed and total employment has shrunk. Rushton remains open even though the public utility that owns it has closed several other mines. Rushton has survived because of its relative efficiency. Its future remains uncertain, however, because underground coal costs more than twice as much to mine as strip mine coal. A sizable percentage of the coal that Rushton ships each month to electric generating stations is "pass-through" coal that Rushton purchases from local strip mines. Nevertheless, Rushton's owners recently invested in modernizing its mining equipment and have plans for opening two new working sections.

Rushton now employs 210 people compared to 250 in the mid-1970s. Many of the middle-aged miners who were at Rushton in the mid-1970s have since retired. Most of the replacements have been drawn from the mines closed by Rushton's owners. By contractual agreement, these workers were given hiring priority at Rushton. These mines were geographically close to the steel industry, which has a strong craft orientation and identity with specific job classifications. Newcomers with this orientation resisted multiskilled work and job rotation.

The men at the luncheon credited the autonomous program for contributing to the exceptionally favorable labor relations climate at Rushton. The union leadership is more stable now than it was in the mid-1970s. The grievance procedure is followed consistently. No wildcat strikes have occurred at the mine for several years. Some people had feared that Rushton's good labor relations would deteriorate with the influx of workers from mines with labor relations that were poorer but more typical for the industry. Apparently the opposite occurred. The men reported that Rushton's good climate "rubbed off" on the new workers. They also reported that these newcomers had heard before they were hired that there was "something special about Rushton as a place to work."

Senior mine management has changed considerably in the last 12 years. The men at the luncheon viewed the new mine manager as more participative and more cooperative. One man said he was "one hundred percent behind safety." Unlike his predecessor, the new mine manager meets weekly with all of his key subordinates and monthly with the chairmen of the union's Mine and Health and Safety Committees. The men thought that the mine manager would support a new autonomous work program if he were approached about it. However, they viewed his immediate subordinate, the mine superintendent, as "more hard-line" and "quicker to react." Senior management also included former section and shift foremen who had opposed the program in 1975.

The mining technology at Rushton has changed dramatically since the mid-1970s. Three of the sections use rip head miners, which are much more productive than those used previously. A new type of lighting equipment on the miners makes the section "as bright as an office." A working face can be advanced by 30 feet before bolting is required. By agreement between the government, union and management, temporary support timber no longer has to be set. Twin boom bolters can drill two holes and place two bolts simultaneously. As a result, approximately 1,000 tons of coal per shift can be mined, much more than the productivity of the 1970s. By contrast, the support work required outside the immediate work face remains fairly labor intensive and slow, i.e., laying track and wire, building brattices, etc. As a consequence, it is very difficult for support work to keep up with the rapid extraction of coal. As the mine currently is not permitted to remove pillars, there is no temporary halt in advance work that would permit support crews to catch up.

At the time of our experiment the national average for coal production was 350 to 400 tons per day. In Rushton, that for the poorest nonautonomous section was over 500, suggesting that Rushton was among the better producing mines. Autonomous A averaged over 700 tons. This suggests that the discrepancy between what the more powerful continuous miner and the rest of the system can do is even greater in 1990 than in the mid-1970s. Productivity is still thought of in terms of the machine rather than the system of which it is a part.

Rushton still has four operating sections, but now two additional "reserve" sections with mining equipment in them are used when one of the four regular sections breaks down. The face crews move to a reserve section while equipment in their regular section is being repaired. One consequence of this practice is that crew members have no sense of ownership in the reserve sections or in their regular sections. Cleanup and rock-dusting tends to be poor. It may be hazardous for crews to work in a section that another crew has worked in previously or that has been left unattended for some time.

The retreat from self-containment of skills within work groups is nearly complete. The section foreman's responsibilities now end at the feeder. A central support group is assigned all tasks beyond the feeder, e.g., move power, lay track, wire, etc. It appears, however, that the support group is overwhelmed by more work than it can handle. The differential rate of productivity growth for coal extraction versus support work has been cited already. The new system for directing air to and from the sections has doubled the number of brattices that must be built for a given amount of coal extraction. Support personnel often are "borrowed" by section foremen who now only have one support person on their crews. The sections are supposed to get a substitute worker from the general crew to fill in for absentees, but this does not always happen. The support person on the second and third shifts builds brattices almost exclusively. Overtime work usually is required to maintain the pace of advances at the face.

Technological change and the retreat from self-containment and multiskilled work have shifted the burden of making manpower and resource deployment decisions from crew members and their section foreman to the shift foreman. Theoretically, the new technology and curtailment of the crew's territorial responsibility should lead to the transfer of workers from the face to support work. The men at the luncheon said that this might have happened if the crew members were still multiskilled. Only a marginal reduction has occurred, however, because most face crew members are not willing to perform tasks that fall outside their regular job classifications. These men also thought that moving crew members and foremen between reserve and regular sections diminished their familiarity with current conditions in either section and impaired their ability to make effective decisions.

These organizational arrangements explain why the men at the luncheon viewed Rushton as being "shorthanded" in spite of substantial increases in productivity and why senior management believes that those currently working cannot be spared for more than the minimum of eight hours of training per year required by the BCOA/UMWA contract. The lack of training contributed to the deterioration of the system of paying top rate to any miner who learned all jobs at the face. This provision remained in place until the mid-1980s, but was dropped after many miners who had qualified for the top rate refused to switch jobs with others. The men at the luncheon said that those miners "just saw it as an easy way to the high rate." The minimum time in the classroom precluded any opportunity to sanction the values or practices of multiskilled work.

Compensation both for workers and managers has improved considerably over the past 12 years. For example, the average miner is paid $128 per day under the current BCOA/UMWA contract or approximately $35,000 per year if overtime pay is included. The basis for calculating bonuses for managers, however, impairs cross-shift cooperation. The bonuses, which can exceed $4,000 per year, are calculated on the basis of productivity per shift (with a penalty for citations and accidents). This practice strongly reinforces the shift mentality that the research team tried hard to discourage during the experiment.

Reflections

Twelve years is more than adequate time to acquire perspective on the Rushton experiment and to understand better why it failed to serve as a model for diffusion to the mine as a whole. Some of the reasons were related to major contextual changes in the mining industry in the mid-1970s. Other reasons were related to the actions of the research team, either resulting from its own judgment or from acquiescing to conditions set by the agencies that funded the experiment.

The contextual factors that made the Rushton experiment possible in the first place began to deteriorate soon after the experiment began. Support at the national level from the UMWA became virtually nonexistent after Arnold Miller was politically weakened following negotiation of the 1974 national contract. This contract was initially rejected by the UMWA International Board, but eventually ratified narrowly by the union membership. The extreme bimodality in the age distribution of union members in the mid-1970s contributed to the narrow ratification. Older workers wanted better retirement provisions, and younger workers wanted larger pay increases. The contract satisfied neither.

The union membership had been enfranchised only recently to ratify the contracts that its officers negotiated. This, perhaps, contributed to rising expectations among union workers and to testing their new political strength. Wildcat strikes increased in frequency every year throughout the 1970s, reaching a peak during negotiation of the 1979 contract. The unsettled state of labor relations in the industry was reflected in relations between Rushton management and workers during and following the experiment. Several wildcat strikes occurred immediately after the vote, ostensibly on issues that were unrelated to the experiment. This may have been an unconscious way of reestablishing union solidarity that had eroded seriously during the experiment.

Other contextual changes affected support for the experiment. For example, Warren Hinks and a partner had held a substantial equity position in Rushton when the experiment began. They sold their interest shortly afterward to the large public utility that owned the remaining interest. Rushton management at all levels was uncertain about Hinks remaining president or the public utility becoming more directly involved in management of the mine. Although Hinks remained president until 1981, his role in daily decision making decreased, while that of the public utility increased. Those managers who supported Hinks' vision of autonomous work grew less confident of seeing it realized, while those who did not support it grew more confident that they could persist in managing as they wished without fear of disciplinary action.

The experimental paradigm set by the funding agencies as a condition for receipt of funds seriously hampered the research team's effectiveness and unleashed some of the dynamics that eventually led to the negative union vote. The experiment consisted of designating some sections of the mine as control groups to be compared to the experimental group on performance at the end of one year. The research team had reservations from the start about the scientific merits of using this method in this setting, believing that one part of a small mine with a highly interdependent work force could not be sealed off from the "contaminating effects" of another part. They permitted its use as a concession for funding, but underestimated the intensity of the social and psychological dynamics that would be released by its use. The envy, anger and rivalry generated between the autonomous sections and the rest of the mine soon overshadowed the search for a better way to work and a better future.

The research team unwittingly contributed to intensifying the negative feelings generated between parts of the mine when it supported the initiation of the second autonomous section. The rationale for support was to avoid the encapsulation and rejection process that often accompanies small demonstration projects undertaken within a larger organization. An unanticipated consequence of the initiation of the second autonomous section was that many relatively inexperienced miners were able to earn the top pay rate very quickly. The disturbance of distributive justice made a difficult situation worse and virtually eliminated any chance that the union membership would vote to continue the autonomous experiment.

Discussions at the luncheon meeting in April 1989 suggested that a much more favorable labor-movement climate exists today at Rushton than existed in the mid-1970s. The current union and management leadership deserves part of the credit, but the improvement also reflects a maturing of labor relations within the industry as a whole. The climate today appears much more favorable to the introduction of autonomous work than was the case earlier. It is a less radical innovation today than it was earlier. This favorable background would allow union and management some margin for error as they explored innovative work practices and tried to implement them. The Rushton experiment offers many lessons for those undertaking such an innovation today. Among these lessons are that active roles must be created for all stakeholders in future forms of work. The roles of participant, evaluator, observer and sanctioner of an experiment may be played by the same or different persons as the experiment evolves. No person need be confined to playing only one role if everyone in the organization is encouraged to experiment and learn continuously.

Postscript

The public utility that owns Rushton announced in January 1991 that the mine would close the following June and that two of its other mines would close in 1992. The company said that Rushton's remaining two million tons were too expensive to mine. The men who came to lunch in 1989 had been hearing for 10 years that the mine might close if productivity did not improve, but they had somehow hoped this might not happen. As reported earlier, productivity had increased four-fold over the previous 12 years, while pay rates had increased two-and-a-half times. Although any single-factor measure of productivity should be viewed cautiously, these numbers indicate that productivity per payroll dollar had improved significantly during these years. This improvement apparently was not sufficient for Rushton to remain economically viable to its owner.

It is tempting to speculate what might have occurred had the experiment in autonomous working survived and spread throughout the mine. The improvement in performance during the critical period might have been maintained and even amplified with the introduction of new technology into the mine. If so, Rushton's current economic outlook might have been different. Two hundred and fifty employees might have been able to work for another three to five years and the closing of Rushton, although inevitable, might have proceeded with more time to plan for the retraining and job placement of its employees.

References

Alexander, C. 1964. *Notes on the Synthesis of Form*. Cambridge, Mass.: Harvard University Press.

Cassidy, S.M. (Editor). 1973. *Elements of Practical Coal Mining*. New York: American Institute of Mining, Metallurgical and Petroleum Engineers.

Faltenmayer, E. 1974. "It's Back to the Pits for Coal's Future." *Fortune*, 89:137–39; 244–52.

Goodman, P.S. 1979. *Assessing Organizational Change: The Rushton Quality of Work Experiment*. New York: John Wiley.

Herbst, P.G. 1962. *Autonomous Group Functioning: An Exploration in Behaviour Theory and Measurement*. London: Tavistock Publications.

Trist, E.L., G.W. Higgin, H. Murray and A.B. Pollock. 1963. *Organizational Choice: Capabilities of Groups at the Coal Face Under Changing Technologies: The Loss, Rediscovery and Transformation of a Work Tradition*. London: Tavistock Publications. Reissued 1987, New York: Garland. Chapters 13, 14 revised, Vol. II, "Alternative Work Organizations: An Exact Comparison," pp. 84–105. Chapters 19–22, Vol. I, "The Assumption of Ordinariness as a Denial Mechanism: Innovation and Conflict in a Coal Mine," pp. 476–93.

Eric Trist and Charles Dwyer

The Limits of Laissez-Faire as a Socio-Technical Change Strategy[1]

Over a period of 10 years, from the late 1960s to the late 1970s, some 70 projects aiming to improve the quality of working life (QWL) involving the use of semiautonomous work groups were carried out in several locations of a diversified manufacturing concern of considerable size.[2] By the time the recession of the mid-1970s was over, almost all these projects had faded out. It was widely assumed in the corporation that the recession itself was the main cause of the fade-out; work groups had been dismembered beyond remedy by bumping and layoffs. One or two executives in central personnel were not so sure that the explanation was that simple and asked us to conduct an independent inquiry into what had happened. They felt the findings might help them to determine what policies might best fit the needs of the 1980s or even beyond.

We were given access to the extensive documentation that existed in the company concerning these projects. We paid field visits to the seven locations involved where, in addition to work observation, we carried out an interview survey and held group discussions with senior plant managers, general foremen, foremen and workers on the background of a comprehensive questionnaire. Between 600 and 700 workers had participated in the projects, some of which were large, that had taken place at these locations. As a result of the visits, during which we interviewed 100 employees evenly split between management (including supervision) and the work force, we compiled analytical reports on each site, which we checked out with those concerned on a subsequent visit. At this time only two of the projects were still active and, soon afterward, one of these was terminated. The only remaining active project was different from the rest in that it was a greenfield site, a small quasi-independent operation designed from the beginning on socio-technical princi-

[1]A modified and shortened version of Chapter 8 in *The Innovative Organization: Productivity Programs in Action,* edited by R. Zager and M. Rosow. New York and Oxford: Pergamon, 1982.

[2]In this extensive project the assistance is acknowledged of Joseph McCann and John Selsky, then Ph.D. students at the Wharton School, University of Pennsylvania, and Dr. Bob Drehr, then of Drexel University.

ples. The projects that faded out all represented attempts to introduce work groups piecemeal into existing work establishments.

Several levels of skill, including white-collar as well as blue-collar personnel, were involved throughout the work group projects. In almost all cases, some improvement took place, even if slight. In a number of cases the degree of improvement was considerable, in a few substantial. Usually, work group projects were initiated in their own areas by interested line managers in order to obtain better results in situations which had sometimes become critical. These managers had learned something about the promising results obtained in many industries with forms of job enrichment involving semiautonomous work groups. They wanted to find out if they, too, could secure improvements. They made full use of central personnel as internal consultants. By and large, the efforts they made, though thoroughgoing, were individual efforts. There was little active support at the plant manager level or active interest on the part of senior management above plant level. Foremen varied in their reactions. Team members were usually positive.

The Locations Perspective

ISOLATED PROJECTS

The first semiautonomous work group emerged during 1967 in the engineering development group at *Location A,* whose manager gradually gave extended responsibility to a group of nine draftsmen who evolved into full-fledged designers. The experiment was successful. The groups persisted for four years until the manager left in 1971.

The development group project was concerned with transforming a group of draftsmen from detailers into designers. The manager believed that this was necessary to secure economies and increase productivity and, as far as possible, the capacities of the draftsmen. More than 90 percent of the assignments came to be handled by them, leaving the engineers free to concentrate on large projects and theoretical work. Occasionally, an individual would lack the creativity or was too inflexible fully to make the required change. Individual differences therefore had to be taken into account.

A change in management style to a more participatory mode was entailed, with the manager no longer acting as a "boss." The project began in the "job enrichment" tradition but transcended it in that there was the involvement of the entire group in unit activities and an explicit change in the nature of the managerial role toward a participatory mode. The change in job content was major and involved an altogether higher level of responsibility for group members, continuous learning about larger organizational issues, interpersonal relations and ways to improve the work group's performance. In one case, patents were filed for a design developed by the group. The union did not object to these projects and was viewed as informally cooperative.

The same concept was extended to a wire shop, a model shop and an optical shop where the program cut operating costs drastically and improved morale and productivity. The designers filed only two grievances on matters that were quickly corrected. Yet the project was allowed to lapse when the initiating manager departed in 1971.

The second project in 1969 also took place at Location A in a unit making a heavier type of equipment. It was initiated by the operations manager. A group of 12 skilled welders and fitters were given responsibility for the planning, scheduling and control functions necessary for their work. So great was their involvement that they attended a skills-improvement seminar (with their foreman) during a strike which took place soon after the team was formed. The experiment was judged "remarkably successful" by those concerned because it had changed the labor relations climate and saved 50 percent in overhead. Declining business caused the team to be disbanded in 1972. No attempt was made to restart it later.

The success of the welding team stimulated a wider development in 1971 in an area making a complex type of product at *Location B*. This occurred in a crisis situation in which the department was under threat of closure. The manager of manufacturing engineering was the initiator. Dramatic reductions were obtained in the time required to build complex products. In one case, while planned time was 1,600 hours, actual completion time had been more than 2,000 hours; this was now reduced to 1,300. In another, there was a 42 percent productivity gain. In still another, a 30 percent productivity gain was accompanied by a 33.3 percent reduction in quality rejects.

One project led to another and a works council was formed in 1973 to cover all 60 employees in the area. Despite these successes, groups were discontinued in 1974 when the initiating manager left. The effort at Location B was a more comprehensive endeavor than that attempted at Location A and is as impressive as anything then reported in the literature concerned with a complete but small complex operation. Yet it failed to impinge on plant or higher management.

The pattern revealed by these successful initial developments may be summarized as follows. The nature of the work was complex, the workers skilled and the union cooperative, or the objections of union officers were ignored by those involved. The initiator was an interested line manager, below the level of plant manager, who was in difficulties over his bottom line. He involved central personnel in a consultative role. The projects grew in scope but were limited to the area of the initiating manager. Though they persisted, with substantial economic success, for three or more years, they faded out when he left. In organizational pattern and value base, these sporadic efforts were alien to the prevailing managerial culture.

MULTIPLE PROJECTS

The second pattern to appear was that of multiple projects in one plant that developed intensively over a short time period and then faded. It began at Location A. Seven groups were introduced in processing between January and March 1972 by the manager formerly involved with the welding group. Three more groups were later added in other product areas.

These projects began to become "experiments" in a more self-conscious sense. Hard data on performance were sought, with before-and-after measures and control groups. There was a concentration on measurement. Central personnel was more prominent, though the initiation of projects by interested managers persisted. The workers tended to be less skilled. Various operations of a more routine kind began to be included.

This pattern "exploded" at *Location C,* where no fewer than 13 groups were introduced during 1972 and five more in early 1973. While almost all these efforts were modestly successful, they were short-lived.

The write-up concerning work groups at Location A had come to the attention of the personnel manager of Location C in mid-1971. He discussed it with a member of central personnel and the shop operations manager, who had become enthusiastic about the possibilities apparent in work groups and was beginning to implement them in his area. The personnel manager began a program of foreman training. The training consisted of role modeling in group relations skills. The shop operations manager attended the meetings, and general foremen seemed supportive and took part as group leaders in some of the off-site training. The plant manager remained neutral with respect to work group experiments. Many foremen felt that it was the shop operations manager's idea and that it was merely one more management gimmick that would terminate when the manager moved on. Numerous "management techniques" had been tried over the years and most had been perceived as failing—dying out within a few months.

The foremen who had been through the training were asked to volunteer to try work groups in their areas. Only four or five did so, but their groups were regarded as quite successful. Unable to obtain volunteers for more groups, the shop operations manager selected a number of foremen who were *told* to try the work group approach.

In due course, the shop operations manager was moved to another location, and the personnel staff turned their interests to other functions. The business climate worsened, causing layoffs and bumping as well as pressures for production and reinforcing supervisors in their desire to revert to older and more comfortable supervisory styles. The groups faded.

Yet the groups had been modestly successful during their 18 months of existence. Efficiency measures were available for 11 of the 12 groups started in 1972, and the results were positive for all except one: four represented increases of up to 4.9 percent; two up to 9.9 percent; and four over 10 percent. The negative result was 7.5 percent. Measurement periods were between six and 12 months.

The 1972 program was developed with enthusiasm, which was caught in a report by the personnel manager reflecting the excitement of those leading the endeavor. He and the shop operations manager had started thinking about work groups some three years earlier when they stood looking at the picket line, which formed religiously every day in spite of the inclement weather. They had wondered how they might motivate the employees to work that enthusiastically after the strike was over.

It is amazing that something that began so well should have ended so dismally. The interviews are retrospective and took place three years later. Yet vivid feelings were expressed and negative attitudes make a strong contrast with the positive picture in the personnel manager's earlier report.

There were widely divergent views among management as to what work groups were, their desirability and under what conditions, if any, they might be reinstituted. The most knowledgeable person remaining on site was the personnel manager. While he was still enthusiastic about the concept of work groups, he did not believe that it could be reintroduced successfully. There was inadequate management support, some of the foremen involved were opposed and there was fairly widespread employee disillusionment based on experience.

Knowledge about work groups was not widespread among management, but those who were concerned with the experiments expressed a cautious optimism. As one moved to the foreman level, the sense of having had a positive experience decreased, and the range of views widened. At one end were views such as "It was a game," "No one took it seriously" and "I already had a work group in operation and calling it a group didn't change anything." At the other end, there was at least one foreman who was enthusiastic, who supported the concept strongly in his own area and who believed that it was effective. There was also resentment expressed by some that the work groups were imposed by the shop operations manager and, as such, they were resisted or given only reluctant cooperation. One employee's comment reflects this perception—"All of a sudden we were a work group." The concern that imposition did take place was accompanied by a strong belief that the concept could not be successfully forced. There must be both a shared sense of the need for, and the desirability of, work groups along with a shared sense of ownership of them.

Several employees expressed the feeling that "it was not clear what was going on. Nobody would define what work groups meant." At best, the employees saw the work group concept as an opportunity to "treat people like people, to be honest and open with employees, to facilitate communications, to listen to what employees had to say, to keep them informed and to develop mutual respect."

By far the most intense responses came from a group of six women, all of whom had been members of work groups and most of whom were long term employees. Some indicated quite favorable experiences—"It worked for us"—and regretted the dissolution of the groups. For some, the dissolution was the consequence of their operation's moving overseas. For others there was the quite clear belief that the groups were allowed to fade out by the inaction of hostile or indifferent foremen or were simply abolished by the management when lines were reorganized.

Concerns were also expressed that the groups had a great deal more to do, including paperwork and much of the foreman's job, with no increase in pay, and that some members had to "carry" other employees who would not cooperate in group activities. In short, it would take a great deal of effort over an extended period of time to convince these employees of the desirability of reinstituting work groups. They said they would require unambiguous evidence that there was serious, significant and sustained support of the concept throughout the management ranks (particularly at the foreman level), a clearer concept of what a work group was supposed to be and do and a long term commitment to maintaining the groups through difficult times.

The employees compared present conditions with the plant atmosphere five years before when the first groups were started. They had found the atmosphere then very positive, supportive and pleasant. They indicated that in the past they looked forward to coming to work but now they hated to come to the plant each morning. They felt that the engineers were a particular source of difficulty, for example, "They tell you what to do whether it's right or not and you have to do it." "They are never on the line." "They take the credit while we do the work." "They look down on us and make us feel stupid." "Even though they are often wrong, we can't correct them." Similar points were made about management, for example, "They don't come out into the plant very often." "They have no faith in the workers." "They try to push off everything they can on us." "They don't give us any support, they don't care." "We are dumb people to them." "You can't talk to the managers."

The employees during the experiment were drawn from the surrounding area, which is a small city/rural environment. They were not hard-line unionists nor a group ideologically in conflict with management. However, compared to a period three years earlier, they saw themselves in a significantly less desirable work environment. Union officials had been briefed regarding the formation of several groups. Among the officials mentioned were the president of the local and the shop committee chairman. No objections appear to have been raised.

A manager who had recently come to the location and who had had extensive experience with work groups at Location A began to develop production measurement groups in his area of responsibility. These had many of the characteristics of the work groups. The strategy was to get them more naturally assimilated into the area.

Those interviewed reported attitudes typical of employees whose hopes have been raised only to be dashed. They showed acute sensitivity to any suspicion of management manipulation, while the management interviewees showed the strength of foreman resentment over coercion.

That there should be those willing to try again is testimony to the durability of the belief that there is something inherently worthwhile in work groups. Restarting in such an environment, however, is clearly more difficult than starting where such past experiences have not taken place.

The pattern of multiple experiments exploded with even greater intensity in *Location D,* where, between the spring of 1973 and the fall of 1974, 19 work-groups were introduced. For almost all of them, some degree of success was reported. Yet, as at Location C, they faded.

If their demise was linked to the recession, our interview material suggests that the negative character of the organizational context was also relevant. An organizational climate survey had been carried out to explore attitudes concerning work groups and greater employee participation in decision making. Most of the 21 general foremen and 71 foremen taking part were negative in varying degrees. No systematic attempt was made to deal with these attitudes.

The Location D effort was the most deliberately experimental of the programs. Sophisticated attention was given to research design despite rough operational conditions. Measures of results obtained were numerous and rigorous, putting an extra load on foremen. Control groups did not know that they were control groups, even when under the same foreman as experimental groups. There was no lifting of the pressure for production while the groups were finding their way and settling in.

A resident consultant from central personnel was much in evidence. He was there at the request of the plant manager who, like the other managers mentioned, was looking for new ways to improve performance in a situation that was no better than marginal from an economic point of view. He was familiar with what had happened at Locations A and C.

Location D was the first plant at which initial interest at the plant manager level was reported. With his sanction it was possible to conduct experiments in all areas of the plant. This showed that semiautonomous work groups could make improvements under a wide variety of technical conditions. The plant manager, however, did not continue to give the support he provided at the beginning. He was too preoccupied with the immediate economic problems of the plant. Sustaining the groups once they were established would have taken time he did not have. A lot of additional work was created for foremen through extra record keeping and training. The needs of the groups did not fit in with many traditional operating procedures and measurement practices. New problems of compensation began to emerge. The problem of coping with these wider issues was too great given the immediate operational pressures which worsened as the recession deepened. The projects, therefore, remained too much under the "ownership" of the consultant, despite his assiduous attempts to transfer this ownership to management.

After numerous interviews at all levels, it became evident that the primary process problems during group operation were found at their "boundary," to some extent with the group's links to upper and to lower levels, but primarily at the interfaces with support groups—maintenance, personnel, materials suppliers, work planners, instructors and timekeepers. Because these units did not take part in group goal-setting efforts, were not included in group meetings and were not evaluated along with the groups, they had little reason to respond in a timely manner to group needs. Group members were allowed to contact these units directly, but several respondents indicated that these support units sometimes continued to deal exclusively with the foreman rather than with group members.

Location D was the first nonunion plant in which work groups were tried. There is, however, little evidence that unions were serious obstacles to the formation of work groups at any of the unionized locations. There was a surprising amount of cooperation by the stewards directly involved, even when there were misgivings or outright objections by other union officers. Improved performance from group methods would help, they hoped, to keep jobs that were threatened.

Management preference on the sites studied was to proceed with a minimum of formality in order to avoid raising difficult issues with the bargaining unit. This was in keeping with the way in which projects arose in the areas of interested managers rather than through a plantwide effort which would bring the union committee as a whole into play. Nevertheless, the emergence of a works council at Location B represented a move in the direction of more formal labor/management cooperation in the areas of quality of working life and productivity.

Location E was a twin plant site where eight work groups were rather rapidly introduced during 1974 in the packaging areas. Each foreman had between 50 and 80 people under his control and the areas were considered "problematic." The packing area jobs were all entry-level positions, the work force was young and the employees had short service. There was a constant flow of workers, high turnover and constant bumping. The work load was dictated by the production rate of the rest of the line. The workers were expected to pack whatever was produced.

Entry areas of this kind, where the work is entirely unskilled and where exposure to disruption of all kinds is greatest, are not auspicious sites for work groups, especially in an inaugural phase. Management apparently had little idea of what it was getting into and had no strategy for assessing the conditions needed for success. There was some training of foremen in terms of role modeling and team building, but this was done in parallel with the setting up of the work groups rather than as a preparation for them. Group members were not offered training.

Groups were introduced on three shifts in the packing area in one plant and on two shifts of a similar area in the other. In one plant the majority of the first shift favored the group approach, but the union steward encouraged resistance. This was due to an antagonistic relationship he had with the shift foreman. When a new foreman was assigned to the packing area, a group approach was reintroduced at the initiative of the employees. Following a series of meetings, several work changes were initiated, and a trip was made to the other plant, which had what was considered to be a more organized packing area. Following a shutdown, there was a 50 percent turnover. This, together with a series of drug problems, brought the group approach activities on this shift to a halt.

Acceptance of the group approach was better on the second shift and enthusiastic on the third. Meetings were held for several months. However, the activities of these two groups also stopped after a shutdown and the high turnover (70 percent on the second shift) that followed.

In the other plant, work groups were introduced in January 1974 in the packing area on both shifts. During the initial period of two to three months, one team worked well. Better cooperation between incentive and day-work employees was noted. There was greater autonomy and participation; cooperation was in evidence in a new arrangement of the packing area. According to our interviews, however, these gains were short-lived. After start-up, the groups experienced a number of "personality clashes" as older and younger workers were brought together under the bidding system. Group activity faded under strict work-rule adherence when bumping brought an infusion of higher-seniority workers into established groups; nor was the piecerate system conducive to a more cooperative group model.

There was little reference to any training. The comments were that whatever was done was not very successful. The members themselves were seen as generally cooperative, especially in the beginning and on two of the shifts. One shift was considered very problematic: it was a young, antagonistic work force with poor work habits and a lot of absenteeism, and it was "very much into drugs." This latter group did begin to develop as a more disciplined, cohesive team after a foreman change. This was a promising result considering the poor quality of the group. However, by then layoffs, plant shutdown and turnover had decimated the original group.

Location E represents the most extreme case of the introduction of work groups in a negative organizational context, at an inauspicious moment. Management appears to have regarded the groups simply as tools to be "slotted in" wherever convenient—where they might help out with one or two immediate headaches. The work groups at this location were begun when the phase of multiple experiments had already passed its peak in the other locations and when the disruptive effects of the recession were already in evidence. Groups started under these circumstances at an inexperienced site had little chance of surviving.

Yet the groups themselves were promising, despite personality conflicts in two teams and poor timing for their introduction in another. The disrupting forces were largely external. Realization of this seemed to be the basis of the not altogether unhopeful attitudes of the respondents concerning restarting teams under more settled conditions.

This pattern of multiple projects, intensively developed at one site only to fade after some 18 months (even though moderately successful), suggested to us that the laissez-faire approach adopted contained a strategic error. There was no systematic organizational support, no preparedness for systemwide implications, no working through to an overall concept to which plant management as a whole could become committed. The failure to persist of these economically successful, intensive, multiple experiments represented to us the limits of laissez-faire as a change strategy.

A Training Framework

The projects so far described were initiated under conditions of strain as regards maintaining production at an economic level. In some cases, the economic situation was one of crisis. This was apart from the recession, which came later. It constituted a main reason for the initiating managers to try something new and for the workers to cooperate to preserve their jobs. But *Location F* was expanding in 1972 when work groups were started. The need was to take full advantage of a positive business opportunity. This also provided a situation which could encourage innovation.

What was done differently at Location F compared with other sites was to embark on a management training and development program before work-groups were introduced. This went considerably beyond the "role training" offered to foremen at Location A and elsewhere. Not only foremen and general foremen but management personnel above this level were included. In three years, no fewer than 150 members of staff went through a 13-week program (three hours a week) designed by an external consulting firm. The introduction of work groups was not delayed until all 150 staff members had completed the program.

The aim was to change managerial style toward a more open and participatory mode. Such a change is consonant with the philosophy of work groups. The scope of the training program indicated a not inconsiderable management interest for moving in this value direction. It provided a wider support base than existed on other sites, even if this was not so throughout the entire plant.

Another difference was that Location F did not follow the pattern of rapidly introduced multiple experiments. Only two groups were formally instituted. A third had spun off naturally and was not known as a work group. The training program also led quite a number of foremen informally to allow their teams considerable freedom of a work group type.

No attempt was made to secure elaborate measures, which were a strain to collect; to insist on control groups, often difficult to identify; or otherwise to create a climate of self-conscious experimentation. The process was one of slower and more natural assimilation.

The problem was to discover why the rate of diffusion was not faster. Three years is a long time. At one point the union was the obstacle. This inclined management to keep the work group idea implicit and to rely on the training of the foremen to work things out informally.

Yet, for one group, output was up 31 percent and rejects down 37 percent in the first year. This has been maintained with several innovations. In the other group doing sophisticated work with nonexempt personnel, overtime was reduced from six to three hours a week for the whole of the first four and a half months of operation in the new mode, with two members off sick. In spite of this the groups were allowed to die.

Something more is needed than either the pattern of multiple experiments or the training framework provided. In the first instance, intensive development of multiple experiment failed to arrest fade-out. In the second, extensive preparation through a well-designed training program failed to occasion widespread diffusion.

A Greenfield Site

This location represented a development of a different kind. It was a new plant (1973) designed from the beginning on work group principles with an organizational structure and management philosophy consistent with them. Though a very small operation (fewer than 100 personnel in all), it was an entity in itself. This is a very different situation from being a component in a larger established operation. That it should have been brought into existence at all suggested that, for the first time, someone in the line above plant level had some interest in testing (in the comparative safety of so small an operation) the validity of moving toward the full organizational alternative now available to the conventional manufacturing setup. Yet some anxiety was voiced concerning future support from management above plant level. All personnel were salaried, the management structure was "flat," specialist staffing was minimal and far-reaching responsibility had been delegated to the groups. Like a number of other new plants set up along innovative lines in the United States, it was nonunion. There are, nevertheless, an increasing number of cases in which unions have participated in the design of such plants.

Location G weathered its own start-up and survived the recession. It outperformed a sister plant that is older and more conventional. People said they liked working there but they were, of course, the kind of people who like to work in this way, as were the managers who had chosen to develop the plant along these lines.

A relatively large and heterogeneous manufacturing corporation cannot depend too heavily on the odd new plant it sets up from time to time in order to discover its preferred organizational path into the future. It seemed significant, therefore, that small steps were being taken spontaneously to restart workgroups—at Location C, for example, where a good deal of participation had continued informally. Moreover, one or two managers formerly associated with work groups appeared to be intent on introducing them in other locations where they were now working. Interest in setting up such groups "when the time was ripe" had been expressed by three small plants. The supply of initiating managers had far from dried up. Such managers were beginning to comprise a network of increasingly experienced individuals who, though dispersed, remained in informal contact.

Despite severe setbacks and the phenomenon of project fade-out, the work group concept had survived the recession.

Interview Survey Perspective

This perspective treats the findings of the interview survey as a whole across all sites (except one which was not available for interview).

It was important to interview management members as well as work group members—not only the foremen directly involved but also general foremen and plant and personnel managers. Roughly equal numbers of the work force and management were interviewed in a sample of 100. Some nongroup members were included as their perspective also was relevant. Though Location D was overrepresented, it is doubtful if this is unduly distortive.

The 80 questionnaire items are grouped under headings which describe six broad areas: program design, implementation, internal processes, support, evaluation and termination. Managers were interviewed individually, while members of the work force were sometimes interviewed in groups with a member of the research team first taking the group through the questionnaire, then discussing matters arising with them. With managers, this type of discussion took place during the administration of the questionnaire.

The level of cooperation among the interviewees was high but their experiences of work groups were "cold"; the groups had ceased functioning two to three years previously. Not unnaturally, since the experiences were being recalled from so far in the past, some respondents could not answer a number of the questions. Also, there were those who did not feel able to express an opinion on some of the broader issues. This was particularly true of work force members. Therefore, varying numbers gave answers though most respondents answered most questions.

For the present analysis, the four points of the scale have been collapsed to two—those agreeing and those disagreeing. Each of the six sections is introduced by an overview statement. The questions pertinent to the section are then given, along with the number of respondents agreeing or disagreeing. A short commentary is added which makes use of the qualitative material. A correlational analysis was carried out, but because of the small numbers and the dubiousness of assuming normal distributions the results are inconclusive. Therefore it has been omitted from the present discussion.

Despite the limitations of the data, the interview survey discloses a number of important findings and a great deal of suggestive material. It gives a picture of how work groups were experienced by those who took part in them or were closely associated with them in a managerial capacity. Under the circumstances, the extent of the recall is remarkable, as well as the strength of the views and feelings expressed, leaving no doubt as to the impact of work groups on those who had experienced them or the importance that they attached to the concept. This picture complements that obtained from site visits that is described in the first half of this paper. Many of the views commonly put forward in the literature were voiced by this group of operating people, who between them seemed to have learned the alpha and omega of work group functioning. Too little of this knowledge and wisdom was used by those responsible for initiating and running the programs. The corporation did not know of the wealth of experience that had been built up. The process of organizational learning had scarcely begun.

PROGRAM DESIGN

Strong views were expressed concerning the principles on which work groups should be designed.

Voluntarism. Involvement in work groups should be voluntary. Nothing good would come out of attempts to force people to participate.

Selectivity. The best strategy is to select suitable areas rather than to proceed plantwide from the beginning.

Diffusion to the whole plant. On the other hand, there was concern about experimental groups becoming privileged, especially in the work force where any form of divisiveness is feared. The prospect of diffusion to the plant as a whole should be kept under consideration from the beginning. Ultimately, having part of a plant on work groups and part not is likely to produce difficulties regarding equity.

Inclusion of management in evaluation. Plant management and general foremen as well as foremen and group members should be considered as part of a total effort. Therefore, the performance evaluation of these higher ranks should include a judgment on how well work groups within the scope of their responsibility are doing.

Payment. Additional pay for group members as compared with nongroup members was not recommended. Special pay would give rise to envy and jealousy and would be disruptive. However, pay schedules should be sensitive to employees acquiring new skills and be adjusted accordingly.

Sharing in savings. When productivity increases or cost savings are obtained, the benefits should be shared between the company and all employees concerned—both workers and management—and on a plantwide basis.

Recognition of individual performance. Though work groups focus on group efforts, the individual needs to be recognized too. Contributions to group are often differential.

Allowance for group differences. The differences in performance among work groups tend to be considerable. This must be accepted. It means that no program can remain uniform.

IMPLEMENTATION

Implementation is concerned with how well the program design is placed in operation within the actual workplace. Some principles stated were:

Training. The amount and adequacy of training given key participants (unit workers, foremen, general foremen and others) on group concepts and processes were viewed as critical. The training needs of foremen and group members were also significant concerns. While perceived as adequate, the training of foremen was, upon closer inspection, uneven and too short, according to the interviews. Group members' training was seldom provided, although it is crucial if truly effective groups are to develop.

Feedback. Provision has to be made for adequate feedback to group members and management (i.e., methods for providing information about group performance). Effectiveness has to be periodically checked and reported to group members if motivation is to be maintained and corrective actions taken.

Site selection. The selection of appropriate work units and plant sites is a key factor in long term success.

Goal clarity. Clarity of both management's and the group's expectations (goals) regarding the use of work groups is essential for success, as is their congruence and compatibility.

Start-ups. Start-ups were felt to have been rather ineffective. While there was agreement that group member selection and site selection was good, greater attention to these factors would be needed for future efforts.

Group meetings. Interviews indicated great interest in ways to improve group meetings; the inclusion of support groups in these meetings is one way of improving them and the development of group skills another.

Performance. Additionally, while management felt that they had adequate information on group performance, work group members believed that they themselves did not have adequate information on results. In terms of group goals, there was much greater agreement that goals were clear. Work group performance was perceived to be good by twice as many respondents as those who felt performance was not good.

INTERNAL PROCESSES

This area is concerned with internal group activities and attitudes toward these activities. The adequacy of group meetings, the attendance of key "others" (general foremen, management, support units and so on) and their roles in these meetings were key elements. The importance given to goal setting, the level of conflict (internally and interunit) and the level of interest in groups once they had been operating for a while were also stressed.

One of the most important findings of the entire study was that it is essential for both short term and long term group effectiveness that support units, such as maintenance, be included in group meetings. Also, management's role in regulating and smoothing relationships between units needs to be more explicit. Management should also be willing to alter plant rules and policies that inhibit the functioning of work groups. This was rarely done.

Many people lost interest in maintaining their work groups once they had operated for a while. This was said to be caused by unresolved problems such as:

- constraining rules and regulations;
- "support units," such as maintenance and engineering, that did not support the groups;

- feelings that the commitment and support of management were diminishing;
- poor communication horizontally and vertically.

These were all external constraints. Work groups did not often break down for internal reasons. It was said that there was little inter-member conflict and excellent group spirit, and that group meetings were open and on the whole constructive.

Some operating principles suggested were:

Line management involvement. Successful work groups cannot, it was said, be solely promoted by the personnel department. Line management has to be directly involved in monitoring, evaluating and helping to solve problems.

Group meetings. Provision of a place and sufficient time to hold meetings was regarded as essential. A minimum level of group skills for members is "a must."

Group decision making. Decisions directly affecting a group should be placed before it to get advice and, when possible, a solution. When this is not possible, the reasons why a decision affecting the group was made should be provided.

Role clarity. A clear understanding of each member's role, the foreman's role relative to the group and the place "others" (management, support units) have in supporting the group was regarded as essential.

Inclusion of others in meetings. There is a need to include foremen, general foremen, management and nongroup members (e.g., support units) in group meetings with varying degrees of frequency to share information and solve problems at an inter-group level.

Lateral communications. Communications among groups, group/nongroup units and foremen allow information and new idea sharing. Ways to encourage these types of communication need to be created.

SUPPORT

This area is concerned with how much underlying support there was for the work group idea. The majority of respondents believed, despite all the obstacles, that work groups were feasible in their locations and that with some effort they could be maintained. This latter belief was one of the most emphatic opinions given in this inquiry. It implied that the basis of underlying support did indeed exist, while the termination of most of the groups indicated that the support was not effectively mobilized. Some of the key constraints have already been listed; they were in the organizational context rather than in the groups themselves. Respondents felt that as one went up the management ladder the clearness with which support was offered diminished. This confirmed the answers to corresponding questions in other sections.

An emphatic opinion was that management's attitude to work groups should be thoroughly assessed before any program was embarked upon. If management acceptance and commitment were not obtained, the work group concept had little chance of success.

People thought of support in two ways:

- as commitment to work groups because of their inherent benefits and the chance they offered workers for a more active involvement in the organization; and
- as interest in work groups solely because of their positive effects on productivity.

Work group members and foremen tended to interpret support in the first sense; general foremen and management tended to interpret it in the second sense. A basic misunderstanding about the goals and purposes of the programs usually existed between higher and lower levels. These attitudes were not irreconcilable. In the long run, a successful program depended on their reconciliation.

Three important principles surfaced regarding support:

Creating support for work groups. Acquainting work units, foremen and management with the benefits of using work groups should be undertaken through training programs, discussion with others with group experience, films and so on.

Commitment to the work group idea. Assessment of tangible, long term support must be made before implementation. Voluntary adoption of the group mode by a work unit is one sign of support. The commitment of resources (time, money) is another.

Maintaining support. More than just commitment is needed to keep groups viable. Ongoing training, timely, adequate feedback on performance, clear goals, and role clarity for those involved are also needed. Rewards for goal accomplishment and incentives for participation need to be present and explicit.

EVALUATION

Evaluation addresses the types, source, frequency and effectiveness of the measures of performance used by work groups. In addition, this dimension includes a set of questions about changes in work behavior and attitudes associated with the work group program.

The perceptions of the respondents with respect to work group performance measures revealed a great deal. For instance, a majority of respondents felt that performance criteria were clear, although 39 percent felt they were not clear.

There was a decline in these feelings about measurement clarity from the management level to the work group level, which indicated a problem in maintaining communications down the line. Management and supervisory levels felt that group members knew how well they were doing better than they did. Supervisory levels felt they were communicating feedback to a greater extent than members were receiving it. There was, as a result, little association between how clear respondents perceived the performance measures to be and how well they perceived themselves to be functioning.

Respondents perceived the same types of performance measures as those being used. Emphasis was placed on the standard economic measures, such as productivity and efficiency, scrap, absenteeism rates and quality control. What may be an indication of a participative attitude was the fact that two or more levels appeared to have determined these measures. The respondents disagreed on how often these measures should be taken. Performance was apparently assessed with varying frequency and emphasis. The actual measures were regarded as good.

Three important points should be considered regarding evaluation.

Criteria development. Group members, foremen and management should develop performance criteria collectively; ownership of the measures and results would thereby be shared.

Feedback. An important part of evaluation is providing results to the groups. Feedback must be timely and constructive. Thought should be given beforehand, preferably when criteria have been developed, as to how this information is to be provided.

Inclusion of others in evaluations. Survey results indicated that other individuals and groups (foremen, general foremen, management, support units) should be included in work group evaluations. How this might be done could be negotiated with these individuals and groups. As noted elsewhere, evaluation of individual performance in terms of contribution to the group effort is also needed.

TERMINATION

This area is concerned with the perceptions of respondents in regard to the reasons why the groups stopped functioning, how they felt about termination and what they felt would be necessary for the groups to be started up again.

A number of important observations from the data can be made. Three out of four respondents, especially at lower levels, did not want work groups stopped. Interview material showed that layoffs and personnel changes were not the only reasons why groups terminated. In many instances the teams simply "fell apart" after a while. They did not receive the ongoing committed interest and effort that they required if they were to be assimilated into the fabric of the workplace. This effort and interest diminished after a period of initial enthusiasm. Yet more respondents stated that they would like to have the teams started up again. Given what we believe to be moderate levels of success overall, this response illustrates the viability of the work group concept and its ability to gain and maintain broad-based support.

Several foremen felt caught in a bind. Two sets of objectives that could not be satisfied simultaneously were being communicated to them from their superiors:

- get the work groups functioning;
- maintain performance levels.

This placed a considerable burden on the foremen because an additional set of responsibilities (establish the groups) was added to their regular duties (performance maintenance). Several foremen felt that they were receiving neither the moral nor the resource support effectively to address this new set of demands. Moral support—interest and involvement in the functioning of the groups— did not come from their superiors; resource support did not come from equipment, maintenance, personnel, suppliers of materials or plant planners.

Many respondents felt that, initially, there was much enthusiasm for the program among group members but that their interest declined as the program continued. Other experiments with work groups have shown that, over time, the groups increase employees' autonomy, participation and interest on the job. The combination of the two factors noted (lack of moral support and lack of resource support) was a major reason for the attenuation of interest in sustaining the groups and brought about their dissolution. The difficulty in establishing a new work structure without the support that was seen to be required made people give up and programs fold.

Finally, what would it take to start the groups again? Respondents seemed confused on this point, but clearly there was a need for commitment from management as well as from workers themselves. The interview survey suggested the following requirements:

- A clear and coherent program design.
- Thorough preparation of management and training of foremen and group members.
- A selective implementation effort.
- Continued, concerted management support.
- Plantwide diffusion of new concepts and ways of operating.
- Some special assistance from inside or outside the plant at the group and foreman levels during implementation and periodically thereafter to develop skills.

Further Developments

A CORPORATE REVIEW

During the fall of 1978, a review of the material summarized in this chapter was held at corporate headquarters. Four functional vice-presidents were present as well as a number of other staff people. No line managers were present, however. Half a day was set aside to consider whether a new beginning should be made with work group projects with explicit corporate support or whether it would be best to remain inactive or even to discourage fresh attempts.

The findings occasioned considerable interest, as few of those present had been aware of the extent of the group activities that had been taking place or of the positive results obtained, more often than not, in spite of the tendency of the projects to fade out. The location perspective suggested that, if work-groups were to be started again in the laissez-faire manner that had characterized them in the last ten years, they would in all likelihood fade out again. The perspective of the interview survey suggested that, if they were restarted in a more strategic manner, with corporate support, the wealth of experience about the do's and don't's that had been accumulated by the managers and workers immediately concerned would provide a solid foundation on which to build the type of future effort that could become self-sustaining. A persistent belief in the potential benefits of work groups, for both job satisfaction and productivity, lingered in a number of participants (especially the workers) despite the vicissitudes and disappointments encountered.

We suggested that the work group by itself was too small a unit to bring about lasting organizational and performance improvement. The data made it plain that all the systems of an operating plant, or a similar self-standing workplace, were involved in one way or another in work groups. The organizational context had to change at the same time if the enduring results for job satisfaction and productivity possible through semiautonomous groups were to be realized. This implied the working out of a new philosophy of management based on participative principles in which each level within a plant would have to some extent to redefine its role as regards the others. A number of operational practices, control systems, measurement procedures and reward systems would also require modification. A new type of cooperative relationship with the union would have to be evolved in areas not previously thought to belong to labor relations. Work improvement through QWL had to be envisaged as a long term effort. For plants to be secure in venturing along this road, they would have to know that there was stable commitment to it in the corporation above plant level.

Many of those present were inclined to accept these views at least to some degree. Work improvement through QWL was indeed a long range strategic undertaking requiring a large investment of management time and energy and a large investment in the training and development of the work force as well as of those in the supervisory and plant-management ranks. This was a daunting prospect. The company, some of those present pointed out, had other formidable priorities in the technological field regarding new products and new manufacturing processes. The changes entailed would strain the capabilities of operation managers for the foreseeable future. These managers could not be asked to undertake a major parallel task, especially as their views on QWL were contradictory. The company's systems of management practice, they said, had stood the test of time and, in labor relations at least, both sides knew where they stood.

Several leading corporations had been evolving large scale programs in QWL in the last few years. "Let them do the pioneer work " was a view advanced by some strong voices. "We'll hang well back in the pack watching what they are doing and learning from it. Then, if and when the time is ripe for us, we'll mobilize the very considerable internal and external resources we can command and move forward quickly on a wide front."

Though this was not a decision taking meeting and there was a wide range of opinion, it was apparent that no one was about to make any policy proposals to get QWL supported at the corporate level. No formal encouragement of QWL projects was to be expected for the present from those in high-level staff positions, whatever their personal view. Any prospect of corporate sanction seemed a long way off.

An Innovative Affiliate

Nevertheless, this meeting did not signal the end of work-innovation projects even in the shorter run. A supporter appeared in a high-level line manager. The chief executive officer (CEO) of a large affiliate, which did more than 2 billion dollars of business a year and which had considerable autonomy, took up the challenge. He had been convinced for some time of the importance of the value changes taking places in the wider society, especially in the attitudes of the younger generations entering the work force. He was preoccupied with the need to press forward with organizational as well as technological change if the involvement and commitment of employees at all levels were to be obtained. He regarded this commitment and involvement as essential to assure the levels of innovation and productivity he deemed necessary for the survival of the business in a world of increasing competition, complexity and uncertainty.

He had appointed one of his senior vice-presidents to make a critical assessment of innovative projects across the whole field of human resources in North America, Europe and Japan. The first author of this paper met this vice-president at an intensive QWL workshop and was invited to work out with him a strategy for assessing the willingness and preparedness of managers in the affiliate to undertake projects in work innovation. The vice-president felt it was essential to start with the senior executives, functional as well as operational, around the CEO, but he did not think it would be appropriate to begin with a meeting of these key individuals as a group. They were not ready for it. Accordingly, the first author held long, unstructured interviews of two to three hours with each of the 12 most senior executives.

These interviews disclosed a widespread awareness of the situation described by the CEO, a willingness to move in a direction which would integrate the human and technical needs of the enterprise, but very great differences in their beliefs regarding whether it was appropriate for them to do so in the immediate future of their own businesses. Some had all-absorbing priorities in products or markets; others had a union which was implacably adversarial and had just elected a new leadership of the same kind; others had too many managers of the old school to want to proceed very far until more of the younger generation were in positions of greater responsibility. Yet the conviction was general that QWL was the right direction in which to move in the longer term.

In a report to the CEO, the first author suggested a strategy of selective development in contrast to laissez-faire. Laissez-faire had failed in the corporate parent and the findings were discussed in the report which the CEO circulated to his own senior managers. To assess the acceptability of the new strategy and to begin to define its operational meaning, the CEO asked each of his two group vice-presidents to hold meetings in retreat with his senior managers. Each of these meetings was scheduled for a day and a half. The CEO himself would attend as required, as would the first author.

These meetings confirmed the need to proceed with work innovation, whether called QWL, some other name or no name. Each senior manager would be responsible for developments in his own area. The method was adopted of listing the constraints and opportunities in each section of the business. Through this, an attempt was begun to identify specific criteria for site selection. When a site seemed appropriate to senior management, the question of its desirability and feasibility would be taken up with local management. Nothing would be forced. Only if there was a genuine wish to proceed on the part of local management would action steps be taken. Then the question of involving the union would arise in those plants that were unionized.

More internal resources would have to be developed. One of the ablest of the younger plant managers and one of the ablest of the younger personnel managers, both of whom had begun to accumulate experience in this field, were appointed to nourish developments in work innovation throughout the affiliate and to assist selected sites.

As regards external resources, one independent center and one university center have been involved, together with a consulting firm with special experience in the problem solving methods which have been developed in Japan.

During 1979 two projects were launched, one of which has survived severe market vicissitudes. Both have now become substantial, and a third project has been started.

These and other projects in this affiliate, and emerging endeavors in other divisions of the corporation, are picking up the efforts of an earlier network of activist managers. How they fare will constitute the story of the eighties as distinct from the story of the seventies with which this paper has been concerned. It will reflect the growing strength of the QWL enterprise worldwide as evidenced by the international conference on "QWL in the '80s" held in Toronto at the end of August 1981.

The economic climate has indeed changed. Improvements in productivity have become imperative, but we now know that employee involvement and commitment—desirable for their own sake—are essential for the achievement of such improvements. At the first annual conference of the Philadelphia Area Labor/Management Committee, held in November 1981, Rex Reed, the vice-president for labor relations and corporate personnel of Michigan Bell, put it this way in his keynote address: "The time has come to change the managerial culture of America"—to one of participation and power sharing.

The case reported in this paper shows some of the complexities of trying to take the first steps toward this basic cultural change in an endeavor in which every corporation must find its own path. A great deal has been learned, even if there is still more to learn. Meanwhile, the more experiences of what has so far taken place that are publicly shared, the more rapidly will organizational learning accumulate in industry as a whole.

Bill Westley and Eric Trist

Socio-Technical Projects in the Canadian Federal Public Service[1]

Trist:

Now, I'd just like to say a very brief word about the events which have taken place in the field of quality of working life (QWL) since 1976, when the original three experiments supported by the Treasury Board took place. If I look at the world of QWL in Canada and in other countries, we have passed beyond a stage where we were mainly concerned with pilot projects often called "experiments." This turns out to be rather an unfortunate word. People thought they were guinea pigs. It was tentative and exploratory but it was, in a sense, very real from the beginning. We've moved from this phase of starting in little places and just finding out whether it was going to work at all or not, what might be in it and so on—getting through the uncertainties and ambiguities—to a phase of systemwide organizational change in pretty large units. We quickly found that just to do something in one small place in a department or agency didn't work out and it was usually phased out. We had to take on the much larger system and to look at QWL not as something merely for people on the shop floor or in the office, but something which concerned everyone, at all levels and in all functions.

QWL has to do with a transformation of organizational life, a new paradigm of organizational life which seems to be emerging in all western counties. I have been very struck with this in the last two or three weeks. I have been to two meetings in New York concerned with innovation and productivity and the relation of these to QWL. I haven't been working continuously in the United States for three or four years as I have been mostly in Canada, and I was impressed with the change. Various U.S. organizations like General Motors, U.S. Steel, AT&T—places like that; one or two representatives from smaller States; then local government; then the federal government. The unions were represented at quite a high level in these industries—the UAW, the Communi-

[1]This report was presented to the Conference on Quality of Working Life in the Federal Public Service convened by Labour Canada and the Treasury Board in 1981.

cation Workers of America and the Steel Workers. Among a number of leaders of industry, it is now taken for granted that a change toward something—which none of us see too clearly yet—has happened. We've got to get on with it, in a strategic way, a businesslike way.

Here in Canada, we started late but have been on the move relatively rapidly and, as some of you may know, the second International Conference on QWL will be held in Toronto. Canada is the host country and I think has earned that right through the developments that have taken place in the last three years. This International Conference is a very different type of conference from the first one, which was held at Columbia University in 1972; the people present then were, with one or two exceptions, academics. There were about two hundred of us. We were concerned with problems of theory and method. It was at that conference that the term QWL was coined. We had to find something that wasn't as narrow as "job enrichment" or as wide and unsuitable for North America as "industrial democracy" in the European sense. Something new had to emerge, and it was then that the idea of linking the quality of one's experience at work with the quality of one's life as a whole was becoming an international concern. People were concerned that no matter how we might be improving economically, we didn't seem to be getting on all that well from the point of view of the quality of our experience of life. It was felt that the quality of life in the workplace, where we spend a third of our time, was of vital importance. At that time, it was appreciated widely, for the first time, that large numbers of people in the workplaces of the western world were having anything but a high quality time. Low QWL was having a negative effect on productivity and industrial relations. The conference we are planning for Canada at the end of August is not mainly an academic conference. It will be a signal to the world that the leadership in this field has passed from people like Bill and myself to those whom we call "real-world people" such as yourselves. I mean that the leadership is passing to managers and to union people and to representatives of various government agencies throughout the West. I hope that this conference will clearly make that signal and I am very proud that it should be in Canada.

As he has done the bulk of the work in the present project, I will now ask Bill to make the main report.

Westley:

I have learned a tremendous amount about the Public Service, about the way people work, their qualities, their imagination. I have not had that experience before, and I want to express my gratitude to you all. It was a good experience, and it wouldn't have been possible without a lot of sincere help from all of you.

I want to say one other thing before getting into the detail and that is to reiterate one point that Eric has made. What we see now is a massive movement, particularly in the private sector, into QWL programs. This is not simply a predisposition to "do good." It represents a solid need for control and for motivation which organizations have been losing and which they find that they can regain through QWL programs. In industry, this is seen as a way of running organizations. It is not seen simply as a goodwill gesture to the workers. I think it would be worthwhile mentioning that Proctor and Gamble build all their new pulp and paper plants entirely according to socio-technical QWL principles and they regard themselves as having a serious competitive advantage over all other companies in the field. This demonstrates that when you get people involved, use their human resources and move to a new management paradigm, important things happen in the control and running of the workplace.

QWL Projects in the Federal Public Service

Our reconnaissance of QWL in the Federal Public Service included interviews with at least 75 people in 17 different organizations (departments, agencies, unions). These included people as high as the Deputy Minister, as well as the groups of employees involved in the QWL programs. Throughout, we were received courteously, given ample time and had frank and open discussions. Many people we talked to were eager for further information about QWL. Some were desperate for help in keeping their projects going.

We found nine projects in the Federal Public Service. They vary as to whether they were the first, second or third wave projects and in the degree in which they have represented change. We classified these projects into six categories:

Canceled: one project. This was a project which had been started, moved along; then there was a management decision to cancel the project.

Redesigned: one project. This is a project which took off in one form, seemed to falter and then the management redesigned it into a new package and it has been moving forward since then.

Arrested: two projects. These projects started off strongly with steering committees, design teams and consultants. They progressed to a certain point and then stopped. They still exist, but they are incomplete. For example, in one of the projects, they moved to the point of having project committees and setting up a certain amount of consultation with employees. At that point, they seemed to run out of energy and nothing new happened.

Incipient: three projects. This title does not refer to people thinking about having projects, for in some cases the projects were well advanced. Instead, it refers to QWL-type programs which are not recognized as such, or programs which, though called QWL, are only in the stage of union/management collaboration. Thus, in one case there was a group of eight people under a foreman who had developed some QWL redesign and team work. But the managers didn't see this as a QWL program; they saw it as part of a program to upgrade productivity and efficiency. Another case was a project where the organization felt strongly that it had a big quality of working life program under way. But, while they had made a good beginning in an extensive set of management/labor committees and a QWL committee, they had as yet no plans for redesign. This is what I meant by incipient projects.

Stable: one project. A stable project is a mature project which has gone through all the stages of analysis and development and seems to be a permanent part of the structure.

Growing: two projects. A growing project is one in which there is vigorous management support for the expansion of QWL in the department or agency. I should point out that we only had two of these and the redesigned project was one of them.

This gives you a brief overview of what we found. In each of these cases, incidentally, I talked to people who were involved—employees, supervisor and manager. Whenever possible, I talked to union leaders. We talked about the project and what they thought about it. Most of what I am saying today is based on these discussions.

Accomplishments and Shortcomings

First, the accomplishments. These are six characteristics of QWL in the Public Service that are of great importance:

You have always operated with labor/management steering committees, and it's been a very important part of trying to build the confidence, the trust and the collaboration necessary for success.

The projects have had unusually strong union support. In Canada, the Public Service Alliance of Canada is the only union that has issued a policy statement supporting QWL. This is a tremendous advantage to a QWL program.

Many projects agreed to allow innovation. This is more important than one might think. In the midst of detailed regulations and contracts, unions and managements said, "Okay, we will turn these people loose for a while and let them do something very different and then we will review what they have done." This has resulted in some very interesting developments.

There has been a recognition of the need for job redesign. What I mean is that in some places QWL programs are seen purely in terms of working conditions and do not involve the redesign of jobs for real and durable change. The job should be redesigned to increase the amount of responsibility or autonomy, variety, challenge, mobility and learning on the job itself. These are qualities of jobs which are the criteria of redesign and this has been recognized in the Public Service.

There have been changes in the conditions of employment like flextime. I don't know whether they are QWL changes in the strict sense, but they certainly accompanied it. The Public Service employs a lot of single parents. For them, flextime and other changes in the conditions of employment become very important life variables. The fact that they have been introduced is a real advantage.

There have been, fairly consistently, changes in the supervisor's role. The idea has been recognized—the idea that what supervisors used to do can be done by employees for themselves has been widely accepted.

In complex systems like federal departments and agencies with a heritage of intricate regulations, these are solid accomplishments.

Next, the shortcomings:

The most important and consistent shortcoming of the Federal Program has been the lack of clear management commitment and training. There has not been a single department that we have encountered that has an unambiguously clear management commitment or reasonable management training. This has had important consequences. First, management cannot and will not provide the support, guidance and leadership necessary to successful QWL change without the training which provides in-depth knowledge.

Secondly, managers consistently fear QWL systems and do not see their advantage to management. They think it will result in loss of control. They assume that it's going to be costly, full of people out of their control and that they are going to be blamed. All they see are people doing things in ways which they are not accustomed to. Since no one has shown them how to manage people in a QWL system or how to get outcomes, they don't understand that the QWL program produces higher degrees of control in terms of outcome. In other words, it gets results. Under the circumstances, it's natural that they should be afraid and, when they are afraid, they backlash against programs.

Thirdly, this lack of commitment and training produces conflicting ideas of QWL within the hierarchy of an organization. We found that people had very different views of what QWL is, what commitment means, what the outcomes should be and so on. During our discussions, many of the managers were naturally quite hostile to QWL. They felt, for example, "this is simply management by committee." However, when they understood that it was a real management tool and suitable to their needs and plans, they became more interested.

Training

There have been only two kinds of training available so far—awareness training to appreciate what QWL means and introductory workshops which explain the basic concepts. They tell a manager what QWL is, but they do not teach him how to manage a QWL system. But the knowledge is available.

In industry, managers are being trained to manage in terms of socio-technical principles. This is a QWL training that enables a manager to grasp the complex confused system he's involved in, so that he can allocate the responsibility, understand how to divide functions and responsibilities, understand how to use information systems and how to allow autonomy in the developed program. This is a management skill. It is not merely a way of managing QWL; it is a new paradigm.

The Special Character of Work in the Federal Public Service

I came armed with prejudices like many other citizens. I would encounter somebody in the customs office who would not wait on me and be furious. I had many of the typical complaints of an ordinary citizen. When I came to Ottawa, I came feeling that government had developed into a set of unwieldy bureaucracies which employed too many people. I was not sure what they were doing or how well they were doing it. But as I began my work and came to know the people in Ottawa, my impressions changed.

I am a trained sociologist, the kind of sociologist who goes into the middle of an environment and spends a long time sensing what it's like around him and then tries to put words around it. I trust my reactions. In Ottawa, the first thing I became aware of was that everywhere I went there were lots of people. I was never so bumped and jostled in my life. For a while, this was confusing to me; it was like the New York subway, but I was not in subways but in office buildings. Then I realized that what I was experiencing was a labor intensive environment, one in which people were moving briskly to do their jobs. This is certainly not the image I had before. I had thought that working for the Public Service was a leisurely activity. Instead, I found people working hard. I also became aware that these people were exceptionally well qualified in terms of education and intelligence.

Then I began to hear people talk about their work in ways which I had not heard before. Their talk implied a significance to their work which I certainly hadn't encountered in industry. I realized that what was significant in their work was that it was connected to the major social purposes of our society. In Canada, whenever we have a major value or a social purpose, what do we do about it? We create a public agency! These departments or agencies are the structural articulations of the values of society. The Canadian International Development Agency (CIDA) exemplifies this tendency. We lead the world in offering a proportion of our income to help the rest of the world. Why do we do this? Nobody forces us to. It was a definite value decision, and we are putting a lot of money into it. I began to realize that if this was really what Government was all about, its purposes were the basic social purposes of society. I got very excited about this. I said, "Well, you know, I'll bet that lots and lots of people come here for that reason. They want to work in something that's socially meaningful."

Then I said, "Well, that's really interesting, I never thought about that before!" My view had been that we ought to run the Government as inexpensively as possible, and I never really thought about effectiveness. But I realize that, if these are major social purposes, our major concern is not cost. I don't mean that we are not concerned with cost, but we set up an agency because we want it to accomplish something, not to make money. If you have a problem in health, justice—any area like this, you want it to be effective. This was the second revelation to me. It was an enormously moving experience.

Then the third thing I ran into was confusion. I kept running into confused people at every level. Some people in new agencies at high levels knew what they were doing, but most people didn't. There was a gap between the work and the social purposes. For me, in my work in QWL, this is a crime. The most difficult thing to do is to attach people to social goals. If you go to the business world, getting people committed to the goals of business is probably the most difficult thing to do. But here, the social goals are loud and clear. The people are dedicated and intelligent, why aren't they connected?

I came out of it feeling that I wanted to see the Government grow, and I was no longer an advocate of shrinking government. You may not be aware of it, but Eric and I are highly aware that technological displacements are occurring at such an enormous rate that our problem is going to be what to do with unemployed people. The old problem was: how will a small production population support growing numbers of young and aging people? Now, with technological change, the problem has disappeared. With modern technology, a tiny fraction of people can support an enormous population. What will you do with the load of population? What should they do but work with major social purposes? So my view, for what it's worth, is "let the Government grow." I don't suppose you ever heard anybody say that before.

Images of QWL in the Federal Public Service

As I talked to people, I began to pick up images of QWL in the Public Service, and I want to share some of these images with you.

One image was that it was a failure. Many people felt it was just not working. What is the fact? The one program which people thought was a failure had been canceled by the management group. Eric and I agree that that program was an outstanding success; there's no question about it. If you talk to those people today, the redesigned work system is intact. They are the most turned-on, enthusiastic, thinking group of people you've ever met; it's just unbelievable. The organization had decided that it cost too much. The reason for it costing too much was a design error, a serious design error, but the program was a great success. And a lot of people think it is a failure. It is not a failure. In human terms it is a great success.

Secondly, some people thought that QWL was a success but only for low level jobs, like data entry clerks. The fact of the matter is that it has succeeded with professionals. If you would stop and reflect on it at all, you'd realize it's almost the ideal prescription for a group of professional jobs. Professionals are, by definition, internally controlled persons with a wide range of competence. If you can just build jobs in such a way that they can use those skills and that competence, they will work well. There isn't any question about the fact that QWL is, if anything, more suitable to professionals than to nonprofessionals.

The third image I got was: it's government by committee. This is a reasonable fear because, in the early stages of a QWL program, during the process of analysis, there are a lot of meetings. People keep coming to meetings. There are committees formed; there is analysis, and it seems almost interminable. Actually, it is not: it only lasts about a year and a half to two years, then you are over the hill. But, meanwhile, some people regard that as an interminable process. The critical thing to realize is that, as the group matures, it creates responsible people who move toward autonomy. When they can be autonomous, meetings will be no longer necessary, at least as far as the manager is concerned. The group may meet, but the manager does not need to be there, so his meeting time drops sharply. I have no hesitation in guaranteeing to the managers that when they have a mature QWL program in place, they will have more productivity, not less.

The fourth image was that QWL is a form of worker control of management. What is the fact? The fact is that the workers take more responsibility and make more decisions about their work, decisions which were previously made by supervisors. Thus, QWL is almost always welcomed by managers and supervisors because if you talk to them, they often complain about having to make all the decisions for their subordinates. This changes when the subordinates make those decisions. There isn't any question about the fact that some power, or authority, is transferred down the system. But it is power that never should have been that high in the system in the first place, because it's using up the time of managers. In a modern world, managers need tremendous amounts of time to deal with the complexities of the external world. They don't have it.

Finally, there was an image that QWL involves a loss in productivity. This is a complicated question, but the fact is that, in some projects, there is a loss of productivity—a temporary loss of productivity. If you have professional people who are working reasonably well to start with, and you take them off the job to go to meetings or to do an analysis, their productivity has to drop. At the point when the analysis is finished and they return to work, the productivity curve should go right back up again. What's interesting is that there are some projects I encountered where there was no loss of productivity at all. I asked somebody about this, and they said to me that the people who volunteered for the design team were hot shots anyway and they were compulsive about getting their work done, so that they did just as much work as they always did and still went to committee meetings. So you see, it varies.

In the long run, there should be no loss of productivity at all. In most cases, in 80 percent of the cases, in an industry where you do a complete QWL program along socio-technical lines, there is an increase in productivity.

Evaluation

QWL represents a major change in how jobs are designed and work systems are managed. Therefore, people are interested in how they can evaluate their success. I will approach this in terms of three criteria: motivation, effectiveness and efficiency.

First, motivation. In looking at the program in Ottawa, I have no hesitation in saying that, exactly to the degree that QWL change was introduced, employees became devoted, enthusiastic, interested and made creative contributions. Whether the program is regarded by any of you as a success or a failure, in my experience it is a success for the majority of those involved. Now what do I mean by "to the degree that . . ."? Some programs only went as far as consulting employees but did not change jobs or organization structure. A committee was formed, and the committee met regularly to be consulted by the supervisor or the manager. What was remarkable to me was how enthusiastic those people were, how much they got turned-on by just being consulted. However, in those cases, the people who were not on the committee and didn't experience consultation were losing interest. That's what I mean by "the degree." The people who got involved in the consultation began to feel more human, more mature, more seriously treated and felt involved.

When a program went as far as redesigning the jobs, giving the employees autonomy and withdrawing supervision, employees responded by accepting more responsibility and becoming self-disciplined. In one case, the employees now take such responsibility for their own work that when they began to appreciate that technological change was causing a loss of jobs, they initiated the study themselves. They went to management and asked for a training program which would allow them to be retrained to absorb the other jobs. Management didn't have to think about it at all! The whole thing was laid out there on the shop floor, by semi-skilled people! That's people taking responsibility for their own lives! In a full change program, when employees were given increased responsibility and autonomy, they were strongly enthusiastic about their work. So I have to end up by saying that every single government project was a success in terms of motivation. In other words, you got a return on the investment you made. Sometimes the investment was small, sometimes it was large. I don't mean money, I mean in terms of the amount of change implemented.

Now, to turn to effectiveness. Effectiveness to me is measured by the degree to which the department or agency achieves its mission. That's a complex question. I don't know how many agencies have a clearly defined, collectively agreed-on mission. In QWL programs it's critical that the whole management group come to a mission exercise and that the mission be translated into goals and goals into performance or achievement indicators. I use the term mission because it's the only thing that encompasses something as grand as a department or agency in terms of goals. Within complex agencies, this mission appears as a set of sub-goals for the different subsystems. With this in mind we can define effectiveness as the degree to which the subsystem meets its sub-goals. For many subsystems in the Federal Public Service, the goal is service, and the key factor is the employee who meets the public. They determine effectiveness. They are providing the service. We know that in all QWL programs, there is a substantial increase in effectiveness when socio-technical redesign occurs. The outstanding story, which you probably all know, comes out of Bell Telephone. It was written many years ago by a man called Ford, who wrote a book called *Motivation Through the Work Itself* (1969). He described the complaints department in Bell. This work was so complicated that they only hired college graduates, and it took a long time to train them. But they had something like a 70 percent turnover. Work was organized along typical production line patterns with a supervisor allocating the work load to each one of these employees every day. Ford simply redesigned that situation. Each employee was given a territory and dealt with all complaints coming from that territory, dealing directly with the customers, and with the people in the company needed to solve the problems. The turnover dropped to something like five percent. Those customers belonged to somebody in the organization; they didn't belong to anybody before.

When people have the autonomy to deal with a customer and feel a sense of ownership of the customer and the resource they provide to them, you are going to improve your effectiveness. Quality of working life job redesigns are customer-driven. Where a work system is redesigned to emphasize service to the customer and is guided by its effectiveness in doing so, effectiveness definitely increases.

Finally, there's the boogie man of all areas—cost. How much does it cost? Does it cost more to operate a QWL designed unit? Costs usually increase during the change period because productivity drops due to the diversion of time to analysis and training and because of consultants' fees. The only long range increase in cost that we found is for training. Training increases because QWL programs require that people be growing and changing. That is part of the basic motivational system of any organization. The changes usually improve efficiency because of

- reduced costs for supervision as workers become self-supervising;
- reduced absenteeism; in industry there have been large decreases in absenteeism, sometimes from as high as 16 and 17 percent to three percent;
- reduced turnover; if you like your work and find it fulfilling you come to work;
- reduced waste; as people get more interested in and committed to their work, there is less waste.

These are just the most precise and easily defined ways in which QWL can increase efficiency in the Federal Public Service. Less precise, but more important, are increases in efficiency arising from employees' attention, thoughtfulness, creativity and resourcefulness. If people share the goals, understand the costs and like their work, they will find many ways to reduce costs.

You may be aware that there are a number of evaluation studies about QWL projects in the Federal Public Service. I have read practically all the evaluation studies on all the projects. I am a person who is absolutely against "before and after" survey measures for evaluation purposes. Let me give you a simple example of why. One of the things that happens in QWL programs is that everybody's standards change. At the beginning of a program you ask employees, "Are you satisfied with your job?" They might say, "Moderately satisfied." Six months later, after they have learned that the jobs can be made more creative and that there should be mobility, in response to the same question they sometimes reply, "No, I am very dissatisfied with my job." Does this mean that QWL is showing negative results?

I have seen some good surveys. A lot of you have used the Michigan survey. You'll see that some attitudes become more positive and other attitudes become more negative. Many of the changes may well be statistically significant. But this doesn't mean that they are psychologically or socially significant. Statistically significant results can occur from a few people changing position in a profile of 40 and that simply isn't significant as far as I am concerned. Surveys are wonderful ways to learn about your organization to start off. If you give them back to people who can use the data themselves it can be kind of exciting. But that's what they are for, not "before and after" studies. Productivity in its normal sense is a very complex phenomenon. Every agency should look carefully at what it really means, what can it use, what can it work with.

How Should QWL be Evaluated in the Public Service?

This may well be a question you are asking in view of the criticisms leveled against surveys. My reply is in terms of its dominant concerns and needs. The Federal Public Service has its own culture and obligations so that in answering this question I have tried to imagine myself the Deputy Minister or director of a department or agency. As such I would be concerned with running a department, with the problems of maintaining a decent reputation, with getting work done, with dealing with the Minister as a political figure, etc. Obviously, I don't understand it well enough, but that's the position I try to take, and I have chosen three criteria affecting this position: the public image, effectiveness and industrial relations.

First, the public image. I would want my department to have a good reputation, to be seen as one which was doing a good job, was a good place to work and a good place to get service from. I would want the public to say, "That's a good department, people want to work there." The industrial experience has been that QWL improves reputation by creating an image of a good place to work. In one Montreal company, before they started the program, they had difficulty recruiting workers. Two years later, when the program was in place, they had a thousand people on their waiting list. The image of that industry as a workplace changed in that community. That is not an unusual outcome. Modern, highly educated people don't want to work in traditional departments. They love working in redesigned departments.

Second, if you go back to my discussion on effectiveness and if you take the service criteria, the people who are on the leading edge of your organization should be providing the kind of service to the public which is effective in getting it done. But, more importantly, they should like relating to the public. If we ask what is it about work that affects how people treat the public, we find that if people feel misunderstood—that somebody's on their back all the time—and frustrated, they are *not* inclined to be nice. If they do get angry and are in a situation where they have little power, being low on the totem pole, there is only one person they can take it out on because he or she has no authority over them and that's a member of the public. This is because the public can hurt the Minister, but it can't hurt the employee. So, if somebody's angry and feeling bad, they are going to give bad service to whomever they encounter.

On the other hand, if people feel good, feel rewarded by their job, feel valuable, they meet the public with the sense that they are doing good work, they belong to an agency that people like. They will enjoy giving service. When citizens encounter an agency where they get efficient, effective service and meet competent, pleasant people who are interested in their work, they begin to say nice things about the agency to their friends and relatives. Where do you think reporters get their leads when they start to give you a hard time? They get them from employees and citizens. The whole question of reputation hinges around your capacity to deliver a program which adequately meets people's needs, fulfills their self-image, lets them grow. The differences are really astonishing. In my view, making an agency a good place to work can have a tremendous impact on the image of the Public Service.

Second, effectiveness. Well, effectiveness, as I said before, means the delivery of a quality service and this, in turn, is linked to something else: the people carrying out the work should take seriously the goals of the organization. Just what is it they are supposed to be doing? Is it their goal? Do they take ownership of it? Within every organization there is always a struggle between private and organizational goals. Every one of us has it all the time, for example, between our home life or our careers and doing a good job. But most people don't know how to do a good job for they don't know what the goal of the agency is. They don't know what they are supposed to be doing. Try it out. Take a little questionnaire and send it around, asking people about the mission, the goal of the agency; you'd probably get very upset. The point is that the goals are not shared; sometimes they are not consistently articulated. Even where they seem to be shared, people may use different performance indicators, differences which imply different goals. Goal-setting isn't a matter of doing it once; it isn't a matter of writing a pamphlet. It's a process that has to be kept in motion. Effectiveness depends on two things: the commitment of people willing to deliver quality service and people knowing what they should do. Any good socio-technically redesigned system automatically builds that in. It has to be done.

Finally, industrial relations. One of the things we know is that the world is so complex and the needs of people are so complex that there's a huge area of needed collaboration between workers and management, between management and the unions. The potentiality for these differences in needs becoming differences in goals, deepening into serious social cleavages and conflicts, is now so great that it is a major achievement to maintain a modest amount of cooperation between the levels and functional divisions of an organization. If the cleavages become deep and competitive, and adversarial relations predominate, managing the differences can consume large amounts of organizational energy.

If there is much conflict—particularly when it is unadmitted and under cover—people will engage in defense work, allocating time and resources to covering up and maintaining face. If this is the case, the gulf between workers and management will be large, and distrust will prevail. It will then spill over into collective bargaining, which has been designed to deal with legitimate conflicts of interest.

QWL programs, because they are collaborative and because they build a shared collaborative work system, do build trust and bridge differences. In fact, this is one of the early and striking gains from a QWL program. Thus, QWL improves industrial relations in the office and even in the bargaining session.

Trist:

Though it would not be appropriate for us at this stage to make any specific concrete suggestions as to what might be attempted, we should like to indicate more generally the directions that future developments might take. The aim of any sustained implementation scheme would be to establish conditions that would enable as many projects as possible to grow and diffuse throughout departments and to reduce to a minimum those that get held back. We postulate that QWL involves systemwide change geared to the longer rather than the shorter run if significant operational benefits are to be attained and maintained.

Two strategies may be suggested, which are complementary and which may with advantage be developed simultaneously. One concerns what may be undertaken inside departments and represents an intradepartmental strategy. The other concerns what may be undertaken between departments and represents an interdepartmental strategy. It is postulated that one will reinforce the other. To make this reinforcement possible is the great advantage of a sectoral approach.

Bill will deal first with what might be involved in a systemwide program covering all levels and functions within a department. I will conclude with a sketch of what might be involved in the interdepartmental context.

Westley:

Until recently, QWL programs have focused on the office employee or shop floor worker. These have often had "experimental" status. Thus, often with the support of a steering committee, one or two sites would be selected, and the technical and social systems in these sites would be analyzed by a team consisting of a diagonal slice of that part of the organization (manager, supervisor and workers of various kinds). Predictably, this has led to conflicts between the change site and the rest of the organization which has not changed. Recent work has suggested that, for change to be really effective, one must adopt a total systems approach within an organization.

At McGill University, we have recently developed a program that we call "Action-Learning: The Four Key Roles." This program is aimed at the simultaneous involvement (not just support) of policy managers, operational manager, supervisors and employees. Each group is asked to operate in a team setting and to go through a specialized action-learning program to analyze and redesign their own work roles and work role system. Naturally, the substance of their analysis will differ for these different roles, but their efforts must be coordinated. In fact, a well designed QWL program should be constructed so that the work of each group supports the work of the other groups. For example, the policy managers' action-learning program should be designed to specify both the mission and the human resource management philosophy of that organization, which in turn is translated into goals to be provided to supervisors and to workers. Thus, each key role uses material developed from the analysis of the other key roles.

The result of these four simultaneous action-learning programs is that a total organization, as a system, adapts to the challenges of its environment and of its people, and develops a redesigned system adequate to meet these challenges. It also means that the managers, for example, will find a redesigned role for themselves which is not only compatible with the QWL program in the office or on the shop floor, but uses QWL as an intrinsic part of managing the organization. We have found that managers going through these programs experience QWL in a new and more vital fashion, saying, for example, "Now I finally understand why this is necessary."

In programs without action-learning for the other key roles, managers often find themselves burdened with managing the old system in terms of the metaphor of the new system. They call this "management by committee," and they are right. It imposes upon such managers an intolerable burden and explains why they so frequently reject QWL change programs.

The development of QWL in the Federal Service needs such total organization programs for its departments and agencies. It needs them if the agency is collectively going to establish clear goals, improve public reputation and achieve a high degree of organizational effectiveness. Since QWL is so successful in the office or on the shop floor in the Public Service, it stands to reason that the addition of this total system approach could materially strengthen the operations and management of Federal Agencies.

Trist:

As regards the interdepartmental context, we have the advantage of having two critically relevant bodies already in existence, namely, the Senior Steering Committee and the Core Group. Our suggestion is that the activities of these two bodies be expanded in ways appropriate to their roles.

The role of the Senior Steering Committee is, in relation to the Treasury Board, to formulate the general policy of the Federal Public Service in the QWL field. For this purpose, it needs to meet sometimes alone and sometimes as a Joint Steering Committee with the presidents of the unions concerned. Presumably the latter would also at times wish to meet alone.

Committee membership would need to be kept to a high level: Deputy Ministers (DMs) or their equivalent, with relevant Assistant Deputy Ministers.

Questions are likely to arise sooner or later that will involve the political side and may require legislative change. Issues of job classification and compensation are cases in point, as are questions of overall budget allocation and what to treat as development (capital) expense and what as operating expenses. The present system is based on the old paradigm and, in the long run, will need extensive overhaul.

For the foreseeable future it may be expected that the Senior Steering Committee would have to meet as a joint committee with the union presidents at least once a year.

It would also need to meet not less than once a year with the Core Group—to be directly informed of the state of projects; the types of problems being encountered; the evaluation of strategies and outcomes; and the kinds of action required of it. Great uncertainty has been experienced in the Core Group concerning its relations with the Senior Steering Committee and the role of the latter. An annual joint conference with a lunch or dinner would do much to symbolize the importance of the interaction and affirm the continuing commitment of senior management.

It is assumed that the Secretary of the Treasury Board and the Deputy Minister of Labour are the core members of the Senior Steering Committee—along with the Chairman of the Public Service Commission. Thereafter are the DMs of departments with active QWL projects. From time to time, this group might like to have an extended meeting of the kind hosted by the Deputy Minister of Labour this week.

Occasionally, either the more restricted or the more extended group may care to invite distinguished outsiders to make presentations, or discuss informally and in private, their experiences in developing strategic QWL programs: senior executives of large corporations or of leading unions; key officials of foreign governments or international agencies such as the ILO; academics or consultants with recent experience of topics of particular relevance to the Federal Public Service.

Among these topics would be the microprocessor revolution and its implications for the office of the future, both with respect to job design and the substantial reductions in personnel made possible. Another topic might be work-sharing and the spread of part-time employment.

There would be an advantage in asking Ministers to attend some of these meetings as it will be necessary to keep the political as well as the administrative side updated regarding major changes likely to take place in the world of work in the decade now beginning.

The aim would be to develop a shared appreciation of the likely policy consequences at the highest levels of the Federal Government, which has now on more than one occasion—for example, in speeches by the Minister of Labour—committed itself to support QWL in the country at large.

The Core Group, composed as it is of management and union representatives from departments with ongoing projects, can function as an invaluable exchange for the comparison of QWL experiences in the Federal Public Service as a whole. On the one hand, it has a dissemination and nurturant role; on the other, a training and development role. It is the medium through which impending policy issues may be brought to the attention of the Senior Steering Committee.

With the Senior Steering Committee meeting once or twice a year, the Core Group might meet quarterly, given that the number of projects is likely to increase. In addition to being concerned with issues arising, exchange of information and preparation of briefs for the Senior Steering Committee, these meetings should be actively concerned with promoting training and development.

The Core Group should keep itself updated in the field as a whole, using the QWL units in the Treasury Board and Labour Canada as immediately available resources. Both units have built up libraries of reference material which are underutilized.

Departments need to be encouraged to develop in-house consultants. The Core Group, using the Treasury Board Unit, should actively concern itself with their development. There should be funds for such people to attend outside courses and workshops.

The Core Group would need a small budget, say $15,000 per annum, to hold special events and invite appropriate external resource people to them.

There would be great advantage in holding a residential retreat of two or three days every year at which the state of the art in QWL in the Federal Public Service could be surveyed, special topics discussed and future development adumbrated. A number of large corporations hold such events. Members of the Senior Steering Committee might attend at least one session of this conference.

Core Group events of this kind are postulated as leading to the development of a QWL network in the Federal Public Service which could become highly interactive, with the more experienced aiding the less experienced, on informal as well as formal lines, and the knowledge of all being increased. Various Core Group events would tend to become peer-group gatherings of this network. Such meetings provide ideal conditions for mutual learning as has been demonstrated in the United States where several interplant QWL networks exist in the private sector and, until funding was withdrawn by the present Administration, one—called Project Network—was successfully launched in the public sector. Recently, New York State has decided to proceed along these lines, quite extensively.

The development of interdepartmental activities depends on the development of intradepartmental activities which will entail a substantial investment in training at all levels, as Bill has suggested, if projects are successfully to be sustained and diffused.

These activities will need to be fostered on a collaborative basis by an institution such as the Core Group. The Treasury Board Unit will need to provide assistance at a sufficiently senior level to command attention.

Funds should be made available, whether by departments or by the Treasury Board, to use external as well as internal third parties. It will be some time before the Federal Public Service builds up enough internal expertise to be self-reliant. In any case, it will need to keep a window open on the outside world.

The developments envisaged are systemwide throughout the Federal Public Service and are long range. They are aimed at securing substantial results. The cost of not embarking on such a course is likely to be considerable by the end of the decade. While departments will participate voluntarily, strong and active leadership is required by the Treasury Board and Labour Canada in their complementary roles.

Reference

Ford, R.N. 1969. *Motivation Through the Work Itself.* New York: American Management Association.

Fred Emery and Einar Thorsrud

The Norskhydro Fertilizer Plant[1]

The initiative for this experiment arose from the Norskhydro Company. This is one of Norway's largest companies, with over 1,000 employees in the four production complexes it directly manages at widely separated sites around the country. As a science-based industry—electrochemical and petrochemical—it has long prided itself on being a progressive influence on the Norwegian scene. A new president was appointed at the beginning of 1967. He quickly started discussions with the Heroya Workers Union (HAF) at the main complex, with a view to thrashing out a new approach to productivity. The sort of thinking that was brought into these discussions can be illustrated by a statement from the president in 1968:

> A tremendous and worldwide increase in knowledge has created a new foundation for the use of knowledge and ability in solving the problems of society and production.
>
> Many people say that modern development in technology puts man out of function. This is not true. The individual will not lose his importance. In industry the requirements of individuals increase. They must increase their competence and initiative, and the value of machinery, raw materials and processes which the individual person is given responsibility for, is steadily increasing. More than ever before, the crucial matter behind the progress in society, in industry and for the individual person is to make proper use of man's abilities and initiative.

On the same occasion two of the leading shop stewards, Tor Halvorsen and Arne Johnny Nansen, wrote on behalf of their Union (HAF):

> The idea of participation represents nothing new in HAF. For a long time we have understood that we must participate in order to obtain great results within industry. The best results are never reached after a one-sided evaluation. Today all positive forces must be released in a constructive participation. Today only the best results are good enough.

Independently of, but parallel to, these discussions, the management and

[1]This chapter is based mainly on unpublished follow-up reports by Jon Gulowsen.

shop stewards met representatives from the Hunsfoss plant in a national labor-management seminar and discussed in concrete terms the experiences from that experiment. With the agreement of the Joint Research Committee, the management decided that the company would start up its own experimental studies and itself finance whatever assistance it needed from the research team.

As the first experimental site, the company chose a new fertilizer plant being constructed at Heroya. This offered the very great advantage of not having to first overcome an established management system and old customs and practices. It had the further advantage that the existing fertilizer plant, which was alongside it, would provide some basis for comparing performance. The overall purposes of the experiment were to be the same as for the earlier experiments. Increased productivity was not expressed as an aim in itself, but it was stated that the project could not be accepted if it ran contrary to the normal long-term development of productivity.

The Action Committee

From the start it was clear that the experiment should proceed via the active collaboration of management and the local union. A declaration of the project was drawn up and signed by both these parties. An important clause in the bulletin they issued gave protection to the experimental area:

> If it is convenient or necessary to change the organisation, the division of functions or the payment system from the usual pattern within the company, this may be done within the experimental area provided such changes are granted to have no immediate consequences outside the experimental area.

Of course, the agreement did not allow a completely free hand. The overriding constraint was that the experiment should come up with forms of participation that would be economically viable in fertilizer production *and* that would act as a demonstration model for the rest of the company. Getting an experimental success by extending special advantages to the workers in the experiment was thus not an acceptable solution.

To carry through the agreement, an Action Committee was decided upon. Drawing on the experiences of the earlier experiments, it was felt that such a special body would be needed to help the change process and to cope with the temporary load on communication channels that the experiment would create. The specific needs that were identified were:
- contact with the local management and authority within the area;
- contact with the workers to secure their confidence;
- drawing upon technical competence in the fertilizer production;

- contact with the personnel department in order to secure information from within the company as well as to make a future diffusion easier;
- contact with the research workers.

To meet these needs the following people were appointed to the action committee:

- the head of the fertilizer department (chairman),
- one representative from the local trade union,
- a charge-hand from the old factory,
- a representative from central management,
- a representative from the local personnel department,
- a representative from the Work Research Institute.

The last mentioned provided the ongoing link to the resources of the research team.

In the event, the Action Committee was not the prime source of the new job design, but it did carry out most of the preliminary reality testing of the ideas. In all its other functions, the committee proved invaluable. Two of its members were continuously present in the fertilizer plants. They maintained effective two-way communication so that many of the misunderstandings and difficulties that plagued some of the earlier experiments were dealt with before they started trouble. They not only kept the committee aware of the atmosphere in the plants but were able to feed in ideas, observations and suggestions from the operators and supervisors.

The Action Committee launched the project by organizing a meeting, which was attended by nearly 100 percent of all employees in the old fertilizer plant (recruitment for the new plant had not yet begun). At this meeting committee members outlined the objectives of the experiment and the ideas behind it. The interest displayed and the quality of the discussion directly reflected the high morale of the plant. As the men themselves were anxious to point out, there had been important steps toward participative management in the preceding year. So they felt they knew what the experiment was driving at, and, from their own experience, they knew that this was a way to get a good cooperative atmosphere and better production.

Following the mass meeting, the Action Committee moved to protect the experiment from outside influences that would have reduced the range of experimental choice. With the support of the operators, they prevailed upon the plant manager to postpone, and eventually cancel, a manpower study that an external consulting firm was supposed to carry out and also to postpone the introduction of UMS (a standard time system for planning and paying maintenance work).

As the experiment took shape, the Action Committee became increasingly immersed in the urgent task of recruitment, training and the wage system. We will return to this after dealing with the critical phase—the emergence of a design for operating the new fertilizer plant.

Design Proposals

Although the new plant had a vastly improved layout and included some important technical innovations, both plants were largely automatic, heavily instrumented and equipped with centralized controls. The sheer volume of dry and liquid materials being transported through the many stages of production meant a high but variable load of maintenance work and constant monitoring at many points.

The operators have little manual work but must move across large areas, that can include many physical levels. At intervals they visit one of the control rooms which are natural centers of communication. It is characteristic of this kind of process technology that work is fairly relaxed when production is high and stable. The workers are only kept busy performing a limited number of routine tasks. However, things become very hectic when production starts to go out of control.

To an outsider, the dimensions of the factory are very impressive. One can go through large parts of the factory without meeting anyone. Process flow, layout and the information system create divisions in the factories. Each of the units has a separate control room and is manned with up to five operators. Both factories have their own small mechanical workshops which can handle the majority of the day-to-day maintenance tasks.

The old factory consisted of two geographically separated areas, and the workers were divided into two sub-groups. Each of these sub-groups was supervised by a charge-hand who acted as a troubleshooter. The charge-hands reported to the shift foreman.

Most of the maintenance was done by a local maintenance group which reported to the department management. However, breakdowns on night shifts were handled by a shift pool of maintenance workers. These people did not report to the department management. A low status group of day workers did the necessary cleaning and laboring.

At an early stage in the construction of the new factory, in fact many months before the new approach was started, an experienced production engineer had designed the organization and manning scales for operating the plant. His ideas were based on the traditional methods of work organization and on the technological specifications of the new factory. Although his ideas were never put into practice, we will examine his model since it shows the way many engineers in that and many other companies thought, and still think, about work organization.

The engineer's original model included the following proposals. Every shift should be under the supervision of a foreman who would be in charge of the whole factory. Technical specifications suggested that the factory could logically be divided into three areas; therefore, the shift group should also be divided into three corresponding sub-groups, each of them under the supervision of a charge-hand. The operators within each group would be allocated three different grades of skills, with the charge-hands on the highest level. Two highly skilled operators would be in charge of the central control room. A special day force, reporting to a day foreman, would be responsible for cleaning, laboring and transport activities. Maintenance would be organized as in the old factory.

When the participation experiment commenced in March 1967, the total research group, with Professor Louis Davis (on sabbatical at the Tavistock Institute), visited the old factory and studied the plans for the new one. This group interviewed many of the people in the department, collected data and made a socio-technical analysis. A meeting between representatives from management, supervisors, the workers in the department and the social scientists produced another organizational model that was suitable for both factories.

This model was based on, among other things, an analysis of the maintenance data from the old factory. These data suggested that various kinds of repair work were significant parts of the daily work load throughout the factory. In fact, it proved to be difficult to separate maintenance from normal process operations. Since the new factory appeared to be divided into a number of separate geographical units, it was suggested that each shift should consist of sub-groups structured in the following way.

Each sub-group should include at least one worker who possessed versatile maintenance skills. The idea was that each sub-group should possess the skills and the working capacity necessary to tackle most of the production variances that occurred in their area. The model did not include charge-hands. The basic idea of the model was to provide conditions for increased self-sufficiency and autonomy at group level and better opportunities for learning and work satisfaction for individual group members. The different implications of the two approaches can be readily seen in the manning table given in Table 1.

This reduction of 40 percent needs to be closely examined, as it highlights the differences in organizational principles. The reduction had nothing to do with lowering the targets for level of plant efficiency nor with burdening the workers; the management would not allow the first, and the unions would certainly not allow the latter. The reduction stems from a difference in principle. In the first design, an overriding principle was that every necessary task had to be identified as the responsibility of a particular individual. The individual was then pinned to the geographical area where "his or her tasks" were located. Each person's own specified work load had to be so gauged that coping with normal peak load could be expected. In this plant it was easy to calculate, from the performance data of the old plant, that most of the operators would have nothing to do but watch a great deal of the time, even though their neighbors might be experiencing a temporary overload. The shift charge-hands

TABLE I   Manning Levels for the New Plant (1967)

	Initial proposal based on classic scientific management principles	Subsequent proposal based on semiautonomous groups
Plant manager	1	1
Production assistants (clerks)	2	2
Superintendent	1	1
Day foreman	1	0
Shift foreman	4	4
Maintenance foreman	1	1
Shift charge-hands	12	0
Shift-operators (12 x 4)	48	40
Maintenance workers	12	8
Day laborers	12	0
Total	94	57

provided a floating reserve of multiskilled workers. They and the foremen could temporarily reallocate duties to help with crises, but even this was limited by the fact that individuals tended to know only their own jobs. The next level of backup was provided by the maintenance staff and the day laboring gang. These people took the load of these kinds of tasks off the operators and theoretically allowed for maximum utilization of operators on operating tasks.

We started, as in earlier experiments, from the principle that groups take responsibility for as many of the necessary tasks in their area as possible. It would be up to the group to deploy and re-deploy themselves so as to cope with variations in task loads and to ensure adequate monitoring over the processes still running in control. To operate effectively in this way, the members of the group would need to be multiskilled to the point where they could at least lend a hand with any of the tasks coming up in their area (as were the charge-hands in the previous design). Because of the sheer physical size of the plant, it was recognized that a shift would normally operate as three small sub-groups. It seemed that a shift crew of 10 would be sufficiently flexible to cope with the operating tasks, with many of the less skilled maintenance tasks and with all of the cleaning and moving tasks. The management and union representatives accepted the desirability of the shift crew coping with these other tasks. Too much downtime was due to waiting for maintenance or to someone failing to use a spanner before trouble actually occurred. Similarly, spillage was not unrelated to the operators' carefulness and alertness. However, both parties felt it would be prudent to set shift staffing at 11. They also felt that it might be difficult to recruit two skilled maintenance workers per shift to work in the teams as operator-maintenance workers. (They were right. The plant finished up with only one per shift.)

It was expected with the new system that the shift foreman would for the most part be acting-in for the manager and superintendent, not acting as a supervisor. And, of course, there would not be a set of charge-hands to organize.

One final feature of the design should be noted. Everyone on a shift could expect to be skilled up to the level of control room operation. An understanding of automated process plant operation requires a close and up-to-date view of things from the center and from the floor level. Under the classic one worker/ one job approach, control room operators tend to be wedded to their "white collar job" and its attendant status.

Thus, instead of the traditional status differences among unskilled day laborers, ordinary operators, control room operators and charge-hands there would, in our design, be only differences in currently proven competence. Achievement of higher competence was expected to be largely up to the individual. There would be no waiting until a vacancy occurred at the next level and, even then, having no prior chance to prove fitness to compete for the vacancy.

Developments in the Design

Two months after the meeting that considered these alternative designs one of the engineers in the division brought forward "new" proposals based on discussions within the local management group.

- Process workers would each be responsible for cleaning in their own work area.
- There should be no low-skilled daytime groups in the factory.
- Each shift should have a charge-hand in addition to the foreman. This charge-hand should have some competence in instrumentation as well as being capable of acting as a troubleshooter for the whole factory.

These proposals accepted the suggestion that a day cleaning squad be avoided. In other ways, it was a rearguard action. The reversion to individual/task area responsibility and to charge-hands would have eliminated the notion of semi-autonomous groups. The "job enlargement" entailed in doing one's own cleaning would probably not have been seen by the union as "job enrichment."

The Action Committee gradually came to their own conclusions regarding the design of the organization. There should be no charge-hands or low status day workers in the factory. Shift operators should be urged to work in pairs or in larger groups within their own group territory. The shifts should, if possible, be staffed with some maintenance people. (The number of maintenance people who applied for jobs in the factory was limited. Thus each shift, which numbered about 12 operators, had only one or two maintenance workers when the factory started up.)

Using these ideas as their point of departure, the different shift groups subsequently developed their own ways of working the new organizational patterns. The major differences were in the degree of multiskilling they were prepared to accept and the size of geographical areas they were prepared to man. The older workers showed less interest in increasing their skills and, not unnaturally, more interest in minimizing walking and climbing stairs.

Prior to the shift groups doing anything, or even existing, the Action Committee had a lot to do themselves, and a lot to work out with others, so that the proposals for semiautonomous group manning could become operational.

Wage System and Bonus

It was obvious that the new manning proposals offered considerable economic advantages to the company, provided they worked. It was equally obvious that some new wage system would be needed to bring advantages to the operators and to go on doing so in the likely event of the new system continuing to create further advantages for the company.

Previous experiments gave some leads to the Action Committee, but they were not seen as providing any model that could simply be copied. Before the committee could move, an overall site productivity agreement was finally settled in April 1967. This agreement offered all the workers on the site, including the old fertilizer plant, an opportunity to earn more. It included a manpower analysis which was to be taken care of by a consultant firm, and the introduction of piece rates for maintenance work according to a so-called Universal Maintenance System (UMS).

At a plenary meeting, the workers in the fertilizer factory questioned the applicability of this productivity agreement to the project area. They saw the principles as irreconcilable because the manpower analysis started from the principle of one person/one job with unshared responsibility. They also questioned the competence of outside specialists.

With this background, the workers suggested that their own manpower analysis should be taken care of by the Action Committee. This was done in cooperation with the local management. The proposal, which suggested a reduction in the manning of the old plant from 72 to 60 workers, was unanimously accepted. Later the maintenance group was reduced from 12 to eight people.

The old fertilizer plant, after this event, followed more or less the same pattern as was developed by the new plant when it gradually started to operate on the new basis during the early autumn of 1967.

Next the Action Committee, aided by the local management, worked out a bonus scheme for all operators in the old fertilizer plant. This bonus was based on the following criteria:

- Production volume of acceptable quality.
- Control over raw materials lost, particularly nitrogen.
- Other costs which could be influenced by the workers.
- Total number of man-hours for production, including service workers' time.

The central idea behind the bonus scheme was to pay the workers according to factors which they themselves could influence; factors which at the same time were important for the factory. Since the bonus included all workers in the factory, it was expected to stimulate cooperation. The payment and the working conditions for each individual depended upon the joint effort of the whole factory staff: operators, maintenance, clerks and supervisors. The bonus scheme represented the first step toward a new wage system for the new factory. It soon became clear that more drastic changes would become necessary.

The traditional wage system put people in a position where it was not in their interest to help each other, and hence it acted against cooperation and mutual aid in the work situation. It did less than nothing to encourage a way of work that could provide opportunities for learning from each other, for sufficient variation, for the development of work groups and for operators to get to know the whole process. In other words, chances for satisfaction of the psychological job requirements were small.

In order to improve the chances for satisfactory psychological work conditions, the Action Committee devised a new wage system. In close cooperation with the local shop stewards, it was decided that each worker should be paid according to proven competence. Both theoretical knowledge and practical experience from production could contribute to higher wages. By learning all the jobs in the factory, the process operators could advance from wage class no. 2 to class no. 6 and then get the same wages as skilled maintenance workers. The wage system presupposed that the workers were given the chance to rotate through all jobs in the factory.

It was hoped that this would reward the workers for learning from their work and, step by step, developing more flexible interdependent work patterns. It was agreed that the local shop steward and the general foreman should be responsible for the evaluation of the competence of the workers. This wage system was a major innovation. For management, it was a challenge. Would lower manning rates and better performance offset the added costs of training and paying extra for having a reserve of competence on the job?

Recruitment to the New Factory

The workers who became superfluous—through their own rationalization—in the old factory were guaranteed jobs in the new plant. But it was necessary to recruit more people. A lot of discussion took place about how the vacant positions should be advertised. It was agreed that any such advertisement should create only those expectations that were in line with the intended design of work. The final advertisement was as follows:

> We need workers to take care of process and maintenance in the new fertilizer factory (process workers, maintenance workers, plumbers and instrument makers). The company is going to try to develop new kinds of cooperation to the benefit of employees as well as the company itself. Therefore, we want to get into contact with employees who are interested to:
>
> learn and develop themselves further through the work
>
> take responsibility
>
> become active members of a work group
>
> participate in the training of others
>
> participate in developing jobs and ways of cooperation which create conditions for personal development through the work.
>
> It may be necessary to alter many of the usual norms within the organization, such as formal organization and contents of the different jobs. At the moment, it seems likely that work groups with optimal competence within maintenance and process control will have to be formed.

No financial incentive was mentioned. The advertisement generated more than enough applications. Selection was based on interviews by a representative from the personnel department, the general foreman of the factory and the trade union representative in the Action Committee. Concerning wages, the operators were assured that they would not lose anything compared to their old level while they were training until the new factory was started. No other guarantees were given.

This procedure differed significantly from established routines in the personnel department of the company. The 20 workers who were selected according to the procedure that has just been described made up the first group to join the staff for the new factory. The majority of the remaining part of the staff came from the old factory and joined somewhat later. This group had not been through special selection.

Training

Traditionally, process operators in Norskhydro, as in most other companies, have received little systematic training and education. They have generally had to prepare themselves for the performance of relatively simple routine tasks by working together with a more experienced worker. The narrow specialized jobs gave little opportunity to understand the process as a whole and did little to stimulate further learning. Only half of the 20 new men had even this much experience of process work. So the Action Committee immediately took the initiative to set up a training scheme. A course of 200 hours of theoretical training was started in cooperation with the company school and the local shop stewards. Practical experience and training went on in the old factory and later in the new factory as equipment was being installed. Due to lack of time to commissioning date, only the first group went through the whole training program. The rest of the workers, all experienced, were given a shorter theoretical training program lasting 40 hours.

The character of the training was dictated by the desire to staff the factory with multiskilled operators having a broad knowledge in process maintenance work. They were therefore provided with learning opportunities in chemistry, process knowledge, instrumentation and maintenance work. The interest in the training program was great, and the operators constantly probed the connection between the theory and their future work. Supervisors and technicians on the factory staff participated in the course both as teachers and as students.

The training scheme, which was built up for the workers in the fertilizer department, represented a "new deal" in the training policy within the company. Previously, the company school had mainly been occupied with training craftsmen in craft skills: plumbers, welders, mechanics, etc. The majority of those trainees were under 20.

The new training scheme was a first step toward creating in the company the status of a "skilled process worker." The need for adult training was stressed, and new organizational and pedagogic principles were applied: "The school must go into the factory; the factory must become the school." In particular, it was believed that education for working as semiautonomous groups should be based on semiautonomous learning groups. As the pressure for multiskilling built up on the site as a whole, there were signs of the education being routinized. We are not in a position to judge whether the principle was ever firmly established in the company school or, if established, whether the observed tendencies remained central.

The Operation of the New Principles in the New Plant

The critical test of the new principles of organization was in this case quite simple. What was judged to be a good design by traditional "scientific management" principles stated that about 94 people were needed for the plant to be efficiently operated. The alternative design, based on self-managing multiskilled shift teams, predicted that 56 people could operate the plant with at least equal efficiency and with greater satisfaction to the people concerned. The modified design went into operation with 60 people, one extra operator per shift. The difference in staffing levels was still so great (60 to 94) that there could be no rational doubt that different principles were at stake. Differences in technology, personnel, etc., were nowhere near comparable in the magnitude of their possible effects on work satisfaction or efficiency.

Two questions arise:

Did the much lower manning level with semiautonomous groups manage to achieve the level of efficiency that would be expected with a traditional design?

Did the workers benefit accordingly from the system (or was the per capita improvement in efficiency taken from their hides)?

Let us reply very briefly to the first question, turn to the second question, and then return to the first.

The new mode of operation was obviously economically viable by management's standards. They encouraged the old fertilizer plant to move over to the same principles of operator self-management and encouraged their other plants on the site to move in the same direction. Although this has been achieved only to a limited extent, it is explicit company policy to push in this direction. Over seven years of operation (1967–74), there has been no question of going back to the old principles of organization. This managerial attitude was not due to Norskhydro having money to throw away, to sustained union pressure or to public opinion. We will return to the question of what evidence could have been so convincing to management.

The most obvious and most easily measured advantages to the workers were those flowing from being multiskilled, being able to increase their skills and being able to use and be paid for these additional skills. Less easy to measure were the advantages of the workers being able to make so many of the decisions about the deployment of their capabilities. Even less obvious were the advantages that accrue from disappearance of the "donkey jobs" of day laboring and the erosion of the "labor aristocracy" of control room operators and charge-hands (as welcomed and further pushed for by the paper machine operators at Hunsfoss).

The plant was commissioned in 1967. By late summer 1969, the average operator was being paid extra for competence in 5.4 out of the 8 possible task skills in the plant. One shift lagged noticeably behind in multiskilling and rotation of jobs, and they were also noticeably dependent on their shift foreman. These were older workers, and this seemed to be their preferred style. In the overall pattern this was not disruptive.

Observations made at this stage also showed that the average operator was involved in two to four different task areas during a shift. In the traditional system, the operator was only rarely involved in more than one area and then had to be paid as if it were overtime. Multiskilling was obviously the new norm. Even the "laggard shift" had an average of more than three skills. Flexibility in the use of these skills was markedly higher than in the old system and indicative of the new style of working.

A measure of the attitude of operators was taken after they had had some months of working the new system (Table 2). Because of the work pressures in the factory, only 33 of the 52 operators and maintenance workers could be taken off the job to be interviewed at the start and only 22 in December 1972. Some of these respondents had worked in other equally traditional jobs but not in fertilizer production, and others were in the maintenance section which was only marginally affected. The differences are striking enough to offset the inadequacies of the data.

TABLE 2   Changes in Attitudes of Workers Between Previous Job and December 1967 in the New Plant

		Yes	No
Do you have adequate responsibility for determining your work?	Old job	14	19
	New plant	24	1
Are there good chances to learn on the job?	Old job	10	21
	New plant	25	1
Is there adequate variety in the job?	Old job	16	17
	New plant	22	4
Does the job give you a sense of security?	Old job	13	20
	New plant	22	8
Do you feel satisfied with the job?	Old job	18	13
	New plant	26	0

Of critical significance is the fact that all but one worker on the new plant said that they could now determine how they did their jobs. As social scientists, we did not think it necessary to run statistical tests of significance over these figures; they were very obviously highly significant. After day-to-day experience of the new form of organization for more than four months, the workers thought they had more control, better chances to learn, more optimal variety, more satisfaction and more security.

Our systematic observations on the new plant continued through 1972. Some changes were occurring. The younger people with the higher levels of competence were expressing some dissatisfaction with lack of further challenge and applying (successfully) for new jobs in other parts of the company. The labor market, particularly within their own company, was becoming very rosy. Thus, while labor turnover was practically nil during the first two years, it now resembles the turnover for operators in the other chemical plants on the site.

It is sometimes asked whether the effects we are describing here could not have been achieved just by making the same changes in wages and bonuses. This seems an appropriate point at which to confront such queries. Quite simply, what good would it have done the new plant to have paid for a high level of skill if this were used only within one individual's area of responsibility? What good would a group bonus have done if the workers did not have the rights and responsibility of self-management? We suggest that self-management of the work groups is the key, not the lock to be turned by forms of monetary reward. This is rather obvious when we consider older forms of group working, where money rewards sustained brutalized forms of subcontracting within which employees had even fewer rights for self-determination and less legal protection against exploitation.

Self-management was not complete and was never intended to be so. However, there was no felt need nor any expressed desire for the return of charge-hands. In fact, when one foreman retired, no one was formally appointed to replace him—one operator was informally asked whether he would look after the things the foreman used to do (answering the outside phone, etc.). Observation of a typical shift cycle confirmed the "decentering" of the foreman on all but the one shift mentioned above (Table 3).

Returning now to the company's apparent satisfaction with semiautonomous group working, the most obvious fact is that the plant worked. It did not collapse from undermanning, and it did not have to be kept on its feet by special support systems. The evidence allows us to go beyond this simple statement of the key fact. The plant did not only work, it worked better than could have been expected on the traditional system of manning.

The bonus scheme was based on savings in inputs as well as increase in outputs. Adequate records of these were not brought into being until 1969, the

TABLE 3   Persons Consulted by Operators About Problems

	Foreman	Other operators	Both
Shift 3	7	2	0
Shifts 1, 2, 4	8	11	4

need for such data not having been recognized. In the two years 1969–70, the bonus increased about 50 percent.

Production data for each of the three main lines exist from commissioning time. They show increases between 50 and 100 percent despite the low manning levels. The downtime percentage for the plant's operation was probably the most critical indicator. Downtime was the most costly experience the plant could have. It was expected from experience of this type of plant that downtime would vary between 10 and 30 percent (usually more than 20 percent). In the new plant with the new form of organization, the downtime has been kept within 5 and 10 percent, much less than half. This was achieved by the increased concern of the operators, not by increased effort.

With the savings on inputs, these reductions in downtime (with such low manning levels) might well explain the continued managerial interest.

Diffusion of Project Results at Corporate Level

Diffusion must be seen in the specific context agreed upon at the time the project was launched. It was Norskhydro, in collaboration with its related unions, which took the responsibility for the project and for evaluating the results. The Joint National Research Committee agreed to the project plans in general and to the involvement of the research group.

When the new fertilizer plant had been in operation for a few months, the Action Committee presented a progress report to a joint meeting of company and union representatives. A decision was quickly made to start preparations for similar projects in other plants. Six months later the company magazine published the results from the fertilizer project and stated that the new principles of work organization would constitute a shift in company policy. It soon became clear that this was easier said than done. One was obviously not dealing with an experiment and a simple transfer of results but with all the complexities of changing the largest private industrial organization in Norway.

This occurred at a time when Norskhydro and its unions faced two serious challenges, which diverted most of their resources away from the Industrial

Democracy project. First, Norskhydro became a major partner in the North Sea Oil activities. Second, there was a national struggle over membership in the European Economic Community with a referendum deciding that Norway was not going to join. This caused considerable reorientation within the company, and its major union was divided politically to the extent that it could not mobilize its members in anything but traditional bargaining issues.

In view of these limitations, it is perhaps understandable that diffusion from the fertilizer project has been slow. One project in the carbide plant was just getting off the ground, after considerable resistance from the supervisor, when market conditions caused the plant to close down. An extensive project started in the magnesium plant, which has included major technological improvements and retraining activities. Projects in a large mechanical workshop and in the transportation sector were hung up on primitive bargaining over a new structure.

In 1970 a new wage agreement, based on the model from the fertilizer project, was signed for the whole company, granting all workers the right to get training on the job and in special courses integrated in a guaranteed promotion ladder. A special incentive system (UMS) for maintenance workers, causing a split between process operators and special tradesmen, was gradually abolished. A two-year program was set up to retain 350 foremen for alternative supervisory roles. Most of them had had no formal education beyond the age of 15, and their average age was now above 50. In 1973 and 1974, a series of middle management seminars have been run to initiate small organization redesign projects. Still, no further real breakthroughs have occurred at the productive level to match the policy declarations of the company in 1968. Some of the reasons for this can perhaps best be understood if we explore on a more general level the trade union and management involvements in projects of this nature.

Other reasons might have to be sought at the level of the research team. At Hunsfoss, after a very different start-up at the chemical pulp plant, the machine operators on the paper machines took things very much into their own hands. They first worked out what they needed to do and then checked it out with the researchers and with the operators at Porsgrun fertilizer plants. At the Hemya complex, despite the very successful start-up of the fertilizer plants, we implanted a resident expert, which tended to stifle local initiative. The carbide plant experiment stopped because the market for carbide closed down. The magnesium plant experiment developed very slowly in the face of a massive technological redesign. The unions in the central workshops and in transportation would not consider redesign of jobs until they had settled outstanding scores with management, by arbitration.

We should perhaps at this stage have implemented the lessons of the Hunsfoss paper mills; namely, we should have pulled out the resident expert and provided advice on call.

Trevor A. Williams

Visual Display Technology, Worker Disablement and Work Organization[1]

In Australia, as in other countries, new office technology has been adopted widely and rapidly in recent years. Associated with the introduction of visual display units (VDUs) there was, in the first half of the 1980s, a remarkable increase in disablement among employees who operated them. In the Australian Public Service between 20 and 30 percent of keyboard and clerical employees were reported to be suffering from musculotendinous disorders known collectively as repetition strain injury (RSI). Disablement on a similar scale was being reported in the private sector, and there was also evidence of visual and neurophysiological damage. Unless prevented or apprehended in the early stages of development, many of these injuries can become crippling and persist for long periods of time, if not the duration of a person's life. The economic costs of lost production and workers' compensation payments reached serious proportions. There was a possibility that manufacturers and suppliers of visual display equipment might face legal liabilities. VDUs were discarded by some organizations. Late in 1984, the Australian government established a Task Force on Repetition Strain Injury in the Australian Public Service, and concern about RSI increased considerably in the private sector (*Business Review Weekly,* 1984). There was a strong perception of the sudden increase in injury as definitely related to the introduction of VDUs into the workplace, an issue which was not unique to Australia.

The evidence for a relationship between VDUs and worker disablement came largely from observed association. The human and economic costs of occupational injury made prevention and control an urgent priority. At the same time, the relationship between VDUs and RSI was not well understood. A technology had been introduced that was forcing human adaptation and giving rise to disorders in human functioning (Corlett and Richardson, 1981). There were considerable economic pressures to adopt new technology, but the introduction of VDUs may have pushed technological innovation to the limits of current knowledge about its effects on human beings.

[1]A revised version of "Worker Disablement and Work Organisation," *Human Relations,* 38:1065–84, 1985.

Furthermore, there was a growing belief that injury was significantly affected by the design of work organization. Medical practitioners were advocating a search for solutions in work organization design on the grounds that substantial advances in medical knowledge and treatment would be too slow and that work redesign offered a means of prevention rather than cure (Ferguson, 1984). Ergonomists, who had made their own contribution through the design of workstations, were suggesting that further progress toward preventing injury depended on such factors as the volume, flow, speed and duration of keyboard work, which were determined by the organization of work. Moreover, developments in technology were allowing scope for choice in work organization design. Decisions about work organization were becoming less constrained by technological parameters than they had been by some of the energy-based technologies of industrial production (Buchanan and Boddy, 1982; Eason and Sell, 1981; Turner and Karasek, 1984).

This paper discusses current knowledge about the relationship between VDUs and worker disablement as a basis for examining the role of work organization in this relationship. It considers alternative basic work organization designs in relation to new technology and their likely consequences for occupational injury. The findings from a study of two Australian government departments with significantly different levels of reported occupational injury are examined and compared in terms of their work designs and VDU applications. The findings are consistent with the expectation that organizations which introduce new technology while retaining conventional bureaucratic work designs will experience greater occupational injury among workers than organizations in which work design provides employees with more variety and scope to control their own task performance.

Visual Display Technology and Worker Disablement

Most concern about worker disablement from VDUs in Australia has focused on RSI. This term refers to injuries to the upper limbs, shoulder girdles and neck attributed to:

- static loading, or isometric contraction, of the neck, shoulder and upper arm muscles to support and fix the arm in a position of function;
- dynamic loading, or repetitive movement of the forearms, hands and fingers (and sometimes upper arms) to execute a task;
- force used to execute a task.(Browne et al., 1984)

The term RSI is applied to a large number of musculotendinous disorders. The same symptoms can arise synchronously from different causes: they can be associated with recreational as well as work activities, and they can be related to personal stress and tension. The injuries can occur in some individuals engaged in a given activity but not in others. Hence, RSI is not precisely defined medically. It can have multiple causes, and its relationship to working with VDUs is not clearly or precisely understood (Browne et al., 1984; Ferguson, 1984). Nevertheless, RSI became extraordinarily prevalent among VDU operators, and outbreaks frequently followed the introduction of VDUs.

Several factors were considered to increase the risk of RSI and aggravate its symptoms. The main factors identified were

Biomechanical. Incorrect posture; the number, speed and frequency of repetitive movements; the amount of force used; extreme movements; faults in workstation equipment and task design; muscle tension associated with stress; operator adjustments to protect injured limbs; and individual susceptibility to strain injury.

Work organization. Excessive duration of work without rest; bonus and incentive schemes; inadequate training; work rate; work load; work flow; fragmentation and specialization of tasks; work monitoring; and work output norms.

Reporting and management. An unsympathetic climate in the workplace; anxiety about job security; failure of supervisors to recognize and act on signs of injury; lack of education about RSI and information concerning reporting procedures; lack of alternative work; language barriers; lack of management information and policy; inadequate availability of medical services; incorrect or delayed diagnosis; and inappropriate management of injury. (Browne et al., 1984; Ferguson, 1984; Stone, 1983)

In this prevalent view, RSI is primarily a physiological phenomenon. The symptoms of pain and weakness in muscles and tendons and their presumed origins in biomechanical functioning and the demands of task performance suggest a basically physical interpretation of what is happening in the interaction between operators and VDUs. Similarly, apart from RSI, there is concern that working with VDUs can adversely affect visual functioning, but attention so far has been largely confined to the physical effects of "visual fatigue." This is generally regarded as muscle strain caused by prolonged convergence of the eyes at the point of attention and by alteration of the shape of the lens to focus on a near object (National Health and Medical Research Council, 1983). Physiologically oriented research and interventions have made important contributions to the understanding and prevention of injury associated with VDUs. It is not the intention here to devalue those contributions, but it is necessary to go further.

The physiological view of RSI points to demands of task performance as contributors to injury but not as characteristics of the technology. An obvious question is why RSI did not become widespread with the introduction of typewriters. It was a technological innovation that required considerable experimentation and learning and adaptation of postures, movement and techniques for efficient operation while avoiding discomfort and strain. These lessons may have been overlooked in the introduction of VDUs. Many operators may not have received adequate keyboard training, and there have been numerous cases where important ergonomic considerations were neglected. Also, keyboard work on VDUs is less varied and more repetitive with fewer opportunities for operators to move around in their work when compared with typists. Rapid introduction of the technology and possibly inferior equipment would aggravate such difficulties. Nevertheless, these factors do not seem sufficient to explain the epidemic proportions that RSI reached. There appears to be some important qualitative difference between the technology involving even the advanced electromagnetic typewriter and the electronic VDU.

This possibility has been raised by Fred Emery (1984) in relation to tenosynovitis, potentially a very serious injury that is attributed to the drying up of synovial fluids in the tendon sheaths, caused by abrasion and inflammation. This may be explained physiologically by the fact that electronic keyboards, while reducing the force required to activate the keys, also make possible much faster keystroke rates than do conventional typewriters. A threshold may have been transgressed which previously was not known. However, it may be that the synovial fluids in the tendon sheath are not being replenished sufficiently because the touch pressure on the keys is too light to provide the feedback to the brain necessary for replenishment to occur. Alternatively, skin and bone joint stimulation may be projected directly into the human nervous system at a precortical level. If so, this would have emerged during human evolution under feedback conditions given the more familiar and much firmer uses of the hand such as grasping or prodding, rather than the feather stroking of an electronic keyboard. Either way, the feedback conditions of at least some electronic keyboards are outside the range in which the human perceptual system, in this case the haptic or touching subsystem, evolved. Emery notes that keyboard operation may constitute prolonged inactivity for the knuckles and wrist joints, which weakens the cartilage and makes it susceptible to damage from other activity. The symptoms of damage observed in cartilage research are very similar to those of tenosynovitis (F. Emery, 1984). Emery's line of inquiry does not preclude the effects of excessively fast keystroke rates but directs attention beyond physiological questions to the interaction between technology and human perceptual functioning.

As with RSI, the prevalent view concerning the effects of VDU operation on visual functioning concentrates on physical effects. Merrelyn Emery's research on television, which she has extended to VDUs, shows that more is involved. Many VDUs contain the same cathode ray tubes as television receivers. The main differences are that working with VDUs entails closer viewing distances and longer viewing periods. Hence, the effects found in television viewing are expected to be more pronounced in VDU operation (M. Emery, 1985; F. Emery, 1959/Vol. I).

The cathode ray tube emits radiant light in contrast to the reflected light in which the human perceptual system evolved. The general effect is to induce high levels of attention (fixation) and recognition of symbols but reduction in cortical activity with resultant lower consciousness and alertness. In VDU operation this may raise two problems. First, the effect of viewing the screen is lower alertness and recall—but the task often requires alertness, recall and understanding. Second, a small percentage of the population is extremely sensitive to the radiant light of the cathode ray tube, "TV epilepsy." It is presumed that the rest of the population is normal—but there may be a spectrum of individual reactions to radiant light ranging from no or very little disturbance to neurophysiological functioning through mildly abnormal reactions to extreme reactions (Burch, 1984; M. Emery, 1985). If this is the case, a considerably larger number of individuals may experience more or less persistent mildly adverse effects from radiant light.

In several studies of VDU operators, a core of symptoms has been identified. Compared with individuals not working with VDUs, operators have been found to experience more difficulty in getting out of bed; eye strain; blurred vision; shoulder pain; neck pain; red eyes; irritability; frontal headaches; lower back pains; worsening of vision; and reduction of energy (M. Emery, 1985). These symptoms may arise, not only from the physical effects of VDU tasks, but from neurophysiological effects as well. The hypothesized relations between VDUs and miscarriages or birth defects do not have to rest on the considerable but controversial body of argument concerning radiation effects. The disturbances that radiant light may evoke in some individuals could be sufficient to induce biological malfunctioning (Burch 1984).

The physiological perspective on VDUs directs attention to the repetitive nature of operators' tasks and to their constrained movements as principal sources of strain and injury. Tasks may involve data or text entry, data inquiry or dialogue between the operator and the system. These differences affect whether the operator is viewing hard copy or the screen or both and, in turn, the sources of musculoskeletal loading and potential strain. The effects of task demands can be aggravated or mitigated by the design of equipment and by the techniques that operators use. Individuals vary in their susceptibility to both musculotendinous and visual strain and, hence, the extent to which they are at risk when working with VDUs. Task analysis to determine the types of physical loading involved, ergonomic design, operator training and individual assessments are measures which can be taken to reduce the risk of injury among operators (Department of Employment and Industrial Relations, 1984; Joint Committee of Public Accounts, 1984). The studies by F. Emery and M. Emery suggest that VDUs represent a more fundamental technological discontinuity, particularly the introduction of the electronic keyboard and the cathode ray tube, that creates perceptual and neurophysiological problems in the relationship between people and technology. Ultimately, the problems which they identify require change in the technology itself, more selective and appropriate application of technology and development of technology that is compatible with the evolution of the human species.

From both perspectives—human and technological—work organization may have important consequences. From the physiological perspective, the basic issue is the performance of repetitive tasks in constrained positions that gives rise to dynamic and static loading. The longer and faster the operators work, the greater is the risk of injury. Duration and speed of work can be varied, but in what ways and with what effects depends on how the work is organized. Time is also an important factor in the effects of VDUs on human perceptual and neurophysiological functioning. From this perspective, the issue is the duration of people's interaction with a technology that evokes maladaptive responses in them. Reducing and regulating the time that they spend in this interaction would not be a complete answer, but it is important. Moreover, although the immediate concern here is with occupational health and safety, the introduction of new technology raises wider issues in the future of work and its organization—whether the essential features of conventional industrial organization will be perpetuated and intensified or whether, with new technology, work will undergo basic socio-technical redesign.

VDU Technology and Work Organization Design

The role of work organization design in the interaction between VDU technology and workers is brought into sharp focus by considering the two basic work design alternatives postulated by Emery (F. Emery, 1976; Emery and Emery, 1974/Vol. II, Emery and Thorsrud, 1977; Emery and Trist, 1972/1973). One alternative, which Emery calls bureaucracy, is to subdivide work to a point where those performing the component tasks cannot control their own activities or coordinate with others performing related tasks. Control and coordination are imposed on task performance through hierarchical structures. The other alternative, participative democracy, is to integrate related tasks and create organizational units whose members are able to control their work, in cooperation with each other, to meet both the performance requirements of the organization and their own needs.

This choice applies not only to work organization but to the design and application of technology. With computer technology, application systems can take the form of batch processing or work unit processing. In batch processing, all processing of a particular type is completed before the next processing stage commences. Processing cycles tend to be short and repetitive, and the system encourages subdivision of tasks. There is little requirement to provide operators with a coherent model of the system's operation, because operators at each stage are concerned with only one or a very few steps in the process. In work unit processing, all processing of a particular item or transaction is completed before the next one is handled. Work is carried out in modules that lend themselves to decentralized processing structures in which operators can have a high degree of interaction with the system, tend to be involved in complete operations and have scope for intervention in, and control over, the process (Turner and Karasek, 1984).

Consideration of the basic work designs and computer application designs gives the array of socio-technical alternatives shown in Figure 1. The work organization and computer application dimensions represent the same socio-technical choice from two perspectives. Thus, Turner and Karasek (1984, pp. 665, 671) note, "when a new system is implemented, intentionally or not, labor is reallocated between man and machine. . . . Task allocation decisions on the part of a system designer are tantamount to defining the human's job." However, maintaining a distinction between the work organization and system design dimensions serves to emphasize that there are two related but distinct choices about technology and work organization, and that a choice on either dimension could take precedence over the other. The choices can be, and often are, made separately or at different stages in the process of introducing new technology. The technical system may be defined first with little or no attention to the effects on work organization and on employees in their jobs. This approach assumes that human and organizational adjustments to accommodate the new technology will follow from the way in which the technical system is designed. The alternative is to integrate technical and human requirements from the start in the design not just of a new technology but of a new socio-technical system (F. Emery, 1980/Vol. II; Herbst, 1974/Vol. II; Williams, 1983, 1988).

The choices of social and technical design in the introduction of visual display technology have a direct bearing on the extent to which work is repetitive and on control over the volume, flow, speed and duration of keyboard work. In the bureaucratic/batch system, the tendency toward maximum subdivision of work increases the repetitiveness of tasks, and employees have little control over their work. Also, much faster keystroke rates compared with typing tend to be reflected in output norms not only of managers and supervisors but also of the operators. Management's expectations of higher productivity are usually the main reason for introducing VDUs, and the technology makes it possible to monitor precisely the volume and accuracy of each employee's output. Moreover, when operators are engaged in a small number

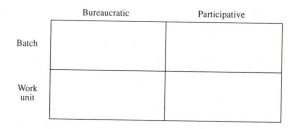

	Bureaucratic	Participative
Batch		
Work unit		

Figure 1. Socio-technical alternatives

of repetitive tasks, their keystroke rates tend to increase progressively, and this can be encouraged by incentive schemes. Hence, the bureaucratic/batch system enables higher productivity to be pursued through highly subdivided tasks and monitoring and control of individual performance. It entails no fundamental change from conventional work organization, and batch processing is easier to program than the alternative of work-unit processing (Turner and Karasek, 1984).

Most Australian organizations introduced visual display technology while retaining conventional bureaucratic work designs. In response to the growing incidence of worker disablement associated with VDUs, a variety of measures have been adopted. These include ergonomic analysis and design; upper limb and visual acuity assessment to identify individual susceptibility; and improved operator training. There is a trend toward discontinuing output incentives and machine monitoring. Rest breaks and exercise programs have been introduced. It is becoming accepted that employees should not work full time on VDUs and that their jobs should include nonkeyboard tasks. These are measures to reduce the disabling effects of VDUs without changing the basic work organization or the technical processing system.

However, problems have been encountered with these measures. Ergonomic analysis and design have been accepted by managements and unions as important but limited in their capacity to prevent injury. Assessments of individual susceptibility are recognized as in the interest of employees but are rejected by unions as a basis for excluding people from employment involving VDUs. The importance of operator training is acknowledged, but there is growing concern that operators generally have so little knowledge and understanding of the systems they are working in that their work is meaningless.

The other measures appear to be more promising. It is within management's prerogative to restrict or eliminate work incentives, overtime and machine monitoring of performance. In practice, pressures for production undermine these policies. Also, the electronic keyboards are designed for fast keying, and keystroke rates tend to increase despite limits imposed by management or established by agreement with unions, and attempts to enforce the limits may be resented by the operators. Similar problems are encountered with rest breaks and exercise programs. In many organizations rest periods have been introduced to be taken by operators at regular prescribed intervals. Again, this may conflict with production pressures. Operators, who are located throughout the organization in sections where other staff do not operate VDUs, may suffer ridicule and embarrassment if they take the rest breaks. Operators can become frustrated at having to take breaks at exact times when this interrupts the rhythm or completion of their work. When rest breaks and exercise programs are established by management, although they are intended for the good of the operators, they may be perceived by the latter as further regimentation of their working lives.

One further recourse is to give nonkeyboard as well as keyboard tasks to employees. However, in bureaucratically designed work organization, the scope for combining keyboard and nonkeyboard tasks to create meaningful jobs for individuals is limited due to the highly fragmented nature of most tasks and the inability of employees to control their work and to coordinate with others (Australian Public Service Board, 1984).

Not only is worker disablement from VDUs more likely in bureaucratic/ batch systems, but the organizational characteristics of these systems make it difficult to adopt effective measures to prevent disablement. The workers are performing repetitive tasks and lack control over the factors affecting their work. Therefore, hierarchical controls offer the only means of regulating the effects of VDUs on the people operating them, but the work organization design itself constrains or defeats these measures.

The alternative is to develop participative democratic work organization designs in conjunction with introducing new technical systems based on batch or work-unit processing. Although RSI became a generally serious problem for the Australian public service, the prevalence of reported RSI varied between departments from zero to 38 percent.

From the above analysis, it would be expected that departments that differ significantly in their levels of reported RSI would display different characteristics of system and work organization design. They may, of course, differ in other respects, but the purpose of the study reported below is to establish whether departments with relatively high and low levels of reported RSI had adopted different approaches to systems applications and work design. The central hypothesis is that departments with relatively high reported RSI will have introduced batch processing systems while retaining traditional bureaucratic work organization. Departments with relatively low RSI are expected to have developed work designs and systems applications with participative work-unit attributes (although the combination of participative work design with batch processing should also be reflected in lower prevalence of injury). In contrast to bureaucratic/batch systems, participative work design should provide operators with greater control over their work and the RSI risk factors; more varied work; more opportunities for learning; more scope to help and support each other; and more involvement in the production of meaningful outcomes.

RSI, New Technology and Work Design: A Comparative Study

The prevalence of RSI among Australian government employees in December 1986 was estimated by dividing total reported RSI by total staff numbers in each department, location and employment designation group. (Data were taken respectively from *Census on Repetition Strain Injury in the Australian Public Service,* quarterly December 1984 to June 1987; and the Public Service Board *Statistical Bulletin,* 1985–86.)

The incidence of RSI was evenly distributed between clerical and keyboard designation groups, with 48 percent occurring among clerical employees and 52 percent among keyboard workers. But there were over seven times more clerical than keyboard staff employed in the Australian public service. RSI was, therefore, largely a keyboard problem in the public service.

The differences between departments that are of greatest interest concern the prevalence of reported RSI in keyboard designations. Departments with comparatively high and comparatively low keyboard RSI were selected to study their systems applications and work organization designs to establish whether and in what ways the departments were different in these respects. Two departments have been studied sufficiently for the findings to be reported.

The difference in RSI prevalence between these two departments (14.6 percent for Department A and 8 percent for Department B) is statistically significant at the one percent level (Table 1: $chi^2 = 18.14$, p = .01 for one degree of freedom). The expected RSI frequencies are those that should have occurred if there was a simple direct relationship between keyboard work and RSI such that the number of RSI cases reported in each department was a function only of the number of keyboard staff employed. The discrepancy between the expected and the actual observed frequencies suggests that other factors may be involved, and the discrepancies are large enough to warrant further investigation.

Initially, a senior manager in each department was contacted to explain the study and seek approval and cooperation for research to proceed. Information on the main systems applications was obtained, and sections of the depart-

TABLE I   Departmental Differences in RSI Incidence[a]

	o	e	$o - e$	$(o - e)^2$	$(o - e)^2/e$
Department A					
Non-RSI	1221	1251	30	900	0.72
RSI	209	179	30	900	5.03
Department B					
Non-RSI	610	580	30	900	1.55
RSI	53	83	30	900	10.84
				$X^2 = 18.14$; $p = .01$	

[a]RSI frequencies: o = observed; e = expected

ments were visited to study their functions and work organization using the framework of socio-technical analysis and, where appropriate, the complementary method of role analysis.

In *Department A* there were 209 cases of reported RSI among 1221 keyboard staff, or 14.6 percent of all employees in keyboard designations. The department is responsible for the administration of a high volume of transactions with the public (Figure 2). On a daily cycle, branch offices prepare input data that are transmitted to central computers in the national office for overnight processing, and the branches receive, print and distribute output from the national office the next day. Transactions from the public are received and recorded by a control section that sends them either to the appropriate sections for examination prior to computer processing or directly to the Automatic Data Processing (ADP) input section, which enters data from the transactions for transmission to the central computers. An output control section receives output back from the central computers for printing and distribution within the department or to the members of the public who originated the transactions. Around this system, sections deal with inquiries, investigations, appeals and complaints and perform corporate service functions. Several sections specialize in particular categories of transactions and handle inquiries and complaints; they also receive and examine transactions before sending them to the ADP input section (via computer terminals or physical delivery) for entry into the system.

All current systems applications are based on batch processing against central data bases. The processing work is routine, and the function of the ADP input section is simply to key the entry of data into the system. Transactions are received in the section and jobbed into batches, which data processing operators collect for keying. The system automatically rejects invalid input. The

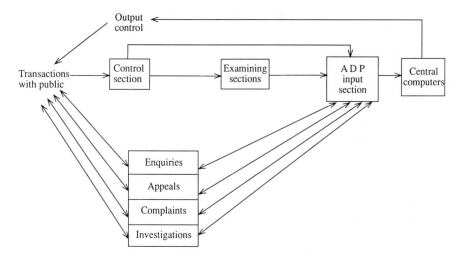

Figure 2. Main transactions processing operations in Department A

operators have very little discretion and are employed full time on keyboard entry which, in practice, is now limited to five hours per day because, due to RSI, operators are restricted to 50 minutes of keying per hour. Of the 209 cases of reported RSI in the department, 134 cases, or 64 percent, involved data processing operators. An interview with management confirmed that, while RSI had occurred in other keyboard designations (notably typists), the major problem had been with the data processing operators. Due to seasonal fluctuations in ADP input staffing levels, it was not possible to obtain an accurate estimate of the percentage of all data processing operators reported as suffering from RSI. However, the situation in this department is consistent with the general pattern in the public service. In December 1986, 17.4 percent of data processing operators had reported RSI, followed by word processing typists with 11.5 percent. The figure for data processing operators had been as high as 24 percent, and they were clearly the occupational group most at risk.

It is worth noting that, while RSI was a serious problem, particularly in the ADP input section, VDUs were used extensively in other sections of Department A where the incidence and prevalence of RSI were negligible. In sections dealing with inquiries, complaints, investigations and the like, there was no full-time keyboard entry work, and the new technology was used to support staff in their dealings with the public and to extract information from the system. However, in sections which handled specialized transactions, including on-line entry of data into the system, the logic of conventional work design may have suggested a division of work between keyboard operators doing all the data entry and clerical staff dealing with the public and updating information for entry into the system.

In one large section, the temptation to adopt this form of work organization was resisted, and an alternative work design was deliberately developed. The section was created in the early 1980s to deal with certain members of the public who may apply to the section for exemption or special treatment. A form is sent to the person who completes and returns it. The returned form is examined, and the person may be contacted for further information or clarification. When the information on the form is completely reconciled, it is keyed into the system. Forms are processed in batches proceeding first through the clerical and then through the keyboard entry stage. Work is organized on an individual job basis, with staff collecting work from central locations and taking it to their workstations. However, the work of the section is so arranged that each employee's duties are 50 percent clerical and 50 percent keyboard. Keyboard tasks include making corrections and updating information as well as data entry. While on keyboard work, staff may receive calls from people they have been dealing with during the clerical stage. Some staff found themselves keying their own clerical work, and this has been established as common practice. The VDUs are monitored for usage, but individual staff are not monitored and appeared to be broadly rather than closely supervised.

At the time this section was studied, RSI prevalence had reached crisis proportions in Department A, but there was only one reported case among the 131 staff in this section. The sufferer was new to the section and may have been injured previously while working as a full-time data processing operator. The variety of keyboard and clerical tasks and the scope for people to move around in their work appeared to be important factors in the virtual nonoccurrence of RSI. Formal rest breaks from keying had not been introduced, management preferring to establish a general understanding that staff should take rest breaks when they needed to. Staff were aware of RSI and appeared to have sufficient control over, and variety in, their work that they could take responsibility for avoiding injury, rather than have management attempt to avoid injury for them through imposed safety practices.

Department B had 53 reported cases of RSI among its 610 keyboard staff or a prevalence rate of 8 percent. The department had two main functions. One was to monitor developments in sectors of the economy, provide information and policy advice to the government and operate an information service for the public. The other function was to plan and implement assistance programs, which also included public information services. The first function employed a high proportion of middle to senior level staff in ongoing contact with industries, conducting research and preparing policy information and advice. These project officers were supported by relatively small numbers of clerical and keyboard staff. Although formally employed in keyboard designations and engaged in word processing, keyboard staff generally had a range of tasks including filing, preparation and distribution of documents; handling transfers of information within and between sections; and collection of basic data. The organization of work around projects allowed support staff to relate their tasks to functions and outcomes. Most managers interviewed said that support staff were encouraged to get involved in projects although they did not do any contact work. The roles of keyboard staff contained mixtures of keyboard and clerical tasks, there was a trend toward increasing use of personal computers by project officers and keyboard staff normally spent no more than 50 percent of their time keying.

The second function employed a greater number of keyboard and more junior clerical staff and required more routine keyboard entry into central information banks. This function was more decentralized geographically, with many staff working in branch and local offices throughout the Australian states. While staff performed data entry tasks, they also had clerical work, there was considerable direct contact with the public and the work involved interrogating the information banks for assistance in their work as well as entering data into the banks. The main problems with the second function appear to have been the design of systems to meet central requirements and inadequate consultation with staff in branch and local offices who encountered difficulties in using the systems effectively. Nevertheless, reported RSI in Department B was among the lowest for keyboard staff during the crisis period.

Reported keyboard RSI in the public service has been declining for some time, as shown in Table 2; comparable figures for Departments A and B are given in Table 3. In response to the emergence of RSI as a serious occupational health problem, departments implemented a variety of measures. These were surveyed by Crawford (1987) and, although confined to the Australian Capital Territory, her findings provide some indication as to the pattern of departmental responses (Table 4).

The general impression is that departments responded with a variety of measures but that some measures were more likely to be adopted than others. All departments had established some form of RSI reporting procedure: 75 percent or more sought ergonomic advice on equipment and furniture; had appointed officers responsible for RSI management; provided counseling for RSI-affected staff; introduced education and training in RSI prevention; employed external consultants (mainly medical practitioners, physiotherapists and ergonomists); and had introduced rest breaks and exercise programs. Departments were less likely to have conducted workplace investigations where staff were diagnosed as suffering from RSI or to have made changes in work design. Workplace investigations, where undertaken, were more likely to result in changes to equipment and furniture than to work design.

TABLE 2   Decline in RSI, 1985–1987

	Dec 1985	Mar 1986	Mar 1987	Change (%)
Typist	577	558	378	−34.5
Secretary	373	271	150	−59.8
Data processing operator	593	545	380	−35.9
Word processing typist	441	372	260	−41.0
Other keyboard	43	25	22	−48.8
Total keyboard	2027	1771	1190	−41.3

Crawford's findings suggest that critically examining and changing the design of work organization was the least preferred alternative in departments' responses to RSI. It must be acknowledged that the incidence and prevalence of RSI in all employment designations have declined and that the measures most widely adopted appear to have contributed to this general reduction of occupational injury. At the end of the reporting period, RSI remained an occupational health problem affecting more than 1,000 keyboard staff in the public service (Table 2). In the case of Department A, it is evident from Table 3 that there had been relatively modest improvement in the most seriously affected employment designation of data processing operators. In the ADP input section, furniture and keyboard equipment were of an advanced standard, boards displayed the times of scheduled rest breaks and the physical environment was pleasant and comfortable, but RSI among the department's processing officers declined by only 17.7 percent, while it had been reduced by 35.9 percent in the public service as a whole (Table 2). This is consistent with the contention that measures such as rest breaks and improved operator training, equipment, furniture and physical working environment can help to reduce occupational injury but, in themselves, are not sufficient to eliminate the problem.

In the area of activities where Department A had the most serious prevalence of RSI, the characteristics of bureaucratic/batch socio-technical design were clearly evident. The systems application was based on linear sequential work flows broken down into discrete processing steps. The work organization and the technical design allowed operators little discretion in their task performance, and the tasks were simple and repetitive. Within Department A, the greater task variety and operator control over task performance and the virtual

TABLE 3   Decline in RSI by Department

	Department A				Department B			
	Dec 1985	Mar 1986	Mar 1987	Change (%)	Dec 1985	Mar 1986	Mar 1987	Change (%)
Typist	49	55	43	−12.2	34	37	32	−5.9
Secretary	2	3	2	0.0	16	13	2	−87.5
Data processing operator	147	128	121	−17.7	1	1	0	0.0
Word processing typist	13	19	13	0.0	17	16	8	−52.9
Other keyboard	6	5	7	1.7	0	0	0	0.0
Total keyboard	217	210	186	−14.3	68	67	42	−38.2

TABLE 4   Remedies for RSI

Measure	Yes		No	
	N	%	N	%
RSI reporting system	42	100	—	—
Ergonomic advice	39	93	3	7
Officer responsible	38	90	4	10
Counseling	37	81	5	12
External consultants	34	81	8	19
Education, training	34	81	8	19
Exercise programs	32	76	10	24
Rest breaks	29	69	12	29
Job design	27	64	15	36
RSI policy	27	64	15	36
Workplace investigations	23	55	19	45

nonoccurrence of RSI in the special transactions section provides one point of contrast. This might be described as a participative/batch socio-technical design. Department B also had a significantly lower prevalence of RSI throughout its keyboard designations and areas of operation. There was no full-time keyboard entry work; keyboard staff had a range of tasks and a substantial proportion of their work enabled them to identify their efforts with meaningful projects and outcomes. These findings are consistent with the central hypothesis that departments with relatively high prevalence of RSI were more likely to have adopted bureaucratic/batch socio-technical designs and that departments with relatively low RSI were more likely to display participative work-unit characteristics.

Comparisons between two organizations do not, of course, provide unequivocal confirmation of the hypothesis. If the findings held for a larger number of departments with more nearly similar functions and operations, this would provide a somewhat stricter and more comprehensive test. However, the Australian government's concern about new technology and the design of work organization has gone beyond the initial preoccupation with RSI to encompass a wider range of issues in public sector performance and the quality of working life available to government employees. The government's current policy on work design is stimulating work organization innovations throughout the public service, which do not require further empirical evidence concerning RSI for their justification. Improving occupational health and safety is one objective of the government's Office Structures Implementation (OSI) program, but the program is also intended to provide employees with greater responsible autonomy, variety, opportunities to attain higher levels of skills and knowledge, job satisfaction and career prospects. The original research focus on new technology, work organization and worker disablement has also shifted to the broader question of relationships between new technology and the democratization of work.

From Occupational Health to Industrial Democracy

Following lengthy consultation with departments and unions, the broad change intended by the OSI program is the integration of the previously separate keyboard designations, clerical assistant grades and the bottom five grades of the clerical administrative structure into a single structure within which jobs will contain mixtures of keyboard and clerical skills and career paths will be more open to all staff. More than 70,000 office staff employed in 48 different, and often narrow, classifications will be integrated in one structure with five levels, in which traditional work divisions are supposed to disappear along with long-standing barriers to career mobility (Australian Public Service Board, 1987).

For Department B, the integration of keyboard and clerical tasks does not represent a radical departure from its existing work organization. The main problem for Department B arises from the gap between the senior grades of the project officers and the junior grades of support staff. Although there are no strict formal educational requirements, many project officers have tertiary qualifications, and they all have considerable experience in both analytical work and high-level industry contact. Some support staff have attained more senior positions, but the qualitative differences between analytical and contact work and support tasks currently present a barrier to advancement from lower to higher positions, which the department will have to develop strategies to remove.

In Department A, the work organization conformed closely to the traditional public service office structure and was a more typical object of the changes required by OSI. The department established an OSI implementation team nationally and in each branch, which initially concentrated on reviewing existing job classifications and resolving anomalies created by moving to the new five-level structure. Next, OSI working parties were set up to examine the

existing work organization of sections; develop alternatives which were presented to and discussed with the staff who would be affected; and propose
agreed changes to management through the OSI implementation team that now
had a coordinative role in the planning and implementation of change. A
working party usually included management and union representatives, employees working in the section and a member of a services section concerned
with matters such as industrial democracy or equal employment opportunity.
At this stage the department also commenced keyboard training for clerical
employees.

The main transactions processing operation, which was the principal source
of RSI in the department, was selected as one of the first target areas for change
under the RSI program. Four sections previously described were involved in
the operation, each performing a discrete part of the process. The whole
operation entailed 31 manual or machine processing tasks and seven filing and
storage tasks. These tasks were divided between the four sections with further
subdivisions within sections such that staff each performed one or a small
number of tasks repeatedly on a succession of transactions.

The working party identified several alternative arrangements, one of which
was preferred by the great majority of staff in the existing sections. The
preferred work design integrates the four sections into one section with each
employee completing the entire processing cycle on transactions.

The new work organization was tried initially in a pilot unit operated by 17
employees from the existing sections and a supervisor. These employees were
volunteers and, prior to the pilot unit, received training in keyboard operation
or clerical processing depending on which designations they had worked in
before. Although the broad intention was that each employee would perform
the entire processing cycle on transactions, this was qualified in two main
ways. First, some types of transactions required different levels of knowledge
and experience, and there was a division of work between more junior staff
processing the simpler transactions and staff in higher grade classifications
processing the more complex transactions. Peak work loads for these different
transactions varied, and there were periods when junior staff were unable to
share the work of senior staff, whereas in other peak periods senior staff were
able to process some of the simpler transaction types. The simpler transactions
comprised the bulk of the processing with the result that employees at different
seniority and pay levels spent considerable periods doing the same work. This
caused some friction between members of the pilot unit, with junior staff
questioning the status differences and higher level staff resenting the perceived
erosion of their seniority.

Second, while employees were involved in the entire processing cycle, they
did not complete the cycle for each transaction that they handled. Rather, one
employee performed all tasks entailed in receiving a transaction through to

entering it into the system for processing, but it was likely that another employee would deal with the checking, reconciliation and distribution of the processed transaction. At least in part, this was due to the pilot unit's inability to control the flow of output from the central computers, in the national office. Staff collected batches of processed transactions as they came back from the central computers, and it would have been coincidental if the same person who performed the input tasks on those transactions also performed the output tasks on the same transactions. The work redesign in the pilot unit was providing staff with greater variety of tasks and increased opportunities for learning and advancement based on acquiring new knowledge and skills. However, branch office dependence on the central computers was a factor which inhibited staff identification with the whole transaction as the object of their task performance. The pilot unit's lack of control over the entire cycle also affected its performance. The cycle was taking between 10 and 30 days to complete, but the unit only took three days to complete its work on each transaction. The unit supervisor thought that most transactions could be processed in one day if all of the processing was done within the unit.

The pilot unit was not given any production objectives. Its purpose was to try the new work organization design and to improve and refine procedures. Within the scope of the unit's control over its operation, this is being achieved, for example, by eliminating tasks made redundant when employees perform sequences of related tasks previously performed separately by different people. Initially, error rates were high while staff were learning new tasks. Average keyboard speeds were 40 percent slower than in the ADP input section, but staff in the unit were productive for whole work periods whereas ADP operators only worked five hours per day due to rest breaks. Despite the tension between different seniority levels, employees in the unit have remained enthusiastic about the new work design and have successfully tackled the learning challenges involved. In time, this should reduce or eliminate the division of work between staff based on the types of transactions they deal with.

Early in 1989, the first of several processing modules commenced operation with 75 employees, including the 17 who participated in the pilot unit. Three further modules will be established during the year and the old sections phased out, but several issues remain. Beginning with the staffing of the pilot unit, transfer of employees to the new work design has been voluntary. This continues to be the case, but there is some concern about whether all staff in the old sections will be attracted to the new work organization. Because the pilot unit was located in close physical proximity to the sections, staff in the unit continued to interact with their workmates in the sections, and there was a continuing flow of information about the pilot unit's experiences, which may have helped to reduce anxiety.

Employee demand for places in the new processing modules is very strong at present, but this may be for reasons which are problematic. It appears that more staff are attracted to the new work design because of the opportunities to acquire skills and knowledge which can be used to seek promotion and pay increases than are attracted by the prospect of more interesting and challenging work. There is no public service or departmental objection to rewarding employees for attaining higher performance capabilities, but the processing modules are already having difficulty in meeting the expectations of staff (supported by their unions) that they will be promoted as soon as they have acquired the new skills and knowledge. In the longer term, this has important implications for the department's and the public service's employment structure. The immediate problem for Department A is that employees are transferring to the processing modules to gain new skills and knowledge and then seeking further transfer to higher level positions elsewhere if their promotional expectations are not met immediately within the modules.

Other issues concern constraints on the new work design. The effects of branch office dependence on central computers may be reduced or eliminated through a major computer reequipment program. Department A is exploring the possibility that a significant proportion of transactions could be entered into the system directly from outside private computers or public access terminals. This could substantially reduce transactions processing within the department. A more radical but feasible step would be to abolish the department's ongoing transactions with the public in their present form and to replace them with onetime determinations of transaction status, which would change only in accordance with changes in actual status or in government policy. If the current technological change program does not go this far, increasing the control that the processing modules in branch offices have over the processing cycle would seem to require the provision of local computing facilities to perform the same functions for the modules as are currently performed by the central computers, with records of transactions being transmitted to central computers rather than having them involved in the actual processing cycle. Other sections of branch offices could have access to the national system, local systems or both.

The future of the transactions processing modules is affected by current uncertainty about the future of the transactions processing function in Department A. If the function continues to be performed as at present, or with a reduced volume of work due to direct entry of transactions from outside terminals, it will be necessary to resolve the issues raised by the present division of work among different transaction types; the lack of control by the modules over the processing cycle; and employee expectations of advancement. There are other issues concerning access to high security areas of the department that also constrain the new work design at present. However, considerable progress has been made in the directions intended by the OSI program. There are an increasing number of OSI work redesign initiatives in the department, but it was in the main transactions processing area that traditional work organization and the application of new office technology had interacted to create the most pressing problems and need for change.

Conclusions

The Australian experience with, and response to, RSI has several ramifications. First, an important development may have occurred in the "appreciative system" of the society, or the way in which the phenomenon is collectively perceived, evaluated and acted upon (Vickers, 1965). The disorders known generally as RSI (or occupational overuse syndrome) in Australia are present and prevalent in other countries although known by different names, but Australia is unusual in the extent to which RSI has been recognized as probably or definitely related to work involving VDUs. There has, of course, been a general trend in industrial countries toward greater emphasis on occupational health and safety (Corlett and Richardson, 1981), and this may partly account for the Australian response to RSI. Other factors have been suggested as more peculiar to Australia; e.g., VDUs may have been introduced there more rapidly compared with other countries. It is more clearly the case that the recognition of worker disablement from VDUs is an achievement for the individuals and groups who sought to have it recognized. This recognition is due also to the strength and attitudes of Australian trade unions which took a leading role in gaining acceptance of RSI cases as legally compensable. The unions have rejected negotiating danger money for keyboard work and, while demanding medical services for their members who work with VDUs, have insisted that the ultimate aim must be to eliminate RSI from the workplace. Although there are suspicions of RSI as mass malingering, these carry little credibility among most employers. The association between VDUs and worker disablement may be disputed for a long time, but it has become an important social and political reality.

The human and economic costs of RSI created strong pressures for rapid effective resolution of the problem. What was known medically and ergonomically about the problem pointed to work organization as an important factor. Several measures have been increasingly adopted by organizations to counter the evident disabling effects of VDUs. The most commonly introduced measures are ergonomic design; susceptibility assessments; operator training; discontinuation of work incentives; rest and exercise periods; and providing mixtures of keyboard and nonkeyboard tasks. Such measures can have some effect in reducing worker disablement, but there is a more fundamental issue. Most Australian organizations adopted visual display technology while retaining bureaucratic work organization design. This increased the repetitiveness of the work and the control imposed on workers, making them vulnerable to injury. When measures were then introduced to prevent disablement, the same bureaucratic work organization design limited the effectiveness of these measures. Management was trying to prevent and control injury *for* workers without changing the basic characteristics of work organization that were contributing to the occurrence of injury in the first place.

Effective and stable prevention of worker disablement requires more fundamental redesign of work organization. The high prevalence of RSI particularly among data processing operators in Department A, where traditional bureaucratic work organization had been retained while introducing new technology, is consistent with the contention that bureaucratic/batch designs increase the risk of occupational injury and also constrain the effectiveness of attempted countermeasures. The virtual nonoccurrence of RSI in the special transactions section in Department A and its low prevalence in Department B are associated with socio-technical systems in which task variety and employee control over work are considerably greater.

The Australian government's Office Structures Implementation (OSI) program is broadening the public service's approach to new technology and work design. The OSI is a vehicle for the government as an employer to put into practice the kinds of work organization initiatives which it advocates. These policies encompass not only formal consultative procedures but also workplace issues including work design and employee participation in decisions about their work. While the main transactions processing operation in Department A provided a case where bureaucratic/batch design was associated with comparatively high worker disablement, the new work organization design (in addition to making the work less hazardous) is establishing directions for the democratization of work and for the design of new technical systems to support democratic work.

References

Australian Public Service Board. 1984. *Job Structures for Keyboard Work: New Directions?*

———. 1987. *Statistical Bulletin* No. 75.

Browne, C.D., B.M. Nolan and D.K. Faithfull. 1984. "Occupational Repetition Strain Injuries: Guidelines for Diagnosis and Management." *Medical Journal of Australia* (March 17).

Buchanan, D.A. and D. Boddy. 1982. "Advanced Technology and the Quality of Working Life: The Effects of Word Processing on Typists." *Journal of Occupational Psychology,* 55:1–11.

Burch, W.M. 1984. "VDT Hazards—An Hypothesis." Joint Committee of Public Accounts, 225th Report, *Occupational Health and Safety Aspects of VDUs,* Vol. 2. Canberra: Australian Government Publishing Service.

Business Review Weekly. 1984. "Keyboard Cripples: The Avalanche Looms." November, 17–23.

Corlett, E.N. and J. Richardson. 1981. *Stress, Work Design and Productivity.* New York: Wiley.

Crawford, M. 1987. *Survey of Repetition Strain Injury Prevention and Management Strategies in the Australian Public Service.* Canberra: Australian Government Publishing Service.

Department of Employment and Industrial Relations. 1984. *VDUs at Work.* Canberra: Australian Government Publishing Service.

Eason, K.D. and R.G. Sell. 1981. "Case Studies in Job Design for Information Processing Tasks." In *Stress, Work Design and Productivity,* edited by E.N. Corlett and J. Richardson. New York: Wiley.

Emery, F.E. 1959. "Psychological Effects of the Western Film: A Study of Television Viewing." *Human Relations,* 12:215–32. Rewritten version, Vol. I, "Latent Content of Television Viewing," pp.574–85.

———. 1976. *Futures We Are In.* Leiden: Martinus Nijhoff.

———. 1980. "Designing Socio-Technical Systems for 'Greenfield Sites'." *Journal of Occupational Behaviour,* 1:19–27, Vol. II, pp.192–201.

———. 1984. *Tenosynovitis or Repetition Strain Injuries.* Submission to Task Force on Repetition Strain Injury in the Australian Public Service. Canberra.

Emery, F.E. and M. Emery. 1974. *Participative Design: Work and Community Life.* Canberra: Centre for Continuing Education, Australian National University. Revised, Vol. II, "The Participative Design Workshop," pp.599–613.

Emery, F.E. and E. Thorsrud. 1976. *Democracy At Work.* Leiden: Martinus Nijhoff.

Emery, F.E. and E.L. Trist. 1972/73. *Towards a Social Ecology: Contextual Appreciation of the Future in the Present.* London/New York: Plenum.

Emery, M. 1985. *The Social and Neurophysiological Effects of Television.* Canberra: Australian National University, Ph.D. Thesis.

Ferguson, D. 1984. "The 'New' Industrial Epidemic." *Medical Journal of Australia,* March.

Herbst, P.G. 1974. *Socio-Technical Design: Strategies in Multi-Disciplinary Research.* London: Tavistock Publications. Chapter 2 revised, Vol. II, "Designing with Minimal Critical Specifications," pp.294–302.

Joint Committee of Public Accounts. 1984. 225th Report, *Occupational Health and Safety Aspects of VDUs,* Vol. 2. Canberra: Australian Government Publishing Service.

National Health and Medical Research Council. 1983. *Occupational Health Guide: Visual Display Units.* Canberra: National Health and Medical Research Council.

Stone, W.E. 1983. "Repetition Strain Injuries." *Medical Journal of Australia.* December.

Turner, J.A. and R.A. Karasek. 1984. "Software Ergonomics: Effects of Computer Application Design Parameters on Operator Task Performance and Health." *Ergonomics,* 27:663–90.

Vickers, Sir G. 1965. *The Art of Judgment: A Study of Policy Making.* London: Chapman and Hall.

Williams, T.A. 1983. "Technological Innovation and Futures of Work Organisation: A Choice of Social Design Principles." *Technological Forecasting and Social Change,* 24:79–90.

———. 1988. *Computers, Work and Health.* London: Taylor and Francis.

Louis Davis and Stu Sullivan

A New Type of Labor-Management Contract Involving the Quality of Working Life[1]

Introduction

In the North American tradition of evolving theory from practice, this paper reports what may become a significant innovation in union-management relations. This pragmatically evolved development may be crucial to the evolution of new forms of union-management collaboration. Reported are the extremely rare events of union participation in the design of a new chemical plant organization and the evolution of a new form of union-management contract developed through collective bargaining and responding to the organizational philosophy that guided the design. This philosophy stated the key criteria to be incorporated into the organization design as:

Employees are responsible and trustworthy.

Employees are capable of making proper decisions given the necessary training and information.

Groups of individuals can work together effectively as members of a team.

Advancement and growth to individuals' fullest potential and capability.

Compensation on the basis of demonstrated knowledge and skill.

Direct, open and meaningful communication among individuals.

Information flow directed to those in position to most quickly act upon it.

"Whole jobs" to be designed to provide maximum individual involvement.

System that provides direct and immediate feedback in meaningful terms.

Maximum amount of self-regulation and discretion.

Artificial, traditional or functional barriers to be eliminated.

Work schedules that minimize time spent on shift.

Early identification of problems and collaboration on solutions.

Errors reviewed from "what we can learn" point of view.

[1]This paper was first published in the *Journal of Occupational Behaviour*, 1:29–41, 1980. The authors gratefully acknowledge the very considerable assistance provided by Norman Halpern, Consultant, Shell Canada, Ltd.

Status differentials to be minimized.

During the past few years, suspicion and distrust have surrounded the issue of union-management collaboration in the development of work environments and conditions that could provide a rewarding relationship between work and the needs, expectations and goals of those who do the work. Both unions and management were, and largely are, immobilized by the uncertainties of departing from the 200 year old tradition of

- instrumentalism, i.e., work as an instrument to support the goals of satisfying personal needs of individuals outside the workplace;
- the external behavior control of workers to achieve the goals of the organization or of its managers.

This immobility characterizes all western societies at this stage in their evolution. It has led to partially appropriate responses that are either political (*mitbestimmung*, or union representation on boards of companies in western Europe) or economic (Scanlon Plans, earned time bonuses, etc., in the United States) (Davis, 1979). In deep and meaningful ways, such responses to the new realities of demands to enhance the quality of working life (Yankelovitch, 1979) can be seen as either an avoidance of the need to develop a new relationship between union and management that is responsive to the evolving new demands in the work place, or as a recasting of the expressed needs and expectations into conventional responses of more money, fewer hours, etc. All this is taking place in the face of deep changes in Western societies surrounding the meaning and purpose of work and the relation between society's members and the work of society. Such challenges signal the transition of modern societies from the historical period of the last 200 years, the industrial era, to an evolving post-industrial era.

The attempts of a future-oriented union and a future-oriented management to develop a new relationship between worker and work confronted them with the need to evolve a new and more appropriate relationship pushing beyond the terms of historical union-management relations. Both the union—Oil, Chemical and Atomic Workers International Union (OCAWIU)—and the management—Shell Canada, Ltd. (Shell)—came to perceive the formal collective agreement as an instrument that would support or hinder the evolution of new workplace relationships, i.e., as a part of the "social support system." The collective agreement that emerged from the process of free and open collective bargaining was informed by the shared perception that the contract, as an enabling instrument, would become the central social system support instrument or general constitution supporting the evolution of specific adaptive and collaborative practices.

The recent joint design in Canada of a complex chemical plant for the manufacture of polypropylene and isopropyl alcohol and its organization, followed later by the bargained labor-management contract, serve as a crucial learning opportunity. This design is a triple first: the first joint technical and social design of a highly complex continuous, automated process plant and its interrelated social system or organization; the first joint design undertaken with participation of both union and management; and the first labor-management contract bargained in response to an organization (and job) design which is an alternative to bureaucracy (Davis, 1977). As with other firsts crucial to the evolving post-industrial era, such as the engineering design in Volvo's auto assembly plant at Kalmar, Sweden (Gyllenhammer, 1977), this development will have to be considered in all future union-management relationships based on other than adversarial relationships.

To aid our learning from this signal development, we need to explore the background to the organization design of this new plant, the specifics of the design and the content of the labor-management contract. A detailed report of the design has been published (Halpern, 1985).

Background to the Design

The background to the design starts in the early 1970s when the manufacturing division of Shell began studies of its own way of managing its workers and utilizing their capabilities. Substantial recommendations were made, some of which were implemented and many of which seemed to be waiting for 1975 when the design of the polypropylene-isopropyl alcohol plant was to begin. The recommendations of the earlier studies pointed to the need to enhance the quality of working life of refinery and chemical plant workers. Such workers, with good pay and working conditions, were found to be seeking greater control over the decisions affecting their lives in the workplace and were inhibited from fully utilizing the considerable skills and experience they had acquired. The usual roles of a traditionally operated organization, enlightened though it may be, imposed needless restrictions on workers. Typical of their comments were

> I operate a five (or 10) million dollar machine but have to obtain approval from the foreman for an overtime meal when I am asked to stay at work beyond my usual departure time.

> I have to wait for the foreman to arrive to sign off on a maintenance request. All he does is add his signature to the form after he asks me if the work is needed.

The primary concern of Shell management and a major concern of OCAWIU were the physiological and psychological problems associated with shift work.

In the early 1970s, the issues of remuneration, security, control over workplace decisions, shift work, development of self and participation in governance of one's work life, taken together, came to be called the quality of working life (QWL). By the time the design began, the participants were well aware of this concept and that it could be strongly affected by organization and job designs.

Design Process

When the design of the polypropylene-isopropyl alcohol plant was to begin in 1975, the manager, who had undertaken earlier studies, was asked to become the internal advisor for the purpose of organization design. In this way the issues of QWL were brought into the design process. Sensitivity to QWL issues led senior managers to appoint a concerned and knowledgeable operating manager or superintendent for the future plant. In the tradition of the company, this manager would also have the responsibility for designing the organization, coordinating the engineering and bringing the plant into production. Prior to the appointment of the Design Team, the internal advisor helped prepare the operations manager by reviewing the company's own past studies and examining innovations recently introduced by other companies in the industry. The new operations manager or superintendent was given the sanction to undertake the design of the new organization without regard to the prevalent bureaucratic/scientific management structures and job designs. He had the freedom to recommend viable alternatives developed by the Design Team suitable to the requirements of the new plant and the new work force.

The appointment of the external consultant led to the introduction of the socio-technical systems design approach and to the formation of a Design Team and a Steering Committee consisting of senior executives from all relevant segments of the corporation. The Design Team's membership changed over time as it proceeded to design different levels and parts of the organization. By the end of the process it consisted entirely of local managers and union leaders, while, at the start, it had as members the internal and external advisors, the superintendent, the assistant superintendent, various experts, the superintendent of the related refinery, the managers of the overall manufacturing site, employee relations and corporate industrial relations and, somewhat later, the local and regional leaders of the OCAWIU. Labor-management relations had been and continue to be very good.

The technology and technical system chosen called for continuous processing using various vessels, reactors and remote control of chemical reactions that could be physically dangerous if not properly done. Equipment and instrumentation costs required a massive capital investment amounting to approximately two million dollars per employee. The characteristics of the technology, size of investment and the small number of employees (150) led to the recognition that economic success would depend on the willingness and dedication of these employees. The recognition that higher levels of technology, frequently accompanied by very large capital expenditures, increase the dependence of organizations on their workers, rather than the opposite as predicted by engineers, was crucial to the design process. This awareness, plus a prior history of examining and searching for work relationships that would reflect the high level of responsibilities placed on workers, led to dissatisfaction with the bureaucratic-scientific management structures prevalent throughout the industry.

The design process began without the union. The Design Team understood very well the increased dependence on workers caused by advanced technology and was conscious of the need to consider the impact of the new plant on the adjacent existing refinery. The initial process centered on examining what constraints had to be accepted by the initial Design Team and on exploring answers to the question: "What kind of society are we going to build in the new plant?" These explorations of social and organizational values led to the formulation of a general charter, or organizational philosophy, that served as a guide to design and subsequent operation of the plant. The organization philosophy strongly emphasized cooperation, participation, self-regulation, autonomy, variety and careers as essential features of the future plant society. Security was not specifically mentioned.

Union-Management Joint Design Process

There was considerable discussion regarding union jurisdiction. Some people expected that the refinery union would have jurisdiction over the new plant when completed; others thought the union would not. Some said this did not matter since it was management's prerogative to design and organize work. Others were concerned with the negative consequences of placing a completed design before the union as a *fait accompli*. The consultant to the Design Team questioned whether excluding the union was contrary to the organization philosophy and to the congruency principle of socio-technical systems design, which calls for design methods to be congruent with the features of the organization (Cherns, 1976). All came to see that success of the future operation of this costly, leading-edge technology plant was in various ways bound up with participation by the union.

Finally, following considerable examination, the Design Team recognized that the union would represent the future members of the plant and invited it to join as a partner in developing the design of organization, jobs, rewards, training and controls. Such participation of the union as a basis for successful operation is contrary to conventional wisdom about advanced technology, large corporations and engineering and management processes.

The union accepted with two stipulations:

- that it be a full partner in the design process;
- that it maintain a high profile.

These conditions were quickly accepted. The participation of the union representatives provided the means for capturing and utilizing organizational learning at the shop floor level. Initial concerns were soon forgotten as the high quality of union contribution unfolded, and managers congratulated themselves on their statesmanship.

Later, the external consultant had an opportunity to interview the Canadian national director of the union. He was asked to indicate why he supported his union's participation in the design process in the face of the history, in North America, of rejection by many unions of QWL activities. His reply is very instructive. He said,

> We would be poor union leaders indeed if we did not utilize the opportunity given us by management to participate in providing for satisfaction of quality of working life needs for workers. If you think that only managers have problems with our members as their workers, then you are unaware that we have many similar problems with our members, particularly younger members. We must grasp each opportunity that becomes available to learn how to find the means of responding to quality of working life issues raised by our members if we are to be a strong viable union.

What was the role of the union in the design process? What was their contribution to the design? Would the design have been the same without them? How were they beneficial to future union members who would be joining the new organization? These questions are difficult to answer because of the relationship that evolved. Quickly managers accepted the union leaders as equals and vice versa. Each contributed as an individual whose membership on the Design Team was highly valued. The team called on its members as experts on the basis of their reputations, knowledge and experience. Many proposals were generated through synergistic interaction among team members, whether union or management. Proposals for features of organization and jobs were examined by both union and management for secondary and unintended effects on members at all levels. The union representatives' greatest contributions seemed to be centered on proposals regarding the knowledge and skill modules for advancement, maintenance, working hours, shift teams and their rotation. Additionally, the union representatives helped develop the team coordinator role, shop steward role and the Good Work Practices Handbook.

Design Process and Outcomes

Before proceeding with the outcomes of the design process, i.e., the organization and job designs, we need to examine the QWL background conditions in North America influencing labor-management cooperation. In 1975 there was great concern, uncertainty and mistrust regarding QWL. Most union leaders, while acknowledging that life in the workplace needed improving, saw attempts to improve the quality of working life as dominated by management initiatives undertaken for productivity improvement purposes. They felt they were excluded from domains of concern which had traditionally been theirs. Further, QWL developments tended strongly to emphasize direct participation of workers without considering the effects on the representative role laboriously earned by unions. The consequence was either outright rejection of QWL undertakings by most unions or conflict with management over so many specifics as to inhibit the start of undertakings.

The design process proceeded to analyze the central character of the technology with which the prospective social system would have to interact. This analysis, conducted with the aid of technologists, examined the proposed and existing manufacturing process, finding that, although continuous and automated, it operated with a substantial number of uncontrolled variables. For a variety of reasons, the newest similar plants exhibited a very low level of utilization. In response to these findings, the Design Team opted for organizational forms that would maximize learning and improve response time in dealing with disturbances as they arose. The more that members of the organization could learn to control variables, the greater would be their ability to regulate the process and to increase plant utilization, thus enhancing economic success. Each percentage increase in utilization would yield large economic returns. The computer is off-line, i.e., the computer is not in the control loop for a number of variables. This requires operators to make control decisions, which facilitates learning. The necessary computer programs were designed so that operators could use the computer in the mode of evolutionary operations. In terms of what was known about relevant variables, the closed loops programmed into the computer actually are the maximum from an optimizing point of view, as contrasted with a controlling point of view. The computer answers queries put to it by the operating personnel regarding the short run effect of variables at various control levels, but decisions are made by the operators. Operating personnel are provided with technical calculations and economic data, conventionally only available to technical staff, that support learning and self-regulation. In this manner, operator learning is enhanced. By thus utilizing the experience of operators, computer programs can be updated to further enhance learning and so on interactively.

The choice of a learning organization model affected the structure of the organization, jobs, rewards, etc. It supported the structural decision to treat the entire plant as one organizational unit without any internal boundaries so that wider system learning would take place. It influenced the decision not to create specific jobs or positions with fixed boundaries and job descriptions. The choice made was to have the work to be done belong to a team as a whole. The team could assign, daily if necessary, the needed tasks to its members on the basis of both their skills and competence and the physical allocation of the operating units. The needs for organizational learning were seen to be best supported by unrestricted individual learning, and thus a system of open progression was designed with pay or rewards based on acquisition of knowledge and skills.

The organization structure was most strongly influenced by application of the concept of the organization as consisting of self-maintaining (sociotechnical) organizational units supported by the requirements for learning. Two sets of criteria were applied:

- The location of the boundaries of organizational units so that organization members have identifiable outcomes, control inputs, possess the requisite response capabilities in numbers, skills, competences and information.
- The socio-technical criterion (Cherns, 1976) that the identification of response to and access to the source of a disturbance, interruption or variance are within the same boundary.

Additionally, the structure was influenced by simultaneously considering it to be a minisociety and a transforming (work performing) agency. The minisociety consideration brought into focus functions such a problem solving, coordination, social system maintenance, conflict resolution, individual advancement, equity, workplace justice, shift work, etc.

The design selected treated the entire plant and its processes as one organizational unit. One team of 18 people plus a team coordinator operates the entire process including laboratory, shipping, warehousing and many aspects of maintenance on each shift. The teams needed for 24 hour, 365 day operation would be supported by some planners, engineers and managers as well as a team of 14 maintenance craftsmen-instructors and two laboratory specialists on days. The organization design was further influenced by societal issues stemming from strong negative pressures about shift work. The Design Team sought to minimize shift work and to share equally the positive and negative aspects of working life. The design provides for six shift teams. Each team rotates and controls, in turn, all the work activities of the plant. Based on the 37.5 hours a week schedule of the plant, 4.5 shifts are required for continuous around-the-clock operation. The design selected calls for 1.5 shift teams, on average, to join on days with the following groups: 14 maintenance craftsmen-instructors, 2 laboratory specialists and 2 warehousemen-schedulers. The shift team joins with the maintenance craftsmen to become the maintenance work force while obtaining cross-skill training in maintenance crafts. In this manner, a maintenance response capability becomes available on all shifts for emergency situations, with a concentration of maintenance capability during days. The six shift team arrangement provides for the members of all shift teams to spend approximately 53 percent of their work time on days. Should a future experiment with the 12-hour day work out, 72 percent of each member's work time would be spent on days as compared with 33 percent in a conventional shift arrangement.

Not unexpectedly, the organization structure is flat, having three levels— the shift teams and their coordinators, operations managers and plant superintendent. The day foreman level present in conventional refineries and chemical plants is omitted since these people are now staff technical advisors. Within the teams the structure is deliberately amorphous, permitting the team to assign tasks to its members as required. Additionally, for organizational continuity, various leadership functions, including planning and coordination, have been assigned to the team members. Team members have received training to perform a variety of social system maintenance functions including problem solving, confrontation, conflict resolution, norm setting, etc. Each team has a shop steward who is one of its members. This is particularly useful since very few rules exist and the labor-management contract language is permissive, leaving to team members the determination of their day-to-day working lives. A Good Work Practice Handbook (GWPH) was developed, with union input, which serves as an administrative guide governing specific job-related activities such as overtime meals. What is frequently described in labor-management contracts, making them rigid and subject to legal quibbling concerning work related activities, is now in the GWPH. The collective agreement thus remains as the enabling document it was originally intended to be. The team coordinator, staying with the team as it rotates through the shifts, serves as the intershift team link and the link with management. The coordinator's major functions are to provide boundary protection for the team, acting as a mediator or buffer between them and demands from the environment; to provide technical expertise and training on the processes; and to serve as the management representative on the shifts, sometimes being the only such representative present. In addition to the shop stewards, the union structure has a five-person executive committee including the union officers in the plant.

Members of the teams do not have specific job titles or assignments but rather grade levels or competence levels based on the knowledge and skill attained. Advancement depends on qualifying examinations and performance tests covering specific groups of knowledge and skill modules. This arrangement supports open progression and satisfaction of individual differences through the many career paths available. Each team member must acquire all the process or operations knowledge and skill modules, which are present at every wage grade level. Beyond this there are choices available for individuals to combine knowledge and skill modules from six specialty areas with operations modules to make up each individual wage grade level. The specialty area skills include maintenance crafts, quality laboratory testing, warehousing and production scheduling.

The various combinations provide six career paths among which an individual can choose. The specifics of the paths chosen depend on joint organization needs and individual desires. The interests of the plant and of the individual member come together in the provision and support of training that is always available, reinforced by the system of wage payment and reward. The more groups of knowledge and skill modules learned, the higher the wage level. Each member may move at his or her own pace right to the top level. While there is an expectation that everyone would attempt to reach the top level that they are capable of achieving, time limits are not imposed for doing so. No one is forced to move, and failure to learn and advance cannot impede anyone else's progress. These norms were developed by team members at the start of plant operation.

Collective Agreement

As the organization design was completed (some specifics were added later), recruiting, selection and training were designed. At this time the union representatives took on dual roles, continuing their work on the Design Team and engaging in the collective bargaining process of a labor-management contract for the new plant. Participating in the bargaining for management were the manager of the manufacturing center, the chemical plant superintendent and the employee relations manager. The union negotiating committee was composed of the local and regional officials who were serving on the Design Team, joined by five of the craftsmen-instructors who had been transferred from the refinery to the chemical plant to form the maintenance team.

After hard bargaining, a first-of-its-kind labor-management contract was developed. As indicated earlier, this contract is unique in that it is the first labor-management agreement developed in conjunction with the design of a postbureaucratic organization giving specific emphasis to achieving high quality of working life for its members. Both union and management representatives at the bargaining table understood the basic nature of the new organization, with its emphasis on self-maintenance, learning and participation, its flexible work assignments and its evolutionary structure based on specifying only what is critical to organizational functioning, i.e., minimal critical specifications (Herbst, 1974/Vol. II; Cherns, 1976). They understood that the design was, in effect, a skeleton structure that would be further evolved from subsequent experience. This learning was the opposite of their prior experiences in bureaucratic organizations, where all aspects of structure and relationships were completely specified. They agreed that the survival of the organization and enhancement of the quality of working life for its members would come from the detailed structures and practices that would be evolved by those in the organization, from the participation of members in solving the problems of the organization and from the feedback and utilization of organizational and individual learning.

Both union and management appeared to conclude that protecting and developing the organizational form would best discharge their responsibilities and advance the satisfaction of their own needs and the needs of those they represented. Their shared understandings led to agreement that flexibility and support should be the central features of the labor-management contract. The contract emphasizes and reflects flexibility and is itself an evolutionary document providing enabling conditions consonant with the organization design. It was as if the principle of minimal critical specification had been applied by the negotiators. Both sides made some signal concessions in support of developing the collective agreement. Management did not insist on the customary management rights clause in the contract, accepting general rights stated in law. At the same time it accepted mandatory deduction of union dues as necessary for continuity of the union. The union for its part did not require a seniority clause, except for layoff, since open progression was one of the central features of the organization. With provision of continual training and objective qualification examinations, each worker has an equal opportunity to advance to the highest level that the individual's aspiration, capacities and energy allow. Under these conditions, the union saw no need for the usual seniority clause.

An examination of the agreement indicates how flexibility and support were translated into contract language. The agreement—unconventionally—begins with a unique foreword that sets the tone for what follows. The complete text of the foreword is as follows:

> The purpose of the agreement which follows is to establish an enabling framework within which an organizational system can be developed and sustained that will ensure an efficient and competitive world-scale chemical plant operation and provide meaningful work and job satisfaction for employees. Recognizing that there are risks involved and that there are many factors which can place restraints on the extent to which changes can occur, both management and union support and encourage policies and practices that will reflect their commitment to the following principles and values:
>
> > Employees are responsible and trustworthy, capable of working together effectively and making proper decisions related to their spheres of respon-

sibilities and work arrangements—if given the necessary authorities, information and training.

Employees should be permitted to contribute and grow to their fullest capability and potential without constraints of artificial barriers, with compensation based on their demonstrated knowledge and skills rather than on tasks being performed at any specific time.

To achieve the most effective overall results, it is deemed necessary that a climate exists which will encourage initiative, experimentation, and generation of new ideas, supported by an open and meaningful two-way communication system.

Ten brief sections follow which cover the main issues:

1. *Recognition:* recognizes the union as the sole bargaining agency.
2. *Plant Committee:* states the union's right to have a plant committee for negotiation or otherwise and to have a shop steward on every team.
3. *Grievances:* states only that "there shall be developed and maintained a system to ensure the prompt and equitable resolution of problems at the Plant."
4. *Hours of work and rates of pay:* states that the basic work week is 37 ⅓ hours; that workers are paid on salary, gives the salary levels and describes schedules, shifts and how they may be altered; overtime pay and shift bonus.
5. *Deduction of union dues:* company deducts monthly dues for the union.
6. *Seniority:* states that seniority applies only to layoff and defines seniority and conditions of recall.
7. *Vacations:* the vacation entitlements by years of service are given.
8. *Statutory holidays:* the ten holidays are described, as are statutory holiday pay conditions.
9. *Safety and health:* "the union, in consultation with team representatives, may appoint two representatives on the Safety Committee." Meetings of this committee have been called for purposes of safety or to investigate accidents involved in injury to employees.
10. *Termination of agreement:* gives dates of the term of the agreement and time required for notice of termination or revision.

The contract has not been too kindly received by various leaders of other unions in the region. It has become the subject of widespread discussion as a forerunner of the type of relations that can be developed in support of new forms of organization and QWL.

Social System Support

The first year of the collective agreement was taken up largely by training of new employees, team formation, equipment testing and some plant commissioning. Actual operation of plant by work teams looks as if it will begin during the second year of the collective agreement. Late in the first year when all workers were on site, the stresses of having no rules or norms and no specific contract language led to some extended developmental meetings between the union executive committee and plant management. Out of these meetings evolved a collaborative social system support mechanism to deal with grievances as called for in Section 3 of the collective agreement. A Team Norm Review Board was established composed of six employee representatives, one from each team and one from the maintenance group, three management representatives and the union vice-president. Consensus is required in reaching Board recommendations and in introducing new norms. The Board audits team norms. It cannot discipline. In the event that a team member's problem is not resolved at team level, i.e., face-to-face with the team coordinator and shop steward, the member may appeal to the Board to adjudicate the issue. To date, the Board has been an effective vehicle for problem solving and for developing guidelines at shop floor level.

Later in the first year, a Joint Information Committee was established to aid with the very considerable task of communicating and sharing information among teams that operate around the clock every day of the year. This Committee is composed of one team coordinator and one team member from each team, making 14 members. It should also prove to be an important part of the social system support mechanism by which the organization maintains itself.

The union's view of developments that took place during the first year of the collective agreement is revealed in part of an article written for publication by the National Director of the union. Reimer (1979) states,

> Our program with Shell Canada, Ltd., at the Sarnia Chemical Plant has received much notice. Programs of this nature and others of course require continuing attention. However, one can already observe that in this "open society" operation, where people speak up more frequently, there is less fear in the plant and indeed higher attendance at Union meetings. The nature of the operation tends to keep the people more informed and the meetings where decisions are made affecting their welfare have a higher priority. I understand there is very little absenteeism and the quality of training and the versatility in the plant are concrete attainments. The more the worker is trained, the higher is his income and management can put him to better use. Our Collective Agreement has a statement of purpose and is about five short pages in length. We expect that nothing will be written into the Agreement arbitrarily and that if anything is added, it will have

stood the test of time. It is interesting to note that in this Agreement, management does not incorporate the traditional Management's Rights clause.

The first year under the collective agreement came to an end and negotiations for renewal were completed. Management and union agreed that, with the exception of changes in salaries, the contract finally signed would remain the same as the collective agreement described above.

Conclusion

The design process and the resulting design, as well as the collective agreement, for this nonbureaucratic chemical plant indicate that there is another path available better suited to the post-industrial era. This path is marked by a cooperative process and by the objective of a high quality of working life for all members of the organization. Once again we see a demonstration of the powerful outcomes of substantive collaboration as compared with confrontation in union-management relations. It may be that only by such collaboration will a high quality of working life be truly provided for the members of organizations.

The collective agreement informs us that the "contract as an enabling document" is essential to evolutionary design and thus to a postbureaucratic form of organization. Counterintuitively, we are instructed that high technology increases dependence on workers for economically successful operation. Increased reliance on workers further emphasizes the obligation during design to examine the needs, aspiration and goals of members, i.e., their quality of working life. The joint union-management process more easily satisfies this examination and the development of useful responses. It also demonstrates that shared responsibility for the development of a new organization evolves through union-management collaboration.

We may well close by examining a duality of questions. First, would this innovative collective agreement have been developed without the prior experience of the joint union-management design process? Second, would the new form of organization have survived without the collective agreement as an evolutionary and enabling document?

The answers to these questions are inferential. The long period of working together, the trust developed, the shared experiences, the agreement on organizational philosophy and the early exposure to socio-technical systems concepts and QWL concepts had their effects. Undoubtedly, union and management had developed a substantial set of shared understandings that serve as a basis for considering their individual and joint needs as well as those specific to this new form of organization. At this period in the life of the new organization, given both the fragility of any new social system and the open evolutionary form of the design, it would appear doubtful that this new form of organization can survive for very long without the collective agreement as an enabling and supporting instrument. It was planned to do a follow-up review after operations stabilized.[2]

Arrested Development[3]
Louis Davis

A unique labor-management contract was negotiated in 1978 at the opening of a new chemical plant designed on the basis of socio-technical systems concepts (Davis, 1982). It was the first such contract in the chemical industry. In addition to the usual purposes of formalizing relationships and protecting the interests of labor and management, the parties saw, and constructed, the contract as an "enabling instrument." In support of this purpose, the contract is a skeletal document enacting the socio-technical systems design principle of "minimal critical specification" (Herbst, 1974/Vol. II), i.e., specifying only that which is crucial to the functioning of the organization at the outset and leaving the remainder to be jointly evolved.

This recently conducted review found some unexpected developments. To understand these we need to take into account that the plant is both a production organization in its own right and a branch of a larger company. Most of the requirements and demands to which the plant's members must respond originate, primarily or secondarily, in the higher levels of the company. The structure of the organization and the roles of its members have developed in consequence, given the freedom allowed by the contract.

Management and union staked the future of the plant and of their relationships on an organization design supported by their unique labor-management contract. The central features of the contract were, and continue to be, first, minimum restrictions on union-management collaboration and participation from all levels of the organization in decision making. Such collaboration and participation allows the organization design to evolve based on shared learning. Second, the norms or guide coordinator lines for discipline, safety, advancement, training, etc., which determine what life is like in the daily functioning of the organization, are developed jointly. The start-up design provided the structure for collaboration to keep evolution going, capture experience, maintain flexibility, develop "norms," provide the means for justice in

---

[2]In 1989, this operational review was undertaken at the plant to explore predicted performance.
[3]A requested update, 1989.

the workplace and develop ownership of the design. Last, participation at all levels on all issues of organizational functioning and individual needs was the basis for developing the most effective union-management relationships.

With a contract emphasizing and depending on collaboration and participation, two tests can be used to evaluate its effectiveness. First, is there an increase in the degree of collaboration/participation on the part of all members at all levels in planning, problem-solving, norm setting, justice, etc.? Second, is the continuing design of the organization structure and roles of members taking place through collaboration and participation? If so, then the original intent of the signatories has been achieved.

However, such relatively simple tests do not fit the complex relationships of an organization. This is particularly so where participation occurs at the governance level through plantwide standing committees and at the operational level through semiautonomous work teams. Beginning with the view of the contract as an "enabling" instrument to support the operational philosophy, i.e., charter or constitution, of the new organization and to support the interest of the parties, there are other criteria for judging the contract's effectiveness. Among these are

- Providing flexibility, i.e., ease of making agreed to changes.
- Supporting further evolution of the organization structure and its roles.
- Maintaining the organization's operating philosophy.
- Enhancing the careers and rewards of members.
- Enhancing relationships between workers and superiors and between union and management.
- Providing just and equitable treatment of all members.
- Enhancing bottom-line performance.

The outcome of this operational review is reported in terms of plant performance and of internal development of the organization and the roles of its members. The plant's performance has met and exceeded the goals set for the mature state of operation as initially designed. Ten years after start-up of full operations, the plant is operating at approximately 200 percent rated capacity, producing at outstanding quality levels. Its product is cost-competitive in the world market. The number of employees has remained unchanged since the end of the start-up phase. During the start-up period, there were additional temporary technical experts, on leave from other plants, serving as facilitators to provide technical training and troubleshooting. All the facilitators left, returning to their organizations, during the second and third years of operation. Approximately one half of the current employees were not present at start-up. The largest turnover took place at the end of the second year. The overwhelming majority of team members have advanced to the highest pay level through acquisition of the knowledge and skills called for in the "learn more" wage system.

Having reviewed the impact of the labor-management contract on the performance of the plant's external goals, let us turn to the internal functioning of the plant, i.e., its management, structure, roles, governance, union-management relations, etc. As stated above, the intent behind the original organization design was to put in place the minimum necessary structure and to leave the completion of the design to subsequent collaboration. How well and to what extent the organization structure and internal relations have evolved collaboratively are then also tests of effectiveness.

There was, however, an early departure from the participative mode. In 1981, the second year after full operational start-up, each of the six operating teams of 20 people was assigned an additional "team coordinator," also referred to as "team leader," to provide more technical training. Until very recently, then, each team had two coordinators (leaders). With the removal of the second team leader in mid-1989, the number of members on each team returned to that called for in the original design.

From a collaboration/participation point of view, the addition of the second team leader was seen by team members as unilaterally imposed by plant management, as was the tradition elsewhere in the factory. Although helpful early on, the second team coordinator was seen later as an impediment to participative decision making and to development of self-regulating work teams.

Labor-Management Contract

During the 11-year period of plant operation, there have been very few changes in the contract other than wage rates. Two years after start-up, severance language was added. Nine years later, in the present contract,
- a recognition clause was added;
- the Philosophy Statement was moved from the Foreword into the main body of the contract; and
- joint consultation was specified as the means of decision making.

The Good Practices Handbook continues as the only central documentation specifying guides and behavioral norms. The handbook continues to be changed and has more norms, regulations and guidelines, including advancement, overtime equalization, discipline, role descriptions, etc. Some of these are seen to be out of date and unnecessary.

Learning and Advancement

The employee advancement program, based on pay for knowledge and skill that the team members are certified to have obtained, has performed very well.

In 1989, the eleventh year of operation, approximately 90 percent of employees are at the top level of skill and wages. The advancement plan's requirements and operation are guided by the Training Advisory Board, one of the participative plantwide standing committees. The progression plan began on the first day of full operation, which followed six months of basic skill training for all. Two years later process skills were separated from other skills and reduced in complexity, making it easier to advance but resulting in reduced flexibility of team members. There are pressures to extend the career ladder by adding some technical work now done by technical staff. Union and management are uncertain over the future direction of further organizational evolution. The result is inaction at the Joint Union-Management Committee. The maintenance crafts team—the only function-based group—was, and is, outside the advancement plan and has been demanding equitable treatment. There are indications that evolutionary design is not taking place.

Shift Teams as Self-Regulating Units and Their Members

As originally designed, one team operates the entire plant on each shift as part of 24-hour, 7-day continuous running. One exception is the maintenance/craftsman/instructor team, which works on days only. On a rotating schedule each operational team joins the maintenance team for instruction and repair work.

Members see the team structure as a prized feature of the organization, even though they are not themselves intensely engaged in team governance activities. Except for participation in their teams, a majority see the plant as quite traditional in operation. Teams meet every two months for four to eight hours to review issues and problems. Small groups within teams meet as needed. Team members decide whether they wish to bring personal problems to the team or to the team coordinator. Day-to-day problems can be dealt with by anyone and reported through a new "event handling" procedure. The team coordinator handles minor infractions before they become disciplinary issues. The teams deal with disciplinary issues, forwarding up those they cannot resolve. Teams get involved in what are seen to be "big" or "hot" issues. Day-to-day issues are forwarded to standing committees, who poll team members rather than receive teams' recommendations as originally planned. The original organization design which called for one team to operate the entire two-product plant was abandoned. Now each team has two groups, one for each product, whose members work together only when they rotate into the warehouse. However, all are still informed, sharing knowledge because there is one control room.

Team members are reasonably competent to participate in team self-regulation and in committee activities, which are part of their larger roles. Nonetheless, since the start-up training given 12 years ago, there has been no follow-up or refresher training for team members in social system skills such as team membership, conflict resolution, interpersonal dynamics, etc. Neither have team-building exercises been provided to assist in the development of more robust teams. Recently, plant management has rediscovered socio-technical systems and is beginning some team coordinator training and giving more control to the teams.

Union-Management Relations

The union plays a role in governance of the plant at many levels. The organiza-tion design called for six work teams, one maintenance team, technical and administrative staff and five plantwide standing committees. The standing committees are the Overtime Equalization Board; Team Norms Review Board; Training Advisory Board; Joint Health and Safety Board; and Joint Union-Management Committee. The first four are advisory to the Joint Union-Management Committee, whose approval is required for implementation of recommendations. The union is represented on each of the boards and standing committees. With the exception of the Joint Union-Management Committee, they are largely inactive or meet pro forma. In addition, each team has a shop steward member. The shop stewards have been very passive, failing to exert any leadership of their teams and have acted in traditional ways on disciplinary matters. The plant's union leaders have attempted to stimulate the stewards without success. Training for this role has not been provided.

Grievances, one of the major areas of conflict between unions and manage-ments, are of minor consequence here. There has not been an arbitration in the 11-year history of the plant. Most issues are handled at team level.

During the last five years, the union has acted as the champion of the philosophy which undergirds the structure of the organization and its mode of operation. During the most recent contract negotiation, the union was prepared to strike to support its demand to have the Philosophy Statement included in the main body of the contract. Management agreed to the inclusion.

Looking to the future, the union is concerned that about half the work force see the "system" as traditional except for high participation taking place in self-regulation of teams. With only one third of people active in various committees and many saying that they have not gained anything special from the system, plus minimal stimulation of, and training in, self-regulating team operation, there may be growing apathy toward participation.

Management sees the union's concerns as too narrowly focused on its members. Excluded from consideration by both union and management are staff personnel. The union's relations with management have become active in the attempt to clarify the role of union officers. Union-management relations are seen as good and as close despite the fact that they have not led to further organizational evolution as intended. Missing is close and meaningful interaction both with teams as miniorganizations and with employees as team members. The more's the pity since the organizational structure was designed to function in this manner. Management's interaction with individual employees takes us back to the previous Tayloristic form of organization.

Conclusion

The labor-management contract has proven to be a leading instrument in enabling collaboration and participation. However, while enabling—in contrast to hindering or restricting—it is inadequate by itself for it does not, perhaps cannot, specify commitments to further evolution of the organization and roles of its members. Additionally, even with a contract that supports and stimulates collaboration, there is the long-standing North American history of union-management relations with its belief system concerning the roles and positions taken by the parties—that managements have rights and are proactive, while unions are parochial and reactive, hobbling development. So while collaboration and participation are quite high at the Union-Management Committee level, this is insufficient for stimulating change and evolution without an appropriate shared worldview suitable to the conditions of the 1990s. And, most importantly, management is not providing needed leadership.

Overall, the structure of the organization, roles of its members and union-management relations have not evolved beyond what was essentially present at start-up 11 years ago; in fact, there has been some slight regression. The organization remains in a state of arrested development as reflected in the inactivity of the standing committees, in the substantial amount of unilateral decision making and in the relatively rare meetings of the work teams to solve problems, plan and deal with their self-regulation and the governance of the plant.

The most likely explanation for this state of affairs, seen elsewhere, is the failure of senior managers to acquire and transmit the necessary understanding of the underlying conceptual bases and paradigms on which the plant's organization is structured. This necessary understanding, while only a requirement in traditional organizations, becomes crucial where organizational concepts are so different from those of the conventional bureaucratic/scientific management with which managers are familiar. Socio-technical systems concepts, on which this organization is based, confront managers with a discontinuity in beliefs and practices rather than gradual change. This requires that senior managers invest energy and time to learn and understand the new concepts and to pass on the concepts to their successors. Such understanding is essential for giving appropriate sanction and continuing support for a new form of organization and style of management.

Without in-depth understanding, only token support for further evolution is likely to be provided by top management. When, as in this case, the new form of organization achieves outstanding bottom-line performance, the lack of adequate grounding on the part of senior management easily leads to the "black box" approach: "We have this successful organization, we do not understand why (i.e., what is happening inside the black box?). Therefore we had best keep everything as it is to assure continuation of the desirable results. That we might achieve better outcomes by further evolving based on learning from experience is only a prediction."

Finally, the system of developing managers in the company also contributes to the low level of organizational evolution. These practices exist in all parts of the company and were in use prior to the opening of the new plant. They become part of the plant's practices.

The careers of managers require rotation and transfer. Each young manager must go through all the positions, transferring to a succession of plants where they are made available. Thus, in the plant under review, new managers are sent into the plant each on his or her four-year cycle. They have *not* been selected for compatibility with, or capacity for, this self-regulating organization, nor have they been prepared through training for a role with such different requirements. Upon arrival they try to learn, from colleagues and subordinates, the basic elements of the (socio-technical) system and what is required of them. In the meantime, they continue to operate and make decisions in the traditional mode. By the time they learn enough, through self-instruction, they move on to the next posting. If a manager fails to move to a new posting every four years, then it is musical chairs for him or her, dropping off the career ladder. Future progress is stymied. "If I am to progress, I must leave the plant neat and tidy and not messy with organizational change."

Summary

The new and still unusual labor-management contract satisfied the expectations of the parties. It permitted and supported a team-based form or organization based on the principle of team self-regulation through participation. The performance of the teams and the plant is very high by conventional bottom-line measures. The contract also fostered good, merit-based advancement and monetary rewards; good working conditions; and high commitment to the organization. Although it was written to support evolution of the organization structure and its roles, little evolution has taken place. The content of the contract and its implementation provide a necessary basis; however, in themselves they are insufficient. The intervening variable is leadership of managers and union officials—leadership that is congruent with the organizational philosophy. Many employees at all levels have a mixed view of the organization. As stated by some, "The operation of this plant falls between traditional and participative management. For some issues and problems it is more one than the other. We expected more participation in operations and in governance of the plant as inferred in the philosophy and in the social-systems training we received at start-up. Nevertheless, this is a very pleasant place in which to work and we are staying."

Finally, the lesson repeated in other settings, is that top management support at the outset of an organizational innovation is absolutely necessary. However, support only at the outset is insufficient. For long-term development, corporate top management's continuing commitment to maintaining and further evolving the organization in fulfillment of the organizational philosophy is needed. Particularly crucial is the selection and preparation of new managers, supervisors and staff who will be moved into the organization over time. Given the performance achieved as measured by bottom-line criteria, this somewhat negative assessment may be seen as unwarranted. Our focus, however, is on the failure to fulfill the expectations set at the outset, i.e., the failure to achieve the potential provided in the organization design supported by labor and management.

References

Cherns, A. 1976. "The Principles of Sociotechnical Design." *Human Relations,* 29:783–92.

Davis, L.E. 1977. "Evolving Alternative Organization Designs: Their Socio-Technical Bases." *Human Relations,* 30:261–73.

———. 1979. "Individual-Organization Conflict." *California Management Review* (Winter).

———. 1982. "Organization Design." Chapter 2.1 in *Handbook of Industrial Engineering,* edited by G. Salvendy. New York: Wiley.

Gyllenhammer, P. 1977. *People at Work.* Reading, Mass.: Addison Wesley.

Halpern, N. 1985. "Organization Design in Canada: Shell Canada Sarnia Chemical Plant." In *People and Organizations Interacting,* edited by A. Brakel. New York: Wiley.

Herbst, P.G. 1974. *Socio-Technical Design: Strategies in Multi-Disciplinary Research.* London: Tavistock Publications. Chapter 2 shortened and revised, Vol. II, "Designing with Minimal Critical Specifications," pp. 294–302.

Reimer, C.N. 1979. "Oil, Chemical and Atomic Workers International Union and Quality of Working Life—A Union Perspective." *Quality of Working Life: The Canadian Scene* (Winter).

Yankelovitch, D. 1979. "Work, Value and the New Breed." In *Work in America: The Decade Ahead,* edited by C. Kerr and J. Rosow. New York: Van Nostrand-Reinhold.

Collaborative Action
Research

Action research provides the basic methodology for most socio-technical studies, as these are concerned with identifying organizational change processes as they occur and with understanding their unexpected developments and the constraints that often limit and even negate them, i.e. change and the conditions under which change occurs or fails to occur. Organizations have to be willing to allow the necessary contacts to take place. The client as well as the research team is active. This gives rise to a process of co-learning between the client and the research team. The emphasis on learning has led the writer and some of his colleagues to prefer the term "action learning" to "action research."

Unit Operations, the scheme put out by Arthur D. Little for technological analysis of the chemical industry, recommended itself as a takeoff point for socio-technical operational analysis. After intensive research, however, Emery and his colleagues found that the analytic unit for a socio-technical system had to be itself a socio-technical system.

The first widely practiced method for undertaking action research inquiries in bringing about socio-technical change has been called the nine-step model. In the light of work at Norwegian plants and a new Shell refinery in England, Emery presented the method at a conference of socio-technical academics held in Lincoln, England, in 1967. This method was used in training the managers and union representatives in the yearly courses presented by Davis and his colleagues at UCLA throughout the 1970s and, indeed, subsequently. The group undertaking the design has first to make an overall scan of the problems likely to arise and then an analysis of the unit operations of the technology. The method goes on to identify the variances in these which must be coped with if improvements are to be made. Special attention is paid to the key variances involving the social system, and a separate analysis is made of workers' perceptions. The implications for maintenance and user and supplier departments (inside or outside the company) are examined. Finally, account is taken of the effect of general policies on the constraints and opportunities within the company. Proposals for change may arise at any point but need to take all these factors into account. This procedure has been found remarkably effective in continuous process plants for which it was originally designed.

It became necessary to specify how tasks might best be converted into jobs to be undertaken by workers so that they would experience a jointly optimized product. Emery's hypotheses in this regard are presented.

In Australia, the Emerys have moved forward to Participant Design Workshops that immediately involve those concerned in job redesign on the grounds that they know more about their jobs than anyone else. They have been successful in simpler heavy industries where there is great hostility to any procedures which smack of academia.

In Norway and Sweden, as the 1970s wore on, the question arose of introducing national legislation to ensure that jobs were designed in accordance with the six recognized criteria proposed by Emery as needing satisfaction for a high quality of working life. Workers were given the right to demand the presence of such criteria and to refuse work which did not exemplify them. These questions came to the fore in the design of new plants. Emery and Thorsrud used them in designing a new plant for Norskhydro.

Murray pioneers a new way of reaching engineering designers. Simulation is used in projects involving group and organizational factors which are part of formative training so that experience of them, rather than merely information on them, is built into engineering education.

Trist emphasizes the need to include all levels of the work force in socio-technical change. The effectiveness of socio-technical changes is linked to the level at which they are initiated. Local initiation often leads to fade out unless unusually well protected. Central mandate for socio-technical change is not sufficient alone but must be worked through with intermediate levels. There can be innovative subsidiaries and innovative divisions, but in the end all divisions and functions have to be involved. Trist emphasized this in his keynote address to the conference on Work Improvement and Industrial Democracy of the European Economic Community in 1974.

Entirely new problems arise in the design of advanced technology using microprocessors and computers. There is great danger at present that these industries will produce large numbers of narrow, unproductive jobs. Pava's account of change in an organization with advanced computer and microprocessor technology shows that newer factors are involved than those encountered in continuous process and manufacturing technologies. Trist comments on the general implications of Pava's analysis.

Though the search conference is reserved for Volume III, it was felt that a brief introduction to it might be a suitable last contribution to Volume II. A statement taken from a report by Morley and Trist on a search conference on day care in Saskatchewan is provided.

Fred Emery

Socio-Technical Unit Operations Analysis[1]

This analysis is based on a study with the aim of devising a conceptual scheme for the analysis of worker/machine/equipment relations within the more common unit operations, presupposing a classification of unit operations and a systematic description of their characteristics. The other members of the project team were Hans van Beinum of the Tavistock Institute; Louis Davis, visiting from the Department of Engineering, University of California, Berkeley; and P.G. (David) Herbst, on loan from the Institute of Industrial Social Research, Technical University of Norway, Trondheim. An associate was Per Engelstad, a chemical engineer with a postgraduate diploma in Sociology, Institute of Work Research, Oslo.

A determined effort to build on the Arthur D. Little (ADL) concept of unit operations convinced us that this would not answer our problems, although it seemed useful for machine tool development. We found it necessary to develop concepts and scales for total production systems.

The two Tavistock Documents to which this report is ancillary (Davis and Engelstad, 1966; Herbst, 1966) report the main findings of the study group but do not give an overview of how the group works. In this report we have indicated the initial perspective of the study group and its subsequent development.

Initial Perspective

The support of the Social Science Research Council was sought to enable Davis and senior members of the Tavistock staff to prepare a theoretical paper called *Unit Operation Analyses of Socio-Technical Systems.*

This project represented for us a direct and vital continuation of work previously supported by the Department of Scientific and Industrial Research (DSIR). Their grant in 1958 enabled us to formalize the concepts and generalizations arising from the Institute's earlier work on socio-technical systems. In

[1]Reprinted from *The Democratisation of the Work Place.* London: Tavistock Institute Document, 1966.

this report, *Characteristics of Socio-Technical Systems* (Emery, 1959/Vol. II), we presented a conceptual scheme for measuring the "degree of mechanization/automation" and drew attention to the independent dimension of the unit operations required for production, maintenance and supply. Marek and Emery (Marek, 1962) subsequently collaborated to measure in detail the variations in degree of mechanization/automation in engineering and power generation plants. The measured differences appeared to be sensibly related to observed differences in what was required of the operators and supervisors. This work, which DSIR sponsored for many years, has been continued for three years in Norway (on behalf of the Norwegian Trade Union Congress and Employers Federation) and in active collaboration with the Technical University of Norway, Trondheim (Thorsrud and Emery, 1964). There was at that time no interest in the Britain in active collaboration with socio-technical experiments.

Our three Norwegian field experiments have revealed that

• It is possible to formulate general principles for designing jobs and work organizations so as to increase human satisfaction with, and involvement in, the work (Thorsrud and Emery, 1964).

• It is possible with current tools adequately to analyze a technology so as to determine how jointly to optimize the social and technical systems (Marek et al., 1966).

• It is *not* possible systematically to argue from experience with one type of technology to another, at least not in the detail needed to decide on specific changes in job organization or technology.

• It is *not* possible for social science findings in this field to be widely diffused to, and applied by, management and unions unless socio-technical analysis can be so conceptualized as to be free of some of the restriction to types of technology and to be comprehensible to the professions most readily available to industry.

It is urgent that we find a solution to these theoretical questions. The Norwegian project is moving from the experimental stage to diffusion and will, we hope, become a challenge to British industry's thinking about the utility of social science. Already a major British refining company has adopted what is essentially the Norwegian approach to joint optimization of social and technical systems; it has involved all of its top and middle management, through a series of residential conferences and has decided to establish its own field experiments (Hill and Emery, 1971/Vol. II).

Davis and his coworkers had quite independently arrived at the same conclusions as a result of their socio-technical experiments in U.S. industry (Davis, 1966). Exchange of working papers led to Davis taking leave of absence from Berkeley so that, in cooperation, we might be more successful in solving this problem.

Our present line of thinking is that there is a finite number of unit operations that is significantly smaller than the number of different productive technologies. Many of the technologies differ only in the way they combine members of this more limited set of unit operations. If principles can be evolved for worker/machine/equipment relations for the most common unit operations, then a useful beginning will have been made to generalizing knowledge of socio-technical systems. We should note in passing that such broad classifications as process industries, mass production, etc., are invaluable for a sociology of industry or a psychology of occupations but are next to useless for this task, owing to the wide variety of operations and wide range of mechanization within each plant.

A major contribution to classifying unit operations has been released by Arthur D. Little, Inc. (as part of their government sponsored Automation Project). Furthermore, they have reported on the use of information theory as a common language for both the human and the technical components of any unit operation.

Davis has supervised a series of case studies of different unit operations and, among his coworkers, Crossman (1960) has further developed the use of information theory in worker/machine systems.

By working with van Beinum, we have at our fingertips a fairly wide range of unit operations with which we have had intimate contact. Among the theoretical lines we wish to pursue are the following:

- Evolving a more fundamental, and hence shorter, list of unit operations. This seems feasible. Many of the operations named in the ADL catalogue are, for purposes of socio-technical analysis, identical. In some cases, the differences in name simply reflect differences in the history of the operation; in other cases, they reflect differences which could make no difference in the variances that human beings could cope with.

- Developing a more appropriate common language than information theory for the human and the technical aspects of work. Information theory is too general. A more promising theory is that of directive correlation (Sommerhoff, 1950). Directive correlation can itself be formulated in terms of information theory, but it includes feedback as a special case and it is specifically concerned with the joint operation of processes obeying different laws. Within this theoretical language it is possible to handle not only technical processes but also such concepts as responsibility.

First Stage

Throughout June, Davis, Engelstad and Emery worked directly on the ADL concept of Unit Operations. Engelstad collaborated actively because this was of direct relevance to the continuing socio-technical experiment in Norway.

Two main conclusions emerged from this stage.

First, it seemed perfectly feasible to evolve toward a more fundamental, shorter list of unit operations. Primarily, this meant a classification of "tool" and "material" according to their physical state characteristics (e.g., solid-structured plastic aggregate, fluid or gas). Within the cells thus formed, it is possible to group the ADL unit operations and to detect their essential commonalities in terms of the interstate processes involved. However, this led us in the direction currently being pursued in machine tool research. It was not the direction in which we wished to go, even though there were useful payoffs in a technical analysis that identified logical models of basic processes such as paring off surface layers of solid structures and segregating liquid-aggregate, liquid-liquid mixtures.

Second, analysis in terms of unit operations failed to encompass many of the critical variances for which production design (or redesign) decisions have to be made. Such an analysis could not indicate to the designers whether, for instance, they should automate workers out of a system, whether they should opt for a segmented, externally controlled task structure (à la conveyor belt assembly) or whether they should trade off a deliberately degraded technical system for greater on-the-job learning. The critical variances excluded by unit operations analysis were those emerging from the environment within which the production system had to survive economically and from the human input which is *always* essential to this survival. This last statement is very strong and should be explained. We were unable to identify, or even conceive of, any production system, no matter how happily automated, that did not require for its integrity as an economic unit a human element for command and "re-programming" (design and maintenance).

These conclusions could have been reached on theoretical grounds. We preferred to reach them by detailed analysis and discussion of existing production systems and the process of industrial design (for this latter we are very much indebted to the special knowledge Davis brought to the group). The document by Davis and Engelstad reports the steps leading to the second conclusion. We did not prepare a document on the first conclusion as this was going into areas beyond our competence.

Second Stage

Discussions throughout July were extended to include Herbst and van Beinum. The general direction that we took is shown in Herbst's document. After the critical work of the first stage, we proceeded on the assumption that the *basic unit for socio-technical analysis must itself be a socio-technical unit and have the characteristics of an open system.* In design terms this represents the last level at which decisions can be taken for joint optimization of the human and technical systems with respect to environmental requirements. Failure to recognize this may lead to design decisions being made solely on technical and economic cost criteria with consequent inefficiencies due to excess operating costs, difficult maintenance, lack of growth in system performance, high overheads for control and supervision or lack of adaptability to market shifts. Examples of each of these can readily be given from current design practice.

For theoretical purposes it is necessary to identify the conceptual dimensions of such a unit. At a fairly crude level one can postulate that they share the properties of open systems generally, i.e., that they can achieve "steady state" only by maintenance of direction and a steady rate of progress in that direction, and that, like coupled systems, they are governed by the principle of joint optimization. A more precise and systematic way of expressing these characteristics is Sommerhoff's theory of directive correlations. This deals explicitly with coupled systems when at least one of the systems has the properties of information absorption and retention processing and of self-selected response variability. These properties are characteristic of living systems but are also built into many servo-controlled mechanisms (e.g., a radar controlled anti-aircraft gun). Interaction between different systems can be conceived of only with the principle of *contemporaneous causation,* i.e., a past event cannot be a cause because it is past and no longer exists; a future event cannot be a cause because it does not yet exist. Only systems that exist together can interact. However, independent systems[2] cannot be conceived of as coupled together unless at time, t_o (Figure 1), there is a movement of information at least from one system to another (such a movement could be regarded as a minimal interaction, provided that one recognizes that this usage extends the dimension of interaction far beyond the lower limits of what were until recently considered the significant energy exchanges).

This information can only remain "potential information" unless capabilities exist for processing it together with existing "memories." This condition would appear to open the way for an infinite regress, i.e., no information unless there is prior information. We accept that the regression may be beyond the time span of an individual human but believe that it is finite at least within the span of a *species* emerging and adapting to a physical environment that has in itself an informational structure. Even when processed within memoried categories (a further assumption), the information would be "useless" unless it in-formed action at some later point in time (t_1) which could correspond with,

[2]We are not discussing sets of systems or conditions that are "epistemically dependent," i.e., where the value taken by one conceptually determines the values that will be given to others. In substantive terms, we are discussing neither the relation of parts within the same system nor the relation of a part to the whole.

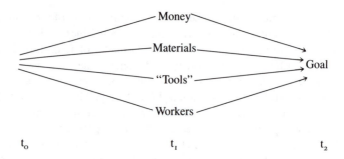

Figure 1. Directive correlation of production factors

and be contemporaneous with, what had in the meantime issued from processes internal to the other system. It is still not enough to warrant a coupling of two or more systems that there should be an informational flow at t_0 which shapes the interaction at t_1. The interaction at t_1 must give issue to a state of affairs at t_2 that is of the sort that we typically described in terms of "goals" for the cognizing system. Although there is a communicable intuitive content to the notion of a "goal state," it is worthwhile to attempt to explicate what we mean in this theoretical context. We do not mean to refer only to subjectively perceived goal states that might be reflected in emotions or organizational morale. Our reference is to changes in the objective probabilities of the cognizing system persisting as a system. If the state of affairs resulting from interaction at t_1 neither endangers nor promotes survival of the cognizing system, then we may be observing a chance interaction, not a coupling.

This last stage again presupposes information transfer and processing. Unless the initial information imports, the response and the resulting state of affairs (t_2) are registered and processed within memoried categories of system states, response tendencies and object characteristics, there can be no change in the probabilities of future survival, i.e., in response capabilities given similar initial inputs.

The situation with which we are concerned is represented in Figure 1. Following on the preceding discussion of the abstracted characteristics of directive correlation, we may be able to specify the necessary conceptual dimensions of socio-technical units. The goal state can often be conceived of as a product/cost relation where the product is specified in terms of quantity and quality and the cost is assumed to include some allowances for product distribution (at least for those instances where product variations entail differing distribution costs, e.g., costs for overcoming novelty or for sustaining freshness or finish). This in itself might appear to reinstate an intolerable degree of indeterminacy insofar as the cost element of the goal state cannot be related to survivability without some specification of market prices. For our purposes we assume that the problem does not exist insofar as the designer of a production system should be given the costs per unit of given quality within which the designing must be done. We will take it that our problems of conceptualization are within this limit.

If the goal state can be specified in the ways indicated in the preceding paragraph then we can identify one of the dimensions relevant to survivability (what Herbst refers to as viability). There must be a specification of a product/cost relation (or some determinate transform thereof) that enables the results of the interactions of people, tools, money and equipment to be recognized as such and judged harmful or beneficial. For the latter judgment to occur there must be "knowledge of results" and a frame of reference.

Working back through our general statement of directive correlations, there must be also

- A choice of responses, which of necessity means that some of the responses are potentially less beneficial or more harmful than others but are, in the absence of past experience, equally likely to occur.
- A knowledge of which initial states in people, tools, money and materials are likely to presage subsequent states.
- An input of information about the state of all variables (people, tools, money and materials) in time for the necessary thinking to be done and the interaction to be shaped by human intervention.

Within this framework we can postulate the following as the dimensions for analyzing our basic socio-technical units:

- specification of objectives;
- knowledge of results;
- judgmental criteria for results;
- range of responses;
- process knowledge;
- stimulus access and timing.

As we have formulated it, the process of judging one socio-technical unit against another (or against itself at a different time) is obviously relative to the objectives that are being specified and the complexity of the other processes involved in the directive correlation. The first is not properly part of our problem. As already stated, the designer cannot start unless the objectives are specified. The second source of indeterminacy can be regarded as also outside our problem area because the designer can pursue given objectives only from the basis of present knowledge; there can be no hope of reducing complexity below the level of current knowledge about what will lead to what.

We are henceforth assuming that economic analysis will determine the objectives to be pursued and that technical knowledge will determine the range of alternative unit operations (in the original A.D. Little sense) that will contribute to achieving these objectives. We shall ignore, at least for the moment, those process characteristics of people and money that reveal themselves during the course of a directive correlation.

Accepting these two limitations to what we are trying to explain, we can now observe an important, interesting convergence. The criteria by which we think socio-technical units should be judged are very similar to those that the Ambers (1962) devised for judging the degree of automation of a production process. The Ambers proposed that the degree of automation should be judged by the human attributes that were mechanized. They further proposed that these attributes should be ordered as follows:

- none;
- energy (for material transformation);
- dexterity (for material/tool orientation);
- diligence (for habitual performance of dexterity);
- judgment (of what is beneficial or harmful);
- evaluation (of multiple judgments);
- learning (of what follows what);
- reasoning (of what could follow what);
- creativeness (to change existing range of responses);
- dominance (commanding a change in goals).

They assert that the last named attribute would be a property of the machine vis-à-vis people, if it possessed all the preceding properties. With regard to the other attributes (apart from creativeness) they specify related system properties and identify examples, even if only embryonic.

The convergence is not accidental. Their studies were concentrated, as were ours, on productive systems that are, or have been, socio-technical systems and hence could theoretically become, or have become, purely technical systems. Their concern is opposite to ours, namely to measure general characteristics of the technical system, but they have, implicitly, drawn their criteria from properties possessed by the total production system.

The conclusion we wish to draw is simple. Given the objectives and the current technical knowledge, the design of a production system must be subordinated to achieving the highest possible level of overall system properties. As implied, the level cannot justifiably be higher than that which can increase goal attainment other than by the learning that could conceivably take place on existing knowledge. Does this conclusion follow from what has been stated? We think it does, because each of the levels specified by the Ambers corresponds to an interdependent part of the directive correlations we call production (allowing for diligence as a property reflected in speed and precision of response). A shortfall in any of these parts can reduce goal achievement.

This brings us to our last point, which should take us back to where we started. If we are usefully to generalize from lessons learned from a particular socio-technical system, we should seek to do so in terms of the level of overall system performance that is being sought. That is, it will be more relevant if we have been trying to raise the total system to a level involving diligence (or learning or creativity) than if the technical unit operations involved were in drilling, pressing or distillation.

Possible Outcomes of the Discussions

Two documents and the present reflections have arisen from the discussion of unit operations. Insofar as these discussions took place between key members of three different research teams, we cannot predict the further outcomes. The current understanding is that the teams will continue these lines of thought in their local settings (within their own budgets) and seek joint publication in the very near future. As much as we are averse to premature publication, we are convinced that these matters require an early airing to a much wider audience than can be reached by the circulation lists of the three institutions. Although these three documents represent fairly adequately our progress in June/July, we shall circulate the further documents we expect to emerge and shall expedite publication of whatsoever will usefully extend the universe of discourse.

References

Amber, G.H. and P.S. Amber. 1962. *Anatomy of Automation*. New York: Prentice Hall.

Crossman, E.R. 1960. *Automation and Skill*. Department of Scientific and Industrial Research, Problems of Progress in Industry No.9. London: Her Majesty's Stationery Office.

Davis, L. 1966. *The Design of Jobs*. London: Tavistock Institute Document; *Industrial Relations*, 6:21–45. Revised in *Design of Jobs*, edited by L.E. Davis and J.C. Taylor. Harmondsworth: Penguin Books, 1972.

Davis, L. and P. Engelstad. 1966. *Unit Operations in Socio-Technical Systems: Analysis and Design*. London: Tavistock Institute Document.

Emery, F.E. 1959. *Some Characteristics of Socio-Technical Systems*. London: Tavistock Institute Document 527. Revised in *The Emergence of a New Paradigm of Work*. Canberra: Centre for Continuing Education, Australian National University, 1978. Also in *Design of Jobs*, edited by L.E. Davis and J.C. Taylor. Harmondsworth: Penguin Books, 1972; Vol. II, "Characteristics of Socio-Technical Systems," pp.157–86.

Herbst, P.G. 1966. *Socio-Technical Unit Design*. London: Tavistock Institute Document.

Hill, P. 1971. *Towards a New Philosophy of Management*. London: Gower Press, 1971. Excerpted, Vol. II, as P. Hill and F. Emery, "Toward a New Philosophy of Management," pp.259–82.

Marek, J. 1962. *Effects of Automation in an Actual Control Work Situation*. London: Tavistock Institute Document.

Marek, J., K. Lange and P. Engelstad. 1966. *Wire Mill of the Christiana Spigerverk.* Document of the Institute for Industrial Social Research, Technical University of Norway, Trondheim; also Tavistock Institute Document.

Sommerhoff, G. 1950. *Analytical Biology.* Oxford: Oxford University Press.

Thorsrud, E. and F.E. Emery. 1964. Appendix 3 in *Industrielt Demokrati.* Oslo: University of Oslo Press. Reissued in 1969 as F.E. Emery and E. Thorsrud, *Form and Content in Industrial Democracy.* London: Tavistock Publications.

Fred Emery

The Nine-Step Model[1]

Purpose of the Model

This analytical model has been developed as a practical tool to help line managers implement the concept of joint optimization in their own departments or sections. It is hoped that it will enable managers to examine their existing technical systems and their existing organizations to gain insight into the technical and social systems, and to improve the level of performance.

The Model in Practice

As the model has been tried out on a number of different production systems, certain lessons have emerged:

- Care must be taken in selecting the appropriate area for analysis. Existing organizational boundaries are not necessarily the most appropriate ones. In practice, it is all right to select a production system as defined by current organizational boundaries, bearing in mind that one result of the analysis might be an indication that the boundaries should be adjusted. Departmental management should not select too large or too complex an area for analysis, at least initially. In most cases, a department is too large a unit for full study within a reasonable period of time with the resources available. Greater progress can be made by selecting smaller units, if possible.
- For analysis, it is helpful to concentrate on the production system as it is currently operating; otherwise, some confusion may creep in with reference to the way it "used" to operate or how it "might" operate in the future.
- A practical difficulty is the tendency to collect too much detail. An effort should be made to identify only key information under each step heading and to avoid getting caught up in an abundance of detail.
- To initiate and carry through an analytical process and to carry out an

[1]Presented to an International Meeting on Socio-Technical Systems, Lincoln, England, 1967.

ensuing action program will require a high degree of effort and commitment. It will also require the participation of people at all levels in the production system concerned. It seems highly desirable, therefore, to set up a small action group headed by the production system manager, with representatives from various levels and with such outside help as may be required.

Analytical Model for Socio-Technical Systems

STEP 1: INITIAL SCANNING

The objectives of this step are to identify the main characteristics of the production system and of the environment in which it exists and to determine, if possible, the main problems and where the emphasis of the analysis needs to be placed. This can be done through a carefully structured briefing of the action group by a departmental manager. The briefing should cover the following ground:
- The general geographical layout of the production system.
- The existing organizational structure and the main groupings within it.
- The main inputs into the system, with specifications where appropriate.
- The main outputs from the system, again with specifications where appropriate.
- The main transforming processes that take place within the system.
- The main types of variance in the production system and their sources, e.g., the nature of the raw material, the equipment or breakdowns.
- The main characteristics of the relationship between the production system and the department in which it exists.

STEP 2: IDENTIFICATION OF UNIT OPERATIONS

The purpose of this step is to identify the main phases in the production operation. Unit operations are the primary segments or phases in the series of operations that have to be carried out to convert materials at the input end of the system into products at the output end. Each unit operation is relatively self-contained and each effects an identifiable transformation in the raw material. A transformation in this sense is either a change of state in the raw material or a change of location or storage of the material.

The actions necessary to effect the transformation may be carried out by machines or by people, but we are not concerned at this stage with either the characteristics or needs of the machines (e.g., maintenance needs or operating characteristics) or the characteristics and needs of the people (e.g., psychological needs). Attention is entirely on the series of transformations through which the raw material goes. Where possible, the purpose of each unit operation needs to be identified in terms of its inputs, its transformations and its outputs.

STEP 3: IDENTIFICATION OF KEY PROCESS VARIANCES AND THEIR INTERRELATIONSHIPS

The objectives of this stage are to identify the key process variances and the interrelationships between them. A variance is a deviation from some standard or from some specification.

It is necessary to emphasize that, at this stage in the analysis, we are concerned with variance that comes from the raw material or from the nature of the process itself as it is currently or normally operating. We are not concerned with variance that comes from faults in the technical equipment or plant (e.g., breakdown or malfunctioning); nor are we concerned with variance that comes from the social system (e.g., maloperation or human error).

We also are not concerned with the total range of variance. From other studies it has been found that there are a large number of variances in any production system that have either no effect or a comparatively minor effect on the ability of the production system to pursue its objectives. It may be necessary, however, to take some such variance into account in subsequent attempts to reach a higher level of joint optimization, but at this stage we are concerned only with those "key" variances that significantly affect the capability of the production system to pursue its objectives in one or more of its unit operations. The sequence of actions necessary is as follows:

- Identification of all variances in the system (arising from the nature of the raw material or from the nature of the process) that, in the opinion of the action group, are worthy of note. The main sources of information are the manager and supervisors of the system, who draw on their knowledge and experience. It is necessary to go through the process of identifying variances several times to ensure that all the main variances have been included.
- Drawing up a matrix of the variances identified. This matrix shows any clusters of variances—control problems—and also shows where information loops exist or are necessary in the production system. It will also help in the selection of key variances (e.g., variances that have an effect through a series of unit operations are likely to be considered key to the control of the process).

The identification of the key variances can be done in two stages.

(1)   The department or unit manager and appropriate assistants should

make a list of what they consider to be the key variances, drawing on their experience and knowledge of the production system.

(2)   The action group should work with this list, checking it against the matrix of variances and against the following four criteria. A variance should be considered key if it significantly affects:

- quantity of production;
- quality of production;
- operating costs (use of utilities, raw material, overtime, etc.);
- social costs (e.g., the stress, effort or hazard imposed on the employees).

The first three dimensions are concerned with the system's *production objectives*. It is possible to move now to an analysis of the social system; to examine the way in which it contributes to control of variances and so to the attainment of the production system's objectives; and to examine the extent to which the social system's own needs are met.

STEP 4: ANALYSIS OF THE SOCIAL SYSTEM

The objective of this step is to identify the main characteristics of the *existing* social system. Its complex sets of interrelations and groupings, both formal and informal, do not need to be described. By structuring the analysis carefully, it is possible for the analytical team to draw out sufficient amounts of the relevant information to enable it to begin to develop job-design proposals relatively quickly. The following steps are the minimum necessary:

- A *brief review* of the organizational structure where necessary, filling in a little more detail than was included in Step 1 on number of levels, social groupings and types of roles.
- Preparation of a *table of variance control* to show the extent to which key variances are presently controlled by the social system. It is possible to identify where key organizational and informational loops exist or are required by using such a table. It answers the following questions: Where in the process does the variance occur? Where is it observed? Where is it controlled and by whom? What tasks must the controller do to control it? What information does the controller have from what source to carry out these control activities? Hypotheses that are formed should be noted for subsequent discussion and possible validation.
- *Ancillary activities* such as descriptions of the workers' roles in the production system should be noted. Activities connected with the control of key variances will be listed in the variance control table. It is likely, however, that there will be a number of ancillary activities. Identifying these and trying to relate them to the control process may well lead to the

identification of additional key variances. On the other hand, it could conceivably lead to the elimination of these ancillary activities altogether.

- *Spatial and temporal relationships* such as the physical or geographical relationships between the various roles in the production system (i.e., distance or physical barriers between workers) and their relationship over time must be mapped out.
- *Flexibility,* i.e., the extent to which the workers share a knowledge of each other's roles, can be identified on a mobility chart. It may be necessary to carry out this step in two phases: an initial analysis of rotation and a more detailed analysis of the extent to which the workers carry out the essential tasks associated with the roles. The chart should cover a period of two or three months. Therefore, it is good to start recording this information in the early weeks of the analysis process.
- The *payment system* and how it is related to various roles in the production system must be studied because it has an impact on job rotation, group working, etc.
- The *psychological needs* of employees can be tested to see if their roles meet these needs. An adequate/inadequate rating for each employee's main activities is sufficient. For this purpose, the action group will need to rely on management perceptions of the roles. To learn the workers' perception for their roles, it will be necessary to set up some machinery for the collection of their views.
- *Identify areas of maloperation* to establish causes, where possible.

STEP 5: PEOPLE'S PERCEPTIONS OF THEIR ROLES

This step, although it is part of an analysis of the social system, is dealt with separately partly because of its importance and partly because of the method of carrying it out. Its purpose is to learn as much as possible of the people's perceptions of their roles, *specifically the extent to which they see the roles as fulfilling their psychological needs.* This can be accomplished by having a personnel worker in the action group, either for this particular purpose or as a full member.

Two interviews can be arranged with appropriate groups of workers, the first within the first six weeks of the analysis and the second toward the end of the process, when job-design proposals are being finalized. Both interviews must be highly structured, designed with open-ended questions based on psychological needs and, in the case of the second interview, on the developing job-needs design proposals.

With this step, an analysis of the production system itself is complete, and it is to be expected that a number of redesign proposals or hypotheses will have emerged.

The analysis now considers the impact on the production system of a number of "external" systems, e.g., maintenance, supply and user systems, personnel policy, etc., that will influence any hypotheses that have emerged and that may well bring about further redesign proposals.

STEP 6: MAINTENANCE SYSTEM

This step is *not* concerned with the examination of the maintenance system or organization as such but solely with the extent to which that system has an impact on the particular production system being analyzed and with the extent to which the maintenance system affects the capability of the production system to achieve its objectives. These objectives are to determine:

- the nature of the maintenance variance arising in the production system;
- the extent to which that variance is controlled;
- the extent to which maintenance tasks should be taken into account in the design of operating roles.

This analysis of maintenance variance is not in any way subordinate to the analysis of process variance carried out in Step 3. Both are necessary to an understanding of the characteristics of the production system. It may be that in some cases, variance of a greater order comes from the maintenance system than from the production system itself, in which case one would expect greater emphasis on this stage.

To collect information on maintenance activities, the analyst must begin with the first month of the project and continue for two or three months. The collection of additional data and the burden of collection placed on operating and maintenance staff should be kept to the minimum consonant with achieving the objectives of the analysis.

STEP 7: SUPPLY AND USER SYSTEMS

This step is *not* concerned with identifying the characteristics of the supply and user systems themselves, but with the way in which these environmental systems affect the particular production system. The objectives of this stage are:

- To identify the variances that are passed into the production system from the supply and user systems.
- To examine, where appropriate, the extent to which these variances could

be controlled closer to their source, or their effect on the production system could be diminished.

In general, the analysis across the boundaries of the production system should be kept at a fairly general level initially and should go into greater detail only if there appears to be a real possibility of effecting an improvement, e.g., a better control of variance or more appropriate flow of information.

The result of this step might be either a diminishing of the variance arising in the production system from across its boundaries or, in some cases, a *redefining of the production system's objectives* to ensure that they realistically take into account both supply and "marketing" constraints.

STEP 8: WORK ENVIRONMENT AND DEVELOPMENT PLANS

The purpose of this step is to identify those forces operating in the wider departmental or work environment that either affect the production system's ability to *achieve* its objectives or that are likely to lead to a *change* in those objectives in the foreseeable future. It has two main steps:

- *Development plans.* The identification of any plans, either short or long term, that have a high probability of being implemented *for the development of the social or the technical systems.* These clearly would have to be taken into account in the development of any redesign proposals.
- *General policies.* The identification of any general policies or practices that impinge on the production system, if these have not been taken into account in the examination of the maintenance system and the supply/user systems. Examples are the general method of promotion, which affects the social system, or the utilities supply and control system operating throughout the plant, which affects the technical system.

It should be emphasized that we are not concerned with the characteristics of these environmental systems as they exist in themselves, but only insofar as they affect the ability of the production system to pursue its objectives. In the analysis of most production systems, these environmental factors will constitute "givens" rather than areas to be included in proposals for change.

STEP 9: PROPOSALS FOR CHANGE

The purpose of this step is to gather all the hypotheses and proposals that have been developed during the analysis process, to consider their viability and to make them the basis of a subsequent action program.

As was mentioned earlier, it is likely that hypotheses will be formed as the analysis of the technical system is being completed. These proposals will probably be expanded, eliminated or modified as further information is gathered about the social and environmental systems.

Those hypotheses that remain must be tested, as much as it is possible on a theoretical basis, against appropriate criteria before being developed into viable proposals. The actual criteria will vary and will require careful design, but these criteria must relate to the production system objectives and must cover:

- The production objectives of the system in terms of quantity, quality and general operating costs. This covers proposals specifically aimed at increasing the control over, or diminishing variance in, the production system.
- The social objectives of the production system, such as those aimed at increasing the extent to which psychological needs are met in role design or at diminishing the costs borne by the work force (e.g., stress, hazard or heavy labor).

Many proposals will, of course, lie in both areas. For example, proposals aimed at increasing the level of responsibility at the lower levels would meet psychological requirements and might lead to shorter lines of communication and more effective variance control. In addition, any proposals for the redesign of the social system must be tested against emergency and crisis needs. In the case of a process unit, this would entail the ability to shut the unit down in the event of a loss of power or feed, or of a major fire.

Organizational Objectives and Role Analysis

This model has been developed in conjunction with the socio-technical model as an alternative method of analysis for departments in which no continuous process exists, e.g., service or advisory departments. Like the socio-technical model, its purpose is to help managers analyze their existing organizations as they currently and normally operate, and to develop proposals for change when this seems likely to lead to improved performance. The model is still in the development stage.

Step 1: General Scanning

This step should provide a general introduction to the outputs, inputs and transformation processes in the department, i.e., its objectives, its work and its organizational structure and location within the organization, as well as to the geographical layout of the department. Scanning is necessary so that more detailed investigations at a later time can be seen against an overall background. In general, the amount of detail collected should be kept small. If this analysis is undertaken by an action group, it is probably useful for the departmental manager to describe each process itself rather than to explain its purpose.

Step 2: The Objectives of the System

It is important to arrive at a clear definition of objectives because this provides a rational datum against which to judge all activities in the department. In practice, the identification and statement of objectives pose difficulties because:

- the objectives stated may be too general;
- they may be multiple, but only one or two may be identified;
- they may be nonmeasurable;
- they may refer to several time periods;
- they may be partly derived from higher or other system levels;
- they may be outputs that the system wants to minimize rather than to maximize, e.g., waste;
- they may involve changes of the internal structure of the system rather than outputs from the system, e.g., change in assets;
- they may not be well enough recognized to be formulated.

To cope with these problems, the following method of analysis is proposed. Consider all major *outputs* of the department, whether they be processed raw materials, communications or workers. Then try to identify all *inputs* and follow these inputs to determine the steps they go through to become outputs. Make sure that no significant output has been missed. Then test outputs to determine whether they are objectives by presenting them to the manager of the next higher system level and asking him or her whether these are, indeed, the outputs required. Also, some inputs come into the department to maintain or develop the assets, and part of the objectives of a department will be directed toward these two activities. The assets of a department include its plant and equipment, the money over which the manager may have authority and the workers.

When considering a department's outputs, a problem may arise because it may not be possible to describe an output such as a communication (written or verbal) meaningfully unless some indication is given of its necessary contribution to an overall decision that is made outside the boundaries of the department. In such cases, it is useful to draw up a table with the following headings:

Description of output

To whom sent

Overall decision it was intended to support

Required contribution of the department's output to this decision
Consequences of substandard performance on the social and economic cost
   (both inside and outside the department)
This analysis will determine the resources that are within the boundaries of
the department and those that the manager needs to bring in. Because department-
mental objectives are more clear, it should be possible to hypothesize the
responsibilities, authorities, information/communication links with others and
key methods and procedures that are appropriate and to match them against
those that already exist.

STEP 3: ANALYSIS OF THE ROLES IN THE SYSTEM

An analysis must also be made of each role in the system to arrive at the role
objectives and to relate them to the overall departmental objectives. This
process should start with the manager's role and work down through the
system.

STEP 4: GROUPING OF ROLES

This analysis will identify the necessary role-interaction links insofar as the
current process exists and will lead to hypotheses about the clustering of these
roles in respect to their geographical and temporal distribution and status
dimensions.

STEP 5: MEASUREMENT OF ROLES AGAINST PSYCHOLOGICAL REQUIREMENTS

After identifying the inputs, transformations and outputs of each role, it is
useful to measure the manager's perception and the workers' own perceptions
of how much each role meets the workers' psychological requirements. The
workers' perceptions of their own roles can be learned through individual
interviews, preferably conducted by someone outside the department.

STEP 6: DEVELOPMENT OF CHANGE PROPOSALS

In the course of the preceding steps, various hypotheses for change will have
emerged. These should be refined into proposals for the redesign of jobs or
organizations, e.g., a change in authorities or methods of grouping, or it may
be that by this stage analysis will have indicated a need for a reformulation of

department objectives. Proposals for change will, of course, have to be related to the overall environment of a department.

STEP 7: MANAGEMENT BY OBJECTIVES

Once the objective of the department and its constituent roles have been determined, attention should be given to developing performance measures, to setting targets (either jointly with a manager or by oneself as consultant) and to feeding back these results to the person occupying the role. However, because important areas of role output may not be readily measured, care should be taken to ensure that these areas are in some way included in performance targets so that role output is not distorted.

Eric Trist

A Socio-Technical Critique of Scientific Management[1]

The term "scientific management" begs two questions—what is "science" and what is "management." If, philosophically, the answers are plural and ambiguous, historically, the answer is singular and clear. Scientific management refers to the movement concerned with work measurement inaugurated by Frederick Taylor (1911) at the end of the first century of the first industrial revolution. Since then it has become the vast enterprise known as production or industrial engineering. Since then has also begun the second industrial revolution based on an information technology rather than simply an energy technology. With this second industrial revolution "management science," growing out of operation research, is becoming as intimately associated as scientific management has been with the first.

The distinction between the two has been well drawn by Russell Ackoff (1970):

> The first industrial revolution was made possible by the development of machines that were capable of replacing man and beast as sources of physical work. This substitution of machines for animals was called mechanization. The development of the relevant technology and its effective use in production processes required knowledge and understanding of the nature of physical work, i.e., what aspects of it could and could not be efficiently mechanized, and how men and machines could separately and collectively work together. At about the turn of this century, the need for mechanization attracted scientists and engineers from a variety of disciplines whose interests covered some aspects of the work process. As a result, work study was initiated. As knowledge and understanding were accumulated and systematized, those who were engaged in such research institutionalized and professionalized their efforts under the name of industrial (or production) engineering. Thus industrial engineering provided the intellectual fuel which powered the process of mechanization.
>
> The second industrial revolution, which is still in its infancy, was started by

[1]A paper contributed to the Edinburgh Conference on the Impact of Science and Technology, 1971.

two technological developments. The first involved the development of machines which could observe, or, in other words, which could convert the objective properties of objects and events into symbols representing those properties. Radar and sonar, developed in the United Kingdom in the late thirties, were such machines.

The second and more important technological development occurred in the mid-forties. Its product was the electronic digital computer, which can be described as a symbol-manipulating machine. These two developments made it possible to mechanize mental work which consists of observation, or symbol generation, and symbol manipulation. Mechanization of the particular type of mental work that we call decision making or control came to be known as automation.

In the first industrial revolution, the knowledge and understanding of the processes to be mechanized were called industrial engineering. Again, in the second industrial revolution, which began in the late thirties, scientists and engineers from a variety of disciplines rose to the challenge. The interdisciplinary activity which resulted came to be known as operational research or O.R. As operational research and the new technology developed, additional fields of related study emerged: these included information theory, decision theory, control theory, cybernetics and general systems theory. Here, as so often had been the case in the past, "engineering" preceded "science." Operational research workers adapted available scientific concepts, methods, techniques and tools to their tasks and improvised some new ones. Others were subsequently developed in the communication, decision, control and systems sciences.

Thus O.R. bears the same relation to the second industrial revolution as industrial engineering to the first. This explains why there was so much debate in the early days of O.R. about their similarities and their differences. At that time the distinction between the two revolutions was not clear.

Along with a number of others, the writer holds the view that the more complex, fast-changing, interdependent but uncertain world growing up in the wake of the second industrial revolution is rapidly rendering obsolete and maladaptive many of the values, organizational structures and work practices brought about by the first. In fact, something like their opposite seems to be required. This is nowhere more apparent than in the efforts of some of the most sophisticated firms in the advanced science-based industries to decentralize their operations, to debureaucratize their organizational form and to secure the involvement and commitment of their personnel at all levels by developing forms of participatory democracy.

Nevertheless, the classic efficiency cult, which Taylorism has come to symbolize, remains the prevailing value of contemporary industry. The majority of those pursuing the second industrial revolution are as much obsessed with it as were those who pursued the first, including many operational research workers who treat systems in much the same way as most industrial engineers treat jobs.[2] It will take some time before the minority, who have already learned to think in much wider terms, will secure an extensive hearing. By then much will have happened in the way of violence, alienation and poor performance that could have been avoided—if the world were a more rational place.

What then are the characteristics of the philosophy of work called scientific management? It has been summarized by my colleague Louis Davis (1970/ Vol. II) as follows:

- The man and his job are the essential building blocks of an organization; if the analyst gets these "right" (in some particular but unspecified way), then the organization will be correctly defined.
- Man is an extension of the machine, useful only for doing things that the machine cannot do.
- The men and their jobs—the individual building blocks—are to be glued together by supervisors who will absorb the uncertainties and variabilities that arise in the work situation. Furthermore, these supervisors need supervisors, and so on *ad infinitum,* until the enterprise is organized in a many-layered hierarchy. In bureaucratic organizations, the latter notion ultimately leads to situations in which a man can be called a "manager" solely on the grounds that he supervises a certain number of people, and without regard to the degree of judgment or decision-making responsibility such supervision requires.
- The organization is free to use any available social mechanism to enforce compliance and ensure its own stability.
- Job fractionation is a way of reducing the costs of carrying on the work by reducing the skill contribution of the individual who performs it. Man is simply an extension of the machine, and obviously, the more you simplify the machine (whether its living part or its nonliving part), the more you lower costs.

This whole conception is now often referred to by social scientists as the "machine theory of organization."

Industrial organizations built on these principles had their heyday in the mass production plants of the interwar period. Daniel Bell (1956) sums up the pattern as follows:

These three logics of size, time and hierarchy converge in that great achievement of industrial technology, the assembly line: the long parallel lines require huge shed space; the detailed breakdown of work imposes a set of mechanically paced

---

[2]Among industrial engineers who thought along very different lines were James Gillespie in Britain and Adam Abruzzi in the United States.

and specified motions; the degree of coordination creates new technical, as well as social, hierarchies.

There is less need in the present context to elaborate on the extent to which the concentration, atomization and control of work was carried than to point to the nature of the penalty paid for the benefits gained. If the benefits gained included more productivity at less cost in the short run within the enterprise itself, the penalties paid included more alienation in the longer run, which spread into the larger society only to react back on the more immediate economic sphere. For some time this was masked in the classic forms of industrial struggle as organized labor sought better conditions for the mass of semiskilled and unskilled workers—more pay, shorter hours, improved amenities, etc. After a period of initial resistance, unions began to learn how to use work-study as a bargaining method in their own interest. This was not a matter inherently related to ownership of the means of production. Lenin admired Taylor and entertained high hopes of what scientific management might do for industry in the Soviet Union.

But as the first signs of the affluent society began to appear, as the Great Depression faded into the background and a new level of economic well-being established itself after World War II, it became evident that something of another kind was wrong, whatever the amount of take-home pay or even security of employment. A first glimpse of what this might be had been obtained in the Hawthorne Experiments carried out by Elton Mayo's followers in Western Electric's plants in the Chicago area at the height of the scientific management wave (Roethlisberger and Dickson, 1939). These were the first extensive studies made in industry by social scientists as distinct from psychologists, concerned with more limited psychophysical problems. They led to the curious and belated discovery that workers were human even in the workplace and that they responded to being treated as such. This led to the rise of the human relations movement which, in sophistication of theory and method, has reached a degree of elaboration as great as scientific management, though it has never matched it in extensiveness of application.

The direction of development taken by the human relations movement was one which concentrated exclusively on the enterprise as a social system. The technology was not considered. Workers were to be treated better but their jobs would remain the same—similarly with supervisors or, for that matter, managers themselves. As Peter Drucker (1952) put it:

It has been fashionable of late, particularly in the "human relations" school, to assume that the actual job, its technology, and its mechanical and physical requirements are relatively unimportant compared to the social and psychological situation of men at work.

What this statement means is that nobody thought the job itself could be changed. It was regarded as invariant. The technological imperative was taken for granted. It was logical, therefore, to concentrate attention on what were considered, however mistakenly, to be the only variable aspects.

The need to pay attention to the social and psychological aspects as a matter of practical personnel policy was generally recognized when full employment conditions were established after World War II in countries such as Britain. Full employment, more than anything else, gave rise to personnel management. The "stick" was unavailable; the "carrots" on offer were often indigestible and always limited. The game of economic rewards continued to be played according to the rules of wage-bargaining between management and labor, where expectations of a fair deal were based on the power balance between the two parties. The recent history of productivity bargaining shows how much it is still played this way. But wage matters apart, attempts were made to set up good relations between all groups and types of personnel in the company, most especially between management and workers. So far as greater loyalty and trust could be established, labor turnover would be reduced and industrial disputes made less likely.

As the management/worker interface was mediated by the foreman, a massive movement took place in supervisory training. How far was person-centered supervision better than task-centered supervision, two-way communication better than one-way communication, persuasion better than coercion, a democratic style of leadership better than an authoritarian style of leadership? How could one change supervisors from one way of behaving to the other? It was soon known that it was of no avail to change the attitudes of foremen if those of management did not change as well (Likert, 1958). So began a far-reaching movement in management training, which later broadened first into management and then into organizational "development" as more of the complex interdependencies and dimensions of the enterprise as a social system were taken into account (Bennis, 1966a, 1966b).

Certain beliefs about the nature of humanity and its basic needs and motivations in the work setting began to gain currency that were the opposite of those held in the scientific management school. Abraham Maslow (1954) introduced his need hierarchy, which postulated that as the more primitive needs for food, sex and security became satisfied, higher needs concerned with group belongingness, self-esteem and self-fulfillment would become more salient. Emphasizing that this would be so even in the workplace, Douglas McGregor (1960) contrasted two models of "industrial man" that he called Theory X and Theory Y. The first represented the traditional management view of workers which had grown up with the first industrial revolution. They were fundamentally "no-goods"—lazy, irresponsible, selfish, etc. They therefore required external control. The second model represented an emergent view: that workers were ordinary, good human beings at work as much as they were at home or as citizens. They had a need for achievement, to take responsibility, to be creative themselves and to take cognizance of others. They were therefore capable of internal control. Basically, they were self-motivating and self-supervising.

Later, we shall return to a facet of utmost significance—that these views made their impact at a time when advanced industrial societies, especially the United States, were becoming not only more affluent but were already well into the second industrial revolution with the very different tasks and roles that the newer technologies were beginning to create. These roles demand involvement and commitment, initiative and the good use of discretion at the bottom of the enterprise no less than in the middle and at the top. This connection was not made by anyone within the human relations approach.[3] Nevertheless, a view of the human side of the enterprise developed that was incompatible with the machine theory of organization. But no one attempted to alter the character of the jobs themselves, which continued to be designed according to the principles of scientific management. In the United States social science attention shifted to the problems of higher management with its increasing needs for flexibility and adaptability in facing change and uncertainty (Trist, 1968). While at this level democratic social climates with transactional forms of relationship between superior and subordinate were tried out, as being best suited to the ends of the enterprise, for the same economic reasons, the shop floor continued to be set up and operated in terms of the values and concepts of the first industrial revolution, elaborated and refined by the principles of scientific management.

Quite early in the post World War II period, 1948–51, the Tavistock Institute undertook an intensive action research study of the London factories of the Glacier Metal Company (Jaques, 1951/Vol. I). Concerned with group relations at all levels, it led to the establishment of a new type of representative structure. Enlightened personnel policies and wage practices were implemented with unusual thoroughness. Yet the underlying alienation of the ordinary worker persisted. The "split at the bottom of the executive chain" remained. The only major factor that had not undergone change was the task or work organization deriving from the technology. This had remained in the old modality. What would happen if this modality itself were changed?

An opportunity to begin finding this out arose at the same time in the then recently nationalized coal industry, where strikes, labor turnover and absenteeism were persisting unabated despite the changeover to public ownership and the introduction of many improvements in pay and working conditions. In the

---

[3]Among British social scientists, however, the connection between technology and organization was central for such writers as Woodward (1958) and Burns and Stalker (1961).

first of what turned out to be a very long series of researches, the writer and a colleague, a former miner, were able to observe at a pit in the Yorkshire coalfield what happened when the method of work organization was changed from the traditional form of job-breakdown to one in which autonomous groups interchanged tasks and took responsibility for the production cycle as a whole. The new groups were formed by the men themselves (Trist and Bamforth, 1951/Vol. II). More extensive experiments using what became known as the composite method were made in East Midland Division between 1951 and 1953, initiated by V.W. Sheppard (1951), who was later to become the National Coal Board's Director General for Production and eventually Deputy Chairman. The gains in productivity and job satisfaction were both substantial, the former being up between 20 and 30 percent for less cost and the latter, apart from expressions of opinion, manifesting itself in decreased absenteeism, negligible labor turnover and an improved health record (Wilson et al., 1951). During further studies in Durham Division, 1954–58, an opportunity arose to carry out a crucial experiment in which the performance of two identical coal faces, using an identical longwall technology—one organized in the conventional and the other in the composite way—were monitored over a period of two years. The composite face was superior in all respects (Trist et al., 1963).

Meanwhile, another Tavistock research worker, A.K. Rice, had applied composite principles in another industry in another country—the textile industry in Ahmedabad, India (Rice, 1958; 1953/Vol. II; Miller, 1975/Vol. II). As soon as the idea of a group of workers becoming responsible for a group of looms was mentioned in discussing the experimental reorganization of an automatic loom shed, the workers spontaneously took up the idea, returning the next day with a scheme which was accepted and immediately tried out. Early success was followed by vicissitudes due to many factors which were investigated, but thereafter a steady state of significantly improved performance was attained. Higher wages were earned and the internally led loom groups, which carried out their own maintenance, offered "careers" from less to more skilled roles, while Hindus and Muslims worked together. The system spread to ordinary looms. Though supported by the local trade union, it came under political attack. Agitators from all parts of the country were brought into Ahmedabad by the Indian Communist Party which, like communist parties elsewhere, opposed innovation that it could not fit into its "operational model"—though Marx himself might have been more appreciative, to judge from his neglected observations on machines and their relations to workers. Members of the work teams and their families were threatened with physical violence if they continued the new system. Attempts were made to set the Hindu and Muslim workers against each other. The attack failed. The workers stuck to a system that was very largely their own creation and that enabled them to enjoy a quality of work life as well as a level of income which they had not previously known.

While their own change experiments were proceeding, the Tavistock workers were able to ascertain that sporadic developments along the same lines had taken place in the telephone industry in Sweden, in the building industry in Holland and in the appliance manufacture and chemicals industry in the United States. There was another way to organize productive work than the prevailing way. There was *organizational choice*.

In the United States, recognition grew that quantified external control and job fractionation had been carried too far, and job enlargement received extensive trial (Walker and Guest, 1952). A distinction was made between extrinsic job satisfaction (which included the pay packet) and intrinsic satisfaction deriving from the quality of the job itself. This was recognized as a major factor affecting motivation (Herzberg et al., 1959). But such recognition implied altering the way jobs were *designed* (Davis, 1957; Davis and Canter, 1955). This meant changing the technological organization, the systems which the human relations school had left intact and which the scientific management school had continued to design according to the atomistic ideology that had characterized nineteenth-century science.

From the beginning, the Tavistock workers had felt that a new unit of analysis was required. This led the writer to introduce the concept of the *socio-technical system* (Trist, 1950; 1981/Vol. II). The problem was not of simply "adjusting" people to technology nor technology to people but of organizing the interface so that the best match could be obtained between them. Only the socio-technical whole could effectively be "optimized." In the limit, the socio-technical whole comprised the enterprise as a whole—in relation to its environment—as well as its primary work groups and intervening subsystems (Emery and Trist, 1960). It was necessary to change the basic model in which organization theory had been conceived.

Using Sommerhoff's (1950) theory of directive correlation, Emery (1966/Vol. II) has formulated the matching process in terms of joint optimization:

> Where the achievement of an objective is dependent upon *independent* but *correlative* systems, then it is impossible to optimize for overall performance without seeking to *jointly optimise* these correlative systems.
>
> Any attempts to optimise for one without due regard to the other will lead to sub-optimal overall performance, so even if an effort is made in an industrial situation to follow the traditional pattern, i.e., to optimise the technical system and hope the social system will somehow sort itself out, then sub-optimisation is certain to result. This is also the case when attempting to optimise each system, but independently, ignoring interaction effects.

It is important to remember that this principle applies where the systems are *independent* but *correlative*. . . . It does not necessarily apply where one system is, in fact, a *part of another*, e.g., a sales section of a company is part of a social system governed by the same laws as the rest of the social system. Where this is the case . . . the chain may be seized by the key link and the rest follows. Socio-technical systems, however, are composed of two distinct systems which, although correlative, are governed by different laws.

Pulling together the findings of a number of investigations, he has offered a set of general socio-technical principles for job design (Emery, 1963; 1966/Vol. II). As these go to the heart of the matter they will be quoted in full:

> The judgment that it is possible to redesign jobs in this way rests upon the evidence that men have requirements of their work other than those usually specified in a contract of employment (i.e., other than wages, hours, safety, security of tenure, etc.). The following list represents at least some of the general psychological requirements that pertain to the content of a job (to what a person is called upon to carry out in his job from hour to hour and from year to year):

> The need for the content of a job to be reasonably demanding in terms other than sheer endurance and yet providing a minimum of variety (not necessarily novelty).

> The need for being able to learn on the job and go on learning. Again, it is a question of neither too much nor too little.

> The need for some minimal degree of social support and recognition in the workplace.

> The need to be able to relate what he does and what he produces and to his social life.

> The need to feel that the job leads to some sort of desirable future (not necessarily promotion).

> These requirements are obviously not confined to any one level of employment. Nor is it possible to meet these requirements in the same way in all work settings or for all kinds of people. Complicating matters further is the fact that these needs cannot always be judged from conscious expression. Like *any* general psychological requirements, they are subject to a wide range of vicissitudes. Thus, where there is no expectation that any of the jobs open to a person will offer much chance of learning, that person will soon learn to "forget" such requirements.

> As already indicated, these requirements, however true they may be, are too general to serve as principles for job redesign. For this purpose they need to be linked to the objective characteristics of industrial jobs. The following is the preliminary set of such principles with which these studies started. They repre-

sent the best we were able to achieve by way of generalising upon existing findings. They are not, we hope, final:

At the Level of the Individual

Optimum variety of tasks within the job. Too much variety can be inefficient for training and production as well as frustrating for the worker. However, too little can be conducive to boredom or fatigue. The optimum level would be that which allows the operator to take a rest from a high level of attention or effort or a demanding activity while working at another and, conversely allow him to stretch himself and his capacities after a period of routine activity.

A meaningful pattern of tasks that gives to each job a semblance of a single overall task. The tasks should be such that although involving different levels or attention, degrees of effort, or kinds of skill, they are interdependent; that is, carrying out one task makes it easier to get on with the next or gives a better end result to the overall task. Given such a pattern, the worker can help to find a method of working suitable to his requirements and can more easily relate his job to that of others.

Optimum length of work cycle. Too short a cycle means too much finishing and starting; too long a cycle makes it difficult to build up a rhythm of work.

Some scope for setting standards of quantity and quality of production and a suitable feedback of knowledge of results. Minimum standards generally have to be set by management to determine whether a worker is sufficiently trained, skilled or careful to hold the job. Workers are more likely to accept responsibility for higher standards if they have some freedom in setting them and are more likely to learn from the job if there is feedback. They can neither effectively set standards nor learn if there is not a quick enough feedback of knowledge of results.

The inclusion in the job of some of the auxiliary and preparatory tasks. The worker cannot and will not accept responsibility for matters outside his control. Insofar as the preceding criteria are met then the inclusion of such "boundary tasks" will extend the scope of the workers' responsibility and make for involvement in the job.

The tasks included in the job should include some degree of care, skill, knowledge or effort that is worthy of respect in the community.

The job should make some perceivable contribution to the utility of the product for the consumer.

At Group Level

Providing for "interlocking" tasks, job rotation or physical proximity where there is a necessary interdependence of jobs (for technical or psychological reasons). At a minimum this helps to sustain communication and to create mutual understanding between workers whose tasks are interdependent and thus lessens friction, recriminations and "scape-goating." At best, this procedure will help to create work groups that enforce standards of co-operation and mutual help.

Providing for interlocking tasks, job rotation or physical proximity where the individual jobs entail a relatively high degree of stress. Stress can arise from apparently simple things such as physical activity, concentration, noise or isolation if these persist for long periods. Left to their own devices, people will become habituated but the effects of the stress will tend to be reflected in more mistakes, accidents and the like. Communication with others in a similar plight tends to lessen the strain.

Providing for interlocking tasks, job rotation or physical proximity where the individual jobs do not make an obvious perceivable contribution to the utility of the end product.

Where a number of jobs are linked together by interlocking tasks or job rotation they should as a group:

> have some semblance of an overall task which makes a contribution to the utility of the product

> have some scope for setting standards and receiving knowledge of results

> have some control over the "boundary tasks."

Over Extended Social and Temporal Units

Providing for channels of communication so that the minimum requirement of the workers can be fed into the design of new jobs at an early stage.

Providing for channels of promotion to foreman rank which are sanctioned by the workers.

It is clearly implied in this list of principles that the redesigning of jobs may lead beyond the individual jobs to the organisation of groups of workers and beyond into at least the organisation of support services (such as maintenance). There is reason to believe that the implications are even wider and that they will in any organisation be judged to be much wider and reacted to accordingly.

Since these principles were formulated, a good deal of experience has been gained with more advanced technologies that depend on processes of continuous production and a high level of automation and computerization. As a result, a nine-step analytical model for socio-technical inquiry has been gradually taking shape (Emery, 1967). Though never formalized, the model may be summarized as follows:

1. An initial scanning is made of all the main aspects—technical and social—of the *selected target system,* i.e., the department or plant to be studied.

2. The *unit operations* are then identified, i.e., the transformations

(changes of state) of the material or product which take place in the target system, whether carried out by workers or machines.

3. An attempt is then made to discover the *key process variances* and their interrelations. A variance is any deviation from a standard or specification. A variance is key if it significantly affects: (1) the quantity of production; (2) the quality of production; (3) the operating or *social* costs of production.

4. A table of variance control is then drawn up to *ascertain how far the key variances are controlled by the social system*—the workers, supervisors and managers concerned. Some of the most important variances may be imported or exported. Investigation of this is one of the most critical steps. Another is to check *how far existing work roles satisfy the six basic psychological requirements*. Attention is then paid to ancillary activities, spatiotemporal relationships, the flexibility of job boundaries and the payment system.

5. A separate inquiry is made into the *workers' perception of their roles*— and of role possibilities as well as constraining factors. Here is a mine of unsuspected knowledge as much as of unsuspected feeling.

6. So far, concern has focused on the target system. It now changes to *neighboring systems,* beginning with the support or *maintenance system.*

7. Inquiry continues into the boundary-crossing systems on the input and the output side, i.e., the *supplier and user systems* which comprise adjacent departments. How do the structures of these units affect the target system and in what state are relations across these interfaces?

8. The target system and its immediate neighbors must now be considered in the context of the *general management system* of the plant or enterprise, particularly as regards the effects of *general policies* or *development plans either technical or social.*

9. Suggestions for change may arise at any point in the analysis, which proceeds by a recycling rather than a strictly sequential procedure, but only when all stages have been completed does it become possible to formulate *redesign proposals* for the target system or to take up wider implications.

This analytical model, which uses an open systems approach similar to that of Katz and Kahn (1966), is not intended as a procedure for the sole use of research workers. It is intended also for operating people in plants where management and workers together have decided to undertake change in which explicit use will be made of socio-technical principles. It has therefore been prepared as a training method. Recently, Davis and the writer, along with other colleagues, held the first university course in the method at the Graduate School of Business Administration of the University of California, Los Angeles. Some 20 managers, industrial engineers and personnel people attended for an intensive period of three weeks. They were drawn from Alcan's smelting plants in Quebec Province, Canada, where socio-technical experiments have been in progress for some two and a half years with the operators and the union now thoroughly involved (Davis and Trist, 1969).

Though toward the end of the 1950s the Tavistock research group had extended its inquiries to examples of the more advanced technologies, these had remained descriptive studies. No further opportunities to conduct operational field experiments arose in a British setting. The next major developments took place in Norway in conjunction with what has become known as the Norwegian Industrial Democracy Projects (Thorsrud and Emery, 1964). This has given a new dimension to socio-technical studies, relating them to central questions of value change as the era of the post-industrial society is brought nearer by the technologies of the second industrial revolution.

The project began in 1961 and is still proceeding. It grew out of a crisis between the Norwegian Confederation of Employers and the Norwegian Confederation of Labor over a sudden increase in the demand for workers' representation on boards of management proposed as a way of reducing alienation and increasing productivity. What is remarkable is that the two Confederations (later joined by the Government) should have requested the assistance of social scientists in order to gain a better understanding of what ordinarily would have been treated as a political problem. But, having helped establish a group, directed by Einar Thorsrud, which had earned their trust, they requested it to undertake research relevant to their problem. Through the ramifications of the project, the group concerned has had to move from Trondheim to Oslo where it now comprises the Institutes of Work Psychology. From the beginning, it drew on the Tavistock's Human Resources Centre as a collaborating organization. Another remarkable feature of the project has been the extent to which research plans have been drawn up in conjunction with representatives of the sponsoring Confederations. This was a necessary condition for success, since the objective could not be limited to undertaking isolated socio-technical experiments. It was, first, to secure an understanding in the leadership of both sides of Norwegian industry of the relevance to problems at the national level of a socio-technical philosophy of work; and, thence, to establish the conditions which would allow this philosophy to diffuse through Norwegian industry at large.

The first phase of the project consisted of a field study of what actually happened in the five major concerns where workers were represented on the boards. These were either government owned or partly government owned enterprises obliged by law to have workers' representatives. The results showed that very little happened except at the symbolic and ceremonial level. There was no increase in participation by the rank and file, no decrease in work alienation, no increase in productivity. The overall state of industrial relations being stable with a stable framework of political democracy, little was added simply by adding a workers' representative to the board of directors. These results, which were compared with experiences in other countries, were widely discussed in both Confederations and in the press. These discussions opened the way for the second phase of the project, which was to search out ways for securing improved conditions for personal participation in a worker's immediate setting as constituting "a different and perhaps more important basis for the democratization of the workplace than the formal systems of representation."

This led to the idea of socio-technical experiments in selected plants in key industries, which, if successful, could serve as demonstration models for diffusion purposes. The selections were made by the members of the two Confederations serving on the research committee in consultation with sector committees of the industries concerned. No pains were spared in developing at all levels an understanding of, and in securing an acceptance of, the experiments in the plants proposed, which had to be respected organizations carrying weight and which, moreover, had to be seen as foreshadowing the future direction of Norwegian industrial development without being too far out. To obtain this breadth and depth of sanctioning and centrality of societal positioning was regarded as essential. Its absence in other contexts had prevented the spreading of proven innovations.

The first experiment was carried out in the metal-working industry, a sector regarded as critical but requiring considerable rehabilitation. A rather dilapidated wiredrawing plant in a large engineering concern was chosen on the grounds that if improvements could be brought about here, they could be brought about anywhere. Productivity increased so much that the experiment was suspended. The workers concerned had begun to take home pay packets in excess of the most skilled workers in the plant. A very large problem had now to be sorted out. If this experiment confirmed earlier findings regarding what could be accomplished when alienation is reduced, it showed up for the first time the magnitude of the constraining forces lying in the wage structures and agreements negotiated according to the norms of the prevailing work culture and accumulating historically. The difficulty of changing such structures, in considerable measure, accounted for the failure of earlier pilot experiments to spread out through the system.

The second experiment was in the pulp and paper industry, also regarded as a critical sector, but where the problem was not so much to upgrade performance with old technologies as to gain control over new. A sophisticated chemical plant was selected where the basic work was information-handling—the core task in the technologies of the second industrial revolution. The requisite skills are perceptual and conceptual; the requisite work organization is one capable of handling the complex information flows on which controlling the process depends. To do this requires immense flexibility and capability for self-regulation. In the experimental plant a number of the key process variances were not being controlled by the social system nor had some of the most important variances been identified. The research team had to engage those concerned in evolving a form of organization that brought as many of the variances as possible under the control of the primary work groups. After much resistance and many setbacks, a process of continuous learning began to establish and to maintain itself as improvements were effected first in one area, then in another.

The model was established of an "action group" consisting of operators actively using supervisors, specialists and managers as resources—rather than passively responding to them simply as bosses—in order to fashion an optimum work organization for a new technology as they were learning the know-how of its operation. This model was now taken up by Norskhydro, the largest enterprise in Norway, which manufactures fertilizers and other chemicals for the world market. The model was first used to refashion an old plant, then to develop the entire organization and operating procedures for a new one (Thorsrud, 1968).

The success of the Norskhydro experiments has been widely publicized throughout Scandinavia. It marked the beginning of the third phase of the project concerned with the diffusion process itself. In Norway, the Joint Committee which originally sponsored the project was transformed into a National Participation Council and a new Parliamentary Commission on Industrial Democracy was formed. In Sweden similar developments have recently taken place at the national level, but it will be some time before a critical mass of concrete experience with the new methods can build up. The situation is similar in Denmark. Meanwhile, in Norway, the most significant recent developments have taken place in the shipping industry in the manning of bulk carriers (Herbst, 1969; 1974/Vol. II).

Undoubtedly there are features in the culture of the Scandinavian countries and in their situation, Norway most particularly, which have enabled them to act as the laboratory of the world in developing a new concept of industrial democracy based on socio-technical theory. In large countries which are more authoritarian, where the first industrial revolution has left a deeper imprint or where the culture is more fragmented, much greater difficulties are to be expected. In Britain, there are signs of the trail being taken up again by specific but important firms. The refining side of Shell, for example, invited the Tavistock Institute to assist it in developing a new management philosophy based on the principle of joint optimization (Shell Refining Co., 1966; Hill, 1971/Hill and Emery, Vol. II). In Ireland, the national transport undertaking (CIE) undertook an extensive project (van Beinum, 1966). Sporadic developments continue here and there in the United States (Seashore and Bowers, 1963; Myers, 1964).

The underlying change which has taken place is that in the science-based industries of the second industrial revolution, workers are not workers in the sense of the first industrial revolution. They are no longer embedded in the technology, contributing their energy or even their manipulative skill to it, but they are outside it, handling information from it and themselves becoming sources of information critical for its management. This change of position and role makes them, in fact, managers, different in degree but not in kind from those who traditionally have carried this title. For the task of management is the regulation of systems and the function of managerial intervention (decision) to establish control over the boundary conditions. Such is the type of activity in which workers now primarily engage, as fact-finders, interpreters, diagnosticians, judges, adjusters and change agents; whatever else they do is secondary. In Jaques's (1956, 1960) terms, the *prescribed* part of their role has become minimal. The "program" is in the machine; the *discretionary* part has become maximal—the reason for the workers' presence is to assess the performance of the program and, if necessary, to change it, either themselves or in conjunction with others at higher levels. No longer is there "a split at the bottom of the executive chain" that separates managers and managed. Everyone is now on the same side of the "great divide," and whatever fences there may still be on the common side would seem best kept low. A general change is, in consequence, taking place in all role relationships in the enterprise. This is the underlying reason for the bureaucratic model being experienced as obsolete and maladaptive, and also for a possible new role beginning to emerge for trade unions (van Beinum, 1966).

To maintain in a steady state the intricate interdependences on which the science-based industries depend requires commitment to, and involvement in, their work from the workers on the shop floor (those who are left) as much as from anyone higher up (and there are fewer of these at intermediate levels). External supervision may correct errors that have been made, but only internal supervision can prevent their occurrence. The amount of error which capital intensive continuous production plants can tolerate is small compared with plants based on technologies which are labor intensive and discontinuous. There is a straight economic reason for this; work stoppages have become too costly, whether they result from machine breakdown due to incompetence or carelessness or from labor trouble due to bad internal relations or external pressures. But if anything at all has become clear about automated plants it is that they do not work automatically. They are the creation of those who run them as much as of those who build them; design continues as operation commences and operational experience informs further design which, from the beginning, has to be developed as a socio-technical process. Moreover, this socio-technical creativeness must be maintained because the change-rate is both rapid and continuous. The autonomous work group setting out on an expedition of learning and innovation from which there is no return would appear to be the organizational paradigm that matches and that is "directively correlated" with the information technology. The advance of technology itself has reversed the world of Frederick Taylor.

Though a great deal of industry does not yet belong to the information technology and though some of it will never belong, the part that does has already become the "leading part." Its influence on the rest may be expected to increase. Moreover, in all contexts there is organizational choice. This is likely to be more frequently exercised in the direction of the new paradigm now that the old paradigm is no longer taken to be a law of nature. Marshal McLuhan (1964) seems to be right in thinking that automation means "learning a living."

The transition to a new concept of the world of work may be slow, unpleasant and difficult, but intolerance (whether in the form of rebellion or dropping out) of narrow and overprescribed jobs is mounting. The contemporary malaise deplored by the "silent majority" may itself be a main force which will hasten beneficial change, for the technological excuse for any job to be inhuman rather than human is rapidly diminishing. Those who wish to be "human" will have more of a chance in the future than many have had in the past.

References

Ackoff, R.L. 1970. "The Evolution of Management Systems." *Canadian Operational Research Journal, 8.*

Bell, D. 1956. *Work and Its Discontents.* New York: McGraw-Hill.

Bennis, W.G. 1966a. *Changing Organizations: Essays on the Development and Evolution of Human Organization.* New York: McGraw-Hill.

———. 1966b. "Theory and Method in Applying Behavioral Change." In *Operational Research and the Social Sciences,* edited by J.R. Lawrence. London: Tavistock Publications.

Burns, T. and G. Stalker. 1961. *The Management of Innovation.* London: Tavistock Publications.

Davis, L.E. 1957. "Toward a Theory of Job Design." *Journal of Industrial Engineering,* 8:19–23.

———. 1970. "The Coming Crisis in Production Management Technology and Organization." International Conference on Production Research, University of Birmingham; *International Journal of Production Research, 9* (1971): 65–82. Excerpted, Vol. II, pp.303–13.

Davis, L.E. and R.R. Canter. 1955. "Job Design." *Journal of Industrial Engineering,* 6:3–6.

Davis, L.E. and E.L. Trist. 1969. "The Socio-Technical Project in Alcan." Unpublished.

Drucker, P.F. 1952. "The Employee Society." *American Sociological Review, 58.*

Emery, F.E. 1963. *Some Hypotheses About the Ways in Which Tasks May Be More Effectively Put Together to Make Jobs.* London: Tavistock Institute Document.

———. 1966. *The Democratisation of the Work Place.* London: Tavistock Institute Document. Vol. II, "Socio-Technical Unit Operations Analysis," pp.559–68.

————. 1967. "Statement on Socio-Technical Analysis." International Conference on Socio-Technical Systems, Lincoln, England.

Emery, F.E. and E.L. Trist. 1960. "Socio-Technical Systems." In *Management Science, Models and Techniques*, Vol. II. Oxford: Pergamon Press.

Herbst, P.G. 1969. "Socio-Technical Design in Ships." Unpublished. Institutes of Work Psychology, Oslo.

————. 1974. *Socio-Technical Design: Strategies in Multi-Disciplinary Research.* London: Tavistock Publications. Excerpted in Vol. II, "A Learning Organization in Practice: M/S *Balao*, pp.409–16.

Herzberg, F., B. Mausner and B. Snyderman. 1959. *The Motivation to Work.* New York: John Wiley.

Hill, P. 1971. *Towards a New Philosophy of Management.* London: Gower Press. Excerpted in Vol. II as P. Hill and F. Emery, "Toward a New Philosophy of Management," pp.259–82.

Jaques, E. 1951. *The Changing Culture of a Factory.* London: Tavistock Publications. Reissued 1987, New York: Garland. Chapter 4 revised in Vol. I, "Working-Through Industrial Conflict," pp. 379–404.

————. 1956. *The Measurement of Responsibility: A Study of Work, Payment, and Individual Capacity.* London: Tavistock Publications.

————. 1960. *Equitable Payment: A General Theory of Work, Differential Payment, and Individual Progress.* London: Heinemann; New York: John Wiley.

————. 1990. Vol. I. "Working Through Industrial Conflict: The Service Department at the Glacier Metal Company," pp.379–404. Revision of Chapter 4 of *The Changing Culture of a Factory.*

Katz, D. and R.L. Kahn. 1966. *The Social Psychology of Organizations.* New York: Wiley.

Likert, R. 1958. "Effective Supervision: An Adaptive and Relative Process." *Personnel Psychology,* 11:317–32.

McGregor, D. 1960. *The Human Side of Enterprise.* New York: McGraw-Hill.

McLuhan, M. 1964. *Understanding Media: The Extensions of Man.* New York: Harper.

Maslow, A.H. 1954. *Motivation and Personality.* New York: Harper and Row. 3rd ed. 1987.

Miller, E. 1975. "Socio-Technical Systems in Weaving, 1953–1970: A Follow-Up Study." *Human Relations,* 28:349–86. Revised in *Organizational Democracy and Political Processes,* edited by C. Crouch and F. Heller. Chichester: John Wiley, 1983. Revised, Vol. II, "The Ahmedabad Experiment Revisited: Work Organization in an Indian Weaving Shed, 1953–70," pp.130–56.

Myers, M.S. 1964. "Who Are Your Motivated Workers?" *Harvard Business Review,* 42:73–88.

Rice, A.K. 1953. "Productivity and Social Organization in an Indian Weaving Shed: An Examination of the Socio-Technical System of an Experimental Automatic Loomshed." *Human Relations,* 6:297–329. Condensed, Vol. II, "Productivity and Social Organization: An Indian Automated Weaving Shed," pp.106–29.

————. 1958. *Productivity and Social Organization: The Ahmedabad Experiment.* London: Tavistock Publications. Reissued 1987, New York: Garland.

Roethlisberger, F.J. and W.J. Dickson. 1939. *Management and the Worker: An Account of a Research Program Conducted by the Western Electric Company, Hawthorne Works, Chicago.* Cambridge, Mass.: Harvard University Press.

Seashore, S.E. and D.G. Bowers. 1963. *Changing the Structure and Functioning of an Organization: Report of a Field Experiment.* Ann Arbor: University of Michigan Press.

Shell Refining Co. Ltd. 1966. *Statement on Company Objectives and Management Philosophy.* London: Shell Centre.

Sheppard, V.W. 1951. "Continuous Longwall Mining: Experiment at Bolsover Colliery." *Colliery Guardian,* 182.

Sommerhoff, G. 1950. *Analytical Biology.* London: Oxford University Press.

———. 1969. "The Abstract Characteristics of Living Systems." In *Systems Thinking: Selected Readings,* edited by F.E. Emery. Harmondsworth: Penguin Books.

Taylor, F.W. 1911. *The Principles and Methods of Scientific Management.* New York: Harper.

Thorsrud, E. 1968. Papers on the project at Norskhydro. Unpublished. Institutes of Work Psychology, Oslo.

Thorsrud, E. and F.E. Emery, 1964. *Industrielt Demokrati.* Oslo: Oslo University Press. Reissued in 1969 as F.E. Emery and E. Thorsrud, *Form and Content in Industrial Democracy.* London: Tavistock Publications.

Trist, E.L. 1950. "The Concept of Culture as a Psycho-Social Process." *Proceedings, Anthropological Section, British Association for the Advancement of Science.*

———. 1968. "The Professional Facilitation of Planned Change in Organizations: Review Paper." *Proceedings, International Association of Applied Psychology, XVIth International Congress.*

———. 1981. "Socio-Technical Ideas at the End of the '70s." In *Adapting to a Changing World.* Ottawa: Labour Canada. Revised in Vol. II, pp.324–37.

Trist, E.L. and K.W. Bamforth. 1951. "Some Social and Psychological Consequences of the Longwall Method of Coal-Getting." *Human Relations,* 4:3–38. Shortened, Vol. II, "The Stress of Isolated Dependence: The Filling Shift in the Semi-Mechanized Longwall Three-Shift Mining Cycle," pp.64–83.

Trist, E.L., G.W. Higgin, H. Murray and A.B. Pollock. 1963. *Organizational Choice: Capabilities of Groups at the Coal Face Under Changing Technologies: The Loss, Rediscovery and Transformation of a Work Tradition.* London: Tavistock Publications. Reissued 1987, New York: Garland. Chapters 13, 14 revised, Vol. II, "Alternative Work Organizations: An Exact Comparison," pp. 84–105. Chapters 19–22, Vol. I, "The Assumption of Ordinariness as a Denial Mechanism: Innovation and Conflict in a Coal Mine," pp. 476–93.

Van Beinum, H. 1966. *The Morale of Dublin Busmen.* London: Tavistock Publications.

Walker, C.R. and H. Guest. 1952. *The Man on the Assembly Line.* Cambridge, Mass.: Harvard University Press.

Wilson, A.T.M., E.L. Trist, F.E. Emery and K.W. Bamforth. 1951. *The Bolsover System of Continuous Mining.* Tavistock Institute Document.

Woodward, J. 1958. *Management and Technology.* London: Her Majesty's Stationery Office.

Fred Emery and Merrelyn Emery

The Participative Design Workshop[1]

The second major form of learning environment we designed and evolved was the Participative Design Workshop. In its publicly recruited form, it was known as the Development of Human Resources Workshop (the DHR). As with Searching (Morley and Trist, 1981/Vol. II; Emery and Emery, 1978/Vol. III), the workshop allows of great flexibility. Participative design may be used discretely or as a phase of a Search to answer the question, "How do we organize ourselves to make sure it all happens?"

When people are accepting responsibility for learning, planning and orientating themselves about their own affairs, it is obvious that to implement and complete the task they will need, in most cases, to design or redesign a continuing form of organization that will also promote ideal-seeking behavior. If a bureaucratic organization is created, the incompatibility of such a structure with the recently experienced structure and process of the planning community will destroy the momentum of that work and recreate the conditions which the Search Conference attempted to change. Most existing organizations are structured according to Design Principle One. A Search Conference is structured on Design Principle Two. Therefore, those who are Searching need the conceptual tools with which to design an organization on Principle Two. Here we discuss how we can design our organizations so that they meet human as well as technical and economic requirements—how they become socio-technical organizations.

Bureaucratic structures and the systems of management associated with them have been unable systematically to provide for the personal growth and development of their members, in particular the large numbers at the base of the pyramid. To rectify the current situation, which is still dominated by bureaucratic structures, large and small, we need knowledge of (1) democratic structural alternatives; and (2) how effectively to introduce them. There is no longer any real question as to whether these alternatives are workable.

Investigations began in the field of "work" and enabled social scientists to identify a number of important determinants of job satisfaction. These factors

---

[1]Revised version of the original, *Participative Design: Work and Community Life*. Canberra: Centre for Continuing Education, Australian National University, 1974.

are called "psychological job requirements." Also clarified are the genotypical features of these alternatives as opposed to the phenotypical characteristics. Phenotypical features of a bureaucratic structure would include such factors as impersonal relations between officials, a functionally specialized division of labor and the "paper war." These phenotypical features in some ways hide the deeper genotypes, which are those characteristics that must be changed if an organization is to move from one design principle to another. Unless people can perceive the genotypes behind the shifting, graduated faces of phenotypes, they may constantly be in the position of tinkering without changing the design principle. This is the fundamental criticism leveled at sensitivity training and "job enrichment," which may temporarily relieve the symptoms while the disease gallops along.

The participative design workshop provides an environment for conceptual and experiential learning about the genotypical features of the democratic organizational alternative. For this learning to be as meaningful as possible it is necessary to include:

- material about the genotype of bureaucratic structure;
- an experience of democratic structure;
- some experience of using tools and strategies for the introduction of such a democratic structure.

Design of the Development of a Human Resources Workshop

The final form of such a workshop is illustrated in Table 1.

As with Searching, the basic assumption is that the most adequate and effective designs come from those who do the jobs in question. It is only from people pooling their various—usually fragmented but always detailed—knowledge that a comprehensive and relatively stable design can come. It is only when the people involved work out their own designs that the necessary motivation, responsibility and commitment to effective implementation is present. The aims of the design are spelled out to the participants in the statement of psychological requirements, and they then proceed to

- analyze how the job is now done;
- assess how far this falls short of meeting the human requirements;
- redesign for a better way of doing the job (if such is felt to be needed);
- work out how the new design could be implemented through a participative learning process.

In Table 1, we have assumed that, following the negotiations and prebriefings described above, four natural teams are present, from one or more organizations or groups. The teams may be *deep slices* through the existing hierarchy of the organization or section. Given a small discrete or well-defined

TABLE I   Development of Human Resources Workshop

Step	Action
1.	Plenary. Final briefing, expectations, exploration of extended social field
2.	Small groups Desirable futures Probable futures Connections are made to democratic structure
3.	Plenary. Briefing on conceptual tools
4.	Mirror groups A + B redesign A, C + D redesign D
5.	Plenary presentation of designs
6.	Mirror groups A + B redesign B, C + D redesign D
7.	Plenary presentations
8.	Team groups and/or plenary. Future strategy and process

section or unit, say four to ten persons, it is best that everybody in that unit work together on the design. The size of the group may be increased by the desirable, if not necessary, inclusion of the union representative, first line supervisors and other management. Given a large unit, it is necessary to ask it to select an appropriate number of its members to become the design team for learning purposes. The "deep slice" is a strategic response whereby knowledge held by each hierarchical level is contributed to system design. It is obviously not a feasible alternative to have separate groups working on part solutions or aspects of a design.

Stages 1 and 2 follow the design of the Search Conference.

Stage 3 consists of a concise briefing, in everyday language, of the criteria by which the quality of a job may be judged, relating this to the two basic forms of organizational design, followed by a set of simple tools to analyze their current form of organization, which provide clues to finding an effective democratic design.

At *Stage 4,* two teams coalesce into one group to analyze and redesign the organization of one team's project. Teams are matched for maximum heterogeneity. This serves two purposes. The first is that the greater the difference between the organizations of A and B, the more closely the Bs will have to question A if the Bs are to gain sufficient information to help toward a redesign. During this process it is inevitable that the Bs must question A's hidden assumptions about the necessity of some aspects of the status quo and thereby help A *unlearn*. The second purpose reflects the need to recognize that the basic choice between organization design principles is always present, regardless of the nature and purpose of the organization itself. These groups work autonomously within the workshop structure, thus experiencing the alternative they have come to explore.

Stage 5 is self-explanatory. Team B and Team D present reports on A's and C's organizational redesign.

Stages 6 and 7 repeat the process, reversing the roles of A and B, and C and D.

Stage 8, the final session, picks up loose ends, points of future process and strategy.

The Briefing—Conceptual Tools for Organizational Design

The most important thing to remember when delivering this briefing is that it will be most effective when it is simple, brief and visual. To save time in your presentation, have already prepared and mounted on the wall at least three large sheets of paper. The first should look something like Figure 1. You then speak about it in more or less detail and with various emphases depending on the membership. The following is designed primarily for places of paid employment. It can be adapted for families, communities, etc.

These are the six most important psychological criteria for job satisfaction. The first three concern the content of the job. Satisfaction with differing levels of these criteria will vary between individuals and within individuals over time.

- Adequate elbow room: the sense that they can make decisions and don't have some boss breathing down their necks. But too much autonomy can leave people feeling lost.
- Chances of learning on the job and going on learning: such learning is possible only when people are able to set goals that are reasonable challenges for them and get feedback of results in time for them to correct their behavior.
- An optimal level of variety: people can vary the work to avoid boredom and fatigue and gain advantages from settling into a satisfying rhythm of work.

The next three criteria relate to the climate or environment of the workplace. These aspects can always be improved.

- Getting help and respect from their workmates: this includes all forms of support and tolerance of individuality.
- A sense of how one's activity contributes to bettering the overall social

Criteria for Satisfaction in Work

Should be optimal for the individual	1. Elbow room—decision making 2. Learning—(a) setting goals (b) getting feedback 3. Variety	
Can't have too much	4. Mutual support and respect 5. Meaningfulness—(a) socially useful (b) able to see relation of own contribution to overall product 6. Desirable future, not dead-end job	

Score items 1–3 from −5 to +5
Score items 4–6 from   0 to 10

Figure 1. Visual for first set of concepts

condition, making or doing something essential for the welfare of others. Part (b) is related to the satisfaction gained from seeing how your little bit is of consequence to a larger scheme of things. (Assembly work has become so fragmented that many workers do not know the final product to which they are contributing.)

• A desirable future; not necessarily promotion, but not a dead-end job: hopefully one that will continue to allow personal growth or some sort of career path.

These psychological requirements cannot be met by simply fiddling with individual job specifications, using such means as job enlargement, job rotation, rest pauses or humane supervisory contacts. If the nature of the work allows room for improvement, this will be best achieved by locating responsibility, for control over effort and quality of personal work and for interpersonal coordination, with the people who are actually doing the job. This is the group solution. It is a structurally different arrangement of people, tasks and supervisor.

The second sheet is shown in Figure 2. Model A defines the dominant bureaucratic form of organization also known as "scientific management."

The building block for this type of organization is the one person/one shift unit. Controls might be sloppy or tight but the principle or genotype is the same. The organizational module is the supervisor and his or her section, with responsibility for control and coordination being jealously defended as the prerogative of the supervisor. The module can be indefinitely repeated upward to the managing director. It is based on the premise that human beings can be

A. Design principle one: redundancy of parts
   Bureaucratic structure

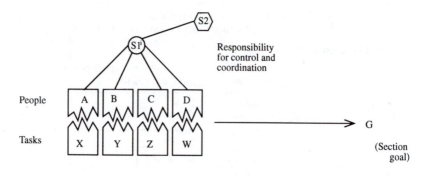

People

Tasks

Responsibility
for control and
coordination

G

(Section
goal)

B. Design principle two: redundancy of function
   Democratic structure

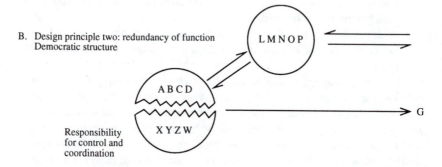

L M N O P

A B C D

X Y Z W

Responsibility
for control and
coordination

G

Figure 2. Visual for second set of concepts, organizational genotypes. (Elements are defined in the text.)

used as redundant parts. When individual tasks have been fragmented to the point where each of them demands almost no skill, unskilled workers are, in fact, simply slotted in and out as if they themselves *were* machines. The first level supervisors (Sl^i, Sl^{ii}, . . .) control the relation between A and X, B and Y and coordinate all the individual tasks to ensure an adequate performance or product (G). A, B and C are denied responsibility for control and coordination.

In this structure there is little opportunity for decision making, learning or variety. The tighter the job specifications, the more control the supervisor has over the subordinates.

But in this structure there will be an almost universal tendency to develop an "informal system": one designed "to beat *the* system." A, B and C may, for instance, evolve their own rules and norms for production. Cliques will form around a common basis of trust such as race or religion whose purposes are not related to achieving either quantity or quality of production. They will institute alternative mechanisms of coordination that suit them personally. In a tightly run section where it is difficult for an informal system to take root, the structure will inherently foster a competitive atmosphere between A, B and C. Each of them will feed only that information to S which makes them look good relative to the others.

We can then begin to see why a redefinition of individual jobs has no real chance of changing things, why it is so much favored by some managements and arouses suspicions of some unions. Enrichment of individual jobs usually entails switching bits of task X from A to B. This can easily degenerate into "robbing Peter to pay Paul." This is, of course, very difficult to do if Peter happens to be in a craft union.

Such manipulation leaves the communication pattern basically unchanged. If person A, confronted with new circumstances, believes that he or she needs some help from person B, he or she must still direct the request up to the supervisor who may or may not direct it back down to B. Communications, both between workers and S1 and between cliques (A and B) and (C and D), are characterized by the "them and us" phenomenon. They operate as a filter and amplifier and are essentially error producing. Only the supervisor's interests relate to the overall achievement of G (the section goal), and S1 has an S2 looking over his or her shoulder. The "us's" will amplify what makes them look good, and they will hear as little of the downward communication as suits them. S1 will be anxious to hear and remember what will sound good to his or her supervisor, including excuses for malperformance. There can be little mutual support and respect in such a situation.

The power structure is similarly unchanged. Regardless of any loosening up of the system in easy times, or the appointment of a friendly, "human" supervisor, with the return of crisis and the demands to tighten up the usual operation of managerial prerogatives will enable the individual jobs to be screwed back to tight, specialized, supervisable performances that will yield a guaranteeable performance level.

The alternative democratic organizational module has markedly different potentials. The first and obvious feature is that it is not restricted to just redistributing jobs X, Y and Z between A, B and C. Responsibility is handed back to A, B and C so that they may share and allocate *among themselves* the requirements for control and coordination of their task-related activities. They take responsibility for X, Y and Z plus all the task interdependencies, XY, XZ, YZ, XYZ. The group must share the tasks of monitoring and controlling the contributions of its own members and organizing their mutual support to cope with individual and task variations. They are now all jointly responsible for the achievement of G. In this module individual "job enrichment" is qualitatively different. Individuals can negotiate an optimal degree of variety and autonomy for themselves and renegotiate it according to changing circumstances. As a desirable flow ensues in the workplace, the individual is provided with a human scale organization, a work "home" and "family" territory whereby people feel that they fit into the organization, no matter how large it may be. It is now in all their interests to help each other and to begin to appreciate individual differences. Because this structure is explicit and formally agreed, the quality of work life cannot easily be degraded.

Communication and power within groups take on markedly different characterstics. They are not basic variables of organizational design but secondary or derivative characteristics of the underlying or genotypical structure. It is a waste of time teaching people to "communicate" if they have to continue to communicate through a bureaucratic medium.

Changes in organizational design, therefore, affect the nature of communication and power, but the reverse does not hold. Provided we have a *group* which has accepted responsibility for a *group* task, then they will seek to make their life easier, or more productive for their ends, by

- communicating quickly, directly and openly the needs for coordination arising from task or individual variability;
- allocating tasks, rewards and punishments to control what they consider to be fair contributions by members.

Such groups can get a sense of an overriding group responsibility only if they have at least four members. With three it is too often unstable, simply a matter of interpersonal relations—two against one. If the groups are kept to eight or under they are less prone to "group emotional" behavior. Larger groups can be effective if they share a deep-rooted culture and if the parts of the group task are highly interdependent.

These groups can be only "semiautonomous," or self-managing, not fully autonomous as they often were in cottage industry. They may be using materials and equipment which others own. In any medium to large organization, there are complex interdependencies between sections or groups. The groups may also be working in conditions where others are responsible for observing social legislation. Many circumstances indicate that varying degrees of autonomy will be agreed to for different groups, starting with less and gaining more as taking responsibility is learned and practiced. People cannot be expected to accept responsibility as a group unless goals are explicit, realistic and challenging and they get feedback as a group. They must feel that the membership and possible leadership of their group are to some degree under their control. Group integration and sharing will be low unless there is sufficient multiskilling to allow flexible allocation of work within the groups. Steps toward setting up self-managing groups require more explication of goals, methods and responsibilities than is usual. This is essential for learning and democratic control.

A modified form. The democratic group implies that a fair degree of multiskilling is possible, and hence that people can make real decisions about helping each other or swapping jobs. However, there are important areas of work where multiskilling is not feasible because of the training time involved in special skills and knowledge. Each highly skilled person has his or her own special contribution to make and, while the overall success of a project depends on the effective coordination of their activities, we cannot expect to achieve this by each person becoming expert in all areas. The management of enterprises confront the same dilemma.

Beneath the managing director are usually functional managers for such things as production, finance, marketing, R & D, personnel and administration. They are typically chosen for their expertise, and it is not expected that the production manager will be as good at financial matters as the finance manager. They, in turn, expect to be judged and rewarded for their expertise in their function.

Organized bureaucratically, these work sections show the same shortcomings as are described above. Concern about this has been manifested in the rash of efforts at "matrix" and "project" organizations for R & D work and "team building" for management. A more prosaic but effective solution uses the same principle of locating responsibility for coordination clearly and firmly with those whose efforts require coordination.

A management example is given in Figure 3. In the bureaucratic state (A) the dynamics of competition are identical with those discussed with respect to (A) in Figure 2.

In the team concept (B) the functional manager is judged and rewarded, or punished, as much for his or her effective coordination as for his or her ability to propose and implement policies in that division of the organization. If an unresolved conflict arises between the managers, the managing director must sort out whether it is because one or more of them are incapable of, or unwilling to find, a suitable compromise or whether the framework of policy that he or she is responsible for is inadequate. In the first case, he or she must decide on some reeducation or redeployment; in the second, he or she must move from the normal operating mode where he or she is relatively free from

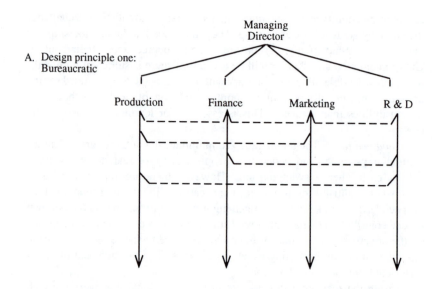

A. Design principle one:
Bureaucratic

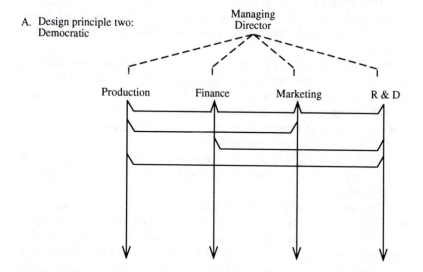

A. Design principle two:
Democratic

Figure 3. Visual for third set of concepts, modified where multiskilling is not feasible. (Elements are defined in the text.)

ongoing intra-organizational commitments, into a policy-forming or Search mode. The managing director and managers as a group need remain in the mode only long enough to create an adequate framework of operating policies.

Respecifying job responsibilities in line with (B) would seem to be a simple matter. In fact, it seems from experience that only time and a few unpleasant but exemplary experiences are needed before the changed nature of team responsibilities is grasped.

A final point should be made about this modified design. This concerns the emergence of leadership. The bureaucratic system (A) makes it very difficult to identify a potential leader because people are paid for putting their best efforts into their specialties. In a genuine team structure (B) it is relatively easier to see who is best capable of grasping and using constructively the concept of supra-individual goals. It is the ability to work in this way that would indicate a potential for overall leadership.

There is one other concept which is of use in the participative design of organizations. It is the concept of the "jury system" as a replacement for representative forms of coordination in large organizations or systems. It has, however, not yet become an integral part of this initial briefing phase of a design workshop, although it could become one. It is considered under the heading of *strategy*.

Operational tools. The use of these analytical tools will help teams obtain a profile of the current structure and function.

Following the conceptual briefing, time should be available to introduce three ways in which the concepts are converted into practical tools.

1. First show the team how to convert the six criteria into a table, which *through discussion* they will fill in and then analyze. An example of such a table is given in Table 2.

    Individual names may replace the classifications across the top. Remember that criteria 1–3 are scored from − 5 to +5 (too little or too much) so that 0 indicates about right; and criteria 4–6 are scored from 0 to 10, indicating none to extremely good. While a psychometrician would berate this process as subjective and unscientific, it has substantial power to promote better understanding of persons, tasks and interdependencies. Once the table is complete it is immediately obvious where the organizational structure is causing particular problems.

2. Once this analysis is completed to the group's satisfaction, they should begin to look at how the work flows through the section to gain an appreciation of interdependencies, imbalance and size of total task.

Within this analysis, tasks should be assessed in terms of training or skilling requirements, and any natural breaks in the process or flow should be noted in case the section should need to be divided into more than one self-managing group. The group often finds it useful to set up a skilling table such as that

TABLE 2   Example of First Stage Analysis (by class of job or skill grouping)

	Typist	File clerk	Receptionist	Accountant, etc.
1 Decision making	−2	−4	3	5
2 Variety	−4	−5	0	2
3 Learning	−2	−3	·1	4
4 Mutual support and respect	3	3	1	0
5 Meaningfulness	3	1	5	7
6 Desirable future	4	2	2	9

shown in Table 2 to help assess future training needs if multiskilling is not currently adequate to allow self-managing group function.

In the example given in Table 3 it is obvious that Alice and Jenny would be unable to replace any others in an emergency, or to rotate to gain job variety. Also skills K and M can only be handled by two individuals which may inhibit flexibility. Although it is rarely essential that there be complete multiskilling in a group, there should be sufficient flexibility built into it to cope with absentees and the extremes of fluctuation in work load at any stage of the work flow. Requirements and priorities for on the job learning and external training will be obvious.

3. Using the visual models presented in the briefing, the team should also attempt to draw up the organizational structure of their workplace as it exists at the moment. This can be one of the most educative tasks for any organization. Some discover that the complexity of reporting lines is beyond their power legibly to convey on paper; others discover that there is almost nothing to draw—laissez-faire.

These three essentially simple tools taken together convey an immense amount of information and can pinpoint areas of weakness to be addressed specifically in a first draft redesign along democratic lines, incorporating all the necessary and unique aspects of their circumstances.

Participative Design Other Than in DHR Workshops

Many more organizations have been through this process than could be accommodated within a diverse multiteam learning environment. Examples range

TABLE 3   Multiskilling

| Individual | Skills required for group task | | | | Number of skills |
	J	K	L	M	
Mary	x		x		2
Jim	x	x	x		3
John	x			x	2
Alice	x				1
Joe	x	x	x	x	4
Jenny	x				1
Number with skill	6	2	3	2	

from two or more teams from different parts of an enterprise working in a modified DHR structure, mirroring each other, to a single team or the whole of a small organization redesigning themselves. Every sort of contingency seems to have been found and accommodated.

Time spans of design work have varied widely, for example, with work being carried out whenever the organization could afford it. Half a day has been found to be sufficient to get the process well under way.

Membership patterns have also varied according to circumstance but, where the organization is larger than a single natural group or demands a hierarchy of objectives, the deep slice plus design for lateral coordination is essential.

In the on-the-job setting it is virtually impossible, particularly when meeting times are at intervals rather than intensive, to separate stages of learning, design and/or implementation. Evolution will begin in practical terms after the first meeting and will continue hand-in-hand with analysis and formal design. In this sense, the process becomes closer to that of a well established democratic organization where day-to-day operation, technical change, coordination and planning are all in a state of constant but orderly flux. As has been described of a Searching community, the process is erratic to a linear mind; ideas and practices will be tried, dropped and recycled with or without variation. Apparently small or trivial adjustments or changes may later be seen to have consequences unpredicted at the time. All this is part and parcel of the very substantial commitment to change of people who are involved at the level of the system.

In cases where a group, or a whole small organization, is attempting redesign, the managers of the learning environment must to some extent take on the role of the mirror groups in the DHR workshop. That is, they must at least spend enough time with the group to get them seriously to question their cultural and organizational assumptions before they begin to redesign. Otherwise, some at least of the conventional "wisdoms" about how things must be done—"in this industry," "with our people," etc.—will be carried over to the new design. These understandings might be totally justified, in which case discussion will serve to build confidence. But those which prove to be unjustifiable are best exposed and replaced. In this context the managers play all of the roles of manager, mirror group and expert consultant. Where to put the emphasis will, at any one moment, be a question of judgment using the primary criteria of which perspective will contribute most to the long term learning of the group.

Instances where participative design needs no more than a brief introduction to the structural alternatives, as sometimes happens toward the end of a Search, should always be concluded by giving a more adequate opportunity for exploration. Should people wish to take the process further, it is best that they be aware of what it entails.

Those Searches which have been planned to include sufficient time for an adequate experiential introduction to organizational design have proved particularly successful. The Search has set the context, the climate and the motivation for asking, "How do we organize ourselves to achieve these purposes?" At this stage the community has become a self-managing learning environment in its own right, and its members will pick up and use new concepts rapidly, adapting them to their own circumstances.

Participative design workshops can also be part of any smorgasbord or cafeteria type conference for people who have come simply to shop around for ideas. Workshops, in distinction to a Search, are sufficiently self-contained to serve this type of learning purpose. Groups of strangers can be formed within such a format with the first task of sharing experience of their organizations. From this discussion they choose one theme for analysis and subsequent redesign. This can be in no way more than an introduction but, as stated above, as long as there is some experiential manipulation of the concepts, a two- to three-hour session can lay the groundwork for further learning and diffusion.

The question of continuing support from the management team is usually raised at some point. We have always assured support in the form of further workshops or interventions during implementation but stress that any such support is entirely dependent upon invitation. Need for continued support has ranged from zero to quite intensive follow-up. Implementation has sometimes flowed so smoothly that after some time without contact we have assumed that nothing ever eventuated. At times Murphy's law appears to operate, and in these cases much fundamental groundwork must often be laid, or re-laid. One of the temptations for a group returning from a participative redesign workshop is to become so enamored of their solution that they attempt to impose it on others rather than repeat the participative learning process itself. This is a very real danger and the point cannot be overemphasized in the final strategy session.

References

Emery, M. and F. Emery. 1978. "Searching: For New Directions, In New Ways . . . For New Times." In *Management Handbook for Public Administrators,* edited by J.W. Sutherland. New York and London: Van Nostrand.

Morley, D. and E. Trist. 1981. *Children Our Number One Resource: A Report on the Saskatchewan Search Conference on Day Care.* Saskatoon: Co-operative College of Canada, 1981. Excerpted Vol. II, "A Brief Introduction to the Emerys' 'Search Conference,' " pp. 674–78.

Fred Emery

Legislating for Quality of Work Life[1]

First, there is a question of terminology: the U.S. phrase "quality of work life (QWL)" has introduced yet further complications to the area of concerns known previously as "worker participation." Improvements in lighting, heating, safety and canteen provisions could obviously improve quality of work life, but these would not require any form of worker participation, not even prior information that such improvements were about to take place. Changes in individual job specifications so that the specified duties have more variety, more customer contact, etc., require no worker participation. In fact, Herzberg, who gained considerable notoriety for this last kind of improvement in quality of work life, consistently insisted that, not only should the workers *not* be allowed to participate in such respecification of jobs, but neither should even their first-line supervisors.

However, the recent introduction of the notion of "quality of work life" has only extended the range of things that might be considered as relevant, largely to allow U.S. efforts to appear as belonging to the mainstream. What we have now is a wider range of relevant and irrelevant proposals for improving QWL (see Table 1).

For my purposes I am going to define QWL as the quality of the work itself.

Having for so long taken the public position that legislation for work redesign would be ineffective, I find it ironic that the Norwegian parliament is passing just such legislation on the grounds that the six criteria I formulated on QWL[2] provide an adequate measure for effective enforcement.

I would like to explore this notion further, as I think it may indicate that times have changed. At a very general level I have argued in "Organisational Responsibility for Individual Development" (1976) that since "man is not an island unto himself" we have a responsibility to nurture and enhance the dignity of others, if we know how. If we knew of changes in work design that would enhance the dignity of people in their work, then we should seek those changes. If legislation could create such benefits without incurring even heavier costs, the legislation should be supported.

[1]Slightly revised from an unpublished document, 1976.
[2]See pp. 602–3 of this volume.

TABLE I   Quality of Work Life

Industrial democracy	Participative	Self-managing groups Semi-autonomous groups
	Representative	Worker-directors Works Councils Joint consultation committees
Individual job enrichment		
Health, safety, physical milieu		

The 1972 German Works Constitution Act requires the "tailoring of jobs to meet human needs." It is a bit humorless to talk of "tailoring," but the point is that such a requirement could hardly be made to hold up in a court.

I had been inclined to think in terms of laws like traffic ordinances that establish strict criteria such as kilometers per hour, pollution controls that specify parts per million and Factory Acts that specify space and luminosity. Even these kinds of laws pose major problems of policing.

Perhaps we should be looking at the sort of legislation that is required to protect wilderness areas from hard usage. Here we have a situation where the great majority of users would benefit from restrained usage and where traditional policing cannot be effective within any reasonable level of costs. This is not only a matter of staffing and patrolling—with its own damage to the environment—but also of the difficulty of getting effective prosecution in the courts. Effectiveness of legislation is not going to be a simple function of the determination of a legislature to protect the wilderness areas. To be effective, the legislation must base itself on the two conditions we have mentioned, namely, adequate policing and effective prosecution.

It is my belief that these two conditions also exist in QWL and that they share two other conditions that, while not central, have considerable nuisance value. Thus, just as trail bikers are getting a little paranoid about the four-wheel drive people (who tend to be older, more family oriented and of higher economic status) trying to scapegoat them, so we can expect some managerial fears that while QWL brings them immediate benefits, it also brings them one step closer to the guillotine. I think the experience of the Yugoslav Works Councils and of worker-director schemes is ample evidence that such beliefs are unjustified. Nevertheless, they will still be aroused by any attempt to legislate in this field, no matter what party is in power. The other condition could jokingly be called "the Irish factor"—any legislation will be seen as too much legislative interference.

If legislation takes proper account of the two central conditions, these latter two conditions should not be more than temporary nuisances. If patience is shown in the enforcement of the law, they will probably be lesser nuisances for a shorter time.

Now for some suggestions for the form such legislation could take, with the Norwegian Law Section 12 and the ministerial exegesis as a starting point.

The law could establish that if X (or X%) of employees lodge a complaint about the design of their jobs with the appropriate government authority, then that authority will

(a)   Initiate discussions with the employers and unions to see whether they are willing to proceed directly to joint implementation of new job designs.

(b)   If not, the authority will order a QWL survey of the work force in that establishment. If this confirms the complaint then

(c)   The company, not just that particular establishment, will be
   (i)   struck off the list of those eligible for government contracts;
   (ii) put onto penalty rates for contribution to an industry training levy (where legislation for such levies is in force).

(d)   These penalties would be lifted when management, employees and unions are satisfied that they have established a process for change. If this process breaks down, the above machinery of government inter-vention can be reinvoked.

This is a poorly defined procedure. It seeks the advantages that are sought in modern family law procedures, namely, that there may be common interests and, where there are, they should be a formative influence, provided that the interests of third parties are not thus endangered. Some points in the procedure need to be tightened up.

At stage (b) there is the question of what kind of "survey" would confirm the original complaint and hence justify penalties. It would be unwise to attempt to set scientific standards for such a judgment or to use a judge. Jury-type procedures seem more appropriate.

This intuitive model is not meant to be a blueprint but only an example. As an example, we can take it to pieces to see what kinds of things have been built in.

The first feature builds in a sort of threshold. Nothing is legally set in motion unless some employees want change, or their unions push them into a request for change.

Even when there is an employee initiative and an employer rejects it, a second hurdle has to be overcome. A survey has to show, to the satisfaction of a jury, that there is mismanagement of human resources. Only after this auditing function does the law call for economic sanctions against the employer. These sanctions produce bad publicity and they remain until the employer can convince the courts that the situation has been remedied. A repeat survey at the employer's expense is one way of doing this. One would expect that there would be other, less costly, ways evolved—for example, site visits and representations to the courts by employees and their union representatives. Obviously some cases of collusion will arise because the sanctions may be seen to threaten the viability of the firm and hence lead to the loss of jobs. This is, however, no different from situations where wage levels are increased by a court or where pollution laws are enforced.

Note that no policing function is involved—no army of inspectors. If an employer decides that it is preferable to carry the cost of sanctions, then nothing can be done unless extralegal pressures are brought to bear by unions, other employers, employee or consumer boycott, etc.

I really do not think that more than this should be attempted by law. After all, the situation is one that can lead to benefits for both parties. The law would serve its purpose if it brought this fact to their awareness and, in the case of managers and employers, reminded them of their special responsibilities in managing the human resources of the society.

Reference

Emery, F.E. 1976. "Organisational Responsibility for Individual Development." *National Labour Institute Bulletin* (September).

Hugh Murray

Socio-Technical Action Simulations for Engaging with Engineering Designers[1]

The knowledge and experience gained through the academic and professional training of engineers and technicians in the human aspects of their disciplines—or the lack of it—have their influence through the roles they may occupy in three main fields of professional activity: the design of equipment and products, the design of manufacturing systems and the operational management of work systems. In each of these, engineers and technicians are subject to constraints imposed by the organization for which they are working which, in turn, is subject to the requirements of its customers. Engineers, and other professionals to whom they are related in a total system, who fail to take account of human aspects, or who take a restrictive or simplistic view of human attributes, needs and behavior, ultimately have their roots in a training that is dominated by a technological imperative. The equivalent in training for personnel or human resource managers is to ignore the technical characteristics and requirements of production systems.

This paper presents the course of an action research to develop a practical facility—an action simulation in educational socio-technology—for introducing postgraduate engineers with varied disciplinary backgrounds, and other related professional managers and specialists, to a common understanding of the organizational design of manufacturing systems. The range of considerations in the action simulation is conveniently indicated by the (UK) Institute of Production Engineering's definition of manufacturing systems engineering (MSE) as a "... comprehensive production discipline which optimizes the use of men, machines, materials (including information), and money . . . by the simplest integrated combination of processes, machine systems, tooling systems, people, organisational structures, information flows, control systems and computers, with a competitive balance of technology and methodology."

[1]A new paper.

The Presenting Problem

In the mid-1970s training endeavors in the socio-technical approach were changing from formal didactic learning methods to more experiential learning on field sites involving learning by doing, rather than the more simplistic observation of the expert in action or practice in exercises to develop skills of application (van Beinum, 1975; Emery and Emery, 1974/Vol. II). Advances in this direction require the participation of organizations prepared to involve their employees in learning by jointly doing something creative about their mutual concerns. But the possibility of participation in real-life work redesign or design is, for students, the exception. Opportunities to engage at the primary work system level are few; they arise unpredictably in time; they may be geographically inconvenient; variety may be restricted and few can participate. The process of organizational change may be so extended that the likelihood of a student being able to see it through is minuscule. Moreover, the risks to external company participants, students and the training institution attendant upon involving people in training in the real-life problems of others are all too evident, but are probably more apparent than real.

This was essentially the situation facing staff at the Cranfield Institute of Technology who were trying to develop more effective methods of introducing postgraduate students of industrial engineering and production management to socio-technical methods in work system design (Emery et al., 1967; Kember and Murray, 1991). Conventional teaching methods involving formal lectures, researched case studies, seminars on personal work experiences, field observations and surveys and, exceptionally, "possible" future work related changes had failed to provide useful, practical socio-technical learning opportunities of a kind analogous to the technical experience of, for example, engineers and ergonomists in laboratory or workshop. There were special exercises and experiments, but these were concerned with either aspects of technical task performance using real objects (e.g., electrical equipment assembly) or exercises typical of methods used in social system training to illustrate particular aspects of group organization (e.g., different kinds of communication patterns). Lacking were opportunities for gaining hands-on experience of integrated socio-technical operations in quasi-real life production settings which could be experimentally manipulated and critically evaluated.

To overcome the obvious problem of physical access, in limited time, to a significant variety of operating work organization designs and to lay the base for practical training in design and change under protected conditions, the only viable course was to develop, as a socio-technical laboratory, one or more perceivably realistic, face valid, practical simulations of typical manufacturing systems. In these simulations students (and others) could occupy active work roles appropriate to various organizational designs and scenarios. This would have the advantage that, unlike field engagements, all students could have direct experience of much the same situations—as well as intentionally contrasted experiences.

It was uncertain to what extent it was possible to design a learning system to enable trainees to experience, both cognitively and affectively, the diverse nature of the interdependence between the social, the technical and the influence of organizational context and contingencies and, in addition, to develop a stance toward design that is seen as collaborative and explorative between disciplines rather than exclusive and prescriptive. The antecedents for such a learning system were two-fold—technical simulations including management games both for predictive purposes and for training (Elgood, 1984) and experiential methods in social systems training (Bridger, Vol. I; Miller, Vol. I).

In the organizational field, these approaches had been substantially oriented toward management task performance and, as such, had implicitly contained elements of a socio-technical nature, but in neither had this been more than marginal. With some notable exceptions (Shackel and Klein, 1976) in which simulations featured both the technical and the organizational, the primary focus of simulation methods was "technical," as in computer-based complex decision making exercises. The human content of the simulated situation might be limited to persons as cyphers; the role relationships and organization structure of the decision makers might be ignored or, at best, simple and mutually affective relationships between the operators of the system and the operands in the system simulated might be overlooked. Technical simulations involving organizational role playing as an explicit area of concern were more common at the level of the individual, relatively rare at the primary work group level and exceptional at departmental and company wide levels.

Experiential methods of social system training were, and are, many and varied, but those of particular relevance for action simulations are task-oriented and deal with inter-personal relations in the "here and now" and make some use of laboratory-like experiments and application exercises relating to external situations. Sometimes the latter method engaged directly with people actually involved, but more usually there was recourse to representation through role playing. Social systems training of this kind is typical at the small group level but may also deal to some extent with inter-group relations and with social aggregate phenomena. Task-oriented social system training explicitly represents the technical system as human tasks; the physical reality of the technology is absent or, rarely, presented in simulated form.

That a specifically social-technical form of experiential learning might be derived from simulation and task-oriented social system methodologies was supported by the example of a noncomputer business game—"The Happy

Hunting Indian Band Corporation" of British Columbia Research, developed from "The Enterprise Corporation" game (source not known). The game, built around a simulated production process and organization, producing "space-craft" by folding printed paper blanks, was designed to provide participants with affective and other experience in a traditionally organized work system and opportunities to redesign the organization of the whole system. The scope for alternative production methods, work organization structures and company environment scenarios was evident and in action the game was capable of making lasting impact. Its artificiality, however, limited its use to making "points" rather than helping to solve problems. Construction kit materials (e.g., "Lego") had a similar use in simulating assembly and "on-off" production processes but did not present a sufficiently acceptable technical challenge to which engineers could respond. Without an adequate technical "anchor" they found themselves trying to deal with (to them) uncomfortable, intangible issues like frustration, warped communications, bad feelings, dissatisfaction—issues they saw as the concern of others with different disciplinary backgrounds.

Practical Parameters and Conceptual Basis for Action Simulations

Realistic action, or role playing, simulations of productive work organizations can be designed to provide four incremental levels of experience for students:
- In operative, supervisory and managerial roles in one or more types of manufacturing system, each with one or more varieties of primary work unit organization.
- Carrying out social-technical analyses of such systems, monitoring and making comparative evaluations of production, behavioral and attitudinal data.
- Participative re-design of work systems, e.g., to meet changed requirements.
- Implementation and operational evaluation of organizational changes.

The particular kinds of simulated system that need to be developed depend on several practical considerations:
- Whether the course (or simulation-based experience) is self-contained and continuous, or discontinuous (e.g., one day a week), or linked to some other course. The latter two considerations may constrain choice of product and production process.
- The time orientation of participants—to gain understanding of the past, an ongoing experience, or as a preparation for the future? The difference

between the first and second is between "there and then" and "here and now" in terms of the interpretation of experience. The third, which has connotations of prototyping a new design, is about discovering the nature of the future in the present, which may require the relaxation of some reality constraints.

• The likely setting in which a simulation is to be used—classroom, laboratory, workshop, factory—may technically constrain what can be attempted. Artificiality arising from a mismatch between technology and environment may affect the perceived reality of the simulation.

When it comes to choosing possible production systems for simulation, their technical characteristics have to be assessed in relation to the foregoing considerations. Table 1 illustrates ten decision areas that may be used in searching for production systems to simulate or in assessing the compatibility of design options with each other and with training objectives. In designing a manufacturing simulation with a low level fabrication or assembly technology, the most important requirement is for a nontrivial, realistic, obviously engineered and seemingly required product. The technical production process should be sufficiently complex to permit alternative methods of production and alternative forms of organization to be devised, yet not so demanding of operative skills that they cannot be acquired rapidly by most people.

A second main requirement is that the work roles and work relationship structures of different primary work units should be relatable within a common conceptual framework that permits of systematic and objective comparison in the same terms, e.g., a typology based on activity relationship, role differentiation, task dependence and goal dependence (Herbst, 1974). The possibility of, for example, measuring work relationship structures and interaction patterns within and between groups affords some comfort to "hard" scientists in a "soft" field.

The third requirement is that simulated primary work units be embedded in an appropriate simulated organization structure of management, supervisory and specialist roles, which controls the running of the primary unit in line with its own policies through creating different operating conditions (e.g., raw material supply, demand for product, labor supply, etc.). This calls for both prepared scenarios and a creative response to unplanned events during their running (e.g., absences, disputes). The simulated wider organization needs to be more realistic than ideal in its structure and functioning. Simulated primary units can also be ideal, internally consistent types or—as in real life—internally inconsistent in some respects, giving rise to undesired consequences, e.g., a misfit between the structure of a wages system and task performance requirements. In each case the criteria underlying the particular design decision need to be explicit.

TABLE I   Manufacturing System Action Simulation: Examples of Technical Design Options

Decision area	Design options	Decision area	Design options
Product	Real object with market Real object without market Model (toy) Paper abstraction	Unit operations	Transfer (supply, buffer, stock) Reductive (drilling, milling, cleaning) Additive (assembly, welding, blending) Changes of state (bending, molding, cooling) Inspection and rework
Technology level	Powered tool Powered hand tool Simple tools Manual aids Manual		
		Skill levels	No training required Picked up on job Minimum training Somewhat specialized
Production system	Continuous flow process (liquid/solid) Production line (fabrication) Assembly line Batch	Size (number of persons)	One unit (7–9) Two units (14–18) Three units (21–27) etc.
Throughput time	Instant Cycles possible in shifts (one, two, many) Continuous	Setting up/ down time	Minutes Hours Days
		Materials and components	Reusable Consumed
		Costs: capital	Low Medium High

An Action Research in Prototyping a Simulation

The initial task of designing and building a prototype socio-technical action simulation of a small manufacturing unit was given to a group of graduate students taking a master's degree in Industrial Engineering and Production Management. They had previously opted to specialize in ergonomics and work organization. Teaching was by conventional methods, the limitations of which have already been mentioned. Students each carry out an individual project in the "engineer" role, applying existing knowledge and techniques to solve specific problems, and together, take part in a substantial, industry-based, problem-oriented group project. Ideally, the choice of the group projects would be negotiable, the type of solution open rather than predetermined and the methods used discretionary, rather than preselected (Cherns, 1976). The student roles were those of consultant or action researcher, depending on the nature of the problem. In these terms the simulation design project had both kinds of relationship, with the university institution as client in the shape of their teachers.

The student group which was to design and build the simulation could call on the services of technicians, fellow students as volunteer subjects and teaching staff as "external" advisers. The group was also wholly responsible for creating an organization to manage the group project and carry out the work. The group members were therefore involved in two levels of learning: applying their knowledge from lectures, etc., to designing a real work system for the group project in which they had roles and the task for which the project had been established, designing a simulated manufacturing system (Kember and Murray, 1984). During the course of the project, particularly in the area of alternative organizational options, increased carryover of learning between these levels was observed in both directions.

The members of the project group were three engineering graduates with factory employment experience and two industrial psychologists of whom one had an engineering background. The mixture of disciplines was fortuitous and during the later organizational design phases was important in highlighting the differences between individual cognitive styles and what individuals presented as ideal organizations (Kilmann and Mitroff, 1976).

The broad structure of the project was predetermined by teaching staff and had three phases. The first was an on-site socio-technical scanning and analysis of the systems in a local factory for fabricating and assembling electromechanical controls, followed by more detailed studies of relatively small production units within it. This was to give all group members a common reference experience for Phase 2, the design, construction and testing of a simulated system within given constraints. In the third phase (and subsequently with other project groups), the simulation was to be run with volunteer student groups (and if possible with workers from the field-site factory) both to facilitate further development and to assess whether preliminary hypotheses as to behavior and attitudes exhibited in different forms of simulated work organization were confirmed. For these purposes three types of work organization were prescribed by teaching staff:

- The *unit production* model, in which individual "craftsmen" carried out all tasks required to produce a whole product.

- The *production line,* in which workers, in sequence, engaged in simple, repetitive short cycle tasks.
- "Autonomous" *group working,* in which the self-regulating group could, for example, decide the production method within limits set by the available technology; the allocation of individuals to roles; role exchange; etc. (Gulowsen, 1972)

The initial briefing for Phase 2 covered the reasons for needing to develop a simulation and explained the necessary conceptual and practical parameters. As an introduction to action simulation methodology, the group ran a primary work-group version of the Enterprise Spacecraft game and, in a prototyping model, tried to simulate different methods of organizing the assembly of toy automobiles using Lego materials. An early decision was taken by the group that in order to engage the interest of engineers, the simulation should call for the exercise of hands-on technical skills. Other things being equal, the higher the technology used in the simulation the more attractive it would be. This pointed to a fabrication of solid objects rather than an assembly process, a chemical flow process being too specialized and not within the competence of the design group. The main problem in the simulation construction was deciding on a product item that had substantial versatility with regard to production technique, required multistage manufacturing, had low cost and could be realistically produced under different forms of work organization. Some 16 product ideas were considered and rejected by the project group, and the choice of the ultimate product was a matter of inspiration. The sequence of events, which proceeded in three phases, was somewhat as follows:

- An engineer member of the group recalled that as a child he had made a "flying toy" out of scrap metal. There was a concurrent need for give-away toys for a staff children's party. A group decision was quickly taken to design and develop a product—the "Cranfield Flyer"—like the flying toy. A basic technical method of construction was produced.
- The risk to children of possible poor workmanship was realized. A plastic coating process was invented to cover all surfaces. Coatings in different university colors could be used for "marketing."
- It was recognized that bench hand-tool production methods would be used in reality to produce quantities of objects similar to the core component—a propeller, for example—with varying specifications for experimental work in aeronautics. The propeller was redesigned to exploit this as a "required" range of "real" products.

From the initial decision onward the project group had little doubt about the "correctness" of their choice of product. The choice not only fitted the requirements of the action simulation but it "connected" the simulation to the immediate institutional environment, so that it would be more likely to be perceived as "fitting in"—Cranfield has a history and reputation in aeronautics. Whether this, and continuing helicopter activity on the airfield, gave rise to the engineer's initial suggestion is a matter for conjecture.

Normal bench handtools (e.g., drills, metal cutters, files) were used to fabricate the propeller from an aluminum alloy blank, through a variable sequence of nine operations, taking in all 12 man-minutes per propeller. Work relationship structures and work role descriptions for each type of work organization were drawn up for seven to nine participants. Scenarios and procedures were prepared and iteratively developed in a series of runs of the simulations, using groups representing a wide range of age, cultural background, engineering and industrial experience. A basic 10-session, nominally 30-hour course evolved to provide a learning experience of the primary group in the workplace, where the roles occupied and the organizational structures are studied (Murray and Kember, 1991). Kolb's (1976) experiential learning model summarizes the learning process provided by the course (Table 2). The structure, content and duration of the course, particularly the number and length of simulation runs, are tailored to participant needs.

Several critical experiences contributed to the design. In the first three sessions, the ergonomically poor, low-level technology employed worried some engineers who would press for technical improvements and upgrading, suggesting ways of bringing this about. As these would have organizational and other implications within the wider context, consideration of them was referred to the group's own design session (session 8) and, when judged feasible, suggestions were implemented.

Although most engineers had some experience of both the Individual and Production Line types of organization which represented extremes on a continuum of skill content and variety, they found it hard to conceive of the possibility of variants. To introduce the idea of options, a Modified Line was introduced (session 4) in which simple changes (e.g., in layout) could lead to changes in the work relationship structure.

Some engineers took a skeptical view (in session 5) of qualitative observations on production performance, behavior and attitudes. Subjective estimates of the quality of finished products would be challenged—a common "scientific" defense against accepting interpretations about the significance of organizational changes. (Equipment was later constructed to measure quality.) Similarly, video recordings removed much argument about behavioral observations.

To reduce the likelihood of carbon-copy designs, the production task given to the group in the new design session (8) needed to be changed (e.g., greater product variety, mix changes, anticipated market difficulties), implying the need for flexible and robust designs to be able to respond to uncertainty.

A main problem in the design sessions (8 and 10), particularly for groups

TABLE 2   Outline of the Ten-Session Course Structure

Session	Main activity	Learning process
1	Assessment of skills, preferences and training	Concrete experience
2	Roles in "individual" type of organization	Concrete experience
3	Roles in "line" type of organization	Concrete experience
4	Roles in Modified Line	Concrete experience
5	Feedback, comparative analysis of performance	Observations + reflections
6	Comparative socio-tech analysis of structures	Form concepts + generalizations
7	Instruction in redesign methodology	Form concepts + generalizations
8	Group designs own organization	Test implications in new situations
9	Group runs own design	Test implications in new situations
10	Feedback on performance; redesign, rerun	Test implications in new situations

who had had little exposure to case material, was to detach them from consideration of only line types of organization. In such cases it was important for teaching staff not to infringe on the group's autonomy by intervening at the design stage, but to delay intervention until feedback and redesign. When it was possible to have two or more groups in the same course, they could be balanced or could be compared to reflect certain differences (e.g., in experience or cognitive style). When put into "competition" with each other, engineers were able to see a range of design preferences and solutions and hence actually experience the many options in the way work can be organized with a given level of technology.

An unexplored topic in running an action simulation course is how best to take account of differences in the cognitive styles of participants, i.e., how they prefer to take in information and make decisions. Kilmann and Mitroff (1976; Kilmann 1983) found that individuals with fundamentally differing cognitive styles have fundamentally different conceptions of what constitutes an ideal organization. This idea has profound implications for organizational design.

All individuals use both *sensation* and *intuition* as modes of perceiving at different times, but tend to develop a preferred mode, the strength of which may differ among individuals. This is also the case for the decision making modes, *thinking* and *feeling* (see Myers, 1962).

Individuals who prefer to take in information via the senses (sensation) and who are most comfortable with details and facts may have greater doubts about the fidelity of the simulation model than those who prefer to take in information by means of their imagination, by seeing the whole gestalt (intuition). In an engineering institution which students have chosen to enter and for which the successful outcome is a higher degree, logical impersonal analysis (thinking) may be a more likely way of reaching a design decision than a subjective, personal process (feeling). Nonetheless, in an action simulation, with its novelty, some may well make design decisions based on personalistic value judgments, particularly if this is their preferred style. Combining the two perceiving modes (sensation [S] and intuition [N]) with the two decision-making modes (thinking [T] and feeling [F]) results in four personality types with differing cognitive styles: ST, NT, SF, NF.

To judge from a comparison (Table 3) between engineering and finance/commerce undergraduates (quoted in Myers, 1962), it seems likely in a teaching simulation that the cognitive styles of engineering students may not only vary among themselves, but many differ modally from those in other disciplines. Manifestly, the cognitive style of the engineering designer should be considered in relation to the influences that shape the technical and human organization—but it may be suggested that it should extend equally to all stakeholders who influence and participate directly in the design process. It is not a question only of singling out engineers, or other disciplinary or functional groups, for separate action simulation-based training in work organization design. It is also necessary to provide them with complementary designing experiences other than through role playing other functions, in quasi-real multifunctional organizational settings in which participants can encounter the cognitive styles and organizational ideals of others. Particularly apposite would be use of the strategic choice approach (Friend and Hickling, 1987), which offers a range of practical methods enabling people of different outlook, discipline and skills to analyze interconnected problems and to work adaptively toward decisions.

The original student project group—and others that succeeded it—produced a viable simulation that reproduced the necessary and sufficient conditions for the manufacturing situation it sought to model. The propeller fabrication simulation was right for the immediate needs of the particular institution. Different products and production technologies might be better suited to other colleges, polytechnics, etc., located in areas with different industries. At the beginning, it had been thought necessary to develop simulations of a range of

TABLE 3   Comparison of Cognitive Styles[a]

Student group	Sensation/ thinking	Sensation/ feeling	Intuition/ feeling	Intuition/ thinking
2188 engineering students (Cornell, MIT, RPI, 1962–64)	24%	11%	22%	43%
488 finance/commerce students (Wharton School, 1956 & 57)	51%	21%	10%	18%

[a]Data abstracted from Myers (1962), table p. 64. Columns indicate modes of perceiving/decision making.

other production systems (e.g., for process industry and for assembly), but use of the fabrication simulation was, in practice, found sufficient to facilitate training in the basic aims and methods of socio-technical design. However, other action simulations were developed for use in individual research projects of production scheduling and office-work organization.

Action Simulation of a High-Tech Manufacturing System

A major postgraduate engineering student group project used the work organization action simulation course for general training, prior to assessing the implications for job and organizational structure of a suggested staged introduction of a full flexible manufacturing system (FMS) in an actual company (Cranfield, 1984). Conventional engineering and socio-technical design philosophies were compared, and it became apparent that approaching prototyping in a more socio-technical way would be an economically effective method for exploring the organizational impact of a sequence of technical changes (Kember and Murray, 1988). Useful as the "propeller" action simulation is as an initial teaching and training facility, its low-tech image is a limitation to its attractiveness and usefulness to engineers in an increasingly high-tech computerized world. More and more, the nature of information technology is requiring production and manufacturing engineers to become involved with the design of whole systems rather than with the replacement of single machines.

Against the background of the FMS group project, a further project was undertaken to demonstrate the practical feasibility of an action simulation of an FMS as an example of computer integrated manufacturing that would enable managers and designers to recognize and explore person/machine interface and organizational issues, options and problems before design decisions in the technical system are finalized.

A flexible simulation of an FMS, i.e., one which could cover a range of configurations, was constructed, and a Mark I working prototype of manifest interest to engineers was demonstrated (Cranfield, 1989). The simulation (a small parts FMS that made prismatic components for aircraft) was not a replica, but included features from several installations and the literature (Gerwin and Leung, 1980; Gunn 1982). Something of its nature may be inferred from the sequence of design decisions taken iteratively: product; production process and routes; physical layout; material flow; information flow via computer network; likely variances and where they are generated and likely to be detected; "company" organization; operating scenarios; key variances and control patterns; operator tasks; primary group and support system work roles.

The design had to create a valid perceptual experience for a range of possible participants and call for the exercise of conceptual skills in addition to limited manual activity. In the action simulation itself, what are simulated are the visible and other perceptible aspects of the product and production process and not the actual production process itself (which is supplied in a scenario). The process takes place in "black boxes" which input and output products in course of production and emit appropriate signals. This makes the modular design generic and capable of adaptation to many different kinds of product and production process.

For realism, an FMS action simulation must operate in some representation of the real world of business conditions and requirements, which is mediated through an explicit wider organization structure of roles and positions. Many functions may impinge directly or indirectly—and quickly—on the running FMS (e.g., computer programming, scheduling, personnel, marketing, etc.). Many more "external" people may interface with the FMS than operate it directly, and so socio-technical design of advanced manufacturing systems is relatively more concerned with meso- and macro-system level functioning. For consistency, the technology used, as well as the organization at such levels, may well need to be simulated to facilitate multifunctional design approaches and training.

Conclusions

What has been advocated in this paper is the introduction into graduate level engineering education (and where appropriate into in-house management training) of the integrated socio-technical systems approach to the design and management of work organizations in manufacturing industry. Crucially, in addition to conventional teaching methods, basic training in work design should be experiential, making use of work organization action simulations, initially with low level technologies, to elucidate principles before moving to more advanced simulated or real manufacturing systems. For the better appreciation of differences in cognitive style which affect the design process, some integrated training should take place with other technical and nontechnical disciplines or professionals with whom engineers have to work, or to whom they have to relate in manufacturing work organization design.

Short of such integrated education and training, action simulations can be used as introductory familiarizing or "sensitizing" events for all people likely to be involved in a specific real design or redesign operation. Ideally, the action simulations should be generically as similar as possible to the real options.

Moving from the generic to the specific, a more socio-technical approach to prototyping could be envisaged to enable engineers, jointly with other stakeholders, to explore design options and test out ideas in a way analogous to the use of engineering prototypes; e.g., the organizational implications of conventional computer simulations of manufacturing systems could be tested. A move toward explicit socio-technical prototyping would facilitate the participation of operators and others in the design and commissioning process, the selection of potential operators and the initial stages of operator training—all social system aspects of direct concern to the engineering designer of manufacturing systems.

References

Bridger, H. 1990. Vol. I. "Courses and Working Conferences as Transitional Learning Institutions," pp.221–45.

Cherns, A.B. 1976. "Behavioural Science Engagements: Taxonomy and Dynamics." *Human Relations*, 19:905–10.

Cranfield. 1984. *The Organisational Aspects of Flexible Manufacturing Systems*. Unpublished report. College of Manufacturing, Cranfield Institute of Technology.

———. 1989. *Working Organisation of Computer Integrated Manufacturing Systems*. Unpublished report. College of Manufacturing, Cranfield Institute of Technology.

Elgood, C. 1984. *Handbook of Management Games* (third edition). London: Gower Press.

Emery, F.E. and M. Emery. 1974. *Participative Design: Work and Community Life*. Canberra: Centre for Continuing Education, Australian National University. Revised, Vol. II, "The Participative Design Workshop," pp.599–613.

Emery, F.E., M. Foster and W. Woolard. 1967. "Analytical Model for Socio-Technical Systems." Reprinted in *Socio-Technical Systems: A Source Book* (1978), edited by W.A. Pasmore and J.J. Sherwood. La Jolla, Calif.: University Associates.

Friend, J. and A. Hickling. 1987. *Planning Under Pressure: The Strategic Choice Approach*. Oxford: Pergamon Press.

Gerwin, D. and T.K. Leung. 1980. "The Organisational Impacts of Flexible Manufacturing Systems: Some Initial Findings." *Human Systems Management*, 1:237–46.

Gulowsen, J. 1972. "A Measure of Work Group Autonomy." In *Design of Jobs*, edited by L.E. Davis and J.C. Taylor. Harmondsworth: Penguin Books.

Gunn, T.G. 1982. "The Mechanization of Design and Manufacturing." In *The Mechanization of Work*. A Scientific American book. San Francisco: W.H. Freeman.

Herbst, P.G. 1974. "Production Tasks and Work Organisation." In *Socio-Technical Design: Strategies in Multi-Disciplinary Research*. London: Tavistock Publications.

Kember, P. and H. Murray. 1984. *Project Learning and Organisational Choice for Engineers*. Tavistock Institute Document.

———. 1988. "Towards Socio-Technical Prototyping of Work Systems." *International Journal of Production Research*, 26:133–42.

———. 1991. *Work Organisation for Engineers*. Cranfield, UK: Cranfield Press.

Kilmann, R.H. 1983. "A Typology of Organization Typologies: Towards Parsimony and Integration in Organizational Sciences." *Human Relations*, 36:523–48.

Kilmann, R.H. and I.I. Mitroff. 1976. "Qualitative Versus Quantitative Analysis for Management Science: Different Forms for Different Psychological Types." *Interfaces*, 6:17–27.

Kolb, D.A. 1976. "Management and the Learning Process." *Californian Management Review*, 18:21–31.

Miller, E.J. 1990. Vol. I. "Experiential Learning in Groups, I and II," pp.165–98.

Murray, H. and P. Kember. 1991. *The Cranfield-Tavistock Work Organisation Action Simulation: Tutor's Manual*. Cranfield, UK: Cranfield Press.

Myers, I.B. 1962. *The Myers-Briggs Type Indicator*. Princeton, N.J.: Educational Testing Service.

Shackel, B. and L. Klein. 1976. "Esso London Airport Refuelling Control Centre Redesign: An Ergonomics Case Study." *Applied Ergonomics*, 7.

Van Beinum, H. 1975. Flevo-Oord Summer School. Personal communication.

Eric Trist

Work Improvement and Organizational Democracy[1]

The Sanction of a Central Mandate

It is sometimes maintained that approval from the top is the critical requirement for the successful carrying out of a change program. But even when a central mandate is given, and this is usually hard to obtain, implementation does not automatically follow. The problem is then created of finding a suitable instrument to carry it out.

In Philips Electrical Industries, work-restructuring experiments rapidly convinced the Main Board of the desirability of spreading socio-technical change throughout the corporation. As early as 1965 the Chairman made public his commitment to the new principles so that there should be no doubt about the sanction carried by the central mandate. The Board itself could not carry out the changes. How were they to be accomplished?

The chosen instrument was the Technical Efficiency Organization (TEO), one of the main staff divisions. Responsibility for appreciating the human and social aspects of work organization was assigned to the group also responsible for the technical and efficiency aspects, causing a redefinition of mission in socio-technical terms. The TEO had to add psychological and social science competence to engineering and OR competence. The conflicts between these approaches were internal to the change agent, which had itself to develop the integrated capability required in the plants.

Being a staff division, the TEO could not impose its policies on operational management but had to act as an internal resource, supporting and evaluating projects undertaken by plants and disseminating the findings and experience throughout the concern. A process of organizational learning of the widest kind was thus set in motion. For example, in 1968 the TEO issued a major report called "Work-Restructuring for Unskilled Workers." This, with the sanction of

[1]Part of the keynote address to the Conference on Work Improvement and Industrial Democracy of the European Economic Community, Brussels, 1974.

the central mandate supporting it, had the effect of substantially increasing the number of work-restructuring projects being undertaken.

The Technical Efficiency Organization also undertook research studies of such projects when invited by the departments concerned. This can only take place when operating people have reached the point of wishing to increase their understanding of the complexities involved through systematic and sustained analysis. Too little of this type of evaluation is being undertaken by operating organizations. The TEO made available a wealth of evaluative case histories in which attention is paid to failures as well as to successes, so that there has been a great deal of learning from mistakes.

More than 50 projects of various dimensions are said to be under way. But the diffusion process has been slow, depending on the creation of an internal market for the new approach, which has to be thoroughly understood and wanted by those directly concerned or nothing much happens, even when central support is given.

The Process of Cumulative Innovation

The opposite of central mandate is the accumulation of initiatives from below until, eventually, a central mandate is given. Over the last seven years a process of this kind has been taking place in General Foods.

An innovative manager had designed a new plant on advanced socio-technical principles (similar to those used in Norskhydro) and brought it into successful operation with one or two key colleagues. A high level of work satisfaction was achieved, together with major cost savings. This plant, which was in Topeka, Kansas, received national and, indeed, international publicity.

Despite all this, several attempts to convert existing General Foods plants to more innovative forms of socio-technical organization lagged rather badly for some years. The Topeka model was rejected. Criticisms were many: it required special conditions; it was a greenfield site; there was no union contract in the way; employees were specially selected; etc. Other managers did not want their plants to be compared with Topeka. There was a great deal of envy. Evidence of Topeka's operational success was disregarded. These reactions encapsulated the innovation. Similar reactions have been observed in other organizations undertaking major change programs of this kind. High profile demonstration experiments are far from always effective as foci of diffusion in the organization in which they have taken place. Outsiders are often more receptive.

However, largely through the efforts of the original innovator, Lyman Ketchum (Ketchum and Trist, 1992), several small projects eventually persisted in various plants. Experience of these showed that before a change effort could make any serious headway, the plant manager and his staff had to "work through," and make explicit to themselves, the implicit assumptions on which traditional management and organization are based. This rather emotional "unprogramming" ordeal had to be endured before socio-technical concepts could be learned and the new work ethic internalized. The process had to be repeated at supervisory levels and with the union.

From these experiences emerged what has become known as the Plant Managers' Network. This is composed of several plant managers, interested in carrying through local innovations, who meet informally off-site to compare experiences. This network has become a powerful medium for social learning.

In the last year or so, a program of considerable scope has developed in one of the largest divisions. Beginning with a small new equipment installation, it became plantwide in the largest location and has begun to spread to others. The leading edge of the change effort has, therefore, become divisional.

This development has made a fresh impact on top management at the corporate level where the interest aroused earlier had not survived the antagonism to Topeka. Hard evidence was now to hand that large, and often old, unionized plants could transform themselves and begin to internalize the new work ethic and in so doing improve their operations. The corporate vice-president for operations developed a document entitled "An Operations Philosophy for General Foods." This was sanctioned by the president, who had participated in the drafting, at a recent corporationwide conference of operations management where the document was discussed in detail.

The philosophy not only commits the corporation to socio-technical work design but also to principles such as maintaining labor stability. Operations managers are now testing out how far the marketing and financial sides will, in practice, honor this. A new dialogue has opened.

The Role of the Innovative Subsidiary

Intermediate between central mandate and cumulative innovation is a process in which a subsidiary or division of a large corporation undertakes the role of being an experimental site. This allows the implications of socio-technical change to be experienced at all levels of management except the very top and yet to be contained in one organizational space.

A process of this kind has taken place in the refining side of Shell in Britain, where four out of five refineries have been involved. In the early 1960s, severe problems of overmanning were experienced, together with difficult labor relations and increasing management frustration. The company decided to make an all out effort to bring about changes which would make possible a higher level of motivation and commitment to company objectives on the part of all employees, leading to an enhanced level of performance. The results have been publicly reported for the years 1956–70 (Hill, 1971/Hill and Emery, Vol. II). The fifth refinery was a joint enterprise with Imperial Chemical Industries (ICI). Shell did not want to expose or impose its internal experimental processes to or on its partner.

A small team was set up to study the company's long-standing motivation problem on a full-time basis and to propose long-term plans for solving it. A collaborative relationship was established between outside social science resource people from the Tavistock Institute and internal resource people from the company. One result was a considerable transfer of knowledge and skills into the organization.

A document was produced that stated explicitly the objectives the company would work toward and the management philosophy, or values, which would be used to guide decision making in pursuing them. Key features of the document were a reconciliation of the company's economic and social objectives and the adoption of the principle of joint optimization of the social and technical systems.

At a residential off-site conference, the top management of the company, led by the managing director, committed itself to the objectives and philosophy and to seeking commitment to them throughout the organization. The top management team met under similar circumstances at critical decision points in the program to decide and guide the general course it should take. In order to secure this wider commitment, a complete dissemination program was developed. Through numerous conferences at each location, large numbers of employees at all levels were able to test the objectives and philosophy for themselves. The remaining employees had an opportunity to do this at departmental meetings. Eventually all the employees in the company were included. The dissemination process was dynamic, not stereotyped. Different methods were tried out and each location developed programs that were best suited to its own refinery situation. The dissemination process achieved considerable success in securing a widespread understanding of, and commitment to, the company's objectives and philosophy. It also produced quite a number of highly enthusiastic employees. They represented the critical mass who led the process of implementation.

With few exceptions, trade union representatives, both internal shop stewards and outside officials, reacted very favorably to the company's intentions and offered their support. The dissemination program developed new skills in many people and created a climate in the company that permitted and encouraged trying out new ideas. Although not all the experiments achieved their purpose, they contributed to the overall learning and development and provided a stepping-stone to the next move forward. An important example of this type of innovation was the setting up of joint management/union working parties whose new role and new frame of reference were accepted by the majority of the shop stewards and by all the trade union officials. Although they did not fully complete their tasks, the work they did made a valuable contribution to the productivity bargains that followed.

The outcome of the productivity bargaining, after the expenditure of much time and effort, was also very successful. More important than the content of the bargains, significant as that was, was the manner in which they were decided. Both management and union representatives were dedicated to the bargaining's success and shared to a greater extent than ever before the same frame of reference. The level of participation on the part of shop stewards in the formulation of the bargains and the level of effective communication with the shop-floor employees was exceptionally high. The result was commitment to the content and the spirit of the deals, not merely a collection of unenforceable agreements. A more general result of the new climate and the new collaborative working relationships between shop stewards and management was a vast improvement in the industrial relations situation at Shell Haven, where they had been exceedingly bad. General morale improved accordingly.

The other major field where innovation took place was in the design of jobs. Here again, partial success in one venture did not stop progress but led to the start of another. The process was again dynamic. The pilot projects at Stanlow Refinery created great opportunities for learning and indicated good possibilities for improvement in performance levels. The introduction of two simplified methods of analyzing existing systems provided another great learning experience in which many people in the company were involved. The application of the methods at Stanlow showed good and promising results. As with the earlier pilot projects, they demonstrated how shop-floor employees could contribute significantly to these results. The nine-step method of socio-technical analysis was also found valuable, both as a training tool and in its practical application.

The largest-scale application of the philosophy was in the design of the social system at Teesport, the new highly automated refinery. The principle of joint optimization of social and technical systems was consciously and carefully applied, with highly successful results. A wide variety of other implementation measures were all undertaken within the framework of the philosophy. They included changes in the staff appraisal system and in manpower planning, job enrichment and so on.

The development program was subjected to many countervailing pressures, some internal (such as the retirement or transfer of key people, both in management and among the resource people) and others external (such as the disruption of crude supplies by war and the pressures felt at the Teesport refinery to regress to old norms).

The countervailing forces mentioned above have arrested the progress of the program in Shell (UK). Indeed, a regression is apparent if the early 1970s are compared with the late 1960s, despite the enormous effort made initially. The sustaining of innovation over long time periods is a problem requiring further study.

The United Kingdom initiative has been taken up and developed further in Australia by one of the British refinery managers who went out there. Recently, a major program has been put under way in Holland outside the refining field. Members of the Group Board have been kept informed of what has been transpiring from the beginning of the British project. They have never interfered but have not felt that the process has reached a point where active Group policies were indicated.

The Function of Local Experimentation

The difficulty of effectively obtaining top management commitment in very large organizations has been demonstrated in the accounts that have been presented. Fortunately, a number of cases demonstrate that significant changes can take place on a small scale here and there at the departmental level. They are often spontaneous and unofficial. They do not attract undue attention, which is their protection.

A remarkable case of this kind has been reported from Corning Glass. One or two innovators in the R&D department of one plant began to introduce experimental socio-technical change with the assistance of behavioral scientists. Other departments tried out changes for themselves. There was no pressure.

There is some reason to expect that local experimentation will become more common. The search for a new work ethic and for organizational values and forms that will embody it, is, in the last analysis, a response in the wider society to profound changes taking place within it. Many more people were likely during the mid and late 1970s to pick up the relevant signals from the environment than during the late 1960s and early 1970s—and to act on them. The pioneer projects have shown the way and some of the larger socio-technical change efforts have received a great deal of publicity, as has the alienation phenomenon. What appears to be happening in a number of organizations is the appearance, simultaneously or in close succession, of multiple small change efforts in several different places. The burdensome processes of securing sanction from the top are not undertaken. The managers concerned simply become proactive, assuming that to make the required changes is within their discretion—and union locals do not always inform their higher echelons. This way of proceeding is becoming more possible as the new ethic becomes more familiar. The number of these small endeavors is not only increasing but networks which connect them are beginning to form between as well as within firms. They may also be rendered futile by absence of top support.

The Professional Organization as Change Agent

In Japanese industry in the last 10 years, a grassroots movement has arisen involving a new philosophy of work with special reference to improving product quality by increasing worker involvement, participation in decision making at the shop-floor level and encouraging personal development. This movement represents a dramatic break with the traditional paternalistic culture of the Japanese factory and the Taylorism that the society had imported into this.

Sony has been a leading exponent of the new philosophy and attributes a significant role to it in the firm's remarkable growth, particularly with reference to the ability of their work force to cope with the rapid technological change in their products.

A societal change which may be linked to the movement is that status in terms of age, so fundamental in Japan, is being diminished, though the process is no more than in its first very early phase. The older and the younger generations are nevertheless beginning to merge, at least in the workplace, into a kind of senior/junior, teacher/pupil relationship, performing closely associated jobs in which they assume joint responsibility.

This relationship also extends to the scientist-technician and to people with differing backgrounds and academic disciplines who are brought together to solve problems across technical, business, financial and political boundaries. In these respects Japanese social structure in the work setting is beginning to develop into a series of collective partnerships, involving deep relationships and effective teamwork, supported by free-flowing information, responsible judgment and a good deal of youthful zeal. Where will this lead the society as a whole with its complex and long-evolved culture?

Of special interest is the mechanism of the teamwork, which is carried out through what the Japanese call Quality Control Circles (QCC). These Circles can best be described as groups of workers and foremen who voluntarily meet together to solve shop oriented production/quality problems. They aim at improving daily work and human relations through the "mutual development of the participants." The foreman is usually, but not always, the leader.

The first Circles were entirely spontaneous. Their importance, however, was recognized by a critically relevant national professional association—the Japanese Union of Scientists and Engineers (JUSE). Members of this organization began to nourish the Circles in various workplaces. It soon became JUSE's official policy to give them technical assistance and as more Circles began to form they were registered with JUSE. In this way, a national network was built up which was independent of any particular firm, yet which had great power of organizational entry.

Since June 1962, when the first three Circles were officially registered with JUSE, the QCC movement has had a fantastic rate of growth. The members of the Fourth QCC Team, who toured the United States in September 1970, reported that there were over 400,000 Circles, with over 4,000,000 workers. Since then numbers have grown to more than 500,000 and 5,000,000 respectively. A Circle may have as few as three or as many as 20 members but generally has between 5 and 10 members. Once a Circle is registered with JUSE, it becomes part of the national organization.

Cost savings range from as little as $250 to a high of $500,000 per case per year; savings of $100,000 are frequent and the average runs about $56,000. While 32 percent of the QCC meetings take place during working hours and 44 percent afterward, 24 percent meet under both conditions. When meetings take place after working hours, compensation is offered in 71 percent of cases. While 35 percent of Circles meet once a month, 65 percent meet more often; 80 percent of the meetings are for an hour or more; 35 percent for two hours or more.

Of 1,566 companies surveyed by JUSE, 1,424 (91 percent) were using QCCs. The industries covered included chemicals, electrical, textile, general machinery, wood products and consumer products. Japanese writings on the subject lay stress on a philosophy of happiness and creativeness in work. In fact, features of what we have called the new work ethic are emerging against a very different cultural background.

A prominent feature of Circle activities is the extent to which they are concerned with teaching workers the technical skills of industrial engineering, quality control, etc. That is to say, the professionals have ceased to hoard the knowledge which is their power. They are sharing it. This is a process of work-linked democracy which has no parallel in the West.

Autonomy, Personal Growth and Participation

The projects reviewed indicate that types of organization structure, management methods and job content can be developed that lead to cooperation, commitment, learning and growth, ability to change, high work satisfaction and improved performance. When responsible autonomy, adaptability, variety and participation are present, they lead to learning and behavior that improve the organization and enhance the quality of working life for the individual.

Autonomy means that the content, structure and organization of jobs is such that individuals or groups performing those jobs can plan, regulate and control their own work worlds. Autonomy implies a number of things, among which are the need for multiple skills within the individual or with a group organized so that it can shape an array of tasks; and self-regulation and self-organization, which are radical notions in conventional industrial organizations. Under the principle of self-regulation, only the critical interventions, desired outcomes and organizational maintenance requirements need to be specified by those *managing,* leaving the remainder to those *doing.* Specifically, situations are provided in which individuals or groups accept responsibility for the cycle of activities required to complete the product or service. They establish the rate, quantity and quality of output. They organize the content and structure of their jobs, evaluate their own performance, participate in setting goals and adjust conditions in response to work-system variability.

Research indicates that when the attributes and characteristics of jobs are such that the individual or group becomes largely autonomous in the working situation, then meaningfulness, satisfaction and learning increase significantly, as do wide knowledge of processes, identification with the product, commitment to desired action and responsibility for outcomes. These findings support the development of a job structure that permits social interaction among jobholders and communication with peers and supervisors, particularly when continuity of operation is required. Simultaneously, high performance in quantity and quality of product or service outcomes is achieved. This has been demonstrated in widely different settings.

The content of jobs has to be such that individuals can learn from what is going on around them and can grow, develop and adjust. Relevant here is the psychological concept of self-actualization or personal growth, which appears to be central to the development of motivation and commitment through satisfaction of the higher-order intrinsic needs of individuals. The most potent way of satisfying intrinsic needs may well be through job design. Too often, jobs in conventional industrial organizations have simply required people to adapt to restricted, fractionated activities, overlooking their enormous capacity to learn and adapt to complexity. Such jobs tend also to ignore the organization's need for its workers to adapt. In sophisticated technological settings, the very role of individuals is dependent on their adaptability and commitment. With no one around at a specific instant to tell them what to do, they must respond to the situation and act as needed. The job is also a setting in which psychological and social growth of the individual should take place. Blocked growth leads to distortions, with heavy costs for the individual, the organization and the society. Where the socio-technical system is designed so that the necessary adaptive behavior is facilitated, positive results in economic performance and personal satisfaction have occurred at all levels in organizations.

It surely has always been known, but only lately has it been demonstrated, that part of what a living organism requires to function effectively is a variety of experiences. If people are to be alert and responsive to their working environments, they need variety in the work situation. Routine and repetitious tasks tend to dissipate the individuals. They are there physically, but not in any other way.

Another aspect of the need for variety is less well recognized in the industrial setting today but will become increasingly important in the emergent sophisticated technological environment. Cyberneticist W.R. Ashby (1960) has described this aspect of variety as a general criterion for intelligent behavior of any kind. To Ashby, adequate adaptation is possible only if an organism already has a stored set of responses of the requisite variety. This implies that in the work situation, where unexpected things can happen, the task content of a job and the training for that job should match this potential variability.

Participation of the individual in the decisions affecting his work, in development of job content and organizational relations and in planning of changes is fundamental. Participation plays a role in learning and growth and permits those affected by changes in their roles and environments to develop assessments of the effects.

Implications

The new work ethic has implications for leaders of business and industry, unions and government, some of which will not be easily accommodated, for they require fundamental rethinking of the roles of people in organizations and concomitant modification in organizational form, management, labor contracts and government regulations.

Some of the conclusions are directly contrary to cherished beliefs held at all levels of our society. Widely held beliefs cannot be undermined rapidly—a reason for the slow progress to date. The most significant conclusions and implications can be stated as follows:

- Productivity or efficiency versus the quality of working life is in itself an inappropriate concept. Productivity and quality are not opposite ends of a continuum, but are on two different scales. Enhancing one does not necessarily diminish the other. Under appropriate organizational structure and job design, experience shows that the two are directly related, i.e., both increase together.

- Coercive regulation and control by management begets more coercion. Planning and measuring to achieve and maintain coercive or repressive regulation and control of an organization's members trap both management and unions. They are forced into dead-end situations, with no options for developing suitable social or technical organizations. Urgently required are new ways of measuring outcomes where the social system and its members are considered as resources as much as the technical system and its parts are now. At national as well as company level, the incompleteness of economic theory and supportive accounting systems relegates these concerns to externalities, removing them from organization design and the management decision process. This effect has inhibited considerations of the quality of life.

- Regarding flexibility of technology, the indications are that the opposite of technological determinism is the reality. Results of socio-technical design of factories with sophisticated technology indicate that there is more than enough flexibility on the technological side to suit social system requirements for a high quality of working life. Of course, there are limitations, but the full constraints are not known because almost everywhere engineers are asked to look at and design the technical system independently of any other considerations.

- Self-regulation and control at the workplace through autonomous or semiautonomous jobs and groups yield high levels of satisfaction, self-development and learning and high performance in output and quality. They form the basis for further organizational design to reduce the repressive and coercive character of organizations and resulting worker alienation.

- In all instances where substantial enhancement of the quality of work life has taken place, it was preceded by a rethinking of management ideology about how organizations and individuals work. The ideology of the first industrial revolution regarded man as unreliable, unmotivated and responding only to economic inducements. Men were spare parts in organizations and society. This ideology has had to be reassessed and changed. Though spurred on by the requirements of the second industrial revolution, this reassessment is a slow process and a large undertaking.

References

Ashby, W.R. 1960. *Design for a Brain*. London: Chapman & Hall.

Hill, P. 1971. *Towards a New Philosophy of Management*. London: Gower Press. Excerpted in Vol. II, P. Hill and F. Emery, "Toward a New Philosophy of Management." pp. 259–82.

Ketchum, L. and E. Trist. 1992. *All Teams Are Not Created Equal: How Employee Empowerment Really Works*. Newbury Park, Ca.: Sage Publications.

Calvin Pava

Nonroutine Office Work[1]

Predominantly nonroutine office work often defies traditional socio-technical analysis. Multiple, concurrent, nonlinear conversion processes and professional separation render this approach inapplicable. This paper explores a socio-technical intervention based on the modified procedure. The setting is a software engineering group in a moderate-sized computer systems firm. At the time of the design, the department employed 52 professionals and 12 support staff. The steps taken were as follows:

Step 0: Mapping the Target System

Step 1: Entry, Sanction, Start-up

Step 2: Initial Scan

       Identify the Environment

       Summarize Major Historical, Social and Physical Features

       Formulate the Mission

       Formulate the Philosophy

Step 3: Technical Analysis

       List and Assign Priorities to Deliberations

       Identify Different Forums

       Identify Parties to Each Deliberation

       List Obvious Information Gaps in Each Deliberation

       Analyze Component Office Work Activities for Each Deliberation

Step 4: Social Analysis

       Depict the Role Network

       Summarize Characteristic Values

       Identify Reciprocal Values

       Outline Discretionary Coalitions

Step 5: Work System Design

       Charter Major Deliberations and Discretionary Coalitions

       Chart Responsibility for Major Deliberations

       Design Human Resource Policies that Support Effective Coalitions

Step 6: Approval and Enactment

[1]A revision of Chapter 5 in C.H. Pava, *Managing New Office Technology: An Organizational Strategy.* New York/London: Free Press/Collier Macmillan, 1983.

Step 0: Mapping the Target System

The initial request for organization redesign came from a program team leader in a unit assigned to a large, innovative software development project for a highly advanced system the company was working on. He was concerned that the existing social and technical infrastructure, adequate for smaller projects, would prove insufficient to manage such a large undertaking, and he explored this situation with a consultant.

From the start it was apparent that changing only the organization of a few program team leaders reporting to this single development program leader would not generate much improvement. Instead, a broader change initiative was necessary. At a minimum, the reconfiguration of work would have to embrace the entire software group involved in the computer system development project, perhaps spilling over into hardware engineering. Ultimately, organizing deliberations[2] that spanned all units working on the new computer would result in the tradeoffs necessary for its success.

Step 1: Entry, Sanction, Start-up

The program team leader worked with the consultant to create interest in the proposed design effort. Discussions and instructional materials (cases of redesign in other organizations) eventually persuaded all development program leaders and senior programmers to sanction redesign of the entire software group.

Representatives from different levels and specialties in the software group formed the design team. The team's mandate was to analyze the software group and to propose a more effective social and technical configuration. The team members were also asked briefly to analyze other groups involved in the computer system project and to suggest changes that might be made in their work system.

The development programmer convinced initially skeptical, reluctant top managers to champion the design effort. To do this, the heads of other units involved in the development of the computer system were invited to join a steering committee. This committee would periodically review the design team's work, providing a sounding board and perhaps smoothing the way for redesign of other units participating in the computer development project.

Because of severe time pressure on all team members, it was agreed in advance that the consultant would perform certain tasks on behalf of the design

---

[2]Pava's "deliberations" and "discretionary coalitions" are detailed by Trist in this volume, pp. 662–73.

team; precisely what was initially left open. It was also agreed that the team was to meet once each week for a maximum of five hours and that the steering committee would meet with the design team on a monthly basis, with short updates written weekly by a design team member and the consultant.

Step 2: Initial Scan

The initial scan gets the design team to paint the "big picture"—how the system's software engineering organization has developed and how it currently functions.

IDENTIFY THE ENVIRONMENT

The mission of a work system must be executed in relation to a dynamic environment. Socio-technical theory distinguishes two levels of the environment: the transactional and the contextual. The design team outlined the software group's transactional environment to include hardware engineering, marketing, customer service and divisional organizations. The contextual environment included an increasingly competitive labor market for software engineers; growing customer sophistication in purchase decisions; tight money, with resulting decline in brand loyalty; and stronger competition from innovative software companies. The environmental scan made the design team members more sensitive to the external forces that their work system had to contend with. Specifically, technical elegance alone was no longer sufficient for success. Cost, timely delivery, complementary products and attractiveness to new talent were becoming greater factors in success.

SUMMARIZE MAJOR HISTORICAL, SOCIAL AND PHYSICAL FEATURES

The design team recognized that the software group and other groups involved in the computer system project were too dispersed to permit easy coordination of work. Moreover, the project groups had grown so quickly that there was distrust and misunderstanding between old-timers, who were familiar with each other, and new people, who were not yet considered proven. Finally, the software group had shown a strong tendency to delay "debugging" in past projects. This had led to both premature product release, which exported problems to customers, and delayed product rollout. These outcomes served to generate resentments from the marketing and service organizations.

The initial scan compels design team members to begin viewing their work as a whole, rather than immediately focusing on specific problems or solutions. Also, during these early proceedings, team members begin learning the group dynamics they must master to function effectively as a team. During the initial scan the software group design team settled upon ground rules for conducting its work. Finally, the scan made historical and other trends vivid, opening up areas of discussion hitherto closed and encouraging people to reflect and take action jointly on phenomena over which they had previously exercised little control. This capacity to identify and manage institutional issues was an outcome of the initial scan, which endured longer than any particular substantive finding.

Formulate the Mission

The design team defined the group's mission: to provide advanced system functions and reliable programs that served customer needs at minimum economic and social cost. Mission statements sound glib to some but represent careful consideration. Team members linked specific top-priority objectives in their group's mission (such as advanced functions, reliable programs, customer service and minimum costs) to key elements of the company's strategy. Commitment to providing advanced system functions arose from the advanced nature of the software project, which was intended to deliver a higher level of cost performance than earlier products. Concern for reliability was based on earlier experiences with hasty debugging that had exported software problems to customers and impeded rapid buildup of market share. Serving customer needs was a priority rooted in the firm's renowned orientation to market responsiveness (especially adopting popular features before other firms). Minimum costs were important in light of the firm's tight capital and the need to keep good people from burning out. Emphasis upon programs rather than code was particularly meaningful; it represented a fundamental reconceptualization of the software group's business. Typically, priority had been given to code, or individual lines of commands written into a program. "The number of good lines of code per day" was a standard way of assessing performance in the software group. But the industry trend was that software products were becoming much more complex. As this shift occurred, interrelations between subsections of a program became more critical. To do a good job, system analysts and programmers had to be cognizant of much more than the subsections of code that they were immediately responsible for composing. Reference to a bigger picture was vital, especially in the later stages, as correction of any one part of the program required alteration of other modules. The design team decided to shift everyone's focus by designating good overall programs as the mission of the unit's efforts. The mission statement was reviewed with the steering committee, which proceeded to sanction it.

FORMULATE THE PHILOSOPHY

The design team articulated a philosophy about the way people should be managed in the software group:

- With sufficient understanding and skills, employees are professionally suited to a high degree of self-direction within a framework of mutual honesty and mutual constraint.
- Not all employees seek identical career development. Both specialist and generalist talent are needed by the software group. Multiple paths of development are therefore necessary to create a variety of alternatives. Such development must be supported by individual initiative, joint discussions and periodic formal appraisals.

Like the mission statement, this philosophy may initially sound glib. Yet interpreted in the context of the software unit's history, it diplomatically summarized important value choices. The first clause, calling for professional self-direction with mutual honesty and constraint, was an attempt to strike a firm balance between extreme authoritarianism and participative management, styles between which the group had earlier oscillated. The second clause, referring to career development, sought to legitimize a rising need for different talents as the business grew, a situation that previously had led to petty status distinctions and arbitrary promotion decisions. Hence, the philosophy statement involved human resource issues that were vital to the group's continued success.

Step 3: Technical Analysis

Nonroutine office work predominantly involves multiple, often nonlinear, conversion processes. This part of the analysis proceeds by mapping deliberations; the traditional variance matrix is used only for strictly routine tasks.

LIST AND ASSIGN PRIORITIES TO DELIBERATIONS

Technical analysis of nonroutine office work begins with listing all deliberations in which managers and professionals take part. This is done by having the design team specify what topics must be settled for the unit's mission to be fulfilled. Accordingly, the design team identified over 35 deliberations that went on within the software engineering group and between this group and its environment, including:

- stipulation of system features;
- outline of system documentation;
- PERT (Program Evaluation and Review Technique) timeline development and management;
- test/target machine allocations;
- employee development and advancement;
- declaration of different design editions;
- keeping pace with hardware changes;
- adjudicating model debugging with integrity of initial system architecture;
- reconciling late debugging compromises with initial system specifications.

It took the team some time to decide what constituted a deliberation. Then alternative formulations were tried in order to produce the right balance of parsimony and detail. After the list was settled on, the team rank-ordered the items to ensure that the more important deliberations would be fully analyzed. Less vital deliberations would be analyzed partially or on an as-needed basis. The team chose thus to analyze 18 of the more than 35 rank-ordered deliberations.

IDENTIFY DIFFERENT FORUMS

At this point, the design team was asked to identify the different forums in which each major topic was to be deliberated and to classify these forums according to their level of formality (structured, semistructured and unstructured). A sample of the analysis appears in Table 1.

IDENTIFY PARTIES TO EACH DELIBERATION

Next, a design team will specify who is involved in each important deliberation. First, a list of current participants is drawn up. Second, information taken from the deliberation and information contributed to it are noted for each participant. Third, a revised list noting who ideally should be party to the deliberation is posted, excluding current participants who do not belong and including overlooked parties. Finally, the ideal list is annotated to indicate what information each party brings to the deliberation. These data are set aside for use during the social analysis, which follows the technical analysis. The

TABLE 1   Forums Associated with a Major Deliberation: Stipulate System Features

Type of forum	Topic
Structured	Annual strategic planning cycle Industry reports and periodicals Quarterly marketing reports Beta test site conference and user conference
Semistructured	Conventions and conferences Post-project reviews Division and corporate technical seminars
Unstructured	Troubleshooting customer problems Ad hoc technical discussions and exchanges

software design team used the procedure outlined here, and a portion of this analysis is summarized in Table 2.

List Obvious Information Gaps in Each Deliberation

At this point, the design team was asked to reflect on the analysis already done and to identify obvious gaps or cracks where information goes astray in each major deliberation. To do this, each major deliberation's topic is listed and, reviewing the information collected thus far, the team identifies evident gaps. This often proves to be one of the most useful points in the design process for gathering information. For example, the design team arranged interviews with other people in the software group. Most interviews were conducted by the consultant on behalf of the design team. Table 3 indicates how several major deliberations appeared to the team in terms of information cracks.

Analyze Component Office Work Activities for Each Deliberation

The next phase of technical analysis had the design team scrutinize each important deliberation in terms of its component office work activities in order to highlight less obvious problems and opportunities for improvement. The design team was asked to suggest problems or improvements in a standard list of component office activities applied to every key deliberation. This exercise provided the basis for constructing an information activity matrix. The team's analysis of one key deliberation is shown in Table 4.

TABLE 2   Parties Ideally Associated with a Major Deliberation: Declare Different Design Editions

Ideal participants	Information taken from deliberation	Information contributed to deliberation
Senior programmers	Progress reports and reviews Interface with hardware engineers on pending hardware changes	Overall perspective Adjudication Enforce integrity of architecture
Program team leaders	Progress report and review backup Gauge team capability	Realism of decisions against team realities
Market-segment managers	Beta site and customer reports Knowledge of competitors	Viability of choices against user base and competitor realities
Project document control	Overview all documentation	Implement new additions in archives
Senior system engineers	Familiarity with pending options	Fit against imminent hardware changes

TABLE 3   Obvious Information Gaps in Selected Major Deliberations

Deliberation	Gaps
Stipulate system features	Marketing information overly aggregated—no tangible punch Slow documentation transfer between hardware and software engineering Long-term strategy not clear enough to inform choices Field engineers neither receive nor contribute
PERT development and management	Project managers do not get full information on team Marketing not warned soon enough of delays and release impacts PERT changes poorly distributed
Declare different design editions	No summaries of recent updates Poor integration between existing standards and updates Poor distribution of update documents to software engineers at dispersed locations Bad proofreading of updates

TABLE 4 Component Work Activities of a Major Deliberation: Stipulate System Features

Component Activity	Issue
Type	WP operators find principals inaccessible for questions Erroneous documents
File	Suggested ideas not available in one spot Different drafts lost
Dispatch/receive/sort mail	Company mail sub takes too long to sort mail
Dictate/read/reflect/doodle	Reports not organized for easy scanning Excessive wait for computer time to do financial and time projections
Compose/draft	Multiple authors must wait for each other's copy
Schedule	Meetings impossible to schedule
Meet/travel	Someone always must travel for a meeting No plane to meet if unscheduled
Discuss	No good records of ad hoc technical sessions
Phone	Telephone tag between software and marketing

To summarize, socio-technical theory requires the design team to scrutinize both the technical and the social subsystem of the workplace. Although the technical analysis is now complete, achieving the best fit between the two subsystems demands careful examination of the social network.

Step 4: Social Analysis

In the social analysis, the design team is required to examine closely the network of parties to key deliberations. These parties must effectively function as discretionary coalitions if the work system is to attain informed trade-offs and long-term success.

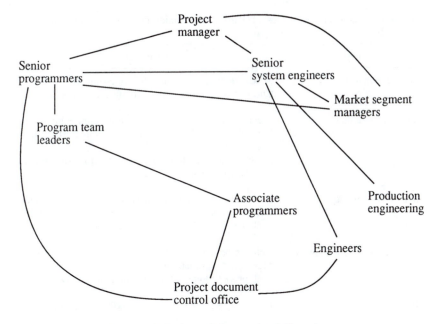

Figure 1. Role network for a major deliberation

DEPICT THE ROLE NETWORK

To begin, the design team sketches the role network for each major deliberation. Earlier analysis helps this task proceed quickly. The list of participants in
each key deliberation drawn up in the technical analysis is retrieved. Often, a
design team will adopt its own diagrammatic conventions in mapping role
networks. For example, different kinds of connecting lines could signify
different sorts of relationships, and size of circles and distance could represent
the relative power and proximity of parties. A deliberation role network drawn
by the software design team appears in Figure 1.

SUMMARIZE CHARACTERISTIC VALUES

Next, the design team is guided to summarize the orientations that typify each
party in the major deliberations. Interviews and informal discussions can be
used to confirm initial impressions. An example of one such listing is given in
Table 5.

TABLE 5 Characteristic Values of Parties to a Major Deliberation: Declare New Design Editions

Party	Orientation
Project manager	Maximize hardware and software change fit Curtail features that intrude on other business lines
Senior programmers	Clearly stipulate closing dates for different editions Prevent system changes from undermining established architecture Delay edition cutoff announcements to maximize maneuvering room
Senior system engineers	Keep software changes from wagging hardware changes Get early maximum information on pending software changes
Market-segment managers	Achieve delivery date targets at all costs Make product reliably improved—no great leaps Link proposed upgrades with competitor moves
Program team leaders	Do not squeeze troops with inflexible design cutoffs
Associate programmers	Get a fair shot at refining initial products Get clear cutoffs on different editions in advance Acknowledge late cuts only if they help team make specs
System engineers	Keep software changes from shaping all hardware design Resist design cutoffs that render previous solutions ineffective
Documentation control	Be sure that everyone receives and acknowledges edition cutoffs
Production engineers	Low cogs

IDENTIFY RECIPROCAL VALUES

The design team must identify divergent orientations of parties who are interdependent by virtue of engagement in the same deliberation. These orientations constitute the reciprocal values that must be balanced in discretionary coalitions. Usually, this identification is done in a separate diagram (Figure 2),

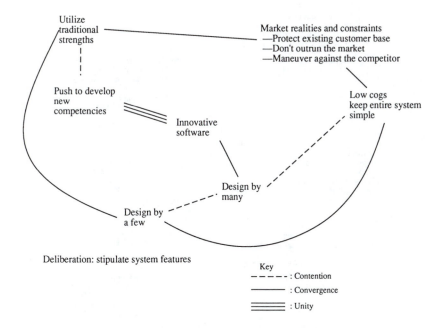

Figure 2. Reciprocal values of parties to a major deliberation

but it can also take the form of value orientations added to the chart of characteristic values.

OUTLINE DISCRETIONARY COALITIONS

Finally, the design team must identify the parties who characteristically take divergent positions. By balancing opposite interests, a discretionary coalition can guide deliberations to produce intelligent trade-offs. Figure 3 indicates how the design team set up a discretionary coalition. Through the social analysis, the design team decides what discretionary coalitions to organize in order to render key deliberations productive.

To summarize, analyzing the social subsystem of nonroutine office work reveals discretionary coalitions needed to run the deliberations identified earlier in the analysis of the technical subsystem. The method of social analysis proposed here illuminates reciprocal points of view needed in deliberation and traces out the parties that champion these perspectives, with emphasis on a mix of viewpoints and players that can render informed trade-offs on a sustained basis.

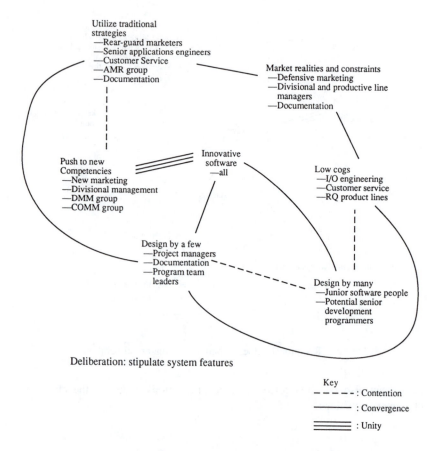

Figure 3. Discretionary coalition organized around a major deliberation

Step 5: Work System Design

The final step of socio-technical analysis for nonroutine office work is to formulate design proposals that best match the technical and the social sub-system. The preceding analysis permits informed judgments about how the work system could be more effectively organized. In addition, socio-technical theory suggests some coherent, fundamental changes in nonroutine office work configurations that are likely to create a high commitment, high performance organization.

TABLE 6   Charter of a Major Deliberation: Stipulate System Features

Mission	To define new product and product enhancement features that contribute to greater share in current and future markets. Vital to attain cost/functionality with timely completion. Cost is more elastic than time. New developments must permit migration from the product series.
Forums	Strategic and operation planning Quarterly marketing reviews Monthly product-line forum Customer service task force Ad hoc coffee room sessions with product marketing Weekly suggestion listing Real-time module and system manager updates
Participants and orientation	See corresponding responsibility chart, notes, and videotape.

CHARTER MAJOR DELIBERATIONS AND DISCRETIONARY COALITIONS

The design team can start to outline a high performance organization by chartering the major deliberations through which discretionary coalitions must strike intelligent trade-offs. Typically, this charter states the topic of a deliberation, its purpose and importance (sometimes linked with a principal organizational strategy) and the various forums through which the deliberation is pursued. At this point, the team may propose chartering deliberations not uncovered in the technical analysis. An example of a charter by the software design team is shown in Table 6.

CHART RESPONSIBILITY ROLES FOR MAJOR DELIBERATIONS

This chart can help the design team to suggest specific forms of contribution for different coalition members. An effective deliberation does not require that every party to it have the same form of involvement; often different forms of participation are best. A responsibility chart is an analytic tool that a design team can use to suggest how different parties can be involved in a coalition. A responsibility chart shows the preferred contribution of each party to a deliberation.

The software design team chose to do only enough responsibility charting to

TABLE 7   Responsibility Chart for a Major Deliberation: Declare Different Design Editions

	Task					
Party	Propose updates	Propose bundling updates	Collate revisions	Verify debug test	Document	Announce
Senior programmers	A	A	I	I	—	A
Program team leaders	R	C	C	R	C	C
Market-segment managers	—	C	I	—	C	R
Project documentation control	I	R	R	C	R	I
Senior logic system engineers	I	—	—	—	—	I

R = Responsible to initiate and carry through; C = Consult; I = Inform; A = Approve; — = No involvement

be able later to teach this technique. The team thought that charting should be done by actual coalition members, perhaps aided by design team members. Practice charts were made both to train team members as facilitators and to serve as instructional material. Table 7 reproduces one such practice chart.

DESIGN HUMAN RESOURCE POLICIES THAT SUPPORT EFFECTIVE COALITIONS

The design team must suggest ways in which myriad other organizational factors can be made to complement the work of discretionary coalitions. Aided by suggestions from their consultant, the software engineering group design team considered four major areas in which changes might be needed and made substantive recommendations for each. Among the suggested changes in each area were:

Compensation. Base greater proportion of bonuses paid to senior engineers and staff above this level upon division performance. Allocate more discretionary funds to interfunctional groups for small joint development projects to promote familiarity and trust across unit boundaries. Cease to tie word processing operator pay to key strokes per hour; this was found to encourage documentation errors.

Promotion and personnel development. Begin planning selective diagonal promotion within specialties to groom people for positions in general management. Develop programs to move all professionals out into the user environment at least twice a year. This exposure could help them appreciate marketing's problems. Provide updates of market developments to engineering professionals on a regular basis. Conversely, inform marketing on a regular basis of new capabilities that could be offered to customers. Quarterly briefings are suggested in order to provide an ad hoc form of training on viewpoints across functions.

Symbolic recognition. Bolster the availability of documentation by creating a more direct reporting relationship between the head of software documentation and the manager of the computer system development project. Too often, limited records impede development. A more direct relation should help make documentation a higher priority in terms of both resource allocation and compliance. Refurbish meeting rooms to make them more pleasant; especially, improve lighting and seating, and install snack machines. Current spartan meeting facilities encourage people to skip meetings. Give market-segment managers larger offices, with meeting tables and enamel writing boards. This improvement would put them on a more level status with senior engineers and allow them to convene ad hoc sessions in their offices.

Ground rules and yardsticks. Begin to inculcate ground rules for the firm's own style and method of operation. Everyone in the firm comes from a different background; thus, everybody has his or her own way of doing things. Develop programs to give people exposure to more common styles of management and to teach them the necessary skills. Initial areas of improvement include conflict resolution and summarizing information in meetings. Establish measures that underscore the importance of entire programs over the sheer value of code. Develop indices of program functionality to encourage an orientation toward performance of programs as a whole. Possible functionality measures include number of program subsections versus number of bugs between modules at late project stages; actual versus targeted performance of the entire program; and actual versus projected costs for the entire development. Developing completely accurate or conclusive indices is impossible, but ongoing efforts to measure effectiveness—the final product overall—will increase commitment to entire program systems and encourage learning.

Suggest structural changes. Specialize the phases of system design more narrowly. Close off bottom-up suggestions at a definite time and then finalize specifications based on the final choice of a few key people (programming team leaders and senior programmers, in consultation with marketing and logic design). Start a liaison group between documentation and software units to assess continually and upgrade documentation routines. This group should report directly to a group of senior programmers. Institute special councils to assess periodically the quality of each deliberation. Each council should include some top managers who would be able to sanction needed changes.

Technical enhancements. Finally, the design team will suggest changes in office technology to assist the major deliberations. First, the team should propose new information handling procedures; these specify how information is to be gathered, recorded, deciphered, circulated, reviewed and reformulated. Although the procedures stipulate what sorts of information and exchange must exist, they may not necessarily spell out how all this information handling is to proceed. At this time, the software engineering group design team recommended a number of new procedures:

- Circulation of software group PERT scheduling charts and monthly update summaries to market-segment managers.
- Regular contact between programming team leaders to chart compatibility between subroutines before entire program modules are put together; also provision of regular access to portions of semifinished programs before release to central files.
- Quarterly updates to the entire software group on market conditions and especially on competitor activity.

Next, the design team suggests new devices to implement existing and proposed procedures. The team should construct a list of procedures that need improvement and identify both high and low technology solutions. The software group design team recommended advanced office technology for some unautomated applications, but a variety of less flashy technical changes also were proposed. Many of these would establish organized information that could later quite easily migrate to advanced communications and computing systems. A sample of the design team's technical suggestions is shown in Table 8.

Step Six: Approval and Enactment

With the design proposal finished, the team organized a special meeting to communicate findings to the steering committee. A number of changes were approved—some proposed by the design team, others suggested by the steering committee. Once a final design was settled, the steering committee and design team formulated a transition plan. The transition plan specified how the proposed design would be made operational. It recommended briefing sessions for all members of the software design group, subsequent revision and approval in the design, training in conflict resolution skills for all coalition

TABLE 8   Selected Technical Recommendations

	Gap or procedure	
Suggested enhancements	*Program Evaluation and Review Technique (PERT) chart tracking*	*Regular Program Team Leader (PTL) contact*
Low technology enhancements	Local copying (protocol for common update notation) Make review part of program team leader sessions: weekly and midcourse project reviews	Bigger boards and tables in PTL offices Polaroids to capture board info.
High technology enhancements	Interface costing estimation for software and PERT programs Weekly updates via electronic mail distribution Digital store and forward voice messaging	Computer messaging to end telephone tag Provide small portable terminals for remote taps Phone conference between Bendrel and Wallace sites (with slow scan TV?)

members and periodic revision. The overall effect was to improve the quality and speed of development work in and beyond the software group. Coordination and problem solving among professional functions improved, deadlines were met with greater frequency and the work setting became less stressful.

Eric Trist

Pava's Extension of Socio-Technical Theory to Advanced Information Technologies[1]

Like many people, I have been waiting for a book that would guide me through the maze of multidimensional issues to which the advent of advanced office technology gives rise. Calvin Pava has written such a book, the first, in my knowledge, to combine in one account the technical and social aspects of office organization; the complete range of activities undertaken from very routine to entirely nonroutine; and the macro-implications for the wider society as well as the micro-implications for the office itself. As the title *Managing New Office Technology* (Pava, 1983/Vol. II) suggests, he is concerned with the management of these interacting aspects and processes, which are not as likely to produce beneficial outcomes simply of their own accord as the apostles of automation would lead us to expect; rather will they require an expansion of management concern to factors in the environment usually regarded as beyond its purview, while extending internally the role of informed choice.

This approach is a far cry from the prevailing perspective, which concentrates attention on the technological aspect so that what the equipment makers propose is solemnly installed with the eager support of data-processing and internal "systems" staffs. Absent is any informed scrutiny of organizational and social aspects. This absence has untoward consequences: the creation at the lower levels of large numbers of poorly designed jobs that lower performance and increase alienation; failure to appreciate the subtle yet profound changes required in managerial and professional roles; the export to the labor market of those made redundant without serious thought to their retraining or future place in society.

What is happening in the office is presented as part of a wider revolution centered on the microprocessor which, during the present and subsequent decades, will establish an information society in the midst of the older industrial society. This revolution is proceeding at an accelerating rate, but there is

[1]Originally published as an Epilogue to C.H.P. Pava, *Managing New Office Technology: An Organizational Strategy.* New York: Free Press; London: Collier Macmillan, 1983.

scant recognition of the depth and scope of the changes entailed. While some general concern has been expressed over the likelihood of unabsorbable unemployment and scenarios have been offered of both extreme centralization and extreme decentralization, little has so far been said concerning new modes of organization which more advanced technologies make possible in the office itself. Unless the potentiality of these alternative organizational modes is realized, the negative effects of following the technological imperative will spill over into the wider society in a way that no external correctives can remedy. Only an internal revolution in the structure and cultural fabric (to use Pava's term) of the office itself can supply the necessary conditions for the realization of beneficial outcomes. Yet internal revolution alone will not be sufficient. For the necessary and sufficient conditions to be realized, wider changes in social values and legislative provision must also take place.

In Pava's book, both these issues are addressed and the interconnections between them are unraveled. He shows how changes in the office can enable the enterprise to reach out proactively into the surrounding society and how changes in the latter can then more easily link back to internal changes. Virtuous as opposed to vicious circles can thence be created, though how much of the former will depend in a far-reaching way on the choices made and the initiatives taken (over the next 10 to 15 years) by those in leadership positions—the managers, in both the private and public sectors.

Fortunately, there have arisen in organizational studies a theory and practice that have disestablished the technological imperative from the long reign of unchallenged rule, which has created the technocratic bureaucracies that still remain the predominant organizational form in advanced industrial societies but which are becoming increasingly dysfunctional in view of the higher levels of complexity, interdependence and uncertainty present in the contemporary environment. I refer to the socio-technical approach that is concerned with discovering the best match between the social and technical systems in any organization in which people must use technology to accomplish their objectives. A full-dress exposition of this approach is given in Pava's book, one of the very few comprehensive accounts to be offered. Not unnaturally, socio-technical studies originated in productive organizations, but more recently a large amount of empirical work has been undertaken in administrative establishments. Little, however, has been done to extend either theory or methods of analysis to the particular needs of the latter. Unless this is done, the chances are small of avoiding the bad consequences of introducing advanced technology into these settings. Yet in an appropriate extension lies the best hope of developing an office of the future that at one and the same time will be human and high performing.

The present book makes very substantial advances on what has so far been accomplished toward this end. In order to do this its author has had first to enlarge the notion of technology—to break it free of hardware constraints. The introduction of more advanced devices and procedures has had the paradoxical effect of etherealizing them in the form of what he has called "deliberations." Next, he has had to clarify types of organizational form hitherto only dimly perceived—to break socio-technical theory free from the monopolizing idea of the autonomous work group. Third, he has had to extend the methods of work analysis from those suitable for single linear conversion processes to those that can meet the demands of concurrent multiple nonlinear conversion processes. These additions occasion the introduction of a new conceptual language. Terms such as deliberations, discretionary coalitions, saturated interdependence, artificial rationality, micromyopia and stakeholder comanagement are not jargon but names for new referents essential for the field's advance.

These innovations stem from Pava's having chosen to deal with the full range of activities that take place in office settings and therefore to include managerial and professional work rather than to restrict himself to the more routinized aspects of information processing. These latter are the type of activity commonly thought of as being carried out by most office workers, but conceptually they are no different from the type of routine work carried out by most factory workers, for both belong to the same major technological family which Thompson (1967) called the long-linked technology. In this technology the various steps of a conversion process follow each other in a linear sequence which has one outcome; there may be several such processes each with its own outcome going on in parallel, or in succession, where the output of (a) is the input of (b); but the underlying logic is the same. This being so, it is not surprising that routine factory work and routine office work can be treated within the same socio-technical paradigm, so that work redesign for both can follow the pattern of the self-managing work group.

As the level of entirely nonroutine activities is approached, this pattern becomes infeasible. Conversion processes are multiple, concurrent and nonlinear; skills are too complex to permit cross training; the work culture is that of the individual professional or manager who yet must collaborate with colleagues. By saying that the technological system for such work consists of deliberations, Pava has pinpointed the fact that the technology involved has become cognitive. The conversion processes entail the transformation of equivocal, ill-defined, ambiguous, conflicting issues into problems that can be dealt with. Since the topics to be deliberated vary immensely, so do the requisite resources, which tend to be assembled in temporary systems. These are the characteristics of Thompson's (1967) intensive technology but, valuable as his distinction has been between this technological family and those of the mediating and long-linked technologies, Thompson did not identify its core content. This is what Pava has done.

In introducing his idea of deliberation, a generic concept that covers a whole miscellany of unprogrammed activities, he has identified a dimension of professional and managerial work that has so far gone unrecognized. This dimension has been obscured by a too exclusive concentration on decision making. Deliberations are not in themselves decisions but their hinterland, which constitutes the world of cognitive technique. Deliberations provide a new unit of analysis, the equivalent for the intensive technology of unit operations for the long-linked technology. They involve determining the full range of pertinent topics, analyzing their components and ensuring their examination through a series of forums (structured, semi-structured or unstructured), in which all the relevant parties present their various perspectives so that optimum trade-offs can be achieved. This technology comprises a methodology for what McWhinney (1980) has called the resolution of complex issues.

The combination of advanced computer and communications technology, referred to by the French as télématique, creates conditions that potentially increase very substantially the capacity for deliberation. Far higher levels of complexity can be comprehended, prodigious amounts of information rapidly summarized and retrieved, many alternatives compared without incurring intolerable fatigue and all these data and analyses checked and shared with an immediacy hitherto impossible. When the generations now being brought up on the computer begin to engage in managerial and professional activities, this capacity for deliberation should be strengthened beyond its present range. Any such strengthening will be fully utilized in coping with the complexities and uncertainties emanating from an increasingly turbulent environment (Emery and Trist, 1965). Automating the routine advanced technology will accomplish a figure/ground reversal of attention and effort from instruments to operations. The bulk of a manager's time and energy can now be spent on addressing the issues rather than in laborious preparation to get to the point. The possibility is therefore imminent of being able to deliberate more topics at a higher level of competence and of doing more of the work that at present tends to be left undone because it is either too difficult or too time-consuming. One may even hope that the urgent will less often drive out the important.

Deliberation is a social as well as a cognitive process that proceeds in terms of what Pava has called discretionary coalitions, the temporary groups or network nodes formed by whatever parties are necessary to conduct particular deliberations. The salience of discretionary coalitions constitutes a figure/ground reversal in the organizational sphere parallel to that in the technical sphere, which pushes physical instruments into the background and gives the foreground to cognitive techniques. Unless the organizational changes take place, the technical possibilities will remain unrealized.

In conventional technocratic and bureaucratic organizations the structural foreground is occupied by static positions that delineate the responsibilities of the officeholders and their authority to discharge them. These positions carry ownership of expertise and access to privileged knowledge in ways that falsely politicize the resolution of complex issues, which depend on pooled knowledge and interpositional collaboration. Complex issues are the rule rather than the exception in nonroutine office work. The discretionary coalitions brought into existence by deliberations yield a novel organizing principle in relation to which the static positions of the organization chart become scaffolding and retreat into the background.

These coalitions form and reform themselves according to the needs of particular deliberations. Their purpose is to obtain the best outcomes from the inputs of multiple perspectives. The issues are not owned by any one position but by the coalition. This minimizes false politics and maximizes true negotiation among parties carrying divergent but relevant values. The goal is optimum trade-offs leading to the best informed choices.

In reading Pava's account of this process I was forcibly reminded of my experience as a staff officer in World War II. During wartime the environment is changing so rapidly and in so many unexpected ways that military organization has constantly to redeploy itself to ensure that the relevant resources are brought to bear on the issues arising. One therefore found oneself moving from setting to setting and conferring with a wide range of people of varying rank about different matters even during the course of a single day. Given the rapid change and high uncertainty now prevailing, the business environment is becoming more like a wartime environment. The need is greater therefore in nonroutine work to bring discretionary coalitions into the foreground. For this to happen, easily and reliably, the alternative organizing principle which presupposes openness and trust rather than possessiveness and suspicion needs to be explicitly recognized. This explicit recognition is demanded by Pava's analysis. The logic is difficult to avoid—if difficult to implement—given the inheritance of older and opposite ways.

That there might be other forms of nonhierarchical organization than autonomous work groups was first recognized in the socio-technical literature by Herbst (1976/Vol. II), whose discussion of alternatives to hierarchy identified the additional forms of matrices and networks. In the former, the skills and competences were only partially interchangeable. Matrices were neither autonomous work groups nor bureaucratic hierarchies; rather were they what Schwartz and Ogilvie (1980) have called "heterarchies." They compose project groups that form the basis of Pava's product line-market-segment organizations prominent in the hybrid form of office work. Herbst treats certain distinctive properties of networks such as the lack of need among their members to be copresent in space and time and their ability to foster and maintain fields of directive correlations over long periods. Lacking a concept of deliberations, however, he was unable to identify discretionary coalitions as the type of network formation that is brought into existence by the unprogrammed but interactive character of a great deal of day-to-day managerial and professional work.

Concerned with the lower levels of organizations employing long-linked technologies, early socio-technical studies concentrated on self-managing work groups. Though the concept of self-regulation was extended to every organizational level so that the organization as a whole was seen as a series of mutually articulated self-regulating systems, which made it both flatter and leaner, this model did not spell out the nature of the self-regulation required at the high levels. The implicit assumption that it proceeded throughout on the basis of self-managing work groups with interchangeable skills and pooled identity was obviously untenable; but no alternatives were offered. Emery's (1976/Vol. II) concept of senior functional managers maximizing their contributions to the whole rather than their own domains, though seminal, is still a work group analogue. The concept of discretionary coalitions in relation to deliberations offers for the first time an operational approach to the analysis of managerial and professional work in a nonhierarchical perspective. However much the hierarchical scaffolding may still be in the background, it is the unprogrammable sequences of coalitional formations that must become salient at the higher levels of any organization if it is to succeed in coping with substantial degrees of complexity, interdependence and uncertainty. This is consistent with project organization of the matrix type at the middle levels and with self-managing primary work groups at the lower levels. Taken together, these three forms provide a complete organizational alternative to the traditional technocratic bureaucracy. Furthermore, it would seem that deliberational coalitions are likely to become increasingly pervasive further down in the organization.

Pava's analysis offers a more general organizational theory than that pertaining to office work, though a great deal of an organization's nonroutine unprogrammable work goes on in office settings. The concepts of deliberations and discretionary coalitions provide the tools for a socio-technical analysis of managerial work modeled in Emery's (1967; 1976/Vol. II) alternative design principle (the redundancy of function rather than the redundancy of parts). How to use these tools is illustrated in an analysis of the activities of a design team in a software engineering group, which are traced through step by step. Emphasis is given to obtaining a revised perspective on "the bigger picture" in which the unit is embedded, through environmental scanning and redefinition of mission, taking into account the production of programs rather than codes. The thoroughgoing search process entailed is undertaken before the step-by-step analyses of the technical and social systems themselves are made on lines which differ considerably from the procedures used for long-linked technologies, though the theory is the same. Attention is paid to the difficulty of obtaining enough time from senior executives, which puts an extra load on the consultant, but care is taken to involve all parties so that organizational learning can become as complete as possible. Any organization that experiences such a process will undergo deep change in its cultural fabric and structural form.

The offices of many organizations cover the entire range of activities from very routine to completely nonroutine, with a good deal of their work taking place at the hybrid level. The organizational changes outlined in Pava's models are all in the same direction so that the outcome is a self-consistent alternative to the technocratic bureaucracy. If the top or middle levels remain in the old paradigm while the bottom level changes to self-managing work groups, or if badly designed jobs are left at the bottom while at the top and in the middle discretionary coalitions and project groups become salient, dysfunctional dissonance may be expected, giving rise sooner or later to unmanageable conflict or irreversible estrangement.

In addition to a change in salience from physical to cognitive technology and from staff-line hierarchies to discretionary coalitions, Pava suggests that advanced office technology is tending to produce a third figure/ground reversal—from a preoccupation with efficiency to a greater concentration on effectiveness. Efficiency is concerned with the best use of resources inside the organization. The more automatic its attainment, the less need efficiency consume human attention, which is then freed to grapple with the complexities and uncertainties of the environment that are rendering organizational survival ever more problematic under conditions of turbulence. Effectiveness therefore needs to become a prominent concern in the work of those at every organizational level, even those concerned with the highly routinized activities of Pava's order-taking and customer-service examples.

Though Chester Barnard (1938) introduced the distinction between efficiency and effectiveness early in the development of organizational theory, most of the effort since then has been devoted to perfecting internal controls whose elaboration has proceeded in terms of scientific management. That this has been overdone is now widely recognized, and self-managing work groups have gone far to redress the balance and produce higher efficiency, while simultaneously increasing job satisfaction. Advanced technology can vastly increase the efficiency of office work, but this should not be the main goal, which is rather making use of efficiency gains to improve effectiveness.

To a far greater extent than previously recognized, achieving this goal will entail managing the organization proactively in collaboration with its stakeholders, external as well as internal. The list of stakeholders, actual and potential, is lengthening as society changes. Pava gives an account of how stakeholder groups gain in both self-awareness and public recognition as they progress in status from unorganized interests to interest groups, to claimants and to stakeholders proper who have power as well as voice. The point is forcibly made that the enterprise can no longer wait until such groups are pounding on its door. Early detection of those likely to become important is required. Early two-way engagement with them needs to be undertaken so that goals can be harmonized where possible and unnecessary conflicts avoided. The idea of stakeholder comanagement is a relatively recent one, but it is likely to gain hold as environmental interdependencies increase. Advanced technology in the office can greatly assist this aspect of the management of effectiveness.

The process, however, needs to be two-way. Other organizations, particularly government (at all levels) but also unions and professional and educational organizations, must reach out toward the enterprise from their own bases. For example, all the responsibility for the unemployment likely to follow in the wake of the microprocessor revolution cannot be taken on by the enterprise alone. Legislative provision will have to be made for retraining and reallocation on a scale not so far contemplated and with an imagination not so far shown, even though the enterprise itself must do very much more.

The three figure/ground reversals which have been discussed are parts of the same fundamental change process which society and the enterprise are undergoing in relation to each other. The advent of advanced office technology makes these reversals obtrude massively into the managerial and institutional levels of organizational life as distinct from the technical levels, to use Parsons's (1960) terminology. So long as these reversals could be kept within the technical core they did not radically change the character of the organization as a whole. Now that advanced office technology has brought them into the levels where multiple trade-offs have to be negotiated and value changes fashioned in relation to the wider stakeholder environment, a paradigm shift is heralded.

The office revolution is the final stage of the organizational revolution. In place of the technocratic bureaucracy that matched a less complex, less interdependent but more stable environment, there is arising a reticulist form of organization adapted to more turbulent conditions. To attain and maintain a level of effectiveness that will make the difference regarding survival, this emergent form must strengthen its capacity to conduct deliberations, assemble discretionary coalitions and deploy project teams and primary work groups supported, but not dominated, by its more static form of organization or its array of procedures and devices, however sophisticated. The paradox is that greater technological sophistication will throw more rather than less weight on how the human side performs, albeit that there will be fewer human beings around. The recent survey of corporate excellence by Peters and Waterman (1982) suggests that this trend is already apparent in many of the best run American companies, where the organizational complexities inherent in multiple interfacing and flexible deployment are rendered endurable by the relatively simple structures of a more static kind on which they rest. By the end of the decade it will be evident that the ascent of the S curve of systematic organizational change has been undertaken in earnest.

The office revolution, though radical, will not take place abruptly or across the board. It will occur incrementally and unevenly, though the rate will accelerate. This is in keeping with Pava's (1980) more general theory of planned change as a nonsynoptic process which he has called "normative incrementalism"—normative because value change is at the heart of substantial as distinct from marginal innovation (Burns and Chevalier, 1978). The great advantage of normative incrementalism is that it gives full scope for learning to take place over the extended time period required for a paradigm shift to establish itself. Many improvements will be made in diverse settings and pioneers and early adapters will learn from each other's, as well as their own, experiences—against the moving ground of a changing environment.

Nevertheless, the learning process can be hastened by the provision of good maps and step-by-step guidelines. These are provided in Chapters 4, 5 and 6 of Pava's book in the examples of projects that the author has personally conducted with routine, nonroutine and mixed types of office work. Attention is drawn to the need to set any proposed change in its larger context, both environmental and organizational, and to be case-specific regarding how far linear work analysis is appropriate or how far modified procedures more suitable for nonroutine components should be introduced—or a mixture of both. A distinction is drawn between analysis and design. The latter does not issue automatically from the former, though it is founded on it. Design has its own perspective and involves sensitive negotiation with all stakeholders. The importance of their inclusion is critical when it comes to implementation, for unless user ownership has been established, resistance is to be expected. The opportunity for organizational learning will not have been given. Involvement is a factor on which both democracy and enlightenment are conditional. Moreover, design does not finish when operations begin; in one sense it is never finished and depends for its elaboration on operational experience. User contributions become the basis of further discovery and engender the excitement that renews commitment. Design proceeds best by "minimum critical specifications" (Herbst, 1974/ Vol. II), which provide the most valid criteria for decision making under conditions of uncertainty.

The book, therefore, is a "practicum" as well as a "theoreticum." Without the theoretical framework the cogency of the practical steps would not be appreciated but, unless these steps had been set out, the practitioner would be left without a "how to" tool kit. Of special importance is the identification of a limit, beyond which the conventional nine-step model of socio-technical analysis becomes infeasible, and the development of an alternative, which can take over as the level of routineness associated with single conversion processes diminishes. The nine-step model has become something of a fetish with a number of practitioners, but it was not intended as a universally applicable methodology. It grew out of the experiment at the Hunsfoss Paper Mill in the Norwegian Industrial Democracy Project (Emery and Thorsrud, 1976; 1992/ Vol. II) and was then offered as a training tool for departmental managers in the Shell Philosophy Project (Hill, 1971/Hill and Emery, Vol. II). It arose, therefore, in relation to continuous process technology. In experiments with office units in the same project, another method was tried that was more suited to these settings, but it was no more than an embryonic sketch. The nine-step model has proved far more widely applicable than its original use with continuous process technology suggested, but its range seems best restricted to the long-linked technological family. Pava's work has given us a modification appropriate to intensive technology. A lot of socio-technical work being done in banks, insurance companies and retail establishments, much of it related to the introduction of computers, is concerned with secondary technologies rather than the primary technology which affects the quality of the exchanges themselves (their effectiveness). A satisfactory socio-technical solution would entail the involvement of those on both sides of the reciprocal relationships in question—joint client/provider and buyer/seller design teams that would, among other things, look at the service consequences of distant rather than face-to-face transactions and of computer identification of individual customer information.

Several lines of future development are already in their early stages. Some of these are noted in Chapter 7 of Pava's book, such as the dedifferentiation of the factory and office as both become increasingly characterized by computerized tool stocks. This will tend to phase out the distinction between blue- and white-collar work. Even more far-reaching in its consequences will be the diminishing need for workers in related activities to be colocated. Under some circumstances they may work at home, under others in widely separated parts of the enterprise. There will be increased scope for work to be contracted out to small entrepreneurial groups and for customer self-service. These opportunities seem so great that a very substantial process of decentralization is likely to set in. Fears of greater centralization, warranted while computers remained large and expensive, are likely to prove less warranted now that the microprocessor has begun to take over. Foreshadowed is a spatial distribution of work very different from that at present obtaining, with far-reaching consequences for society as a whole.

As regards the scale of unemployment to be expected when the new technologies are fully established—unless new industries are capable of absorbing it—the ensuing crisis will be met only by a redefinition of work that dissociates the concept of work from the fact of employment and recognizes the value of alternative forms of social contribution. Though there are signs of some movement in this direction, the full crisis is still some distance off, so that we have a few years in hand to prepare for the radical changes involved in moving toward "a partially employed but fully engaged society" (Trist, 1981).

Meanwhile, there is one short-term certainty: that, if the technological imperative continues to be blindly followed, the worst consequence will supervene not only in the creation of badly designed jobs at the more routine levels, but in managerial failure to seize opportunities that will remain unseen unless processes of deliberation and forms of discretionary coalition are introduced that are far more effective than those operating in most contemporary organizations. The question is whether we let the present condition continue and so lose the advantages of advanced office technology or, by countervailing it, gain them. The choice is ours. In Pava's words:

> This choice may be exercised by design or default. Design represents attempts to move beyond past errors. Default is the unknowing ratification of unacknowledged history. Socio-technical analysis represents one way to design instead of default.

These brief sentences sum up the message of his book.

References

Barnard, C. 1938. *The Functions of the Executive*. Cambridge, Mass.: Harvard University Press.

Burns, T. and M. Chevalier. 1978. "Policy Fields." In *A Management Handbook for Public Administrators*, edited by J.W. Sutherland. New York and London: Van Nostrand Reinhold.

Emery, F.E. 1967. "The Next Thirty Years: Concepts, Methods and Anticipations." *Human Relations*, 20:199–237.

———. 1976. *Futures We Are In*. Leiden: Martinus Nijhoff. Chapter 4 reproduced in part, in Vol. II, "The Second Design Principle: Participation and the Democratization of Work," pp. 214–33.

Emery, F.E. and E. Thorsrud. 1976. *Democracy at Work*. Leiden: Martinus Nijhoff.

———. 1993. Vol. II, "The Norskhydro Fertilizer Plant." pp. 492–507.

Emery, F.E. and E.L. Trist. 1965. "The Causal Texture of Organizational Environments." *Human Relations*, 18:21–32.

Herbst, P.G. 1974. *Socio-Technical Design: Strategies in Multi-Disciplinary Research*. London: Tavistock Publications. Chapter 2 shortened and revised Vol. II, "Designing with Minimal Critical Specifications," pp. 294–302.

———. 1976. *Alternatives to Hierarchies*. Leiden: Martinus Nijhoff. Chapter 3 slightly revised in Vol. II, "Alternatives to Hierarchies," pp. 283–93.

Hill, P. 1971. *Towards a New Philosophy of Management*. London: Gower Press. Excerpted, Vol. II as P. Hill and F. Emery, "Toward a New Philosophy of Management," pp. 259–82.

McWhinney, W. 1980. "The Resolution of Complex Issues." Unpublished manuscript.

Parsons, T. 1960. *Structure and Process in Modern Societies*. Glencoe, Ill.: Free Press.

Pava, C. 1980. "Normative Incrementalism." Ph.D. dissertation, University of Pennsylvania.

———. 1983. *Managing New Office Technology: An Organizational Strategy*. Excerpted in Vol. II, "Nonroutine Office Work," pp. 644–61.

Peters, J. and R.H. Waterman. 1982. *In Search of Excellence: Lessons from America's Best-Run Companies*. New York: Harper and Row.

Schwartz, P. and J. Ogilvie. 1980. *The Emergent Paradigm*. Stanford, Calif.: Stanford Research Institute.

Thompson, J.D. 1967. *Organizations in Action: Social Science Bases of Administrative Theory*. New York: McGraw-Hill.

Trist, E.L. 1981. "QWL in the '80s." Closing address, International Conference on QWL and the '80s. Toronto. Vol. II, pp. 338–49.

David Morley and Eric Trist

A Brief Introduction to the Emerys' "Search Conference"[1]

The main method for shaping the field in action research, later developed into action learning, involves active collaboration between clients and social scientists. This collaboration depends on joint agreements being worked out and revised as occasion warrants. Only material agreed on by both sides is published. The Search Conference, as designed by the Emerys, is one of the main techniques used. Projects involving search conferences are expected to last for a time, often a very considerable time. It is expected that differences between the parties will arise but that most of these will be resolved.

Search conferences have been found to create conditions under which the multiple dimensions of complex issues can be cooperatively explored (to a far higher degree than is usual) by members of the many and often divergent groups concerned. During the 1970s between 300 and 400 search conferences were held in Australia, where the method was taken and elaborated by the Emerys after its small beginnings in the Tavistock. In the last five years some 30 search conferences have been held in Canada in organizations and settings of many kinds. The Faculty of Environmental Studies at York University has become interested in the method as a means of securing widespread public participation in the appreciation of complex issues, of evoking new ideas for their creative solution and of instigating processes of social learning which, in the long run, will increase the capability of the society to manage itself in the uncertain, rapidly changing environment with which it is confronted.

A search conference depends, first of all, on getting the various parties at interest, the *stakeholders,* together under some acceptable auspices in which there is enough trust for them to agree to meet. The participants come as representatives of their organizations or as individuals concerned with wider domains. As individuals they are much freer to undertake exploratory work. The purpose of the search conference is to gain new understanding, to generate new options and, through these, to create the possibility of more cohesive

---

[1] Taken from D. Morley and E. Trist, *Children Our Number One Resource: A Report on the Saskatchewan Search Conference on Day Care.* Saskatoon: Co-operative College of Canada, 1981. A full account will be given in Volume III.

relationships among many who have hitherto not been able to cooperate, through apparent incompatibility.

The role of the staff of a search conference is purely facilitative. They manage the learning process, not the substance; a ground rule is that they must not interfere at all in the content of the discussions. In this way, the participants experience full ownership of what is produced and take full responsibility for it. As it is "theirs," they are more likely to feel commitment to it and therefore to follow it up in their back-home settings or directly to suggest steps which will allow it to come to fruition.

This is of special importance when many of the participants are grassroots people without positions of prominence in any organization and who sometimes have never aired their views in public before. In many circumstances the membership of a search conference is a mix of such people along with organizational leaders at several levels. In the search conference atmosphere they all have equal status.

When the membership is less than 20, the search conference can proceed through all its phases in one total group. When it is larger—say, 40 or 60 members—most of the work is done in small working groups of 10 or less, which report back their detailed work for general discussion in plenary sessions.

To permit thorough exploration of multifaceted issues, search conferences require a considerable commitment of time. Participants are required to come for the whole of the time. Partial attendance is disruptive. It is difficult for a search conference to complete its task in less than two and a half days. A longer time period is preferred—three to four or even five days.

Moreover, new thinking of the type required cannot be done under conditions of distraction, where the telephone can disturb or immediate demands of the office intrude. Therefore the conferences are best held under what is called "social island" conditions—in a residential establishment at some distance from the participants' workplaces and homes, where supporting services are available. The technology includes plentiful supplies of flipcharts, felt pens and masking tape and secretarial services to permit outline records of each day's proceedings to be available to all participants the next morning.

A brief record needs to be kept of meetings, decisions and other events with their dates, so that a log becomes available on the course of the process for all concerned. A log-keeper could function for, say, ten weeks. These records give the outline of a learning process—invaluable for analysis and comparison.

The search conference depends on a basic assumption that the future can to a considerable extent be influenced by human intervention. There is no such thing as *the* future; there are a number of possible futures. The job is actively to bring about the one desired, rather than passively to be overwhelmed by one preferably avoided.

On the one hand, a search conference is future oriented, usually taking at least a 10 to 15 year time horizon. This is to unlock people from their immediate short-term preoccupations. On the other hand, it seeks to have people relate the issue or problem with which they are concerned to the wider society, to set it in its context, to take the wide as well as the long view. However, the wide and long views must always be brought back to the present and to the focal problem; toward the end of the conference the task has to be faced of agreeing on action steps.

The conference begins by having participants share their views on the main issues and trends deriving from the past, which they feel are likely to go on influencing the future during the next 10 to 15 years, and to identify new issues and trends, which they feel are likely to emerge in this period. No one has a privileged insight into the future. Therefore, everyone's views carry equal weight. Scanning the wider environment in a futures perspective is generalist work. What influence people's actions are their beliefs and perceptions. It is these which need to be shared publicly so that mutual ignorance of what participants think is replaced by public knowledge. The material evoked by the facilitator is recorded on flipcharts without criticism or debate.

If small groups are necessary, they elect reporters to summarize the groups' work for plenary sessions. All the flipcharts are hung around the walls so that they can be inspected by everyone. This holds for all sessions. In this way, the participants find out what kind of world they think is coming up, how far there is a shared view of this and what kind of large scale forces they will have to take into account in resolving the issue which concerns them or the organization they wish to remodel.

The second phase of the conference focuses on the issue or organization which is the concern of the members. They are asked to build a picture of its present state and to analyze how it came to be this way. They are then asked what is likely to happen to it, given the picture of the large environment, if no changes are made. What is the degree of match or mismatch?

This usually leads to a consensus that change is required, but the question of change is not approached directly. The third phase is concerned with forming a picture of what the participants consider to be a desirable future for the organization, issue or domain with which they are concerned. They are encouraged to think constraint-free, to dream but to remain credible—not to become, in a false sense, utopian. Nevertheless, their task is to generate a common vision that can motivate people to "invent" means of pursuing it that they would not otherwise have thought of.

The fourth phase brings the participants back to the present. Having generated their vision of a desirable future, what are the constraints which they see in the way of attaining it? They must take into account here what they have said both about the present state of their local organization or issue and of the trends coming up in the wider environment. But what also are the opportunities, many of which may lie unrecognized? Some of the best opportunities may be found by facing up to the constraints. Identifying a desirable long-range future usually has the effect of narrowing the field of constraints and widening the field of opportunities.

So far, the conference has proceeded in the same general mode in the same small groups, which are usually mixed groups composed of a cross section of the kinds of people present. They may meet also in homogeneous groups to discuss constraints and opportunities from a different set of perspectives.

For the fifth and last phase—the consideration of action steps—a basic change is made in the mode of procedure. First of all, in a key plenary session, a set of themes is identified in terms of which it is agreed that action of various kinds is required; these form the topics for study by a number of theme or task groups. These groups are not the same as the initial search groups but are composed of those most interested in a particular theme. The facilitators are then withdrawn, and the new groups proceed entirely autonomously, thinking out their action steps in the light of what has been learned from all the previous sessions. The action steps are usually in terms of broad strategies geared to longer term, rather than shorter term, courses of action, though some of the latter which are urgent may be included. There is great variation in search conferences regarding how far task groups go in working out action steps. Unless thorough work has been done on the desirable future and on constraints and opportunities, no new path into the future will have been identified. Work on the proposals for action steps will tend to take two or three sessions, at least.

A recent innovation in search conference procedure has been to invite senior people from the domain of concern—politicians, senior government officials, senior corporate executives and key interest group leaders—to attend the final plenary, to hear the presentations of the task groups and to take part in the discussion. This makes the participants more accountable to the key decision makers in their constituencies and exposes these decision makers to the innovative thinking of the conference. Experience so far suggests that this step increases the likelihood of implementation, but whether to take it requires careful consideration. If it is taken, a "dummy run" of the presentation may be made in-house before the visitors arrive. Many conflicts often have to be resolved before the conference can turn to the outside world.

A search conference requires careful preparation and planning—jointly undertaken by the staff and the sponsoring organizations—regarding who should be invited, how public it should be made, etc. A search conference is not an isolated event but an episode begun long before and continuing long afterward. It is of the utmost importance to ensure that means are found to keep the various groups in contact, to report back the proceedings effectively and to encourage the conditions that will allow a long-range shift in the field to take place, for search conferences are about substantial or fundamental change, not marginal or superficial change. Very often it is some time—many months or a year or more—before their impact becomes apparent. They have the delicate but necessary task of opening up new paths, of encouraging innovation without usurping the role of the organizations from which their members come. They have, rather, to change the relations between these organizations so that, within a new framework, they can accomplish what they were previously unable to do.

Contributors

Ken Bamforth, M.A. (deceased). Lecturer in Industrial Management, director of field projects, Department of Industry, Leeds University; leader, social project staff, Ellis Group of Companies, Bradford, Yorkshire; Postgraduate Fellow, Tavistock Institute; face worker (filler), Elsecar Colliery, Yorkshire.

Albert Cherns, B.A. (Hons.) (deceased). Professor of Social Sciences and Head of Department of Social Sciences, Loughborough University; Fellow, British Psychological Society; Governor, British Steel Industry's Ashorne Hill College; Member, Tavistock Institute Council. Senior appointments in the Department of Scientific and Industrial Research; Secretary of the Heyworth Committee that recommended the establishment of a British Social Science Research Council.

Louis Davis, M.S. Professor Emeritus, University of California at Los Angeles, Anderson Graduate School of Management and Chairman, Center for Quality of Working Life. President, The Davis Group Inc. Formerly Professor, University of California, Berkeley and Chairman, Human Factors in Technology Program; Visiting Senior Fellow, Tavistock Institute of Human Relations; Lucas Professor, University of Birmingham; Consultant, OEEC Marshall Plan.

Charles Dwyer, Ph.D. Associate Professor, Graduate School of Education, University of Pennsylvania. Formerly Chairman, Wharton Center for Applied Research; Director, Management and Behavioral Science Center, Wharton School.

Fred Emery, Ph.D. Fellow, British Psychological Society; Elton Mayo Award, Australian Psychological Society. Formerly Senior Fellow, Center for Continuing Education and Research School for the Social Sciences, Australian National University; Chairman, Human Resources Centre, Tavistock Institute; Senior Lecturer in Psychology, Melbourne University.

Merrelyn Emery, Ph.D. Lecturer, Centre for Continuing Education, Australian National University.

David (P.G.) Herbst, Ph.D., D.Litt. (deceased). Member, Norwegian Royal Society of Sciences; Fellow, Royal Statistical Society. Senior Staff, Work Research Institute, Oslo. Formerly Professor of Psychology, University of Oslo; Senior Staff, Tavistock Institute.

Gurth Higgin, Ph.D. (deceased). Professor Emeritus in Continuing Management Education, University of Loughborough. Formerly Chairman, Human Resources Centre, Tavistock Institute.

Paul Hill (retired). Industrial consultant. Formerly Director, Human Relations Division, MSL International Management Consultants; senior personnel roles with Shell International in Venezuela and the United Kingdom.

Lisl Klein, Ph.D. In consulting and research practice. Formerly Senior Staff, Tavistock Institute; Lecturer in Industrial Sociology, Imperial College of Science and Technology, London; Consultant to German Federal Ministry of Research and Technology; Social Sciences Adviser, Esso Petroleum.

Eric J. Miller, Ph.D. Fellow, Royal Anthropological Institute. Director, Tavistock/Leicester Conferences on Group Relations; Senior Staff, Tavistock Institute.

Gareth Morgan, Ph.D. Professor of Management, York University, Toronto. Fellow, International Academy of Management. Formerly Professor of Organizational Behavior, Pennsylvania State University; Professor of Organisational Behaviour, University of Lancaster, England.

David Morley, Ph.D. Professor, Faculty of Environmental Studies, York University, Toronto. A principal of the Adapting by Learning (ABL) Group; Coordinator of the York/Habitat project associated with the United Nations Centre for Human Settlements (Habitat) Information Office for North America and the Caribbean, located at York University.

Hugh Murray, Ph.D. (retired). Fellow, British Psychological Society. Formerly Chairman, Centre of Organisational and Operational Research, Tavistock Institute; Senior Psychologist, Army Operational Research Group.

Calvin Pava, Ph.D. Consultant in organization design and planning. Formerly Assistant Professor, Harvard Business School; Professor of Telecommunications, New York University.

Alexander Pollock, M.A. Member, British Psycho-Analytical Society; Fellow, British Psychological Society. In psychoanalytic consulting practice. Formerly Senior Staff, Tavistock Institute.

A.K. Rice, Sc.D. (deceased). Chairman, Centre for Applied Social Research, Tavistock Institute. Co-founder, A.K. Rice Institute, Washington, D.C. Formerly Deputy Chairman, Industrial Welfare Society, London.

Stu Sullivan. Ontario Coordinator, Energy and Chemical Workers Union; Vice-President and Chairman, Energy and Environment Committee, Ontario Federation of Labour. Formerly Chairman, Board of Governors, Lambton College; Staff Representative, Oil, Chemical and Atomic Workers Union; founding member, Energy and Chemical Workers Union.

Gerald Susman, Ph.D. Fellow, American Psychological Society. Robert and Judith Klein Professor of Management and Director, Center for the Management of Technological and Organizational Change, Pennsylvania State University. Formerly Study Director, National Academy of Sciences.

Einar Thorsrud (deceased). Director, Work Research Institute, Oslo. Formerly Chairman, International Council for the Quality of Working Life; Associate Professor and Director, Institute for Industrial Research, Trondheim; Director, Industrial Democracy Programme, Norway; prominent in the resistance movement during World War II.

Eric Trist, O.B.E., Ph.D., LL.D. (Hon.) (retired). Fellow, International Academy of Management; Fellow, Academy of Management. Formerly Member, Psychological Committee, British Social Science Research Council; Professor Emeritus of Organizational Behavior and Social Ecology, Wharton School, University of Pennsylvania; Professor under the same title at York University, Toronto, and UCLA; Founder Member and Chairman (1958–1962), Tavistock Institute.

William Westley, Ph.D. (retired). Professor Emeritus, McGill University. Formerly Professor and Chairman, Department of Sociology, McGill University; Director, McGill University Industrial Relations Centre; President, S.T.S. Associates.

Trevor Williams, Ph.D. Senior Lecturer, Department of Management, University of Wollongong, Australia. Formerly Visiting Scholar, Tavistock Institute of Human Relations; Adviser to the Task Force on Repetition Strain Injury in the Australian Public Service, 1985.

Subject Index

Name Index

This book was set in Linotron Times. Times is a modified book version of the original Times New Roman, a newspaper typeface, commissioned in 1931 to be designed under the supervision of Stanley Morison for the London *Times*.

Printed on acid-free paper.